TH ☑ O9-ABH-081
ST. MARY'S COLLEGE OF MARYLAND
ST. MARY'S CITY, MARYLAND 20686

A WAR IMAGINED

by the same author

THE PATTERN OF HARDY'S POETRY
THE EDWARDIAN TURN OF MIND
EDWARDIAN OCCASIONS
THE AUDEN GENERATION
FLIGHTS OF PASSAGE: REFLECTIONS OF A WORLD WAR II AVIATOR

edited texts

FURTHER SPECULATIONS by T.E. Hulme
THE AUTHOR'S CRAFT AND OTHER CRITICAL WRITINGS
by Arnold Bennett
ROMANCE AND REALISM by Christopher Caudwell
THE COMPLETE POETICAL WORKS OF THOMAS HARDY
THOMAS HARDY (Oxford Standard Authors)

A
WAR IMAGINED

*The First World War
and English Culture*

SAMUEL HYNES

ATHENEUM
New York 1991

Maxwell Macmillan International
New York Oxford Singapore Sydney

For Arthur Crook
and
Juliet Wrightson

Copyright © 1990 by Samuel Hynes

First American Edition 1991

All rights reserved. No part of this book may be reproduced or transmitted in
any form or by any means, electronic or mechanical, including photocopying,
recording, or by any information storage and retrieval system, without permission
in writing from the Publisher.

Atheneum
Macmillan Publishing Company
866 Third Avenue, New York, NY 10022

Library of Congress Cataloging-in-Publication Data

Hynes, Samuel Lynn.
    A war imagined: the First World War and English culture / Samuel
Hynes.—1st American ed.
      p. cm.
    Includes bibliographical references and index.
    ISBN 0-689-12128-8
    1. World War, 1914–1918—Influence.   2. Great Britain—
Civilization—20th century.   I. Title.
D523.H96   1991
940.3—dc20   90-21873

Macmillan books are available at special discounts for bulk purchases
for sales promotions, premiums, fund-raising, or educational use.
For details, contact:

Special Sales Director
Macmillan Publishing Company
866 Third Avenue
New York, NY 10022

10 9 8 7 6 5 4 3 2 1

Printed in the United States of America

CONTENTS

Acknowledgements   ix
Introduction: A Gap in History   xi

PART I   THE LIGHTS GO OUT: 1914–15
    1 The Wars Before the War   3
    2 The Arts Enlist   25
    3 The Home-Front Wars   57

PART II   THE TURNING POINT: 1916
    4 Running Down   99
    5 A Turn of Speech   109
    6 The New Look of War   120
    7 Dissent at the Turn   145

PART III   WAITING FOR DAYLIGHT: 1917–18
    8 Dottyville   171
    9 The Death of Landscape   189
    10 The Lives of the Martyrs   203
    11 The Last of the Home-Front Wars   216
    12 The Beginnings of 'Post-War'   235
    13 11/11/18   254

PART IV   THE WORLD AFTER THE WAR: 1919–25
    14 Monument-Making   269
    15 Anti-Monuments   283
    16 The War Becomes History   311

17 'A Botched Civilization'   337
18 The Wars After the War   353
19 The Generation Wars   383

PART V MYTH-MAKING: 1926–33
20 The Ten Days' War   407
21 The War Becomes Myth   423

Epilogue   464

Notes   470
Index   508

ILLUSTRATIONS

Plates

(between pages 114 and 115)

1 Barribal, 'The Man of To-day', a tailor's advertisement from *Colour*, November 1915
2 Will Dyson, 'Wonders of Science'
3 Will Dyson, 'Kultur Protector'
4 Stephen Phillips's *Armageddon*: Satan consults his generals
5 Walter Sickert, 'The Soldiers of King Albert the Ready'
6 'To the Death', *Chums*, August 15, 1914
7 'Roll of Honour', *The Times*, July 8, 1916
8 *Battle of the Somme*: the faked attack
9 Muirhead Bone, 'Battle of the Somme: Mametz Village and Wood'
10 The manuscript of Siegfried Sassoon's 'Atrocities'
11 C. R. W. Nevinson, 'The Doctor'
12 C. R. W. Nevinson, 'Returning to the Trenches'
13 C. R. W. Nevinson, 'Paths of Glory'
14 'Paths of Glory' censored
15 William Orpen, 'Dead Germans in a Trench'

(between pages 306 and 307)

16 'Aren't the Old Men Splendid?', a tailor's advertisement from the *Cambridge Magazine*, November 2, 1918
17 The temporary Cenotaph (Sir Edwin Lutyens)
18 C. R. W. Nevinson, 'He Gained a Fortune but He Gave a Son'
19 Max Beerbohm, 'Mr Lytton Strachey trying hard to see her with Lord Melbourne's eyes'
20 Max Beerbohm, '"A Chiel" 1914–1918': Eminent Lady: 'I wonder what dear sweet Colonel Repington always carries that funny little note-book with him for.'

21 Paul Nash, 'The Menin Road'
22 Wyndham Lewis, 'A Battery Shelled'
23 John B. Souter, 'The Breakdown'
24 Scene from R. C. Sherriff's *Journey's End* (stage version)
25 William Orpen, 'To the Unknown British Soldier in France', first version
26 'To the Unknown British Soldier in France', second version
27 Stanley Spencer, 'The Resurrection of the Soldiers'

Reproduced in the Text

H. G. Wells, 'Mr Osborn's Dream of Himself', p. 23
Obituary notice of Henri Gaudier-Brzeska, *Blast*, 1915, p. 66
Broadsheet, 'Christ and Peace', p. 82
H. G. Wells, holograph page from *Mr Britling Sees It Through*, p. 133
Dedication page, *New Paths*, 1918, p. 240
'Reconstruction', Sanatogen advertisement, *New Statesman*, December
    1918, p. 264
H. G. Wells, 'Winston Doing Everything', p. 413

ACKNOWLEDGEMENTS

A book like this one, written over many years, accumulates many debts, which I must try to acknowledge here. Two foundations, the John Simon Guggenheim Memorial Foundation and the American Council of Learned Societies, have supported me through sabbatical leaves. Princeton University has been liberal with released time and with research assistance. Members of the faculty and staff of the Princeton English Department have also been helpful: I particularly thank Beth Harrison and Marilyn Walden. In London, staff members of the Imperial War Museum have been endlessly patient and efficient. The British Library, the Bodleian Library, the National Art Library of the Victoria and Albert Museum, and the University of London Library at Senate House have all been valuable resources, generously offered.

Many individuals — friends, acquaintances, and total strangers — have been helpful, among them Martin Anderson of the Toccata Press, Lord Annan, Melanie Aspey of *The Times*, Alan Bishop, Ted Bogacz, Carolyn Burke, Richard Cork, Milein Cosman, Laura Cowan, Rob Cowley, the late Richard Ellmann, Roy Foster, C.J. Fox, P.N. Furbank, Paul Fussell, Sandra Gilbert, Nicholas Grene, Graham Halton of *Musica Viva*, Barbara Hardy, Sir Rupert Hart-Davis, Robin Hartley of Heal's, Michael Holroyd, Joanna Hynes, Sheelah Hynes, Lisa Jadwin, the late Hans Keller, Sebastian Knowles, Cecil Lang, David Large, James Longenbach, Richard Ludwig, Norman MacKenzie, Suzanne McNatt, Jane Marcus, Tim Materer, Luke Menand, Tom Moser, Deborah Nord, William Ostrem, C.C. Pond, John Poole, Anthony Preston, Miranda Preston, Dean Rapp, Mary Schmidt, Elaine Showalter, Martha Senkbeil, Robert Spoo, Jon Stallworthy, the late Lola Szladits, Frances Whistler, Charles Wintour, Nonie Wintour, Jacek Wisniewski, and Robert Wohl.

The author and publishers would like to thank the following for permission to reprint copyright material: the Imperial War Museum for material from unpublished MSS in their collections; the London School of Economics and Virago Press for extracts from the *Diaries of Beatrice Webb* edited by Norman McKenzie; the Literary Executor of Vera Brittain and Virago Press for the poem 'The Superfluous Woman' from *Testament of Youth*; A.P. Watt Ltd on behalf of the Literary Trustees of Robert Graves for the poem 'A Dead Boche' from *Fairies and Fusiliers*; Faber & Faber Ltd and New Directions Publishing Company for 19 lines from 'Hugh Selwyn Mauberley' from *Collected Shorter Poems* by Ezra Pound; Gerald Duckworth & Co. Ltd and the Estate of Sir Osbert Sitwell for six lines from 'The Modern Abraham'; the Estate of Siegfried Sassoon and Sir Rupert Hart-Davis for the poems 'Victory', 'The Hero', 'The Poet as Hero', 'Banishment' and seven lines from 'Repressions of War Experience'; Unwin Hyman Ltd for an extract from *Images of War* by Richard Aldington.

Thanks are also due to the following for permission to reproduce copyright illustrative material: the British Library for plates 2, 3 and page 82; Sheffield City Art Galleries, plate 5; Raymond Mander and Joe Mitchenson Theatre Collection, plates 4 and 24; Times Newspapers Ltd, plate 7; *Daily Mail*, plate 17; the Trustees of the Imperial War Museum, London, plates 8, 11, 12, 13, 15, 21, 22 and 26; Mrs Eva Reichman, plates 19 and 20; the University of Hull Art Collection, plate 18; Royal Academy of Arts, plate 23; the National Trust Photographic Library, plate 27; the Estate of Siegfried Sassoon and the Humanities Research Centre, University of Texas at Austin, plate 10; Chatto and Windus and the University of London Library for a drawing from *Mr Britling Sees It Through* by H.G. Wells, page 133; A.P. Watt Ltd on behalf of the Literary Executors of H.G. Wells for sketches from *Boon* and *Meanwhile* on pages 23 and 413; the Department of Prints and Drawings and the Trustees of the British Museum, plate 9; the National Library of Scotland, plate 6; Philadelphia Museum of Art, plate 1; the Tate Gallery, plate 14; University of Princeton Library, page 240.

The author and publishers have made all efforts to obtain necessary permissions with reference to copyright material, both illustrative and quoted; however, should there be any omissions in this respect we apologise and shall be pleased to make the appropriate acknowledgements in any future edition.

INTRODUCTION

A Gap in History

The First World War was the great military and political event of its time; but it was also the great *imaginative* event. It altered the ways in which men and women thought not only about war but about the world, and about culture and its expressions. No one after the war — no thinker or planner, no politician or labour leader, no writer or painter — could ignore its historical importance or frame his thought as though the war had not occurred, or had been simply another war.

Even as it was being fought the war was perceived as a force of radical change in society and in consciousness. It brought to an end the life and values of Victorian and Edwardian England; but it did something more fundamental than that: it added a new scale of violence and destruction to what was possible — it changed reality. That change was so vast and so abrupt as to make the years after the war seem discontinuous from the years before, and that discontinuity became a part of English imaginations. Men and women after the war looked back at their own pasts as one might look across a great chasm to a remote, peaceable place on the other side.

This sense of radical discontinuity of present from past is an essential element in what eventually took form as the Myth of the War. I use that phrase in this book to mean not a falsification of reality, but an imaginative version of it, the story of the war that has evolved, and has come to be accepted as true. The construction of that story began during the war, and grew in the years that followed, assimilating along the way what was compatible with its judgements, and rejecting what was not. The Myth is not the War entire: it is a tale that confirms a set of attitudes, an idea of what the war was and what it meant.

A brief sketch of that collective narrative of significance would go something like this: a generation of innocent young men, their heads full of high abstractions like Honour, Glory, and England, went off to war to make the world safe for democracy. They were slaughtered in stupid battles planned by stupid generals. Those who survived were shocked, disillusioned and embittered by their war experiences, and saw that their real enemies were not the Germans, but the old men at home who had lied to them. They rejected the values of the society that had sent them to war, and in doing so separated their own generation from the past and from their cultural inheritance.

This story has been told in many ways: in histories of the war, in fictions and memoirs, in poems, in plays, in paintings, in films; but its essential elements remain much the same. They constitute a set of abrupt disjunctions — between generations, between fighting soldiers and those who controlled their lives, between the present and the past — which can be reduced to two terse propositions: the old betray the young; the past is remote and useless.

That Myth of the War was given its fullest definition in the years around the end of the Twenties, when the great war memoirs and novels, and the first full edition of the poems of Wilfred Owen, were published. No generation since then has questioned its validity, and it remains the accepted interpretation of the war, repeated in texts written by authors who did not experience the war, but who inherited its myth. Here, for example, is George Orwell, in *The Road to Wigan Pier* (1937), explaining the origin of his schoolboy radicalism during and just after the war:

> Essentially . . . it was a revolt of youth against age, resulting directly from the war. In the war the young had been sacrificed and the old had behaved in a way which, even at this distance of time, is horrible to contemplate; they had been sternly patriotic in safe places while their sons went down like swathes of hay before the German machine guns. Moreover, the war had been conducted mainly by old men and had been conducted with supreme incompetence.[1]

And here, writing twenty-five years after Orwell, is Stephen Spender:

> The immediate reaction of the poets who fought in the war was cynicism. The war dramatized for them the contrast between the still-idealistic young, living and dying on the unalteringly horrible stage-set of the Western Front, with the complacency of the old at home,

the staff officers behind the lines. In England there was violent anti-
German feeling, but for the poet-soldiers the men in the trenches on
both sides seemed united in pacific feelings and hatred of those at
home who had sent them out to kill each other.[2]

These passages are distillations of what the best war writers were saying
in the years when Orwell and Spender were coming of age, and it is not
surprising that they accepted that myth as truth. It continues to be
accepted in our own time. In novels, films, television documentaries,
popular histories, the story remains the same; we live still in that myth.

We live with the consequences of the First World War in another,
more comprehensive way. The sense of a gap in history that the war
engendered became a commonplace in imaginative literature of the
post-war years. Poets and novelists rendered it in images of radical
emptiness — as a chasm, or an abyss, or an edge — or in images of
fragmentation and ruin, all expressing a fracture in time and space that
separated the present from the past. And this was the case not only in
writings about the war, but in Modernist works that are not a part of
what we would ordinarily call war literature — in *Women in Love*, *The
Waste Land*, and *Mrs Dalloway* for example. The gap in history had
entered post-war consciousness as a truth about the modern world.

And not only in imaginative literature, but in critical writing too.
F.R. Leavis, writing in the early Thirties, described his time as one
'when the gap in continuity is almost complete', and Spender, seeking in
the 1950s to describe the unique quality of the characters in the
Twenties novels of Huxley and Hemingway, wrote that they were 'cut
off from history, as well as from thought and religion'.[3] More recently
Paul Fussell, in his influential book *The Great War and Modern Memory*,
has described the war as 'perhaps the last to be conceived as taking place
within a seamless, purposeful "history" involving a coherent stream of
time running from past through present to future'.[4]

That sense of radical change is the subject of this book: how English
culture was transformed, and English imaginations were altered, by
what happened between 1914 and 1918, and how that process of change
determined what England after the war was like and what *modern* came
to mean. The war is at the centre of this story, but as the agent of change
and not as a narrative of military actions. And the story does not begin
in 1914, nor end in 1918, but extends back into the Edwardian world
before the war, and forward into the modern, post-war world, ending
in the early 1930s, with the Myth of the War fixed, Modernism

dominant in the arts, and a new world war beginning to enter consciousnesses as a possibility, to make them once more different.

Any reader who happens to know my earlier books, *The Edwardian Turn of Mind* and *The Auden Generation*, will see that this one fits between them and completes a trilogy that is a cultural history of England from the death of Queen Victoria to the beginning of the Second World War. I didn't set out to write a trilogy twenty-five years ago, and the three books are not systematically continuous; but they share one conviction — that art and history are not to be separated, that art exists in time and is shaped by the events of time. Surely there has been no period in modern history when that was more true than the years that I deal with here.

PART I

THE LIGHTS GO OUT
1914–15

I see no end that we should like; Futurism, Suffragettism,
exaggeration of the Ego have been symptomatic of this
cataclysm . . . The clock of civilization has been put back
two centuries and we take it for granted.
  Charles Ricketts to Sydney Cockerell, October 1914

CHAPTER I

The Wars Before the War

I

The best-known and most often quoted response to the beginning of the First World War is surely Sir Edward Grey's: 'The lamps are going out all over Europe. We shall not see them lit again in our time.' The remark is Grey's least official utterance — it is not clear when or where he said it, or indeed if he said it at all[1] — but it survives because it expresses an essential feeling of the time. It says nothing about historical causes or national ideals or military goals; nor does it touch on victory or defeat: it simply says that there had been light, and now there was darkness.

Grey's sense of the end of something known and knowable, and the beginning of its unimaginable dark opposite, was shared by many of his contemporaries, and was expressed both in public and in private writings. The nature of what had ended was variously defined, depending on what the writer most valued: the deaths of Socialism, Christianity, avant-garde ideas, and tradition were all announced and mourned for. What the mourners felt in common was simply that something of great value, something vaster even than the peace of Europe, had come to an end on August 4, 1914.

This feeling was poignantly expressed in a letter that Henry James wrote to a friend on the first day of the war:

The plunge of civilization into this abyss of blood and darkness by the wanton feat of those two infamous autocrats is a thing that so gives away the whole long age during which we have supposed the world to be, with whatever abatement, gradually bettering, that to have to take it all now for what the treacherous years were all the while really making for and meaning is too tragic for any words.[2]

James saw that even if the war had been instigated by the German and Austrian emperors, its historical causes were more complex than that; to understand it, one had to see it as the inevitable consequence of *all* the historical past. He found this a bitter truth: for it seemed to force upon him the recognition that the values on which his long life as an artist had been based — his belief in liberalism, in progress, in art itself — were not only casualties of war, but were among the war's causes. His image for the war, like Grey's, was of a plunge out of light into darkness.

Civilization, James's term for the light that had failed, is a word that appears again and again in responses to the beginning of the war. One finds it in Parliamentary debates, in newspapers, in private diaries and letters, in reported conversations. Civilization is threatened, is toppling, is mutilated or destroyed; the clock of civilization has been put back. Indeed the topic was so much discussed in Bloomsbury, Virginia Woolf complained, that it had become boring. 'Then we went through London,' she wrote in a letter in the second week of the war,

> — and oh Lord! what a lot of talk there was! Roger, of course, had private information from the Admiralty, and had been seeing the German Ambassadress, and Clive was having tea with Ottoline, and they talked and talked, and said it was the end of civilization, and the rest of our lives was worthless.[3]

This apocalyptic sense of an ending is everywhere in the accounts of those first days of wartime, and though Virginia Woolf could be ironic about it, it was clearly deeply disturbing for most people. Like James, they had believed, or had *wanted* to believe, that English society was fundamentally stable, and that it was evolving in a progressive direction. War could not occur to interrupt that process, because war was uncivilized. And now suddenly war had come, and had brought that dream of order to an end. It came not simply as an interruption of peace, but as a contradiction of the values that they had thought made Europe one civilization.

One can get a sense of what that pre-war civilization had been if one considers the situation in the arts in London in, say, 1912. That was the year of Edward Marsh's first *Georgian Poetry* anthology, and of Pound's *Ripostes*. The first English production of *The Seagull* opened that year, and there were new plays in London theatres by Galsworthy and Bennett. D.H. Lawrence's *The Trespasser*, Wells's *Marriage*, and Conrad's 'The Secret Sharer' were all published in 1912, and so was Constance Garnett's translation of *The Brothers Karamazov*. Orage's

New Age was the leading journal of art and letters, and Harold Monro's *Poetry and Drama* was announced as about to begin publication. In the art galleries the Camden Town Group, led by Walter Sickert, held its third show, and Roger Fry mounted his Second Post-Impressionist Exhibition, with paintings by French, Russian, and English artists. The Futurists exhibited at the Sackville Galleries that year, and the Russian Ballet danced at Covent Garden, and over at the Queen's Hall Henry Wood conducted the first English performance of Schönberg's *Five Pieces for Orchestra*.

Even in such a sketchy account of the year's artistic activities as this one, a reader must be struck by the variety of things that were going on: Georgians and Imagists, Impressionists and Post-Impressionists, realistic novelists and experimental ones, Englishmen and foreigners, were all evidently flourishing. And flourishing together — Lawrence and Rupert Brooke appearing together in *Georgian Poetry*, Wyndham Lewis exhibiting both with the Camden Towners and the Post-Impressionists, French and Russian painters among the English ones in Fry's show. Groups existed, but they were not separated from each other, either by generations, or by class, or by the little wars of cliques and factions. On the contrary, there was an extraordinary degree of interconnectedness among them: everyone seemed to know everyone else, and most of them got on very well. They appeared in the same journals — Sickert, Bennett, Lewis, and Pound were all published in the *New Age*, and they went to the same parties — at Ottoline Morrell's Thursday evenings in Bedford Square, and at T.E. Hulme's Friday evenings in Frith Street. If some thought themselves more modern than others, their Modernism did not isolate them, or make them hostile to the more conservative tastes of society at large. And society, though it might laugh at Post-Impressionist paintings, or frown at Wells's ideas of the relations between the sexes, or even weep in pain at Schönberg's dissonances, nevertheless went to see Fry's exhibitions, and bought Wells's novels, and even turned up at the Schönberg concerts, and made no attempt to suppress any of them.

Taken together, these examples of art and toleration suggest a nation of remarkable civility, and one can see why men like Grey and James chose *light* as their image of the pre-war world, and why later writers referred nostalgically to those years as the 'Edwardian afternoon'. But nostalgia is bad history; if one looks further one sees that in fact the afternoon was not as serene and sun-bathed as it seemed: there were many clouds in the Edwardian skies. Irishmen, women, and workers, for example, were all exerting pressures against established society and its mores. In 1912, the year I have just summarized in such pacific artistic terms, there was a prolonged miners' strike, Suffragists began their campaign of destroying property by breaking London shop-windows, and the government once more tried and failed to get a Home Rule bill for Ireland through Parliament. Society may still have seemed stable to the guests at Lady Ottoline's and the audiences at the Proms, but they would surely have been aware that that stability was threatened.

By the spring of 1914 the sense of threat had greatly increased. Ireland was in a state close to civil war: British officers at the Curragh announced that they would refuse to obey orders to act against Ulster Unionists, and both Unionists and Republicans engaged in gun-running on such a scale that the armed civilians in Ireland were said to outnumber the British troops. One can measure the seriousness of the situation by the degree to which the language of warfare had entered the rhetoric of public discussion — Sir Edward Carson, the Unionist leader, ranting to Belfast volunteers of 'a clean war and a clean fight', and Winston Churchill telling an audience that 'bloodshed no doubt is lamentable ... but there are worse things than bloodshed, even on an extensive scale.'[4] Such language suggests that the antago-nists had reached the point at which they desired battle almost for the sake of the battle, as a release of the feelings that could find no other resolution.

The Suffragists were also waging war that spring, both in their rhetoric and in their actions. Mrs Pankhurst told the court at the end of her trial in 1913 that

> this movement will go on and on until we have the rights of citizens in this country, as women have in our Colonies, as they will have throughout the civilised world before this woman's war is ended,[5]

and in 1914 that woman's war was accelerating to new levels of violence. Houses, churches, and public buildings were burned, works of art in public galleries were slashed, and women rioted at Buckingham Palace.

During that spring there were also serious troubles with the trade unions — strikes in schools, coal-mines, and the building trades, and a threat from the 'triple alliance' of railwaymen, transport workers, and miners of a general strike in the autumn. When Lloyd George, then Chancellor of the Exchequer, addressed a City gathering of bankers and merchants in July, he saw neither stability nor sunlight in the immediate future for England.

> I should not be doing my duty here as Finance Minister if I did not utter this word of solemn warning — that the prospect of an equitable settlement of these dangerous disputes is complicated and darkened, undoubtedly, by the situation in Ireland. Should there be civil strife in that land, and Heaven avert it, in the course of the next few weeks, when that industrial trouble which I have referred to is maturing, the situation will be the gravest with which any Government in this country has had to deal for centuries.[6]

A civil war, a sex war, and a class war: in the spring of 1914 these were all foreseen in England's immediate future, and with a kind of relish. Rhetorically speaking, they were already being fought; the language of war had become, by then, the language of public discourse.

Anyone in touch with modern art in England during the early months of 1914 would have sensed a similar belligerent spirit at large — more aggressive and provocative, and considerably less 'civilized' than English art had been in the past. F.T. Marinetti, the founder of Italian Futurism, was in London that spring to publicize his movement. Futurism was a brand of modern art that celebrated machinery, noise, speed, and violence, and wholeheartedly condemned the past. 'We wish to glorify War,' the first Futurist manifesto proclaimed, '— the only health-giver of the world — militarism, patriotism, the destructive arm of the Anarchist, the beautiful Ideas that kill, the contempt for women.'[7] Marinetti spent the spring lecturing and reciting his works and quarrelling with English Modernists; there was an exhibition of Futurist paintings in London in May, and a 'Grand Futurist Concert of Noises' in a London music hall in June. But everything about Marinetti's Futurism was a concert of noises, and while he was on hand, aesthetics became a mode of warfare.

At the same time that Marinetti was bombarding England with Futurism, an English modern movement of comparable violence was forming around Wyndham Lewis and his friend Ezra Pound. Lewis and Pound called their part of the whirl of modernist energy Vorticism, and for a time there was a movement of sorts in England with that collective name — enough of a movement to earn a place in the history of English art, and even to have a retrospective exhibition in a London public gallery sixty years later.[8] But the importance of Vorticism was not so much in its principles, which were never very coherent, nor in its achievements,

which were scattered, as in the mere fact that it existed when it did, and
as it did. To take note of it is simply to remind ourselves that in the last
months before the Great War began, the preliminary skirmishes of
another war were taking place. It was partly an art-war, and some of its
weapons were works of art; but it was more than that. It was a war
declared by a violently adversarial avant-garde against *all* English
institutions and traditions: one of its slogans was 'END OF THE CHRISTIAN
ERA', and that is not a statement about *art*, but about an entire culture.

Vorticism was a new kind of movement in the violence of its
aggressiveness and the range of hostilities, but it had other characteristics as well that distinguished it from movements that had preceded it in
English art: it cut across the arts, seeing in all of them the same potential
energy, to be expended against English traditions, and the English past;
and it defined itself in generational terms, and opposed itself specifically
to the previous generation. 'There has been a generation of artists,'
Pound wrote in February,

> who were content to permit a familiarity between themselves and the
> 'cultured' and, even worse, with the 'educated,' two horrible classes
> composed of suburban professors and their gentler relations. This
> time is fortunately over.[9]

In its place Pound saw a new generation, which he identified particularly
with the works of Lewis:

> Mr Lewis has got into his work something which I recognise as the
> voice of my own age, an age which has not come into its own, which
> is different from any other age which has yet expressed itself intensely
> . . . And we have in Mr Lewis our most articulate voice. And we will
> sweep out the past century as surely as Attila swept across Europe.[10]

The most important characteristic of the movement is in that last
extraordinary image of Pound's — the image of the artist as Attila the
Hun. Pound made the point even more explicitly in the same essay: 'In
Mr Lewis's work one finds not a commentator but a protagonist. He is
a man at war.' Here again, the rhetoric of discourse is the rhetoric of
war.

Vorticism's most war-like act was the publication of *Blast*, the first
issue of which appeared in June 1914. Everything about it was belligerent: its colour ('steam-calliope pink', Pound called it),[11] its typography
(large, black, and sanserif), its artwork (mostly Vorticist abstractions),
its poetry (satires by Pound). It contained two 'manifestoes', of which

the first was not really a manifesto at all, but simply two lists, the first beginning 'BLAST' and the second 'BLESS' — as though Lewis and his friends were drawing the battle-lines for their war with society, or perhaps taking a muster of their troops. The 'Blasted' are primarily establishment figures of the time; the 'Blessed' include many artists, but also belligerents in the other wars against society: a trade unionist, an Ulster rebel, militant Suffragettes. They are not blessed, I take it, because of their causes, but because they are opponents — and potentially violent ones — of English society.

The second manifesto is more what one expects a manifesto to be — declarative and propositional — but very bellicose in its language. Consider its first ten propositions, which appear as follows:

1. Beyond Action and Reaction we would establish ourselves.
2. We start from opposite statements of a chosen world. Set up violent structure of adolescent clearness between two extremes.
3. We discharge ourselves on both sides.
4. We fight first on one side, then on the other, but always for the SAME cause, which is neither side or both sides and ours.
5. Mercenaries were always the best troops.
6. We are Primitive Mercenaries in the Modern World.
7. Our *cause* is NO-MAN'S.
8. We set Humour at Humour's throat.
   Stir up Civil War among peaceful apes.
9. We only want Humour if it has fought like Tragedy.
10. We only want Tragedy if it can clench its side-muscles like hands on its belly, and bring to the surface a laugh like a bomb.[12]

The sense of these sentences is not always clear; what *is* clear is the imagery and language of warfare. The manifesto seems to declare a war without a meaning, with the combatants undefined and the cause No-Man's, a war to be fought for the sake of its violence.

Lewis's signed contributions to the first *Blast* support one's sense that he was himself deeply involved in this fantasy of a war against unnamed antagonists. Two of his drawings are titled 'Plan of War' and 'Slow Attack'; his play, 'The Enemy of the Stars', is a violent conflict ending in a murder, and his set of aphorisms, 'Vortices and Notes', includes this remark:

Killing somebody must be the greatest pleasure in existence: either like killing yourself without being interfered with by the instinct of self-preservation — or exterminating the instinct of self-preservation itself!¹³

When one considers the historical location of *Blast*, in the early summer of 1914, the whole thing may seem simply ignorant, self-indulgent fooling: young men talk this way when war has no reality for them, but is only a virile figure of speech. But Vorticism was more than that: its violence, offered as the defining characteristic of a young generation of artists, was something new to the English art-world. In choosing to break violently with the past, and with contemporary society, in choosing pure opposition without connections, these young artists were declaring a kind of war against their world such as was already being fought, or threatening to be fought, by other partisans on other fronts: by Suffragists, Irish nationalists, Ulster loyalists, trade unionists. They were saying that for the social and cultural conflicts that they saw around them, *war* was the appropriate metaphor.

It is not really surprising, then, that when the Great War came, many of the same Englishmen who had believed in the pre-war dream of civilization looked back and saw that it had not been true, that the symptoms of a nation's sickness had been there all along, and that *this* war was simply the final eruption of all that restlessness and discontent. England, it seemed, had many enemies, including some at home, and in some English minds those enemies became conflated and confused, so that opposition to one — to modern art or votes for women — came to seem as patriotic as opposition to another, to Germany itself. England's war, and the world after the war, would be profoundly different because Englishmen perceived the war against Germany as a war against all those other enemies too — a war in defence of civilization, against a barbarous, many-headed enemy.

II

To many English artists, the coming of the war was initially felt as a sudden and catastrophic end to the life of art and thought. 'It is over with all our ideas,' Roger Fry wrote to a friend in August 1914, 'and all the really important things for many years,' and many other artists and writers felt this same sense of an abrupt and total stop — a kind of paralysis of the imagination. There are numerous accounts in letters and

journals of the time of inability to work at all during those August days.
'I can't keep still, and I can't work,' Galsworthy complained; 'can do
nothing' (E.M. Forster); 'live in a sort of coma, like one of those
nightmares when you can't move' (D.H. Lawrence); 'the passage of
events . . . has immobilized my mind' (Edmund Gosse); 'the general
uneasiness and tension of minds seems to take all the strength out of me'
(Rupert Brooke).[14] It was as though the declaration of war, simply by
being uttered, had destroyed the conditions under which art could be
created. Reality had changed, in fundamental ways that called into
question the assumptions on which art, and civilization itself, had been
based. 'The subject-matter of one's effort,' Henry James wrote to a
friend,

> has become *itself* utterly treacherous and false — its relation to reality
> utterly given away and smashed. Reality is a world that was to be
> capable of *this* — and how represent that horrific capability, *historically*
> *latant*, historically ahead of it? How on the other hand *not* represent it
> either — without putting into play mere fiddlesticks?[15]

How represent this new vision of reality? That seems to be a formal
question. But behind it lies another and more difficult one: how
understand it? James saw that the coming of war invalidated the old
assumptions about art and civilization. Before the new reality could be
represented, it would have to be understood. The past would have to be
reassessed, and history revised, before a theory of art could be
formulated that would accommodate it to this horrific present.

This process of historical revision would occupy English artists and
critics throughout the war, and for many years after. Out of that reassessment would come post-war Modernism and the dominant moods
of the inter-war years; it would be the most important and most wide-
ranging cultural change in modern English history.

The process began at the war's beginning, with the essential questions
that James had posed: how was one to understand this new reality?
Could it be rendered in art? And if so, how? These were questions that
many writers worried over in the early months of the war — worried
over, and wrote essays and lectures and reviews about, addressed to
audiences who must have felt the same anxieties.

You can see Edmund Gosse worrying over these questions in an essay
on 'War and Literature' that he wrote in the early autumn of 1914.
Gosse's place in the Edwardian literary establishment was as secure as
anyone's could be: if there had been a laureateship for men of letters, he

would certainly have had the job. He was not only an endlessly productive critic and editor, he was also a friend of everyone who was influential, from poets to peers. Until early in 1914 he had been Librarian of the House of Lords, a post that suited his taste for books and his taste for titles equally well. He had left that office, on reaching the statutory retirement age of sixty-five, with the greatest reluctance. That good official life had come to an end; and now the war had brought an end to the whole Edwardian world of which it had been so comfortable a part. The two endings — his own, and the era's — must have merged in his mind. It was a judgement, he thought, a judgement of that life of indulgent civility: it had all been *too* pleasant.

And so Gosse began his meditations, in 'War and Literature', with an odd metaphor of decadence and purgation:

> War is the great scavenger of thought. It is the sovereign disinfectant, and its red stream of blood is the Condy's Fluid that cleans out the stagnant pools and clotted channels of the intellect. I suppose that hardly any Englishman who is capable of a renovation of the mind has failed to feel during the last few weeks a certain solemn refreshment of the spirit, a humble and mournful consciousness that his ideals, his aims, his hopes during our late past years of luxury and peace have been founded on a misconception of our aims as a nation, of our right to possess a leading place in the sunlighted spaces of the world. We have awakened from an opium-dream of comfort, of ease, of that miserable poltroonery of 'the sheltered life'. Our wish for indulgence of every sort, our laxity of manners, our wretched sensitiveness to personal inconvenience, these are suddenly lifted before us in their true guise as the spectres of national decay; and we have risen from the lethargy of our dilettantism to lay them, before it is too late, by the flashing of the unsheathed sword.[16]

Like James, Gosse looked back at pre-war England and found a misconception there. But whereas for James the war was the ultimate manifestation of the follies of the past, for Gosse it was the disinfectant that would cleanse the present — and not simply present art, but all of 'our' self-indulgent, hedonistic, luxurious habits. All of the English Edwardian past seemed to come under Gosse's censure — or at least all of the comfortable part, which was what he knew.

Gosse's theme was not a new one in English thought, though he was the first writer to bring it into the discourse of war. The idea that there was in the nation an excess of wealth and comfort, and that that excess threatened some essential quality of English life, had been around for a long time. One finds it in Victorian social critics like Carlyle, Disraeli, Arnold and Ruskin, and Carlyle even gave it a name: it is the 'Condition of England' problem. In the Condition of England theme, as these writers developed it, there is both social guilt and nostalgia; they looked around them at an England becoming plutocratic and industrialized, and they saw a growing underclass of urban poor who were left out of England's affluence and ignored by England's rulers; but they also looked back, and saw a lost rural England that had been simpler and more decent and, somehow, more English.

One can find both the guilt and the nostalgia in later, Edwardian versions of the theme: most explicitly in C.F.G. Masterman's *The Condition of England* (1909), but also in important novels of the time like Wells's *Tono-Bungay* (1909) and Foster's *Howards End* (1910). But not in the writings of establishment figures like Gosse, until the war. What the war did was to make the condition of England a social disease for which war was the cure. War, with its male asceticism, its discomforts and deprivations, was the physical opposite of Edwardian luxury. But in its demand for dedication and sacrifice it was also the *spiritual* opposite. So Gosse could be positive about the situation in France: war would purify and cleanse; war was good for England. It was a view that was widely held at the war's beginning. It is, for example, the point of Rupert Brook's war sonnets. Consider the octave of the first sonnet, 'Peace':

> Now, God be thanked Who has matched us with His hour,
> And caught our youth, and wakened us from sleeping,
> With hand made sure, clear eye, and sharpened power,
> To turn, as swimmers into cleanness leaping,
> Glad from a world grown old and cold and weary,
> Leave the sick hearts that honour could not move,
> And half-men, and their dirty songs and dreary,
> And all the little emptiness of love![17]

This is Gosse versified, without the Condy's Fluid. One can see why the poems, with their Condition of England viewpoint, were popular; for they seemed to confront and acknowledge the suffering that war would bring to the nation, and to give that suffering value. And the same could be said of Gosse's essay.

Having established the social benefits of war, Gosse went on, somewhat apologetically, to ask himself what effect the war would have on the lives of men of letters — men like himself. To answer that

question, he looked back again into history, and found the past instance
that seemed most similar to the present one: what had happened to
literary men in France during the Franco-Prussian War. His examination
of that historical example was not encouraging: 'most of the elderly
authors', he wrote, 'were struck dumb with consternation,' and for
French writers in general 'the horrible months, the interminable,
desolated, mutilated months, were mere tracts of intellectual wilderness.'[18] The creative imagination was paralysed, and all literary composition 'of the higher kind' was suspended.

It is a gloomy and highly emotional account, and no wonder: history
was repeating itself, another intellectual wilderness was forming, in
which there would be no place for his little bookish essays and his social
skills: the life of letters would simply cease. Gosse thought that a few
more serious books would trickle from the presses, but they would be
the last. 'What we must really face,' he wrote,

> is the fact that this harvest of volumes, be it what it may, will mark
> the end of what is called 'current literature', for the remaining
> duration of the war. There can be no aftermath, we can aspire to no
> revival. The book which does not deal directly and crudely with the
> complexities of warfare and the various branches of strategy, will,
> from Christmas onwards, not be published at all.[19]

Gosse, in his essay, had looked into history twice, and had found two
endings there. One was for him bad news: the war had brought to a
close those pleasant, belletristic days in which he had flourished. But the
other he saw as good news: it had also ended the flabby decadence of
peace. Gosse was the first English writer to look back from wartime and
to see that Edwardian England was dead. He did not follow the
implications of that thought very far; but in the years to come others
would. They would see that if the past were indeed dead, then the
future, the world after the war, would have to be a new beginning. The
continuity of history had been broken.

At about the same time that Gosse was writing his views of war and
literature, another man of letters of the old school was thinking about
war and art. Selwyn Image was just Gosse's age; like Gosse he had
grown up under Victoria, and had flourished under Edward VII. In his
youth he had been a follower of Ruskin, and he had gone on to make a
minor reputation as an artist and poet. Since 1910 he had been Slade
Professor of Fine Art at Oxford, and it was there at Oxford that he
delivered, as his first lecture of the autumn term, 'Art, Morals, and the

War'. The lecture had not, in fact, been written for Image's Oxford students; he had already given it several times in the weeks since the war began, to audiences as diverse as the Women's Diocesan Association and the Architectural Association, and it seems rather more appropriate for such general groups than for a lecture hall full of fine arts under-graduates. For Image had very little to say about art, and much to say about the justice of the English cause in war. Nevertheless he seems to have felt obliged to speak to his students on this unacademic subject before he could deliver the lectures that he had announced for the term — on Jean François Millet, and on the Art of Lettering in Decoration. It was as though before he could talk about Millet, he had first to reassure himself and his audience that war and Millet were compatible, and that civilization, as represented by lectures on the Art of Lettering, had not ended, and need not end, with the declaration of war.

'We have to remind ourselves,' Image told his audience of potential soldiers,

> with what stoicism we can muster that the effect of war upon art has never been wholly bad, nay, has on occasion been quite the reverse of bad ... There is some force in the paradox that War and Art are not always enemies, and that Peace is not always Art's best friend.[20]

Image went on to explain, by way of a metaphor, why this should be the case:

> The truth is that for many a day past to some of us it has by no means seemed that the ways of Art, however pleasant, have been altogether salubrious. There has been overmuch excitement and frivolity, overmuch running hither and thither after fools and their folly, overmuch licence and even applause accorded to fallacious theories and practices as destructive as they were ridiculous. To remind ourselves of but one example. How persistently has it been dinned into our ears in certain anti-philistine quarters — sometimes, one must confess, with brilliant and seductive paradox — that Art need have no thought of Morals and Spiritual Purpose, nay indeed, ceases to be Art so far as it *has* thought of them — must concern itself not at all with the vulgar work-a-day likes and dislikes of the general community, but keep retired, dainty, disinterested, apart, from the soiling dust of life's normal courses — a sheltered sensitive-plant fearful of the passing touch! Ah! there is little doubt we need a cleansing purge, a sharp awakening, a recalling to sanity, to a

readjustment of our estimates of things. Well, perhaps it was only
war, a war such as that upon us, a war, as I have put it to you, for the
sake of fundamental ideals, that could give us for Art and conduct
generally the salutary shock.[21]

For Gosse the war had been a disinfectant; for Image it was a purge.
England, like some Edwardian glutton, must take the cure, and would
be the better for it. It is a medical metaphor that would turn up again
and again as men like Image strove to justify war as a social activity —
though the exact nature of the impurities to be purged would vary.

Image's attack was directed at 'certain anti-philistine quarters'. He
named no names, but it seems clear that he was thinking of the artists
and writers he had known in the Nineties, the art for art's sake followers
of Oscar Wilde. You might expect that England's most distinguished
Professor of Fine Art, speaking in 1914, would have regarded Decadence
as a dead issue of the Nineties; after all, Roger Fry's two Post-
Impressionist shows had come and gone, and Futurism and Vorticism
were contemporary art-issues. But Image clearly regarded Decadence as
a current phenomenon, and one that was a continuing and urgent threat
to English morality.

About its currency, at least, he was right: Decadence and Oscar Wilde
were very much alive, as issues, in 1914. Even as Image and Gosse were
uttering their views on war and art, Wilde and his tastes were on trial
(once more) in the Central Criminal Court in London. The cause at
issue was a suit by Wilde's executor, Robert Ross, against Wilde's
erstwhile lover, Lord Alfred Douglas, on a charge of defamatory libel.
But at the heart of the case was Wilde's influence on both litigants:
Douglas's relations with Wilde were debated, and so was Ross's taste
for painted boys. The trial ran on for weeks, and in the end was
dismissed when the jury could not agree that either man was worse than
the other.

This case, a quarrel between two odd and litigious men over the
reputation of a dead homosexual, may seem a digression from Image's
lecture to his Oxford students, but there is an important connection.
Image had described Decadent aesthetics as an urgent moral issue; the
Ross/Douglas trial brought homosexuality once more into public
discussion. The two events mark the beginning of a wartime renewal
of feelings that had surrounded the Wilde case in the Nineties — hatred
and fear of sexual deviance, and a felt need to suppress the art and
ideas about art that were associated with it. Henceforth the higher

morality of war would be invoked as justification for the persecution of homosexuality and the censorship of art. And Wilde would reappear as a symbol of the Condition of England before the war, of the degeneracy and decadence that men like Gosse had also perceived. Image had not created this new morality — he was not a man who initiated ideas — but he had lent it the authority of his professorship.

Image had gone one step beyond Gosse: he had proposed that War was not only good for England, it was also good for Art. In the first months of the war many other critics and literary journalists were saying much the same thing, labouring to formulate a wartime aesthetic in terms of which war and art could be seen to be mutually supportive. Articles very quickly began to appear with titles like 'Art after Armageddon', 'Art and War', 'War and Poetry', and 'The War and the Future of Music' (all published in the autumn of 1914). The general line of argument of these pieces can most easily be made clear with a few examples: *on war and music*, from an article by Sir Charles Stanford, Professor of Music at Cambridge, and Professor of Composition and Orchestral Playing at the Royal College of Music (age sixty-two):

> The unmistakable influence which natural convulsions and inter-national wars have had at all times in awakening the highest forces of musical art is one of the most interesting problems of the historian and the psychologist. The evidence is convincing and cumulative. At no time has a great country failed to produce great composers when its resources have been put to the supreme test of war ... Hence it is as common to find a great artistic movement rising at moments of gravest peril, and even of disaster, as at a period of triumphant success.[22]

on war and poetry, Arthur Clutton Brock, art critic of *The Times* (age forty-six):

> In origin and in fact [war] is and always has been in the main a thing ugly and brutal, and a blot on human character and intelligence. But at worst it has always been a great experience; and, like all great experiences, it has had the power of setting the human spirit free ... It was inevitable, then, that the greatest war of all time should call out the poets.[23]

on war and fiction, S.P.B. Mais, novelist, critic, and schoolmaster (age thirty):

... this is the golden age of novelists. However poor our drama and poetry may be, we have more novelists of ability now than ever we had before at one time.

That this War will produce many more we can scarcely doubt, for times of stress are remarkable for the literary activity which they inspire. Think of the days of the Armada; of Marlborough; think of the French Revolution; never does genius flourish as it flourishes in times of national disaster ...[24]

on war and the visual arts, C.H. Collins Baker, painter and Keeper of the National Gallery (age thirty-four):

Artists will be pretty hard hit by the war, but Art will benefit if the war be great enough to engrave the world's mind deeply ... Given certain conditions, war and periods of precarious existence have always produced a fine temper of intelligence and a rare susceptibility.[25]

I have noted both the professional positions of these writers and their ages, to make a point: that though they shared a positive view of the effects of war on art, and though they all wrote from positions more or less within the 'establishment', they were not all members of one elderly generation. Before the war was over, such men, holding such views, would seem to fighting soldiers to constitute one enemy, the Old Men, and hostility towards them would become a common element in war writing. But here, at the war's beginning, the men who saw virtue in war were not a generation: they shared only two things — their optimism, and their ignorance of war.

These writings from the first months of the war — Gosse's quarterly essay, Image's lecture, the pieces in the weeklies — are best understood as responses to the initial confusion and uncertainty that the coming of war had caused among English artists and writers. The authors I have quoted were of different ages and different degrees of prominence, but they all belonged to one general class — they were persons of intelligence and some creative ability who had succeeded in their professional worlds, and who had drawn comfort and security from the assumption that these worlds were stable and permanent. The war shook that sense of security, called their assumptions into question, and left the world, as James said, in darkness. But these critics did not make the darkness their subject. Rather they attempted to lighten it, to familiarize the war, and so make it both imaginable and endurable.

They did so, primarily, by placing the war in history. They compared this war to others, and so made it not Armageddon, but simply another war. They looked in the histories of those other wars for evidence that art had survived destruction, and of course they found it. Greek art had survived the Persians, Michelangelo had not stopped working when Alessandro dei Medici invaded Florence, Purcell had lived through the English Civil War, Turner and Constable and Wordsworth had out-lasted Napoleon. Far from being the end of civilization, the war would be the end of civilization's illnesses; and when it was over, and England had been cured, there would still be art, and organized society, and men of letters.

In arguing in this vein, these critics were doing something that at first seems very odd in the first days of a patriotic and popular war — they were blaming England for it. Or if not exactly England, then the softness into which England had fallen in the pre-war years. Part of the argument was that English self-indulgence, and English tolerance of disruptive movements like Irish nationalism and Suffragism, had encouraged the Germans to think that England would not and could not fight. A more important part, though, was the assumption that the Germans were right: that Englishmen had abandoned the high austere ideals of conduct that had made the Empire great, and had sunk into a too-comfortable, too-prosperous Edwardian decadence. War became, in this argument, a true English activity, and peace became vaguely foreign. This notion — what Hilaire Belloc called 'the fruitful vision of a re-creative war'[26] — would continue in circulation until enough men had experienced war as it actually was to deny it.

Such critics did not, of course, solve the problem of art and war; they simply denied that it existed. If there was no new reality to be confronted, then there could be no problem of representation; the world was the same, and the old modes of imagining it at war would be adequate. This was no doubt a comforting position to take; it relieved the critics of the difficult task of thinking their way to a new aesthetic, and made them seem patriotic for not doing so. But it was not a productive one (and none of the critics who took it was a creative artist of any importance). No important work of art from the war years can be said to be based on their notions of the relations between war and art, though plenty of negligible war art was, as we shall see.

III

What the new relationship between war and art would have to be, Henry James had seen at once, and with despair. For James was old when the war began — he would die before it was half-over — and though he could perceive the problem that the war posed, he could not turn his insight into art. There was, indeed, only one writer in England then who came near to doing so at the war's beginning — H.G. Wells. Wells may seem an unlikely person to take up a Jamesian theme: we tend to think of him as a journalist-prophet who wrote brilliant science fiction and some rather hasty social novels — a kind of anti-James, in fact. But Wells had admired James, as the correspondence between the two writers shows, and he had shared some of James's faith in the civilizing power of literature. And when the war came, he felt a despair at the failure of that faith that was as deep as James's. In the autumn of 1914, Wells was a divided man — one side journalist, you might say, and the other side James. The journalist was gloriously busy supporting the war: in August 1914 alone he wrote eleven war articles, which before the end of the year were collected and published in a book with a title that became first the war's greatest cliché and then its bitterest irony: *The War That Will End War*. And he continued through the autumn months, with articles like 'The Need for Strength and Clearness at Home', 'The Most Splendid Fighting in the World' (on war in the air), and 'If England is Raided'. They are not very individual, not very Wellsian-sounding essays; indeed the most striking thing about them is the way they seem to speak with a different, 'official' voice — more like the voice of Edmund Gosse than of Wells. Take as an example this passage from 'The Most Splendid Fighting in the World':

> One talks and reads of the heroic age and how the world has degenerated. But indeed this is the heroic age, suddenly come again. No legendary feats of the past, no battle with dragons or monstrous beasts, no quest or feat that man has hitherto attempted can compare with this adventure, in terror, danger and splendour.[27]

How readily Wells assumes the Condition of England position: the world had degenerated in peacetime, but war has restored the heroic age. It is the rhetoric of the most jingoistic journalists, a rhetoric that Wells ought to have despised. And he *did* despise it — only not in the *Daily Chronicle*.

As if that weren't enough war activity, Wells began a campaign, early

in August, to organize an irregular army of the old, the unfit, and the
Boy Scouts: 'Nobody', he wrote, 'wants to be a non-combatant in a war
of this sort.'[28] His first notion was that this rag-tag army would be there
to defend England against the German attacks that he was warning
about in his journalism, but in a few months its function had become
less restricted; it would serve, Wells wrote in October, 'as a guarantee of
national discipline under any unexpected stress'[29] — which seemed to
include revolution and civil war as well as invasion. But whether the
enemy turned out to be Germans, or other Englishmen (or Irishmen, or
women, or even Futurists), it was clear that Wells would be at the head
of his troops.

That was one side of Wells, the ebullient, fanciful, journalistic side.
But there was also the other Wells. In those same autumn months this
Wells, unable to write a novel, turned up 'some old papers' and
reworked them into *Boon* (or, to give the book its full title, *Boon: The
Mind of the Race, The Wild Asses of the Devil, and The Last Trump: being a
First Selection from the Literary Remains of George Boon, appropriate to the
Times*). Wells described *Boon* as 'just a waste-paper basket',[30] but it is a
good deal more than that; it is the first important English war book. It is
not *about* the war, in the sense of describing fighting; it is, rather, an
account, and in its curious form a kind of model, of the problem that
James had perceived — the problem of being a writer at a time when
reality has changed, and for the worse.

Boon is offered to its readers as the posthumous papers of George
Boon, a popular Edwardian writer who has just died, early in the war
but of natural causes. The papers have been gathered and edited, the title
page explains, by Boon's friend Reginald Bliss; Wells's name appears
only as the author of 'An Ambiguous Introduction'. Bliss's editing
consists of stringing the pieces together, with explanatory transitions
and comments by himself, to make what amounts to a history of Boon's
anger at the follies of the Edwardian peace, and the greater follies of the
war.

Wells apparently wrote the first two papers — 'The Mind of the Race'
and 'The Wild Asses of the Devil — in 1911, when he was smarting
from the attacks made on *Ann Veronica*, and his increasing disfavour
with Edwardian literary society. In a preface written after the war, he
described his motives:

He [Wells] had been bored intolerably by the pretentious solemnity
of various contemporary literary artists and critics; he had been

patronised and reproved by them to the limit of endurance, and he
wrote 'The Mind of the Race', a bundle of personalities and parodies,
to relieve his mind.[31]

The personalities and parodies are explicit, and often very personal.
Wells attacked old acquaintances by name, both in his text and in the
clever satirical drawings that accompany it: Shaw, Ford Madox Hueffer,
Conrad, James, Mrs Humphry Ward, Roger Fry, Wyndham Lewis are
all mentioned; so are the *English Review* and the *New Age*, the two most
advanced literary journals of the time. The late Edwardian cultural scene
is elaborately developed, and elaborately ridiculed — including even
Wells himself.

All this is mildly interesting, as evidence that dissatisfaction with
Edwardian culture existed before the war; but if that were all there was
to *Boon* we would not be lingering over it. Wells himself thought that
'there was something more than litererary badinage in this work of the
year 1911', and described that something more as 'the author's deepening recognition, half derisive, half terrified, of the increasing dangerous-
ness of political and international affairs'.[32] That quality — a tone of rage
and despair — seems in fact to have been what Wells added when he took
up his 'old papers' in the autumn of 1914. Like James, he must have felt
that the Edwardian age he had been ridiculing shared the responsibility
for what had happened in August, that it was not simply ridiculous, it
was also culpable. And so he framed the papers in an account of Boon's
last days, and killed off his Edwardian self.

The story of those last days is one of lost idealism — a sour and angry
version of James's grief at what the war really meant. Boon mocks at the
Great Reputations, including his own, and at the pre-war world that had
created and sustained them. 'At least the Germans stand for something,'
he cries from his sick-bed:

> It may be brutal, stupid, intolerable, but there it is — a definite
> intention, a scheme of living, an order, Germanic Kultur. But what
> the devil do we stand for? Was there anything that amounted to an
> intellectual life at all, in all our beastly welter of writing, of nice-
> young-man poetry, of stylish fiction and fiction without style, of lazy
> history, popular philosophy, slobbering criticism, Academic civili-
> ties? Is there anything here to hold a people together? Is there
> anything to make a new world? A literature ought to dominate the
> mind of its people. Yet here comes the gale, and all we have to
> show for our racial thought, all the fastness we have made for our

souls, is a flying scud of paper scraps, poems, such poems! casual
articles, whirling headlong in the air, a few novels drowning in the
floods . . .[33]

Literature has failed England, and Boon dies more out of rage at the
failure than anything else.

Wells also added some satirical particulars, including an extraordinarily savage attack on the profession of letters in wartime London, as

*Mr Osborn's dream of himself as a Prussian
Spartan refreshing himself with Hero's food
(fresh human liver) and drink (blood and
champagne) after a good Go In at some
Pacificist softs.*

personified by E.B. Osborn, a patriotic journalist on the *Morning Post*. Wells devoted some ten pages of abusive prose and five derisive drawings to poor Osborn: 'The embodiment of the Heroic Spirit', he called him, 'one of your gentlemen who sit in a room full of books and promise themselves much moral benefit from the bloodshed in France.' (Wells had no doubt been offended by passages like this one, from an Osborn article entitled 'The Heroic Spirits': 'I myself seek equanimity nowadays chiefly in the company of Greek and Roman poets — men for whom war rather than peace was the natural order of things . . .[34]) Wells hated the idea that war might be considered natural, or even beneficial: 'War', Boon says, 'does nothing but destroy.'

As an act of imagination *Boon* is entirely negative. It is a destructive book, even a self-destructive one; its form is a destruction of form, a broken narrative put together out of unfinished pieces from the repudiated past, by an invented editor who doesn't even understand Boon's rage. Its fragmentation does not become a new kind of form, as *The Waste Land*'s fragments do; it remains in fragments, an evidence of the past life that had failed. One might say that it offered to its time a model of the smash-up of Edwardian values, but it was a model that could be of no use to other English writers in wartime. For all that Wells had to say (and show) about art and war was that they are incompatible; war destroys everything, including poor, foolish, civilized art. The questions that James had posed remained unanswered.

Wells is an important writer for the cultural historian, even in his relative failures, because he was himself always an historian — of the immediate present, or of the moment that had just passed, or on occasion of the future. His ideas were always up-to-date, or a bit beyond, and so were his feelings. It is the feelings in *Boon* that are most important, and two feelings in particular: the feeling that the pre-war world should be not simply forgotten, but rejected, because it had been wrong; and the feeling that between that world and the world-at-war there was a discontinuity, a gap in history that could not be bridged. These feelings would in time become commonplaces that would be fundamental to post-war attitudes towards the pre-war past, but Wells was the first to give them articulate expression in a work of imagination. For that reason *Boon* deserves a place at the beginning: it is the first war book that matters.

CHAPTER 2

The Arts Enlist

I

War, the critics said, would be good for the arts in England. But was it? The immediate effect was certainly negative: a sense of paralysis, a crisis of values, an emptiness where Edwardian culture had been. But it is the nature of war to fill such vacuums with its own values, and ultimately to make the prosecution of war the *only* value. Before long, most English writers and artists were involved in one way or another in the war: Galsworthy raised funds for War Relief, Forster was a fire-watcher and cataloguer in the National Gallery, Brooke enlisted, Henry James helped Belgian refugees, and Gosse, always a great scrounger of manuscripts from his literary friends, turned his acquisitiveness to patriotic ends by begging books, manuscripts, and autographs from the same writers, for sale at Red Cross charity bazaars. Only Lawrence remained aloof and uncommitted.

English writers were also quick to support the war *as writers*. The first 'war poem', Henry Newbolt's 'The Vigil', appeared in *The Times* on the morning of August 5 (the British ultimatum to Germany had expired at 11 p.m. the previous evening). Newbolt had written the lines sixteen years earlier, but he had done so, he told a friend, in mystical anticipation of this moment: 'that they should be printed — after sixteen years — at the exact midnight for which they were written, gives me a strange sense of an Omniscience . . . a not-here dominating the here.'[1] From that day on, there were almost daily war poems in *The Times*, by Poet Laureate Robert Bridges, Kipling, Maurice Hewlett, Edmund Gosse, Laurence Binyon and William Watson, and many less-known and never-to-be-known poets. During August 1914 as many as a hundred poems a day arrived at *The Times*, and though the number declined somewhat thereafter, several thousand had been received by the following August.[2]

Prose writers also hurried into print. Wells poured out his stream of articles on military subjects, and filled in spare moments writing letters to editors. His friend Arnold Bennett was almost as copious. Bennett had begun by thinking the war a mistake for England (like many an Englishman then and a generation later, he thought that Russia was the real enemy); but a week after the war began he wrote in his journal: 'I am in *full* work, and only a defeat of the Allies will put me off work.'[3] Between August 4 and the end of 1914 he published twenty-eight articles on aspects of the war.

Popular journalists like Bennett and Wells would have written about the war without encouragement, but more retiring writers might not; the British government made their participation easier by organizing men of letters on its own behalf. Less than a month after the declaration of war, C.F.G. Masterman, who had been put in charge of a new Department of Information (that is, of British propaganda), summoned a number of writers to the department offices at Wellington House 'for the organization of public statements of the strength of the British case and principles in the war by well-known men of letters.'[4] At the meeting on September 2 were James Barrie, Bennett, A.C. Benson, Hugh Benson, Bridges, Hall Caine, G.K. Chesterton, Arthur Conan Doyle, Galsworthy, Thomas Hardy, Anthony Hope Hawkins, Maurice Hewlett, W.J. Locke, E.V. Lucas, J.W. Mackail, John Masefield, A.E.W. Mason, Gilbert Murray, Henry Newbolt, Owen Seaman, G.M. Trevelyan, Wells, and Israel Zangwill. Rudyard Kipling and Arthur Quiller-Couch, who could not be there, sent messages promising their services. Masterman had identified the pillars of the Edwardian literary establishment (of which he was himself a minor member), and had mustered them, conscripted them almost, into government service.

But he had made one crucial mistake: almost all of his chosen writers were too old for military service. Hardy, the eldest, was seventy-four; Masefield, the youngest, was thirty-six; the average age was just over fifty. From a soldier's point of view they were old men, and as the war went on they would seem less and less to have the right to make moral statements about it. The concept of the Old Men, as the makers of the war and enemies of the young, had many origins; but one was certainly that meeting at Wellington House in September 1914, when those middle-aged and old writers gathered to support a war in which they would not fight.

One effect of Masterman's meeting was a further burst of war writing: Hardy, for example, seems to have gone straight home from the meeting to compose 'Men Who March Away' (the poem is dated September 5, 1914). But a more general, and more significant, consequence of the meeting was that from the earliest days of the war there was an 'official' war literature, a literature that articulated the government's version of the causes and moral issues of the conflict, and supported the government's determination to continue the fighting.

This commitment of writers to the war was not allowed to be a merely private matter; two weeks after Masterman had gathered them, the twenty-five members of his original group were joined by another twenty-five writers in an 'Authors' Declaration', published in *The Times* (and in the *New York Times* the same day). This statement began:

> The undersigned writers, comprising amongst them men and women of the most divergent political and social views, some of them having been for years ardent champions of good will towards Germany, and many of them extreme advocates of peace, are nevertheless agreed that Great Britain could not without dishonour have refused to take part in the present war.

The principal reasons offered were the defence of Belgian neutrality and the prevention of the ruin of France. The declaration concluded:

> For these reasons and others the undersigned feel bound to support the cause of the Allies with all their strength, with a full conviction of its righteousness, and with a deep sense of its vital import to the future of the world.[5]

The new supporters included four women (there had been none in the original group): Jane Ellen Harrison, May Sinclair, Flora Annie Steel, and Mrs Humphry Ward. Other new names included William Archer, Granville Barker, Rider Haggard, Jerome K. Jerome, Henry Arthur Jones, and Arthur Pinero. None of these is a surprising addition: they extended but did not alter Masterman's original intention, that the most respectable and established writers in England should instantly and publicly support the war. No other war in England's history had been defined and defended so quickly, and by writers of such stature.

This enlistment of the literary establishment was a mode of warfare without precedent, and one can't help wondering why the government felt it to be necessary. One reasonable answer is that in 1914 the government depended for its continuance on the support of a more literate portion of the population than ever before. Late Victorian legislation had raised the general level of literacy and extended the franchise: consequently there were more voters in England to be persuaded of the rightness of the nation's cause, and they could be persuaded in writing.

There were also potential soldiers to persuade, for this was to be a war fought by volunteers. And for the first time in English military history they would be *literate* volunteers — young clerks and young artists, students from Oxford and Eton, the sons of peers and the sons of parsons, men from all classes, but sharing a common literacy. In the past it had been different. Until the end of the nineteenth century English armies had been made up largely of illiterate and semi-literate troops commanded by gentlemen. The Boer War was the first English war to be fought after the Education Act of 1870, and many of the men who fought in it could read and write; but one can judge the level of their literacy by the fact that no writing of any importance was produced by the fighting soldiers, and that no one who subsequently became a major writer or artist served among them.[6]

It was clear by the end of 1914 that this war would be different — it would be the most literary and the most poetical war in English history, before or since. One could learn that from the pages of *The Times*, or the *Morning Post*, or the *Daily Chronicle*, or the *Westminster Gazette*, where war poems appeared as regularly as first leaders. Or at any bookshop, where anthologies of war poetry appeared with astonishing rapidity — three in September 1914, another in November, twelve in 1915, six more in 1916. Some of the poets in these volumes were well-known figures from Masterman's group — Bridges, Hardy, Chesterton, Hewlett and Kipling are all in the first wave of anthologies — but most were a good deal less familiar. Who today has heard of Henry Chappell, 'The Bath Railway Porter'? Or of Harold Begbie? Or of Cope, Fagan, Grogan, Gyles, Moberley, Holmes, or Bliss? But there they all are, among the war poets.

By November 1914 there were enough bad war poems in print to inspire an anti-war-poem poem, 'Song: in War-Time', published in *The Egoist*. It begins:

> At the sound of the drum
> Out of their dens they come, they come,
> The little poets we hoped were dumb,
> The little poets we thought were dead,

> The poets who certainly haven't been read
> Since Heaven knows when, they come, they come
> At the sound of the drum, of the drum, drum, drum.[7]

And they continued to come. As the war continued, more and more poems came from serving soldiers, so many that eventually the *Westminster Gazette* had to declare a moratorium on poems from the front.[8]

We later readers think of the war poetry of the First World War as having been written by such soldier-poets, and it is true that the poems we are likely to read and value today were written by them. But the mass of war poetry was not. A recent bibliography of English poetry of the First World War lists over 3,000 works by 2,225 poets; of these poets, less than a quarter were in uniform. Another quarter were women. So more than half must have been male civilians (as war poets from Homer to Kipling had traditionally been). Within months this kind of poetry — the 'official' poems by Masterman's regiment of writers, and the unofficial imitations of them — was already a vast heap of work, similar in conventions, in rhetoric, and in values. This heap would continue to grow throughout the war, and even after the peace.

The swift appearance of so much war poetry could not go unnoticed, and by mid-September of 1914 articles and reviews were appearing in the reviewing journals. Reading through these early pieces, one gets a strong sense of a common critical problem: how does a conscientious critic, who is also as keen a patriot as the next man, judge poetry that is at once patriotic and inept? To their credit, most of the critics stuck to their literary standards. Harold Monro, then editor of *Poetry and Drama*, simply announced to his readers that he could find no war poetry worth publishing, and chided the popular press for having lower standards than he had. 'The war poetry that has appeared in the press,' he wrote,

> does not seem to have represented an exalted, a natural, or even a valuable form of patriotism . . . We get an impression of verse-writers excitedly gathering to *do something* for their flag, and as soon as they begin to rack their brains how that something may be done in verse, a hundred old phrases for patriotic moments float in their minds, which they reel into verse or fit into sonnets — and the press is delighted to publish them.[9]

Reviewers on the more popular weeklies were generally as severe as Monro about the literary qualities of the war poems, but more generous about the patriotic content: the poems were mediocre, unpromising, old-fashioned, stilted, mere metrical prose — the judgements were often quite fierce — but they contained a fine spirit, noble intentions, or at least sincerity. The general conclusion was that nothing good had yet appeared, but that a new age of poetry was surely coming.[10]

Though these critics did not find much war poetry that they could praise, they knew what they were looking for. Monro wanted an 'exalted' form of patriotism, and Clutton Brock said much the same thing more elaborately in describing the duty of war poets:

> it is the very essence of their business to be magnifying mirrors of that fraction of our life which is great and significant. And so, though they are far more aware than they used to be of the ugly and stupid side of war, they will still, and quite rightly, for the most part pass all that by and insist that for them the thing that matters in war is not the waste and loss of the body and the goods of the body, but the escape of the spirit into that eternal world in which bodily death is as nothing compared with the triumph of an idea.[11]

This is a fair statement of what we might call the General Principle of War Poetry at the beginning of the war. It is an idea of poetry based not on the war itself — that is, on *these* men killing *those* men — but on the *idea* of war, which in turn is based on the poetry of the past. Clutton Brock built his argument on examples from the past, from the *Iliad* to 'The Charge of the Light Brigade': poets have always seen war as heroic, therefore it must have its heroic side (could Homer and Tennyson have been wrong?), and it is the duty of poets to magnify that side.

That was reasonable enough advice for poets in 1914: how else could you write a poem about a war that had scarcely begun, except by imitating past examples? That, after all, is what tradition is for. Most of the poets and would-be poets turned to the heroic poetry of the past, and made their poems out of its magnifying rhetoric. And most of their critics saw that what they wrote was bad. But only a few saw that the problem was in part a rhetorical one, that as John Palmer put it, 'language has rather got in their way than helped them to sing as they would wish.'[12] The new age of war poetry would not come until a new rhetoric evolved, a rhetoric that could express a new and radically different general principle — one that rejected the old idealism, the exaltation and the escape of the spirit and all that, and confronted what Clutton Brock had urged poets to pass by: 'the ugly and stupid side of war'.

But not all of the early war poets turned to heroic poetry and high rhetoric for their models; there were other resources in the English poetic tradition, in the Romantic lyric and the elegy, and a few moving poems were written in this quiet, unheroic mode. Later taste in war poetry, based as it is on the style and themes of soldier-poets like Owen and Sassoon, has tended to ignore these earlier works (you will not find them in the major anthologies of war poems). But not all of them are without merit or interest; an ignorant, middle-aged civilian will not write about war in the way that a young subaltern will, but he may write movingly nonetheless. Some war poems of 1914 and 1915 are touching, I think, partly because they are so ignorant, and so wrong in their expectations of what the war will be.

Take, as an example, Masefield's 'August 1914'. It was published in the September 1914 issue of the *English Review*, and is probably Masefield's response to the appeal that Masterman had made to writers earlier in the month. Clutton Brock thought it the finest poem that the war had so far produced, and Ivor Gurney called it 'the best of the war poems'.[13] One might perhaps dismiss Clutton Brock as a conservative and ignorant civilian, but Gurney was in the trenches when he wrote his comment.

What was it in the poem that made it seem excellent both to the critic at home and the soldier at the Front? Primarily, I think, it was its traditional style; in its elegiac evocation of the English countryside and the English past it has more of Gray and Arnold and Tennyson in its slow pentameter lines than of Masefield. It begins:

> How still this quiet cornfield is to-night;
> By an intenser glow the evening falls,
> Bringing, not darkness, but a deeper light;
> Among the stooks a partridge covey calls.

And after further description

> These homes, this valley spread below me here,
> The rooks, the tilted stacks, the beasts in pen,
> Have been the heartfelt things, past-speaking dear
> To unknown generations of dead men ...[14]

These were men who left England 'And died (uncouthly, most) in foreign lands' because they loved the English earth. Masefield's poem is about continuity, linking the soldiers of 1914 with past volunteers and this war with past English wars. Its form is a demonstration of another kind of continuity — the continuity of literary tradition.

'August 1914' is the only war poem that Masefield published; yet of all the Georgian poets he had the fullest experience of war. He worked in military hospitals in France, went to Gallipoli during the disastrous campaign there, and in 1917 spent weeks walking over the battlefields of the Somme offensive. Out of these experiences came three prose books — *Gallipoli*, *The Old Front Line*, and *The Battle of the Somme* — but no published poems. Not that he didn't try to write them. The pocket notebook that he carried during his walking tours of the Somme contains drafts of more than a dozen poems, of which four or five refer in some way to the war. But of these, only one addresses the experience of war directly, in a chronicle of the growth of a man from childhood to his death in the trenches. It is a kind of refutation of the idealism of 'August 1914', and refers to the war as 'this crime, / This hell of evil / This bloody smear on Time'. Clearly Masefield felt deeply what this poem says: yet he never finished or published it.[15]

Why not? one wonders. Was it that by 1917 war poems were being written by men who had fought on those battlefields that Masefield had merely visited? Masefield was a man who was modest about his powers of imagination; when he wrote about the Somme in *The Old Front Line* he explained to his readers that he could only describe the scene as it was after the fighting; 'What it was like on the day of battle cannot be imagined by those who were not there.'[16] Perhaps in the presence of such witnesses he chose to be silent.

Masefield offered another explanation in the introduction he wrote, near the end of the war, for an American edition of his poems and plays. 'When the war began,' he explained,

> I wrote some verses, called *August, 1914*, which at the time I thought of calling *Lollingdon Hill*, from the little chalk hill on which they were written. Some other verses were written in the first months of the war, including some of the sonnets; but that was the end of my verse-writing. Perhaps, when the war is over and the mess of the war is cleaned up and the world is at some sort of peace, there may be leisure and feeling for verse-making. One may go back to that life in the mind, in which the eyes of the mind see butterflies and petals of blossoms blowing from the unseen world of beauty into this world. In that life, if it comes again, one may not be too old to look towards that world of beauty, and to see it and tell of it.[17]

Masefield is here confessing himself unchanged as a poet by the war — still a Georgian, at the end of the romantic tradition, still believing that poetry is made out of natural beauty, and plain, traditional words. Before he knew what war was, he could write a war poem in that tradition — that is what 'August 1914' is; but once he had been there, and seen 'the ugly and stupid side of war', he felt his poetic voice silenced. He could not write war poems on the old principles; and he could not imagine other principles that would make war poetically possible. Rather than write false war poetry, he wrote prose.

'August 1914' is an elegy for the lost peace of the English countryside, and for the men who would leave it to die in the war. It is also an elegy for a kind of poetry. In August 1914 a poet could write about English landscape in frankly emotional terms, could draw upon the traditional English past both for his subject and for his method, taking his place in the continuity of literary history without embarrassment. After the war that would not be possible; for one of the discontinuities that the war would create would be the break with the literary past that would become a principle of post-war Modernism, and would make poets like Masefield casualties of war.

II

One tends to think of the arts of the First World War primarily in terms of poetry; but the other arts were also quick to respond to the presence of war. Almost as quickly as books of war poems appeared in the shops, exhibitions of war paintings opened in London galleries. The first of these shows, titled simply 'Some Modern War Pictures', opened in Bond Street in October 1914. The Battle of the Marne had just ended, and trench warfare had begun, but there were no trenches, no Germans, and no Marne to be seen in Bond Street. Instead, there were paintings of British naval vessels at sea, and of Napoleonic battles. The artists were A. Chevallier Tayler, who did the ships, and R. Caton Woodville, who did the battles.[18] I have not seen any of the paintings from this show, but reviews did make perfectly clear what the artists had done: they had taken two traditional military subjects — the seascape with man-of-war, and the battle-scene with generals — and had simply done them again. In doing so they had also repeated two traditional ideas about war: that arms and armaments are romantic, and that military leaders are heroic. Both ideas would turn up again and again before the war was over, often with official government sanction.

In January 1915 another kind of exhibition opened at the Leicester Galleries (which had been, and would be again, the principal home of modern English art in London). This was a show of war pictures by the painter William Strang, and of satiric drawings by the cartoonist Will Dyson. In both cases the approach was essentially allegorical. Strang's pictures included an etching, titled simply 'War', of a uniformed skeleton beating a drum (an image that goes back to the fifteenth-century Dance of Death woodcuts), and an oil painting, 'Harvest', showing a brightly coloured harvest field with, in the foreground, a man lying shot dead. Dyson's drawings were what you'd expect of a wartime cartoonist: the Kaiser hanging an Iron Cross on a bestial soldier, an airplane full of apes bombing a city (see plate 2).

Like Tayler's ships and Woodville's Napoleons, these pictures by Strang and Dyson were pictures not of war, but of *ideas* of war — traditional images, made out of previous images, to express traditional ideas: one could call them 'war pictures' only if the word *war* is understood to refer to a concept, and not to contemporary events. They belong, that is, to the world of Gosse and Newbolt and Clutton Brock, not to the world of actual men in actual battle. (The same might be said of 'The Man of To-day', a painting by Barribal that the London tailors Pope and Bradley ran in the art journal *Colour* in November 1915 'to assist recruiting', in which war is represented primarily as a change of clothes — see plate 1).

In neither the art exhibitions nor the tailor's advertisement was there any representation of the war that was being fought in France; of course there couldn't be — none of the artists had been there. That fact, like the inherited images of war, was part of the tradition: Uccello had not been at the Battle of San Romano, Antoine Gros had not been at Eylau, Lady Butler had not charged with the Scots Greys at Waterloo. The First World War would see the end of that absentee tradition, and the beginning of another, in which painters did at least their preliminary work *en plain air* — a phrase that would take on a rather different meaning on the Somme from what it had for Monet on the Seine.

Through the following months there were other exhibitions in London that included war paintings — a Sickert in the New English Art Club's show in December, a couple of Nevinsons in the London Group's in March 1915, Belgian war scenes at the International show in May, nine pictures by various hands in the Royal Academy Summer Exhibition — but scarcely any of them impressed the critics. The *Times* review of the Royal Academy show, for example, was headlined 'The

War in Art', and listed the war pictures in the exhibition; but the
reviewer observed that none of them was interesting: 'The war has not
suddenly inspired British art with a new seriousness and simplicity,' he
wrote; 'but no one could expect it to do that, and we shall not give
ourselves the cheap pleasure of rebuking our painters because they are
not new-born since August.'[19]

There was one exception, though; Walter Sickert, the best, and best
known, of living English painters, did seem to have been changed by
the war, to the great excitement of reviewers (and of some critics since).
'We have been waiting with great curiosity,' the *Morning Post*'s reviewer
wrote,

> to see what effect the war would have on British artists. Prior to
> Monday there was no sign of its influence on their ideas or outlook.
> But its effect is now vividly and salutarily apparent in a large painting
> by Mr Sickert, who we never expected would be moved by topical
> events, however stirring . . . But the glamour of physical warfare has
> aroused him from the gloomy analysis of unsavoury types to the
> representation of nobler specimens of humanity. 'The Soldiers of
> King Albert the Ready' may be dismissed by some critics as uncen-
> sored pictorial journalism. To us, however, it suggests unlimited
> possibilities. Mr. Sickert might well become the first great military
> painter of England. . .[20]

This comment is another version of war-as-purification, like Gosse on
Condy's Fluid; the glamour of war, in this critic's view, had saved
Sickert from Camden Town squalor.

'The Soldiers of King Albert the Ready' (see plate 5) is a curious sport
in Sickert's career — a large picture painted at a time when Sickert was
painting small ones, melodramatically composed and lit and strongly
outlined (neither a characteristic of Sickert's work), and with an heroic
public subject, when Sickert's reputation was for obscure domestic
interiors. Sickert painted it partly because he was moved by the
sufferings of the Belgian people during the German invasion of their
country, and wanted to contribute the picture to the Belgian Relief
Fund. But he was also momentarily stimulated by the idea of war as a
subject. To get the details right he worked from photographs, and
from bits of uniform and equipment he borrowed from Belgian soldiers
in London hospitals. 'One has a kind of distaste for using misfortunes to
further one's own ends,' he wrote to a friend. 'But pictures of Belgian
incidents so far as they have any effect can be useful. Besides if military

painters had always been too bloody delicate they never would have got anything done at all.'[21]

At this point, then, in the midst of painting his picture, Sickert was thinking of himself both as a benefactor of Belgians and as a military painter. While the mood lasted he painted one other large painting, 'The Integrity of Belgium', which must have resembled 'The Soldiers', though it is now lost. Two other pictures of the same period (the autumn of 1914) are titled 'Tipperary' and 'Wounded', and sound military enough; but in these instances what Sickert had done was to paint two pictures in his old domestic-interior manner — a woman playing the piano while a man listens, a man lying in a bed with a woman leaning over him — and give them topical titles. To be sure the man in 'Tipperary' is a soldier, and the woman in 'Wounded' is a Red Cross nurse, but the war, the weapons, the precisely rendered uniforms, and most of all the martial spirit have all gone. By the end of 1914 Sickert's brief career as a military painter was over.

English musicians responded to the coming of war even more quickly than the painters did. At the first Prom concert of the season, on August 15, the orchestra played both 'God Save the King' and the 'Marseillaise', and the audience rose to sing both, though apparently with more passion than precision; 'with a little better acquaintance with the words of the former and the tune of the latter,' one critic remarked drily, 'so musical an audience might produce a wonderful effect.'[22] Audiences would get plenty of practice before the war ended: at some concerts as many as five national anthems opened the programme.

Not everyone was moved by them. Virginia Woolf wrote of a Queen's Hall concert in January 1915 that 'the patriotic sentiment was so revolting that I was nearly sick', and Clive Bell complained that 'even at concerts our ears are exasperated by national platitudes and the banalities of our Allies'[23] — though he might have been thinking of the *other* banalities, the third-rate compositions that were thrust into programmes simply because they were by Belgian, or Russian, or French composers.

The banalities were not always old ones. 'Tipperary', a song that had been written in 1912, became popular when soldiers of the New Army made it their marching song. It was sung so often that Ivor Novello's mother found it tiresome, and asked her son to write an alternative (or so one story goes).[24] He obliged by writing 'Keep the Home Fires Burning'; it was performed at a National Sunday League Concert in the autumn of 1914, and was an instant success — and became just as

tiresome in its turn. New patriotic songs began almost at once to
appear in English musical journals[25] and in concert programmes. Lord
Tennyson, the poet's son, found an unpublished poem by his father
titled 'A Call to Arms', which Emily Lady Tennyson set to music, with
some help from Sir Frederick Bridge; it was sung at the Albert Hall
by the Royal Choral Society on October 10. In the same month a
new poem by England's most popular patriotic poet — 'The King's
Highway' by Henry Newbolt — was sung at a Prom concert, in a
setting by Sir Charles Stanford.

Neither Tennyson's nor Newbolt's song seems to have made much
impression on musicians, audiences, or critics. But a new work first
performed in December 1914 did. When Sir Edward Elgar conducted
'Carillon', his setting of a poem by the Belgian poet Emile Cammaerts,
at a concert of the London Symphony Orchestra on December 7, it
was instantly acclaimed. Yet it seems to have nothing in common with
the general run of English patriotic poems and songs of the time.
Cammaerts had written a *Belgian* war poem, and at the end of 1914 that
meant a poem not of conflict but of defeat. The German army had swept
through Belgium in the first weeks of the war, killing and burning, and
had continued south towards the Marne, leaving Belgium a defeated,
occupied country, from which those who could had fled. Cammaerts's
poem begins:

> *Chantons, Belges, chantons,*
> *Même si les blessures saignent, même si la voix se brise,*
> *Plaus haut que la tourmente, plus fort que les canons,*
> *Chantons l'orgueil de nos défaites,*
> *Par ce beau soleil d'automne,*
> *Et la joie de rester honnête*
> *Quand la lacheté nous serait si bonne.*[26]

'Carillon' is an unusual composition — not a sung setting of the poem
but an accompaniment for a spoken recitation, with the orchestra
providing a prelude and interludes between stanzas of the poem, and
falling silent, or nearly so, during the spoken passages. The work begins
in the confident, declarative manner of the Pomp and Circumstance
marches — which is no doubt what Elgar's admirers expected of him —
but it moves quickly into a quite different mood, sombre and elegiac
and marked by descending sequences of notes that are like tolling bells,
and thereafter the two moods intermingle. It was as though Elgar
already understood that the heroic musical tradition would not be

sufficient to express this war — that there would have to be a music of grief, too. As recited by the poet's wife, the English actress Tita Brand, 'Carillon' made a powerful impression on the first-night audience: 'The combined work of poet, composer (who conducted), and reciter was received with almost frenzied enthusiasm by a large audience,' the *Musical Times* reported[27], and there were many curtain calls. What, exactly, was that audience responding to? A melodramatic poem in French by a little-known Belgian? His wife's impassioned performance? The presence of England's greatest living composer on the podium? The idea of suffering Belgium? Or all of these, brought together on one emotional evening in a wartime that was still new and exciting? Certainly the critics didn't share it: 'If this is all that the tragedy of Belgium can bring from a musician,' the *Times* reviewer wrote, 'it seems a small tribute.'[28] But small tribute or large, 'Carillon' was a success. Elgar toured with it during 1915, and performed it many times in London: 'Orchestral concerts in London are at present divisible into two classes,' *The Times* observed in May 1915; 'those which secure large audiences to listen to Elgar's "Carillon", and those which secure small ones for other music.'[29]

Elgar went on to set other patriotic poems — 'Le Drapeau Belge' and 'Une Voix dans le desert' by Cammaerts, 'For the Fallen', 'To Women', and 'The Fourth of August' by Laurence Binyon, and four poems from *The Fringes of the Fleet* by Kipling. These poems were all written early in the war — the Cammaerts and Binyon poems in the first eight months, Kipling's in the autumn of 1915 — but Elgar's settings came slowly; the last of Binyon's was finished in March 1917, the last by Cammaerts in the following month, those by Kipling in June 1917. In the case of 'For the Fallen' the delay was circumstantial: another composer had begun setting the poem, and Elgar abstained for a while, only completing his own version after the competing one had been published. And of course he was busy during those early war years with other things. Still, he seems to have taken a long time to complete such relatively simple compositions.

He was aware that to the poets concerned he must seem dilatory. When at last he finished the Binyon settings in April 1917 he wrote apologetically to the poet:

> I fear I have been a very long time, but the difficulty over the one poem last year put me off somewhat & it has taken me all this time to overtake the first careful rapture.[30]

It had clearly been a trying task.

Elgar had trouble completing the setting of war poems, yet he went on working at them. Why? The simplest explanation is that he was acting out of a sense of duty, a feeling that by making music appropriate to these poems he was contributing to the war effort — raising morale, encouraging the Belgians, cheering on the Navy, doing the sorts of things that Masterman had asked his collection of writers to do. And he had chosen poems that addressed those matters, and did so in the high style of the established tradition of war poetry. That they were poems that spoke to Elgar's sense of himself as an Englishman I have no doubt; he had, after all, written the Pomp and Circumstance marches. But they don't seem to have engaged him as a composer. They would require a popular kind of music, the kind that would reach and move the people, and Elgar did not fancy himself in that role. When his friend Sidney Colvin wrote to him in April 1915, urging him to complete 'For the Fallen', Elgar replied:

> Some of my dear friends appeal to me to work in order that the people — musical people — may have something really good (that is complimentary to me and, inferentially, to the B.P. [British Public] — something they really want — well, they do not want me & never did. If I work at all it is not for them.[31]

Elgar was writing for the B.P., yet *not* writing for them; making war music, yet dissociating himself from the audience for such music. No wonder his settings were slow in coming. When they were finally completed, in mid-1917, Elgar turned away, firmly and finally, from the patriotic and popular, and from the B.P.

III

In the first months of the war, theatre managers scurried to find something military to put on their stages. There were revivals of patriotic plays like *Tommy Atkins* and *On His Majesty's Service*, and new productions of *Henry IV Part One* and *Henry V*, and Granville Barker's staging of scenes from Hardy's *Dynasts*. The first *new* war play to be produced was *England Expects* —, by the actor Seymour Hicks and Arnold Bennett's sometime collaborator Edward Knoblauch, which opened on September 15. The play was described in the press as a 'recruiting drama', and the published announcement of the opening makes that description seem exact.

> The performance [the *Times* report read] will be preceded by cinematograph pictures of the Army in times of peace, as well as the most recent war films. Several prominent actors have promised to recite 'The Charge of the Light Brigade' and other appropriate poems at the various performances.
>
> Recruiting officers will be in attendance at the theatre all day. A free concert and military music will be given in the lobby before each performance. There will be a daily *matinée* and two performances nightly at very low prices, and the entire gallery will be free.[32]

This account suggests that *England Expects* — belongs to the history of recruiting schemes rather than the history of the English theatre, and its reception supports this view: *The Times* announced but did not review it, and its closing date was not recorded. But in its own terms it seems to have been a success. Its crucial scene was one set at the Horse Guards in Whitehall, in which a recruiting sergeant appealed to the audience to join up, after which four actors planted in the stalls rushed to the stage, signed the book, and exited to a patriotic song from the sergeant. The scene was so persuasive, at one performance at least, that a member of the audience clambered up after the four actor-recruits, and had to be sternly sent back to his seat by the sergeant.[33]

It was not until December 1914 that anything one could call a serious, original war play appeared, and then only a very small one, produced under less-than-serious circumstances. J.M. Barrie's 'playlet', *Der Tag*, opened at the London Coliseum on December 21, on a variety bill that also included a play by Sir Arthur Conan Doyle, a ballet, three comedy acts, a family of equilibrists, and a company of trained pigs. Theatre publicity announced that 'The burning words of a great mind on a great subject should render this little play one of national interest',[34] but concentration must have been difficult.

Der Tag is a dream play of a puzzling kind. It opens on a meeting of the Kaiser with his Chancellor and an officer, in which the Kaiser is urged to sign a declaration of war. He delays, the others exit, and he is visited by the Spirit of Culture ('a noble female figure in white robes'), who pleads for peace; he then recalls his officers and refuses to sign the declaration. When they have exited once more the Kaiser seems to fall into a dream — of Reims bombarded and centres of learning sacked. But this is the reality; it was his noble refusal of war that was the dream.

Culture re-enters, 'sorely wounded', to rebuke him for his crime. She hands him a dagger, and leaves. The light of the candle burns low. Curtain.

Virginia Woolf saw *Der Tag* in January 1915, and thought it 'sheer balderdash of the thinnest kind'.[35] The reviewers came to much the same conclusion, though they put it more politely. 'The exact intention of the play remains obscure,' the *Times* man complained:

> Is this Kaiser, whom Sir James presents to us, his idea of the German Emperor as he actually was during those eventful days of July and August, when the peace of Europe trembled in the balance, or is it his idealized Emperor, his view of how the really great man — the Bonaparte, who is constantly thrown in the Emperor's face as the emblem of strength — would have wished to mould the destinies of Europe?[36]

What Barrie meant to say about moral responsibility for the war is indeed obscure, though he seemed to intend that it should be seen as a war between Prussianism and Culture, rather than between Germany and England. One point, however, is clear: Barrie was concerned that his play should state not only the case against Prussia, but the case against England — that is, against the pre-war England that had invited attack. Consider the following passage from the opening scene:

> CHANCELLOR (suavely): Your Imperial Majesty, Britain will not join in just now.
> EMPEROR: If I was sure of that?
> CHANCELLOR: I vouch for it. So well we've chosen our time it finds her at issue with herself, her wild women let loose, her colonies ready to turn against her, Ireland aflame, her paltry British army sulking with the civic powers.
> EMPEROR: These wounds might heal suddenly if German bugles sounded. It is a land that in the past has done things.
> OFFICER: In the past, your Imperial Majesty; but in the past alone lies Britain's greatness.
> EMPEROR: Yes, that's the German truth. Britain has grown dull and sluggish: a belly of a land, she lies overfed, no dreams within her such as keep Powers alive; and timid too — without red blood in her, but in its stead a thick yellowish fluid. The most she'll play for is her own safety; pretend to grant her that, and she'll seek her soft bed again. Britain's part in the world's making is done: 'I was,' her epitaph.[37]

All the anxieties of the pre-war days are there: Ireland, the Suffragists, the mutinous army, and the soft life. And so is the common notion that the war would cure all that: 'England was grown degenerate,' the Spirit of Culture tells the Emperor, 'you have made her great again.'

Der Tag is, in its own dramatic terms, essentially what the paintings of Strang and the cartoon of Dyson, and the poems of Newbolt and Kipling and Brooke were — not a representation of the war, but an allegory about *ideas* of war. That must have seemed the only method open to Barrie in December 1914; the war could not have had any actuality that could be dramatized then, it was simply an abstraction, a dialogue between Emperor and Culture.

A longer and more ambitious war play, by another experienced Edwardian dramatist, opened in London a few months later. Stephen Phillips had made his reputation as a writer of poetic dramas in the early 1900s, with plays on traditional literary and Biblical subjects: *Paolo and Francesca* (1900), *Herod* (1901), *Ulysses* (1902), *The Sin of David* (1904), *Nero* (1906), after which he dropped out of sight. The war must have seemed to him a glorious opportunity for him to restore his faded popularity; he responded with *Armageddon*.

Once more Phillips drew on what he knew — the traditional power of blank verse and the theatricality of epic literature. This time his source was *Paradise Lost. Armageddon* begins in Hell, with a debate of the fallen angels ('Miltonic in origin,' said *The Times*, 'if in nothing else'[38]) in which the war is planned, and Attila the Hun is sent to earth to organize it (see plate 4); it ends in the same place, with the diabolic plans for a diabolical earth frustrated by British virtue. In the intervening scenes Reims is bombarded, a drunken German officer attempts to rape a French woman, a British officer refuses to take revenge on German civilians, and Joan of Arc appears in a vision. It is a curious work, not so much a play as an anthology of wartime clichés about heroes and enemies and the forces of good and evil, written in a mixture of bombastic verse and melodramatic prose. Lest that seem too harsh a judgement of poor Phillips, here are examples of both the poetry and the prose. From the opening scene, Satan speaks:

> For Eden now let Europe make amends!
> Hurl we a massive Fury on the world,
> With engines and artilleries of Hell,
> With wail of women and cities thundered down,
> Until beneath the bellowing, blind world-blow

> Justice shall reel, Love, Pity, and mankind
> Shall build to Force, not Faith, temples afresh.
> Here is Thy sting, O Hell, Thy Victory here.

And from later in the scene, an interview between General von der Trenk, commander of the Fifth German Army Corps, and a French prisoner:

> *Trenk.* What of another force to the westward? Where are they?
> *Prisoner.* I cannot tell, sir.
> *Trenk.* (*Sipping wine and curling moustache.*) Now understand, you dog, we are here to bring you our Kultur. If you will not take it with a spoon, you must take it from the shell. It must be battered into you. You understand that? What?[39]

(Surely the last time in the history of the English drama when a villain was directed to curl his moustache.)

One might think that Phillips's play would have been a certain success, given the mood of the time: its Germans were brutes, its Englishmen and Frenchmen were heroes, and it had the destruction of Reims for a centre-piece. But the London critics were not so foolish or so bloodthirsty as all that: they treated *Armageddon* the way the Germans treated Reims, and the play closed in a week. Whatever a successful war play might be, it clearly wasn't this one.

IV

War novels began to appear early in 1915, some six months after the war began, and from then on were published with greater and greater frequency, until by mid-year they were being reviewed in batches: the *Athenaeum* did seven under the collective title of 'War Novels' in July, and five months later the *Times Literary Supplement* dealt with eleven at once in a review titled 'The War in Fiction'. Many of these books were essentially boys' adventure stories — they had titles like *With French at the Front, In Khaki for the King,* and *A Boy Scout with the Russians,* and illustrated covers, and many illustrations inside — but they were not reviewed as children's literature, but with books clearly intended for adults. They continued the tradition of Henty and his imitators, and must have appealed to the same readership, which included adults as

well as adolescents. They would have been easy to read since, as the
TLS reviewer remarked, they were pretty much the same:

> Most of them are concerned with the Western front; the villain is
> pretty sure to be a German spy — a voluble scoundrel who tells us
> some home truths about our unpreparedness and devotion to sport —
> while the other Germans are a nasty crew with the redeeming quality
> of courage . . .[40]

For writers in this tradition the Great War was simply one more English
battle, with the usual heroes on this side and the usual brave villains on
the other, a battle that would be won by British pluck and individual
courage, with perhaps a cavalry charge at the end. Change the locale and
the nationality of the enemy, and you could write essentially the same
book about any English war.

And many writers did. Take the case of Captain F.S. Brereton, author
of *With French at the Front*. Brereton was a surgeon who had served with
the Scots Guards in the South African War, retired, and rejoined the
army in 1914; he was head of the Committee for the Medical History of
the War, and later of the Medical Section of the Imperial War Museum;
when he retired again in 1919 he was a brevet lieutenant colonel with a
C.B.E. A busy military career, it would seem; yet Brereton found time
to write forty-eight novels, all of them concerned with military
operations, from the Peninsular War to the final attack on the Western
Front. Eleven of Brereton's titles began with the word *With* and a list of
them will give the flavour of his work: *With Wellington in Spain, With the
Dyaks of Borneo, With Wolseley to Kumasi: A Tale of the First Ashanti War,
With Shield and Assegai: A Tale of the Zulu War, With Roberts to Candahar,
With Rifle and Bayonet: A Story of the Boer War, With French at the Front,
With Joffre at Verdun, With Allenby in Palestine, With Our Russian Allies,
With the Allies to the Rhine.* Brereton seems to have covered every British
engagement of the preceding century except the Crimea. For him, wars
were identified with a) commanders, b) geographical goals, and occasionally c) weapons. Those terms changed, and changed his titles;
otherwise, the stories were much the same.[41]

Brereton's first novels of the Great War had certain didactic functions,
however, that the titles don't reveal. You will see one if you go back to
the *TLS* reviewer's remark about the 'voluble scoundrel who tells us
some home truths'; like Barrie's Emperor and Chancellor, Brereton's
villains are there partly to reveal the weakness, the disunity, the softness
of England. His heroes perform another equally didactic function: they

state the English case. So the novels, besides being adventure stories, are instant history books, explaining how England got where she was in 1915, and who is to blame.

John Buchan's *The Thirty-Nine Steps*, another novel of 1915, also belongs to this category of instant history books, and is the best-known example. Unlike the others it is not a war novel, but an adventure story of flight and pursuit, in the tradition of Stevenson's *Kidnapped*, that ends just as the war begins. But its subject is a war subject: it is How England Got There. The book's villains are German spies who are plotting to force a war upon Europe, and its hero, Richard Hannay, is a Colonial who is present to describe both England's case and England's weaknesses (which include Liberalism, Free Trade, a complacent middle class, and 'the Jew'). Buchan was the most prolific, and the most popular, historian of the war — his *Nelson's History of the Great War*, written as the war was being fought, ran eventually to twenty-four volumes. But one might argue that his greatest influence on the way Englishmen thought and felt about the war was through the Hannay novels, which made the war both a moral melodrama and a history lesson for Englishmen.

Books of this kind were histories; but they were also in their way recruiting tracts. I suppose they always had been; probably there were many Victorian youths who wound up on the Northwest Frontier, or at Khartoum or Ladysmith because they had read Henty. But neither Henty nor Buchan nor Brereton was as explicit about enlisting young men as some others were in 1915. Escott Lynn dedicated his *In Khaki for the King* as follows:

PRO PATRIA
TO THOSE TRUE BRITONS OF THE
BULLDOG BREED
WHO, IN THEIR COUNTRY'S HOUR OF NEED,
NOBLY RESPONDED
TO THE CALL TO ARMS,
THE AUTHOR LOVINGLY AND ADMIRINGLY
DEDICATES THIS BOOK,

and followed the dedication with a prefatory letter, addressed to 'Dear Boys, —,' which ends:

It is up to you boys of to-day to see that a similar danger never threatens your glorious Empire again. Those of you who have not yet

donned khaki, see to it that when you are old enough you train
yourselves to defend your homes, your mothers, your sisters, your
country, all that you hold dear ... And believe one whose proud
privilege it has been to wear the King's uniform, that those days you
will spend in khaki or in blue will be amongst the fullest and happiest
of your lives.[42]

Lynn seems, like Brereton, to have had a military career; and like
Brereton he wrote many military adventure novels — thirty-two of
them, including one on the charge of the Light Brigade, another on the
Indian Mutiny, and at least three on the First World War. In this case,
apparently, as in Brereton's, one war was much like another.

Certainly their wars were remarkably alike. Both *With French at the
Front* and *In Khaki for the King* begin in Berlin, from which the English
heroes must escape in order to fight the Germans; both include brave
Belgians and German spies, the retreat from Mons, a cavalry charge, and
a fanciful account of aerial combat. These similarities are not there because
one author copied the other, but because they shared a common war —
not the Great War in its early months (neither seems to have known
much about that), but a common *literary* war, the war of the colonial
adventure novels from which they derived their styles and their novel-
writing imaginations. One gets no sense from either book of actual,
observed military actions — of massed movements of troops, trench warfare, artillery fire, mud and death; they offer instead the old adventures,
rewritten. Only the dates and (sometimes) the place-names are real.

The same literary war was fought, at an even lower literary level, in
popular boys' papers like *Captain* and *Chums*. *Chums* in fact anticipated
the war by some nine months; it ran a serial about a war between
England and Germany, beginning with the December 1913 number.
Once the war began, such stories appeared in every issue, and that is
scarcely surprising. What *is* surprising is the preoccupation with death
and defeat that the two papers shared — with last brave survivors,
impossible odds, and battles fought to the last man. *Captain* even ran a
feature article, 'All That Was Left of Them', recounting famous
historical occasions when English armies had suffered disastrous defeats
— at Albuera, in the charge of the Light Brigade, and on the Northwest
Frontier, among others. *Chums* printed colour illustrations of similar
disasters — as for example the painting of a naval battle reproduced in
plate 6, which was included in the August 15, 1914 issue, with this
caption:

TO THE DEATH

An incident in naval warfare. A British battle-cruiser, crippled in a
fight against overwhelming odds, is making a last desperate attempt
to smash at least one of her foes before she sinks.[43]

The caption implies that the incident had actually occurred. It hadn't;
the first naval engagement involving the loss of a British cruiser was the
Battle of Coronel, fought on November 1 off the coast of Chile. Why
then invent a fictional defeat? Why this fascination with last desperate
attempts? And what effects would such fictions have on the young men
and boys who read them, and who entered the services? Lessons in how
to be the last man alive seem an odd way to prepare troops for battle; but
they were certainly a part of the popular mentality at the war's
beginning. 'To the Death' seems to have been one of the strongest of
popular literary conventions.

These adventurous war stories were instant histories of the war — not
of the actual fighting, but of the causes and the issues, in the simplest
pro-Allies terms. But there were also histories of a more customary kind
being written, often by the same writers. Like no previous public event,
the Great War began to be turned into history almost as soon as the first
shot was fired. Within a year at least seven serial histories were in
progress: both *The Times* and the *Manchester Guardian* published one,
and there were others by John Buchan, by Sir Arthur Conan Doyle, and
by the thriller-writers William Le Queux and Edgar Wallace. There was
a *Children's Story of the War*, and *The War: A History and Explanation for
Boys and Girls*.[44] These were popular histories, most of them sold in
parts at a modest price, and one might say that they were launched
because publishers saw a potential market for them. But the market was
there because the public at large didn't understand the war, was
confused about its causes and frightened by its scale. Perhaps they
wanted to be told that what was happening in their world was not
Armageddon, but simply another war like the others, a matter of
campaigns planned and battles fought, such as could be illustrated with
drawings of cavalry charges. That, in any case, was what they got from
most of these books. If none of them has survived as history, that is
because their familiarizing versions of events, like the stories in the war
novels, have not seemed adequate to the events. In history, as in the arts,
the familiar would have to be made unfamiliar before it would be
accepted by later generations as a credible version of the war's reality.

Two books published during 1915 did get beyond the conventions of
the war-novel genre. *Sergeant Michael Cassidy, R.E.*, published in June,

was the first book by a young officer of the Royal Engineers, Herman
Cyril McNeile. McNeile had been in the army for eight years then, and
would serve to the end of the war, when he would retire as a lieutenant-
colonel. Because he was a regular on active duty, he did not sign his
book with his own name, but called himself 'Sapper', the military term
for an engineer.

Sapper's Michael Cassidy is an Irish regular soldier, one of the 'Old
Contemptibles' who were the first British expeditionary force to cross
into France, and who suffered the first severe losses at Mons and Ypres.
Cassidy has been wounded, and is recuperating in a London hospital,
where he tells tales of his experiences to a sympathetic officer. Most of
Cassidy's tales are military tall stories, some of them broadly comical,
others full of violence. But they are realistic in their treatment of the particulars of war: the trenches, the mud, the constant shells, the dead German
who hangs on the barbed wire, grinning. 'You must mind, sir,' Cassidy
tells his officer-auditor, 'that the war over yonder is different to what you
and I were brought up to.'[45] So it was, and Sapper was the first English
novelist to try to record that difference. Nevertheless, his book is not an
anti-war statement; it is rather a celebration of the qualities of the Old
Contemptibles. At the end of the book most of the Regulars are dead,
and volunteers are replacing them. ''Tis but remnants we have left of
our original army,' Cassidy says on the last page, 'but there has never
been anything in this world to beat it — and there never will be again.'[46]

Through the autumn and winter of 1914–15 another series of soldier's
anecdotes had been appearing in *Blackwood's Magazine*, titled 'The
First Hundred Thousand', and signed 'Junior Sub.' — that is, junior
subaltern, the lowest commissioned rank. These are not so much stories
as barely fictionalized sketches, of a different army than Sapper's; this
one is 'Kitchener's Army', the volunteers who responded to Lord
Kitchener's appeal for 100,000 men at the beginning of the war. The
sketches began in the November 1914 issue with an account of new
recruits attempting close-order drill, and all through that winter and
early spring they dealt with the tribulations of training, in cheerful
incidents that were more like letters home than like fiction. A second
series, from July to November 1915, took the recruits into the trenches,
and over the top at Loos, and there there was pain and dying, though
there was also some humour, and much praise for the new soldiers.

The First Hundred Thousand was published as a book in December
1915, with the author's name 'Ian Hay' on the title page in place of
'Junior Sub'. It says something about its qualities that it was issued in

time for the Christmas trade (my copy of the second impression is inscribed 'To the Family from Miss Gregory, Xmas 1915'). It was a book that gave imaginative reality to the life of the young men who had volunteered, but a *cheerful* reality, full of humour and good-fellowship, that the families at home must have found reassuring. Reviewers, praising the book, found in it both realism and something more. 'The sketches have a continuity and proportion,' the *Spectator* wrote, 'and if they do not afford us a true and memorable record of the development of some of the first recruits of the New Armies into proud and efficient fighting men we do not know where to look for such a record.'[47] And the *Saturday Review* observed that the sketches 'contain all that is irrepressibly brave, comical, devoted, prosaic, glorious, or dull in the lives of thousands of young men who in the last eighteen months have been learning the business and the art of war . . .'[48] What these reviewers were really saying was that Hay had found a means of seeing war and the military life in the best possible light, while appearing to describe it realistically. Look at the adjectives — proud, efficient, brave, comical, devoted, prosaic, glorious, dull — how they manage to validate traditional martial virtues by mixing them with ordinary qualities, making war at once heroic and everyday.

Puzzling over the way Hay managed to do this, the *Saturday Review* man concluded: 'It would seem that "Junior Sub", a practised author, instinctively has repressed all that is formal and deliberate in his craft in order to allow his theme the greater freedom.'[49] It is true that 'Junior Sub'/'Ian Hay' was an experienced writer; he had had a career as a journalist before he joined the Argyll and Sutherland Highlanders, and had published five books, all as 'Ian Hay'. But it is not true that his style was not deliberate: to have no style is a style, too. Hay's was not, in fact, as invisible as all that: it was plain, but he allowed himself archnesses and ironies, and at moments of high emotion he was emotional. What gave his writing the feeling of stylelessness was the directness of the narrative, the use of first-person and present tense, and a lot of realistic-sounding dialogue. It was a style that suited the subject, and later narratives of the war would adopt it. Hay seemed to have given the war a voice.

It was not, however, quite a *new* voice. Sapper had found it, too, if less skilfully and consistently; and behind them both there was Kipling. Sapper's Michael Cassidy is an obvious imitation of Kipling's Terence Mulvaney, the Irish adventurer in *Soldiers Three* (1888), and Hay's Scottish rankers are cut from the same cloth. One might argue further that behind Kipling stands the ur-figure of the entire tradition — Private

Tommy Atkins, the archetypal British enlisted man. Kipling evidently thought so: he dedicated *Soldiers Three* to

> That Very Strong Man,
> T. Atkins,
> Private of the Line.

But Kipling had done more than recognize Tommy Atkins — he had invented him; that is, he had created the literary type, and the style that would make it possible to write about common soldiers without glorifying them, making them simultaneously all the things that the *Saturday Review* found in Hay's book: brave, comical, devoted, prosaic, etc. It may be that Kipling, by writing about British soldiers in this mode, made them like that. One British general thought he had. 'I myself had served for many years with soldiers,' Major-General Sir George Younghusband wrote in 1917,

> but had never once heard the words or expressions that Rudyard Kipling's soldiers used. Many a time did I ask my brother Officers whether they had ever heard them. No, never. But sure enough, a few years after the soldiers thought, and talked, and expressed themselves exactly like Rudyard Kipling had taught them in his stories! He would get a stray word here, or a stray expression there, and weave them into general soldier talk, in his priceless stories. Rudyard Kipling made the modern soldier.
>
> Other writers have gone on with the good work, and they have between them manufactured the cheery, devil-may-care, lovable person enshrined in our hearts as Thomas Atkins. Before he had learnt from reading stories about himself that he, as an individual, also possessed the above attributes, he was mostly ignorant of the fact. My early recollections of the British soldier are of a bluff, rather surly person, never the least jocose or light-hearted, except perhaps when he had too much beer. He was brave always, but with a sullen, stubborn bravery. No Tipperary or kicking football about it.
>
> To Rudyard Kipling and his fellow-writers the Army owes a great debt of gratitude for having produced the splendid type of soldier who now stands as the English type.[50]

Sapper and Ian Hay were surely among the other writers whom the General had in mind; if they did not invent Tommy Atkins, they adapted the Kipling product for the Great War market, and it must be partly because of their work that when someone in the ranks shouted

'Are we downhearted?' the ordinary private cried 'No!' whether he was or not.

Younghusband did not include patriotism, enthusiasm, or a desire to die for one's country among the characteristics of the manufactured Atkins; and rightly so, for neither Kipling nor Sapper nor Hay had anything to say about such Rupert Brookeish emotions. Sapper's Cassidy loves his regiment and his fellow-soldiers, but he has nothing to say about *England* (he is, after all, an Irishman), and Hay's Scots go to war for no higher motive than a patient sense of duty. On this point, at least, art does seem to have imitated life: reading through the diaries and letters of men who fought in those early months, one doesn't find many exalted feelings about the romance of war, or even about England. They were where they were because they felt a duty to be there; but they seem to have known what they were doing, and what the odds were. If they were cheerful, it was no doubt because there was no point in not being cheerful; or perhaps they had read their Kipling. It wasn't because they were ignorant of what lay ahead of them.

Both *Sergeant Michael Cassidy* and *The First Hundred Thousand* end on an elegiac note. Cassidy laments the end of 'our original army', and Hay's narrator bids farewell to his fellow-volunteers in these valedictory sentences:

> And here I propose . . . to take leave of The First Hundred Thousand. Some day, if Providence wills, the tale shall be resumed . . . But the title of the story will have to be changed. In the hearts of those who drilled them, reasoned with them, sometimes almost wept over them, and ultimately fought shoulder to shoulder with them, the sturdy, valiant legions, whose humorously-pathetic career you have followed so patiently for fifteen months, will always be First; but alas! they are no longer The Hundred Thousand.
>
> So we will leave them, as is most justly due, in sole possession of their proud title.[51]

This mourning note is not really surprising at the end of these books: after all, they both deal with disastrous British defeats. Cassidy has fought at Mons, the scene of the first British retreat of the war, and Hay's recruits go into battle at Loos, where the British lost 50,000 men and gained nothing. But it isn't exactly the lost battles, or even the lost men, that are being mourned for: it is rather, I think, the war's lost beginnings. Both books assume that there was a time when good, simple men had fought cheerfully for good, simple reasons, in a war that they expected they would shortly win. By mid-1915 those men were dead, and the war seemed likely to go on for ever. A mood, not quite of disillusionment, but of loss, begins here: a sense that the spirit of the war had ended before the war did. This is not the dominant tone of either book — far from it — but it seems to enter at the end of both, almost in spite of the authors' cheerful intentions. Loss is the great theme of this war: not victory, not defeat, but simply *loss*; and one might argue that in literary terms it found its first muted expression here, as these two cheerful writers looked back at the stories they had told, and saw that the men they had written about were dead.

V

Literature moves us, and shapes our images of reality — that's obvious enough; English men and women learned to imagine the war as they did partly because writers like Sapper and Ian Hay wrote their stories. But not all imagination-shaping texts are *literature* in the customary sense of the word: images of reality arise out of many sources, visual and aural as well as verbal, and among verbal sources out of all kinds of non-literary texts.

Some of the most influential documents in the shaping of English war imaginations were those that recorded, in what seemed factual, documentary form, alleged atrocities committed by the German army in the invasion of Belgium and northern France. These accounts appeared very early in the war, and addressed the subject on several levels of authority and sophistication. Within the first nine months of the fighting there were at least three versions available.

Of these, the first to appear was a pamphlet compiled by William Le Queux, titled *German Atrocities: A Record of Shameless Deeds*. It was issued in September 1914, priced for a mass public at twopence, and purported to be based on Belgian government statements, interviews, and the reports of war correspondents. From those sources Le Queux had gathered stories of massacres, of women used as shields, and of the destruction of Louvain — not as valid or as shocking as later accounts would be, but the first in the field.

Le Queux's pamphlet was followed, in February 1915, by *The Official Book of the German Atrocities*, identified on its title page as 'The Complete Verbatim Report of the Belgian, French, and Russian Commission of Enquiry. Published by Authority' — whose authority was not made clear. This book was longer, and more extreme in the crimes described, than its predecessor had been, and included atrocities committed against French and Russian civilians as well as against Belgians. Its purpose was more than simply the dissemination of 'official' information, as the last paragraph of the introduction made clear:

> It is the duty of every single Englishman who reads these records, and who is fit to take his place in the King's Army, to fight with all the resolution and courage he may, that the stain, of which the following pages are only a slight record, may be wiped out, and the blood of innocent women and children avenged.[52]

It was a work of propaganda, that was obvious; but like the boys' adventure stories it was also a recruiting tract.

By the time the *Official Book* had been published, a government committee had been appointed in England to make a report on atrocity allegations. It was called the Committee of Alleged German Outrages, and was under the chairmanship of the lawyer and political historian Viscount Bryce. The Committee was appointed in December 1914, and published its report, commonly known as the Bryce Report, in May 1915. The report was divided into two parts: '(1) An analysis and summary of the evidence regarding the conduct of the German troops in Belgium towards the civilian population of that country during the first few weeks of the invasion'; and '(2) An examination of the evidence relating to breaches of the rules and usages of war and acts of inhumanity committed by German soldiers or groups of soldiers, during the first four months of the war, whether in Belgium or in France.'[53] The Committee was unanimous in finding the German army guilty of repeated acts of cruelty and atrocity.

The publishing of the Bryce Report had, I think, two effects. First, it fixed in English minds, as 'official' and therefore true, the idea of the German soldier as a cruel savage, living and acting outside the limits of decent human behaviour. The part of the report concerned with the treatment of Belgian civilians confirmed what had from the beginning been a central support for English intervention in the war — the idea that the invasion of Belgium had been an action of inhuman and indefensible brutality. The second part, concerned primarily with behaviour on the battlefield against opposing soldiers, convicted the Germans of breaking the rules of civilized warfare. The idea that such rules might exist and be honoured may seem naive, when one considers the ways in which the First World War was fought, but the Bryce

Report was published just at the time when the war was becoming, to English eyes, barbaric: the first zeppelin raids on London and the first use of gas on the Western Front took place in April, the *Lusitania* was sunk in May. To people who still talked about 'playing the game' the Germans were excluding themselves from the human race. The consequences for attitudes towards the enemy were profound; henceforth it became quite acceptable to express a desire for the annihilation of Germans, the bombing of German civilians, the gassing of German troops. 'The game' was over.

Those were the consequences of the report itself. The appendix to the report must have had another kind of effect. There the interested reader (and how could one *not* be interested?) would find the transcripts of the depositions taken by the Committee from some 1,200 sources — Belgian soldiers and civilians, British soldiers, and the diaries of the German dead, account after account of hideous atrocities, all told in detail. Here are three examples:

Belgian Soldier. At Haelen, about August the 20th, I was with my regiment in the trenches. The next day after the battle we were on patrol duty and when in a wood I saw the body of a carabinier hanging on a tree; the chest and stomach were cut open and the heart had been taken out. [This story is verified in the following deposition, also by a Belgian soldier.]

British Soldier, N.C.O. On 24th October we were in an old café, near La Bassée, Private C . . . and Private D . . . called me to see something. In the garden were some sacks of potatoes. Among them two sacks contained one a man and one a woman apparently cut up. They had their clothes either on or pushed in the sacks with them. The Germans had occupied the village for days before. We had just driven them out. [This part of the deposition is corroborated by Private C . . .]

Plasterer [Belgian]. On the 23 August I went with two friends (names given) to see what we could see. About three hours out of Malines we were taken prisoners by a German patrol — an officer and six men — and marched into a little wood of saplings where was a house. The officer spoke Flemish. He knocked at the door; the peasant did not come. The officer ordered the soldiers to break down the door, which two of them did. The peasant came and asked what they were doing. The officer said he had not come quickly enough and that they had 'trained up' plenty of others. His hands were tied behind his back and he was shot at once without a moment's delay. The wife came out with a little sucking child. She put the child down and sprang at the Germans like a lioness. She clawed their faces. One of the soldiers took his rifle and struck her a tremendous blow with the butt on the head. She fell dead. Another took his bayonet and fixed it and thrust it through the child. He then put his rifle across his shoulder with the child upon it. Its little arms stretched out once or twice. The officer ordered the house set on fire and straw was obtained and it was done. The man and his wife and child were thrown on the top of the straw.[54]

The style of the depositions is quite uniform; as in those quoted, it is plain, circumstantial, and unjudgemental. Since most of them are translations from Flemish, French, or German, one must conclude that this is an official style — chosen for its effect, or perhaps simply as a way of dealing officially with emotionally powerful texts. Whatever the reason, it is a style that seems to give authenticity and authority to a new version of war, and a new set of war images — and most important, a new idea of the enemy. A literary reader might of course have come across such images before, in Homer or Shakespeare; but he would perceive these differently; these were *real*, because they occurred in a government document.

The Bryce Report removed the idea of atrocity from the realm of propaganda — the newspaper cartoon and the recruiting poster — and placed it in sober reality. Thereafter it would be taken for granted by most English people as a truth about the Germans; articles would appear in respectable, conservative journals like the *Saturday Review* and the *Nineteenth Century*[55] assuming everything that the Bryce Report had reported to be factual. And when Arthur Machen's book of war tales, *The Angels of Mons*, was published in August 1915, its fantasies would be taken as fact. Machen's most celebrated invention in that book, the story of the spirit-bowmen who fought with the British at Mons, became an ineradicable part of English wartime mythology; but there are other stories in the volume that are more outrageous, and they come from the Bryce Report or its predecessors — stories of a murdered priest, a crucified baby, a slaughtered child.[56] And they, too, were taken as true.

Whether individual narratives in the report were records of actual events it is impossible to say. Certainly the German troops that invaded

Belgium acted with intentional brutality, executing civilians and burning towns to suppress resistance. The more extravagant tales, of babies spitted on bayonets and priests hanged by their own bell-ropes, have the sound of horror fictions, of the sort that wars commonly generate. But wars have their true atrocities, too, and some of the reported actions undoubtedly did occur. The essential point, though, is that Lord Bryce and his committee believed their evidence to be true, and transmitted their conviction to their readers.[57]

One might say of the Bryce Report that it released into English imaginations a style, a language, and an imagery of violence and cruelty that would in time permeate imagined versions of the war, and become part of the record. No one should have been surprised at the brutality of later accounts of the war; it was all here, in May 1915, in the report of a government committee.

CHAPTER 3

The Home-Front Wars

It is the nature of war to diminish every value except war itself and the values war requires: patriotism, discipline, obedience, endurance. Other values, which in time of peace would be thought civilized — freedom of thought, tolerance, a broad and generous receptiveness to culture — these will be devalued, because they are unwarlike. Even the idea of civilization itself will shrink, from a community of culture embracing the world, to that part of culture that is on *our* side.

War releases other aggressions too — all those hostilities that have been present in peacetime, but restrained — and so when war comes, other, 'little' wars come too: the war of the old against the young, the war of the old-fashioned against the modern, the war of the national against the foreign and of the conforming against the non-conforming. It is not surprising, then, that once the Great War had begun, conflicts of values began, and grew violent, or that qualities that cultivated Edwardians had taken to be the very signs of their nation's civilization were seen to be the symptoms of a national disease.

Diagnoses of that disease varied, depending on what guilts, resentments, private quarrels and self-interests the diagnostician brought to the case. But most Englishmen who confronted the question agreed that whatever the disease was, it was not English; some foreign pestilence had infected English life, English values, the English character over the past decades, and had deflected the nation from its proper course. The war had been sent to put England right; what effect it would have on the continent seemed far less important.

I. *The War Against Modernism*

What was foreign was also frequently what was new, and many diagnosticians of England's illness traced it to advanced ideas from Europe. Here, as an example, is a passage from a wartime lecture by the sculptor W.R. Colton. 'As far as Art is concerned,' Colton said,

> it was high time that war should come with its purifying fire. In some fifty years so-called Art had grown in Europe like unto a puffed-out and unhealthy fungus of enormous size, without beauty, without delicacy, and without health. A wave of diseased degeneracy had submerged Philosophy, Music, Literature, and Art to such a depth that, looking forward, I venture to prophesy that future centuries will gaze back with pity upon this period of mistaken morbidness.
>
> We find, perhaps, in the German philosophers and musicians the first crystallised expression of this viciousness, but unfortunately we, with all other nations of Europe, cannot pretend that we are exempt. The morbid invention of the artistic mind is seen everywhere. We have Oscar Wilde, Aubrey Beardsley, and others. The futurists, the cubists, the whole school of decadent novelists.[1]

Colton's diagnosis is interesting because of its comprehensiveness, but his general point was scarcely a new one: we have seen it in the writings of Ricketts and Gosse and Image, and in Brooke's poems and Wells's *Boon* and Barrie's *Der Tag*. It says that Edwardian England was infected with a European disease, and had become degenerate, slothful, soft, corrupt. The name of this disease you might say was *Modernism*; but you would have to add that for persons like Colton, the Modern did not begin with Post-Impressionism and the twelve-tone scale, but was an infection that went back to Nietzsche and Wagner, and in England, inevitably, to Wilde. Futurism, Cubism, Decadence — they were all one sickness.

The ideas and works of Modernism, both in Colton's sense of the term and in the more recent sense, were all present in England before the war: one could look at Cubist paintings, or hear Schönberg conduct his own works, or read *Dorian Gray* or Nietzsche easily enough in 1914. But once war had been declared, critics began to shuffle such works into one pile, and to see them as constituting a single common enemy that threatened the moral foundations of the nation. To be Modern, they saw, was to be German, and it was right and patriotic that English critics should declare war on Modernism wherever it could be detected.

This war against the Modern was fought by critics, journalists, and politicians, in newspapers and periodicals, in House of Commons debates, and in the law courts; it went on as long as the war did.

The arguments in this polemical war were various, and by no means consistent with each other. the attackers shared only a general sense of who their enemies were. For some, war and modern art were simply two expressions of the same values: 'In an age of brutal strife,' an *Athenaeum* critic wrote, 'the art, if any, will be brutal also, the extremes of Futurism being alone suitable to express its spirit.'[2] If the critic was a moralist, that common brutality would be seen as a symptom of the culture's sickness, as in this comment on a London Group exhibition in 1915:

> Such a display was essential to complete the chastening of our pride in twentieth-century civilisation. The war has shown that its possession does not necessarily endow the man of 'Kultur' with higher moral sensibilities than the barbarian; while the works of Mr. Jacob Epstein and others of the London Group revealed that the aesthetic tendencies of the most advanced school of modern art are leading us back to the primitive instincts of the savage . . .[3]

From this it was only a short step to the view that modern art was the expression of a specifically *German* barbarism; the *Times* review of the same show was headlined: 'JUNKERISM IN ART',[4] which is odd, when you consider that the principal influences on the artists included — Wyndham Lewis, Epstein, and C.R.W. Nevinson among others — came from England's allies, from France and Italy.

When Mark Gertler exhibited his Modernist 'Eve' in a London gallery in December 1915, a label was stuck on her belly by some outraged viewer with 'Made in Germany' written on it.[5] Other critics made the war/art connection in their own eccentric terms: the composer Cyril Scott, being a theosophist, perceived a terrible discord on the Astral Plane, of which Post-Impressionism, Futurism, Cubism, *Blast*, Schönberg's music, and the war were all manifestations. His explanation of this discord was portentously obscure, but his conclusion was clear enough: war and Schönberg were essentially the same.[6]

One could just as easily attack from the opposite direction, taking Modernism to be the spirit of peacetime triviality, which war's seriousness had refuted and dispersed. 'Whatever turn the wheel of English life may take,' St John Ervine wrote in 1915, whatever be the mood of English letters now and onwards; this is certain: that we shall hear no more of the pretty-pretty babblers, with their Bond Street barbarism and their rococo recklessness. The Vorticists and the Imagists and the Futurists and the rest of the rabble of literary and artistic lunatics provided slender entertainment for empty days; but our minds are empty no longer; and we have no time to waste on monkeys on sticks.[7]

Others took the 'decadence' line, and argued that the war would purify English art of its un-English abnormalities — including its sexuality. Here, for example, are two comments from an April 1915 symposium on the effects of war on literature:

Arthur Waugh:
It seems probable ... that the intellectual and literary conscience of the nation will be enormously braced, and that aberrations of taste will no longer be tolerated. Cynicism, self-advertisement, sexuality, perverse eccentricity — there will be no room for some time to come for violences of this kind.

W.J. Locke:
The war's tremendous tempest of elementals should cleanse the sex problem from all the accretions of decadent sophistry of the last thirty years.[8]

The cleansing of the sex problem — or, one might say, the war against sex — was an activity that was pursued with increasing enthusiasm to the end of the war. War may release sexual aggressions, but it also has its puritanical side, and there would be some fanatical puritans at large in wartime England, opposing sexual freedom as they opposed other freedoms. But here, at the war's beginning, it seemed to men like Locke that the war would do its own cleansing, as though it were a purifying force in nature.

The fiercest engagement in the earlier stages of the war against sex was the attack on D.H. Lawrence's *The Rainbow* in the autumn of 1915. The novel was published in late September, and was reviewed widely, and on the whole unfavourably, during October; reviewers called it 'a monotonous wilderness of phallicism' and 'an orgy of sexiness'. Early in November the Metropolitan Police, acting on instructions from the Director of Public Prosecutions, seized the publisher's stock of the book. The case was heard before the chief magistrate on November 13; Methuen, the publisher, apologized for publishing the book, agreed to have a thousand copies destroyed, and paid costs, and *The Rainbow* became an un-book and remained one throughout the war.

After the trial was over, a question was asked about it in the House of Commons: were these proceedings taken under the Defence of the Realm Act? The Home Secretary assured his colleagues that they weren't; *The Rainbow* had been charged under the Obscene Publications Act of 1857. Nevertheless, there was a point in the question: there was a good deal of war feeling mixed up in the case, and it seems unlikely that Lawrence was pursued simply because of his novel's sexiness.

There were, for one thing, Lawrence's other publications of the same time. In October — between the publication of *The Rainbow* and its suppression — the first issue of *The Signature*, a journal edited by Lawrence and Middleton Murry, appeared. It contained Lawrence's 'The Crown', an odd, highly symbolic discourse about the conflict of opposites and the destruction of civilization, in which the war appears only as a kind of metaphor; but it does refer to 'our blasphemy of the war', and when Lawrence's friend Cynthia Asquith read it she was afraid that it might be considered treasonous. In the same month the *English Review* published his story 'England my England', in a version that ends with the grisly trench killing and mutilation of an English soldier by Germans. It is not unreasonable to think that professional reviewers knew of these writings, and that some of them regarded Lawrence as pro-German, or at the least anti-war.

Hostile reviewers of *The Rainbow* did not say that Lawrence was unpatriotic or pro-German — not directly, that is. They said instead that his book was unhealthy, diseased, and decadent; but in the atmosphere of the early war years that amounted to much the same thing, for as we have seen, England's decadence and sickness were widely regarded as a cause of the war. *The Rainbow* was a sex novel, one more symptom of the sex problem that the war had been sent to cleanse, and by writing it Lawrence had managed to subvert the war effort without mentioning it. If this connection of the novel and war seems fanciful, consider this paragraph from the review of the novel written by James Douglas, of the London *Star*:

> The wind of war is sweeping over our life, and it is demolishing many of the noisome pestilences of peace. A thing like 'The Rainbow' has no right to exist in the wind of war. It is a greater menace to our public health than any of the epidemic diseases which we pay our medical officers to fight inch by inch wheresoever they appear. They

destroy the body, but it destroys the soul. 'Cant!' cries the critic. Not at all. It is self-preservation. The poise and balance of the mind are not trivial things. The power to see life as a struggle against putrescence is not a sentimental fad or fancy. Every man and every woman must take sides in that battle, and at their worst they know that they ought to take the side of the angels in their souls. Life can be made very horrible and very hideous but if literature aids and abets the business of making it horrible, and hideous, then literature must perish.[9]

There is no distinction here between the actual war and the metaphorical war against sexuality in fiction. Both were battles for which extreme sacrifices must be made.

Conservative critics might not agree on whether Modernism was brutal or trivial, whether it was like war or like peace, whether it was an aberration or a disease or a form of licentiousness, but they knew its current names: it was Post-Impressionism, Imagism, Futurism, Vorticism. These were the movements that had been so energetically publicized in the pre-war years by Roger Fry, Pound, Marinetti, and Lewis; and now, when the reaction set in, they were the specific targets of attacks. This does not mean that the attackers were always clear on what these movements meant; often they seemed simply to be the names of *isms*, against which the deep English distrust of abstractions could be directed. When John Galsworthy tried to explain, in an essay on 'Art and the War', what was really wanted in art, he wrote:

> What is wanted in a work of art is an unforced, natural, and adequate correspondence between fancy and form, matter and spirit, so that one shall not be distracted by its naturalism, mysticism, cubism, whatnotism, but shall simply be moved in a deep impersonal way by perception of another's vision.[10]

This is not exactly a reactionary statement: Galsworthy was not urging a return to some earlier historical style of art, but to an imagined past (English, of course), in which art had existed in a pure state, undefiled by abstract ideas. There was too much *whatnotism* in the world, that was the trouble. Why couldn't art be simple?

Gosse attacked whatnotism, too — though he called it Vorticism. In April 1915 he added an epilogue to his 'War and Literature' essay, mainly to withdraw the gloomy predictions of the end of literature that he had made six months before. English letters were alive and well, he reported:

No brilliant effusion of talent, no exploration of new fields, can be expected or even desired. But we shall, I think, see a quiet persistence along the old paths, and we may be comforted by the disappearance of a good deal that was merely histrionic. The self-advertising mountebank will grow tired of standing on his head in the empty marketplace. We may probably hear very little more about 'vorticists'.[11]

As far as Vorticism was concerned, this was more an expression of a fond hope than a description of the situation in London that spring. Gosse wrote his epilogue just after the opening of the London Group show that had prompted the *Times*'s 'Junkerism' headline, and just before the opening of the first (and only) Vorticist group show. He must have been hearing a lot about Vorticists as he wrote; but he could hope that he would hear less in the future, that war would drown the Vorticist uproar, and art could resume its quiet, customary ways.

It is easy enough to see why a conservative critic like Gosse should have been anti-Vorticist: it would have been astonishing if he hadn't been. The hostility of A.R. Orage is harder to understand. Orage had made his reputation during the Edwardian years as the editor of the *New Age*, the most modern and iconoclastic weekly of the time. In its prime, the *New Age* had been the principal example of the integration of modern art and thought that characterized English culture of the time; but what policies, what editorial gestures would preserve that integration in wartime? Orage chose to support the war, and that support became his paper's central principle; the iconoclasm faded (how could one be both pro-war and iconoclastic?), his most interesting writers left him, the reproductions of modern art disappeared from his pages, and the *New Age: A Weekly Review of Politics, Literature and the Arts* became little more than a weekly review of the war.

In his own contributions, which were increasingly numerous as his old contributors departed, Orage began to take an aggressively anti-Modernist position. In September 1914 he reported Pound's essay on Vorticism, which had just appeared in the *Fortnightly Review*, but only to dismiss it:

Whether he knows it or not, Vorticism is dead. It was, at best, only a big name for a little thing, that in the simmering of the pre-war period suddenly became a bubble, and is now burst. Of the magazine 'Blast', which was devoted to the propaganda of Vorticism, I doubt whether another issue will appear. Compared with the war it is incomparably feeble.[12]

And in October he added:

> It is to be hoped that the war will put an end to 'Imagism' in poetry and all such nonsense. A great event such as this in the world of action demands of artists and writers equally great efforts in the world of art. Otherwise what good are we? ... But the Imagists and such-like triflers — can they produce a poem to match a rifle, or even parallel in their verse the discipline of the goose-step? They are simply idlers, hiding from one reality in the pretence of another ... Once more I express the hope that they may all perish in the war.[13]

In these outbursts, Orage was expressing a conviction that he shared with many of his countrymen: that art and war, the world of imagination and the world of action, were in competition as alternative realities, and that war and action were the greater and more serious. In taking this position, Orage may have thought that he was coming to the aid of his country in a critical time; but the price of his patriotism was the values that had made the *New Age* important.

One can see from these examples that for many English critics, of many different critical persuasions, the war against Germany rapidly became a war against Modernism. They seem to have intended simply to eradicate from English life something that was undesirable, and especially in wartime — a sickness, a fraud, or a foolish triviality — and so leave England stronger and more English. What in fact they did was to diminish English culture, by declaring everything that was lively and new in the arts to be alien and inimical to the English cause. If pre-war Modernist movements like Futurism, Vorticism, and Imagism did not survive the war as movements, that is surely in part because of the attacks that were made on them during the war by patriotic critics, on patriotic grounds.

The critics accomplished something else as well: they made the war generational. Their attacks on modern art were in effect a declaration of war against the younger generation, the generation that would have to do the fighting. Not the entire generation, of course — there were plenty of young men, in the army and out of it, who thought the way their elders thought about Modernism — but its most gifted and creative members. Gosse and Galsworthy were declaring war on the avant-garde.

And what, meanwhile, was the avant-garde doing? Mainly it was dispersing. Some young artists and writers enlisted at once: Rupert Brooke, the Nash brothers, David Jones, Stanley Spencer, Ivor Gurney, Siegfried Sassoon, Robert Graves, T.E. Hulme, and Henri Gaudier-Brzeska all enlisted in the first month of the war. Others who were pacifists engaged in alternate service that took them out of the main currents of English culture — Forster, for example, spent most of the war in Egypt, and David Garnett went to France with a Quaker relief mission. Still, a considerable number of young men were still around and out of uniform a year after the war began: Wilfred Owen and Isaac Rosenberg did not enlist until October 1915, and Wyndham Lewis, who had to wait until he could be cured of the clap, joined up only in March 1916. And there were those who didn't go at all: Ezra Pound, T.S. Eliot, and D.H. Lawrence among them. Even in the autumn of 1915 one might have thought that there were still enough of such artists at hand to constitute a workable avant-garde. But in fact there was nothing going on by then: the war had virtually stopped the English Modern movement.

You can see one aspect of this process in records of art exhibitions. The momentum of pre-war Modernism had carried over into the first months of the war, and there were important exhibitions in London early in 1915: the London Group, the Vorticists, and the young painters of the Cumberland Market Group (Bevan, Gilman, Ginner and John Nash). But by summer the breaking up was under way, and by the end of 1915 English modern art had almost disappeared from the London galleries.

Something similar was happening in the journals that had been outlets for advanced literature. Harold Monro's *Poetry and Drama* came to an end with the December 1914 issue, *Blast* died the following summer, and the *New Age*, though it continued, ceased to harbour Modernist writers. The reasons for ceasing to publish were clear enough: Monro and Lewis were soon to enter the army, neither had the money necessary to continue publication, costs were rising, and the audience for serious (or adversarial) modern writing was shrinking, as military service and war work absorbed the intelligent young. But one feels another motive at work, too — a feeling that the war had drawn to itself all of society's scattered aggressions, and had made that other struggle, the polemical war of the Moderns, seem merely Art. And so the young departed, and left the field to the middle-aged.

Before Lewis left, however, he issued one last *Blast* — a 'War-Number' published in July 1915. *Blast* no. 1 had also been a war number of a sort, full as it was of the language and imagery of warfare and violent death; and *Blast* no. 2 repeated some of those martial gestures. The front cover carried a Lewis Vorticist drawing of men, rifles and guns, titled 'Before Antwerp', and there were Vorticist war drawings by William Roberts, Edward Wadsworth, and C.R.W. Nevinson elsewhere in the book. Lewis contributed 'War Notes' in his customary belligerent style, and Gaudier-Brzeska sent in a manifesto, 'Vortex (written from the Trenches)'.

But there is one appearance of war in *Blast* no. 2 that is not Vorticist, or metaphorical, and that has no note of belligerent excitement in it. At the end of the pages of Gaudier-Brzeska's 'Vortex' notes is this black-bordered notice:

MORT POUR LA PATRIE.

Henri Gaudier-Brzeska : after months of fighting and two promotions for gallantry Henri Gaudier-Brzeska was killed in a charge at Neuville St. Vaast, on June 5th, 1915.

No work of art in the journal has the force of this simple statement: war-as-fact had overtaken war-as-metaphor.

The other new note in *Blast* No. 2 is its historical content. The first *Blast* had rejected history, blasting 'years 1837 to 1900' and announcing that 'The Present is Art'. But in *Blast* no. 2 the Present is War, and Art is History. Lewis's prose contributions in particular are historical essays, such as a man might write at the end of an era — retrospective accounts of avant-garde painting in Europe and in England before the war. 'Blast is a history book, too,' Lewis wrote to Augustus John in the summer of

1915;[14] and so indeed it had become — a history book, and a part of history. And having become history, it ceased to exist in the present; two further numbers were promised, but none appeared.

The dispersal of the English avant-garde was gradual and incomplete, but it was thorough enough to disrupt and virtually stop the development of English Modernism. More happened in the process than simply the shutting down of journals and galleries: energies were deflected and dissipated, and groups that should have worked towards common goals were separated. The generation that would fight the war was separated from its elders, and the artists who had gone into uniform were separated from those who hadn't, who might otherwise have been their allies in one modern movement. Wilfred Owen, for example, went to his grave thinking of himself as a Georgian, because Sassoon and Graves were Georgians and were with him in the army, but he seems never to have heard of Pound or Eliot, or of *Blast* or the *Egoist*. English culture would be different after the war because, at this crucial point in its development, the avant-garde was scattered and silenced.

II. *The War Against Culture*

In the years preceding the war, English culture had been moving cautiously towards a cosmopolitan awareness of Europe. Modern French art, the Russian ballet, and recent German music had won the approval of at least the more advanced English intellectuals, and could be seen or heard with increasing frequency in London.[15] The war arrested this Europeanizing process, drawing a line across Europe that divided good culture from wicked culture (or more often *culture* from *Kultur* — a word that swiftly entered the English vocabulary as a pejorative term for the enemy's idea of civilization). Good culture ostensibly included England's allies, and there were attempts in art exhibitions and in concerts to favour the Russians and the French; but the general effect of the war was to return the English to what they had always naturally been — an insular race, suspicious of whatever was new, or different, or above all foreign.

The war against *Kultur* was a widespread effort, with official support, to eliminate German influences from English cultural life, and to denigrate German accomplishments. One can get the general tenor of the campaign from the cartoons that Will Dyson exhibited in his

London show in 1915; they were drawings that ridiculed German civilization, German professors, German science, and German art. In a typical example, titled 'Kultur Protector', Goethe, Beethoven, and Wagner kneel before Herr Krupp, exclaiming: 'Hail, Saviour Krupp, how can we ever thank thee?'; a bouquet of flowers laid before Krupp's throne adds the greetings of Heine (see plate 3). One might think that such makers of European civilization would be beyond criticism, even in wartime, but clearly they were not. And Dyson's cartoons were by no means unique in their assaults; at the same time that his drawings were on show, Goethe was being condemned as a megalomaniac in letters to *The Times*.

This cultural war was fought on many fronts, but most fiercely in the two areas in which German influence had been strongest in pre-war England — scholarship and music.[16]

English scholarship, as it existed in 1914, had grown from nineteenth-century German roots: in philosophy, in classics, in theology, in philology, in science and medicine, in psychology, Germany was the place to which English scholars went for their training if they could, and from which they learned their methods and academic standards. It is not surprising that on August 1, three days before the declaration of war, a group of English scholars should have published a letter in *The Times* expressing their distress at the thought that they might find themselves at war with the country to which they owed so much:

> We regard Germany [they wrote] as a nation leading the way in the Arts and Sciences, and we have all learnt and are learning from German scholars. War upon her in the interest of Servia and Russia will be a sin against civilization. If by reason of honourable obliga-tions we be unhappily involved in war, patriotism might still our mouths, but at this juncture we consider ourselves justified in protesting against being drawn into the struggle with a nation so near akin to our own, and with whom we have so much in common.[17]

The protest was signed by professors from Oxford, Cambridge, Aberdeen, and Harvard.

Once war was declared, those mouths were stilled, and a war of professors began; but not at once, and not on all fronts. In the beginning, many scholars strove to preserve the ideal of a scholarly community, and testified to the importance of Germany in creating that ideal. Gilbert Murray was Regius Professor of Greek at Oxford, a distinguished scholar and a respected liberal thinker. Like many liberals, he was appalled at the thought of war between civilized nations, and he was active in efforts to avert such a calamity; even on August 3, the day before war was declared, his name appeared in English newspapers as a member of a Neutrality Committee that still hoped to keep England out of it. But once the war was a reality, Murray saw that that position was untenable, and struggled to find another. That struggle is recorded in his essay 'First Thoughts on the War', written in August 1914. It is a troubled essay, full of moral uncertainty, in which one can discern the voice of the classicist arguing with, and in the end out-shouted by, the voice of the patriot. What, Murray asked himself, was the task of non-combatants like himself in wartime? It was, he decided, to avoid embitterment and brutalization of feeling — to remain civilized.

> It may be a difficult task [Murray wrote], but at least it is not hideous; and some of the work that we must do is. So hideous, indeed, that at times it seems strange that we carry it out at all — this war of civilised men against civilised men, against our intellectual teachers, our brothers in art and science and healing medicine, and so large a part of all that makes life beautiful.[18]

Murray doesn't mention German scholars here, but it is clear that he is thinking about them, and about the debt that English classicists owed to the great Germans of the nineteenth century. And beyond that specific debt, there is the larger vision of 'civilized man', engaged in a humane activity that ignores national boundaries.[19] Murray saw that a European war would necessarily be different from the other wars that England had fought in the century since Waterloo: it would be fought against a nation that shared English ideas of civilization. But he saw no way out of this dilemma, and he gave his support to the war; he was one of the writers who attended Masterman's propaganda meeting in September, and his signature was on the 'Authors' Declaration' that emerged from the meeting.

At about the same time that Murray was setting down his first thoughts, W.P. Paterson, Professor of Divinity at the University of Edinburgh, was gathering scholarly essays for a book that was published in the spring of 1915 as *German Culture: The Contributions of the Germans to Knowledge, Literature, Art and Life*. Paterson made the intentions of the book clear in his preface:

> The Germans are undoubtedly one of the great peoples of history, who, like the English, combine a share of the intellectual and aesthetic

endowments of the ancient Greeks with the practical capacity of the ancient Romans; and they have made a substantial contribution to the common store of civilised humanity. They have made some mark — often a very deep mark — in every higher department of the life and labour of the human spirit. The aim of the present book is to give a somewhat detailed account of what Germany has thus accomplished in the chief spheres of human activity, and an effort has been made to estimate the value of its work without prepossession or prejudice.[20]

Paterson had chosen some distinguished contributors, including Michael Sadler on German education, Donald Tovey on German music, and J. Arthur Thomson on German science, and on the whole they accomplished what he had hoped for. Their essays are learned and judicious, praising where praise is due, generalizing here and there on German national qualities — their thoroughness, their humourlessness — but without malice and without chauvinism. The book was just the thing, one might think, to help the English to preserve a proper sense of proportion in a difficult time. And other, similar books were appearing at the same time: *British and German Scholarship* by the Biblical scholar James Hope Moulton and *German Culture Past and Present* by the socialist-historian Ernest Belfort Bax are both serious efforts to treat German culture justly. But by 1915 it was too late.

The professors' war began on August 20, 1914, when two of Germany's most distinguished scholars, Ernest Hackel and Rudolph Eucken, published a protest in the *Vossische Zeitung* against England's case for being in the war. The protest was quoted in *The Times* for August 25:

> What is happening to-day will be inscribed in the annals of history as an indelible shame to England. England fights to please a half-Asiatic Power against Germanism. She fights not only on the side of barbarism, but also of moral injustice, for it is not to be forgotten that Russia began the war because it was not willing that there should be a thorough expiation of a wretched murder.
>
> It is the fault of England that the present war is extended to a world war, and that all culture is thereby endangered. And why all this? Because she was envious of Germany's greatness, because she wished at all costs to hinder a further extension of this greatness. She was only waiting for a favourable opportunity to break out to the detriment of Germany, and she therefore seized most promptly on the necessary German advance through Belgium as a pretext in

order to cloak her brutal national selfishness with a mantle of respectability.[21]

Against these attacks, Englishmen retaliated with counter-attacks:

> Really the German professor is very marvellous person. Perhaps the world has never seen so curious a combination of childlike artlessness, truculence, and stodgy erudition. An English statesman — was it Gladstone? — once said that there was no animal more dangerous than a mad sheep, and modern Teutonic professorship whimsically suggests sheepishness turned bloodthirsty.

> [German scholars are] williing to spend their lives in narrow and absorbed pursuit of some object which, viewed in cold blood, possesses no very great importance and no particular illumination or beauty.

> ... up to the present there has been no such thing as an original German culture.

> Industry, in fact, not gifts, is what the Prussian Government demands of its learned — and industry that shall provide a population tenacious in acts of war, infinitely courageous in the contemplation of death, and utterly and finally at the disposal of the State, whether the actions of the State be good or evil.[22]

The source of the first quotation is what one might expect: it is from *The Daily Call*, an ultra-patriotic halfpenny paper that had sprung up when the war began. But the others are less easily dismissed: they are (in order) by Gilbert Murray, John Cowper Powys, and Ford Madox Hueffer (who would later call himself Ford Madox Ford): all English intellectuals of reputation, and all engaged in denying that German intellectuals were in any way comparable to themselves.

The case of Hueffer is a particularly interesting one, for he was not only a serious artist, he was also a self-consciously cosmopolitan man of letters, who in pre-war days had been proud of his connections with Germany. He was the son of Franz Carl Christoph Johannes Hüffer, a German musicologist who had emigrated to England, anglicized his name, and become music critic for *The Times*. Hueffer had travelled in Germany with his mistress, Violet Hunt, in 1911 and again in 1913, and he contributed two essays, a preface, and numerous notes to her book, *The Desirable Alien at Home in Germany*, published in 1913. In these contributions Hueffer made much of his Germanness, signing his notes

J.L.F.M.H. — that is, Joseph Leopold Ford Madox Hueffer — and referring to 'my august Sovereign, Ernest Ludwig Grossherzog von Hessen-Darmstadt und bei Rhein'. He had criticisms to make of modern Germany — he thought, for example, that the German university system was 'extraordinarily wrong-headed', and he confessed that 'a year or so ago I should have said that I detested the Prussianism of the congeries of nations that Germany is.' But recent history had changed that: 'Now we have the image of a Germany threatened with immense Slav empires, kingdoms and states . . . And I confess that I should hate the thought that this proud people, full of free passions, should cease to bulk large in the comity of nations . . .'[23] If anyone in pre-war England could have been regarded as pro-German, it was surely Hueffer.

Yet within a few months he was writing *When Blood is Their Argument*, a propaganda attack on German culture, and particularly on German scholars — their industrious but impoverished intellectual lives, their dreary, plodding work, their lumpish pedantry. It was a hasty, clumsy, excessive attack, as even Hueffer acknowledged: 'I have been charged', he wrote in his preface, 'with deliberate unfairness to the traditions of German learning and of German scholarship.'[24] And well he might have been.

Hueffer did have this defence, that he was writing in wartime, at the request of his government: any Englishman might compromise his values under those conditions, and particularly if he had a German name. The book had been commissioned by Hueffer's friend C.F.G. Masterman, the head of the government propaganda office known as Wellington House, who had summoned so many other writers to the cause. Masterman had been troubled by the notoriety of George Bernard Shaw's pamphlet, *Common Sense About the War*, which appeared in November 1914. Shaw had written, with his customary outrageous reasonableness, that there were Junkers on both sides of the war. To Wellington House this seemed shockingly pro-German, and Hueffer's book was commissioned as a counter-attack.

Masterman seems to have been pleased with his friend's work — pleased enough indeed to review it enthusiastically in the *Nation*, praising it as a 'passionate indictment of Prussian "Kultur"'.[25] (That, presumably, had been Hueffer's brief.) But though the officialness of the assignment may be a defence, the shabby reality of the situation remains: Hueffer, the son of a German scholar, the good European, last year's Germanophile, abusing German learning in public for the sake of the war.

The German professoriate was attacked from another direction in November 1914 when Sir Arthur Quiller-Couch, King Edward VII Professor of English Literature at Cambridge, addressed his students on 'Patriotism and Literature'. 'Q' was an odd sort of man to hold the lofty academic position that he occupied. He had come to Cambridge from a career as a writer of romances and literary journalism: his principal contribution to scholarship had been the *Oxford Book of English Verse*, which must be among the most unscholarly anthologies ever published. He was known to Cambridge students as an entertaining lecturer, and to his colleagues as a Professor of English who knew nothing about philology or Old or Middle English, the subjects that were then the weighty centre of English studies.

'Patriotism and Literature' showed both sides of Q's reputation. For entertainment, there was this:

> No foreigner can hope ever to penetrate the last excellences of an unfamiliar tongue ... The Germans are congenitally unfitted to read our poetry; the very structure of their vocal organs forbids it. Imagine the guttural horrors of a Teuton delivery of Tennyson's fairy-like Claribel:
>
> > 'Ad eve ze beedle boomez
> > Azward ze ticket lone,'
>
> and so on. The German who can write even passable English is yet to be found.[26]

Q's un- or anti-scholarly side appeared when he turned from German English to German scholarship. It was the Germans' fault, he said, that literary study at Cambridge was stuck in the medieval past and in linguistics; it was their fault that the General Period paper in the English literature tripos ended at 1832. 'Such is the menace of the German mind on our literature to substitute the dry chaff of historical research and criticism for the living seed of our language and birthright. There can be only one way of exorcising this menace of dusty historicism — the sword in the hand of the young, who will see to it the tumour is cleanly lanced.'

Q was right in one sense — English literary scholarship in the early twentieth century certainly was modelled on German examples. But he used that neutral fact, and the general anti-German feeling of the time, to argue a cause of his own that had nothing to do with nationality, and could certainly not be won with the sword. He disliked old literature (what he knew of it), and philology, and scholarly methods generally, and he liked recent literature and anecdotal criticism. By making what he disliked German, he turned an academic disagreement into a patriotic issue, and so narrowed and cheapened it. 'It is ill', he told his students, 'for the country whose destiny passes into the hands of professors.' He meant Germany; but one might adapt his line, and say that it was ill for scholarship when its destiny passed into the hands of professors like Q.

The war of the professors was not a really serious war; nothing suffered except the scholarly ideals of accuracy and objectivity, nothing was destroyed except the scholar's vision of a community of scholars. For a little while it succeeded in making the word *professor* sound sinister and threatening, but only for a while; no one could believe that for long, not even in wartime. It was bitterly fought while it went on; but in the end it simply ceased to matter. 'Fortunately,' Bertrand Russell wrote in the summer of 1915, 'no country consists wholly of professors, not even Germany; and it may be hoped that more sanity is to be found among those who have not been made mad by much learning.'[27]

Russell's hope was scarcely sustained by the other battle in the *Kultur* war: the war against German music. If you went to English concert halls at all before the war, what you mainly heard were German conductors leading orchestras full of German musicians in performances of music by German composers. Bach, Mozart, Beethoven and Brahms filled the programmes and Wagner was so popular that he had his own evenings at the Proms — on Mondays. At Covent Garden, the spring opera season of 1914 included seventeen performances of *Parsifal*, as well as productions of *Die Meistersinger, Tristan und Isolde*, and *Die Walküre*. No other art was so dominated by another nation's artists.

Once the war began, this dominance quickly came to seem (to some Englishmen, at least) a sinister case of German imperialism, an invasion by craft and stealth of what should have been a solidly British art form. Now that German music was *enemy* music, couldn't something be done? Something was done, and very hastily. The popular Queen's Hall Prom concerts under Henry Wood began their 1914 season in the second week of the war, with a programme that was to include Strauss's *Don Juan*; but when the day came (it was August 15), Tchaikovsky's *Capriccio Italien* was performed instead. The following Monday's concert, traditionally a 'Wagner evening', was changed to a programme of French and Russian music.

Strauss was, to be sure, a special case: he was not only German, he was also Modern, and he was often attacked in the anti-Modern campaigns. Even more than Schönberg he was taken to be the musical essence of what was wrong with the Germans: 'The antagonism excited by the ethos of Strauss's music,' a *Spectator* critic wrote in 1915, 'has been largely justified by recent events. The brutality of *Elektra*, the glorification of the combative superman in *Heldenleben*, and the choice of one of Nietzsche's works as the programme of another of his symphonic poems — all show a spiritual affinity with the Germany revealed in the war.'[28] Sir Charles Stanford put it more succinctly: 'Richard Strauss is the counterpart of Bernhardi and the General Staff.'[29] As for Schönberg, the loathing with which he was regarded is expressed in a remark made at a meeting of the Musical Association in November 1914: 'Yesterday when I was reading a book on the harmony of Arnold Schönberg, the only emotion it raised was a vague hope that Schönberg might be somewhere in the German trenches.'[30]

Strauss and Schönberg presented easy cases: they could be dropped from concert programmes without serious protest. But what about the other Germans? What about Bach, Beethoven and Brahms? What about Mozart? What about Handel? The Prom officials saw that a musical season without them would be unthinkable, and before the end of August the following notice was inserted in the Prom programme:

> [The management] take this opportunity of emphatically contradict-ing the statements that German music will be boycotted during the present season. The greatest examples of Music and Art are world possessions and unassailable even by the prejudices and passions of the hour.[31]

In the weeks that followed, the Proms orchestra played Beethoven, Mozart, Mendelssohn, Strauss, Liszt and Bach; the Royal Choral Society opened its season in October with Mendelssohn's *Elijah*, and followed with *Messiah* and Bach's *B Minor Mass*; and the London Symphony Orchestra's season included Bach, Haydn, Mozart, Beethoven, Schumann and Brahms.

By the end of the autumn season it seemed, to observers of the musical scene, that reason and musical taste had defeated the forces of cultural chauvinism. G.B. Shaw — a man who was always pleased at the temporary triumphs of good sense — was in high spirits when he reported the episode to his German translator:

> In London last August the usual series of nightly cheap orchestral concerts called Promenade Concerts announced patriotically that no German music would be performed. Everyone applauded the

announcement. But nobody went to the concerts. Within a week a
programme full of Beethoven, Wagner and Strauss was announced.
Everybody was shocked; and everybody went to the concert. It was a
complete and decisive German victory, with nobody killed. A nation
which can win victories like that should make a present of all its
weapons and ammunition to its neighbours, and continue calmly to
rule Europe in spite of all the idiots in jackboots who believe in no
pre-eminence but pre-eminence in homicidal efficiency.[32]

But Shaw was premature in announcing victory: culture and taste were
not to conquer as easily or as quickly as that. The campaign against
German music would continue to the end of the war, and would even
win some of the battles. It went on, for example, into the spring of 1915
in two series of concerts — the All-English concerts and the No-
German concerts. The All-English series was a part of the British Music
Campaign, an organized effort to get English music into concert
programmes, and (what was more difficult) to get English audiences
into the concert halls to listen to it. The leaders of this campaign were
two English composers, Josef Holbrooke and Isidore de Lara; both
offered concert series in the spring season in which audiences were able
to hear works by such English composers as O'Neill, Delius, Grainger,
Bantock, Smyth, Stanford, and Cyril Scott — and of course Holbrooke
and de Lara.

The concerts were not received with much enthusiasm. Arnold
Bennett's response seems to have been typical; 'Festival of British Music
at Queen's Hall last night,' he wrote in his journal for May 12, 1915.
'O'Neill and Bantock and Holbrooke music (Humoreske — Fifine —
The Bells) rotten.'[33] The audiences' disapproval was increased by the
fact that both entrepreneurs chose to interrupt their programmes half-
way through, to harangue their audiences on the patriotic importance of
listening to English music — a practice that understandably made people
restive; 'Musicians must realize,' the Times reviewer wrote crossly, 'that
their audiences are not fools or naughty children, to be whipped into
concert-rooms whether they like it or not.'[34]

The No-German concerts were the invention of Thomas Beecham —
twenty-five Promenade concerts during May and June, from which
German music would be entirely excluded. His concerts were received
somewhat more kindly by audiences and critics than those of Holbrooke
and de Lara were: Beecham might play music that they didn't especially
want to hear, but at least he didn't tell them that it was patriotic to listen

to it. The series was generally regarded as an interesting experiment, which ought not to be repeated, and it wasn't. Before long Henry Wood was announcing his Prom season for the autumn of 1915: it would include a substantial number of works by British composers — about a third of the total — and that surely was a victory for Holbrooke and de Lara; but it would also include all nine of Beethoven's symphonies, all four of Brahms's, the Mozart G-minor symphony, and five Brandenburg concertos. And the Wagner evenings would be restored. German music had returned to stay.

The musical wars were not over, however; in the autumn of 1914 English musicians had begun their own campaign, not against German music but against German musicians, and it continued relentlessly into the following year. English orchestras had long depended on German instrumentalists and German conductors; the war gave English players an opportunity to rid themselves of this competition, and call their actions patriotism. At meetings held in November, English musicians agreed that German and Austrian musicians in England were 'enemies really and technically' (whatever that meant), and a resolution was unanimously passed approving the formation of a 'National Association for the protection of British interests in music'. Shortly thereafter, Lyons, the restaurant chain, fired all its German, Austrian, and Hungarian musicians.

There were other ways, too — trivial and silly ways — in which the music wars went on. The German language was found to be unpleasing to the English ear, and so the songs of Schubert, Schumann and Brahms, and arias from German operas, were not sung, or were sung in translation. German names seemed to be equally unpleasing: the conductor of the Torquay Municipal Orchestra, an Englishman with the unfortunate name of Basil Hindenberg, had to make a public announcement that he would henceforth be known as Basil Cameron. Even the printing of Bach's portrait on a programme cover was objected to as 'disgraceful'.[35]

Not everyone, of course, was so foolish. The critic Ernest Newman warned very early in the war against musical chauvinism: 'How', he asked his fellow-musicians, '. . . can we contemplate without alarm and regret a possible set-back to the culture that, be its faults what it may, has given us Wagner and Brahms and Strauss and Hugo Wolf?' And another musician, writing in the same journal (the *Musical Times*), urged his readers not to think of the war in musical terms: 'No one', he wrote, 'has a quarrel with the Germany of Beethoven.'[36] But clearly many musicians *did* have a quarrel with that Germany, and saw advantage in pursuing it; the dream of a British music, played by British musicians for British audiences, remained alive until the war ended.

The war against German *Kultur*, the prospect of which had so troubled the signers of that August letter to *The Times*, had become a war against culture. That this had happened, and happened so quickly, was partly a consequence of the high emotions of the early days of the war. But it was also clearly the intention of the English government that it should happen, and that culture should be made a weapon of the war. Perhaps the propaganda planners at Wellington House saw that in a war like this one, fought against Western European nations linked to England by deep cultural bonds, it would be necessary to loosen those bonds, to make destruction possible at all. Perhaps they saw that England *had* to quarrel with the Germany of Beethoven.

What they did not see was that in warring against that Germany, they were warring against their own past. The qualities that in the propaganda campaign were identified as German — the scientific thoroughness, the belief in quantitative measurement, the rationalism, the trust in the authority of the professoriate, and in music and literature the great tradition of romanticism — these were all as strongly woven into the English as into the German past. So that when the cultural patriots of England laid down their propaganda barrages, they often seemed to be firing, not at the Germans, but at their own ancestors. The immediate result was a diminishment of English culture. Another result, perhaps less obvious but more permanent, was a further widening of that gap between the past and the present, that breach in the perceived continuity of history, which was the war's most striking legacy to the world after the war.

III.   *The War Against Dissent*

The official Parliamentary expression of this principle of cultural contraction was the Defence of the Realm Act (commonly known as DORA), which was first enacted on the fourth day of the war, and was thereafter endlessly amended and elaborated right through to the war's end and beyond. As originally formulated, DORA must have seemed a perfectly reasonable step for a nation newly at war to take. It was only half a page long:

Be it enacted by the King's most Excellent Majesty by and with the advice and consent of the Lords Spiritual and Temporal, and Commons, in this present Parliament assembled, and by the authority of the same, as follows:—

1. His Majesty in Council has power during the continuance of the present war to issue regulations as to the powers and duties of the Admiralty and Army Council, and of the members of His Majesty's forces, and other persons acting in His behalf, for securing the public safety and the defence of the realm; and may by such regulations authorise the trial by courts martial and punishment of persons contravening any of the provisions of such regulations designed —

(a) to prevent persons communicating with the enemy or obtaining information for that purpose or any purpose calculated to jeopardise the success of the operations of any of His Majesty's forces or to assist the enemy; or

(b) to secure the safety of any means of communication, or of railways, docks or harbours; in like manner as if such persons were subject to military law and had on active service committed an offence under section five of the Army Act.

2. This Act may be cited as the Defence of the Realm Act, 1914.[37]

If at first glance there doesn't seem to be anything very threatening to culture in these few sentences, that is partly no doubt because of the official rhetoric in which the Act was couched, and partly because of its extreme generality. But even the regulations that were subsequently written to make the law more specific seemed to have little enough to do with cultural matters. Most of them defined and extended the power of the State over Englishmen's lives. His Majesty's Government could seize property from private owners, restrict the movement of persons, and remove individuals from their homes upon suspicion and without charges; it assumed control over a citizen's right to fell a tree, keep homing pigeons, destroy a stray dog, open a pub, treat a friend to a drink, or consort with a prostitute.

All of these restraints had to do with the limitation of individual freedoms; but what did they have to do with Art? They had, as it turned out, everything to do with Art. For DORA gave the State unlimited power to control the instruments of communication and the transmission of information, and to define what was meant by those terms. Almost as soon as the Act itself had been passed, the government was at work extending the Act's meaning in the area of

information. The first extension added the following words to item
1 (a) of the Act:

> or to prevent the spread of reports likely to cause disaffection or
> alarm.

With the adoption of this phrase, so vague and so inclusive, the
censoring of wartime English thought and expression could begin in
earnest. Other amendments followed: in 1915 it became illegal to send
any written communication to or from the United Kingdom except
through the post; in 1916 the exporting of any written or printed
document to any enemy or neutral country in Europe or America,
except under strict limitations, was also forbidden. Other 1916 amendments made the power of DORA over the arts more explicit: no one
should either by word of mouth or in writing or in any newspaper,
periodical, book, circular, or other printed publication, spread reports
or make statements intended or likely to cause disaffection, or to
prejudice recruiting or training, or produce any play or picture or film
that would do any of these things. In effect, any expression of
opposition to, or criticism of, the war in any art form, and any
communication of such opinions to persons in other countries, had
become a criminal offence. English critics had agreed that war was good
for art; DORA reversed the proposition: art should be good for war, or it
should not exist.

One can get a sense of how DORA worked at the start of the war by
considering the history of *The Devil's Business*, a play by the militant
Socialist Fenner Brockway. Brockway wrote the play in February 1914,
as a satirical attack on the growing international munitions industry; the
setting was a British Cabinet meeting during a war between Britain and
Germany, and the characters were recognizable caricatures of Asquith,
Lloyd George, Grey and Churchill. The declaration of war delayed
publication, and in the interval Brockway revised his text, removing
the specific references to nations and politicians: 'Two civilized and
Christian Powers are at war,' his new version began: 'one is your own:
the other the nation who is your particular aversion at the moment.'[38]
Nevertheless, when it was published in October the police raided both
the National Labour Press in Manchester, where the little pamphlet was
printed, and the headquarters of the Independent Labour Party in
London, where it was being sold, and seized all available copies. The
Manchester authorities found the play unobjectionable, and the copies
seized there were returned, but a London magistrate judged the play to

be an offence against DORA — prejudicial to recruiting, he said, and treasonable — and ordered all the London copies destroyed. And so the play remained, good fun in Manchester, treason in London.

Before the war was over, other books would be burned in DORA's name, and writers (including Brockway) would be imprisoned. Most of the first cases involving written documents, however, were charges not so much against living writers and their works as against the tradition of pacifist thought. In November 1915 one John Bailey, a labourer, was sentenced to three months for writing (not publishing) an article strongly opposed to militarism, 'under the influence of Tolstoi's writings'.[39] And in December, two men were given six-month terms for publishing a leaflet setting forth the Christian doctrine of war, based on the Sermon on the Mount[40] — perhaps the one on page 82, which was in circulation at the time.

The power to impose such penalties for such actions struck some members of Parliament as contrary to the English tradition of free speech, but the government was untroubled by their protests: 'I may say now,' Sir John Simon, the Attorney General, replied in the Commons,

> that as long as the provisions of the Defence of the Realm Act as it now stands on the Statute Book give nothing more than is needed in this national emergency the argument that they are novel and do violence to our constitutional traditions is an argument of very little weight.[41]

For the duration of the war, and for some time after, that certainly seemed to be true.

Though these early cases of dissent passed almost unnoticed at the time, and are now entirely forgotten, they make an important point that the Myth of the War has obscured. In the Myth, opposition to the war came late in England, and was a consequence of the experience of trench warfare: look at Sassoon, we say, look at Owen, look at Blunden. Certainly it was true of these war poets, and of the painter Paul Nash, and of soldier-pacifists like Max Plowman and Miles Malleson (and no doubt of most of the 284 men who were executed during the war for desertion or cowardice), that opposition followed experience; but the war had its opponents from the beginning, including many who never fought. Independent Labour Party members spoke against the war in Parliamentary debates in the first days of August 1914; journals like the *Nation, War and Peace*, and the *Labour Leader* published anti-war editorials; anti-war poems began to appear almost as soon as war poems

CHRIST AND PEACE

"Blessed are the peacemakers: for they shall be called the children of God."—*Matthew v. 9.*

"Ye have heard that it hath been said, thou shalt love thy neighbour, and hate thine enemy. But I say unto you, love your enemies, bless them that curse you, do good to them that hate you."—*Matt. v. 43, 44.*

Do you believe this?

If so, it is your sacred duty to

Work for an immediate PEACE!

LEAFLET No. 2.

THE NATIONAL LABOUR PRESS, LTD., MANCHESTER AND LONDON.   20455 did[42]; Shaw's *Common Sense About the War* was published in November 1914. There was strong opposition in Cambridge, led by Bertrand Russell, who was teaching there, and in Bloomsbury.

Opposition grew in part in reaction to the terms in which the war was supported. The language that patriot-journalists used to demonstrate that war was good for art, for example, sometimes seemed to less bellicose persons to be extravagant, outrageous, inflated, or simply foolish. For example, Francis Meynell, a minor Bloomsburyite of military age but of no military inclinations, was goaded to pacific outburst by the imagery of Gosse's *Edinburgh Review* essay on 'War and Literature' (quoted above, p. 12). His response, 'War's a Crime', was the first (and fiercest) article against the war to appear in a national daily newspaper; it was published in the radical *Herald* on December 19, 1914:

> Our comfortable politicians inform us that this is a war against war, and a war contrived by Germany. Our comfortable theologians tell us that it is a war where killing is no sin. My comfortable friends, with wonderful unanimity, tell me that the sacrifices of this war, borne by others and not by me, put any and all criticism from me out of court. And, finally, the most reptilious doctrine of all is expounded with language that is almost obscene by Edmund Gosse in the *Edinburgh* — the 'red stream of blood is the Condy's Fluid,' the 'sovereign disinfectant' for us all!
>
> Let us consider these things one by one. The war has been a 'tonic' for all of us. Mr. Gosse, no doubt, would point to all the young men with narrow chests who are getting fit — fit to be shot down, or worse, to shoot down others. Let us survey (he would argue) the pleasing sight of Lady Rebecca Isaacstein's new-found love of the poor, dear Poor, demonstrated by her opening of a new club for working women (the necessary funds are being 'collected' from her servants). And then the wonderful absence of Suffragist demonstrations and strikes! And so on.
>
> To you, Mr. Gosse, and to others of your kidney, I say that if you are able to shut your eyes — yes, and nose and ears — to the shrieking, mutilated and stinking horrors of the battlefield, and if you are able to dip your mind in this mental 'Condy's Fluid' of blood, and feel stronger for it, and if you are able to point to any other benefit, not nearly as important as *that* crowning mercy, of course, but important, nevertheless — to you I say that any 'good' born and battened in such vileness, in the slaying and maiming and raping of

innocent people, is the final blasphemy against the Almighty. The
lands are rotted with blood and the seas are swallowing their dead,
and the clean, sweet rivers are full of mangled corpses — amen, amen,
it is all a tonic for Mr. Gosse . . . [43]

There is a good deal of Bloomsbury in this performance: a patronizing
irony and wit, a sense of style and of the wickedness of misusing
language, a display of reason in the face of human folly, a willingness to
defend the individual against the multitude. But there is also anger and
fierce abuse such as Clive Bell would not have allowed himself; Meynell
was Bloomsbury, but he was also young and passionate and radical, and
he was writing at a time when anger and abuse were all around him, and
were called patriotism.

It may seem at first surprising that Bloomsbury — meaning, of
course, Leonard and Virginia Woolf, Lytton Strachey, Clive and
Vanessa Bell and their circle — should have been one of the front-line
positions in the war against the war. In English cultural history
Bloomsbury has come to represent the genteel wing of the avant-garde
of its time — a mixture of aesthetic principles, personal relations, and a
certain fastidious class consciousness. But during the war it was
important for a different reason: Bloomsbury then, from the war's very
beginning, was a continuing demonstration of the fact that opposition
to the war — continuous, principled opposition — was a possible
attitude for intelligent English men and women. Of the men of military
age in the Bloomsbury circle, none entered the army: Bertrand Russell
was tried and convicted twice for his pacifist statements, and eventually
went to prison; Francis Meynell refused non-combatant service and was
imprisoned by the military authorities; he went on a hunger-and-thirst
strike, collapsed, and was unconditionally discharged[44]; David Garnett,
Duncan Grant, and Virginia Woolf's brother Adrian Stephen performed
alternative service; E.M. Forster worked with the Red Cross in Egypt;
Strachey faced an official tribunal and was rejected. Nobody fought.

Of those who remained in free civilian life, some simply got on with
their work, but others — Clive Bell, for example — diverted their
energies to argue their convictions in public. Bell was an art critic; but
he was also a born pamphleteer, never happier than when haranguing
and offending the British philistine, whether his subject was Cézanne or
War. During 1915 Bell wrote two pacifist essays, both clearly calculated
to cause maximum annoyance to his countrymen. The first, a pamphlet
titled *Peace at Once*, opposes the war on the very Bloomsburyish ground

that it would leave the world poorer in the pleasures of life. 'The people who will pay most for the war', Bell wrote,

> ... will be the people who live through the next thirty or fifty years. A few capitalists, certainly, will be enriched; the rest of us will have to pay. We shall all be worse off; that is to say, we shall have to work harder and be contented with less for our work. Our labour will purchase worse food, shorter holidays, smaller rooms, less fun, less ease, in a word, less well-being than it used to purchase ... Life will be harder and more joyless. There will be less money to buy food and a drink for the ordinary man and woman, less to buy milk for babies and warm clothes for children, less for scientific experiments and social improvements, less for pleasure, less for leisure. Life will become less amusing and less healthy, old age more cheerless, death more masterful. Worst of all, there will be less hope. That is what the war will cost.[45]

There can't have been many people in England in 1915 thinking about the war in terms of its effects on fun, ease, and the size of post-war rooms. But Bell was faithful to his convictions: a world without pleasures would be the antithesis of Bloomsbury.

In his second dissenting essay, 'Art and War', Bell appeared in a more familiar role, as a Bloomsbury authority on aesthetic matters. The essay was in effect a rejoinder to all those critics who had been explaining why war was good for art, and what patriotic art should be. Bell's reply was simple: war had nothing to do with art, and art had nothing to do with patriotism; the artist's only duty to his country in wartime was to go on being an artist. Indeed, the existence of a war made that duty even more imperative, for 'a nation that would defend the cause of civilization must remain civilized'.[46]

But Bell was not content simply to argue the importance of art; he took the occasion to abuse, with a fine Bloomsbury disdain, those supporters of the war who used art to strengthen their arguments. They cited the destruction of Reims cathedral by German artillery as the sort of barbarism they were fighting; but what, said Bell, did *they* know? 'Reims is or was a typical thirteenth century building; and, like most thirteenth century buildings, is or was, to my feeling, of no great artistic significance.'[47] Certainly it wasn't worth destroying lives and life's pleasures over. And what right had they, the monied class of England, to rant about the destruction of a work of art anyway?

How dare the people who fill our streets and public places with monuments that make us the laughingstock of Europe, the people who cannot spare a few guineas to save a picture, who cheerfully improve away respectable architecture, who allow artists to perish and put up the Admiralty arch, — how dare such people pose as the champions of culture and expose their wounded feelings in the penny and half-penny papers.[48]

Bell's essay is entertaining, but it is also significant, and especially in the context of his other essay, *Peace at Once*, as an anticipation of the post-war cultural situation. Bell assumed, and took pleasure in, an absolute separation between 'those who care seriously for art' and those who don't; and he associated those who do with other forms of dissent, and especially with opposition to the war. That connection of advanced art with political and social dissent would grow stronger in the later war years, and in the post-war years would define the relations between younger artists and their society.

Bell was a Bloomsbury pacifist; but there were other kinds. By the time his essays appeared in 1915 a number of anti-war organizations existed and were publishing pamphlets and holding public meetings. The Union of Democratic Control, a group of political radicals that included Russell and Ramsay MacDonald, was founded in November 1914; the Fellowship of Reconciliation, a Christian pacifist movement, began in December; early in 1915 the No-Conscription Fellowship, an organization with strong trade union support, got under way. In July 1915 a conference on the 'Pacifist Philosophy of Life' was held in London, and was addressed by Russell and Edward Carpenter. And there were other opposing organizations — the Women's International League, the League of Peace and Freedom, and the Friends' Service Committee for example. It was no doubt partly because of these activities that the powers of DORA had continually to be revised and expanded.

Together these opposing groups made a very odd anti-war army: Socialists, Bloomsbury aesthetes, radical women, trade unionists, Quakers, Christians, a few Cambridge dons. They were alike in one thing only: what they cared most about, whether it was art, or religion, or the intellectual life, or the working class, was not a national but an international principle, and therefore a contradiction of the principle on which war — any war — is fought. Among them they conducted a war-against-the-war, often at considerable personal cost.

And the government fought back with the weapons that it commanded: suppression, prohibition, conscription, and imprisonment.

In terms of the total British population, these opposing movements did not amount to a very large minority. There were no major artists among them, and no significant work of anti-war art came out of any of the groups. Nevertheless, they have their place in the cultural history of the war years: from the beginning of the war they kept alive the spirit of opposition, until it could find imaginative expression in the works of the poets and painters of the later war years. It is important to recognize that opposition to the war did not begin over there at Ypres or the Somme or Passchendaele. Dissent had been *thought* in England before any of those battles were fought, though it was only after the battles that it could be given imaginative form.

IV.   *The Women's War*

The Women's Suffrage movement had been a vigorous, often violent form of dissent before the war, and one might have expected that it would increase in vigour after war was declared. Surely the coming of the Great War would be perceived by militant women as a supreme example of male stupidity, and a conclusive argument for giving the vote to women (and perhaps withdrawing it from men). And so, at first, it seemed likely to be. On August 4, a few hours before the war became official, a federation of women's groups in emergency session in London passed a resolution 'deploring the abandonment of peaceful negotiations, the failure to settle the present international differences by conciliation or arbitration, and the outbreak of war in Europe as an unparalleled disaster.'[49] It seemed a moment when women might mass themselves as a political force — not only the factions of the Suffrage movement, but the anti-Suffragists as well. But the moment passed, and the possibility that war might accomplish what rhetoric had not — the unification of women — faded and was gone. Indeed, the immediate effect of the war was to weaken and fragment the movement, and generally to subordinate women's rights to the needs of the war, often with the active support of the women's own leaders.

The first defection came at once, in the first week of the war, when Mrs Pankhurst, leader of the militant Women's Social and Political

Union, announced to her followers that the organization was suspend-
ing its activities. A year earlier she had defiantly told the court that was
trying her that the women's war would go on until English women had
the rights of citizens; now, with a real war begun, she told her regiment
of women to disband, and turned her remarkable energies to supporting
England's cause. In the autobiography that she published a few months
later, Mrs Pankhurst made that decision seem both triumphant and
patriotic:

> Our battles are practically over, we confidently believe. For the
> present at least our arms are grounded, for directly the threat of
> foreign war descended on our nation we declared a complete truce
> from militancy.[50]

But in fact there was no triumph: women were no nearer having the
rights of citizens than they had been before the war, in fact the war
restricted their rights (as it did the rights of all people) in the name of
patriotism. But the truce was made, militancy ended, and for the first
time in a decade British Suffragists and the British government marched
in the same direction.

What happened was not that Mrs Pankhurst and her followers had
made peace; they had simply shifted their belligerency to a different
war, though, having shifted, they made some efforts to claim that it was
in fact the same struggle. Mrs Pankhurst's daughter Christabel, for
example, on a lecture tour of the United States, told her New York
audience that

> there is something very important in this question of the war from a
> woman's point of view. What if Germany wins? She won't, but if she
> did; that would mean a disastrous blow to the women's movement
> both in Germany and in every other country. Bismarck boasted that
> Germany is a male nation. We do not want male nations.[51]

But a nation at war *is* a male nation; by supporting the war the
Pankhursts had defected to the enemy in the women's war.

Patriotic Suffragists like Christabel Pankhurst and her mother must
have seemed valuable as propagandists in this very propagandist war.
But they had other uses, too. The Suffrage societies had accustomed
women to organizing and being organized, and provided already functioning structures and trained officers for the planning and administration
of women in war work and in the military services. Suffragist volunteers staffed the first women's war service, the Women's Emergency

Corps, and had it functioning on the second day of the war, finding war
work for women. Such organizations multiplied and expanded as the
war went on.[52]

Women's organizations could also be counted on to turn out for
pro-war demonstrations when required. In July 1915, for example,
Emmeline and Christabel Pankhurst led thousands of women in a
Women's War Pageant that marched for miles through the rain to
the Ministry of Munitions, where a delegation expressed their support
of a scheme of conscription for both men and women, and offered
their services to the country. The Minister, Lloyd George, was very
pleased; and so he might have been, since he seems to have financed
the demonstration.[53]

But not all of the pre-war Suffragists were pleased with Mrs
Pankhurst's truce, and there were many who refused to shift wars. Her
daughter Sylvia, for example, went on working with the poor of
London's East End, and agitating for the rights of women. In wartime,
among the poor women with whom she lived, the issues were primarily
economic: women in war work were paid less than men for equal work,
and the wives of soldiers did not always receive adequate dependants'
allowances. But there were also questions of civil liberties. Town
councils and military commanders in England and Wales considered
women as threats to the health of the army, and wanted them banned
from the pubs where soldiers gathered, and even kept off the streets
altogether during hours of darkness, apparently on the theory that if
there were no women at hand there would be no venereal disease. To
accomplish this end they invoked the authority of DORA, the all-purpose
weapon against dissent. Against these injustices Sylvia led her own
delegation to Westminster, but they were not welcomed as her mother
had been, and they met no minister. Still they gained some concessions,
and though women continued to be underpaid, they also continued to
drink in Cardiff pubs.

One can see from these examples how the war deflected women's
energies, both on the right and on the left of their movement, away
from the issue of suffrage, and on to other issues that the war seemed to
make more urgent. The directions of those deflections are made quite
clear in the changes that the titles of two women's journals underwent
during the war: Christabel Pankhurst's *Suffragette* became *Britannia*;
Sylvia's *Women's Dreadnought* became *The Workers' Dreadnought*. In both
cases, the war of women against men had become another war: on the
right, The Great War; on the left, The Class War. In the process, the

women's movement was fragmented and dissipated, and virtually ceased to exist as a political movement.

Obviously the central and most divisive issue of the war for women was the war itself. From the beginning there were those within the movement who felt that women should take a united stand against the war, and that a campaign for peace should be a central part of their activities. When the National Union of Women's Suffrage Societies met in Birmingham in the summer of 1915, this question was raised and discussed; but the meeting voted against undertaking 'political propaganda directed to the promoting of international goodwill and future peace'.[54] It seems odd that a majority of these Suffragists should be against such a proposal, at such a time; nevertheless, they were. And because they were, the peace campaigners broke away, and formed a British branch of the Women's International League for Peace and Freedom, and peace as a women's issue was detached from the main body of the Suffrage movement. But by then there really was no movement, anyway.

What the war had done to Suffragism was to move it from the centre of the English stage to a place at the edge, or in the wings. The gestures that in peacetime had seemed violent and dramatic — the breaking of shop windows and the burning of houses — were being enacted every wartime day on a vast scale in Belgium and northern France; by comparison, the women's war could only appear as a marginal, undramatic, and perhaps unpatriotic indulgence. Women could, of course, enter war work, and some did — though not so many as is sometimes thought, and not on the whole from the middle and upper classes. The Women's Emergency Corps took class for granted in its offer to 'find employment for the Middle Class Worker' and 'work for the Voluntary Helper'. One was paid for employment, but not for work. A sociological study of *Women in Modern Industry* published in 1915 made the same point more elaborately:

> In great part the new demand for labour has been met by the overflow from other industries, though it has been supplemented by the addition of voluntary workers of the class usually termed 'unoccupied', that is to say, not working for wages. There are obvious risks in bringing women from the upper and middle classes into a labour market the conditions of which are usually much against working-women; on the other hand, such an arrangement as was made,

e.g. that amateurs should train so as to replace ordinary working women for the week-end, seems an admirable device to use the superfluous energies of the leisured so as to give the workers time for rest and recuperation.[55]

This passage, with its language of 'unoccupied' women, and amateurs, and leisure, implies traditional notions of women and class — notions disturbed temporarily by war, but not essentially altered. And with those notions came serious problems. At a time when men were engaged in war, how were 'unoccupied' women to feel 'occupied'? Not by entering the labour market. Middle-class women were untrained to do any manual work, and they had been raised to think such work unsuitable for ladies. This did not change significantly during the war; statistics show that half of the 800,000 women who came into industry — mainly in munitions factories — during the war years left jobs in domestic service to do so (and caused a severe servant problem). Most of the rest came from other kinds of factory work.[56]

Volunteer work was of course possible, and in women's diaries and letters one finds accounts of little voluntary labours, like this from the diary of Cynthia Asquith, the Prime Minister's 'unoccupied' daughter-in-law:

> Grace called for me at eleven and took me to Friary House, where we did a two hours 'shift' at making portions of respirators ... Any manual labour has great fascination to me and I simply loved it. It is such fun feeling a factory girl and it gave one some idea of how exciting it must be to do piecework for money. One felt so competitive even unrewarded. I must say I was very glad I hadn't got to do a twelve-hour day — it is quite tiring.[57]

For those who didn't find factory work as exciting as Lady Cynthia did, there were various quasi-military services — the Voluntary Aid Detachment, the Women's Army Corps, the Women's Royal Service, the Women's Air Force, the Women's Police, and the Timber Cutters — though the number of women who entered such services full-time was relatively small, only 43,000 by the war's end, according to government statistics.[58] The VAD, in which women worked as nurses' aides in military hospitals, appealed to many younger women, and some fine accounts of the experience were written. Clearly it was intensely painful to work among wounded, suffering men; but it was also, it seems, frustrating. The impression that one gets from women's accounts is of self-doubt and self-denigration, of being women who can't do what the trained nurses can do, and who feel inferior to men because they can't be *in* the war as men can. 'Living so near the edge of death,' Enid Bagnold wrote of the wounded soldiers she nursed, 'they are more aware of life than we are.' And in another passage: 'They are new-born; they have as yet no standards and do not look for any. Ah, to have had that experience too! . . . I am of the old world.'[59] This sense of a new world, inhabited and known only by men who have fought and suffered, turns up also in the war poets of the later war years; it is interesting to see it recognized and accepted as true by one of the excluded.

If a woman were a writer, she could of course write about the war in fiction, and many did. Most books were patriotic, pro-war stories like Florence L. Barclay's *My Heart's Right There*, which appeared in December 1914. The title, from 'Tipperary', suggests the general spirit of the book; and for readers who might miss the point there was also a Union Jack on the cover, the music of 'Tipperary' on the title page, and a dedication 'To Our Men at the Front'. The story — it's not really long enough to be called a *novel* — tells of a regular soldier who leaves his wife and child for service at the Front, is wounded, comes home for a rest, and then returns to the Front. The narrative is told from the wife's point of view, but of course all the action is the husband's, and the war only exists in the account that he gives of it to his passive wife. The moral of the story is put by the husband as he returns to the war at the end of the book:

> It's a righteous war, my girl; and every man who fears God and honours the King, should be up, and out, and ready to do his share; and every woman who loves her home, must be willing bravely to do her part, by letting her man go.[60]

That version of woman's role was repeated again and again, in novels and poems, in speeches and letters to the editor, right to the end of the war. It is not, of course, really a role at all: it offers women only passivity in a time of action — to let go and wait, and to be, in the sociologist's term, 'unoccupied'.

Florence Barclay evidently found that role an entirely comfortable one, but other writing women didn't, and especially those who had been active in the Suffrage movement before the war. For them, the war brought feelings of helplessness, uselessness, and guilt, and there are many war poems by women that express these feelings. Here is a poem by the Suffragist lecturer and writer Cicely Hamilton:

NON-COMBATANT

Before one drop of angry blood was shed
    I was sore hurt and beaten to my knee;
Before one fighting man reeled back and died
    The War-Lords struck at me.

They struck me down — an idle, useless mouth,
    As cumbrous — nay, more cumbrous — than the dead,
With life and heart afire to give and give
    I take a dole instead.

With life and heart afire to give and give
    I take and eat the bread of charity.
In all the length of all this eager land,
    No man has need of me.

That is my hurt — my burning, beating wound;
    That is the spear-thrust driven through my pride!
With aimless hands, and mouth that must be fed,
    I wait and stand aside.

Let me endure it, then, with stiffened lip:
    I, even I, have suffered in the strife!
Let me endure it then — I give my pride
    Where others give a life.[61]

Hamilton eventually dealt with her non-combatant status in the only way that was open to women — she went to France with a women's hospital unit. But that was not always a simple solution, as the experience of the novelist May Sinclair shows.

In 1914 May Sinclair was an established novelist, just over fifty: a woman with every right to be non-combatant, one would think. But she wanted to be in the war, and in late September 1914 she left England with a Red Cross ambulance unit to work in Belgium as the unit's secretary, treasurer, and part-time nurse. She was attached to a hospital in Ghent, and retreated when the army did. Three weeks later she was recalled to England, ostensibly to raise funds for the unit, and was refused permission to rejoin it in the field. In effect, she had been sacked, apparently for incompetence.

Out of this brief experience came two books: *A Journal of Impressions in Belgium*, published in August 1915, and *Tasker Jevons: The True Story*, a novel, published in February 1916. The *Journal* is a first-person, present-tense narrative of May Sinclair's three weeks in Belgium: how she tried to be helpful, how she was snubbed and ignored by doctors and nurses and left behind when heroic deeds were to be done, or went along and failed to do them, and how in the end she was simply cast aside. *Tasker Jevons* uses the same ambulance-unit material in its climactic chapters, but the story is told by a man, and the experience is given to a man (a novelist clearly modelled on H.G. Wells), and the ending is an heroic one.

Of the two books, the *Journal* is brilliant, moving, and convincing, while the novel is just another war novel, undistinguished and altogether forgettable. Why the difference? It is not, I think, simply a matter of fact versus fancy, but that the journal contains one crucial element that the novel lacks: it is about failure, a woman's unsuccessful attempt to enter the heroic world of war. Not that her book doesn't contain heroines: it does — women who walk on to battlefields in search of the wounded, and who stay at their hospital posts in Antwerp as the city falls to the Germans. But they are heroines of the traditional, nurturing, 'womanly' kind. May Sinclair wanted more than that: she wanted adventure, and 'the illusion of valour'. She wanted to know what being a hero feels like; and, being a woman, she failed.

In the *Journal* she explains the principal reason for her failure in a metaphor that is common in war writing:

> It is with the game of war as it was with the game of football I used to play with my big brothers in the garden. The women may play it if they're fit enough, up to a certain point, very much as I played football in the garden. The big brothers let their little sister kick off; they let her run away with the ball; they stood back and let her make goal after goal; but when it came to the scrimmage they took hold of her and gently but firmly moved her to one side. If she persisted she became an infernal nuisance. And if those big brothers over there only knew what I was after they would make arrangements for my immediate removal from the seat of war.[62]

Before long they did know, and she was removed. The book ends: 'I want to go back.' But she was never allowed to go.

Rebecca West, in a sensitive review of the *Journal*, described its essential qualities exactly: it is, she wrote, 'largely a record of humiliations, and is told with the extremest timidity and a trembling meticulosity about the lightest facts.'[63] That's it: it is a book about humiliation, the humiliation of being a woman at a time when only the things that men do are valued. And yet it has its own values, and Rebecca West recognized that too:

> every page of this gallant, humiliated book [she wrote] makes it plain that while it is glorious that England should have women who walk quietly under the rain of bullets it is glorious too that England should have women who grieve inconsolably because the face of danger has not been turned to them.[64]

Rebecca West wrote of May Sinclair's *Journal* that it was 'one of the few books of permanent value' produced in the first year of the war, and she was right. I think it has two kinds of permanent value: it should have a place in women's literature as a rendering of the situation of women in wartime; and it also deserves to be included among the truth-telling narratives of the war, of which all the others were written by soldiers. It shares with those narratives two qualities important enough to be worth pausing over. The first is its prose style, which is bare, direct, exact, and unmetaphorical (the war-as-a-game passage is an exception, thrust in for a special effect): war is not like anything except itself, and the meticulous witness will not interpret it, or place it in some order of perceptions that gives it meaning, but will simply tell what it is. The second is its structure, which is the formal expression of the same point: there is no order in war except chronology, event followed by event without evident reason. These are both points of *exclusion*: they will turn up again and again, as men try to describe the Battle of the Somme, or the 1918 retreat. It is interesting that the first writer to achieve that style and structure should have been a woman.

May Sinclair tried to be in the war, and failed. And having failed, she fell back on the conventions of fiction, and wrote *Tasker Jevons*, a novel in which a loyal wife follows her husband into danger, where he overcomes fear and becomes a hero, and which ends in a customary celebration of married love and reconciliation. It is a bad novel, bad because the author could not ignore those old, false conventions, could not write a novel that was plain enough, or static enough, or unresolved enough to carry a convincing sense of the reality of a woman's war.

This chapter has been concerned with the home-front wars that began when the Great War began, and were waged by Englishmen against themselves: the war against Modernism, the war against culture, the war against dissent, and the war against the woman's war. These were wars that no one could win: their effects could only be diminishing, estranging and destructive. They made England's wartime culture a poorer thing than it might have been; they interrupted the development of a modern English tradition in the arts, and they suppressed the expression of dissenting ideas, out of which intellectual growth comes. As they worked on English society, a divided culture began to emerge: on the one hand the war culture — patriotic, restrictive, and 'official', and on the other that conflux of opposing faiths — the artists, pacifists, women, and radical Christians who constituted such opposition to the war as there was.

The home-front wars did more than divide a culture; they altered the ways in which English men and women thought about their common past, and therefore about themselves. In the years before the war, the condemnation of the past and its values had been the theme only of the young and avant-garde: 'Blast years 1837–1901' could only have been uttered by a Vorticist who was under thirty. But when the war came, it was not only the young who looked back at Victorian and Edwardian England and found war's causes there; weighty elders, figures of the Establishment joined in the condemnation, and sometimes led it. A judgement of the past is implicit in all those metaphors of disease and purgation that appear in early wartime essays and lectures by men like Gosse and Image: England had contracted its sickness, whatever it was, in the years of peace, and now must bleed for it. In the war years that followed, many another English writer looked back at peacetime to discover there the actions, the values, and the failures of heart and mind that had led to this catastrophe, and to pass judgement on the past. And in the process, they distanced themselves from the world that they judged, and so made the discontinuity of history more apparent, and more absolute.

PART II

THE TURNING POINT
1916

The year is dying of atrophy as far as I am concerned, bed-fast in its December fogs. And the War is settling down on everyone — a hopeless, never-shifting burden. While newspapers and politicians yell and brandish their arms, and the dead rot in their French graves, and the maimed hobble about the streets. And the Kaiser talks about Peace because he thinks he's won.

Siegfried Sassoon, Diary, December 22, 1916

CHAPTER 4

Running Down

Everybody seems to agree that 1916 was the turning point of the Great
War: it was the middle year of the war, and at the exact middle of the
year the crucial battle began that changed British fortunes — it's almost
too symmetrical. But even before the symmetry was apparent, the idea
of the turning point was accepted. The year had scarcely ended when the
Times's War Correspondent put his 1916 dispatches together for a book,
and titled them *The Turning Point: The Battle of the Somme*. In the book
he wrote:

> It is to the Battle of the Somme that historians in future ages will
> point as the turning point in the war. The heroism of the French at
> Verdun will probably always stand out as the most splendid achieve-
> ment of any of the combatants in the whole course of the war. But it
> was in the combined victory of the French and British on the Somme
> that the Allies, after two years of conscious inferiority in equipment
> and organization — but never in *moral* — first showed themselves
> definitely stronger than Germany in land fighting.[1]

Those two years of 'conscious inferiority' had actually been worse than
that, they had been years of disastrous British losses: in 1914 at Neuve
Chapelle and Ypres, in 1915 at Loos and in the Gallipoli campaign, from
which at the year's end they were withdrawing in humiliating defeat.
These losses must have been in General Haig's mind on July 1, 1916, as
he sent his troops over the top along the Somme; after two such years
the war *had* to turn; or failing that, it had at least to be *perceived* as
turning.[2]

In retrospect one can see that there were many turnings there in mid-war, and that perhaps the turn along the Somme (if indeed there was a turn) was not the most important one. Other fundamental aspects of the war were turning, too, and were changing English attitudes towards it. There was, for example, a turn in the ways in which civilians were brought into contact with the war. In other English wars the fighting and dying had been done somewhere else, and had reached England only as news. But beginning in 1915 the Germans carried the war into new regions — into the air over London in zeppelin raids, and under the sea in U-boat attacks on merchant shipping and passenger vessels. To see a zeppelin above your head in Hampstead or Kensington, to open your *Times* and find the names of your civilian acquaintances among the *Lusitania* dead, was to experience war differently; if such things could happen, then everyone was in the war, everyone was a potential casualty. One might argue that twentieth-century war really began in the spring of 1915, when the *Lusitania* went down and the first bomb fell from a zeppelin on London; by 1916 many Englishmen must have felt that war had burst its confines, and was all around them.

Though it didn't take a zeppelin or a U-boat to bring the war into English homes, and into civilian lives. In 1916 there could not have been many people in England, rich or poor, in country or in city, who had not been touched by suffering and loss. By the end of the year British casualties on the Western Front totalled more than a million dead, wounded, missing or captured (roughly half of them from the Somme offensive, just coming to an inconclusive finish as the year ended); add to these 120,000 from Gallipoli, and the casualties on all the other, forgotten fronts — Salonika, East Africa, the Middle East, Italy, South Africa — and you can see that by mid-war virtually everyone in England had reason to take the war personally.

In 1916 other wartime matters were turning, too. At the beginning of the year the army turned from voluntary enlistment to conscription, and 'Kitchener's Army' ceased to exist. The Irish situation turned in April, with the Easter Uprising. In May the naval war turned at the Battle of Jutland, from combat between surface ships to a war between surface ships and submarines. In June leadership at the War Office turned, with the death of Kitchener. And in December the British government turned, when Asquith resigned and Lloyd George succeeded him as Prime Minister. The *Times* man was certainly right — 1916 was the fulcrum of the war; but the turning was a more complex and less encouraging business than he had imagined. After 1916, England and

England's war were different. But not because a great victory had been
won along the Somme.

The image of a turning point will do well enough for some aspects of
the situation of England in 1916, but for others a different image is
necessary, to express the sense one gets of a loss of momentum, a
running down of the feelings and forces that had existed at the
beginning of the war. Most Englishmen had begun the war, whether as
soldiers or civilians, with certain hopeful expectations: that it would be a
short war, that it would be somehow an heroic one, that the fact of its
existence would unify England in one patriotic whole. If they were
liberals or radicals they hoped that it would change England; if they
were conservatives they hoped that it would restore the nation to some
previous condition of Englishness. By 1916 it was clear that none of
these expectations were being fulfilled: the war was not going to be
short, and showed no signs of being heroic; England had neither been
unified nor restored by it, and the idealism that expected such good
effects was becoming harder to sustain. The war spirit was running
down; only the momentum of the war itself continued undiminished.

A similar loss of momentum is evident in the arts in England: creative
energies seemed to sink to a low point in 1916 that one might call (if it
weren't too black a jest for the year of the Somme) a 'dead spot' at the
centre of the war. The momentum of pre-war artistic energy — the
thrust of Modernism that had made the late-Edwardian years so lively
— had dissipated. By the beginning of 1916 the pre-war avant-garde
had been substantially dispersed: 'I appear to be the only person of
interest left in the world of art, London,' Pound wrote to Lewis in June,
and Eliot agreed: 'Nearly everyone has faded away from London, or is
there very rarely,' he wrote in a letter to Conrad Aiken in August. 'The
vorticists are non-existent.'[3] A few survivors might have disputed that
claim but Eliot and Pound were nearly right insofar as their own
generation was concerned. Of the ten male contributors to *Blast* no. 1,
for example, only four were still in town; four of the others were on
active duty, and two were dead.

One can see the state of the arts in wartime simply by reading the
announcements of events in *The Times*. Take July 1, 1916 — the first
day of the Somme offensive — as an example. On that day there were
Italian war pictures on exhibition at the Leicester Galleries, Serbian war
cartoons at the Fine Art Society, and Will Dyson war cartoons at the
Savoy Hotel. The Royal Opera House at Covent Garden, which had
been closed since 1914, was opened for 'Women's Tribute Week', a

week of all-star, twice-a-day patriotic entertainments, with a 'Patriotic Fair' on the side. The Scala theatre was running the Official Programme of the British Expeditionary Force at the Front, followed by pictures of the life of Lord Kitchener (who had just died). At the Coliseum a variety show featured war films. Elsewhere one could find the usual British mixture of high culture and popular distraction: *The Magic Flute* at the Aldwych matinée (with *Tristan und Isolde* in the evening), Barrie's *A Kiss for Cinderella* at Wyndham's, Harold Brighouse's *Hobson's Choice* at the Apollo, *The Bing Boys are Here* at the Alhambra music-hall. What one could not find was anything new, experimental, avant-garde, challenging.

This withering away of the arts, and especially of the modern in art, is also apparent in the fact that it was more difficult to find a serious painting to look at in 1916. By that point in the war many London galleries had shut their doors; others, as we have seen, were showing war cartoons. In January 1916 many public museums and galleries, including the Tate, the Wallace Collection, the National Portrait Gallery, and the exhibition rooms of the British Museum, were also closed. These closures were ordered by the Government Committee on Public Retrenchment, ostensibly as an economy measure: by closing the museums, £50,000 per year could be saved (which, by one calculation, amounted to one per cent of the cost of the war for a single day[4]). But it seems clear that it was a symbolic gesture, a way of showing the world that England was seriously at war.

When an exhibition of contemporary paintings did open, it was likely to be taken as an occasion for directing attention not towards the art, but away from it, towards the war. When a modest exhibition of recent English paintings was organized in Brighton in the autumn of 1916, the Prime Minister's daughter, Elizabeth Asquith, was asked to open it. Her remarks were summarized in the *Morning Post*:

Miss Asquith said the outbreak of war had concentrated all enthusiasms on one subject; all the old crazes and illusions had been shattered into a thousand pieces. The great conflict shut out everything else. Certainly, underneath all we were doing our hearts were at 'the front,' and our thoughts full of the anxieties of the fight we were waging to free the world from the threat of Force, and to leave it a place where all art and all beauty might thrive. What the effect of the war would be on Art no one could tell. Intrinsic values would certainly be restored, and there would probably be a reaction toward form, vision, and restraint. The Twentieth Century, she thought, had already proved itself an artistic ancestor of which future ages would be proud.[5]

This sounds more like a closing than an opening — a closing not just of this show, but of twentieth-century Modernism with its 'crazes and illusions'. The speech is one more instance — this time from a young and advanced woman — of the wartime inclination to regard pre-war Modernism as an historical mistake that had been terminated by the war.

Among the older generation another kind of 'closing down' had taken place. It is striking how few of the great Edwardians had found an adequate wartime voice, or the heart to use it. Some had been distracted into war work, and had spent the first two years being busy but unproductive: Arnold Bennett is a good example, rushing between Wellington House and the Wounded Allies Relief Committee, touring the Front, advising the General in Command of the defence of Essex — and writing no fiction of any quality. Others had lapsed into virtual silence: Robert Bridges was Poet Laureate, yet he wrote only three short war poems in 1914–16, and devoted most of 1915 to compiling *The Spirit of Man*, a wartime anthology that is intentionally *not* about the war (it contains only three war poems among 449 items). The usually prolific Kipling was nearly silent, too, grieving for the loss of his only son, missing and presumed dead at Loos; he wrote only a few articles in 1916, mainly for the Ministry of Information. And there were other silences: no novel by Galsworthy or Conrad or James was published in 1916, no book of poems by Yeats or Masefield or Hardy, not even a new *Georgian Poetry* volume. Even the voluble Shaw seemed closed down; he published only *Pygmalion*, a play written before the war.

In the theatre, the situation was much the same. The *Times*'s drama critic, reviewing the 1916 season, saw the year as one in which the theatre had managed to survive, but without distinction. 'It is many years,' he wrote,

since the London stage has had to face such a variety of obstacles as those which it successfully surmounted in 1916. War conditions, darkened streets, Zeppelin raids, daylight saving, the entertainment tax, the growing competition of the cinematograph theatre and the music-hall, all have had to be faced. But while the theatre has held its own financially in a way that few could have imagined possible in the

early days of the European war, it is doubtful whether artistically the
same can be said.

In reviewing the events of the past year few things strike one more
forcibly than the disappointing output of the leading English drama-
tists. It would almost seem as if the war had had a stultifying effect on
the playwright's imagination.[6]

So indeed it seemed, as he ran through his list of important writers for
the theatre: Sir Arthur Pinero, nothing; Henry Arthur Jones, only a new
production of an old play; Barrie, one fantasy and a few charity-
performance sketches; Bernard Shaw, nothing; Galsworthy, nothing;
Granville Barker, nothing; Arnold Bennett, nothing — and so on, down
the list to lesser luminaries, Sutro, Vachell, Brighouse, Parker, Besier,
Knoblock, all silent. 'The great war play', he concluded, 'has still to be
written.'

But though the great Edwardians seemed to have lost their voices,
writing and publishing went on without them, and by 1916 it was
abundantly clear that Gosse had been wrong when he predicted that the
war would mean the end of 'current literature'. There had been a slight
decline in book-production at the beginning of the war, and booksellers
had worried that no one would buy books in wartime; but both
production and sales quickly returned to near the pre-war rates, and
continued that way throughout the war. The only significant change
was that the war itself became a dominating literary subject: through the
first two years of the war, roughly one new book in five was concerned
with the war in some way.[7] 'It is obvious', a reviewer remarked at the
end of 1915, 'that Germany is unduly optimistic in saying that the
British people are tired of the war: they are not even tired of reading
about it.'[8]

In 1916 they read about it in *Greenmantle*, John Buchan's new Richard
Hannay novel, in a new Brereton adventure story, *With Joffre at Verdun*,
and in Escott Lynn's *Oliver Hastings V.C.* and Ruby M. Ayre's *Richard
Chatterton V.C.* (the Victoria Cross had become a ready way to identify
a war novel, and its hero). There were six more anthologies of war
poetry that year, and new volumes in several of the write-as-you-fight
histories of the war. There was plenty of war writing, all right; but little
that a serious critic could seriously praise.

This failure of imaginations to realize the war was a problem to which
thoughtful critics and artists were beginning to turn their attention.
Some were beginning to see, and say, that the ideas about art and

war that had been repeated at the war's beginning had been ignorant and wrong. 'Some misguided people, I believe, still hold that war is a good thing for the arts,' the young critic Alec Randall wrote in the *Egoist* in February:

> even this machine-made, absolute unromantic war has not convinced them of the contrary. They may still be found writing to the *Times* letters full of panegyric nonsense on young heroes such as Rupert Brooke, whose death was a far greater poem than his life ... War-patriotism is proved to be a very barren emotion, unless brought into relation with the 'grim realities'.[9]

Randall saw that the war was a new kind of human experience that posed new problems for the artist. The existing conventions — romantic and patriotic — had not provided access to its realities. But what new conventions would realize a machine-made war?

Ford Madox Hueffer, on duty at Ypres in September 1916, worried about the question. The Battle of the Somme was then in its third month, and Hueffer was trying to write a piece about it for the Department of Information. His essay, 'A Day of Battle', was not published during the war, and one can see, reading it now, why it would not have appealed to his friends at Wellington House. For it is not so much about the war as about Hueffer's inability to write about it: it is a soldier-novelist's Dejection Ode. 'I have asked myself continuously', Hueffer begins,

> why I can write nothing — why I cannot even think anything that to myself seems worth thinking — about the psychology of that Active Service of which I have seen my share. And why cannot I even evoke pictures of the Somme or the flat lands round Ploegsteert?[10]

He can visualize war scenes, he says — the villages, the dying and dead men, the planes and the shells — 'but, as for putting them into words! No: the mind stops dead.'

Hueffer's efforts to explain why that should be true, why there was an invisible barrier in his brain 'between the profession of Arms and the mind that puts things into words', amount to a theory of the imaginative vacuum that prevailed in 1916, and an explanation of the course that war writing (or at least war fiction) took in England during the war. Hueffer argued that in 1916 there was no tradition of war fiction written by actual soldiers. The circumstances of being a soldier — the limitations that the orders, duties, and responsibilities of war impose upon a soldier's imagination — were inhibiting. A soldier sees everything — including all humanity — as mere matter: a human head seen in a gunsight becomes simply a 'dark, smallish, potlike object', which smashes if your bullet hits it. The Game of War confines the player's mind.

That would presumably be true in any war: to be a good soldier one must adjust one's sense of humanity and forget the rules of kinder games. But there was another difficulty that no war before the Great War would have posed. Hueffer described this problem in terms of landscape. He was at an Observation Point, looking down at the early fighting on the Somme. He could see all the villages and copses that would later be named in historical accounts of the battle — Albert and Martinpuich and Mametz, Becourt Wood and High Wood:

> And it came into my head to think that here was the most amazing fact of history. For in the territory beneath the eye, or hidden by folds in the ground, there must have been — on the two sides — a million men, moving one against the other and impelled by an invisible moral force into a Hell of fear that surely cannot have had a parallel in this world. It was an extraordinary feeling to have in a wide landscape.
>
> But there it stopped. As for explanation, I hadn't any: as for significant or valuable pronouncement of a psychological kind, I could not make any — nor any generalisation. There we were: those million men, forlorn, upon a raft in space.[11]

So for Hueffer in 1916 there seemed to be two reasons for the imaginative vacuum, and for his inability to put the war that lay before his eyes into words: the mere fact of being a soldier narrowed the imagination, and the war was too vast to be understood. Parts of it, like the territory that he saw from his hilltop, might be *described* — the places named, the numbers of men estimated — but the war itself could not be *imagined*. For to imagine it would be to discover its significance; and as Hueffer looked down at it, 'it all seemed to signify nothing'. A writer might experience the war, but he could not verbalize it in a way that would make his experience seem real to a reader who had not been there. And he could not put his experience into a narrative form — a story with causal connections, direction, and a resolving ending — because that would give it the significance it did not possess, or did not reveal. For Hueffer, in 1916, writing a war novel seemed an impossible task.

Nevertheless, war novels were being written, though some critics

wondered whether they could be fully imagined by civilian readers. The
TLS's reviewer of Hugh Walpole's *The Dark Forest* raised that question
in early 1916. Walpole's novel is about the war on the Eastern Front, and
was based on direct experience: he had spent the spring and summer of
1915 working with a Red Cross hospital unit attached to the Russian
army, and had been awarded a medal for courage under fire. But the
reviewer concluded that authorial experience was not enough; for
home-bound civilian readers like himself, *Russia* and *War* were simply
the names of two kinds of ignorance, against which an English
imagination was powerless. 'Though we know', he wrote,

> that our notions [of Russia] are vague, rather sentimental, and very
> unsatisfying, though we know they must be false, we must put up
> with them, for they are all we have. So, too, we are most of us
> ignorant of war, and yet we cannot, of course, even if we would, keep
> our minds empty of notions of war — notions that must be, from our
> inexperience, inevitably wrong, inevitably romantic, too, and tinged
> with sentimentalism, and all the more confused and unsatisfying from
> the reading of accounts of war persistently written in one convention
> or another, the pathetic, the dramatic, the humorous, the shocking,
> or some other convention. We know that war, like Russia, is not as
> we imagine it; but we cannot otherwise imagine either.[12]

The task for artists — for painters and composers as well as for writers
— is in that last phrase: they had to make it possible to imagine the war
otherwise. Not as it was — art does not reproduce reality — but freed
from those conventions ('inevitably romantic') that invoked familiar
responses to familiar actions, and could therefore be felt as courage, self-
sacrifice, patriotism, humour, pity, pathos. The artists' war would be a
war against such abstractions, which make war seem familiar, and
therefore tolerable. They would have to find ways of making this war as
*un*familiar in art as it was in reality, and yet make it imaginable. It was a
task that had not yet been performed as the war entered its third year,
though the problem had been defined.

Hueffer and the *TLS* reviewer, in their different ways, saw the war as
unimaginable. Other men agreed, and went further: the war was
unimaginable, and should be so; to realize it in art would be to give it
aesthetic value. Consider, for example, the testimony of Ben Keeling.
Keeling is a fine example of the generation of potential leaders that was
lost in the war. If he had survived, he would have been an important
public figure — a writer, perhaps, or a politician. He was a Socialist who

had been a Fabian at Cambridge, and had then come to London to work as a political journalist. He was a staff member of the *New Statesman* from its inception, and was known and admired and mourned by the extraordinary people who were associated with that journal — Shaw and Wells, the Webbs, Bertrand Russell among them. Keeling enlisted as a private when the war began, and was at the Front from early 1915 until he was killed in the Somme offensive in August 1916. At his death he had written no book, but his letters were collected and published, with a tender and admiring introduction by Wells. The book constitutes a sad, compelling account of what it was like to be young, gifted, and radical in the years before and during the war.

Keeling was not a particularly aesthetically minded man, but he was an intellectual, and he read the war poetry that was around, and disliked it intensely. 'I am thankful', he wrote in a letter on April 28, 1916,

> that there has been no good war poetry, or very little. There is not much that is poetic about this war. It is bad enough to have to listen to those people who justify war because it gives them a quasi-sensual satisfaction to see humanity crucified after the manner of the founder of Christianity. It would be almost worse to find our intellectual reactionaries — ineligible for the trenches — deriving satisfaction from war as a stimulant of great literature. I am more interested in life than in poetry, and I should regard it as a disaster to humanity if really great war poems began to appear. It would imply that war did really express something essential in the human soul.[13]

All of these writers I have been quoting saw the problem of art and war in essentially the same way. They saw that the war was not an adventure or a crusade, but a valueless, formless experience that could not be rendered in the language, the images, and the conventions that existed. To represent the war in the traditional ways was necessarily to *mis*-represent it, to give it meaning, dignity, order, greatness — an essential and inevitable place in the human soul. But there was as yet no other way to represent it. It was a curious situation for artists: to be in the middle of the most extended and destructive war in history, and to feel that there were no resources in art and the imagination by which its enormity could be rendered.

CHAPTER 5

A Turn of Speech

When Ford Madox Hueffer lamented that he had no words for the reality of war, he was making a point about another kind of mid-war problem, the problem of language. War had created a new reality; and a new reality may require a new language, and devalue an old one. Englishmen had gone to the war with a traditional rhetoric, a set of abstractions that expressed traditional martial and patriotic values, and made the war seem familiar and invested with meaning. One reason for the popularity of Rupert Brooke's war sonnets is that he got all the abstractions into seventy lines of verse: Holiness, Love, Pain, Honour, Nobleness, Glory, Heroism, Sacrifice, England — they're all there. And it's not surprising that the same words should turn up in mourning references to him after his death in April 1915. They are in the Easter sermon on martyr-patriots that Dean Inge preached that year, and in the obituary of Brooke that Winston Churchill wrote for *The Times*, and in the eulogistic reviews of his posthumous book, *1914 and Other Poems*, which was published in June: all the abstractions and the capital letters, revived to mark a minor poet's death.

The traditional language of war continued as the war went on. Popular novelists and patriotic poets used it; so did public figures in their public speeches; so did young men at war, in their letters and their own war poems. They wrote home to ask for copies of Brooke's poems, and quoted them to cheer their families, or to express their own feelings. There was never a moment of the war after *1914* appeared when Brooke wasn't the most popular war poet, and never a moment when, to the majority of Englishmen, including those in the trenches, his rhetoric did not seem the most appropriate way of speaking and writing about the ideals of the war — at least to those back home in England.

It seemed appropriate partly, no doubt, because it was the rhetoric used by war correspondents, and therefore the language in which most Englishmen at their breakfast tables learned about the war. From it they got two things: the Big Picture of the war, not simply the local confusion and the dying, but the significance of it all; and the reiterated values that gave meaning to the terrible casualties. Here is an example of that journalistic rhetoric, from the *Daily Chronicle*'s war correspondent, Philip Gibbs — the opening paragraphs of his first report of the Somme offensive, date-lined July 1, 1916, and headlined 'The Historic First of July':

> The attack which was launched today against the German lines on a 20-mile front began satisfactorily. It is not yet a victory, for victory comes at the end of a battle, and this is only a beginning. But our troops, fighting with very splendid valour, have swept across the enemy's front trenches along a great part of the line of attack, and have captured villages and strong-holds which the Germans have long held against us. They are fighting their way forward not easily but doggedly. Many hundreds of enemy are prisoners in our hands. His dead lie thick in the track of our regiments.
>
> And so, after the first day of battle, we may say with thankfulness: All goes well. It is a good day for England and France. It is a day of promise in this war, in which the blood of brave men is poured out upon the sodden fields of Europe.[1]

The panoramic view, the splendid valour, and the blood of brave men are all there; it all seems directed, coherent, and right. It is lacking in detail, to be sure; Gibbs was not allowed anywhere near the front lines, and was dependent on official sources for his information, so there is no mention of the fact that the British suffered 50,000 casualties that day, including 20,000 dead — the worst one-day losses for any army on either side, during the entire war. For that reality the reader would have to turn to another page of his morning paper, where he would find a 'Roll of Honour' like the one in plate 7 from *The Times* on the eighth day of the battle.

But even war correspondents learned, and altered their rhetoric in the course of the Somme battles. Two weeks after his July 1 report, Gibbs wrote (of the capture of Bazentin-le-Grand):

> If any man were to draw the picture of those things or to tell them
> more nakedly than I have told them ... no man or woman would
> dare to speak again of war's 'glory,' or of 'the splendour of war,' or
> any of those old lying phrases which hide the dreadful truth.[2]

At home, anyone who supported the war was likely to depend on that
rhetoric, and to defend his use of it as validated by the experience of
war. Gilbert Murray, a liberal and a pacifist by nature, but a believer in
the war cause, spoke out for the old rhetoric in an address to the
Congress of Free Churches in October 1915. It was a dark time: the
Battle of Loos had been going on for a month, with no significant gains,
and 20,000 British soldiers dead. Perhaps that grim fact was in Murray's
mind; perhaps he felt that the casualty lists spoke in a new derisive
language that challenged his beliefs. At any rate, this is what he said to
the Congress:

> A thing which has struck me ... is the way in which the language of
> romance and melodrama has now become true. It is becoming the
> language of our normal life. The old phrase about 'dying for
> freedom,' about 'Death being better than dishonour,' – phrases that
> we thought were fitted for the stage or for children's stories — are
> now the ordinary truths on which we live.[3]

For Murray the war had changed language because it had revived old
ideals that were essentially *literary*:

> Romance and melodrama [he went on] were a memory, broken
> fragments living on, of heroic ages in the past. We live no longer
> upon fragments and memories; we have entered ourselves upon a
> heroic age.

Heroic age: it's a phrase that Wells had used in the first month of the war.
It suggests (though neither man would have thought of it in these terms)
that the war had been declared in order that exhausted literary categories
might be revived, and romance and melodrama restored as versions of
the truth.

Murray and Wells weren't the only English writers who found a
restoration of literature in the war. John Buchan wrote in the dedication
to *Greenmantle*: 'Let no man or woman call its events improbable. The
war has driven that word from our vocabulary, and melodrama has
become the prosiest realism.'[4] The dedication is dated August 1916 —
the second month of the Somme offensive.

At the very time that Murray was affirming the ordinary truths of life in wartime, others were rejecting them. In August 1915, Vera Brittain sent a copy of Brooke's *1914* to her soldier-fiancé, Roland Leighton; he responded in September in a letter from the battlefield at Loos, not with a direct criticism of Brooke, but with this description of a captured German trench, which is criticism of another kind:

> This latter was captured by the French not so long ago and is pitted with shell-holes each big enough to bury a horse or two in. The dug-outs have been nearly all blown in, the wire entanglements are a wreck, and in among [this] chaos of twisted iron and splintered timber and shapeless earth are the fleshless, blackened bones of simple men who poured out their red, sweet wine of youth unknowing, for nothing more tangible than Honour or their Country's Glory or another's Lust of Power. Let him who thinks that War is a glorious golden thing, who loves to roll forth stirring words of exhortation, invoking Honour and Praise and Valour and Love of Country with as thoughtless and fervid a faith as inspired the priests of Baal to call on their own slumbering deity, let him look at a little pile of sodden grey rags that cover half a skull and a shin bone and what might have been Its ribs, or at this skeleton lying on its side, resting half-crouching as it fell, supported on one arm, perfect but that it is headless, and with the tattered clothing still draped around it; and let him realise how grand & glorious a thing it is to have distilled all Youth and Joy and Life into a foetid heap of hideous putrescence. Who is there who has known and seen who can say that Victory is worth the death of even one of these?[5]

This is an interesting and complex passage — both a statement about rhetoric, and an enactment of two opposed kinds. One is the rhetoric that Leighton rejects: it is explicitly Brooke's (Leighton quotes with bitter irony from the third *1914* sonnet 'Blow out, you bugles'), and is marked by the big, capitalized abstractions. The other, the alternative rhetoric, is plain, descriptive, emptied of value statements; it names the broken fragments of the trench world, as though reality consisted only in the ruins of things. Here are two languages and two realities — one made of abstract values, the other of shattered objects — mutually exclusive, mutually contradictory. Gilbert Murray spoke of 'the ordinary truths on which we live'; for Leighton, and for many soldiers like him, there were two kinds of truth about war — but only one was true.

It is depressing to see how little Vera Brittain understood what her lover was telling her. Three days after she copied down Leighton's ironic rejection of Brooke's rhetoric she was quoting in her diary from Brooke's 'If I should die', quite without irony. Even after Leighton's death she seemed to have learned nothing. Her diary account of her brother Edward's experience on the first day of the Somme offensive, when he was twice wounded, is entirely in the heroic tradition: Edward's 'beloved Captain Harris' dies of wounds on the battlefield after telling his men to go on, and not to bother about him; and Edward, faced with an understandable panic among his men as the wounded stream back from the first disastrous wave of the attack, rallies them and leads them over the parapet, where they are slaughtered. Only seventeen men and two officers of Edward's battalion survived the assault unscathed, and Vera Brittain reported this statistic in her diary with evident pride and excitement, and with no sign that she understood what those numbers meant in terms of dead and wounded human beings.[6] It isn't that she was stupid, or bloodthirsty, or more irrationally patriotic than her fellow-English, but simply that she still thought in the terms that English society employed to think about the war, even as she suffered personal losses, and nursed the wounded as a VAD.

Still, there were persons in England in similar circumstances who were thinking in other terms, and questioning the heroic rhetoric. A few weeks after Leighton wrote to Vera Brittain about trench reality, Cynthia Asquith learned of the death in combat of her youngest brother, Yvo, and recorded her feelings in her diary:

> Somehow with the others who have been killed, I have acutely felt the loss of them but have so swallowed the rather high-faluting platitude that it was all right for them — that they were not to be pitied, but were safe, unassailable, young, and glamorous for ever. With Yvo — I can't bear it for him. The sheer pity and horror of it is overwhelming, and I am haunted by the feeling that he is disappointed.[7]

A lot has died in this passage besides poor Yvo. All those Rupert-Brookeish ideas about dying have died too, and only pity and horror are left. But more than ideas have died; for like Leighton's letter this is a statement about *style*. Cynthia Asquith's reality has changed; and so language must change too. That such a change would come to a man in the trenches does not seem surprising; but it is worth noting that it also occurred, at the same time, in the mind of an intelligent young woman of the upper class in Cadogan Square.

Of these two rhetorics, one was present from the war's beginning. The other kind emerged only as articulate men experienced the trench world, and tried to record what they had seen there, and women saw the damaged men returning from that world, and experienced loss and grief. Not that the new rhetoric replaced the old: Truth was not revealed once and for all at Loos or Mametz Wood or Suvla Bay. The high rhetorical style continued throughout the war, even in the trenches. But as the war moved into the time of the great battles on the Western Front, the anti-rhetorical way of rendering war began to be more and more evident.

One finds the new kind first in the letters and diaries of soldiers, personal records often not intended even as a communication to one other person, but simply as a way of fixing reality (and perhaps also of contradicting the other rhetoric). Vast numbers of such records survive — some published, others in manuscripts stored in the Imperial War Museum. Here, as examples, are representative passages from three soldiers' texts. First, an entry from the diary of Arthur Graeme West, a young officer of the New Army, on the Somme in September 1916, describing a trench being shelled.

> Men cowered and trembled. It exploded, and a cloud of black reek went up — in the communication trench again. You went down it; two men were buried, perhaps more you were told, certainly two. The trench was a mere undulation of newly turned earth, under it somewhere lay two men or more. You dug furiously. No sign. Perhaps you were standing on a couple of men now, pressing the life out of them, on their faces or chests. A boot, a steel helmet — and you dig and scratch and uncover a grey, dirty face, pitifully drab and ugly, the eyes closed, the whole thing limp and mean looking.[8]

And another shelled trench, this one from the war diary of Major the Hon. R.G.A. Hamilton, a Regular Army officer who commanded an artillery brigade (also on the Somme, in August 1916):

> The infantry were mostly asleep on the floor of the trench, and we had to step over them. It took about twenty minutes to work our way along a hundred yards. They shelled us and the whole area all the time. The heat was terrific and the smells simply too awful for words. The only thing I can at all compare it to was the rhino that G. and I

Reproduction of an original painting by Barribal, produced by Pope and Bradley to assist recruiting

The House of Pope & Bradley is one of the exclusive few in the West End possessing a dual reputation for military and mufti tailoring. The styles of Dennis Bradley, who designs not only all the mufti garments produced, but the materials from which they are made, have created a distinct vogue. The Service connection of the House includes practically every commissioned rank and regiment in the Army, and the experience gained of the exact requirements of Officers who have seen active service is invaluable. The prices charged are on a reasonable basis compatible with the quality. As an indication for Mufti, Lounge Suits and Over-coats range from 4 to 6 guineas, and Dress Suits from 6 guineas. For Service Kit, Jackets 3½ and 4½ guineas; Slacks from 27/6, Riding Breeches from 2½ guineas. Full Kit and Camp Equipment List, and Book on mufti styles will be forwarded upon application to 14, Old Bond Street, W., or 11/13 Southampton Row, W.C.

1   Barribal, 'The Man of To-day', a tailor's advertisement from *Colour*, November 1915

2 Will Dyson, 'Wonders of Science'

3 Will Dyson, 'Kultur Protector': Those Minor Germans, GOETHE, BEETHOVEN and WAGNER: 'Hail, Saviour Krupp, how can we ever thank thee?'

4 Stephen Phillips's *Armageddon*: Satan consults his generals

5   Walter Sickert, 'The Soldiers of King Albert the Ready'

6 'To the Death', *Chums*,
August 15, 1914

7 'Roll of Honour', *The Times*,
July 8, 1916

8 *Battle of the Somme*: the faked attack

9 Muirhead Bone, 'Battle of the Somme: Mametz Village and Wood'

Reading the manuscript image — the poem 'Atrocities':

Atrocities:
A Murder Case

You bragged how once your men in savage mood
Butchered some Saxon prisoners. That was good!
I trust you felt no pity when they stood
Patient and cowed and scared, as prisoners should.

How did you kill them? don't be shy:
You know I love to hear how Germans die,
Downstairs in dug-outs. 'Camerad!' they cry;
And squeal like stoats when bombs begin to fly.

I'm proud of you. Perhaps you'll feel as brave
Alone in no man's land, when none can save
Or shield you from the horror of the night.

I hope those Huns will haunt you with their screams,
And make you gulp their blood in ghoulish dreams.
You're great at murder. Tell me, Can you fight?

10   The manuscript of Siegfried Sassoon's 'Atrocities'

11   C. R. W. Nevinson, 'The Doctor'

12   C. R. W. Nevinson, 'Returning to the Trenches'

13   C. R. W. Nevinson, 'Paths of Glory'

14   'Paths of Glory' censored

15   William Orpen, 'Dead Germans in a Trench'

shot before leaving East Africa, and that was mild in comparison to this. The trench had been blown to pieces in many places and one had to climb out and run across the mounds of thrown-up earth. In many places the men who had been killed a week or ten days ago were lying in the bottom of the trench, and one had to walk and crawl over them. Many had been half buried by the shells, and only their faces or hands or feet could be seen. They had been trampled into the soft earth by the many reliefs who had passed along the trench since they were killed. Many of the bodies were not complete; in one place a pair of legs were lying on a path and no signs of the rest.[9]

And finally, a description by a private soldier of a German dugout, in which the writer had taken shelter during the attack on Thiepval (September 26, 1916):

The dugout had evidently been the quarters of an enemy machine-gun section, among other things. At the top were several enemy dead, and in the top of one of the entrances was an enemy machine-gun, which had been damaged by a shell-splinter or bullet. At the bottom of the steps lay another dead German, the top of his head blown off. Near him was a German telephone, also several reels of telephone wire, which we used later. The interior of the dugout was littered with enemy equipment, clothing, etc. On a 'table' or bench were some freshly-opened tins of some evil-smelling stuff, which the O.C. Coy. said was horseflesh. In the trench outside lay two of our six-inch 'duds,' all bright and shiny.[10]

A New Army subaltern, a Regular Army major, and a Kitchener's Army private — these represent something of the variety of the British army in 1916; yet the reality that they recorded, and their manners of recording it, are very similar. The accounts are composed mainly of *things* — shells, pieces of equipment, mounds of torn earth, disfigured and fragmented human bodies — all rather small-scale, all randomly disposed, and all rendered without judgement or expressed emotion, as though boot, helmet and human face, heaped earth and bodies, telephones and decapitated heads and tinned horsemeat were all morally equal parts of one chaos. There is no attempt at a Big Picture, no inferred order in terms of which those fragmented particulars might have meaning. The accounts are descriptive rather than narrative: like the war itself they do not move in any direction, or reach any objective — they are simply there. The passages are not without feeling, but they are empty of the abstractions that name the big emotions of war, all those capitalized nouns of the high tradition. They are not even belligerent (the word *enemy* in the last quotation is a neutral descriptive term, like *grey*); and they are unmetaphorical, nothing is like any other thing (except, bizarrely, that rhinoceros), but only itself. Yet, without going beyond the naming of parts, all three passages are oddly phantas-magorical, because their reality is.

The emergence of an alternative rhetoric of war had implications that go far beyond matters of style. Writing like this, seeing like this, implies a fundamental separation in the perceiver: it asserts that there is a reality in war that the customary ways of seeing and saying cannot render, and consequently it divides the soldier from the civilian, Front from Home, Us from You, Us as We Are from Us as We Were. This separation had consequences for both war writers and war painters, but it was more than an aesthetic principle: it assumed that the whole of the war experience was unique and beyond the comprehension of those who had not fought: there were two wartime worlds, and an unbridgeable gap lay between them. It was not a matter of the artist's vision, but the soldier's.

R.H. Tawney was neither a poet nor a painter; he was (or would become) one of England's most distinguished economic historians. Yet he wrote one of the first, and clearest, statements of this principle of separation. Tawney was wounded on the Somme in July 1916, and returned to England to convalesce. While there he wrote two articles, both of which were published anonymously in October. One was a two-part account of his experience on the first day of the Somme offensive; the other was 'Some Reflections of a Soldier', an essay in which he tried to describe and explain to a civilian audience the factors that separated him from them.

'It is very nice to be at home again,' Tawney begins his 'Reflections'.

> Yet am I at home? One sometimes doubts it. There are occasions when I feel like a visitor among strangers whose intentions are kindly, but whose modes of thought I neither altogether understand nor alto-gether approve. I find myself storing impressions, attempting hasty and unsatisfactory summaries to appease the insatiable curiosity of the people with whom I really am at home, the England that's not an island or an empire, but a wet populous dyke stretching from Flanders to the Somme.[11]

As the essay develops, Tawney adopts an Us/You opposition:

> . . . between you and us there hangs a veil. It is mainly of your own unconscious creation. It is not a negative, but a positive thing. It is not intellectual, it is moral. It is not ignorance (or I should not mention it). It is falsehood. I read your papers and listen to your conversation, and I see clearly that you have chosen to make to yourselves an image of war, not as it is, but of a kind which, being picturesque, flatters your appetite for novelty, for excitement, for easy admiration, without troubling you with masterful emotions. You have chosen, I say, to make an image, because you do not like, or cannot bear, the truth; because you are afraid of what may happen to your souls if you expose them to the inconsistencies and contradictions, the doubts and bewilderment, which lie beneath the surface of things.[12]

Tawney's point is essentially an ontological one, but with obvious implications for language and art. There is the picturesque popular *image* of war, which is clear and easy to respond to, and there is the *truth*, which is inconsistent, contradictory, and threatening. If you try to imagine how that truth might be rendered in art, you must arrive at something like the fragmented, directionless descriptions of the letters, diaries, and poems that I have been quoting.

One aspect of the popular image of war that Tawney particularly hated was the figure of the soldier — the Tommy, 'a creature at once ridiculous and disgusting', cheerfully killing his fellow-men, rejoicing in a 'scrap', and somehow ennobled by the whole squalid business. There was plenty of this sort of language around at this time, as official England sought metaphors that would make the Somme casualties acceptable. Most audibly, there was Lloyd George, at that time Secretary of State for War. Asked by an American journalist to state in simple terms the British attitude towards proposed peace talks, he replied:

> The British soldier is a good sportsman. He enlisted in this war in a sporting spirit — in the best sense of that term. He went in to see fair play to a small nation trampled upon by a bully. He is fighting for fair play. He has fought as a good sportsman. By the thousands he has died a good sportsman. He has never asked anything more than a sporting chance. He has not always had that. When he couldn't get it, he didn't quit. He played the game. He didn't squeal, and he certainly never asked anyone to squeal for him . . . Under the circumstances, the British, now that the fortunes of the game have turned a bit, are not disposed to stop because of the squealing done by Germans or

done for Germans by probably well-meaning but misguided sympathizers and humanitarians.[13]

One finds the same metaphors in *The Great Advance*, an anonymous collection of interviews with the wounded, taken as they arrived on hospital ships at Southampton, and published in August 1916: 'Believe me, our men are not only all good, they're all gentlemen and sportsmen,' and 'they're such sportsmen!' And from the editor:

> Not all the treacherous tricks and unscrupulous subterfuges of the Boche can eradicate the innate sportsmanship of our British fighters; and remaining, as they do, high-spirited sportsmen when knocked out of the fight, they tell their battles over in the spirit of a man recounting a fast run with the hounds or a good day's work after big game.[14]

You can see how Tawney, just back from the Somme and with his wound still unhealed, might have found this sort of stuff offensive and untrue. 'Oh! gentle public,' he wrote,

> . . . put all these delusions from your mind. The reality is horrible, but it is not so horrible as the grimacing phantom which you have imagined. Your soldiers are neither so foolish, nor so brave, nor so wicked, as the mechanical dolls who grin and kill and grin in the columns of your newspapers.[15]

The figure of the soldier that Kipling had invented, and that Sapper and Ian Hay had brought into the Great War, Tawney rejected as degrading, and inadequate to the reality. Tawney didn't describe the real soldier in precise terms — he was not, after all, a poet — but he helped to bury Tommy Atkins, an imagined trooper whose cheerfulness had died at Loos, or on the Somme.

But the most important point that Tawney made is not about Tommy Atkins, nor about home-front falsehood, but about ideals. 'When, as has happened in the present war,' he wrote,

> men have taken up arms not as a profession or because forced to do so by law, but under the influence of some emotion or principle, they tend to be ruled by the idea which compelled them to enlist long after it has yielded, among civilians, to some more fashionable novelty . . . Our minds differ from yours, both because they are more exposed to change, and because they are less changeable. While you seem — forgive me if I am rude — to have been surrendering your creeds with

the nervous facility of a Tudor official, our foreground may be different, but our background is the same. It is that of August to November, 1914. We are your ghosts.[16]

This is the testimony of a highly intelligent, experienced young officer. And it is testimony that contradicts the later, post-war version of what happened to idealism. In that version, fighting soldiers became disillusioned and bitter, while the civilians at home preserved their easy faith in the abstractions for which the war had been declared. Tawney saw the change as the other way round: men at the Front continued to believe in the ideals for which they had enlisted, because only if those ideals were valid could their sufferings be justified; it was the people at home who abandoned them. The ideals that Tawney clung to were not Rupert Brooke's resonant words, but other, plainer values, for which many men must have joined up: the idea of fighting a war to save others from war in the future; of making a lasting, just peace; of defending humanity and democracy. These were the ideals that the politicians, the patriots, and the profiteers had betrayed; but they survived on the Western Front, and made men like Tawney — thoughtful, observant, decent men — feel like the ghosts of their own pasts.

Tawney's version of wartime idealism, and what happened to it, explains a lot that is otherwise incomprehensible. It explains the tone of righteous anger in soldiers' letters and poems, which is not merely the note of disillusionment; it explains the deepening sense of alienation felt by returning troops (like Tawney's feeling that home was not in England, but in the trenches); it explains why men like Sassoon and Owen left safe posts in England to return to their regiments in France; and it explains why the best war writing, right up to the end of the war, was not emptied of all values, but only of the empty ones.

CHAPTER 6

The New Look of War

I

By the end of 1916 there was a new realism evident in the ways in which some English men and women thought about the war. It had been going on for more than two years then, and most people had been touched by it — young men they knew, sons or brothers, had been killed or wounded, half a million in the Somme offensive alone. It had also reached them in other personal ways: in the letters that men wrote from the Front (for this was a literate, corresponding army), and in the conversation of those men when they came home on leave (for this was a nearby war — you could hear the guns across the Channel when the wind was right). So most English civilians would have had a sense of the particulars of the war — not only the Big Picture of the journalists and generals, but the details of individual experience, the actuality that the soldiers' diaries record.

These are all ways of vicariously experiencing war that earlier civilians might have known to some degree: the particulars of Ladysmith or of Waterloo might have come like that. But there was one kind of knowing that was new in 1914: for the first time in history non-combatants at home could *see* the war. The invention of the half-tone block had made it possible to print photographs in newspapers, and so to bring realistic-looking images into every house in England.

Not, to be sure, without fierce resistance and censorship by the army. Kitchener regarded reporters and photographers as threats to security and encouragements to the enemy, and after the first few months of the war he succeeded in banning them from the Front, and allowed only official army photographers (two regular officers with no previous training as press photographers) to approach the Front. But gradually controls loosened, and enough photographs began to appear in papers like the *Illustrated London News* to fix in civilian minds images of the war: the rutted, muddy roads, the files of grubby men, the big guns firing, the ruined landscape. There were no English corpses (photographing the dead was forbidden), and no scenes of actual combat, but there were clear, particular images of the men who were fighting, and of the conditions in which they fought.

Even more than the still photographs, though, it was the motion picture that made the war imaginable for the people at home.[1] 'War films' appeared in London variety theatres early in the war: there were war films on the programme with *England Expects*— in September 1914, and with Barrie's *Der Tag* in December. What these films included is not known — pre-war shots of British soldiers, apparently, and perhaps some footage taken with the British army in Belgium in the first weeks of the war — but clearly they appealed to audiences eager for a glimpse of the real thing. This was not what the War Office wanted, however; cinema cameramen, like press photographers, were soon excluded from the war zone, and for the next year only propaganda documentaries using home-front materials were made.

But though the army distrusted photographers and newsmen in general, it was becoming clear to the government that the motion picture offered a uniquely powerful instrument of propaganda, and by the beginning of 1916 a Committee on War Films had been organized, and two cameramen had been despatched to the Front. Over the first six months of the year they sent back some half-dozen newsreels for commercial release, after which one cameraman was invalided home. A replacement went out, and the new team joined the British Fourth Army on the Somme, in time to film — presumably for another short newsreel — the offensive that was about to be launched.

It seems an impossible task — two men, with cameras mounted on tripods and cranked by hand, trying to record on film an attack by thirteen divisions along an eighteen-mile front. Their equipment allowed them no mobility: the camera had to remain stationary while action moved past it. Their lenses were ineffectual for either close-ups or long-distance shots, and all scenes were set in a uniform middle ground. With such equipment they could not film the crucial scenes of the attack — the charge up out of the trenches, and the minutes that followed, when the German machine guns loosed their sweeping fire, and the terrible casualties began. (But of course shots of the heaped-up English

dead would have been forbidden by the censor, even if they could have
been made.)

Faced with these limitations, the cameramen did what they could.
They filmed artillery batteries in action, companies of infantry marching
towards the Front, and men in trenches moving to their attack
positions. Then they filmed the wounded returning from the attack, and
the captured Germans. After a few days they returned to England,
where the rushes were shown to the War Films Committee on July 12;
the whole filming, from preparation to screening, had taken about two
weeks.

At this point, someone recognized that what they had was not the
material for a newsreel, but a full-length documentary of what was still
being officially regarded as the war's crucial battle. The films were
edited into one, captions were supplied by the War Office, and *Battle of
the Somme* was released. The first showing, to a selected audience of
journalists, government officials, General Staff officers, and members of
the film industry, was on August 10; the actual battle was then in its
sixth week, and showed no signs of either succeeding or ending.

What the government thought the film would accomplish is clear
from the letter that Lloyd George, newly appointed Secretary of State
for War, sent to be read at that first viewing and to be projected on the
screen at all subsequent showings. 'You are invited here to-day,' Lloyd
George wrote,

> to witness by far the most important and imposing picture of the war
> that our staff has yet procured.
>
> The Battle of the Somme, furious and desperate as it has been, is a
> first and most important phase of what is an historical struggle,
> unique in its scope and world-wide significance.
>
> I am convinced that when you have seen this wonderful picture,
> every heart will beat higher in sympathy with its cause and purpose,
> which is no other than that everyone of us at home and those abroad
> shall see what our men at the Front are doing and suffering for us, and
> how their achievements have been made possible by the sacrifices
> made at home.
>
> Now, gentlemen, be up and doing also! See that this picture, which
> is in itself an epic of self-sacrifice and gallantry, reaches everyone.
> Herald the deeds of our brave men to the ends of the earth. This is
> *your* duty.
>
> Ladies, I feel that no word is necessary to urge upon you the

importance of throwing in the whole ardour and strength of your invaluable aid. Mothers, wives, sisters, and affianced ones, your hearts will beat, your voices will speak in honour and glory of the living and the dead. You are great and powerful. This is your mission.[2]

Three motives are apparent here: to make the battle seem historically significant (a turning point); to justify home-front sacrifices; and to keep women's support for the war at a high emotional pitch. The film that could do all that would indeed be what Lloyd George hoped it would be — the war's epic.

In terms of audiences, *Battle of the Somme* was a success beyond all expectations. It opened on August 21 in thirty-four London cinemas, and in major provincial cities a week later, and by early September it had been booked for more than a thousand theatres throughout England. Wherever it was shown, attendance records were broken. There were queues all day long outside the Scala and Philharmonic Hall, the two principal London halls showing the film. On September 2 it was shown at Windsor to the King and Queen: the King's reaction was that 'the public should see these pictures that they may have some idea of what the Army is doing, and what war means.'[3]

Not everyone agreed. A cinema operator in Hammersmith placed a notice outside his hall which read:

WE ARE NOT SHOWING THE BATTLE OF THE SOMME. THIS IS A PLACE OF AMUSEMENT, NOT A CHAMBER OF HORRORS.[4]

And there was opposition to the film from persons in high places. The Dean of Durham, in a letter to *The Times*, condemned audiences who 'feel no scruple at feasting their eyes on pictures which present the passion and death of British soldiers'[5] (the echo of the Communion Service, implying that each soldier's death was a crucifixion, is interesting); and the distinguished zoologist E. Ray Lankester wrote, also to *The Times*, that

the days when decent people did not hesitate to seek excitement in witnessing the hangings at Newgate and the flogging of the madmen at Bedlam are long past. We have learnt to mistrust and to avoid the emotional disturbance caused by such experiences.[6]

But most civilians — if one can take letters to the press as representative — saw the film as their King did, as a necessary experience of reality, though their reasons for its necessity differed. For one it would make English men and women 'determined to stop the repetition of such a war', for another (the parent of a dead soldier) it was a chance 'to know what was the life, and the life-in-death, that our dear ones endured, and to be with them again in their great adventure', for a third it would open the eyes of 'thousands of ease-loving people, sitting at home and taking their pleasure . . .'[7] A testimony against war, a great adventure, a purge for the pleasure-loving: it's hard to see how one film could be all of these things. The fact that it was suggests that *Battle of the Somme* was less purposive, and less epic, than Lloyd George thought it was.

Nevertheless it was a powerful and convincing image of the reality of the war. This reality is more than a matter of real soldiers in actual trenches; it is expressed in the very structure of the film, even in those aspects that were the consequences of technological limitations and hasty editing. It is, for example, a film without a narrative line, made up of disconnected vignettes, in which guns fire, men march, other men wait, wounds are treated, an English soldier offers a cigarette to a German prisoner. There are no continuing characters, and no defined individuals; all faces are the same face, dirt-smeared under a tin hat, taut with anxiety or nervously grinning. Among these anonymous faces there are no generals, and very little visible leadership. Nor is there any consistent direction to the movements that the men make: guns fire this way and that, troops move up-camera and then down, as though no one knew where the enemy was. And that enemy is never seen, except at the end, as prisoners, and as corpses.

The places in which these massed figure moves are formless and featureless, without living plants or creatures, or any signs that human beings might have lived here before the soldiers came. (The one exception, a brief shot of peasant women cultivating the ruined earth, comes as a shock — no doubt it was intended to.) The only trees are a few splintered trunks, and the one attempt at a distance shot towards the German lines shows only an emptiness that might once have been a farmer's field.

Death in battle is represented only once. It takes place during an attack, as the camera records a line of soldiers clambering out of a trench, and advancing through barbed wire into No-Man's Land. One man crumples at the parapet edge, and slides slowly back down the sloping side of the trench, to lie motionless there; another drops at screen-left; and further out, beyond the barbed wire, two others fall and lie. (For a still from this scene, see plate 8.) For viewers in 1916, this was the most memorable scene in the film. Rider Haggard wrote of it in his diary:

> The most impressive of [the pictures] to my mind is that of a regiment scrambling out of a trench to charge and of the one man who slides back shot dead. There is something appalling about the instantaneous change from fierce activity to supine death. Indeed the whole horrible business is appalling. War has always been dreadful, but never, I suppose, more dreadful than today.[8]

It must have been this scene that stirred Professor Lankester and the Dean of Durham to protest, and it has remained vivid in memory. While I was writing this book I discussed the film with an elderly English friend who had seen it in 1916, when she was a young girl. She remembered only this scene, but she remembered it in exact detail.

The scene, in still photographs taken from it, has remained a classic image of what the Somme was like; John Buchan used two stills from it to illustrate his *The Battle of the Somme: First Phase* (1917), Sir John Hackett used it in *The Profession of Arms* (1983), and English newspapers used it to illustrate articles on the seventieth anniversary of the battle, in 1986.

It is the only scene in the film that was not authentic. The cameras could not follow an actual attack (for one thing, the Germans took any device stuck on a tripod to be a machine gun, and fired on it), and so a fake attack was staged in a safe rear area. It is the one melodramatic moment in the film, the one action that seems to enact the idea of battle and sacrifices, and you can see why historians and journalists instinctively chose it. But in the film it is not the climax, because there is no climax. We see the men who will fight the battle, and later we see the men who have fought it, the wounded and the battle-worn. But there is no real battle, armies don't meet, no advance is visible, nothing really *happens*.

All of these elements have their resonances — though they are not the traditional resonances of war stories — and together they compose a version of war that has great, non-traditional symbolic force. In this film, war is not a matter of individual voluntary acts, but of masses of men and materials, moving randomly through a dead, ruined world towards no identifiable objective; it is aimless violence and passive suffering, without either a beginning or an end — not a crusade, but a terrible destiny. War Office caption-writers tried to make it into a narrative of a conventional one-day battle, which the British had won, but the visual images deny that story.

The Somme film changed the way civilians imagined the war. If it did not have the same effect on men at the Front, that is scarcely surprising. Raymond Asquith, the Prime Minister's son, saw it on the Somme on September 7, a week before he was killed, and assumed that the scenes had all been staged somewhere else, though he conceded that 'casual scenes in and on the way to the trenches are well-chosen and amazingly like what happens'.[9] John Masefield, who saw it in a military hospital in France, also doubted the authenticity of the front-line scenes, while allowing that 'in their general ruin and waste they were like the real thing'.[10] But however like they were to the real thing, they could not be real enough; they could not reproduce the intolerable noise of bombardment, or the stench of decaying men and horses, or the unrelenting misery of rain and mud. They could not make the scenes that they pictured unfamiliar enough — as unlike England, or any other place on earth, as in reality they were.

II

War Office film-makers saw the war in 1916 as a narrative problem: how to make a story out of a disorder of images. Novelists saw it in much the same way. Fiction conventionally moves through time and through problems to resolutions; but how could one represent the war in such terms when one was in the middle of it, at a point of lost momentum and lost conviction, with no end in sight? On the other hand, as Henry James had asked, how could one *not* represent it either? The condition of *middleness* posed many problems in 1916: a morale problem, a propaganda problem, a strategic problem; for novelists it was also an aesthetic problem. It is not surprising that few serious novelists wrote serious mid-war novels. Two, however, did, and their solutions to the problems are worth some attention.

Rose Macaulay's *Non-Combatants and Others* is not a 'war novel' in the usual sense; as the title says, it is about *not* being one of the fighters. Women are the essential non-combatants — 'the sexually unfit,' Macaulay calls them — and the novel is centred on a young woman's wartime life; but the non-combatant category is larger than that, and it would be wrong to call it simply a 'woman's novel'. A clergyman in the novel explains the wider implications of the title:

War's beastly and abominable to the fighters: but not to be fighting is much more embittering and demoralising, I think. Probably largely because one has more time to think. To have one's friends in danger, and not to be in danger oneself — it fills one with futile rage. Combatants are to be pitied; but non-combatants are of all men and women the most miserable. Older men, crocks, parsons, women — God help them.[11]

The war experience of such outsiders — embittering, demoralizing, miserable — is the subject of the book.

A war novel about non-combatants must be a static, passive sort of book, one would think, and especially if such a novel was written in the middle of a war, and is *about* that middle, as Macaulay's is. The war in *Non-Combatants* has neither a beginning nor an end: the novel begins in April 1915 and ends as the year ends, on New Year's Eve. During those nine months a number of people respond to the war in various ways — with patriotic enthusiasm, with indifference, with despair. Men go off to the war, and sometimes return; or don't go, but stay at home hating it. Women work as VADs, or send clothing to Belgian refugees, or knit, or make sandbags. Parsons preach and writers write. Young men and young women meet, flirt, and sometimes fall in love. And the war goes on, indifferent to these human actions, meaningless, destructive, and apparently endless.

There are events in the novel with conventionally dramatic possibilities: Alix, the young heroine, falls in love with a painter (modelled apparently on Macaulay's friend Rupert Brooke); the painter goes to the Front, and his painting-hand is maimed; Alix's brother dies in France of a self-inflicted wound — the first appearance in fiction, to my knowledge, of what would become a common incident in later war literature. Love, injury, death: in another sort of woman's narrative — *Jane Eyre*, for example — these would have had dramatic, resolving consequences; here they don't, they simply happen. War imposes its own pointlessness on the very structure of the novel, making it fragmented, static, and waiting — like war. 'There seems no way out,' Alix thinks; and that is the mood of the book.

Macaulay took one of the epigraphs for *Non-Combatants* from Wells's *Boon* — a passage that begins: 'War is just the killing of things and the smashing of things. And when it is all over, then literature and civilization will have to begin all over again.'[12] The connection claimed is significant: Wells was the only English novelist before Macaulay to get his hatred of war, and its cost to civilization, into a work of imagination (though in a tone quite different from Macaulay's quiet melancholy). He was an historian of his own time, locating his stories in immediate history and among historical persons, and Macaulay was like him in that, too. *Non-Combatants* is meticulously exact in its references to events of 1915: zeppelin raids and DORA, *The Hymn of Hate* and 'When we wind up the watch on the Rhine', the Deptford riots and the fighting at Ypres, the income tax and Socialism — these are all in the text, composing a dense historical present. In the course of making the present historical, Macaulay touches on many of the issues that I have been discussing: the relation of art to war, DORA and censorship, the diminishment and distortion of English culture, the breakup of the women's movement are all discussed, sometimes in ways that make the book seem more like an ironic essay than a novel.

Take the theme of art and war. It was, as we have seen, a much-discussed issue in the first year of the war. Here, Alix discusses it with her brother Nicholas (a book reviewer) and Mr West (an Anglican curate). Nicholas has been reading a book for review, titled *The Effects of the War on Literature*, and quotes a page from it:

> 'The war is putting an end to sordidness and littleness, in literature as in other spheres of human life. The second-rate, the unheroic, the earthy, the petty, the trivial — how does it look now, seen in the light of the guns that blaze over Flanders? The guns, shattering so much, have at least shattered falsity in art. We were degenerate, a little, in our literature and in our lives: we have been made great. We are come, surely, to the heroic, the epic pitch of living; if we cannot express it with a voice worthy of it, then indeed it has failed in its deepest lesson to us. We may expect a renascence of beauty worthy to rank with the Romantic Revival born of the French wars ...'[13]

This is a brilliant pastiche of many editorials and essays; it has the self-denigration, the confession of English decadence, the assumed heroism, even the French references of Gosse's 'War and Literature' — though it might just as well be a parody of Image, or of Boon's enemy, Osborn. It appears in the novel as a parody, but in this sort of writing it is difficult to distinguish parody from the real thing, and I can see nothing in Macaulay's version that Gosse would have disowned.

Nicholas, disgusted by this rubbish, proposes to edit his own Effects of the War series, and to write the essay on Literature himself. 'War's an insanity,' he says:

and insane things, purely destructive, wasteful, hideous, brutal,
ridiculous things, aren't what make art. The war's produced a little
fine poetry, among a sea of tosh — a thing here and there; but mostly
— oh, good Lord! The flood of cheap heroics and commonplace
patriotic claptrap — it's swept slobbering all over us; there seems no
stemming it. Literary revival be hanged. All we had before — and
precious little it was — of decent work, clear and alive and sane and
close to reality, is being trampled to bits by this — this imbecile brute.
And when the time comes to collect the bits and try to begin again,
we shan't be able to; there'll be no more spirit in us; we shall be too
battered and beaten ...[14]

Nicholas is saying what Wells said in *Boon*: war does not create, it only
destroys. It is an important passage in the book; but it is also important
in the larger context of English wartime culture. For it asserts that the
war is not an event in history but a *gap*, an annihilation of pre-war
reality, and that neither art nor life can simply resume the old continuities when the war ends. This is, of course, a primary tenet of post-war
Modernism; it is worth noting that it emerged during the war years, and
in the works of writers like Wells and Macaulay who were not
Modernists in the usual sense of the term.

When the war ends, Macaulay says, English civilization will have to
start again. But what does one do in the meantime, if one is a non-
combatant? Alix leaves the scene with her brother thinking that perhaps
she and Nicholas and Mr West — the woman, the artist, and the priest
— are the natural enemies of war, and should be allies. She has reached
— or created — a turning point, not in the war, but in her attitude
towards the war. From this point in the novel she moves towards a
commitment to active opposition to the war. She has found the right
form for her woman's war to take.

Non-Combatants is, as I said, an unresolved novel. It ends on a wartime
New Year's Eve, in a final chapter that is made of discontinuous
fragments, each separated from the others as the characters are separated
from each other by the war. The final fragment contains only these two
sentences:

The year of grace 1915 slipped away into darkness, like a broken ship
drifting on bitter tides on to a waste shore. The next year began.[15]

No characters, no direction, only the drift towards disaster: it is a powerful image of a society caught in a war it could neither end nor control.

The novel was not well received by wartime reviewers — not surprisingly, since they were on the whole the same people who had argued that war was good for art, and predicted the renascence that Macaulay ridiculed. The *TLS* critic was disappointed by the book's 'restless monotony', the *Westminster Gazette* found its didacticism a serious flaw, the *Outlook* was offended by its 'superior tone', and decided that it was a 'nerve novel', not a war novel, because the soldiers in it were depressed, not cheerful like real-life Tommies. But the criticism that Macaulay must have found hardest to take came in a *Nation* review that was clearly intended to be admiring: 'What surprises us', the reviewer wrote, 'is that a woman and not a man should have written "Non-Combatants" ... because the "ethos," the stamp and tone of "Non-Combatants" is not feminine, but masculine. Most thoughtful people', he went on, 'would, we think, acknowledge that the spectatorial point of view, with its concomitants of irony, detachment and critical analysis, is more often discovered in the author than the authoress.'[16] To write a novel that no man would write, attacking a war that most men supported, and to be called *masculine* for doing so, must have been bitter.

Non-Combatants was published in August 1916. Wells's *Mr Britling Sees It Through* appeared the following month. Like Macaulay's book, it is a 'war novel' about civilians that is also a history of the early war years; it begins in the summer of 1914 and ends at the end of 1915, and it continually relates its fictional events to actual historical ones — to the Irish Question, the anti-German riots, the Bryce Report, the shelling of Whitby and Scarborough.

Mr Britling is also a history of Wells himself, and of his attitudes towards the war. In this sense it is a kind of sequel to *Boon*. Reginald Boon was Wells's judgement of his optimistic Edwardian self — the man who believed in Science and Progress, and wrote books like *The Mind Set Free*; Mr Britling is the Wells of the early war years — the enthusiastic, belligerent public man who advocated arming the Boy Scouts, and wrote *The War That Will End War*, and told his newspaper readers that 'this is the heroic age, suddenly come again'.[17] If *Boon* was written to repudiate the foolish optimist in Wells, *Mr Britling* was written to record another change of mind, the process by which Wells lost his keenness for war. 'This story', he wrote,

> is essentially the history of the opening and of the realisation of the
> Great War as it happened to one small group of people in Essex, and

more particularly as it happened to one human brain. It came at first
to all these people in a spectacular manner, as a thing happening
dramatically and internationally, as a show, as something in the
newspapers, something in the character of an historical epoch rather
than a personal experience; only by slow degrees did it and its
consequences invade the common texture of English life.[18]

It is the story, in short, of a change in the way ordinary people (and an
extraordinary one like Wells, too) understood the war, as it entered their
lives.

The process of this change gives the novel both its structure and its
historical veracity. Mr Britling is subjected to all the innumerable
pressures, all the truths and all the lies that crowd in upon civilian minds
during a war. He reads the newspapers, hears rumours, and receives
letters from his son Hugh at the Front; he hears of atrocities, and has
news of individual deaths. Gradually his enthusiasm and his faith fail
him, and he begins to have doubts about his nation's cause. But it is not
the deaths and the horrors that sway him; it is his disillusionment at the
decline of English idealism. At the beginning of the war, Mr Britling
thinks (or Wells thinks — there is really no distinction in these
meditations), England had seemed inspired.

> Youth and the common people shone. The sons of every class went
> out to fight and die, full of a splendid dream of this war. Easy-going
> vanished from the foreground of the picture. But only to creep back
> again as the first inspiration passed. Presently the older men, the
> seasoned politicians, the owners and hucksters, the charming women
> and the habitual consumers, began to recover from this blaze of moral
> exaltation. Old habits of mind and procedure reasserted themselves.
> The war which had begun so dramatically missed its climax; there
> was neither heroic swift defeat nor heroic swift victory. There was
> indecision; the most trying test of all for an undisciplined people.
> There were great spaces of uneventful fatigue. Before the Battle of the
> Yser had fully developed the dramatic quality had gone out of the
> war. It had ceased to be either a tragedy or a triumph; for both sides it
> became a monstrous strain and wasting. It had become a wearisome
> thrusting against a pressure of evils . . .[19]

In its assumptions about pre-war England, and the first wartime spirit,
this passage sounds like Gosse and his fellow-patriots. But by this time
(Wells carefully dates it as the summer of 1915) that spirit has been

broken, dissipated not by the realities of war but by certain cynical persons at home, who would become stock figures in later anti-war writings — the older men, the politicians, and the charming women.

The process of Mr Britling's disillusionment continues; by September 1915 it is complete. 'I saw this war . . .', he thinks,

> as something that might legitimately command a splendid enthusiasm of indignation . . . It was all a dream, the dream of a prosperous comfortable man who had never come to the cutting edge of life. Everywhere cunning, everywhere small feuds and hatreds, distrusts, dishonesties, timidities, feebleness of purpose, dwarfish imaginations, swarm over the great and simple issues . . . It is a war now like any other of the mobbing, many-aimed cataclysms that have shattered empires and devastated the world; it is a war without point, a war that has lost its soul . . .[20]

Here again, it is not the deaths of men but of ideals that Wells laments. Mr Britling does not oppose the war, or even desire its end; he only regrets that it has become like any other war.

So far, Mr Britling's history has not recorded a turn of mind, but only a long decline, a progressive loss of faith in the war as a cause. But then Hugh Britling is killed in the trenches, and Mr Britling confronts despair. In the last chapter of the novel he tries to formulate a way out — a turn from darkness towards some faith. He is writing a letter to the parents of a dead German boy, a letter of consolation both for them and for himself. He writes that the young men — his son and theirs — did not die in vain, but cannot say why that is true. He blames German imperialism, and finds no comfort in the blaming. He urges a World Republic (a very Wellsian idea), but instead of arguing the case, breaks off with a page of disconnected words and phrases, which Wells reproduces in his text. Mr Britling cannot finish his letter because none of his arguments is an adequate response to the fact of his son's death, and those last scattered words are his confession of failure, and his judgement on the war-makers: 'Lawyers Princes / Dealers in Contention / *Honesty* / Blood Blood / And make an End to Them.'[21]

Then, on the penultimate page, a sudden affirmation comes: 'Our sons', Mr Britling says to himself, '. . . have shown us God.' And the novel ends with images of a peaceful sunrise. Wells's God does not represent a character's willed choice of values, as Macaulay's does; this God is without attributes, has neither priest nor church nor Holy Book: He is simply a name for the will-to-affirm, hope without reasons in a

hopeless time. Wells tied Him to the end of the novel like a hook on a
fishing line, because he could not let it end with Mr Britling's scribbled
words of despair.

Perhaps it was that confessed need to hope that gave the novel the
note of truth. Certainly wartime readers did find in it a true record of
their own feelings: Shaw called it 'a priceless historical document',
Cynthia Asquith praised it for registering 'so many of the different
phases of one's war thoughts and emotions', Sassoon copied the 'war
that has lost its soul' passage into his diary, and Asquith quoted the same
lines in a letter to Venetia Stanley. Four years later, after the war had
ended, Thomas Hardy still considered *Mr Britling* 'the best war book we
have had. It gives just what we thought and felt at the time.' Among
Wells's friends, only Arnold Bennett was critical; he thought that Wells
had been unfair to the British government — an understandable
complaint from an official of Wellington House.[22]

Wells's account of the home-front turn of mind pleased his home-
front readers, that's clear from the reviews and from the book's printing

record — eleven impressions by the end of 1916. But his imagining of Hugh Britling's life as a soldier pleased a tougher audience, the men at the Front, as Tawney testified. His 'Some Reflections of a Soldier' observed regretfully that civilians realized nothing about the inner life of soldiers. To this statement he appended this footnote when he published the essay in October 1916:

> When I wrote this I had not finished reading 'Mr. Britling Sees It Through.' Hugh's letters show that some people at home do realize it.[23]

Those letters are indeed convincing: they could easily have been copied from the actual letters of some intelligent soldier. Wells had not been to the Front when he wrote *Mr Britling*; nevertheless he could invent a soldier's version of existence there that carried conviction with an intelligent veteran of trench life.

Macaulay had not been to France either. Yet she too could imagine that world; indeed her Alix's version of the war is more violently realistic than anything in the letters of Wells's Hugh Britling:

> Whizz-bangs, pom-poms, trench-mortars spinning along and boun-cing off the wire trench roof . . . Minnie coming along to blow the whole trench inside out . . . legs and arms and bits of men flying in the air . . . the rest of them buried deep in choking earth . . . perhaps to be dug out alive, perhaps dead . . . What was it John had said on the balcony — something about a leg . . . the leg of a friend . . . pulling it out of the chaos of earth and mud and stones which had been a trench . . . thinking it led on to the entire friend, finding it didn't, was a detached bit . . .[24]

This is not simply a convincing imitation of a soldier's letter, as Wells's inventions were: it is a vision of trench warfare at its worst moments, in a style that is close to the relentless particularity of the soldier writers I have quoted — Leighton and Graeme West and Hamilton. She could not have read anything they wrote, of course; no doubt she had got the details from a soldier home on leave, as Alix does in the novel. It would have been difficult not to: there were more than a million Englishmen on the Western Front by the time she wrote her novel, and in any week thousands would be in England on leave. And the military hospitals (in one of which Macaulay worked as a VAD in 1915) were full of wounded men. The war had come home to England; even to civilian imaginations it was a part of reality.

At the turning point of the war, during the first months of the Somme offensive, two novels appear that are about turning points in civilian lives in relation to the war. Both focus on a central character who goes through a period of disillusionment and despair, and turns at the end to a new commitment. Neither goes beyond that turn, to its consequences; both novels end inconclusively at the end of 1915, in a condition of *middleness*, the war still controlling and destroying lives, the individual still powerless to check it. In tone these two inconclusive conclusions differ considerably, to be sure: Wells's natural optimism, which he had tried to kill off in the person of Reginald Boon, resurrected itself at the end of *Mr Britling*, whereas Macaulay's ending is more muted: as a Christian, and as a woman, she expected less of humankind. But in their essential perception of the time the two novelists were alike: both saw the loss of faith and the loss of momentum in the nation at war as realities — and realities in England, not in the trenches — and both saw that in these circumstances some new attitude towards the war was necessary, even though it could have no present resolution. Because they saw their historical moment so clearly, their novels remain essential documents of England at the turning point.

III

Macaulay and Wells resolved the problem that Henry James had posed, the problem of how to represent the new reality of war, by making novels out of immediate history, locating their actions precisely in public time and placing within them many references to actual wartime events. It was one way of imagining the war — or at least the home-front experience of war — and it worked well enough. Yet one feels, reading these books three-quarters of a century later, that all those exact particulars are restraints that confine the novels to their historical moments, and restrict meaning and suggestion. There had to be another, more open way of imagining the experience of existing in a world at war.

And indeed another kind of representation was possible, by which a writer might respond to the war without ever mentioning it — a kind of war writing emptied of history, but faithful to feeling. Two of the major works of English literature of the war years — works that most

critics would judge among the most important of the decade — are of
that kind. Lawrence's *Women in Love* and Shaw's *Heartbreak House* were
both written in 1916–17, and both belong as much to those years as *Non-
Combatants* and *Mr Britling* do, though they are rooted there in less
explicit ways.[25]

Neither the novel nor the play is a 'war work' in any obvious sense.
There is no war in progress in either: no soldiers, no battles, and no
enemy. Nor is either located in time in a way that would place it either
in wartime or *out* of it; there are no dates, and no refernces to historical
events of the kind that Macaulay and Wells used. Both works seem
more or less contemporary with the dates of their composition — there
are motor-cars and electric lights, and the manners and ideas about art
and life seem current — but they might as easily be set in the Edwardian
years as in the war years. Both anatomize and condemn essential
elements of English society, and in this they resemble the wartime
jeremiads of writers like Gosse and Image; but social criticism was also
common among the Edwardians — think of *Tono-Bungay* and *Howards
End*, think of the plays of Galsworthy — and *Women in Love* and
Heartbreak House might in these terms be dated a decade earlier.

Yet one recognizes at once that neither the novel nor the play could be
Edwardian, that both belong to the same middle-of-the-war time that
produced *Non-Combatants* and *Mr Britling*. The war is a presence in both
works, though it does not appear as history; it is there, rather, as a state
of mind, expressed in the tone, in the movement of the action, in the
endings, and in a hovering preoccupation with violence and death.

Women in Love is a novel with a complicated history; Lawrence began
it as *The Sisters* in 1913, then detached a part and rewrote it in 1914–15,
publishing that portion as *The Rainbow* in September 1915 (whereupon
it was suppressed by the authorities, as we have seen). In May 1916 he
began again on the remaining portion of the story, working on it all
through that year and completing it at the end of 1917, though it was
not published until 1921.

During those years of composition the war was much on Lawrence's
mind: not as military events — Lawrence paid no attention to what was
actually happening in France — but as the apocalyptic ending of a sick
civilization. 'I think there is no future for England,' he wrote in a letter
in November 1915: 'only a decline and fall. That is the dreadful and
unbearable part of it: to have been born into a decadent era, a decline of
life, a collapsing civilisation.' And in February 1916: 'This world of ours
has got to collapse now, in violence and injustice and destruction,

nothing will stop it.' And in July 1917: 'I believe the deluge of iron rain will destroy the world here, utterly: no Ararat will rise above the subsiding iron waters ... We have chosen our extinction in death ...'[26]

These apocalyptic prophecies were often related to events in Lawrence's own life: the first quotation was written three days after the court hearing at which *The Rainbow* was condemned, and the last not long after Lawrence's second physical examination for conscription into the army, an experience that he found 'horrible', and later described in a vivid chapter in *Kangaroo*.[27] That was the way Lawrence's mind worked: for him, the world began with the self. But his prophecies were more than simply personal bitterness projected upon the world; they were also expressions of a deep conviction, which he shared with many other thoughtful, depressed persons, that the war was simply the final stage in the death of their world.

Women in Love is an enactment of that apocalyptic vision, though that quality is not obvious in a summary either of its locales or of its plot. It is a wide-ranging novel of English life: of artists, teachers, intellectuals, aristocrats, industrialists, and workers, in country houses and miners' cottages, in village schools and bohemian cafés — the sort of novel, in its social amplitude, that Galsworthy or Wells might have written before the war. And its themes seem, at first glance, to belong to the pre-war years too: they include the wars-before-the-war that were fought over women's rights, workers' rights, and avant-garde art. In these shifting scenes, amid all this talk, four principal characters — the Brangwen sisters, Ursula and Gudrun, and their lovers, Rupert Birkin and Gerald Crich — struggle to give meaning to their lives through their relations to each other. A common theme, and one that has nothing to do with the war.

What *does* have to do with the war is the tone of the novel — the desperation and sense of crisis that fills even its most intimate, least world-regarding scenes. In the opening chapter, for example, the two sisters discuss marriage, and find themselves 'confronted by a void, a terrifying chasm, as if they had looked over the edge'.[28] As a reaction to the prospect of matrimony it seems somewhat excessive; but all decisions, all visions of the future in the book have that fearful quality, expressed in similar images, as an abyss, a chasm, a void on the edge of which individuals tremble. Related to these are other images of devastation and ruin: the defaced countryside, the mean and sordid towns, everything 'a ghoulish replica of the real world', expanding to become Birkin's vision of a world of 'universal defilement'[29]; and images of dissolution, flux, and corruption — humanity flowing towards its own annihilation. These images compose a vision of Western society and Western man at the edge of a vast catastrophe — a violation of meaning and order that is beyond the power of individual human beings to alter. It is a vision that Macaulay's Alix and Wells's Mr Britling share, and it belongs to the same dark time in the middle of the war.

Lawrence's characters go further, though; they *desire* the annihilation that the book prophesies. 'So you'd like everybody in the world destroyed?' Ursula asks Birkin:

> 'I should indeed.'
> 'And the world empty of people.'
> 'Yes truly. You yourself, don't you find it a beautiful clean thought, a world empty of people, just uninterrupted grass, and a hare sitting up?'
> The pleasant sincerity of his voice made Ursula pause to consider her own proposition. And really it *was* attractive: a clean, lovely, humanless world. It was the *really* desirable.[30]

It is not only humanity that Lawrence would like to destroy: at its darkest, the novel yearns for the end of the world. (Lawrence's wife, Frieda, wanted to call it *Dies Irae*, and Lawrence himself proposed *Day of Wrath* as an appropriately apocalyptic alternate title.)[31] 'Dissolution rolls on,' says Birkin, who generally speaks with the voice of Lawrence,

> just as production does . . . It is a progressive process — and it ends in universal nothing — the end of the world, if you like. But why isn't the end of the world as good as the beginning?[32]

All through the novel there is this obsession with annihilation and death — not individual death only, but the death of a society, a civilization, the old life before the war, the whole world. The movement of the novel is itself an enactment of this theme — a movement away from social systems and occasions into separateness and emptiness, from the country house and the school house at the beginning to the frozen, empty space at the end, a movement towards dissolution that is an analogy to the war itself.

Excluded from the literal world of the novel, the war enters it metaphorically. There are images of battles and wounds, of artillery fire and exploding shells — the sorts of images that would be unavoidable in an English consciousness in 1916, even one as egocentric as Lawrence's. But there is no war: Lawrence's imagined world is the contemporary world, but the great catastrophe of the time has been omitted from it. In the course of the action the lovers travel about England and Europe without restrictions: there are no trenches, no closed borders and no moving troops to inhibit their freedom. The Battles of the Somme and Passchendaele were fought while Lawrence wrote and rewrote his novel, but they are not fought in his pages. Yet the war is in the book, and Lawrence clearly intended that his readers should feel its presence there. In the Foreword that he wrote in 1919 he explained:

> This novel was written in its first form in the Tyrol, in 1913. It was altogether re-written and finished in Cornwall in 1917. So that it is a novel which took its final shape in the midst of the period of war, though it does not concern the war itself. I should wish the time to remain unfixed, so that the bitterness of the war may be taken for granted in the characters.[33]

That is an odd intention: to remove the novel from history, in order that an emotional response to history may be taken for granted; to write as though the Edwardian peace had continued into the years of the war, yet write with a war-generated bitterness. It was Lawrence's answer to James's question: how represent it? By rendering not the war, but the *bitterness* of the war — as though bitterness were the war's primal reality.

There is much bitterness in *Women in Love*: bitterness about industrialism, about class, about bohemian decadence, about the mechanization of working life, about the failures of man–woman and man–man relations. These are all historical subjects, and Lawrence understood them as such: his world was bitter for historical reasons. When he addressed himself to these subjects, when he ridiculed or condemned artists and aristocrats and industrial magnates, he was doing what many wartime journalists had done — looking for the causes of the wartime condition of England in English society. In this sense, *Women in Love* is very much a novel of its time and place.

But there is one way in which Lawrence differed from other wartime critics of England. The others saw the war as the historical cure for an historical national disease; but for Lawrence its events were signs of the end of the world. If he imagined anything at all after the war, it was a New Heaven and a New Earth — visionary realms drawn not from history but from the Book of Revelation.

This vision was not simply something that Lawrence created for his fiction: it was the way he saw the world at war. When he witnessed a zeppelin attack on London in 1915 (it was while he was rewriting *Women in Love*), he saw it not as an air raid, but as a War in Heaven. 'Last night when we were coming home,' he wrote in a letter to Ottoline Morrell,

> the guns broke out, and there was a noise of bombs. Then we saw the Zeppelin above us, just ahead, amid a gleaming of clouds: high up, like a bright golden finger, quite small, among a fragile incandescence of clouds. And underneath it were splashes of fire as the shells fired from earth burst. Then there were flashes near the ground — and the shaking noise. It was like Milton — then there was war in heaven. But it was not angels. It was that small golden Zeppelin, like a long oval world, high up. It seemed as if the cosmic order were gone, as if there had come a new order, a new heavens above us: and as if the new world in anger were trying to revoke it. Then the small long-ovate luminary, the new world in the heavens, disappeared again . . .
>
> So it seems our cosmos is burst, burst at last, the stars and moon blown away, the envelope of the sky burst out, and a new cosmos appeared, with a long-ovate, gleaming central luminary, calm and drifting in a glow of light, like a new moon, with its light bursting in flashes on the earth, to burst away the earth also. So it is the end — our world is gone, and we are like dust in the air.[34]

This war in heaven would not purge England of its historical weaknesses, and it would not come to an historical end. The end that Lawrence imagined would be apocalyptic

This is what the end of *Woman in Love* is, as Lawrence recognized. 'The book frightens me,' he wrote in a letter in November 1916: 'it is so end-of-the-world'; and in a letter the following July: 'it is purely destructive, not like *The Rainbow*, destructive-consummating.'[35] And so it is. It moves to its end in a series of scenes removed from English society to the empty world of an Alpine winter — cold, deadly, and without form — where Gerald Crich, the industrial magnate, the English man-of-power, freezes to death. More than a man dies there in the snow. Gerald's death, like other crises in the novel, goes beyond particularity to embrace Lawrence's general sense of the end of the world.

Attached to this powerful scene is a curious little coda, some thirty lines long, in which Birkin and Ursula, back in England, quarrel about the need for love. It is a quarrel that is not resolved, and the novel ends on a disagreement between them. It is a very odd ending — after apocalypse, irresolution. Odd, but in its historical context understandable. Lawrence's novel, like the war itself, seems caught in a process of

annihilation that has lost direction and meaning, and cannot be completed or resolved by an act of imagination. In this final irresolution,
Women in Love is like *Non-Combatants* and *Mr Britling* — another novel
written in the middle of a terrible war that would not end. But it is
different, and unique, in this: it is a war novel such as might have been
written by some Old Testament prophet — visionary, violent, and
apocalyptic.

At the same time that Lawrence was writing his apocalyptic novel,
Shaw was writing an apocalyptic play, to which he gave the name of the
country house where it takes place: *Heartbreak House*. That house is
more than simply a setting for a Shavian conversation-piece: it is a
symbol of England — its traditions, its social structure, its values, its
follies, and its fate. Being a country house, it primarily mirrors the
upper classes, though its inhabitants are not easily classifiable in class-
terms: a mad sea-captain, a captain of industry, two fashionable women,
a poor idealist and his daughter, a romantic idler, a diplomat, a burglar.
The poor idealist describes the others (minus the burglar) as 'very
charming people, most advanced, unprejudiced, frank, humane, un-
conventional, democratic, free-thinking, and everything that is delightful
to thoughtful people'. But the romantic idler sees them more clearly: 'all
heart-broken imbeciles,' he says.[36]

At Heartbreak House the residents and their guests talk. They discuss
everything that constitutes their lives — money, manners, marriage,
class, politics, religion; and in the course of discussing they dismantle
and disvalue all those institutions and centres of accepted values
that constituted what an Edwardian Englishman meant by *England*:
Capitalism, Imperialism, the Governing Class, the City. These are what
Heartbreak House stands for; and they are all collapsing: Heartbreak
House is, as various characters observe, a madhouse, a house without
foundations, a sinking ship.

There is only one crucial subject that these characters do *not* discuss:
nobody mentions war. The language and the weapons of war occur:
Captain Shotover, the mad master of the house, invents submarine
magnets and harpoon cannons, and works at other means of destroying
his fellow-creatures; and torpedoes and explosives come easily to the
other characters' minds as metaphors for the general destruction that is
taking place in their minds and in their lives. But war — the war that
was being fought as Shaw wrote — does not. Readers who enter Shaw's
House through the vast portico of the Preface may be misled on this
point, for the preface is entirely and explicitly concerned with the war —

its causes, its conduct, and its consequences. But Shaw wrote it later, after the war (he dated it 'June 1919'), and it belongs to that time in the history of the imaginings of war, and not to the mid-war time of *Heartbreak House*. The play itself is not explicit: in it war is not war, but only a figure of speech.

Only one weapon of war in the play is not a metaphor — or not only a metaphor. In the last act a zeppelin is heard overhead, and in the final moments a bomb is dropped, blowing up Captain Shotover's store of dynamite, and with it the captain of industry and the burglar. It is a real bomb, and with its detonation, and a few comments, the play ends.

Does this one act of belligerency thrust the Great War into the play at the last instant, making it a war play in the sense that *Der Tag* and *Armageddon* are? No, there is no war here in the world of Shaw's play, and no point in trying to place his action in actual history. We will better understand what Shaw was doing if we remind ourselves that he once wrote a book called *The Perfect Wagnerite*. *Heartbreak House* is his *Götterdammerung*, a Shavian apocalypse in which the destruction of an anachronistic, dying system of values comes, and is desired. As in *Women in Love*, the characters invoke destruction: Hesione Hushabye, Captain Shotover's daughter, asks her father: 'Can't you think of something that will murder half of Europe in one bang?' and her husband, the romantic liar Hector, twice calls on the heavens to fall and destroy them: 'There is no sense in us,' he explains. 'We are useless, dangerous, and ought to be abolished.' And in the final speeches, after the zeppelin has withdrawn, the survivors rejoice in the destruction that it has made: 'What a glorious experience!' Hesione cries. 'I hope they'll come again tomorrow night.' And Ellie, the young girl who has learned so much in one heartbreaking night, adds (*radiant*, Shaw notes, *at the prospect*): 'Oh, I hope so.'[37]

Heartbreak House is not, then, a play about war, but a play about human folly, as manifested in the England that stumbled blindly into the Great War. The crucial exchange on this point comes in the third act when Hector asks Captain Shotover what will happen to 'this soul's prison we call England?'

> CAPTAIN SHOTOVER. The captain is in his bunk, drinking bottled ditch-water; and the crew is gambling in the forecastle. She will strike and sink and split. Do you think the laws of God will be suspended in favour of England because you were born in it?[38]

That figure of the drifting ship of state had also appeared in Rose Macaulay's version of mid-war England. It is a symbol not of the war, but of something more vast and more frightening — a world out of control, destroying itself because no one can stop it.

Women in Love and Heartbreak House are apocalyptic, not historical. Or almost so. In Lawrence's novel, near the end, the meticulous reader will find one historical fact, a remark made by the Kaiser in 1915; 'Ich habe es nicht gewollt.'[39] On that single nail one can hang the events of the novel, if one is so inclined, and say that at least the last chapter must take place during the war. There is one historical fact in Heartbreak House too: Randall, the lovelorn diplomat, plays 'Keep the Home Fires Burning' on his flute at the final curtain. That tune was first performed in the autumn of 1914; so here, too, we must be in a world at war. But one historical fact doesn't make a novel or a play historical, and these two works remain in their own apocalyptic category — parables, or visions of what happened to England in the second decade of the twentieth century.

Reading and experiencing these visions, one feels in each a curious central emptiness, a space where the war should be. There should be an articulated cause for the extreme feelings of despair and the desire for annihilation that characters feel, and for the disintegration of order that both works express. But causation is one of the casualties of war: there are no causes here, only symptoms of dissolution. Both works render this dissolution of order as a central theme and a principle of form, in a way that makes them formally difficult and hard to interpret — makes them, that is to say, essentially Modernist, in the manner of the great post-war Modernist texts, The Waste Land and Ulysses and Jacob's Room. But they are not post-war, but peculiarly wartime texts — texts that cannot be closed or resolved, because the only true ending would be the end of the war — or of the world.

Near the end of both Women in Love and Heartbreak House vague hopes are uttered for the future of mankind (the same is true of both Non-Combatants and Mr Britling). Not to do so would be to surrender to absolute despair, and would be intolerable. So Lawrence gives Birkin these thoughts, following on the solitary death of Gerald Crich:

> If humanity ran into a cul de sac, and expended itself, the timeless creative mystery would bring forth some other being, finer, more wonderful, some new, more lovely race, to carry on the embodiment of creation. The game was never up.[40]

And Shaw gives his Hector Hushabye one moment of positive vision:

I tell you, one of two things must happen. Either out of that darkness some new creation will come to supplant us as we have supplanted the animals, or the heavens will fall in thunder and destroy us.[41]

But what comforts are such visions of a world after humanity, in a time of war? Like Mr Britling's God without attributes, they come not out of belief, but out of the darkness that covered English imaginations in the war's middle years.

CHAPTER 7

Dissent at the Turn

I

By 1916, the early idealistic support for the war had leaked away; the war, as Wells put it, had missed its climax. As idealism diminished, governmental controls increased; if people would not be voluntarily patriotic they must be compelled to be so. 'The year opens badly for labour,' Beatrice Webb wrote in her diary on January 2, 1916:

> The Munitions Act and the Defence of the Realm Act, together with the suppression of a free press, has been followed by the Cabinet's decision in favour of compulsory military service. This decision is the last of a series of cleverly devised steps, each step seeming at once harmless and inevitable, even to the opponents of compulsion, but in fact necessitating the next step forward to a system of military and industrial conscription ... The 'servile state' will have been established.[1]

Conscription was the most obvious instance of the principle of compulsion in action; it was not necessary as a means of expanding the army — there were always plenty of recruits — but as a means of controlling dissent among male civilians, and of assuring those who supported the war that other men were not avoiding it. Amendments to the Defence of the Realm Act are another example. In 1916 the exporting of any written or printed document, to any enemy or neutral country in Europe or America except under strict limitations, was also forbidden. But these amendments went further than that. It became an offence to utter, in any form, any opinion that might be construed as prejudicial to the conduct of the war. This prohibition was explicitly extended to include art forms that had not previously been specified: plays, pictures,

films. It was another mid-war turn: a turn in the control of the
instruments of expression, which withdrew authority from the individual creator and placed it in the hands of the police and the Army,
whose officers became the agents of state censorship, and controllers of
the arts.

With this new authority, police and War Office officials began to raid
offices of organizations thought to be subversive. During 1916 such
raids were conducted against headquarters of the National Council
Against Conscription, the Independent Labour Party, the Union of
Democratic Control, and the Woman's Labour League, and pamphlets
and other documents were seized and destroyed, including, from the
Woman's Labour League, a pamphlet published before the war titled
Help the Babies. Questions were asked in Parliament, but to no avail: the
government had its power, and used it.[2]

Not all instruments of control were official. There were ultra-
patriotic journals like the *Daily Call* and Horatio Bottomley's *John Bull*,
and from October 1916 a new one, *The Imperialist*, edited by a member
of Parliament, Noel Pemberton Billing. To editors like Bottomley
and Billing, the Military Service Act, which established conscription,
provided another set of opponents — those men who invoked the Act's
provisions for conscientious objection to military service. *Conchie*
became a term of abuse, and the tribunals at which appeals for exception
were heard often became opportunities to harass and abuse pacifists.
The trial of Lytton Strachey is the best-known example, mainly for his
famous *double entendre*. Military Representative: 'Then tell me, Mr
Strachey, what would you do if you saw a German soldier attempting to
rape your sister?' Strachey: 'I should try and interpose my own body.'[3]
Strachey's appeal was allowed, as were those of other Bloomsbury
pacifists, but less well-connected objectors went to prison. In 1916
thirty-four of them were ordered to France, court-martialled, and
sentenced to death. (Their sentences were commuted to penal servitude
by General Haig, and they were returned to English prisons.)[4]

As control, and the spirit of control, intensified in England, so did the
spirit of dissent, and especially in print. The more the government
legislated to restrict expression, the more dissenting groups expressed
their opposition to restriction. The Quakers continued their pacifist
journal, *Ploughshare*, and the *Cambridge Magazine* published more and
more outspoken criticisms of the war, including anti-war writings by
men in the forces, and a verbatim account of the appeal of James
Strachey, Lytton's younger brother, against the Military Service Act.

Pamphlets and leaflets appeared from many organizations — some political, some religious, some simply anti-war. Francis Meynell, who had become a private press publisher, joined in with a beautifully printed text of Pope Benedict's *Appeal to the Rulers of Europe*.

And as the flow of anti-war literature increased, so did the government's war against it. In May, two women were arrested in rural Hertfordshire for an offence against Section 27 of DORA — the part dealing with the spreading of reports 'likely to prejudice the recruiting and discipline of His Majesty's Forces'. They had been walking from village to village, 'dressed in black cloaks, in accord with Ruskin's proposal for war-time', distributing pamphlets — the Church of England Peace Society's *Our Common Humanity*, the Fellowship of Reconciliation's *To Christ's Disciples Everywhere*, and Meynell's printing of the Pope's appeal. They were convicted and sentenced to fines of £50 or three months in prison. They both chose prison.[5]

At about the same time, an anonymous pamphlet was published by the No-Conscription Fellowship dealing with the case of a conscientious objector who had been sentenced to two years' hard labour for refusing to obey a military order. Six men were arrested for distributing the pamphlet, whereupon Bertrand Russell announced in a letter to *The Times* that he had written it, and that if anyone was to be persecuted he should be the one. The government promptly obliged; he was arrested and tried, also under Section 27, and was fined £100 and costs. When he failed to pay the fine his goods in Cambridge were seized and sold to make up the sum. Because of his conviction he was deprived of his Trinity lectureship in July 1916; and when he set out to restore his lost income by lecturing around England on social and political subjects, the War Office prevented him from entering prohibited areas (which meant practically all places near the sea, including many entire counties).

By the end of 1916, the government's powers to control, restrict and suppress were greater, but so was the pressure to resist those powers. By that time dissent had begun to establish its own canon — the anti-war texts by which isolated opposers of the war could be encouraged and supported. One can find such a canon taking shape in the wartime diary of Graeme West (from which I quoted in the previous chapter). West had gone to France as a private in 1915, and spent five months in the front lines. Early in 1916 he returned to England and entered officer-training; he was commissioned, and was to go back to the Front in August. But before he did so he went on leave, and spent some of that time with his friend, the philosopher C.E.M. Joad. They read *Boon* together; and West read other books too.

> I read a good deal of liberal literature [West wrote in his diary], met some conscientious objectors, moved much among men not at all occupied in the war, and hence suffered a violent revulsion from my old imagined glories and delights of the Army (such as I had) — its companionship, suffering courageously and of noble necessity under-gone — to intense hatred of the war spirit and the country generally. Most particularly Bertrand Russell's 'Justice in War Time' impressed me . . . I so loathed the idea of rejoining the Army that I determined to desert and hide away somewhere.[6]

West's account of his inner struggle to free himself from the war that he so detested makes sad reading. He planned the speech that he would make to his family, explaining why he would not return to duty — but couldn't utter it. He wrote a letter to the Adjutant of his battalion — but could not bring himself to post it. He walked to the Post Office the next morning to send a telegram — and bought two penny stamps instead. Then, 'in a state of cynical wrath against myself and the world in general', he rejoined his regiment. He was ordered back to France, and was killed there in April 1917.

West is an early example of what became a type: the intelligent young man who went to the trenches, and returned converted to pacifism by his experience of war. His efforts to act according to his new convictions failed, and that failure tells us something about the power of authority, and the weakness of individual dissent. But it is also important to note that his views of war, the army, and England had been changed not simply by his experience of trench fighting, but by the 'liberal litera-ture', including Russell's writings, that were available to him then. It was the existence of other men who thought as he did and who had the courage to express what they thought, that *almost* moved him to act on his new-found convictions. Another kind of courage had become imaginable.

At about the time that West was returning to France, a new writer of 'liberal literature' began to publish anti-war work. If Miles Malleson is remembered at all now, it is as a Shakespearian actor, but he was also a playwright and a political radical. He enlisted in the army immediately after the declaration of war, and was sent to Malta, but was invalided home and discharged in January 1915. He became a pacifist, and with his wife Constance was active in the No-Conscription Fellowship, and

moved in the circle of intellectual pacifists that had gathered around
Bertrand Russell and Ottoline and Philip Morrell.

Malleson's first pacifist publication was a pamphlet, *Cranks and
Commonsense*, published in August 1916. It is a straightforward attack on
war and on the 'commonsense' society that causes wars, and a defence
of 'cranks' like himself — the Socialists, pacifists, and radical Christians
who imagined a peaceable civilization. The pamphlet was not suppressed by the authorities, but they must have taken note of it. They
would have noticed that it was published by Henderson's, a Charing
Cross Road bookshop with such a reputation for radicalism that it was
known (and advertised itself) as 'The Bomb Shop'. And they would also
have noticed the announcement at the back of the pamphlet that
Henderson's would shortly publish another little book by Malleson —
Two Short Plays: Patriotic and Unpatriotic. In October, the Bomb Shop
was visited by an officer from the War Office, accompanied by two men
from Scotland Yard, and all the copies of *Two Short Plays* were
confiscated.

Malleson wrote *'D' Company*, the first of the two plays, in October
1914, while he was serving in the army. It is a simple one-act piece —
two corporals and four privates in a barrack-room in Malta. Alf, one of
the privates, is illiterate, and has letters from home that he cannot read;
Dennis — the only educated man there — reads them to him, and Alf
learns that his brother has been killed in France. Dennis has been writing
a letter to his sweetheart, and Alf asks him to read it aloud. It is a tender
letter, but it is also a political one: Dennis has Socialist ideas about the
war and the peace after it. News comes that the company will be sent to
the Front. There is a Mail Call, and letters are distributed. The play ends
with this stage direction:

> *They all sit on their beds, drinking in their letters like a thirsty soldier at a pot
> of beer. Of a sudden all the lights go out. From the blackness comes a howl of
> execration. Howl after howl—and on this the curtain slides down.*

In his preface to the book, Malleson wrote of *'D' Company*:

> It is, in one sense, real: there is scarcely a sentence in it that I did not
> hear, or an episode I did not witness.
>
> It is, in another sense, unreal: it is impossible, even for the purposes
> of realism, to set down here in print the actual language of my
> barrack-room. The three or four unpleasant words that occurred
> extraordinarily often and in the queerest series of combinations and

connections, not only created a certain atmosphere of ugliness that would be necessary for any really true picture of life then, but also supplied a sort of lilt to the conversation that cannot be reproduced without them.[7]

The point, once more, is one of style: for a new reality, a new language, even though Malleson drew back from a completely literal record.

The other play, *Black 'Ell*, was written in 1916. Malleson was once more a civilian by then, and as he wrote in his preface, his view of 'this colossal catastrophe of the war' had changed; the play is explicitly pacifist. In it, a young lieutenant, Harold Gould, comes home from the trenches, where he has won a DSO. His family receive him as a hero, and his father makes the kind of speeches about defending women and children against criminals that tribunals made to conscientious objectors. But Harold is haunted by the men he has killed, and sees all soldiers, Germans and British alike, as victims. His speeches become increasingly violent and bitter, reaching a climax in his last speech, just as a group of his friends burst in to celebrate his military success.

> HAROLD. It's no use ordering me about, because I've done with it. Oh, I know, I know. You all think I'm mad — looking at me like that. [*He has completely lost control of himself; his words rush out in an ever-growing crescendo.*] But there are millions doing it — millions. The young ones doing it, and the old ones feeling noble about it . . . Yes, Dad feels noble because I've killed somebody . . . I saw him feeling noble . . . and you all look at me, because I tell you it's all filthy . . . foul language and foul thinking and stinking bits of bodies all about . . . millions at it . . . it's not me that's mad . . . it's the whole world that's mad . . . I've done with it . . . I've done with it . . . That man in their trenches — he'd had enough . . . he said he was going to refuse to kill any more, and they called him traitor and pro-English, and they've probably shot him by now . . . Well, you can shoot me . . . because I'm not going back . . . I'm going to stop at home and say it's all mad . . . I'm going to keep on saying it . . . somebody's got to stop sometime . . . somebody's got to get sane again . . . and I won't go back . . . I won't, I won't . . . I won't . . . [8]

The speech is melodramatic; but not much more so than Leighton's letter to Vera Brittain, or Graeme West's diary entry describing his will-to-quit, and his failure to act on that feeling. The conflict between duty (or social pressure, or fear of authority) and hatred of the war was

intense and deeply disturbing, that's clear — and more so in the first
years, when there were not yet any examples of opposition by soldiers,
no bitter poems, no public gestures.

Harold's last speech makes the language point again, this time linking
it to the other kinds of ugliness that war creates, the foul thinking and
the stinking bits of bodies. This is an aspect of the war that would recur,
as poets and painters with traditional ideas of art and beauty in their
pasts came face to face with the new, ugly reality, and tried to render it
in their art.

Malleson's book was confiscated under the provisions of the Defence
of the Realm Act (presumably Section 27), but just what in the plays
violated the regulations was never made clear. On October 31, Sir
William Byles, a radical MP, raised the matter in the House of
Commons, asking the Secretary of State for War to explain why the
book had been seized, and to 'point out, for the deterrence of other
authors, what are the incriminating passages, if any, in the book'. H.W.
Forster, Financial Secretary for the War Office, replied:

> The book in question is, I am advised, a deliberate calumny on the
> British soldier. The visit to Mr. Henderson's premises was ordered
> by the competent military authority.

Philip Morrell then entered in:

> Is the hon. Gentleman aware that this book has the approval of men
> very well known in the literary world, and of unimpeachable patriot-
> ism? Has the hon. Gentleman read the book; if not, will he do so?

To which Forster responded:

> I am advised that the book is very properly suppressed, and I am
> sorry to hear that it has the approval of anybody.[9]

The phrase 'competent military authority' seems to have stuck in
Byles's throat; a week later he was on his feet again in the Commons, to
ask the same Minister

> if he will give the name of the competent military authority who was set
> to judge Mr. Miles Malleson's plays and found that the book was a
> deliberate calumny on the British soldier, and then ordered a raid on the
> publisher's premises and the confiscation of all the stock; and will he say
> what are this officer's qualifications for judging delicate literary work?

Forster was unruffled:

My hon. Friend [he replied] treats this matter as one raising the
question of the literary qualifications of the officers referred to. On
questions of what constitutes delicate literary work, there is, of
course, room for different opinions. But the question involved in this
case was not one of literary taste, but of contravention of the Defence
of the Realm Regulations, and I do not feel called upon to go into the
question of the literary qualifications of the officers concerned in the
matter.[10]

Forster's point is an important one: DORA constituted an official alternative to aesthetic judgement. Henceforth any army officer would be a
'competent authority' to judge whether a work should be published or
suppressed, and 'a deliberate calumny on the British soldier' would be
sufficient cause for suppression (even though Section 27 does not specify
such an offence). Whether it was the coarse illiterates of 'D' Company or
the haunted young officer of Black 'Ell who constituted the calumny was
never established.

Two Short Plays was not allowed to become a part of the anti-war
canon — it was not published until 1925, when it appeared under the
title 'D' Company and Black 'Ell — but Malleson was not silenced. Even
before the book of plays was confiscated he had written another
pamphlet in defence of conscientious objection, The Out-and-Outer,
which was published (also by Henderson's) in November 1916, at about
the time that Sir William Byles was putting his questions in the House.
It was not suppressed, and one must wonder what War Office reasoning
allowed polemical pamphlets to appear unhampered, but seized and
destroyed plays. A distrust of the imagination, perhaps, a fear of the
power of literature that was greater than fear of argument? Whatever the
official motives, something important happened with the publication
and suppression of Two Short Plays: opposition to the war became
literary, and literature became a threat to authority.[11]

II

Malleson, in both his plays and his preface, asserted a turn of language, a
new ugliness that the war imposed, and that he tried to render. This is
essentially the change that I noted in the private prose writings of
serving soldiers. It also occurred in war poetry, and at about the same

time. It was a turn that produced what most readers think of as the permanent poetry of the war; virtually no poems that are in the canon — the war poems that are still read, and get into the anthologies — were written before 1916, or in the old high style. *Our* war — that is to say, the myth of the war, based in literature and art, that we credit as truth — really begins here, with this turn of language and rhetoric, half-way through the fighting.

One can see this rhetorical turn in the poems that Siegfried Sassoon published in 1916. Consider first 'To Victory', a poem that was written in the autumn of 1915. Sassoon had gone to France in November of that year, and had joined the First Battalion of the Royal Welch Fusiliers, just out of the lines after fighting in the Battle of Loos. Among the young officers in the battalion was Robert Graves; Sassoon met him, and the two exchanged poems. Graves recalled that exchange in *Good-bye to All That*:

> At this time I was getting my first book of poems, *Over the Brazier*, ready for the press; I had one or two drafts in my pocket-book, and showed them to Siegfried. He told me that they were too realistic and that war should not be written about in a realistic way. In return he showed me some of his own poems. One of them began:
>   Return to greet me, colours that were my joy,
>   Not in the woeful crimson of men slain . . .
> This was before Siegfried had been in the trenches. I told him, in my old-soldier manner, that he would soon change his style.[12]

The poem that Graves quotes is 'To Victory':

> Return to greet me, colours that were my joy —
> Not in the woeful crimson of men slain,
> But shining as a garden: come with the streaming
> Banners of dawn and sundown after rain.
>
>   I want to fill my gaze with blue and silver,
>   Radiance through living roses, spires of green
>   Rising in young-limbed copse and lovely wood
>   Where the hueless wind passes and cries unseen.
>
>   I am not sad: only I long for lustre;
>   I am tired of greys and browns and the leafless ash:
>   I would have hours that move like a glitter of dancers,
>   Far from the angry guns that boom and flash.

> Return, musical, gay with blossom and fleetness,
> Days when my sight shall be clear, and my heart rejoice,
> When the blithe wind laughs on the hills with uplifted voice.[13]

Sassoon sent the poem to his friend Edmund Gosse, who sent it to *The Times*, where it was published on January 15 as 'To Victory (By a Private Soldier at the Front)', and signed with the initials. 'S.S.'. It seems transparently the poem of a man who has had experience of romantic poetry, but not yet of war — it is metaphorical, abstract, and altogether 'poetical'. Yet it must have moved Gosse; and certainly it moved Lady Ottoline Morrell, who wrote its author a fan letter c/o *The Times*, thus beginning a relationship that would have profound consequences for Sassoon.

Later in 1916, Sassoon began to publish poems in the *Cambridge Magazine*. The choice of this journal is significant, for by 1916 it had become a principal voice of dissent in England (it was, for example, the only English journal to publish regular abstracts of news from the European press, including German newspapers). 'The Redeemer', Sassoon's first 'front-line' poem, appeared there in April. In July he fought in the Somme offensive, and in August was invalided home with trench fever. In November his poems again began to appear in the *Cambridge Magazine*, and by then he had mastered a new rhetoric and was writing the poems on which his reputation as a war poet rests, poems like 'The Hero', which was published in the magazine's November 18 issue:

> 'Jack fell as he'd have wished,' the Mother said,
> And folded up the letter that she'd read.
> 'The Colonel writes so nicely.' Something broke
> In the tired voice that quavered to a choke.
> She half looked up. 'We mothers are so proud
> Of our dead soldiers.' Then her face was bowed.
>
> Quietly the Brother Officer went out.
> He'd told the poor old dear some gallant lies
> That she would nourish all her days, no doubt.
> For while he coughed and mumbled, her weak eyes
> Had shone with gentle triumph, brimmed with joy,
> Because he'd been so brave, her glorious boy.
>
> He thought how 'Jack,' cold-footed, useless swine,
> Had panicked down the trench that night the mine

> Went up at Wicked Corner, how he'd tried
> To get sent home, and how, at last, he died,
> Blown to small bits. And no one seemed to care
> Except that lonely woman with white hair.[14]

C. K. Ogden, the editor of the magazine, must have recognized that this was a poem that would offend some readers, and that required a special authority; he identified its author as 'Lieutenant Siegfried Sassoon, M.C.'. (In Sassoon's other appearances in the magazine neither his rank nor his decoration had been mentioned.) And he was right: it *did* offend. Two weeks later the following letter appeared:

> Sir, — Please let me say how deeply at least one average Englishman (I claim to be as much, but nothing more) is pained, not to say disgusted, by the poem 'The Hero,' by Lieut. Siegfried Sassoon M.C. I am sorry that a British officer who has been decorated for his gallantry should have written it, and equally sorry that it should appear in a journal connected with the University of Cambridge.
>
> Even if the poem relates an incident that is true — and it may be — that is beside the point. In an army of millions there are sure to be some 'cold-footed, useless swine,' but the really 'swinish' thing to do is to immortalise the 'swine' in a poem and call him 'a Hero' — if only for the pain caused to mothers, who in the hour of bitter grief, may wonder if the son they mourn was, after all, only a 'swine.'
>
> Believe me, sir, the average Englishman does not like it, and as an old Cambridge man I sorrow to find this sort of thing in the *Cambridge Magazine*.
>
> > Yours, etc.
> > Charles Geake[15]

The 'average Englishman's' question is not a foolish one: why should a man who was willing to fight, and fight bravely, in a war be unwilling to accept one of war's central concepts, the idea of the Hero? Why did he feel the need to defile that concept? Sassoon explained in a sonnet that was printed on the same page, titled 'The Poet as Hero':

> You've heard me, scornful, harsh, and discontented,
>   Mocking and loathing War: you've asked me why
> Of my old, silly sweetness I've repented, —
>   My ecstasies changed to an ugly cry.

You are aware that once I sought the Grail,
   Riding in armour bright, serene and strong;
And it was told that through my infant wail
   There rose immortal semblances of song.

But now I've said good-bye to Galahad,
   And am no more the knight of dreams and show:
For lust and senseless hatred make me glad,
   And my killed friends are with me where I go.
Wound for red wound I burn to smite their wrongs;
   And there is absolution in my songs.[16]

As an answer to Geake's questions, this does not seem at first to be very satisfactory. Geake had protested the *content* of Sassoon's poem, and Sassoon replied with a poem about a change in his *style*. But the change of style was a change of attitude that had been forced upon him by a change in reality. The soldier-poet for whom war had been a set of traditional images had become a man beyond metaphor. Not only had he abandoned the old style: he repented it, and enacted his repentance in this travesty of romantic war and its language. If the title 'The Poet as Hero' is apt, then heroism has come to mean something that it had never meant before, and that poor Mr Geake would never understand.

The change in Sassoon's rhetoric, from 'To Victory' to 'The Hero', was a complete one: he began 1916 as one kind of poet and ended the year as an antithetically different kind. For this change, the experience of the Somme fighting must obviously have been a principal cause; but one must also take notice of the example of Graves, who had had the experience of battle first, and had begun to find a language for it. Like Sassoon, Graves also wrote war poems that were poems about style. One of the poems in his first book of poems, *Over the Brazier* (published in May 1916), is 'Big Words', a poem that consists of a twenty-line speech in which a young soldier accepts death in the old high-rhetorical way, followed by this two-line rebuttal:

   But on the firestep, waiting to attack,
   He cursed, prayed, sweated, wished the proud words back.[17]

The poem works in essentially the same way that 'The Hero' does: style contrasts with and deflates style, reality denies a rhetoric.

What is involved here, it should be clear, is more than a change of style: a rhetoric is rejected not because it is inadequate, but because it is wrong. In these poems of Sassoon and Graves that rejection is

only implied, but in other poems of the same time it is bitterly
explicit.

Take, for example, a poem by Graeme West: 'God! How I hate you,
you young cheerful men!', sub-titled 'On a University Undergraduate
moved to verse by the war'. The undergraduate in his sub-title was
H. Rex Freston, a student who had left Oxford to join the army as West
had, but a year later. Freston went to France at the end of 1915, and was
killed after ten days in the trenches. His friends back in Oxford collected
his poems in a memorial volume titled *The Quest for Truth*, and
published it in August 1916, just at the time when West was struggling
to find courage to quit the war; West must have read the poems then.

Almost all of Freston's poems were written before he left England, and
though many are 'war poems', there is no experience of war in them,
and they are written in the old inspirational style, with lines like 'I know
that God will never let me die', and 'Oh happy to have lived these epic
days'. West hated them, and wrote his poem against their Rupert-
Brookeish ignorance. His anger seems unjust — poor Freston could
scarcely be expected to reform his poetic style and revise his poems in
the last ten days of his life, in a trench on the Western Front.
Nevertheless, the force of West's attack, and the way he makes rhetoric
a moral issue, make his reaction worth noting. His poem begins:

> God! How I hate you, you young cheerful men,
> Whose pious poetry blossoms on your graves
> As soon as you are in them ...

and goes on to set false rhetoric against truth, in the manner that we
have seen in the poems of Sassoon and Graves (and earlier on, in the
prose of Leighton and Cynthia Asquith).

> Hark how one chants —
> 'Oh happy to have lived these epic days' —
> 'These epic days'! And *he'd* been to France,
> And seen the trenches, glimpsed the huddled dead
> In the periscope, hung on the rustling wire:
> Choked by their sickly foetor, day and night
> Blown down his throat: stumbled through ruined hearths,
> Proved all that muddy brown monotony,
> Where blood's the only coloured thing. Perhaps
> Had seen a man killed, a sentry shot at night,
> Hunched as he fell, his feet on the firing-step,

His neck against the back slope of the trench,
And the rest doubled up between, his head
Smashed like an egg-shell, and the warm grey brain
Spattered all bloody on the parados:
Had flashed a torch on his face, and known his friend,
Shot, breathing hardly, in ten minutes — gone![18]

The reality rendered in these lines is essentially that of the soldiers'
diaries — a world of ruined things. One could say that the rhetoric is the
same, too: the objects of war, named and described, without abstraction
and almost without metaphor (there is only the egg-shell). But there is
one element in West's poem, and in Sassoon's 'Hero' too, that is not in
the prose accounts: that is the tone, the bitterness and anger with which
the false version of war is rejected. That tone, which would become the
dominant tone of those versions of war that would enter and constitute
the myth, begins here, in mid-war. It is another kind of turning.

Neither West's poem nor Sassoon's is 'anti-war' in the dissenting,
pacifist sense. Men in the fighting forces simply did not see the war as
something that could be stopped. Some felt that though it was horrible,
it was necessary; others saw it as an unopposable force, like some natural
disaster, a flood or a great gale. In either case, the poets who spoke for
these men did not argue that men should not die, but that they should
not die for empty words, and that those men (and women) in England
who had sent them to die should not be protected by their ignorance of
what war was. The point of the new poetry was a point of rhetoric: of
truth-telling, not peace-making.

With poems like these, written in mid-war, a new tradition of war
poetry began. They were not, to be sure, the first poems to speak
against the lies of war, or to try to render war in plain words — one can
find such poems published in the first months of the year.[19] But they
were the first such poems to be written by men who had fought, and to
have the authority of direct experience. The notion that only those who
fought could speak the truth about war is one that old soldiers have
always had, but it had never been the basis of an aesthetic until the Great
War, when for the first time the soldiers who fought it were also the
artists who rendered it. Then it began to appear — in letters, in
remembered conversations, in poems — not argued, but simply taken
for granted. It is in Leighton's letter to Vera Brittain, in his 'who is there
who has known and seen . . ?'; and in Graves's 'old-soldier manner'; and
in West's angry 'And he'd been to France . . .'; and in the mind of

Sassoon's Brother Officer. It is still the evident principle by which selections are made for anthologies of war poems.

The implications of this aesthetic of direct experience for war art are obvious: true art will be that which renders what has been known and seen, so only soldiers will be qualified to create it. And it will only be understood by those who have shared the experience, so that only soldiers will be able to appreciate and understand it. It is the absolute separation between the men who fight and those they are fighting for, applied to the arts. This separation will be evident in war poems from about this point on, both as a structural principle — an 'I' who has experienced war addresses a 'You' who has not, and as a theme — the 'You' cannot understand, is unworthy, ignorant, insensitive, old, or female, in any case a non-combatant and therefore excluded both from the experience rendered and from the rendering. The result is a curious kind of elitism, not unlike the attitude of the avant-garde artist towards bourgeois society, but set in terms of war.

III

The aesthetic of direct experience came to English painting at about the same time, but by a different route. In the summer of 1916 the propaganda office at Wellington House launched a programme to record the war in art — a programme that would have profound effects on how Englishmen saw the war, and on the future of English art. Masterman, the director of the office, had been visited in the spring of the year by a friend who remarked that Muirhead Bone, the well-known etcher, had been called up for the army, and that his gifts might be better used than in leading an infantry platoon. Masterman went home and asked his wife who Muirhead Bone was; and out of that conversation the idea of Official War Artists was born.[20]

Bone was an obvious choice, even though Masterman had never heard of him. He had made his reputation as an etcher of 'views', mainly of historic European ruins, but he was also fond of foreign landscapes, and especially of those that had an English look to them — views, that is, that reminded him of the Romantic landscapes that are the great achievement of English painting. He was commissioned as a War Artist in August 1916, and went immediately to France. It is an important fact, I think, that he went to war for the first time *as an artist*: he had not learned to see war with a soldier's eye, as would be the case with later war artists, and went to the Front in the same spirit in which he had gone to Rome, and found similar subjects there. He wandered about behind the lines, sketching ruined churches and châteaux, poplar-lined roads, and distant landscapes with sometimes the smoke of battle on the horizon. He drew trenches on only two or three occasions: no doubt they seemed unpictorial to him, being so shapeless and so unarchitectural. Then he went home and drew the Home Front.

Two hundred of Bone's drawings were published, in ten monthly parts, beginning in late 1916 — the first part with an approving foreword by Douglas Haig, Commanding General of British Forces in France. Each part also had an introductory essay and a commentary on each picture by C.E. Montague, a former leader-writer for the *Manchester Guardian* who was an Intelligence Officer attached to GHQ. The parts cost a shilling each, so most English families could afford them, and for many people at home they must have been an important source of their notions of what the war really looked like. Bone and Montague agreed that what it looked like was England; both the drawings and the commentaries imagine the war in familiarizing English terms. Montague's introduction to the first part begins: 'The British line in France and Belgium runs through country of three kinds, and each kind is like a part of England'[21]; and Bone's drawings seem to support that view. (In a way this is what the troops were doing too, when they called their duckboarded paths and trenches the Old Kent Road and Piccadilly Circus.) Drawings like Bone's are official art, not because they are of generals or heroes, but because they are not *strange*.

'Battle of the Somme' (plate 9) is one of Bone's earliest war drawings: it is dated August 1916, just after he arrived in France. Here war is seen as a landscape subject, treated in the most traditional of landscape forms, the hilltop vista. The seated spectator at the left (who seems to be Bone at work) is conventional — you'll find him in Constable landscapes, and in Victorian prints; he represents the viewer of the picture, who is simply another spectator, further back. He confirms that the view that they are both observing is worth looking at, and that the right relation to it is a viewing relation (that's what landscapes are for). It is a drawing that has everything to do with landscape, and nothing really to do with the war being fought there.

Bone's pictures succeeded in England: that is, they achieved what Masterman and his colleagues at Wellington House wanted. They made the war familiar, and they provided images of it from which both the dead and the suffering living had been entirely excluded. But they failed in France. After the first two parts (titled *The Western Front* and *The Somme Battlefield*) appeared, Wilfred Owen mentioned them in a letter to his mother. Owen had only been at the Front for a few days, and he was clearly in a state of initial shock, and groping for metaphors to express his feelings:

> They want to call No Man's Land 'England' because we keep supremacy there.
> It is like the eternal place of gnashing of teeth; the Slough of Despond could be contained in one of its crater-holes; the fires of Sodom and Gomorrah could not light a candle to it — to find the way to Babylon the Fallen.
> It is pock-marked like a body of foulest disease and its odour is the breath of cancer.
> I have not seen any dead. I have done worse. In the dank air I have *perceived* it, and in the darkness, *felt*. Those 'Somme Pictures' are the laughing stock of the army — like the trenches on exhibition in Kensington.
> No Man's Land under snow is like the face of the moon chaotic, crater-ridden, uninhabitable, awful, the abode of madness. To call it 'England'![22]

What Owen is describing here — and by implication demanding of war artists — is a radically *defamiliarized* landscape, absolutely unlike England, or any other landscape on earth. But he is also demanding that it should be a *moral* landscape, a new allegory of the evil, the horror, and the ugliness of war. One can see the problem that such demands posed for the war artist: how was he to paint pictures that would be entirely strange, and yet would express moral judgements? The problem was essentially the same for war poets like Owen; he would have to free his style of the literary images of horror out of Bunyan and the Bible that his letter contains before he could write his great war poems.

Muirhead Bone added nothing to the possibilities of perceiving the war, because he himself saw it as a traditional subject. But in September, 1916, while Bone was still at work in France, an exhibition of war art opened at the Leicester Galleries in London that did alter perception. 'Paintings and Drawings of War by C.R.W. Nevinson (Late Private R.A.M.C.)' was an important show, for it marked the beginning of a new war art, just as the poems that Sassoon was publishing in the *Cambridge Magazine* at about the same time marked the beginning of a new war poetry. Before the war, Nevinson had been Marinetti's only certain English convert; he had co-authored the English Futurist Manifesto, and when Marinetti appeared in public to recite his works, it was Nevinson who made the war-like percussive noises in the background. Most of Nevinson's pre-war work has been lost, but what survives shows that he was a Futurist in his art as well as in his drumbeating: it is abstract and geometrical, and full of the machinery, energy, and 'lines of force' that Futurism favoured.

During 1914 and 1915 Nevinson had been first a Red Cross ambulance driver and then a private in the Medical Corps in France. He had seen no great victories and no generals, and he had not fired a single shot; but he had seen a good deal of the realities of war. He returned to England, as he later wrote, believing that 'war was now dominated by machines, and that men were mere cogs in the mechanism'; and he painted that belief into his pictures, using machinery, energy, and lines of force. He had seen war, and it was Futurist.

The catalogue of Nevinson's show did not make that point, though; clearly the gallery owners were nervous about how the pictures would be received, and had gone to some lengths to suggest that they had been painted in a proper patriotic spirit. So the catalogue was prefaced with an appreciation not by an art critic, but by a general — Sir Ian Hamilton, just back from commanding the disastrous Gallipoli campaign. Hamilton was known as a man of letters, and something of a poet; what he said of Nevinson's pictures was certainly poetic enough. Of a painting of a star-shell bursting above a trench, Hamilton wrote:

> Look at that star-shell! To the soldier crouching in a mine crater, or crawling from cover to cover to cut barbed wire, the sudden ball of fire that fills his dark hiding place with ghostly light is a murderous eye betraying him to enemies in ambush. Here, truer to the truth, it takes on a mystic semblance of the Holy Grail, poised over the trenches, bearing its mystic message to the souls of our happy warriors.[23]

What Hamilton seemed to be saying was that there were two ways of imagining the star-shell's burst. One was the common soldier's, which Hamilton saw as like a frightened animal's. The other was the artist's (and presumably also the poetic general's): it saw the shell in traditional symbolic terms, as the Holy Grail, with a suggestion of the star of Bethlehem added. This, Hamilton said, was the truer vision.

Here is Hamilton on another Nevinson subject, a column of troops returning to the trenches (Nevinson did several versions):

Here too, seeing this picture of the French battalion on the march, the Pacifist himself is compelled to cry 'Bravo!' Force in full cry after Adventure; energy can be carried no further. And so we come away feeling that the Cup of War is filled, not only with blood and tears, but also with the elixir of Life.[24]

Hamilton got some of Nevinson's Futurist point: he saw the force and energy that Nevinson got into all his pictures of marching men: but he once more added 'poetic' images and ideas that are not in any Nevinson picture — the Cup of War, blood and tears, the elixir of life — to make disturbing images familiar. And he ignored — or couldn't imagine — a point that was crucial to Nevinson's vision: the mechanical nature of this war's mass movements. Nevinson's paintings of troops in motion are paintings of *machines* (plate 12).

Nevinson's show was a great success. Everybody came to it: Shaw, Galsworthy, Conrad, Ramsay MacDonald, Balfour, Margot Asquith, Churchill. Walter Sickert praised the paintings in a review, and the critic William Archer (who lost a son in the war) burst into tears when he saw them. Every picture was sold. Yet these were relentlessly Modernist paintings that emphasized the mechanical violence of war.

Why was the show so successful? Not, I think, because viewers were persuaded by General Hamilton. The critics, at least, found its value in quite another direction — in the connection between Modernism and War that Ricketts had so deplored at the war's beginning. Now, at mid-war, that connection was no longer troubling; it was simply a part of reality. Here is the *Westminster Gazette*'s art critic on the show:

It has been argued that Cubism and Futurism, and other neo-violence in art, were in some way a presage of the war, and that if the Quai d'Orsay had condescended to make itself acquainted with the turbulent doings in the Quartier Latin, and had persuaded Downing Street to do the same, we should all have been piling up munitions and organizing big battalions three or four years before it began ... It is evident at least that the modern artistic tendencies are extraordinarily well adapted to the pictorial presentation of war. Had there been Nevinsons in the world at the time of the Napoleonic wars we should possess fewer pictures of a romantic Emperor on a white charger, or of Grenadiers sleeping picturesquely on the snow; but we should have known a good deal more of what war is like ...

And he went on to make Nevinson's point about the nature of modern war:

> Perhaps unconsciously Mr Nevinson has succeeded in all his pictures in finding a symbolic equivalent for this war of vast and cruel mechanism. The soldiers themselves look as though they were the component parts of a formidable engine, drawn together by some irresistible force of attraction.[25]

The *Westminster*'s critic was not alone in his recognition of Nevinson's importance. Clutton Brock in *The Times* saw the same qualities in the pictures, and though they disturbed him he acknowledged their authority and power:

> An army has often been called a machine; but Mr. Nevinson makes it look like one to the eye; and he does this with plausibility, so that we do not protest against his version of it. He does it by a method which has become a commonplace of modern painting, the sharp distinction of planes. He is half a cubist; but his cubism is justified by what he has to say. It expresses a certain emotion in the painter, and, as it seems to us, a certain protest ... In these pictures [reality] is represented as process to which personality is utterly subject, showing itself only in energy or pain; and the result is a nightmare of insistent unreality, untrue yet actual, something that certainly happens and yet to which our reason will not consent.
>
> The pictures are all illustrations, efforts to show us something novel and strange, something which has stirred the artist because it is novel and strange. There they differ from the great art of the world which heightens what is familiar.[26]

These two critics agreed on one essential point: that the war was Modernist. They saw that the violence and the mechanism of pre-war experimental art had been validated as perceptions of reality by the war itself. Not only validated, but made necessary; for if war was a nightmare in reality, then only a distorting, defamiliarizing technique could render it truthfully — art would have to become 'untrue but actual'. Clutton Brock made another point that is equally important: he saw that pictures that render such a nightmare reality will be more than representations — they will be *protests*. This is the point that Wilfred Owen had made in his letter, that the new art of war must offer unfamiliar allegories, new moral landscapes of a new hell.

Clearly a change of consciousness occurred in 1916; it had even

ıative London newspapers. And that change
images: Nevinson's Futurist war paintings
or imagining war in a new, unheroic, anti-
was not for painters alone. John Gould
n's show when he wrote an essay on war
1916 *Egoist,* and he used the pictures as

hat some one seriously took up in poetry the
of one side or the other, but of the whole
art thereof as he has access to. Mr. Nevinson
cient and workmanlike job in his pictures, of
ions concerning war; now why should not a
same thing, pray?[27]

ıin, intelligent man, saw the connection too,
1 October 1916, while he was working in an
e wrote to his wife that he was going to meet
ırnalist H. W. Nevinson:

has made some stir (it is all drawings of the
see things in cubes & vortices, & I withheld
ve been trying to get at what I really see when
alysis yet.[28]

r he had spent several weeks walking over the
turned to the subject:

s in cubes & lozenges & whirlpools; but the
ɔes see, as compared with what is there, is still
on the march, a mile away on these straight
ction, say, perhaps, a broken down lorry, or a
dead horse; not more than that. Then as one
like one of those 'plumps of spears' in Dürer's
l a form, rather than anything human. Then it
ing humping caterpillar, with men in front,
; down the sides, as the arms swing, & round,
ı the top, which gradually become helmets

covering marching fours.

I wish that I could describe these things so as to make people see
them.[29]

We see in these passages a Georgian poet, schooled in a firm, familiar

St. Mary's College of Maryland
Library-Circulation
18952 E. Fisher Road
St. Mary's City, MD 2068ϵ

vision of reality, confronting a crisis of perception, describing it in terms of another art, but locating it also in his own. There before him was the reality of war: but how could he render it, how could he even *see* it, so strange and so changing as it was? Masefield acknowledged that Nevinson had solved that problem of perception with his cubes and vortices and lozenges; but he could not solve it for himself, not in poetry. He could only go on writing plain prose until the war ended.[30]

IV

A new kind of war painting, a new kind of war poem, a new kind of war prose: what do they have in common? In what ways is Nevinson's 'Returning to the Trenches' like Sassoon's 'The Hero', or Roland Leighton's letter to his sweetheart? The answer is best put in negative terms, in what they all eliminated from their renderings. They cast off the traditions of war art — the generals and the plumes, the high abstractions, the images of heroism and glory that made war itself a value-term — in an effort to reduce, to limit, to confine themselves to bare, ruined reality. They were all, in their different ways, after the same thing — a style in which it would be possible to tell the truth about the war.

With this change of style, a new, wartime, opposing art began to emerge. It was an art that put the innovations of pre-war Modern movements to new uses — to creating versions of war that were truth-telling, but were more than that: were acts of judgement and of protest. Of course Modernism had been that before the war: it had been adversarial and antagonistic towards established Edwardian society. But the war had altered the nature of that opposition, giving it a clear and urgent moral basis that it had not had when *Blast* exploded into print in 1914.

The moral basis, that sense of the avant-garde as a force of moral protest against the war, made a link between the soldier-artists and poets and that other army, the pacifists. For they too — Malleson with his cranks and his out-and-outers, the two Quaker women with their leaflets, the No-Conscription leaders with their plain testimonies of belief — were trying to accomplish a revolution of the imagination, the elimination from their worlds of the language, the rhetoric, the images of heroic war. Graves had called his anti-rhetorical poem 'Big Words', and that, you might say, was the common issue: how to get rid of the big words.

If there was the beginning of a new opposing spirit in 1916, it was only a beginning, one more turning point in the history of the middle of the war. There had been very little of the new art and writing visible in England as the year began, and there was not much more at the end — one important exhibition of war paintings had opened and closed, Graves's first book of poems, and a few poems by Sassoon, had been published, and Malleson's plays had appeared only to disappear again. Nevertheless, a turning had occurred, and its motive force was that element of opposition that linked the young artists who were in the war with their apparent opposite, the anti-war activists.

It is tempting to locate this turn at the Battle of the Somme, and to say that on or about July 1916 the character of war art changed. The Somme offensive is a convenient location for that turn, not because it was so stupid and so bloody (plenty of World War One battles fit that description) but because so many of the important war artists and poets were there — including Graves, Sassoon, Blunden, Rosenberg, David Jones, and Ivor Gurney. The point is not that this battle *caused* a new kind of art, but more simply, and less melodramatically, that by the end of the Somme fighting a number of young men, who had come to the war thinking that they were poets and painters, had seen and felt the reality of war, and were finding ways of expressing it in their own terms. They had arrived at the aesthetic of direct experience *through* experience.

To locate that turn at the Somme is an over-simplification, of course. Nevinson's paintings were based on 1914–15 observations; Graves's first war poems pre-date the Somme; the poems of Charles Sorley, which Graves admired so highly, were published in January 1916 (Sorley had died at Loos in October 1915); *Black 'Ell* owed nothing directly to the Somme fighting. Clearly the force of opposition, and the aesthetic that could express that force, were evolving and growing as the war continued, and more men went to experience it. But it was only in 1916 that it began to appear before the British public, in paintings and poems that shocked, but spoke with authority. From this point on it would increase in volume and force, until in time it became the war — the war, that is, as we imagine it.

PART III

WAITING FOR DAYLIGHT
1917–18

'What have we been fighting for? What are we fighting for? Does anyone know?'
>   H.G. Wells, *Mr Britling Sees It Through* (1916)

The night itself is different. It hides a world unknown. If a sun is to rise on that world, then not even a false dawn yet shows.
>   H.M. Tomlinson, 'Waiting for Daylight' (1918)

CHAPTER 8

Dottyville

In November 1917, Charles Morgan, a young naval officer, returned to England for the first time since August 1914. He had been with the Naval Brigade at the defence of Antwerp, and in the October 1914 retreat he had surrendered to the Dutch, and had been interned. So he had not witnessed the processes of change that had occurred during the first three years of the war; he simply arrived to discover what his country had become. 'I have returned to an island,' he wrote to a friend,

> which undoubtedly bears the name of England. Certainly it is not now what once I thought it to be: perhaps it never was. And are all those fine people, with such an infinite capacity for beauty, to suffer for this corpse of England that remains? Is all we loved to be washed out in order that — in order that — what *are* we fighting for? Not for freedom surely, not for peace. All that has been forgotten long enough ago. Now it's revenge, and a little money, and a little territory, and a little spitting into the face of Christ.[1]

Morgan was not reacting against the horrors of the trenches (he had not been there), nor against the idea of war itself (he clearly felt that there were causes worth fighting for), but against what the English cause had become: his anger was essentially moral. If his reaction was extreme, that was perhaps because he had not been around to experience the daily disillusionments and follies that *Mr Britling* so brilliantly records. But many another Englishman felt the change that Morgan felt: in the fourth year of the war the turn that had occurred in the consciousnesses of soldiers had also occurred among thoughtful people at home.

One finds testimonies to this perception of change in many places: not only in radical–pacifist publications, as would have been the case earlier in the war, but in the most 'establishment' records — in *The Times Literary Supplement*, for example, and the *Daily Telegraph*, and the debates of the House of Commons. In August 1917 the *TLS* ran on its front page a 'Parable of the War', by A.F. Pollard, Professor of Constitutional History at the University of London. In it Pollard imagined 'The Prussian' addressing England:

> 'You see,' he says in effect, 'we were right after all, and in practice you admit it by manifold imitation. You have adopted conscription, gagged your Press, suspended your constitutional guarantees and your sacred rights of liberty. You have had to treat conscience, unless it agreed with your own, as an offence against the law, and to penalize with imprisonment and hard labour a literal interpretation of the Sermon on the Mount.'[2]

Three months later, Lord Lansdowne, Unionist leader in the Lords and a former member of Asquith's cabinet, published a long letter in the *Telegraph* in which he asked the question that Morgan had asked: 'What are we fighting for?' and urged a negotiated peace. 'We are not going to lose this war,' he wrote,

> but its prolongation will spell ruin to the civilised world, and an infinite addition to the load of human suffering which already weighs upon it. Security will be invaluable to a world which has the vitality to profit by it, but what will be the value of the blessings of peace to nations so exhausted that they can scarcely stretch out a hand with which to grasp them?[3]

A few weeks after that, Colonel Aubrey Herbert, a Conservative MP just back from the war, rose in the Commons to defend Lord Lansdowne, and to argue for an end to the war. 'I say that our people are prepared to endure to the end,' he said,

> suffering less than the Germans are suffering, as we know, but prepared to endure to the end if we have still got the same ideals that we had at the beginning. What is called pacifism in this country is miscalled pacifism: it is merely a protest against the brutish Prussian attitude of our own Yellow Press . . . which is doing everything it can to unite our enemies against us by saying to everyone of the allies of Germany, 'There is not the slightest use in your trying to make terms

or surrender, because you will have no mercy from us' — and that is
the soldier's friend![4]

These critics — a conservative historian, a Unionist peer, and a Tory
MP who was a veteran of Mons and Gallipoli — spoke from the centre
of English society; and what they said was that the centre no longer
held. The ideas that they criticized were ideas that they would surely
have affirmed in 1914 — that the privileges of peace must be sacrificed if
necessary for the cause of victory, that England must fight on until
Germany was crushed, that there could be no compromise with the
enemy. But three years of fighting had shown the costs of those
convictions: England had made herself Prussian, had imposed ruin upon
her own future, and had surrendered the power of free speech to the
loudest and coarsest voices.

The mood that these statements described was a negative one: ideals
lost, high emotions drained away, and a war that went on and on with a
momentum of its own, and darkened all life with its presence. Faced
with the irresistible force of the war, men did what men do when
circumstances seem both unendurable and unchangeable: they protested, not with any real expectation of altering things, but simply not
to be silent.

The voice of protest became articulate in 1917, and not only from
peers, politicians and journalists. Soldiers protested, too. The story of
Sassoon during that year offers a dramatic example. In the early months
of 1917, Sassoon was in the trenches near Arras with his regiment, the
Royal Welch Fusiliers. He was wounded there in April, and was
evacuated to the Denmark Hill military hospital in London. In May he
was moved to a convalescent home in Sussex, and a month later was
released to his home in Kent.

During the months of his convalescence, Sassoon continued to write
war poems, very like those he had been writing since the Somme. If
there was anything new in them, it was the increasing intensity of the
loathing that Sassoon expressed for all the people who were not directly
engaged in the fighting — for the generals, the old men, journalists, and
civilians at large, all those non-combatants who had not suffered in the
war, but nevertheless had opinions about it. One finds the same loathing
in Sassoon's diary for these months — for the old men 'cackling about
"attrition" and "wastage of man-power",' for the great lady at the
convalescent home who said reassuringly, 'But death is nothing', for the
TLS reviewer who wrote of 'the everlasting glory and exaltation of

war'. They all represented what seemed to Sassoon an empty, ignorant rhetoric; 'This is the sort of thing,' Sassoon wrote, 'I am in revolt against.'[5]

That revolt was expressed clearly enough, one might think, in the fierce anti-rhetoric of the poems, but for Sassoon that was not enough; a diary-entry of the convalescent-home period ends: 'I'd better go back to the First Battalion as soon as possible, unless I can make some protest against the War.'[6] Why weren't the poems a sufficient protest? Perhaps because at that moment Sassoon had some evidence before him that his poems did not persuade or convert readers. His first wartime book of poems, *The Old Huntsman*, was published while he was convalescing, and the reviews showed that readers brought their views of the war to the poems, and found those views confirmed there: the poems were sordidly and horribly realistic if the reviewer was Virginia Woolf, but they were only grimly humorous, rising to conventional lyricism if the reviewer was E.B. Osborn.[7] Clearly Sassoon's poetry was not changing minds.

But if another sort of protest was necessary, what sort should it be? In June, Sassoon travelled to Garsington, the country home of Philip and Lady Ottoline Morrell, to ask their advice. The decision to go to Garsington was in itself an answer. Morrell had been prominent in Parliament as a defender of pacifists and an opponent of censorship, and in the months since the institution of conscription he and his wife had made their house a gathering place for conscientious objectors. Some — Clive Bell, Aldous Huxley, and David Garnett among them — came there to do alternative service as farm labourers; others came to discuss pacifist policy — Bertrand Russell, Miles Malleson, and Clifford Allen of the No-Conscription Fellowship, were all Garsington guests. At such a place, in such company, it was unlikely that Sassoon would be urged to return to the war.

Morrell's advice was that Sassoon should meet in London with Russell and Middleton Murry, and that they should together compose a statement of protest. Lady Ottoline arranged the meeting, and the following document was drawn up:

I am making this statement as an act of wilful defiance of military authority, because I believe that the War is being deliberately prolonged by those who have the power to end it. I am a soldier, convinced that I am acting on behalf of soldiers. I believe that this War, upon which I entered as a war of defence and liberation, has now become a war of aggression and conquest. I believe that the purposes for which I and my fellow-soldiers entered upon this War should have been so clearly stated as to have made it impossible for them to be changed without our knowledge, and that, had this been done, the objects which actuated us would now be attainable by negotiation.

I have seen and endured the sufferings of the troops, and I can no longer be a party to prolonging those sufferings for ends which I believe to be evil and unjust.

I am not protesting against the military conduct of the War, but against the political errors and insincerities for which the fighting men are being sacrificed.

On behalf of those who are suffering now, I make this protest against the deception which is being practised on them. Also I believe that it may help to destroy the callous complacence with which the majority of those at home regard the continuance of agonies which they do not share, and which they have not sufficient imagination to realise.[8]

It is a protest, right enough; but it also seems another kind of statement, a poet's confession of failure. The poet-protester, having published his poems to no avail, turns to prose, and seeks the help of a philosopher and a literary journalist to make his point. And more than that, he makes his protest not simply in words, but in a physical act of defiance, refusing to obey orders — an act that should lead to a court martial.

The protest was printed by Francis Meynell (the young pacifist who had been so enraged by Gosse and Condy's Fluid), and copies were sent to newspaper editors, Members of Parliament, and various literary men, including Bennett, Wells, and Hardy; Robert Graves got one, and so did Eddie Marsh, and Sassoon's art-critic friend Robbie Ross. There must have been a considerable distribution of the broadside before the police called at the Bomb Shop and seized the remaining copies. Certainly there was plenty of publicity: the letter was printed in the radical *Bradford Pioneer* on July 27, and in *The Times* and the *Daily Mail* on the 31st, and was read into the record in the House of Commons on the 30th. 'Well, you are notorious throughout England now you silly old thing!' Graves wrote to Sassoon on the 31st. 'Everybody here [at the Royal Welch Fusiliers' camp near Liverpool] who's been to France agrees with your point of view, but those that don't know you think it was not quite a gentlemanly course to take . . .'[9]

By the time the protest appeared in *The Times* Sassoon had sent a copy to his commanding officer, and awaited a court martial. Instead, he was summoned before a Medical Board, where he was found to be in need of psychiatric treatment, and was assigned to Craiglockhart War Hospital, near Edinburgh.

Craiglockhart was a hospital for shell-shocked officers: 'There are 160 Officers here,' Sassoon wrote in a letter on his arrival, 'most of them half-dotty,' and he date-lined his letter 'Dottyville'.[10] Was Sassoon one of the 'dotty', then? Opinions among his acquaintances varied. Edmund Gosse, who visited him at Denmark Hill, thought that he was suffering from severe shock, and Robbie Ross, who saw him in June, found him in 'a very abnormal state'.[11] And some of the poems of that time seem to confirm their impressions — for example 'Repression of War Experience', written at his home in Kent in July, which ends with these lines:

> You're quiet and peaceful, summering safe at home;
> You'd never think there was a bloody war on! . . .
> O yes, you would . . . why, you can hear the guns.
> Hark! Thud, thud, thud — quite soft . . . they never
>   cease —
> Those whispering guns — O Christ, I want to go out
> And screech at them to stop — I'm going crazy;
> I'm going stark, staring mad because of the guns.[12]

A man is not mad, of course, simply because he writes a poem about going mad; indeed Sassoon cited his ability to write poems during his convalescence as evidence that he wasn't suffering from shock. And many of his friends agreed that he was not mad. Pacifist friends regarded his gesture as both courageous and rational; Edward Carpenter, the old Socialist poet and free-thinker, sent his congratulations, and Lady Ottoline wrote that he had done 'a True Act'. Soldier friends like Robert Graves thought that his views of the war were right, but that his action had been wrong. Clearly the definition of true madness, or of shell-shock, or whatever it was to be called, depended on the definer's attitude towards the war.

These were all lay opinions. When Sassoon got to Craiglockhart he came under the care of one of England's most distinguished psychologists, W.H.R. Rivers, and from him, one might have thought, a clear and definitive diagnosis would come. But in fact nothing so simple happened — in part because there was no body of knowledge on the psychology of war on which such a diagnosis could be based. As Rivers remarked, army medicine had been prepared for infectious diseases and complex surgical cases, but not for the vast range of mental disturbances that modern warfare would cause among fighting men.[13] In 1917 Rivers was the principal English psychologist treating 'war neuroses', but he was only at the beginning of his investigations.

Rivers's principal contributions to the subject were centred on three ideas. First, he proposed that war neurosis was fundamentally different from the mental disturbances of peacetime: 'the neuroses of war', he wrote, 'depend upon a conflict between the instinct of self-preservation and certain social standards of thought and conduct, according to which fear and its expression are regarded as reprehensible'[14] — not a conflict that civilians usually faced. Second, he rejected the idea, implicit in the term 'shell-shock', that the psycho-neuroses of war had physical origins; they were caused, he said firmly, by the mental stresses and strains of service in the trenches and in the air. And third, he distinguished sharply between the neuroses of enlisted men and those of their officers; the men were trained to obey, and their neurotic responses to strain were those — paralysis, mutism, anaesthesia — that removed them altogether from further participation in the war; officers, who were trained to take responsibility, responded with anxiety-neuroses — nightmares, obsessions, hysteria.

It is often said that it was the treatment of shell-shock cases during the First World War that established the authority of Freud in England. But Rivers, the most influential psychologist working on such cases, was anti-Freudian in fundamental ways, and opposed Freud's work in many of his writings. Rivers believed that self-preservation was a stronger instinct than sex, and a commoner source of mental disorders; he could find few cases arising out of the war, he said, that supported the Freudian view of sexuality. He also believed that the sources of neuroses were to be found in recent events, not in those of early childhood. These theories apparently worked with the shell-shocked officers at Craiglockhart, at least in terms of the army's goals; Rivers helped many of his patients to suppress their anxieties, and to return to active service.

But Sassoon was a special case, and a troubling one — troubling enough to have a place in *Conflict and Dream*, Rivers's study of the neuroses of war. He appears there in a chapter on the symbolism of dreams, as 'Patient B', though Rivers explains that he was not really a patient at all, since he 'was not suffering from any form of psycho-neurosis, but was in the hospital on account of his adoption of a pacifist attitude while on leave from active service'.[15] Eventually Rivers did give a psychological-sounding name to what was bothering Sassoon: he told him that he was suffering from 'a very strong "anti-war" complex'. But Rivers didn't seem so much concerned with treating that complex as with understanding it. He read books and journals about the war that Sassoon recommended — the pacifist *Cambridge Magazine*, and Henri Barbusse's war novel, *Le Feu* — and he talked at length with his 'patient'. And as he read and talked, he began to feel that these new ideas constituted a threat to his own position: what would happen, he asked himself, 'if my task of converting a patient from his "pacifist errors" to the conventional attitude should have as its result my own conversion to his point of view?'[16] It is a surprisingly frank statement of Rivers's peculiar role as a war psychologist: he was at Craiglockhart not to cure but to convert deviant thought into conventional channels, and so to restore his patients to duty.

Sassoon's pacifist ideas disturbed Rivers's confidence in that role, and it is not surprising that the 'pacifist' dream that he analysed in his chapter on dream-symbolism was not one of Sassoon's, but one of Rivers's own. In the dream Rivers saw himself back in Germany, where he had studied psychology. He was visiting a German friend, a fellow-scientist, and as he left the house his host called after him that he had made a wrong turn to the right, and that he should turn left instead. He then turned back to the left, and found the door of a laboratory, and behind it another German scientist, wounded and bandaged. To Rivers, the dream seemed very straightforward: *right* was the conservative and national-istic direction, which he had taken in the war; *left* was the liberal and international direction, which as a scientist he ought to have taken. The wounded man was German science, damaged by the war (and by the actions of English scientists insofar as they supported the military).

In the dream, Rivers was made uncomfortable by the fact that he was in uniform. There too he felt a conflict, which his dealings with Sassoon had forced him to confront. 'So long as I was an officer of the R.A.M.C.,' he wrote,

> ... my discussions with B on his attitude towards the war were prejudiced by my sense that I was not a free agent in discussing the matter, but that there was the danger that my attitude might be influenced by my official position. As a scientific student whose only object should be the attainment of what I supposed to be truth, it was definitely unpleasant to me to suspect that the opinions which I

was uttering might be influenced by the needs of my position, and I was fully aware of an element of constraint in my relations with B on this account. So long as I was in uniform I was not a free agent . . .[17]

Something odd had happened in the doctor–patient relationship: the patient had not been converted, but he had disturbed the doctor's dreams.

After four months at Craiglockhart, Sassoon abandoned his protest and returned to general service. 'I have done all I can to protest against the war and the way it is prolonged,' he wrote in his diary on December 19, 1917,[18] and he returned to his regiment with evident relief. Eventually he was sent again to the Western Front, and there, in July 1918, he was wounded once again, this time accidentally by one of his own men, and so ended his military career.

The months of the 'protest' in 1917 had been a time of strain and unhappiness, Sassoon told Graves; but they had also been a productive time. He wrote some twenty poems while he was at Craiglockhart, including many of his fiercest and most moving war poems; it was there, in the company of the war's failures, that he found his fullest poetic voice. Some of these poems deal with the realities of war — poems like 'Counter-Attack' and 'Survivors'; others with the despised civilians — 'The Fathers', 'Does it Matter?', and the cruel 'Glory of Women'. One of them, 'Atrocities', was so brutal that Sassoon's publisher refused to print it ('this was too much for Heinemann,' he wrote on the manuscript — see plate 10); another, 'Fight to a Finish' — one of the home-front poems — shocked Rivers with its violence: he thought it 'very dangerous'. Dangerous to whom? one wonders. Not to the civilians, certainly — Sassoon's war poems broke no bones. To Sassoon, then? It's hard to see that his hatred for yellow-pressmen and Members of Parliament did him any harm. Perhaps the real danger was to Rivers.

Rivers urged Sassoon to return to active service, and in the end Sassoon agreed. He put his feelings about his act of defiance into a sonnet, which he called 'Banishment':

> I am banished from the patient men who fight.
> They smote my heart to pity, built my pride.
> Shoulder to aching shoulder, side by side,
> They trudged away from life's broad wealds of light.
> Their wrongs were mine; and ever in my sight
> They went arrayed in honour. But they died, —

> Not one by one: and mutinous I cried
> To those who sent them out into the night.
>
> The darkness tells how vainly I have striven
> To free them from the pit where they must dwell
> In outcast gloom convulsed and jagged and riven
> By grappling guns. Love drove me to rebel.
> Love drives me back to grope with them through hell.
> And in their tortured eyes I stand forgiven.[19]

The emotions expressed here are not political, and there is no talk of ending the war, or defining war aims, or instructing the ignorant civilians at home. It is a poem about sacrifice — one of many by serving soldiers — in which the leading of men into battle is an act of love, and honour is a possible concept.

The role of Rivers in this rehabilitation seems to have been a beneficent one. Certainly Sassoon thought so. Afterwards, he referred always to Rivers with affection and gratitude. 'I must never forget Rivers,' he wrote in his diary during his last journey to the Front. 'He is the only man who can save me if I break down again.'[20] So by May 1918 he was thinking of his gesture of the previous year not as a protest but as a breakdown, and Rivers not as a doctor but as a saviour.

Sassoon was not the only poet to come to Rivers's hospital in the summer of 1917; Wilfred Owen arrived there in June — not as a protester but as a shell-shock case. Owen had gone to France at the end of 1916, and had been in and out of the line. He had not been wounded, but he had been battered by war: in March he suffered a concussion in a fall, and was hospitalized; in April he was blown into the air by an exploding shell, and was back in the hospital again. The doctor there diagnosed him as a case of neurasthenia and forbade him to return to action; eventually he was evacuated to England for treatment. He remained at Craiglockhart until October, when he was passed for limited duty and assigned to a post in England. In August 1918 he rejoined his regiment in France in time for the final offensive. He won a Military Cross in early October, and was killed in action on November 4.

The Owen who came to Craiglockhart that summer was a less impressive figure than Sassoon. He was nearly seven years younger, and he was not yet officially a hero (quite the opposite, in his own mind, it would seem); and though he had written a great many poems by then, he had not published any. He knew no one in the English literary world, and seemed little aware of what went on there. The poems that he brought with him were the sort that any young man of poetical ambitions and no experience might write — sonnets about love and beauty and death, some of them 'war poems', full of Keats and empty of substance. He set to work at once to write more of the same.

Then, in mid-August, he met Sassoon, and his work began to change. Sassoon patronized him (he was 'little Owen' in Sassoon's letters), and thought his work 'unequal', but he encouraged him, and read and criticized his poems. Owen manuscripts of the Craiglockhart months show corrections in Sassoon's hand, most of which Owen adopted. But Sassoon's influence was more than a matter of a word here and there; Owen learned Sassoon's rhetoric, and for the first time began to write about the trench world in the language of the trenches, as Sassoon did. 'Nothing like his trench life sketches has ever been written or ever will be written,' Owen wrote of Sassoon in a letter to his mother. 'Shakespeare reads vapid after these.'[21] The influence was immediate and entirely conscious; after their second meeting, Owen wrote to a friend that he had written a poem in Sassoon's style, and enclosed a copy of 'The Dead-Beat'. The next day he added sadly that Sassoon had read the poem, and had objected that the facetious middle didn't fit with the serious beginning and end: 'thus the piece as a whole is no good.' Owen accepted the criticism, and revised the poem.[22]

Sassoon did another kind of favour for Owen: he introduced him to his friend Robbie Ross. To Owen, Ross must have seemed a very sophisticated person, as indeed he was: a man who had known and defended Oscar Wilde, an art critic who lived in London and moved in artistic and literary circles, a friend of the Asquiths and other such notables. Ross was generous in entertaining soldier-poets when they came to town; he took them to lunch at his club, introduced them to famous writers, and offered them lodgings in his house in Half Moon Street — Sassoon, Graves, and Owen all stayed there at one time or another during the war. He read and criticized their poems, and he promoted their books; clearly he was a valuable acquaintance to have. But he was also a link with the past, with the decadent and homosexual tradition of the Nineties; and perhaps he kept that tradition alive in the lives of his literary young friends — both as a style and as a style of life, at a time when they were all somewhat uncertain about both.

If you read through the Craiglockhart poems, as identified in Jon Stallworthy's edition of Owen's *Poems and Fragments*, you can see the process by which the romantic imitator of Keats was chastened and

toughened into — not an imitator of Sassoon, but an English war poet
in the same tradition. Look first at 'Anthem for Doomed Youth', a
poem that Keats might have written, if he had commanded a platoon on
the Western Front, and then at 'Dulce et Decorum Est' (drafted at
Craiglockhart, finished later), 'Insensibility' (another draft, slightly
later), 'S.I.W.' (a draft), 'Greater Love' (a draft, possibly from Owen's
next post). As the latter poem shows, Keats never left entirely; it was
just that the war entered as a complicating influence, and as a rhetoric.

What we see here is the emergence of a tradition and a style,
beginning perhaps when Graves met Sassoon, and told him that a taste
of the trenches would change his style, and continuing to this meeting of
Sassoon and Owen. Owen left Craiglockhart with his best poems still
unwritten, or in unfinished drafts; but he had found the tradition in
which he could say what he wanted to say. These poets, who met and
exchanged poems and corresponded about poetry and war, were not of
course the only poets who wrote realistically about it. Rosenberg was
writing, Blunden was writing, though neither knew Graves or Sassoon
or Owen. But these latter three constitute a sort of centre, a line that
defines what was best and most characteristic in English poetry of the
First World War.

Before he returned to France, Owen drafted a brief preface for the
book of poems that he hoped to publish. He left it unfinished, and it was
not published until after his death; nevertheless, it belongs here, as a
document in the wartime history of imagining the war, and one that is
important enough to quote in full, familiar though it is.

> This book is not about heroes. English poetry is not yet fit to speak of
> them.
>
> Nor is it about deeds, or lands, nor anything about glory, honour,
> might, majesty, dominion, or power, except War.
>
> Above all I am not concerned with Poetry.
>
> My subject is War, and the pity of War.
>
> The Poetry is in the pity.
>
> Yet these elegies are to this generation in no sense consolatory.
> They may be to the next. All a poet can do today is warn. That is why
> the true Poets must be truthful.
>
> (If I thought the letter of this book would last, I might have used
> proper names; but if the spirit of it survives — survives Prussia — my
> ambition and those names will have achieved fresher fields than
> Flanders . . .)[23]

Here, near the end of the war, is a war poet's manifesto, which is not about war but about language — a terse statement that simply prohibits the old high rhetoric without even bothering to say why, as though by now that was self-evident. And so it was, to poets like Owen and Sassoon and Graves. It was self-evident, too, to many prose-writers, as we have seen — writers of letters and diaries like Roland Leighton and Cynthia Asquith and Graeme West and the Hon. R.G.A. Hamilton, and an army of other soldiers, and some civilians. What Owen wrote was what they all knew: the truth about war was a matter of language — and especially of the words that you did *not* use.

Another shell-shocked officer, who was also a poet and a protester, was a Rivers patient in 1917. The case of Max Plowman is less well known than those of Sassoon and Owen, but it is an interesting one. Plowman was a 31-year-old journalist when he enlisted on Christmas Eve 1914, and had already begun to establish himself as a writer — a sort of Romantic Socialist, with a mind full of Shelley and Blake, not the sort, one might think, who would rush to the colours. And he would have agreed: a few days after enlisting he was writing to a friend that war was 'insane and unmitigated filth', and that his enlistment was the 'easy way' to deal with the whole problem. Twenty months later, on the Somme, he described the fighting as 'a bloody fool's travesty of life & excitement'.[24] Yet, like others who felt as he did — like Graeme West, for example — he stayed on, until he suffered a concussion in January 1917, and was sent home to be treated for shell-shock. He was at Bowhill Auxiliary, a branch of Craiglockhart, until July; he doesn't seem to have known either Sassoon or Owen there, but he knew Rivers.

During that summer and early autumn Plowman prepared two little books for publication. One was *A Lap Full of Seed*, a book of poems published in October. It is not primarily war poetry, and at that date in mid-war Plowman felt that he had to explain why. 'Of the war poems at the end of the book,' he wrote in his Preface, 'your forbearance and a word. They are few, because warfare itself is comparatively unimportant: the spirit (though not the brain) of man having already outgrown the bestial occupation. They sound one note, that of individual responsibility, because from a personal standpoint I do not know another worth sounding.'[25] There are only eight of them, and all but one are dated in the first year of the war; Plowman had lost interest in the subject long before he saw any fighting.

The other book was an anonymous pamphlet, *The Right to Live*, which Plowman completed shortly after he left the hospital in the summer of 1917. It is a polemic, not against the war as such, but against the society that made war inevitable. Plowman took for granted that the war would go on to the end; he was not concerned to stop it, but to change the world that would come after. The voice of the pamphlet is the voice of the Romantic Socialist, attacking Mammon, mechanism, and materialism, and praising simplicity and spirit — a very English voice, in a native radical tradition, though it is difficult to imagine its audience in February 1918, when it was finally published.

It must have had a few attentive readers when it appeared, however, for by then Plowman had made his own protest, and was under arrest. He had been called for a medical examination on January 1, and told that after one more month of home service he would be returned to the Front. Two weeks later he wrote this letter to the Adjutant of his battalion:

> I have the honour to request that you will lay before the Commanding Officer the following grave & personal matter.
>
> For some time past it has been becoming increasingly apparent to me that for reasons of conscientious objection I was unfitted to hold my commission in His Majesty's army & I am now absolutely convinced that I have no alternative but to proffer my resignation. I have always held that (in the Prime Minister's words) war is 'a relic of barbarism,' but my opinion has gradually deepened into the fixed conviction that organised warfare of any kind is always organised murder. So wholly do I believe in the doctrine of Incarnation (that God indeed lives in every human body) that I believe that killing men is always killing God.
>
> As I hold this belief with conviction, you will, I think, see that it is impossible for me to continue to be a member of any organisation that has the killing of men for any part of its end, & I therefore beg that you will ask the Commanding Officer to forward this my resignation for acceptance with the least possible delay.[26]

It was rather a different protest from the one that Sassoon had made. Sassoon had protested the change in British war aims; Plowman protested war, *all* war.

As soon as the letter reached its destination the offender was arrested and confined to his quarters under guard. He was court-martialled in April, and was dismissed from the army, though without a prison sentence; by early May he was a civilian.

When Plowman sent his letter of resignation to the army, he also sent a copy to Sassoon, whose published letter of the previous year had clearly been his example. Sassoon did not reply; he simply passed the letter on to Rivers, on the evident assumption that dotty officers who resigned their commissions were his problem, not Sassoon's. Rivers replied with a sympathetic note, asking if he could be of any use, and reporting that Sassoon 'has returned to duty & is quite happy in it'.[27] Plowman did not take up the offer; but later that summer he met Rivers again. At that time, being a civilian, he was threatened with conscription, and once more Rivers offered his assistance. This time Plowman was unadmiring: 'He's a very clever liberal-minded person,' he wrote of Rivers to a friend, 'whom I regard as a fundamental ass.' And he explained why:

> His line on the war is that the individual is always more or less in conflict with the accommodations necessary to society & that war merely imposes a greater need for self-restraint upon the individual . . .[28]

That line would do for an officer protesting the war's aims, and even for those others, hysterical with guilt at their failure to function in combat; but it was no good for Plowman, who had seen his war, and had resigned from it altogether.

Plowman, Sassoon and Owen had three things in common: they were all poets, they all fought on the Western Front, and they all were Rivers's patients at 'Dottyville' in 1917. What influence did the latter fact have on their common decision to protest against the war? And what role did Rivers himself play?

A rather unsympathetic one, you might say, judging from his public utterances, his lectures and professional papers. The notion of war expressed there is that it was a necessary and morally right activity, in which men who had been trained to an hypnotic state of obedience, led by officers trained to repress their anxieties, faced fear and overcame it — if they were normal healthy men. If they were not, they were sent to him, and he helped them to control their hysteria.

That was the public Rivers. But the private man, the individual who talked with his patients and read their books and was troubled by their ideas, seems to have been rather different. That Rivers encouraged his patients to confront and to discuss their war experiences, and so to bring them into consciousness (and perhaps into poems). He rejected the idea that men should suppress feelings, and helped his patients to accept and to express 'unmanly' feelings; weeping, he told them, could be a help to grieving men, and there was no shame in breaking down under stress. War was an inherently traumatic experience, and fear was a natural response to it — the problem was a medical, not a moral one. All feelings about war were valid, and were better expressed than suppressed, though in the end men should control those feelings, and should return to the fighting. Whatever value such notions had in the medical treatment of shell-shock, one can see that they would be liberating for war poets — though they might also be fatal.

Some of the feelings that this treatment seemed to encourage — tenderness, for instance, and love of one's men — have been called homosexual when they appear in the poems of Sassoon and Owen. It may well be that Rivers helped Sassoon to understand and to express his own sexual nature; certainly it was while Sassoon was at Craiglockhart that he was first able to tell Ottoline Morrell that he was homosexual, and his diary in the months after his stay there is more frank about his sexual feelings for men than earlier entries are. But sexuality is too simple a concept for the releasing of emotions that Rivers encouraged; it seems rather that he helped his young patients to accept feelings that traditional notions of war had suppressed, and to redefine what it meant to be a man. Take, as an example, this passage from Sassoon's diary for June 4, 1918 (he was back with his regiment in France):

> After all, I am nothing but what the Brigadier calls 'a potential killer of Germans (Huns).' O God, why must I do it? *I'm not.* I am only here *to look after* some men.[29]

Owen wrote in much the same vein in a letter to his mother a month before he was killed:

> I came out in order to help these boys — directly by leading them as well as an officer can; indirectly, by watching their sufferings that I may speak of them as well as a pleader can.[30]

The significance of these private statements, made by officers at the Front near the end of the war, lies not in what they suggest about the writers' sexual impulses — if they suggest anything — but in the change that they express in the idea of soldier and officer, rejecting killing as the definitive act, and substituting relationships based on gentler feelings: caring, leading, watching, pleading.

Dottyville, as an environment and a community, must have played a part in that change. Here were gathered officers who had fought at Ypres and on the Somme, who had wounds and medals and memories of battle, and who had been banished from the world of war, sent to a place 'of wash-outs and shattered heroes', as Sassoon described it,[31] because their reactions to war were unacceptable. Whether these reactions took the form of letters of protest or of uncontrollable weeping made no difference — they were taken to be neurotic or hysterical or worse, and the army set apart the men who felt them until they should be made normal again.

By setting them apart the government acknowledged what had not been acknowledged before — that a connection existed between war and madness. The existence of Dottyville assumed that war as it was being fought then could damage minds and alter personalities; and by the end of the war there was ample evidence that this was true: an estimated 80,000 shell-shock cases occurred in the British forces.

The experience of separation in such an institution changed the ways in which the separated young men thought about themselves, and about their connections with the war and with the society that pursued the war, and about the condition of being a man. If they were poets or prose writers or painters, it also changed their visions of the war in their art. It is not surprising that madness began to appear in the literature and art of the later war years: there are mad soldiers in Sassoon's 'Survivors' and Owen's 'The Chances' (both written at Craiglockhart), and in paintings by Nevinson and Orpen. the mentally wounded — cases of madness, hysteria, or 'nerves' like Owen's — had become part of reality. There is no judgement implied in the representations of such men; they are not cowards or weaklings, but simply instances of another kind of casualty, another victim of war's horrors.

One could make too much, of course, of three men in a Scottish mental hospital. But it is clearly true that at about this time — a point in the war's history between the Somme and Passchendaele — English attitudes towards the war changed. Protests against it began to be heard, both from civilians in high places and from serving soldiers, and a new English war art began to emerge that uttered its own protest simply by recording a new trench reality. That new reality had to do with details that had largely been left out of previous war art: the devastated earth, the corpses, and the wounded — blinded men, gassed men, crippled men, mad men, men with self-inflicted wounds. But it also had to do with feelings that were new to the art of this war: pity and compassion for its victims, anger and hatred for non-combatants.

For that new reality, new forms of art were necessary — a new rhetoric, new kinds of visual order, and the radical exclusion of whatever might suggest the old values of war-in-art. There would be no more plumes and chargers, no more trumpets, no more Big Words; more than that, there would be no heroes and no victories. It would be a soldier's art, addressed to soldiers, taking separateness as a fundamental fact. And that sense of separation, that division between artist and customary audience, would affect not only the war art of the later war years, but also the art that followed, in the world after the war.

CHAPTER 9

The Death of Landscape

Gradually, in the third and fourth years of the war, the new trench reality began to establish a public presence. Expressions of that reality in verse were published, and noticed: Graves's *Over the Brazier* appeared in May 1916, Sassoon's poems began to turn up in the *Cambridge Magazine* at about the same time, and Isaac Rosenberg published two poems in *Poetry* in December. In 1917 there were more books: Sassoon's *The Old Huntsman* in May, Robert Nichols's *Ardours and Endurances* in July, Ivor Gurney's *Severn and Somme* in October, Graves's *Fairies and Fusiliers* in November. It wasn't an overwhelming amount — not if you consider that more than three thousand volumes of First World War poetry were published — but it was enough to give a collective identity to a new tradition, and to puzzle and disturb conservative critics.

It disturbed, for example, Edmund Gosse, whose enthusiasm for the antiseptic effects of war had been so intense in 1914. In October 1917, Gosse reviewed six books of war poems for the *Edinburgh Review*. The six represented the range of poetic attitudes towards the war, from Brooke's *1914* to Sassoon's *Old Huntsman*.

Gosse had no trouble with the traditional stuff — Brooke's poems, an elegy for a dead friend by Maurice Baring, a memorial volume of poems by a dead soldier — but he found it difficult to deal with three others, the first books of war poems by Nichols, Graves, and Sassoon. Nichols's *Ardours and Endurances*, Gosse wrote, was 'in several ways the most puzzling and the most interesting' of the books; what was puzzling was that Nichols didn't write in the way that Gosse expected war poets to write.

He has no military enthusiasm [Gosse complained], no aspiration after *gloire*. Indeed, the most curious feature of his poetry is that its range is concentrated on the few yards about the trench in which he stands. He seems to have no national view of the purpose of the war, no enthusiasm for the cause, no anger against the enemy. There is no mention of the Germans from beginning to end; the poet does not seem to know of their existence.[1]

This is an acute, though somewhat limited description of Nichols's title-poem, a sequence of thirty lyrics that takes the soldier-speaker by stages from enlistment into battle and its aftermath. Nichols was in fact a transitional poet, part Brooke and part Sassoon. He had Brooke's tone of the reformed decadent, for whom war would be a purification — a mighty winnowing or a clean flame. And he had Brooke's note of endless self-regard, that fascination with one's own sensitive responses to war which is absent from the best of the later war poets. And he used words like *Honour* and *The Brave* without irony. But unlike Brooke, Nichols had had some experience of the trenches; only for three weeks, in 1915, but enough to make it possible for him to introduce Sassoon-like details from the Front — dead snipers in trees, bodies trodden into the mud, that sort of thing.

What Gosse said of Nichols is certainly true: he had no enthusiasm for the war, and no hostile feelings towards the enemy. That is an important element in the war art from this point on; the enemy, if there is one, is at home, not on the battlefield. Gosse's other point is equally important: the scale of war art in those poems has shrunk to the actual scale of the fighting — a few soldiers in a trench, with a few yards of emptiness beyond.

But it was Sassoon's *Old Huntsman* that most challenged Gosse's sense of what a war poem should be, and compelled him to take note of the changes that time had brought to the mood of the genre.

Lieut. Sassoon's own volume [Gosse wrote] is later than those which we have hitherto examined, and bears a somewhat different character. The gallantry of 1915 and the optimism of 1916 have passed away, and in Lieut. Sassoon's poems their place is taken by a sense of intoler-able weariness and impatience: 'How long, O Lord, how long?'[2]

These changes Gosse seems to have understood as historically true and acceptable. What he couldn't accept was the bitterness that went with them. 'The bitterness of Lieut. Sassoon,' he wrote, is not cynical, it is the rage of disenchantment, the violence of a young man eager to pursue other aims, who, finding the age out of joint, resents being called upon to help to mend it. His temper is not altogether to be applauded, for such sentiments must tend to relax the effort of the struggle, yet they can hardly be reproved when conducted with so much honesty and courage.[3]

'The rage of disenchantment' — that comes close to describing what had happened, not only to Sassoon but to Charles Morgan and Colonel Herbert, to Lord Lansdowne and Professor Pollard. But though Gosse could see and understand it, he could not accept it as normal and general. He had to neutralize Sassoon's rage by putting it into literary terms, describing Sassoon in the language of Hamlet, and so making him a tragic hero, isolated and made ineffectual by his bitterness. Such a figure, Gosse seemed to say, was all very well for a poem or a play, but an army of Hamlets wouldn't do, however one might applaud the courage of their testimony. And anyway, Sassoon was probably wrong: 'he may not always have thought correctly,' Gosse concluded, 'nor have recorded his impressions with proper circumspection, but his honesty must be respectfully acknowledged.'[4]

For all his patriotic fervour and enthusiasm for war, Gosse was an acute critic. He saw that war poetry was changing because the war had changed, and he saw that those changes could best be described in negative terms — as disenchantments, derangements, and rejections of the past. But he remained a traditionalist, both in his literary tastes and in his war politics, one of the Old Men — and not surprisingly; he was seventy-two when he wrote the review. And so, though he perceived the change, he had to deny that a radical and irreversible process was occurring, and a new style for a new reality emerging before his eyes.

If one looks at the war art of the later war years — and this is true not only of poetry, but of painting and prose too — one sees how fundamental this change of tradition was. Language and images change, traditional conceptions of space and time are disordered, and connections to what had been living traditions — especially the Romantic tradition — are denied. Viewed historically, these disorderings and denials seem necessary responses to the war, but in individual cases they present themselves as abrupt and conscious breaks with repudiated traditions, acts of will by which a style is created that denies its own past, and in which the act of denial is often a part of the work's statement.

One can see this process in two short poems, one by Graves, the other by Rosenberg. First, Graves's 'A Dead Boche', a poem that records an incident in Mametz Wood during the Battle of the Somme:

> To you who'd read my songs of War
>   And only hear of blood and fame,
> I'll say (you've heard it said before)
>   'War's Hell!' and if you doubt the same,
> To-day I found in Mametz Wood
>   A certain cure for lust of blood:
>
> Where, propped against a shattered trunk,
>   In a great mess of things unclean,
> Sat a dead Boche; he scowled and stunk
>   With clothes and face a sodden green,
> Big-bellied, spectacled, crop-haired,
>   Dribbling black blood from nose and beard.[5]

A shocking, ugly poem: but if you stop to think about it, the situation is actually a conventional Romantic scene: a man alone in a wood, leaning against a tree. But it isn't a vernal wood, and the Boche is receiving no impulses from it. Romantic nature is present in parody, and the force of the poem depends in part on the fact that it *is* present.

The dead Boche is in the title and in the centre of the scene, but the poem isn't really about him; it is about the issue of style that the presence of corpses and shattered trees in woods raises. The poem is addressed to a distanced audience — a 'you', someone who reads poems about war, and who has certain rhetorical expectations. Graves rejects that rhetoric, and offers instead an alternative anti-rhetoric — a rhetoric that is appropriate to the reality of war, with its dead men and its dead nature. It is a rhetoric of pure description, without metaphors and without abstractions, naming no values, not even implying any. The scene that Graves creates in his second stanza is as close to the unmediated actuality of war itself as language can get. And that certainly was what he was aiming for: 'the ideal,' he wrote to Sassoon in September 1917,

> is to use common and simple words which everyone can understand and yet not set up a complex by such vulgarities but to make the plain words do the work of the coloured ones . . .[6]

What Graves did in 'A Dead Boche' was to take a Romantic convention and thrust war into it, turning landscape into landscape-with-corpse,

and making the plain words of war do the work of the coloured
words of Romantic poetry. You find something similar in Rosenberg's
'Returning, we hear the larks':

> Sombre the night is.
> And though we have our lives, we know
> What sinister threat lurks there.
>
> Dragging these anguished limbs, we only know
> This poison-blasted track opens on our camp —
> On a little safe sleep.
>
> But hark! joy — joy — strange joy.
> Lo! heights of night ringing with unseen larks.
> Music showering our upturned list'ning faces.
>
> Death could drop from the dark
> As easily as song —
> But song only dropped,
> Like a blind man's dreams on the sand
> By dangerous tides,
> Like a girl's dark hair for she dreams no ruin lies
>   there,
> Or her kisses where a serpent hides.[7]

The most striking thing about this poem is what Rosenberg has done
with the skylark — Shelley's skylark, but also Shakespeare's and
Hardy's, the Romantic image of the creative imagination in Nature. He
introduces this image, and the related Romantic word for this kind of
experience — joy — but only to set them against the denying reality of
war. War has added an element to the Nature in which larks sing: it has
added death (as it added the dead Boche to Graves's wood), and that
addition disturbs the poem — disturbs both its natural world, so that the
lark becomes a night bird, and its rhetoric, so that what begins as a
'realistic' war poem ends in a phantasmagoria in which inherited images
from Romantic poetry — dreams, tide, hair, kisses — are rhetorically
tangled and blurred.

   Shelley's skylark loses its Romantic power in Rosenberg's poem; and
so, elsewhere, does Shelley himself. He appears in Owen's 'A Terre',
where a blinded soldier says:

> 'I shall be one with nature, herb, and stone,'
> Shelley would tell me. Shelley would be stunned . . .[8]

and more elaborately in Graves's 'Sorley's Weather', where the poet, at
home on leave and comfortably indoors with a fire and his favourite
books, rejects that cosiness for the rain that blows outside:

> Yet rest there, Shelley, on the sill,
> For though the winds come frorely,
> I'm away to the rain-blown hill
> And the ghost of Sorley.[9]

Sorley is the young war poet Charles Sorley, killed in action in France in
October 1915. His book of poems, *Marlborough and other Poems*, was
published posthumously; Graves read it and wrote to a friend: 'It seems
ridiculous to fall in love with a dead man as I have found myself doing
but he seems to have been one so entirely after my own heart in his loves
and hates, besides having been just my own age . . .'[10]

In 'Sorley's Weather' Graves was choosing between two poets —
Shelley and Sorley — but he was doing something more. He was
choosing between traditions, rejecting Romanticism (and its cosy
descendant, Georgianism) and allying himself with a new war tradition.
Not only choosing it, constructing it: making Sorley, the first dead of
the war poets who mattered, into a kind of ancestor, from whom the
line of descent would run to Graves, and from Graves to Sassoon, and
on to Owen — a curious genealogy of men of the same generation, a
'family' of war poets who among them shaped the tradition of war
poetry, not only for their war, but for the next.

As the new tradition of war poetry began to take shape in the third year
of the war, so also did the new war painting, though slowly and with
difficulty. By 1917, most of the promising young painters were on
active service, in widely scattered posts. Henry Lamb was working as a
medical officer in Palestine, Wyndham Lewis and William Roberts were
in the artillery in France, the Nash brothers, Paul and John, were in the
infantry at Ypres, Stanley Spencer was in the hills near Salonika and his
brother Gilbert was in a hospital in the Sinai. Only Eric Kennington and
Nevinson were in England; they had both seen army service in France,
and had been invalided out. Masterman set about finding out who these
young painters were, and where they were, seeking advice from men
of reputation in the art world — the painters Bone and William
Rothenstein, Robbie Ross the art critic, and collector Arnold
Bennett.

The method by which Masterman chose his Official War Artists had a number of important consequences. First, by choosing primarily artists who had had experience in the fighting war, he was making it certain that they would be young painters, and therefore probable that they would be Modernists. And second, he was determining that their paintings would not be made out of the stock images of past military art, but out of direct experience. He imposed no limits on what that rendered experience should be: when Nevinson asked if there were any subject that he should avoid, Masterman replied 'No, no ... Paint anything you please.'[11] A third consequence followed from the late date at which the War Artist programme was begun, and the further delays in making appointments: it became inevitable that the version of war painted would be a late version, from the years when, as Gosse put it, the gallantry and the optimism had passed away.

In this selection process, what I have been calling the aesthetic of direct experience seems to have become a matter of official policy. Masterman could scarcely have hit upon it for aesthetic reasons: he seems to have had no aesthetic sense at all where the visual arts were concerned. What his method implies, rather, is a sense of the war itself — that it was unique and unimaginable, and therefore had to be experienced before it could be truly rendered, and experienced if possible as a combatant.

It does not follow, however, that the pictures produced by the war painters were literal representations of war. It is an evident paradox that though Masterman sent experienced soldier-artists to the fighting fronts to render the war directly, yet the best of their paintings were not realistic in the ordinary sense of the word. We have seen how Nevinson's Futurism made another version of reality possible; but he was not the only war artist of whom this was true. Paul Nash wrote home from the Front: 'I begin to believe in the Vorticist doctrine of destruction almost,'[12] and Wyndham Lewis, who was already a Vorticist, found that

> War, and especially those miles of hideous desert known as 'the Line' in Flanders and France, presented me with a subject-matter so consonant with the austerity of that 'abstract' vision I had developed, that it was an easy transition.[13]

In all of these cases the point is the same: a Modernist method that before the war had seemed violent and distorting was seen to be realistic on the Western Front. Modernism had not changed, but reality had.

The pictures that these young Modernists painted of the war are mainly 'landscapes' — paintings, that is, of the surface of the earth — but with some fundamental differences. Space is derationalized and defamiliarized here: the earth is seen from a great height, or from a position at ground level or below, or from an improbable position in mid-air; and the background is left empty, or disappears, so that distance doesn't run out to a horizon line, but simply disintegrates. On the earth, in these pictures, there are no examples of architecture, no aesthetically pleasing ruins, no signs of previous habitation. More than that, there are no natural forms — no trees that retain the shape of trees, no natural bodies of water, not even natural shapes in the earth itself. Human figures are either altogether absent, or are rendered as tiny, insignificant figures, or are distorted and mechanized. There is no appreciative 'spectator' to these scenes, as there is in Bone's 'Battle of the Somme': you might say that he isn't there because if he were he would be killed; but he's also not there because these are not scenes for which appreciation is an appropriate response.

Nothing in these pictures reminds one of the English landscape tradition; the world that they render is beyond landscape. 'No pen or drawing can convey this country,' Nash wrote home in 1917,

> ... Sunset and sunrise are blasphemous, they are mockeries to man, only the black rain out of the bruised and swollen clouds all through the bitter black of night is fit atmosphere in such a land. The rain drives on, the stinking mud becomes more evilly yellow, the shell holes fill up with green–white water, the roads and tracks are covered in inches of slime, the black dying trees ooze and sweat and the shells never cease.[14]

This is a very pictorial description, but it isn't a landscape; it is rather an *anti*-landscape in words, very like the anti-landscape that Owen described in his letter about Bone's 'Somme Pictures'. It is as though the war had annihilated Nature, and with it the whole tradition of Romantic landscape. One of Nash's war paintings, of Passchendaele, is titled simply 'Void', and his first post-war exhibition was called 'Void of War'.

The best of the English war painters solved the formal problem of how to paint the annihilated Nature of war by adopting the anti-naturalistic conventions of Modernism. But a further problem remained that was not formal. A painter might see the war as a Modernist painter, but he could not avoid feeling it as a man. 'I am no longer an artist interested and curious,' Nash wrote to his wife,

I am a messenger who will bring back word from the men who are fighting to those who want the war to go on for ever. Feeble, inarticulate, will be my message, but it will have a bitter truth, and may it burn their lousy souls.[15]

And how do you paint *that*? War itself might be Vorticist, but anger and pity are not, and cannot be.

Nash's solution to this problem was not a polemical one. He continued to paint his geometrical, unpopulated landscapes, without any visible expression of anger or pity. But this does not mean that he was not painting his feelings about war; he was simply doing so in a more subtle way. Before the war, Nash had been developing as a painter of symbolic landscapes rather in the manner of Blake and Palmer, and if you keep that in mind, then his trench-scapes seem bitter comments on his own Romantic vision, and on the whole Romantic tradition in painting. And to make sure that his viewers did not miss his point, he began to give his paintings titles that bitterly and ironically evoked the lost landscape tradition: 'Meadow with Copse' (a shell-pocked No-Man's Land with a few shattered tree trunks), 'Landscape: Year of Our Lord 1917' (where the irony is in both parts of the title), and 'We Are Making a New World' (more shell holes, more dead trees, and a sun that rises from — or sets into — a bank of blood-red clouds).

Nevinson's solution was more direct. He began to paint figure-paintings that were not in any way geometrical or abstract or Futurist — of a child killed in an air raid, a shell-shocked soldier, a doctor at work in a first-aid station. These pictures seem intentionally clumsy and representational, compared to his Futurist paintings, but Nevinson considered them both important and new — not in technique (which seemed not to matter to him) but in what they said. Of 'The Doctor' (plate 11) he wrote, in a letter to Robbie Ross:

I regard this picture quite apart from how it is painted expresses an absolutely NEW outlook on the so–called 'sacrifice' of war which up to the present is only felt by privates and a few officers who are to all purposes inarticulate, and whose outlook I could only divine through my constant and intimate experiences with them as an orderly for two years, that queer insight that I found I got through nursing them just fresh from the lines and mostly quite helpless.[16]

In other pictures Nevinson shifted his attention to the non-combatants at home, and painted satirical portraits with titles like 'War Profiteers' (two painted, over-dressed young women, perhaps prostitutes), and 'He Gained a Fortune But He Gave a Son' (a portly, prosperous-looking man, no doubt an industrialist — see plate 18). These are pictures that express the soldier's hostility towards civilians, including women; in their technique they anticipate the post-war works of George Grosz more than any English painter, but in their subjects and their tone they are close to the poems of Sassoon.

Nevinson did not abandon trench scenes altogether, but in the last years of the war he sometimes painted them in a more representational style than he had formerly used. That style go him into trouble in March 1918, when a new exhibition of his paintings opened in London. Among the pictures was one title 'Paths of Glory', which was labelled and hung, but which no one saw: it was covered with brown paper, and marked 'Censored' (see plates 13 and 14). It is a picture of the Front, as one might see it from the parapet of a trench — the shell-torn dead earth, the barbed wire — but on that dead earth are two dead English soldiers. It is the first war painting by an English painter that I know of that is a realistic picture of dead men: not war, but what the dead really look like. Nevinson had committed two offences in exhibiting this picture as he did: he had violated a DORA regulation forbidding the representation of the dead; and by labelling it 'censored' he had violated another regulation (or so he was told) that forbade the unofficial use of that term. A few months later William Orpen exhibited a painting of even deader soldiers — that is, of corpses in a more advanced state of decomposition — without any official opposition. But his picture was titled 'Dead Germans in a Trench' (plate 15); apparently it was all right to paint the dead, so long as they were German dead.

Like the war poets, these painters began, in the last year or so of the war, to establish a new tradition of war painting, though it developed more slowly. There were publications of their pictures — *Modern War Paintings* by Nevinson in 1917, and *British Artists at the Front*, containing pictures by Nevinson, John Lavery, Nash, and Kennington, in 1918. And there were exhibitions: Nevinson's second show in March 1918, Nash in May, Kennington in June, Orpen in July. By the end of the war's fourth year, in August 1918, an interested person in London, at least, could have seen a fair number of war paintings in the new tradition.

In these paintings that interested viewer would have seen the end of two traditions. The more conservative painters represented the end of the notion that war was a studio subject, based on slight observation or on none, and the beginning of a new realism that came out of direct experience — not of painting a war but of fighting one. It was this realism, and this experience, that Robert Graves praised in Kennington's work, in the introduction that he wrote for the catalogue of Kennington's 1918 show:

> This is no series of superficial war impressions that Mr. Kennington has recorded: here is no genteel amusement at the gaudy slap-dash camouflage on a big howitzer; no discreet civilian wonder at distant shells bursting along a chalk ridge or the long procession of ammuni- tion lorries moving along the pavé road; no old-maidish sympathy for convalescents at the base hospital. Mr. Kennington is not the embarrassed visitor in a strange drawing room nor the bewildered old lady at her first football match: he is a soldier, and at home in trench and shell hole, knows what is happening, what to see, where and how to see it; more important still, he has the trench point of view, and cannot forget how in the dark days of 1914 he gulped his rum and tea, fried his bacon, filled his sand-bag, ducked under his first bullet, stared into black night across the parapet and endured terror and misery as a private in the infantry.[17]

In this view, the artist is not separable from the soldier: as in much war poetry, the assumption is that only those who have suffered can imagine truly.

Other painters — those who had been experimental painters before the war — recorded another kind of ending: the end of Romantic Nature, and of its visual expression, the Romantic landscape. On the Western Front, Nature was dead — not simply in the sense that growing things could not survive the destruction there, but in the sense that the Wordsworthian idea of natural benevolence had died. And if Nature was dead, then landscape-painting was dead too. The paintings of men like Nash, Nevinson, and Lewis are not landscapes; in some cases — Nash's, for instance — they are more like elegies for the death of landscape.

Arnold Bennett, who wrote the catalogue introduction for Nash's 'Void of War' show, saw a new set of conventions in the pictures that made them the antithesis of conventional landscapes:

> Lieutenant Nash has seen the Front simply and largely. He has found the essentials of it — that is to say, disfigurement, danger, desolation, ruin, chaos — and little figures of men creeping devotedly and

tragically over the waste. The convention he uses is ruthlessly selective. The wave-like formations of shell-holes, the curves of shell-bursts, the straight lines and sharply-defined angles of wooden causeways, decapitated trees, the angle of obdurate masonry, the weight of heavy skies, the human pawns of battle, — these things are repeated again and again, monotonously, endlessly. The artist cannot get away from them. They obsess him; and they obsess him because they are the obsessions of trench-life.[18]

This is an acute description not only of Nash's paintings but of the new tradition of war painting generally: its first element *disfigurement*, the gross violation of that natural beauty that had been the first principle of traditional landscape painting; then *danger* and *desolation*, responses to the visual scene that are new and strange in a painter's world; and finally *ruin* and *chaos*, two terms that acknowledge a formless, devastated earth.

Bennett said that the disfigurements of the earth obsessed Nash because they were the obsessions of trench life, and many letters and diaries of men at the Front support that judgement. It is striking how often the words *landscape* and *nature* appear in those writings, in passages that take note of how these concepts have been transformed by war. It may be the unnatural presence of danger and death that effects the change: 'It's curious', the poet-philosopher T.E. Hulme wrote, 'how the mere fact that in a certain direction there really are the German lines, seems to alter the feeling of a landscape.'[19] Or it may be the felt contrast, not of war and peace, but of war and landscape: 'Every pleasant landscape now seems to suggest the horrors of war by contrast' (Ben Keeling).[20] Or the unnatural deadness of a front-line spring: 'Spring we do have here, but in an abortive sort of way. The felled trees bloom, but for the last time, and forget-me-nots spring up among the ruins. But everything is sad, and our few flowers are like wreaths among so much desolation' (Herbert Read).[21] Or it might simply be a recognition that a man with his head down in a trench is deprived of the ordinary person's opportunities to look at the world, as C.E. Montague explained:

> At most parts of the line a man in the front trench is cut off from landscape. To look at a tree behind the enemy's lines may be to give a mark to a sniper hidden in its boughs. By day you see the upper half of the dome of the sky, and, through loopholes, a few yards of rough earth or chalk, then the nebulous wire and, through its thin places, perhaps a few uniforms, blue, grey or brown, lying beyond, among the coarse grass and weeds.[22]

Which is to say, very discreetly, that such landscape as a soldier can see is altered by the presence of death in it.

Out of these reactions, two recognitions emerge: first, that those qualities of the physical world that the words *landscape* and *nature* once designated have been altered by war; and second, that the relations between man and the earth implied in those terms have also been changed. Natural beauty and natural benevolence have withdrawn from the ravaged scene; and man is no longer secure and at ease there. Nature may remain, in the soldier's mind, in the poem or the painting, but it remains as an absence — the quality, the value, the experience of human belonging that once existed, and should exist still, but that has been displaced by the war. Just as Shelley and Keats are named in war poems in order to be rejected, so Nature appears in poems and in paintings in order to be disfigured, annihilated, made irrelevant to the reality of war.

Disfigured Nature was a trench reality that changed the war artists' world. Wilfred Owen described that change in a letter from the Front in 1917:

> I suppose I can endure cold, and fatigue, and the face-to-face death, as well as another; but extra for me there is the universal pervasion of *Ugliness*. Hideous landscapes, vile noises, foul language and nothing but foul, even from one's own mouth (for all are devil ridden), everything unnatural, broken, blasted; the distortion of the dead, whose unburiable bodies sit outside the dug-outs all day, all night, the most execrable sights on earth. In poetry we call them the most glorious. But to sit with them all day, all night . . . and a week later to come back and find them still sitting there, in motionless groups, THAT is what saps the 'soldierly spirit.'[23]

Ugliness is the subject of this passage, but it is more than the subject: it is the visual and verbal reality out of which the war world was made. War poetry would therefore have to be made out of ugliness too, if it was to be the truth-telling medium that Owen wanted it to be. War is the end of beauty — and the end of beauty's conventions: that was one of the truths that had to be told, and one of the things that Owen's war poems are about. One could say essentially the same thing about paintings like Nash's 'Landscape: Year of Our Lord 1917': it is a painting made out of ugliness, and it is a kind of truth-telling picture, a testimony. These two elements — the ugliness and the testimony — shape the new war art of the last years of the war.

The movement that was beginning to take form might be called a

ne avant-garde, but it was not avant-garde in the usual sense of
rm. These poets and painters were working in opposition to the
al views and values of society, true enough, but in terms of war,
not in terms of art. No wartime painter was as advanced in his technique
as the pre-war Futurists and Vorticists had been; 'Experimentation is
waived,' Wyndham Lewis wrote in the introduction to his post-war
exhibition of war pictures: 'I have tried to do with the pencil and brush
what storytellers like Chekhov or Stendhal did in their books.'[24] The
principal war poets allied themselves not with the new avant-garde of
Eliot and Pound and Imagism, but with the Georgians: Owen wrote to
his mother: 'I am held peer by the Georgians; I am a poet's poet.'[25] And
Sassoon and Graves appeared in Marsh's *Georgian Poetry* volumes. The
prose writers — diarists and letter-writers, for there was no war fiction
yet to correspond to the poems and paintings — seemed not to be aware
of form at all.

Certainly there was a change in imaginations, and certainly that
change arose out of direct experience of war, and had consequences for
the forms in which the war was imagined. If those forms seemed
Modernist, avant-garde, even Vorticist, as they did in many war
paintings, it was because the war seemed to confirm the experimental
visions of pre-war art. But they were modern in a different way. 'There
is nothing there [at the Front] you cannot imagine,' Lewis wrote to
Pound: 'but it has the unexpected quality of reality. Also the imagined
thing and the felt are in two different categories.'[26] The merely
imaginary had become felt reality. On the whole, the painters
responded to that reality in more experimental ways than the poets did;
but painters and poets had this in common, they shared a new reality
that was fundamentally different from what civilians saw, and from
what they had seen before the war. That difference distinguished the
soldier from the civilian; it also distinguished the new war art and war
poetry from previous expressions of the modern kind.

CHAPTER 10

The Lives of the Martyrs

The new art of war was most evident, during the war's last years, in poetry and in painting. One does not find it so readily in imaginative prose of the time, though, for reasons that seem at first obvious enough. The Ministry of Information had not removed prose writers from the Front and made them Official War Novelists; and there weren't many opportunities to write extended imagined accounts of war while in the trenches. But there must have been more to it than that. Perhaps, as Ford had concluded, the war was simply too vast and shapeless to be put into a story; or perhaps the individual soldier's range of vision was too narrow and confined to *see* the war (that was Montague's point about trench-landscape). The lack of a usable tradition must also have been part of the problem; Henty and Kipling were of no help to a man, however gifted a potential novelist, crouched in a trench at Ypres.

Or perhaps the difficulty was that war, while it was being fought, did not seem to be narrative at all, did not seem, that is, to be a continuous and coherent action that moved through related events to a conclusion. One can find support for this thesis in the war novel that Englishmen read most during 1917–18 — a book written not by an English writer, but by a Frenchman. Henri Barbusse's *Le Feu* is the story of an ordinary infantry squad on the Western Front, first in billets and then in battle, told with exact, unsqueamish particularity. It is a realistic novel, in the great French tradition; but it continually violates that tradition. It begins in an unrealistic 'vision', and ends in surrealism, it shifts the person, tense and number of its narrative voice, and it repeatedly protests the incapacity of its own method to render the reality of its subject coherently, because incoherence is the essential principle of that reality. Here, as an example, is Barbusse's account of a pause during a battle:

> We stay there, jumbled together, and sit down. The living have ceased to gasp for breath, the dying have rattled their last, surrounded by smoke and lights and the din of the guns that rolls to all the ends of the earth. We no longer know where we are. There is neither earth nor sky — nothing but a sort of cloud. The first period of inaction is forming in the chaotic drama . . .[1]

Later in the same battle the survivors leave the body of one of their men:

> We leave poor Cocon, the ex-statistician, with a last look, a look too short and almost vacant.
> 'One cannot imagine —' says Volpatte.
> No, one cannot imagine. All these disappearances at once surpass the imagination. There are not enough survivors now.[2]

At the end of the novel, a fatigue party wanders out into the night in an episode that becomes surreal in its fantastic description: heavy rain drowns men on both sides, and mud leaves the opposing armies indistinguishable. The dawn that follows is a symbolic dawn — the dawning of the conviction that war is 'hideous morally as well as physically', and that there must be no more. After which the troops prepare to 'begin war again'. It is a middle-of-the-war ending, like that in Rose Macaulay's *Non-Combatants*.

In formal terms, the shifting narrative style may be a flaw; but if it is one, it is a flaw that many war books shared. It was as though the very act of trying to understand the war, in order to render it in language, engaged the rendering imagination in a continuous process of re-definition — as though the self that recorded changed as the truths it confronted emerged. In Barbusse's case you might argue that the tradition in which he was working — that of the realistic novel of Zola — was adequate as a method for behind-the-line scenes, but inadequate to the challenge of life in battle, where reality became more-than-real. Nash and Lewis had observed much the same thing in painterly terms.

Le Feu is also important for its politics. Barbusse was a Socialist, and the last 'dawn' pages of his novel are a Socialist sermon against war, and for the international cooperation of the working class. These are not new ideas — the Independent Labour Party had been saying these things in England since the war began — but they had not previously been

expressed in a popular work of fiction, one that carried the note of
authority in its account of the war itself.

Le Feu was a highly subversive book, and it appeared at a crucial point
in the history of English attitudes towards the war. It was published in
France in 1916, and won the Prix Goncourt; it appeared in England as
Under Fire, in July 1917, the month during which the Third Battle of
Ypres, commonly known as Passchendaele, began. It was quickly
recognized as important: Robbie Ross described it to a soldier-friend as
'the book your contemporaries talk about most'.[3] Sassoon read it at
Craiglockhart in August, and lent it to Rivers; later he used a passage
from it as the epigraph for *Counter-Attack*. Owen read it, and adapted
some of Barbusse's images for his poem 'The Show'; Wyndham Lewis
read it at the Front, and praised it in a letter to Pound.[4]

But perhaps the most significant response to *Under Fire* was that of
C.E. Montague. In the autumn of 1917 Montague was writing his
preface to the official publication of Muirhead Bone's *Western Front*
drawings, and he felt obliged to defend Bone against the charge that
Bone had not drawn the real war, war 'at its centre'.

> And if you ask who has drawn war 'at its centre' [he wrote], you may
> be referred to M. Barbusse, who has written a book in which war is
> all mud and blood and an agony of fatigue, as it is to some men; and
> the fault of Mr. Bone's art, from this view, is that in drawing our
> front he had drawn too much of its life and too little of death and
> wounds. And then perhaps it is hinted that we are all in league to hide
> from our friends at home some extreme, mysterious horror which is
> 'really' war, war 'as it is,' something which, if it leaked out, would
> make the world lay down its arms on the spot, and the nations kiss
> and be friends.[5]

This apologia is more than simply an attack on Barbusse: it is a response
to a growing conviction among civilians that there was a real war, a war
of death and horror, that was fundamentally different from the official
version, and that had been withheld from them. By the time Montague
wrote, that reality had begun to find expression, and to reach the
English public: the first war poems of Sassoon and Graves had appeared,
and Nevinson had had his first exhibition, and the first of the personal
memoirs had been published. But in the most popular medium — prose
fiction — there had been as yet no truth-telling English example:
Under Fire was the first novel to reach the English public with an
unameliorated rendering of the horrors of the war. To soldier-readers

on both sides it was a faithful testimony[6]; to reviewers it was 'a magnificent tract'[7]; but to the world of official opinion, for which Montague was a spokesman, it was a threat.

Another book by a Frenchman was as important to Englishmen in the late war years as Barbusse's, though in a different way. Georges Duhamel's *Vie des Martyrs* was published in France in 1917, and appeared in England, as *The New Book of Martyrs*, in March 1918. Duhamel was a poet and playwright who was also a doctor; he served as a military surgeon on the Western Front throughout the war, and he made his book out of that experience. Unlike Barbusse, Duhamel did not question the necessity of the war, and he had no apparent politics. He was simply a compassionate observer, who recorded the lives of the common soldiers who came under his care. There are no 'war stories' in the usual sense in his vignettes; Duhamel was not interested in battles, but only in the human wreckage that emerged from them. Nor is there any action: how could there be, in existences so devastated by injury and pain? The 'lives' in his book are narratives only in a peculiarly passive sense: the men are martyrs, and they do what martyrs have always done — they suffer, and they die.

Duhamel set down his motives for writing the book in two passages. In the opening chapter he addressed his reader — the ordinary civilian, such a one as might have just come from visiting wounded soldiers:

> Are you sure that you recognise them? You have just been looking at them, are you sure that you have seen them?
>
> Under their bandages are wounds you cannot imagine. Below the wounds, in the depths of the mutilated flesh, a soul, strange and furtive, is stirring in feverish exaltation, a soul which does not readily reveal itself, which expresses itself artlessly, but which I would fain make you understand.[8]

And at the end, he spoke to the soldiers themselves:

> it is also my mission to record the history of those who have been the sacrificial victims of the race, without gloss, in all its truth and simplicity; the history of the men you have shown yourselves to be in suffering.[9]

In these passages there are two ideas that are important in the history of imaginings of the war. In the first it is the notion that men who have fought and suffered have been transformed beyond the understanding of those who have not: this is the Us/Them separation that one finds in many war writings of the war's later years, here put into medical terms. In the second, it is the conception of the common soldier not as hero, or man-of-action, or even defender of anything, but simply as sacrificial victim, the man who has endured.

The importance of Duhamel's book was recognized in England even before it was translated. Middleton Murry reviewed the French edition in the *Times Literary Supplement* in June 1917, and drew a lesson for Englishmen from it.

> Those who are watching French literature with the sensitive atten-
> tion that comes of old sympathy begin to be aware of a profound
> change in it. They respond reverently to the tremors of a painful
> birth; the echoes of a grim and terrible perturbation of the human
> consciousness perturb them too. Even though they try to hide the
> truth from their souls by a sleek assumption of foreknowledge, the
> moment comes when they must allow that the full discovery of pain
> and death, which has been given to this generation above all others,
> is pregnant with consequences that may shape the creative mind of
> man.
>
> And then they turn with disappointment, that will not be resigned,
> to the literature of England. Are we blind, will our lips not move, are
> we afraid? Shall there not be in England too that bravery of the spirit
> without which the bravery of the body will pass with the body into
> forgetfulness?[10]

What Murry was saying was that the war had changed reality, but it had not changed English literature. In fact a change *had* begun (at Craiglockhart, for instance), but it was not yet very noticeable, and it had not yet found expression in English fiction. Englishmen who wanted that new reality turned, therefore, to two French examples, which seemed to render war as it really was, as a history of endless, helpless suffering.

Like *Under Fire*, *The New Book of Martyrs* was widely read in England in the last year of the war. Robert Nichols read it in January 1918, and thought it 'great stuff'[11]; Sassoon read it in May in billets near Arras, and thought Duhamel the equal of Barbusse. It is clear from passages that Sassoon copied into his diary that he found in Duhamel a confirmation of his own attitudes towards the war. In one diary entry he quoted lines from his own poem, 'Autumn':

> Their lives are like the leaves . . .
> O martyred youth and manhood overthrown,
> The burden of your wrongs is on my head

and followed them with these sentences from *The New Book of Martyrs*:

> It was written that you should suffer without purpose and without
> hope. But I will not let all your sufferings be lost in the abyss.[12]

What Sassoon's poem has in common with Duhamel's book is obvious:
they are both about martyrdom. It is an idea that was becoming current,
in various forms, in the latter half of the war. Clearly a profound change
was occurring, in some minds at least, as to the essential nature of
war.

What had changed most was the sense of the difference in scale and in
power between the individual soldier and the war in which he was
caught. The war itself had come to seem the only source of energy in its
world: guns roared, bullets flew, armies moved; but individual men
could only suffer. Years later, Wyndham Lewis would describe the
Hemingway hero as 'the man things are done to'[13]; that phrase exactly
describes the soldier-figures who huddle in the poems and prose
writings, and even the paintings, of the last years of the war: men who
lose their nerve, men who inflict wounds on their own bodies, suicides,
cowards, mental cases, and hysterics, men who are sent to Dottyville,
the *damaged* men; and the others, the silent, passive sufferers who simply
endure. They are in the poems of Sassoon ('Died of Wounds', 'A
Ballad', 'Suicide in the Trenches') and Owen ('The Dead-Beat',
'S.I.W.', 'Mental Cases'). Diaries of serving soldiers suggest that such
cases were common in the trenches; the diarists record the suicides and
the S.I.W.s (self-inflicted wounds) because they are part of the story, but
generally without condemnation. Here, as an example, is a passage from
the unpublished diary of a private in the London Regiment ('The
London Scottish'):

> 29 June 1916: I was 20 yd. from one of the Kensington's 13th Regt last
> week, when he shot himself through the foot, just to get back to
> England out of it, of course he will get about 84 days field punish-
> ment for it, after the wound has healed up. I went over and fetched
> assistance to him and extracted the empty case out of his rifle, what a
> feeling he will have later on if it takes a long time to heal up, and to
> know he done it himself, but still he is not the only one that as [*sic*]
> done likewise.[14]

In the later years of the war, such personal records began to be published in England, composing a new genre of war writing that had a considerable role in the creation of the growing sense of 'war at its centre' that made Montague so nervous. You might call this new genre war memoirs of the dead: it consists of those volumes of letters, diaries, and journals of men killed in action that were edited by friends or relatives, and were published primarily as memorials, but in some cases also as testimonies against the war. I have quoted from two such books: *Keeling Letters and Recollections*, and Graeme West's *Diary of a Dead Officer* (both published in 1918). There were many others, published late in the war or after the Armistice. Such books have certain common qualities: randomness of focus, shifting attitudes towards the war, an abrupt, unfinished termination — the qualities that you would expect in the records of a young life that came to a sudden end.

One example, however, is different: a complete narrative that moves through experience to judgement and a fully realized ending. Bernard Adams had been a Greek scholar at Oxford (he took a First Class degree in Classics), but his goal was to do missionary work in India, and to prepare for that vocation he had run a hostel for Indian students in London before the war. In short, he was a scholarly, intelligent, religious, dedicated man. When the war began, Adams joined the Welch Fusiliers, and served as an officer with Sassoon and Graves. He went to the Front in October 1915, and was wounded in June of the following year and sent back to England to recover; so he missed the big-name battles of the first two years — Ypres and Loos and the Somme. During his convalescence he wrote *Nothing of Importance*, sub-titled 'A Record of Eight Months at the Front with a Welsh Battalion October, 1915, to June, 1916'. Then he returned to France, where he was wounded in an attack in February 1917, and died the following day.

Sassoon read *Nothing of Importance* soon after it was published in September 1917, and wrote to Graves about it: 'If you and I had rewritten and added to it it would have been a classic; as it is it is just Bill Adams — and a very good book — expressing his quiet kindliness to perfection. He saw a lot through those spectacles of his.'[15] Indeed he did see a lot — his book is the clearest and most intelligent account of ordinary trench life that I know; Sassoon and Graves might have made it more dramatic, and more literary, but they could not have made it better than it is. But what is most interesting about Adams's book is

not what he saw, but how he told what he saw, and how the telling
changes as the very act of writing leads him to contemplate the meaning
of his war.

Adams defines the formal nature of his book in a sentence in his
preface: 'It is the spirit of the war as it came to me,' he writes, 'first in
big incoherent impressions, later as a more intelligible whole.'[16] He gets
that process into the first part of the book, where he tells of his first
impressions of war, by dividing himself into two voices: one is himself
as a young officer on his first tour of duty in France, who keeps an
excited diary of what he sees; the other is the man who is writing the
book, a man who has been changed by his war and his wound, and who
comments, ironically but kindly, on his first self's innocence. He
quotes, as an example, his early diary entry of a German shelling, then
adds, in his old soldier's voice:

> As I read some of these sentences, true in every detail as they are, I
> cannot help smiling. For it was no 'bombardment' that took place on
> our left all day; it was merely the Germans potting one of our trench-
> mortar positions![17]

The innocent self's facts are true, but the feeling is wrong; the spirit of
war has not yet come to him. Or take this exchange, further along in the
book, between the experienced Adams and a new young officer:

> I met Edwards by the dug-out as he returned from inspecting the
> Lewis guns.
>   'Remember,' I said, 'I told you the "First Hundred Thousand"
> leaves out bits? Did you see those R.E.'s who were gassed?'
>   Edwards nodded.
>   'Well,' I said. 'That's a thing it leaves out.'[18]

Adams's quiet narrative puts those bits back in; gradually he corrects the
official, popular version of trench war, revising himself as he goes, as
though his book were an edited text. As he does, his style becomes grim
and realistic, in the flat, descriptive manner of other trench narratives
that I have cited — Keeling's, or Tawney's, or Hamilton's. But it also
becomes introspective and self-questioning, as those other texts rarely
do. 'As I write,' he says half-way through the book,

> I feel inclined to throw the whole book in the fire. It seems a
> desecration to tell of these things. Do I not seem to be exulting in the
> tragedy? Should not he who feels deeply keep silent? Sometimes I

think so. And yet it is the truth, word for word the truth; so I must write it.[19]

At the end of the book, where the young officer thinks about the spirit of war from the distance that his experience and his wound have created, the tone moves beyond realism, and becomes testimony:

It is hard to trace ultimate causes [Adams thinks]. It is hard to fix absolute responsibility. There were many seeds sown, scattered, and secretly fostered before they produced this harvest of blood. The seeds of cruelty, selfishness, ambition, avarice, and indifference, are always liable to swell, grow, and bud, and blossom suddenly into the red flower of war. Let every man look into his heart, and if the seeds are there let him make quick to root them out while there is time; unless he wishes to join those glittering eyes that look down upon the arena.

These are the seeds of war. And it is because they know that we, too, are not free from them, that certain men have stood out from the arena as a protest against war. These men are real heroes, who for their conscience's sake are enduring taunts, ignominy, misunderstanding, and worse. Most men and women in the arena are cursing them, and, as they struggle in agony and anguish, they beat their hands at them and cry 'You do not care.' I, too, have cursed them, when I was mad with pain. But I know them, and I know that they are true men. I would not have one less. They are witnesses against war. And I, too, am fighting war. Men do not understand them now, but one day they will.[20]

This seems a surprising conclusion for a man who is about to return to the Front. There is no mention of the enemy, or of war aims, no suggestion of a real motive for returning. Instead there is praise for conscientious objectors, and the odd assertion that he and they share a common cause.

Like *Under Fire*, *Nothing of Importance* is a book that moves from style to style. Nevertheless, it has a wholeness about it that the style-changes do not diminish (and that the other, posthumous collections of soldiers' writings cannot, by their nature, have). It is a complete, concluded record of an intelligent man's growth through experience to a true knowledge of war. At the end, the reader is certain of two things: that Adams understands the war, and that he will die in it. That confluence of understanding and expected martyrdom gives the last pages a tragic cast that is very moving. It is as though they were already posthumous, even as they were being written.

The figure of the soldier as martyr or victim is common in the writings of serving soldiers in the last years of the war; but one finds it also in the war writings of civilians. An early example is Paul Sandomir — the brother of Alix, the central character in Rose Macaulay's *Non-Combatants* — whose death from a self-inflicted wound is treated with sympathy and without judgement, both by Alix and by the young soldier who tells her the story. A later, and more complex one is Christopher Baldry, in Rebecca West's *Return of the Soldier*, which was serialized from January 1918, and published as a book in June. West's novel is a special example of an established English genre: a 'country house' novel, but a wartime one that is dominated by women. The action never departs from its Thames Valley setting, and is doubly distanced from the war: Baldry is a shell-shocked officer who has lost his memory, and has forgotten the war; and the narrator is a woman, his cousin, who must compose her vision out of second-hand images, though she does so vividly:

> Of late I had had bad dreams about him. By night I saw Chris running across the brown rottenness of No Man's Land, starting back here because he trod upon a hand, not even looking there because of the awfulness of an unburied head, and not till my dream was packed full of horror did I see him pitch forward on his knees as he reached safety — if it was that. For on the war-films I have seen men slip down as softly from the trench parapet, and none but the grimmer philosophers would say that they had reached safety by their fall.[21]

(The war film is obviously the faked scene in *Battle of the Somme*; but the hand and the unburied head must have another source — a letter or a war diary, or some returned soldier's tale, perhaps.)

Chris Baldry's amnesia is more than simply an example of the effect of war on a sensitive nature: it is a symbol of the pastness of the pre-war past. He comes home, not to the wartime present and his waiting wife, but to a pre-war past when he was happy with another woman. He has recovered that past by forgetting the present that has erased it: it is paradise regained, an Eden of love and peace. The story of *Return of the Soldier* is of how Chris's wife, with the help of a psychiatrist (one of the first, surely, in English fiction), compels him to leave that Eden by forcing memory upon him, and so returns him to the present reality of war, and to his proper social role as 'the soldier'.

At the end of the novel, at the moment of his 'return', his wife anxiously asks the narrator to look out of the window at her husband, once more restored to himself: 'Jenny, Jenny!' she cries. 'How does he look?'

'Oh ...' How could I say it? 'Every inch a soldier.'

She crept behind me to the window, peered over my shoulder and saw.

I heard her suck in her breath with satisfaction. 'He's cured!' she whispered slowly. 'He's cured!'[22]

Cured is a bitterly ironic word here; and so is soldier. A decent man has been cured of happiness and peace, which can have no place in a world at war; his cure is something that has been done to him, against his will, in order to return him to the reality of suffering and perhaps death.

This view of the soldier as a victim is perhaps not surprising in a novel by an intelligent, radically thinking young woman in the last year of the war. But it turned up in other places in 1918 that are surprising: for example, in John Bull, the newspaper run by Horatio Bottomley. Bottomley was a rabble-rousing former MP whose recruiting speeches had helped to fill Kitchener's Army, and had made him famous, and his paper was what he was — jingoistic, loud, inflammatory, and very popular. Yet in February 1918 he took up the case of a young officer whom he ought to have despised — a man who had been charged with desertion in the face of the enemy, and who had been court-martialled and shot. 'Shot at Dawn' the banner headline in John Bull read: 'A Trench Tragedy. Plea for the Boy Officer.'[23]

It is a pitiful story. The accused was one Edwin Dyett, a twenty-one-year-old sub-lieutenant in the Royal Naval Division, who had volunteered for the Navy at the beginning of the war, and had been fighting on land ever since — at Antwerp in the first weeks of the war (where he must have served with Rupert Brooke), then in Gallipoli, and after the withdrawal there, on the Western Front. There, in December 1916, he had taken part in an attack and had got lost in No-Man's Land. When another officer found him and ordered him to join a party moving forward, he refused; the next day he was found in a dugout behind the lines. He was charged with desertion, court-martialled, and convicted, with a recommendation for mercy. Ten days later he was told that he would be shot the next morning; the sentence was carried out as scheduled. He was apparently a weak, nervous man who accepted the army's standards of behaviour sufficiently to despise himself for his weakness; but he behaved well before the firing squad. 'Yes,' he said, 'I can face this, but I couldn't face the Boche.'[24]

Bottomley's concern with the case was primarily as an argument for court-martial reform (and, one might perhaps add, as a circulation booster); but it is nevertheless striking that in the last year of the war a journalist so dedicated to defeating and punishing the Germans could think and write sympathetically about a young man who had been shot for cowardice.

Philip Morrell carried the 'Shot at Dawn' issue of *John Bull* into the House of Commons a few days later when he appealed to the government to give special medical treatment to shell-shock cases instead of shooting them. The government's spokesman replied:

> considering the extraordinary numbers that are at the present time in the British Army, of all classes and creeds, the number of executions has been the most remarkably small in the history of the world.[25]

Exact figures of military executions throughout human history are hard to come by, but insofar as this statement implies unusual British clemency in the First World War it was untrue. During the period from the first day of the war until the end of March 1920 the British shot 345 men. The French executed about the same number, or perhaps slightly fewer — half as many as the Italians, who dealt harshly with deserters after the rout at Caporetto. The Germans executed forty-eight. Not all of these men were convicted of military crimes; about ten per cent of both the British and the German executions were for murder.[26]

The facts of the British executions were not withheld from the victims' families, but were communicated in bluntly worded form letters. Distraught families appealed to their MPs, questions were asked in the House[27], and so gradually the knowledge that English soldiers were being shot by English firing squads must have spread among the civilian population, as well as among troops in the field. In the process, the executions became not only events in the history of the war, but also in the history of the ways in which the war was imagined. Cowardice, desertion and fear became as much a part of the story as heroism, and the coward (or shell-shock victim, or frightened boy) became a possible literary figure, and his fate a possible plot. When Kipling wrote his 'Epitaphs of the War', he included one titled 'The Coward':

> I could not look on Death, which being known,
> Men led me to him, blindfold and alone.[28]

It must have seemed to Kipling that without an executed coward the story of the war, and the cast of its characters, would be incomplete.

Nearly two decades after the war had ended, W.B. Yeats refused to include poems by Owen in his *Oxford Book of Modern Verse* because, he said, 'passive suffering is not a theme for poetry'.[29] Historically speaking, he was wrong, of course; the First World War had changed all that. Even before the war ended, passive suffering had become a theme not only for poetry, but for novels, memoirs, diaries, letters, plays, paintings — for whatever art-forms were at hand through which to express feelings about war. Those wartime expressions were the beginnings of a new myth of war that radically transformed traditional ideas and values. Once the soldier was seen as a victim, the idea of a hero became unimaginable: there would be no more heroic actions in the art of this war. And if entire armies could be imagined composed of such victims — if indeed every army was an army of martyrs — then Victory too must fade from the story, and war become only a long catastrophe, with neither significant action nor direction, a violence that was neither fought nor won, but only endured.

CHAPTER 11

The Last of the Home-Front Wars

As the war entered its fourth year, a few men — all of them soldiers, most with experience of the trenches — began to find the forms and images that would express what they had known, 'war at its centre'. There were not many of them yet: a few poets, a few painters, two French novelists, a playwright (suppressed), a couple of memoirists (dead). They did not constitute a movement, in any organized sense, certainly not an avant-garde; still, there were signs of a radically different kind of war art — an art without heroes, without a tradition, and without Nature, in which men were martyrs and the earth was a devastated anti-landscape.

As this opposing art of war grew, so also did other forms of opposition: the voices of pacifists and peacemakers, of critics and Christians, became more audible. Sometimes these were the voices of soldiers — the voices of Sassoon's protest, of Adams's sad conclusion and Graeme West's failure, of Plowman's resignation from all war, of Colonel Herbert's plea for peace. Sometimes they were the voices of civilians: of Bertrand Russell, of the radical politician E.D. Morel, of Sylvia Pankhurst. One, at least, was the voice of a journal: the *Cambridge Magazine* went on reporting European news and the trials of conscientious objectors.

Opposition to the war was more widespread and more articulate in the last year of the war than it had ever been before; and by what seems almost a natural law, as the voices of opposition swelled, the voices of censure and suppression grew more clamorous too. It was on this essential issue of freedom versus control that the last of the home-front wars was fought. There had been others in the early days — the war against Modernism, the war against German culture, the women's war — but they all seemed to have ended, won or abandoned or simply forgotten in the excitement of the Greater War. Modernism, critics said, had come to an end, neither victorious nor defeated, but simply overtaken by history.[1]

Modern art, German culture, and rioting women posed no threats to the progress of the war in 1917–18. But dissent did, or at least seemed to. Pacifists were refusing to serve in the army, and were persuading others to refuse; advocates of a negotiated peace were weakening the nation's resolve to fight on to total victory; and a permissive, un-English decadence in high places was corrupting English society. Or so patriots said. So the war against dissent went on, and grew fiercer, more vindictive, and more punitive. Morel was arrested under DORA in August 1917 for sending a Union of Democratic Control pamphlet to a neutral country, and was sent to prison for six months; Russell was tried under DORA in early 1918 for an article on 'The German Peace Offer', and also was imprisoned for six months; Sylvia Pankhurst was tried and convicted in October 1918 of the DORA offence of 'attempting to cause mutiny, sedition or dissatisfaction among His Majesty's Forces or civilian population' (the occasion was a Socialist speech that she made in Derbyshire) and was fined thirty pounds and costs.

The *Cambridge Magazine* was never prosecuted, but it was repeatedly attacked in the patriotic press: 'its methods are very German and very cunning,' W.H.D. Rowse wrote in the *New Witness*, adding as a clincher that 'it champions the notorious Russell as a martyr', and G.K. Chesterton declared the magazine to be pro-German, pacifist, and intellectually snobbish; a letter to the *Morning Post* from Fight for Right, a conservative pro-war group, described the *Cambridge* as 'remarkably free from any exhilarating belief in the victory of the Allies' arms or predominating righteousness of their cause', and concluded that it was 'a subtle and powerful instrument of Pacifist suggestion'.[2] Pacifists were regarded with such repugnance and distrust by patriotic Englishmen that in June 1918 Parliament voted to exclude them altogether from post-war political life; the Representation of the People Act disqualified conscientious objectors from voting for a period of five years after the end of the war — the only legislative act of modern times to reduce the British electorate.

With the nation in this mood of belligerent anti-pacifism, it is not surprising that the war against pacifists was also fought on the stages of London theatres. Twice in the autumn of 1917 plays were produced that

were frankly and blatantly acts of propaganda against current pacifist
thought. Neither has survived, even as a footnote to the history
of English drama; still, their particular badnesses are historically
interesting, and the ideas that they express are a part of the story of the
English imagination in the war's fourth year.

Henry Arthur Jones was sixty-six when his new play opened in the
autumn of 1917. He had had a long and intermittently successful career
as a playwright, though by 1917 his principal successes were well behind
him, back in the Nineties with the other New Woman plays. Jones
called his new play *The Pacifists: a Parable in a Farce in Three Acts*, and
described it on the title page of the published version as 'showing how
certain citizens of Market Pewbury acted upon the exalted principle of
peace at any price, and how the town fared in consequence.' In the play
the local butcher tyrannizes over the town, enclosing the commons,
soliciting another man's wife, and locking an old lady in a coal-
cellar. The townsmen are afraid to resist him, and the policeman has
rheumatism. In the end they hire a pugilist from another town, who
ducks the butcher in the canal, and peace is restored.

A parable in a farce, Jones said it was: and that is the trouble. The farce
overwhelms and trivializes the parable, and makes it a play about how
to deal with bullying butchers. Jones seems to have anticipated the
problem: a month before the play opened he published his dedication to
it in *The Times*, explaining there what it was really about, and who his
targets were:

> To the tribe of Wordsters, Pedants, Fanatics, and Impossibilists, who
> so rabidly pursued an ignoble peace, that they helped to provoke
> a disastrous war; who having provoked a disastrous war, have
> unceasingly clamoured against its effectual prosecution; who throw
> dust in their own eyes, lest they should perceive the noonday truth;
> whom neither history, nor reason, nor thundering facts can teach;
> whom to convict of having been woefully and blindly wrong in the
> past, does but drive to be wilfully and madly wrong in the future;
> who might justly be regarded as pitiable figments of farce, if their
> busy mischief were not still seeking to bring about the tragedy of a
> delusive and abortive peace.[3]

But you don't turn a farce into a parable by writing about it in *The
Times*, or give a foolish play the weight of tragedy by mentioning
tragedy and disaster in a dedication. *The Pacifists* was the first flop of the
1917–18 theatrical season, and the worst: it closed after ten days. 'I had a

great failure with *The Pacifists*,' Jones wrote to a friend, ' — no other
English dramatist except Shakespeare could have achieved so complete a
failure. It was condemned as quite unworthy by the Press, and the
public never got within miles of its meaning — or of the theatre. Yet it
delighted a lot of cultivated men — such as Edmund Gosse and Henry
Newbolt and Sidney Lee and a score of others on that level.'[4] By *that
level* Jones clearly meant his friends' level of cultural sophistication, but
one might better give the term another meaning, and say that if
the play delighted anyone, it was elderly, belligerent patriots and
imperialists like Gosse and Newbolt, and that it did not reach the
Wordsters, Pedants, Fanatics, and Impossibilists to whom it was
dedicated, because in fact Jones did not understand them, and had
nothing to say to them.

Loyalty, the second anti-pacifist play of that autumn season, was
written by a far more obscure writer, but it fared a good deal better.
Harold Owen was a London editor and journalist, and the author of two
books: *Women Adrift: The Menace of Suffragism* (1912) and *Common Sense
About the Shaw* (1915), a polemical attack on Shaw's pamphlet about the
war. You will get a fair sense of Owen's social views from the title of
the first, and of his attitude towards the war from the dedication of the
second:

TO

THE MEMORY OF

THE HEROIC DEAD

WHO HAVE FOUGHT AND DIED FOR US

WHILST FOOLS AT HOME CONTEND.[5]

Jones had failed by trying to treat pacifism farcically; Owen succeeded
by treating it melodramatically and polemically. *Loyalty* is set mainly in
the London offices of the *New Standard*, a newspaper owned by an old
radical, and written for by pacifists and Socialists, though it is edited,
rather improbably, by a very conservative young man. The action runs
from the summer of 1914, just before the assassination at Sarajevo, to
the summer of 1916. During that time the young editor stands for
Parliament, goes off to the war, and is wounded; the newspaper
proprietor's son is captured by the Germans and murdered; and the
proprietor is converted from Socialist pacifism to a fierce English
patriotism.

But *Loyalty* is scarcely worth reading for the plot; you must read
it, as Dr Johnson read Richardson, for the sentiments. They are the

sentiments that most Englishmen felt in 1917, and that was one reason for the play's success. Here are a few exemplary passages:

> *On Englishness* [Frank Aylett, the young editor/MP, speaks]:
> I shall stand for English ideas — for English traditions — for English feeling and English manners and English sense and English policy, based on English character.
> *On English Decadence* [Anthea, wife of Frank Aylett, discusses English problem plays with her husband]:
> Yes, *why* is it? So gloomy, and problemmy, and full of discontent? [Aylett replies]: Oh, it's all part of the general movement . . . the effect of these long years of peace and fat prosperity.
> *On Class* [Aylett]:
> No. The common people never have ruled . . . and never can!
> *On Women* [Anthea]:
> . . . a woman does not believe in a cause . . . she doesn't *want* to believe in a cause — so much as in the man who upholds it.
> *On the War* [Sir Andrew]:
> I promised to return and work for Peace . . . And I *will* work for Peace — for a peace that passeth their understanding [i.e. the Germans] — for a peace that shall crush infamy to the low earth from which it springs . . . for the peace that comes (*his hands uplifted and trembling*) when Justice has been done — for a justice that shall know no mercy — and condone no crime — for a justice that shall rise higher than that mountain of infamy and fall upon it![6]

The most striking thing about *Loyalty*, however, is not its text, quotable though it is, but its history. According to Owen, it was accepted for production within three days of its completion, by the first management to which it was submitted, went into rehearsal within a week, and was produced (anonymously) three weeks later. It was reviewed in every important London daily and weekly, sometimes admiringly, sometimes not; the *Court Journal* called it 'undoubtedly the best war problem play so far produced', and Chesterton made it the subject of a patriotic sermon in the *New Witness*[7], but other, more judicious critics were less impressed. The *Times*'s critic got both the play's weakness and its strength into one paragraph when he wrote:

There is really no individuality, which is only another way of saying there is no genuine art, in his play. He has thought and felt for himself, no doubt, but as his thoughts and feelings are, in the nature of the case, identical with those of the vast majority of his country-men, the effect is as though he had dished up so many leading articles from the newspapers during the last three years and doled them out among his players.[8]

In spite of its sound doctrine, *Loyalty* ran for only three weeks. Six months later, Owen published the text of the play, explaining in an introduction that though he had felt sure that the play would run 'long enough to achieve the one object I had in writing it — to smash Pacifism', he had failed in that aim:

That object was certainly unachieved, for Pacifism rose to its crescendo, and so supplied a complete justification of the public purpose of the play, in the months after 'Loyalty' was withdrawn. So there is nothing for it but to try again, as every little helps, and, having put it in a play, to bring it now to book.[9]

But Owen had not failed entirely: he had interested persons in power. Colonel Repington, the *Times*'s military correspondent, noted in his diary in June 1918:

Lady L. [ondonderry] keen about the play *Loyalty*, which is antipacifist. I told her that Sutherland [Sir William Sutherland, the Prime Minister's secretary] would square all the Government Press to boom the play, and that I would do my best for the independent Press. S. laughingly agreed.[10]

And the play *was* boomed in that last summer of the war: the printed version was widely reviewed, and in July the Queen ordered a command performance, under the patronage of the King and the Queen, and attended it with the Queen Mother.

By the time that performance was given, Owen had nearly finished a new book — *Disloyalty: The Blight of Pacifism*. There is in this book a spirit that is absent from his play: a strong sense of crisis, and even of impending defeat. This was partly occasional: Owen began writing his book just as the Germans launched their final, all-out offensive on the Western Front in March 1918, and he made much of the threat of a Hun invasion, and of its sure atrocious consequences. 'I suppose it is pretty common knowledge', he wrote,

that Englishwomen, on that black Saturday when Haig's message to the Army shocked even Pacifists to silence, calmly spoke of what they would do to themselves and their children 'if the Germans came' —

for so well known are the demoniacal attributes of 'the German people' that they are dreaded worse than death.[11]

'Haig's message' refers to the Field Marshal's April 13 Order of the Day to his troops, which read:

To all ranks of the British Army in France and Flanders.

Three weeks ago to-day the enemy began his terrific attacks against us on a 50-mile front. His objects are to separate us from the French, to take the Channel Ports, and destroy the British Army.

In spite of throwing already 106 divisions into the battle, and enduring the most reckless sacrifice of human life, he has as yet made little progress towards his goal. We owe this to the determined fighting and self-sacrifice of our troops.

Words fail me to express the admiration which I feel for the splendid resistance offered by all ranks of our Army under the most trying circumstances.

Many amongst us now are tired. To those I would say that victory will belong to the side which holds out the longest.

The French Army is moving rapidly and in great force to our support.

There is no other course open to us but to fight it out. Every position must be held to the last man: there must be no retirement. With our backs to the wall, and believing in the justice of our cause, each one of us must fight on to the end.

The safety of our homes and the freedom of mankind depend alike upon the conduct of each one of us at this critical moment.[12]

Whether Haig's message stiffened military spines or not is not clear; but it certainly caused hysteria among English civilians. The atrocity literature of the early war years had done its job.

But Owen's gloom was more than a reaction to one Order of the Day. It expressed a feeling that had spread among Englishmen since the days of the Somme and *Mr Britling*, until it had reached even such unquestioning patriots as Owen — a feeling that the English people no longer believed in the rightness of their cause. As an expression of this mood, Owen quoted from a *Daily News* editorial, published at the end of 1917, and addressed to Lloyd George:

The spirit of the nation is darkening. Its solidarity is crumbling. We began this war with a splendid faith in our aims and with a unity of moral purpose that was priceless . . . but our faith has grown dim . . .

The nation needs a new lead. It is for you to give it. Restore to it its
faith in itself and in its cause.[13]

This is the mood of Charles Morgan's depressed return to England, of
Sassoon's protest, Pollard's parable, and of Lansdowne's letter. It was a
mood that many Englishmen had come to share privately and even, if
they were courageous, to express publicly; but it had reached a new
intensity and acceptance when it could be uttered in the public voice of a
London daily newspaper, in a direct appeal to the Prime Minister.

What the *News* asked of Lloyd George was that he restore England to
the bright idealism of 1914; but no politician could accomplish that, in
the last year of the war. Nor could it be achieved by launching attacks
upon pacifists, as though they were the cause of a contagious defeatism.
They weren't; they were only a symptom. England had lost its direction
before it had won its war, and it had no course but to struggle on to the
end, in increasing bitterness of spirit.

Among home-front wars, the war against the pacifists was a prominent one. But there was another war, against another kind of dissent,
that was also fiercely fought. That was the home-front war against sex,
and especially against what one might call dissenting sex — that is,
homosexuality. To some minds, homosexuality seemed subversive,
even German. Lord Alfred Douglas (of all people) thought so. Writing
in his own occasional journal, *The Antidote*, in 1915, Lord Alfred quoted
with approval this paragraph by Austin Harrison, from a Sunday paper:

> When we hear of German brutality in Belgium, of their employment
> of chlorine, of the *Lusitania* and the bombardment of open towns,
> there should be no matter of surprise. For years the Germans have
> cultivated a wholesome brutality as part of the military training, and
> latterly this brutality has found national vent in sexual perversion.
> Such things do not make men gentle, humane or noble.

After which, Lord Alfred offered this warning:

> Here is something for Mr. Harrison and all other parties concerned to
> remember:
>   It is just as important to civilization that Literary England should be
> cleansed of sex-mongers and pedlars of the perverse, as that Flanders
> should be cleared of Germans.[14]

One might argue, of course, that Lord Alfred Douglas was not
entirely rational on the subject of sexual perversion. But what about

John Buchan? When he invented Ulric von Stumm, the villain of his novel *Greenmantle* (published in October 1916), he made him a huge, brutal German officer; but he gave him rather surprising private quarters:

> That room took my breath away, it was so unexpected. In place of the grim bareness of downstairs here was a place all luxury and colour and light. It was very large, but low in the ceiling, and the walls were full of little recesses with statues in them. A thick grey carpet of velvet pile covered the floor, and the chairs were low and soft and upholstered like a lady's boudoir. A pleasant fire burned on the hearth and there was a flavour of scent in the air, something like incense or burnt sandalwood. A French clock on the mantelpiece told me that it was ten minutes past eight. Everywhere on little tables and in cabinets was a profusion of nicknacks, and there was some beautiful embroidery framed on screens. At first sight you would have said it was a woman's drawing-room.
>
> But it wasn't. I soon saw the difference. There had never been a woman's hand in that place. It was the room of a man who had a fashion for frippery, who had a perverted taste for soft delicate things. It was the complement to his bluff brutality. I began to see the queer other side to my host, that evil side which gossip had spoken of as not unknown in the German army. The room seemed a horribly unwholesome place, and I was more than ever afraid of Stumm.[15]

All that Stumm seems really guilty of is a rather rococo taste in interior decoration; but to Buchan this is perverted and queer, because it is appropriate only to women, and Stumm is a man engaged in the most 'manly' of activities — war. It makes Stumm not only unsoldierly, but frightening in Hannay's eyes: a soldier with such tastes is a monster as well as a villain.

The army agreed with Buchan: homosexuality was unsoldierly, and the *Manual of Military Law* set severe punishments for sexual contacts between men. Under 'Acts of Indecency', the Manual reads:

> It is a misdemeanour punishable with two years' imprisonment for any male person, *either in public or in private*, to commit or be a party to the commission of any act of gross indecency with another male person, or to procure or to attempt to procure the commission by any male person of any such act; and it is also a misdemeanour to do any grossly indecent act in a public place in the presence of more persons

than one, or to publicly expose the person, or exhibit any disgusting object.[16]

For sodomy, the punishment was more severe: a minimum sentence of ten years, and a maximum of life. Officers convicted of either offence were cashiered from the service before being sentenced.

In spite of the severity of the penalties, a certain amount of homo-sexual activity clearly went on; in the course of the war and the year following (the period covered by official statistics), twenty-two officers and 270 other ranks were court-martialled for indecency. One such case is described in the letters of Raymond Asquith, the Prime Minister's son, who was appointed to serve as the defendant's legal counsel. The case was tried in August 1916, in the early weeks of the Somme offensive; the defendant, an officer in the Grenadier Guards (like Asquith), was the sixth generation of his family to hold a commission in the regiment, and the son of an officer who had been killed in action earlier in the war. He faced five charges of 'homosexualism'.

Asquith expected to lose. 'The case was quite hopeless from the beginning,' he wrote to his wife,

> but most of the witnesses were fearful liars and in other respects tarred with much the same brush as the accused, so it was possible to have a certain amount of fun cross-examining them. One of the 2 principal ones was a queer fellow in the Irish Guards who had been, I think, a quack doctor in peace time and a soldier of fortune whenever there was any kind of a war going on, a tiresome officious puritanical creature full of the missionary and detective spirit and apparently with a bee in his bonnet about the corruption and decadence of the English upper classes and particularly of Etonians.
>
> The other was a nephew of Robert Ross, lately a scholar at Eton, who aroused everyone's suspicions by knowing Latin and Greek and constantly reading Henry James' novels. He was not ill-looking but with an absurdly cushioned figure and a rather hysterical temperament more like a girl than a boy. He was the accomplice who turned King's Evidence.[17]

Two ideas were at work, in Asquith's account, that would defeat his case: the notion that the English upper classes were corrupt, and the notion that public-school boys were effeminate aesthetes. Both relate to the idea of English decadence as a cause of the war, which had first appeared in the war's early months, and had been a commonplace of

English war talk since then. The war was to have been the Condy's Fluid that would cleanse society of its decadence; but here, two years later, and with the war's greatest battle in progress, that cleansing had not occurred. Instead, the infection had burst out here, where one might least expect it, in the officer-class that was charged with directing the war, and in the most elite of regiments.

Asquith's account suggests that it was not simply a homosexual officer who was on trial, but his class, and the behaviour and taste of that class. And the standards by which the case was tried were the standards of manhood and soldiership that war required, if it was to be won. The conflict was not unlike that which Rivers faced, as officer and psychiatrist, and which confronted many of his patients at Craiglockhart — not necessarily in sexual terms, but in terms of martial values vs. the human feelings that obstruct those values. Dottyville was one solution to that conflict; prison was another.

Sexual deviance was a crime against the army. It could also be seen as a crime against a civilian society at war. Deviants could be attacked on patriotic grounds, and were. The most notorious case of such an attack was the one carried out by Noel Pemberton Billing, MP for East Hertfordshire, against the dancer Maud Allan and, once he got going, against most of fashionable English society. Billing, an Independent Member of Parliament, was an eccentric, belligerent man of passionate convictions. Up to the time of the Maud Allan case he had devoted most of his energies to arguing the cause of air power, and badgering those government officials who were responsible for English aviation. From October 1916 he edited his own weekly journal, *The Imperialist*, which fought the air-power fight, but also attacked Jews, German music, Pacificism, Fabianism, Aliens, Financiers, Internationalism, and the Brotherhood of Man. In 1918 the journal began to carry on its masthead the phrase 'The Voice of the Vigilante', and in February changed its title to *The Vigilante*, identifying itself as the organ of a patriotic movement of that name that Billing had founded the previous year.

On January 26, 1918 the *Vigilante* published an article by Billing titled 'The First 47,000'. The number, Billing explained, was the number of English perverts whose vices were known to the German secret service (it was also, of course, a parody of the title of Ian Hay's *First Hundred Thousand*). There was a Black Book, he claimed, in German hands, in which those names and their perversions were recorded, and that list was used to blackmail English men and women in high places into betraying their country and helping the Germans to win the war. In mid-February Billing made the same claims in a speech in the House of Commons. A few days later an article appeared in a popular newspaper, *The Referee*, in which the list was referred to, not as one man's undocumented fantasy, but as fact — a classic example of the life of rumour in wartime.

At about the same time that Billing was making his claims in Parliament, the theatrical producer J.T. Grein was planning a performance, by his Independent Theatre, of Oscar Wilde's *Salomé*, with the dancer Maud Allan in the title role. The performance would be private, and admission would be by subscription, since the play had never been granted a performance licence; Grein's announcement therefore included the address of the secretary of the Independent Theatre Society, to whom subscriptions were to be sent. A few days after the announcement appeared, the *Vigilante* published this item:

The Cult of the Clitoris

To be a member of Maud Allen's [*sic*] private performance in Oscar Wilde's 'Salome' one has to apply to a Miss Valetta, of 9, Duke Street, Adelphi, W.C. If Scotland Yard were to seize the list of these members I have no doubt they would secure the names of several thousand of the first 47,000.[18]

Miss Allan sued for libel. In the Magistrate's hearing that followed, Grein and Miss Allan argued that *Salomé* was a work of art, and that, as Grein put it, 'War and art have nothing to do with one another.'[19] Billing replied that 'this exhibition as given by these people directly ministers to sexual perverts, Sodomites, and Lesbians,' and that 'the practising of these vices, holding as they do, their devotees up to blackmail, has an international significance which is not calculated to prosper our cause in this war.' 'They have chosen,' he went on, 'at a moment when our very national existence is at stake, to select the most depraved of the many depraved works of a man who suffered the extreme penalty at the hands of the law for the practising of this unnatural vice, or one form of it.'[20] The Magistrate allowed that a case existed, and committed Billing to stand trial. (In the midst of all this, between the first and second Magistrate's hearings, the play had its one private performance, and got mixed, rather nervous reviews.)

The trial that followed was a scandal — made so by Billing's outrageous behaviour in the conducting of his own case, and by the weak-witted incompetence of the judge, Mr Justice Darling. It was at no point a trial of the accused on the charge of libel; it was, rather, yet another trial of Oscar Wilde, and of 47,000 putative English perverts. Billing refused to follow, or even to hear instructions from the bench, introduced evidence as he wished, and generally behaved like the prosecuting attorney — at the same time playing with great gusto the role of the brave patriot exposing himself to the whims of the law in defence of his country against a sinister German plot. He produced two witnesses for the defence (one of them an officer dismissed from the army on grounds of insanity) who claimed to have seen the Black Book, and who were willing to reveal some of the names they had seen there: these included both Herbert and Margot Asquith, Colonel Aubrey Herbert, Lord Carnarvon, Lord Haldane — and Mr Justice Darling.

In his summing up, Justice Darling ignored the charge against himself and went to what he took to be the heart of the matter:

> Oscar Wilde wrote filthy works, as you know: he was guilty of filthy practices: he was convicted in this Court and suffered imprisonment, and social extinction, and death in due course . . . Well, gentlemen, it is possible to regard him as a great artiste, but he certainly was a great beast; there is no doubt about that.[21]

The jury withdrew briefly, and returned to find Billing innocent of the charges.

That the case could be tried in the way it was, that the slurs and libels and paranoid accusations that Billing hurled about so freely could be allowed in an English court, is evidence of the power of certain emotional issues in wartime. Homosexuality was one of them: throughout the war the sexual practices for which Wilde had become the representative figure in English minds were considered a threat to English well-being, indeed to English survival. That idea was present in the Grenadier Guards courtroom where Raymond Asquith lost his case, and it was present in English journalism. At the time that the Billing trial was taking place, other English journalists were circulating their own conspiracy theories, reporting 'the moral and spiritual invasion of Britain by German urnings [that is, homosexuals] for the purpose of undermining the patriotism, the stamina, the intellect, and the moral of British Navy and Army men, and of our prominent public leaders',[22] though they reassured their readers that British defensive measures were being taken:

> At the headquarters of the London District Command, at the Horse Guards in Whitehall, some of the best intelligence officers in the world have been engaged since the war began in handling the difficult

problem of the infection of Londoners, especially including soldiers, by the doctrine of the German urnings ... [23]

The metaphor of infection is by now a familiar one; the only difference in this later version is that it was now a German disease, like measles.

The campaign that Billing had launched, and that much of English society supported, was a war against homosexuals, but it was more than that: it was also a war against art. Grein had said that Art had nothing to do with War: Billing replied that it had everything to do with it. Art could be Decadent — that is, foreign and unhealthy — and if it were, it could infect the nation, and destroy its will to fight. The idea of an army defeated by performances of *Salomé* is hard to take seriously; so is the idea of a covert force of deviants turning English soldiers into cowards and English politicians into collaborators. But these notions were taken seriously — by an English jury, and by the general public. In 1918, Oscar Wilde was still alive in English imaginations; and his art was still identified with the crime for which he had been convicted, more than twenty years earlier.

You can see how ideas of decadence and censorship worked together in English minds in another incident from the spring of 1918 — the reception of Arnold Bennett's novel, *The Pretty Lady*, which appeared in April, just when Billing was appearing before the Bow Street magistrate and Maud Allan was appearing before her private audience in *Salomé*. *The Pretty Lady* is a home-front novel, set almost entirely in the West End of London, and concerned with civilian lives there. The lady of the title is Christine, a French prostitute driven to London by the war. There she meets G.J. Hoape, a wealthy, self-indulgent, middle-aged bachelor who busies himself with war committees, and who makes her his mistress. When she compassionately befriends a drunken, shell-shocked soldier, G.J. casts her aside and turns his mind back to the war and his committees, and the novel ends.

Bennett was modest about his intentions in the novel: 'The Pretty Lady', he wrote in a letter, 'is not a moralising or a shaft against moralising or against anybody or anything. It is just *a* novel about the war. And I leave it at that.'[24] Certainly it is that: it offers a vivid picture of London's war (there is a brilliant account of a zeppelin raid, for example), and London wartime society, with its charities and its committees, is rendered with a fine, cold disdain. But reviewers saw more in the book, saw it as an important historical document. It was an 'ironical satire', the *Athenaeum*'s critic wrote, that would 'perhaps be the historic picture of London in the times of the Great War',[25] and the reviewer in the *Nation* made the point even more expansively:

> one may imagine this novel acquiring a kind of immortality as representing, in days to come, the manner in which the Great Catastrophe crashed in upon a society whose life may well seem then frankly to have been incredible.[26]

These things were said in praise; but there were other readers for whom Bennett's vision of social decadence was threatening and wicked. '"The Pretty Lady" is a damnable book,' the *Sunday Chronicle*'s critic announced. 'It has no justification in art or in ethics. It is decadent, ignoble, and corrupting — a "bully" among books, a smiling *souteneur* to lure young men and women to evil, hundreds of pages of pimpishness.' He compared Bennett to the German soldiers who, according to atrocity reports, spat on the church altars of Belgium, and concluded:

> This book ought to be banned under the Defence of the Realm Act as a work calculated to destroy the moral of the people. It is an abomination which will degrade any decent bookstall.[27]

DORA was not, in fact, invoked; but other modes of censorship were. The book was boycotted by booksellers in Bath and Cambridge, and banned by W.H. Smith's chain of shops, and it was attacked by two church organizations, the Catholic Federation and the Catholic Truth Society (Christine was not only a whore, she was a Catholic whore). As a result, the book sold very well.[28]

The historical importance of this incident, in the war's last spring, lies in the sense that readers found in Bennett's novel not only of the decadence of society, but of the end of that society, and in the desperate efforts of a conservative part of society to deny that sense, by suppressing whatever work of art expressed it. It was more than simply the spirit of Billing loose in the land; it was a national mood that Billing had been clever enough, or lucky enough, to have tapped.

This conflation of decadent art with sexual and moral issues affected the situation of modern art in England generally. For it spread a blurry discredit over any new work that departed from the traditional English main stream, and made all Modernism seem not only *un*-English but *anti*-English. If modern art was something that turned men into perverts, and hence into cowards and traitors, then the less of it in England the better. Billing didn't, of course, create these feelings — they had been around since the Wilde trials, and no doubt long before that; but he exploited and intensified them, and so helped to widen the division in English culture between what was modern and what was English.

On the night when the Billing case verdict was announced, Charles Ricketts sat at a concert with the painter Henry Lamb, and in the intervals discussed the significance of the trial. He reported their conversation to Robbie Ross in a letter. Lamb said: 'Nothing will be altered, the brute philistine is the big gut of the nation, it is disturbed and we are all mad and suspicious just now.' Ricketts thought that it might be the first act of the Revolution. 'No,' Lamb replied, 'the country will always be the same.'[29] If this were true — and it seemed to be — then the war had simply given the majority of Englishmen an opportunity to be what they had always been — xenophobic, homophobic, and art-hating — and to call it patriotism.

Billing's campaign was a campaign against 'vice' and against art; but it was more than that: it was also a campaign against the upper classes. For it is clear that it was a part of his intention to exploit what he perceived as a common distrust of the social and political 'establishment' (the same distrust that we saw in the trial of the Grenadier Guards officer). Cynthia Asquith was told by a friend that shop-women were saying, 'We always knew it of the Asquiths, and we're so glad they're being exposed,' and Arnold Bennett wrote:

> there can be no doubt that Mr. Pemberton Billing had a very great deal of support from plain people throughout the country. These people said: 'He is not attacking; he is defending himself. And what has he to gain from his attempt to expose an alleged huge conspiracy of vice and pro-Germanism? Nothing. Hence he must be a patriot.'[30]

In this respect, the trial must be seen as both a symptom and an aggravation of a hostile division between classes that intensified as the war went on, and that would have important consequences in the years after the war.

If ordinary people believed in the German plot as described by Billing, how did members of the ruling class regard it? For some, it was simply a joke. Duff Cooper wrote to his wife, Diana, from the trenches:

> No one here speaks or thinks of anything but the Billing case. Even my Commanding Officer — the most regular of regular soldiers — greeted me when I met him for the first time today not 200 yards from the front line trenches with — 'What did you think of Fripp's

evidence [Fripp was the personal physician of King George V]. I
should have thought he knew more about clap.'[31]

And Diana responded with her own story:

> Lord Albemarle is said to have walked into the Turf and said, 'I've
> never heard of this Greek chap *Clitoris* they are all talking of.'[32]

But others took it more seriously, as a sinister conspiracy — a plot to
smear Asquith and so prevent him from returning to office, or a
Suffragette plot to discredit his wife, Margot. After four years of war,
ordinary English citizens and their rulers were equally willing to believe
in conspiracies and plots; they had all been lied to, officially, for so long,
one might conclude, that they had forgotten what common sense and
reason sounded like, and were ready to believe anything, so long as it
was melodramatic enough.

While the war against deviants went on, the other war went on, too,
and disastrously. At the time that Maud Allan was filing her suit, and
Billing was attacking perverts, Jews, and Art, the Germans were also
attacking, and the English, in spite of Haig's 'backs-to-the-wall' Order,
were retreating. (The one performance of *Salomé* took place on the day
after Haig issued his Order; a review of the play and the text of Haig's
Order appeared in the same issue of *The Times* on April 13, 1918.)
Sassoon, back with his regiment in France, put the trial and the retreat
together in one diary entry:

> The papers are full of this foul 'Billing Case.' Makes one glad to be
> away from 'normal conditions.' And the Germans are on the Marne
> and claim 4500 more prisoners. The world is stark staring mad . . . [33]

And so it seemed to be, in the spring of 1918, in the fourth year of the
war.

These two home-front wars — the war against pacifists and the war
against homosexuals — came together in one court case in October
1918, when the author and publisher of a new novel, *Despised and
Rejected*, were brought before a London magistrate, accused of an
offence under DORA; the novel, it was charged, made 'statements likely to
prejudice the recruiting, training, and discipline of persons in His
Majesty's forces'. The author was named on the title page as A.T.
Fitzroy, but was in fact Rose Allatini, an Italian-born woman living in
England. She had previously published one book, a thesis-novel about
mercy-killing, under her own name, and would go on to publish twelve

others, under various pseudonyms, over the next thirty-seven years, without notable success. The publisher was C.W. Daniel, proprietor of a small radical press that published books of a pacifist tendency. Both defendants pleaded not guilty.

The offending novel is the story of a young man, Dennis Blackwood, who as he grows to manhood learns that he is a) an artist, b) a homosexual, and c) a pacifist, and sees these three conditions as somehow related: he will not destroy because he is an artist, and he will not kill other young men because he is homosexual. He is put into prison with other conscientious objectors, and mistreated there, as COs indeed were (during the war seventy COs died in prison). At the novel's end he is still imprisoned: it is another example of an unresolved wartime novel.

Despised and Rejected is very reticent in its accounts of the homosexual passions of its characters — there is a good deal of yearning, but very little touching — but it is frank in acknowledging that such passions exist in both men and women, and postulates that perhaps such persons are 'the advance-guard of a more enlightened civilisation'.[34] It also contains passages in which Dennis and his friends discuss their pacifist views at considerable length, and argue them against supporters of the war — parents and other Old Men. It was these discussions that constituted the offence, the prosecution said.

The defendants replied that no offence had been committed; the book was a novel, not a tract, and though some characters expressed pacifist views, others took the opposite position. Furthermore, the title did not refer to the hero's pacifism, but to his abnormal sexual inclinations. The prosecutor responded that Daniel had previously been fined for printing a pamphlet 'of a frankly pacifist nature', and that he was 'a person who assisted those who desired to propagate the pacifist idea by printing for them these pamphlets'. *Despised and Rejected*, he concluded, was a pacifist pamphlet disguised as a novel. The presiding magistrate observed first that although the question of whether the book was obscene or not was not before him, he did not hesitate to describe it as morally unhealthy and most pernicious (thus convicting it of an offence for which it had not been charged); he then went on to conclude that it was also pacifist, and found all the offences proved. Indeed, he added that he had had considerable hesitation as to whether he ought not to send the publisher to prison.[35] In the end he did not, but simply ordered him to pay a fine, and had the books destroyed (burned by the public hangman, Virginia Woolf said).[36]

This is an odd case, that in its very oddness is appropriate to represent the condition of England in the last month of the war. A book that is charged with an offence against DORA is defended as being really about homosexuality, and is found guilty of both offences, though only one is charged. At that moment in history, with the Germans retreating and the end of the war in sight, official England still feared and forbade both sexual deviance and pacific thought, and punished them when they appeared; whereas Rose Allatini saw them as somehow connected, two aspects of a better civilization that the future might bring. It was a strange prediction to make at such a time, but a comprehensible one, if you stop to think about it: masculinity in 1918 was manifested in two ways — in heterosexuality, and in war. Allatini's hero stood against both, and was punished. But perhaps the future, the world-after-the-war, would be more liberal, and more peaceable.

The Allatini case takes its place with the Billing trial as an expression of the mood of England at the war's end — a mood of anger, fear, and mistrust that made the last of the home-front wars both bitter and ridiculous. The most important consequence of these wars was surely their effect on post-war English culture. They intensified and solidified what was worst and most repressive in wartime English society, and by so doing helped to create a post-war sub-culture of outsiders, composed of an odd mixture of persons — opponents of the war, artists, homosexuals — whom the war spirit had identified as subversive. Established English culture had had its opponents before the war, and advanced art had been moving towards confrontation in movements like Futurism and Vorticism, but not with such disparate ideological allies. Oscar Wilde had seemed dead in 1914, and pacifism had scarcely been born. But in 1918 both were alive and vocal.

CHAPTER 12

The Beginnings of 'Post-War'

For military historians, the fourth year of the war is notable for the Third Battle of Ypres, or Passchendaele, in which British troops attacked from the end of July 1917 into November, suffered some 300,000 casualties, and gained nothing, and for the German offensive in the spring of 1918, which took them once more to the Marne, and lost them the war. For the historian of English culture, it is the year in which the new war culture began to define itself to the civilian population, in books by Sassoon and Graves and Nichols, in war paintings by Nevinson and Nash, in the first plain-speaking soldiers' memoirs, in anti-heroic war novels about damaged men and martyrs.

But the war culture was not the whole of English cultural life in 1917–18: *The Portrait of the Artist as a Young Man*, *Prufrock and Other Observations*, Dorothy Richardson's *Honeycomb*, and Lawrence's *Look! We Have Come Through!* were all published in England during 1917. So was Virginia Woolf's *The Mark on the Wall*, her first story written in her post-war style, and the first publication of the Hogarth Press. In 1918 the first chapters of *Ulysses* and Pound's first Canto appeared in periodicals. In the field of modern art, Roger Fry arranged his first anthology-show of paintings and sculpture since his two Post-Impressionist exhibitions in 1910 and 1912: 'Works Representative of the New Movement in Art' opened in the autumn of 1917.[1] This show, of French and English artists working 'in the new direction', included none of the great Post-Impressionists of the two pre-war exhibitions, and no Vorticists: by 1917 the Post-Impressionists were history and Vorticism was dead (or, even worse, it was provincial).[2] The show scarcely acknowledged the existence of the war, either as an historical fact or as an influence on art; there is no mention of it in Fry's catalogue introduction, and the only exhibited work that refers to it is a collage by Fry, titled 'German General Staff' — an image of three figures in cloaks and *pickelhaube* helmets derived from a newspaper photograph of the Kaiser and his generals, and apparently intended as a joke.[3]

After the emptiness of the mid-war years, Modernism was re-emerging. But not the same Modernism that had existed in the pre-war years: 'in 1917,' the music reviewer for the *Annual Register* wrote at the year's end, 'the old order had almost disappeared, the shadow of peace times had well-nigh evaporated, and things were — or seemed to be — starting off from a new basis.'[4] And the same might have been said of the other arts, too. The names of Joyce and Eliot and Woolf had not been known in England before the war; nor had many of the names in Fry's catalogue — Brancusi, Mark Gertler, Juan Gris, Nina Hamnett, Jean Marchand.

There were new names, too, in the new journals that began to appear in the later years of the war: *Wheels* at the end of 1916, *Art and Letters* in 1917, *New Paths* in 1918. There one finds the early work of writers who would become the characterizing figures of the Twenties — Edith Sitwell, Nancy Cunard, Aldous Huxley, Eliot. All of these new names — the painters, the novelists, the poets — belong neither to the pre-war art world nor to the world of the war; they are the post-war Modernists. In the fourth year of the war, one might say, Post-war had begun.

These writers and artists, and the editors of the journals in which they appeared, and the older writers and artists who appeared there with them, had one thing in common — they were non-combatants. Some had tried to enlist and had been rejected (like Eliot and Pound); some were physically unfit (Lawrence and Huxley); some were of an older generation (Frank Rutter, Charles Ginner, and Harold Gilman, the editors of *Art and Letters*, were all over forty when the war ended); some were women; some were of the right age and state of health, but had managed to avoid the shooting (Middleton Murry spent the first two years of the war looking for a safe billet, and then did something in the War Office that left him plenty of time to write, until he was invalided out in 1917). But whatever the reason, they had spent the war years doing their own work and advancing their careers. And, one must add, advancing modern art; for though the arts had been quiet during the war, they had not been stationary.

As the war approached its end, and the writers and artists who had fought in it began to return to England, they found these non-combatants in control of things — in the editorships and journals and galleries that made reputations. This is not surprising — who else would do the work and keep the arts going in wartime if not civilians? Still, it must have seemed to the returning men that their sense of the injustice of the war had been confirmed, that civilians had profited while soldiers sacrificed their lives. They also found that while they had been away, four years of change in the arts had taken place without them. Feelings of dislocation, of exploitation, and of lost time must have been very common. In October 1918 Herbert Read recorded in his diary the feelings of the returning Wyndham Lewis: 'He is very bitter about the war: he feels that four years of the most vital period of his career have been torn from his life.'5 Many men must have felt that way in 1918.

These returning soldiers are very little represented in the new journals; it is the non-combatant civilians who fill the pages there. Nor is the war much in evidence; it was still going on, but it had nearly ceased to be a subject for new art. There are very few war poems in the wartime volumes of these journals, and virtually no war paintings among their reproductions. When the war does enter a poem, it does so retrospectively: the poems are not about fighting, but about the dead.

Yet though the war was not present as a common subject in these journals, it was there, as a mood. One can feel it in the first number of *Wheels*, published in December 1916. That was the dark middle of the war (the Somme offensive had just come to a bloody and inconclusive end), and the poems in *Wheels* are full of that darkness, and of death. You could make a depressing little anthology of dark and deathly images from that first number, none of them from poems explicitly about the war, but all full of its mood. It might include some of these lines:

> All the dim terrors dwelling far below
> Interr'd by many thousand years of life,
> Arise to revel in this evil dark . . .

> To-night I hear a thousand evil things
> Between the panels and the mouldering floor . . .
> Armies of corpses hid behind the wall . . .

> The fabric of the air is torn apart:
> The world is dead. There is no world at all.
> The light is dead. There shall be no more light.

> He woke in darkness. 'Twixt him and the skies
> Darted the black things of the middle night . . .

> Now is the evening dipped knee-deep in blood
> And the dun hills stand fearful in their places.[6]

An Oxford reviewer got the mood of the volume very well. 'This verse', he wrote,

> does not dance with joy, but shivers with fear, creaks with menace, droops with despair. It is the work for the most part of very young people, and it is quite unbearably old. Its revelation is the grim fact that the dead are less dead than the living, that where the war has spared it has slain.[7]

This tone, these old-young people, and these living dead, constitute a wartime mood; they will all continue into the post-war world, where they can be found, for example, in *The Waste Land* and *The Green Hat*, and in many other texts. But it is a tone that one also finds in the more fraught poems of the Nineties — that is, a decadent tone; one shrewd critic compared *Wheels* to *The Yellow Book*.

The war is also present in *Art and Letters* (begun in mid-1917), not as a mood but as a motive. An editorial in the first issue explained that it was because of the war that the journal had ventured to appear when it did:

> Friends serving at the Front . . . remind us that there are educated men in the Army who would gladly welcome an addition to the small number of publications which appeal to them. Engaged, as their duty bids, on harrowing work of destruction, they exhort their elders at home never to lose sight of the supreme importance of creative art.[8]

Here art is not the beneficiary of war's epic grandeur, but its antithesis — the civilization that war destroys. *Because* war is a part of reality, art must also continue to exist, and its importance must be affirmed, for the sake of the future. The editorial makes *Art and Letters* both a wartime journal and an after-the-war journal; but in both worlds, the war will be a presence.

New Paths appeared for only one issue, in the summer of 1918. Like the other new journals it anticipated the coming post-war literary scene, as its title suggests and its younger contributors confirm, but it also expressed most explicitly the *other* end-of-the-war theme, the end of a culture. The programmatic side of this sense of endings and new beginnings appears in *New Paths* in a set of articles that survey the present state of the arts: 'Some Tendencies in Contemporary Poetry', 'The Young Novel', and 'Tendencies in Present-Day English Art'.[9]

These are essays, on the one hand, of historical location: they suggest that a survey is appropriate because the arts have simultaneously come to the end of an era. But they are also concerned to chart what is new, what tendencies exist that will continue out of this moment in history into the future. The war is the source of both impulses: here, at the end of a catastrophe to civilization, survivors map the ruins and locate the routes out, the new paths that lead to whatever it is that comes after such a war as this has been. As a subject, as a sub-genre in the arts, the war gets relatively little attention in these essays: discussion of war art tends to come at the end, as a kind of afterthought, a category that must be mentioned for the sake of completeness, but not because it is intrinsically important. War is not a part of the history of the arts, but a gap in that history, a chasm that divides the past from the future.

New Paths also included poems by soldier-poets — not many, only a couple by Aldington and one by Osbert Sitwell, but enough to make it also a wartime journal. These are 'war poems', but of a different kind from those of Sassoon and Owen, not poems of the immediate experience of war, but of retrospection. Here, in the last summer of the war, most of the fighting and dying had been done; the poems are about what is left — the bitterness, the anger, and the grief. Aldington's 'The Blood of the Young Men' is an example. It is very clearly an end-of-the-war poem; most of the young men are dead, and the few who are left speak not of battles, but of remembered horror, and of their losses. This is the poem's final stanza:

> Go your ways, you women, pass and forget us;
> We are sick of blood, of the taste and sight of it;
> Go now to those who bleed not and to the old men,
> They will give you beautiful love in answer!
> But we, we are alone, we are desolate,
> Thinning the blood of our brothers with weeping,
> Crying for our brothers, the men we fought with,
> Crying out, mourning them, alone with our dead ones;
> Praying that our eyes may be blinded
> Lest we go mad in a world of scarlet,
> Dripping, oozing from the veins of our brothers.[10]

A number of the motifs of life during the war that emerged in wartime are here: how women at home failed men at the Front, how the Old Men flourished while the young bled, how the fighting men were alienated from the civilian world. These are the motifs that continued into the peace, and became the conventions of the Twenties — of the war literature written then, but also of literature having nothing explicitly to do with the war. Here, in Aldington's end-of-the-war poem, you can see the actual war slipping backwards, out of the present into the past, into the Myth of the War.

This sense of the moment, of balancing on a point in history where past (the war) and future (the post-war world) intersect, is most explicitly expressed in the dedication of the first (and only) number of *New Paths*, published in May 1918:

DEDICATED

TO THE MEMORY OF

RUPERT BROOKE
GAUDIER BRZESKA
GERARD CHOWNE
DIXON SCOTT
A. NOEL SIMMONS
C. H. SORLEY
EDWARD THOMAS
PELHAM WEBB

and to all those gallant gentlemen who, but for
having died in the service of their country,
would have been pioneers along
the new paths of literature
and art

War and post-war co-exist here, but in a curious way: war in the naming of the dead, those young artists and critics whose deaths are now a part of history; post-war in those new paths that will lead beyond the war, into a new culture. There is, in effect, no present, only a myth of gallant gentlemen, and a promise of a new but unspecified future. That co-existence, which is visible in one way or another in all of these new journals, expresses an important truth; as the war neared its end, a momentum in the arts towards a new, post-war world grew, and the war as a subject faded. But war nevertheless remained in imaginations, as a mood, as a motive, as a sense of the vast absences where gifted young men had been. The arts in England, and the imaginations that conceived them, would strive towards newness after the war, but they would carry the war with them — its images, its absences, and its survivors. In the world-after-the-war, the war would continue to be a part of consciousness.

The intersection of ending and beginning, the art of war and what comes after, did not only occur in literary journals at the end of the war. One finds it also in the cultural occasions of late-war society. Consider, as an example, the party that Sibyl Colefax gave on December 12, 1917. Lady Colefax was a celebrated London hostess — an 'indefatigable lion-hunter', Cynthia Asquith called her[11] — and for this party she gathered an impressive pride of lions. Not entirely the usual, social sort, though, for this was to be a charity poetry reading. For the organizing of it, and the issuing of invitations to poets, she turned to Robbie Ross and Robert Nichols, and for the introducing and speech-making to Edmund Gosse. Poems by a number of war poets were read: Nichols's by himself, Graves's by Gosse, Sassoon's by a young poet named Irene McLeod, Osbert Sitwell's by himself. But it was not only war poets who read: Ross had summoned most of the 'post-war' poets whom I have mentioned, and they read too.

The two groups seem to have resented and distrusted each other: Gosse was reassured by the presence of 'sound Georgians' like Nichols and Sassoon, but unsure about the Sitwells, whom he had only just heard of, while Huxley resented Nichols 'thrusting himself to the fore as the leader of us young bards'.[12]

The reading seems to have gone well enough, however. Here is Cynthia Asquith's account, from her diary:

Went with Mamma to the Poets' Reading at Mrs. Colefax's ... All the poets were young and most of them had fought in the war. It was very moving. I liked Nichols enormously, with his bright, intensely alive, rather stoat-like face. He read again in the same intensely passionate dramatic way: I like it, but a great many people don't. As well as his own, he read two — as I thought — very beautiful poems by Sorley who was killed at twenty years of age. Gosse was in the chair and acquitted himself quite well. Three Sitwells, all looking very German — Osbert, Sacheverell, and Edith — all read from their works. The author of 'Prufrock' read quite a funny poem comparing the Church to a hippopotamus. There was a young man called Huxley, and a very remarkable, fierce, rapt girl called McLeod who read her own clever poems beautifully. Siegfried Sassoon didn't appear, but his poems were read by this girl. Mamma was very much moved by the war poems. I was very, very glad I went.[13]

Arnold Bennett was also there; he thought Miss McLeod was a good reader, and the Sitwells were *très cultivée*, but the best thing was Eliot reading 'The Hippopotamus': 'Had I been the house, this would have brought the house down.'[14]

It was a very mixed gathering: Victorian Gosse in the chair, Decadent Robbie Ross behind the scenes, Edwardian Bennett in the audience, and Georgian war poets on the stage, along with three who had no wartime reputation, but would give definition to the post-war period: Eliot, Huxley, and Edith Sitwell. Fifty years of literary history and poetic taste were there that night — a summary of the strains that would run, at the end of the war, out into the peacetime literary scene.

The poets who read could scarcely have been more various: from Sassoon the purely Georgian, untouched by modern experiments, to Edith Sitwell the fantastic mannerist, to Osbert Sitwell, elegantly mocking, to Eliot the learned innovator. They did have one element in common, though: they were all, in their different ways, satirists. And though not all of them satirized the war, the war was the soil out of which both wartime and post-war satire grew. And it was in satire that post-war culture found its particular bitter voice. You might say that satire was post-war culture's principal inheritance from its wartime past.

Satire is an opposing mode, and it grew in England as opposition to the war grew. One can find occasional examples in radical journals during the early months of the war,[15] but it was not until after the Battle of the Somme that the satiric tone became generally audible. Then Sassoon's war poems began to appear in the *Cambridge Magazine*, and Osbert Sitwell's in the *Spectator* and the *Nation*. These two in particular were immediately recognized as satiric poets: Gosse, in his *Edinburgh* essay on war poets, called Sassoon 'essentially a satirist', and the *Nation* reviewed Sassoon and Sitwell together under the head 'The Young Satirists'.[16]

Very little satire came from the anti-war dissenters, the pacifists, and the conscientious objectors; their opposition was of the more sober and persuading kind. But satire does not set out to persuade: it emerges when the feeling of opposition is strong, but the chances of changing circumstances are weak — it is the anger and the bitterness of the helpless. Most of the anti-war satires written in the last years of the war came from men who had fought, had come to oppose the fighting, and had yet returned to fight again (as Sassoon and Owen and Graves all did). What they wrote were not arguments for stopping the war, but expressions of their hatred of a war that could not be stopped by any opposition.

Satire may be angry and bitter, but it is also a distancing mode. It separates the satirist and those he speaks for from those he attacks — the *Us* from the *Them*, or from *You*. And so it was an appropriate mode in which to express the soldiers' feeling of alienation from the country for which they were fighting, the feeling, as Tawney put it, that 'between you and us there hangs a veil'. That veil would not be lifted when the war ended: the separation that satire implies would continue into the next decade, making the Twenties a decade of satire and social division.

Satiric war poems appeared with increasing frequency in the later years of the war; but it was not only in poetry that the satiric mood of the time found expression. Nevinson's 'Pictures of War' exhibition in 1918 included two satiric paintings: 'He Gained a Fortune, But He Gave a Son' and 'War Profiteers', and Nash began to give satiric titles to his devastated anti-landscapes of the Front.[17] And among the troops in the trenches, the anonymous soldiers' songs became more satiric too, more of 'The Old Barbed Wire', and less of 'Tipperary'.

There was even a 'satirical anti-war opera' being written during these years — Havergal Brian's *The Tigers*, begun in 1916 and completed in 1920. Brian was a self-taught working-class composer, who enlisted in the army at the beginning of the war and was invalided out nine months later; he was working for an armaments firm in Birmingham when he began his opera. The libretto of *The Tigers* satirizes militarism, patriotism, and English society; the score parodies Strauss's *Ein Heldenleben* and Wagner's *Walküre* and *Götterdämmerung*. It has never been performed in its entirety[18]; nevertheless, it was there, one more expression of the end-of-the-war mood.

It is important to take note of what was being rejected in these wartime satirical gestures. The subjects attacked were such as would have seemed unapproachable at the war's beginning: patriotism,

women, mothers, generals, heroes, the Church. Then the older generation at large, those elders who, in the minds of the young, had declared
war in order that their sons might fight and die in it. And finally, the
myths and conventions of the past — particular conventions like those
of Romantic landscape, but more generally the idea of continuity, of a
past that was connected to the present and could therefore transmit
inspiration and meaning. One can see, to revert to the poets at Sibyl
Colefax's party, that the other satirists there, those like Eliot and Edith
Sitwell who were not war satirists, were nevertheless linked to the war
poets by these common rejections, and that they would all enter the post-
war world with the same sense of radical disconnection from a dead,
dishonest past.

In the spring of 1918 a book was published which seemed as satirically
post-war as any of the poems in *Wheels* or at Lady Colefax's party, but
which was offered to the world not as satire, but as history. The author,
Lytton Strachey, was a member of the war generation (born in 1880, he
was older than Sassoon, but younger than Edward Thomas), but he had
opposed the war from the beginning, and he appeared at the war's end, a
man without war experience, and unburdened by its history, the first
post-war historian, and the creator of a new, post-war literary kind —
satiric history. (For Max Beerbohm's Strachey-as-historian see plate
19.)

Eminent Victorians seems, at first glance, an odd book to claim
for post-war Modernism. With its mannered prose style, its studied
paradoxes, and its arch rhetorical questions, it seems more *fin de siècle*
than *fin de guerre*, the languidly ironical work of a latter-day Oscar
Wilde. And indeed the connection is a real one, for Strachey certainly
belonged to that 'decadent' opposition that had persisted through the war
in spite of the outcries of patriots. It is generally thought to have been
Strachey who, when asked why he was not fighting for civilization,
replied: 'I am the civilization for which you are fighting,' a remark as
Wildean in its arrogance and wit as anything that Oscar said.[19] And his
book has those same qualities.

Those qualities make *Eminent Victorians* the first important post-
war book. Ostensibly a set of four brief biographies — of Cardinal
Manning, Florence Nightingale, Arnold of Rugby, and 'Chinese'
Gordon — it is in fact something more ambitious and more subversive
than that. Strachey began his Preface with the statement: 'The history
of the Victorian Age will never be written: we know too much about it';
but that is what his book set out to do, to write a moral history of the

age through four representative figures. If we understand that 'Victorian Age' means not simply the years of Victoria's reign, but the whole spirit of England-before-the-war, then we can see how important Strachey's book was in 1918, and why it was so influential in the years that followed. There at the end of the war, Strachey looked back at the recent English past, and saw that it was a remote and distant time, separated from the present by a great chasm. That past might offer amusing objects for satire, examples of human folly and error, but it had nothing to do with us, on *this* side of the war. The book is a paradigm of the common post-war sense that the war had made history discontinuous, had opened a gap in history that made the past unreachable and irrelevant.

Eminent Victorians is paradigmatic in another sense: it is anti-heroic and deflating in its treatment of its subjects. It has a heroine, Florence Nightingale, a powerless woman who defeats the male world of stupidity and power; but it has no heroes. The three men portrayed (*caricatured* might be a more exact word) represent three powerful shaping forces in English culture before the war: religion, public-school education, and Imperial service. These were all forces that had led young men to war (you will find them all invoked and celebrated in the war poems of wartime anthologies); they would be rejected and ridiculed in the world-after-the-war. Strachey's book offered a model for that mocking, denying stance: it was very much a book for the Twenties.[20]

It was also a book for 1918. It was widely and admiringly reviewed, and went through four editions in six months. It was read by soldiers in France (Sassoon, Duff Cooper, and Maurice Baring all read it there), and by civilians at home (Roger Fry read it on holiday, Bertrand Russell read it in prison and Herbert Asquith praised it in a lecture at Oxford). Only a few readers — the elderly and conservative mostly — found it hard to take; Cynthia Asquith noted in her journal that her old friend the *Times*'s drama critic Charles Whibley thought it 'mere journalism', and ungrammatical journalism at that, and Mrs Humphry Ward, the queen mother of the anti-Suffragettes, attacked it in the *TLS* as unpatriotic.[21]

One striking thing about *Eminent Victorians* is that though it was written during 1915–17, it contains no reference to the war, but maintains a scrupulous aloofness from contemporary events. Or so it seems. There is however one lapse — a metaphorical, but nonetheless bellicose one — in the Preface, where Strachey writes that the wise historian will not adopt the direct method of strict narration, but will adopt a subtler strategy: 'He will attack his subject in unexpected places; he will fall upon the flank, or the rear; he will shoot a sudden, revealing searchlight into obscure recesses, hitherto undivined.'[22] And the book ends on war, too; the last sentence reads:

> At any rate it had all ended very happily — in a glorious slaughter of twenty thousand Arabs, a vast addition to the British Empire, and a step in the Peerage for Sir Evelyn Baring.[23]

The subject of this sentence is the Battle of Omdurman in 1898; but that sardonic tone, and that juxtaposition of slaughter and political advancement, must have seemed to some English readers in 1918 to have a more immediate reference.

The historical wars that Strachey's book describes were Victorian wars — the Crimean War, and the War against the Mahdi. But the war that he declared in his Preface, the historian's war of surprise, was fought against Victorianism itself — that is, against England-before-the-war. *Eminent Victorians* was an important campaign in that war; but it was not the first. There had been skirmishes even before the Great War began: a daring raid on the twentieth century by Quiller-Couch, for example, who put both Pound and Joyce into his *Oxford Book of Victorian Verse* in 1912, and the counter-attack in *Blast* no. 1, which BLASTED 'years 1837 to 1900'. 'We will sweep out the past century,' Pound wrote in June 1914, and young poets continued to exclaim against the past during the war: Graves wrote to Eddie Marsh in 1915 that when the war was over he and other young Georgians would 'try to root out more effectively the obnoxious survivals of Victorianism', and Wilfred Owen wrote to his mother in 1917: 'The Victoria Cross! I covet it not. Is it not *Victorian*? yah! pah!' And Alec Waugh's scandalous *Loom of Youth*, in attacking the public-school system, also attacked 'the rotten conventions of the mid-Victorian era', and announced that 'their day is over'.[24]

The wartime war against Victorianism is only one aspect of the feeling of radical separation from the past that was such a defining element in the war experience. Another version of that feeling is the theme of the Old Men — the conviction that the war had empowered the elderly to send the young to their deaths. This recurs from early in the war until the end (and after), and is expressed by many people, not all of them soldiers, as the following examples show:

> To many of us, I am sure — for I can judge of others by myself, the greatest trial that this war has brought is that it has released the old

men from all restraining influences and has let them loose upon the world.

letter from 'A Temporary Subaltern' to *Cambridge Magazine*,
May 1915.

War — as we presently understand it — is the sacrifice of the young and the innocent on the altar erected by the old and middle-aged . . .

Richard King in *The Tatler*, October 1916.

They [young men] have seen old men, who may have sacrificed nothing, and may even have increased their prosperity in the war, sitting on Tribunals and breaking up the homes and loves and livelihood of the young.

editorial, *The Nation*, February 1917.

To many of us the greatest trial that this war has brought is that it has released the old men from all the restraining influences and has let them loose upon the world.

Mrs Victor Rickard, *The Fire of Green Boughs*, June 1918[25]

To these examples one might add two war poems on the same theme, both from 1918: Osbert Sitwell's 'The Modern Abraham' and Owen's 'The Parable of the Old Man and the Young'. Both use the Biblical story of Abraham and Isaac, but alter the ending to draw a wartime moral. Sitwell's poem ends:

> And if I had ten other sons to send
> I'd make them serve my country to the end;
> So all the neighbors should flock round, and say:
> 'Oh! Look what Mr. Abraham has done.
> He loves his country in the elder way;
> Poor gentleman, he's lost another son!'

In Owen's version, God urges Abraham to offer the Ram of Pride instead,

> But the old man would not so, but slew his son,
> And half the seed of Europe, one by one.[26]

The theme also turned up in war painting, in Nevinson's satirical 'He Gained a Fortune But He Gave a Son' (see plate 18), and even in a 1918 tailor's advertisement — Pope & Bradley again (plate 16; compare with plate 1).

A pacifist magazine, a society paper, a Liberal weekly, a popular women's novelist, two soldier-poets, a Futurist painter — the range of these citations demonstrates how widespread the idea of the Old Men was. And the fact that Mrs Rickard cribbed her sentence from the pacifist *Cambridge Magazine* — even then under attack from the patriotic right — and gave it to a sympathetic soldier in her novel suggests that the idea had reached beyond the minority opposition, and was acceptable to the general public.

In common British usage, and especially when capitalized, Old Men was and is a generation term. But it was a class term as well. Wartime and post-war explosions of wrath against the Old Men were not directed at Old Farmers, or Old Postmen, after all: the term meant those men beyond service age who had the power to send young men to their deaths — directly, if they were generals or admirals or politicians, indirectly if they were journalists or bishops.

One should add, perhaps, that it was also inevitably a gender term. There were pro-war women, women who handed out white feathers and bullied young men in civilian clothes, and who spoke at recruiting meetings, and plenty of belligerent mothers (you find them in wartime novels like May Sinclair's *The Tree of Heaven* and Rose Allatini's *Despised and Rejected*); but there were no Old Women, because women were not perceived as having power. It is one more example of the exclusion of women from the drama of war.

Victorian Old Men represented the power of the past over the present, and wartime hostility to them was an expression of the growing belief that the stupidities and follies of the Victorian past had caused the war. That, essentially, is what Henry James had said on the first day of the war; and it was said again and again as the war went on. If that were true, then the pre-war, Victorian version of history was wrong, and history would have to be re-invented. History was not a story of liberal progress, with a continuous happy ending; the ending was the war. And so the story would have to be re-told to accommodate that disaster. *Eminent Victorians* is one response to that felt need.

Another response can be found in novels of the late war years that one might call 'war-generation histories', novels such as *The Loom of Youth*, *The Tree of Heaven* and Wells's *Joan and Peter*. These novels might seem to have little in common, but they have this — they are all historical novels. In this context, *historical* means two things: first, these are novels that are precisely located in actual time and place, through dates, through historical events, through references to actual public figures; they are stories that could only happen *then*, in the last days of Victorianism. But they are also historical in another sense: they are concerned with the forces of change at work, the social, political, moral, religious, philosophical ideas that brought England to a war, and Victorianism to its death.

The impulse to write such a revisionist history must arise from a sense of the absolute and catastrophic ending of an age. Ford Madox Ford described that impulse in *The Good Soldier*, an early and brilliant example of this literary kind written in the last months before the war began:

> You may well ask why I write. And yet my reasons are quite many. For it is not unusual in human beings who have witnessed the sack of a city or the falling to pieces of a people to desire to set down what they have witnessed for the benefit of unknown heirs or of generations infinitely remote; or, if you please, just to get the sight out of their heads.[27]

Perhaps there was another impulse as well; the felt need not to record the catastrophe, but to bury the dead. That seems to have been Wells's impulse in *Joan and Peter*, a novel that begins in the Nineties, and ends in 1918, during the German offensive. Near the end of the book, the character who speaks for Wells has this advice for the title characters:

> Listen when the old men tell you facts, for very often they know. Listen when they reason, they will teach you many twists and turns. But when they dogmatize, when they still want to rule unquestioned, and, above all, when they say '*impossible*,' even when they say '*wait — be dilatory and discreet*,' push them aside. Their minds squat crippled beside dead traditions . . . That England of the Victorian old men, and its empire and its honours and its court and precedences, it is all a dead body now, it has died as the war has gone on, and it has to be buried out of our way lest it corrupt you and all the world again . . .[28]

But whether the novelist looked primarily backwards or forward, the central point is the same: an age has ended, history has gaped and fallen away from the present.

By the end of the war, there were many novelists writing to set down what they had witnessed — sometimes to judge the past, sometimes to bury it and confront the future. One of the most successful of them was a novelist who is now quite forgotten, as his novel is: Stephen McKenna, whose *Sonia* was a best-seller in 1917. McKenna was a member of the war generation, born in the late 1880s, educated at Westminster and Christ Church, Oxford; he did not serve in the army, but spent the war years in Whitehall, in the War Trade Department. He developed a powerful sense of an ending there, and of a 'vanished generation' — his own.

Sonia is the story of that generation — or rather of the educated, upper-class part of that generation — beginning with their public-school days, and taking them through their years at Oxford, on to London, and then into the war, which some fight and some (principally the narrator) do not. Reading it now, one is likely to conclude that it is no more than a workmanlike novel of its time, put together out of the materials of other, better books — *Stalky & Co.* for the school days, *Sinister Street* for Oxford, *The Light That Failed* for the blinded hero, with an atrocity story of a crucified soldier that must have come out of the Bryce Report, or perhaps William Le Queux's version.

What was it, then, that made this commonplace, derivative book a popular success in 1917? The answer lies, I think, in passages like this one, in which the narrator explains the political situation in the spring of 1914, when O'Rane, the novel's Irish hero, enters Parliament. The threat of war, he tells us, was discounted then:

On the other hand, the condition of England was a matter for considerable searching of heart. A spirit of unrest and lawlessness, a neurotic state not to be dissociated from the hectic, long-drawn Carnival that continued from month to month and year to year, may be traced from the summer of the Coronation [i.e. 1911]. It is too early to probe the cause or say how far the staggering ostentation of the wealthy fomented the sullen disaffection of the poor. It is as yet impossible to weigh the merits in any one of the hysterical controversies of the times. Looking back on those four years, I recall the House of Lords dispute and a light reference to blood flowing under Westminster Bridge, railway and coal strikes characterized by equally light breach of agreements, a campaign in favour of female suffrage marked by violence to person and destruction to property, and finally a wrangle over a Home Rule Bill that spread far beyond the walls of Westminster and ended in the raising and training of illegal volunteer armies in Ireland. Such a record in an ostensibly law-abiding country gives matter for reflection. Sometimes I think the cause may be found in the sudden industrial recovery after ten years' depression following the South African War. The new money was spent in so much riotous living, and from end to end there settled on the country a mood of fretful, crapulous irritation. 'An unpopular law? Disregard it!' That seemed the rule of life with a people that had no object but successive pleasure and excitement and was fast becoming a law unto itself.[29]

The key phrase here is 'the condition of England': it links McKenna's book to a tradition of English social criticism that runs from Carlyle (who coined the phrase) and Disraeli to Masterman and E.M. Forster (whose *Howards End* is an important Edwardian example). What McKenna did in the quoted passage was to rewrite pre-war history, so as to explain the war, finding its cause in the affluence and dissolute luxury of the Edwardian era, and in the disorders of the pre-war 'wars' — the strikes, the suffrage militancy, the Irish crisis. It is an account that makes the war an inevitable national punishment and purge.

McKenna's book was published between the end of the Battle of the Somme and the beginning of Passchendaele; it could scarcely have a firm historical conclusion, any more than *Non-Combatants* or *Mr Britling Sees It Through* could. It ends, rather, on an either/or, with the blinded O'Rane speculating whether England will revert to its old ways — 'the old politics and the old sport and the old butterfly society of London, and the waste and the cruelty'[30] — or whether it will accomplish a moral revolution.

> Is it a great thing to ask? To demand of England to remember that the criminals and loafers and prostitutes are somebody's children, mothers and sisters? And that we've all been saved by a miracle of suffering? Is that too great a strain on our chivalry? I'll go out if need be, but — but *must* we stand at street-corners to tell what we have seen? To ask the bystanders — and ourselves — whether we went to war to preserve the right of inflicting pain?[31]

And there, in that string of unanswered questions, the novel ends. It hardly amounts to a resolution, but it seems to have been what English readers wanted in 1917 — a mixture of religious suffering and chivalry that could still make the war appear moral, and the dying sacrificial. McKenna had imagined the world-before-the-war as a corrupt society ripe for social revolution, and the world-after-the-war as an opportunity for a moral revolution. The war itself he treated as destructive and cruel; but he did not satirize it, he did not make it meaningless, and he did not blame those who commanded it for the lives that they had squandered. *Sonia* is a war novel that Marshal Haig or Lloyd George might have read without discomfort.

Nevertheless, McKenna made some assumptions in his book that link

him to Strachey and to Wells, and to many other writers of the late war
years. He assumed, for instance, that the causes of the war were to be
found in pre-war England, and not in a conspiracy of continental
dynasts, and that those causes were social and moral. And he assumed
that the England in which those causes had operated was lost, dead,
entirely separated from the wartime present and the post-war future.
Pre-war was back there, on the other side of the great fracture of the
war: it was a myth, a story that had come to its tragic ending.

Other English men and women looked back, in the later war years, to
the world before the war, and found their own myths there. Shane
Leslie, an aristocratic young Irish landowner, wrote a memoir of his
early life while he lay wounded in a military hospital, because he
realized, he said,

> that I had witnessed the suicide of the civilization called Christian and
> the travail of a new era to which no gods have been as yet rash enough
> to give their name, and remembering that, with my friends and
> contemporaries, I shared the fortunes and misfortunes of being born
> at the end of a chapter in history.[32]

Clive Bell, Bloomsbury aesthete and pacifist, looked back to that time,
too, though the myth he made was different. 'In the spring of 1914,' Bell
wrote in the *Cambridge Magazine*,

> society offered the new-comer precisely what the new-comer wanted,
> not cut-and-dried ideas, still less a perfect civilisation, but an intel-
> lectual flutter, faint and feverish no doubt, a certain receptivity to new
> ways of thinking and feeling, a mind at least ajar, and the luxurious
> tolerance of inherited wealth.

Searching for an historical analogy of that time, Bell found it in the
France of Louis XVI:

> Society before the war showed signs of becoming what French
> society before the Revolution had been — curious, gay, tolerant,
> reckless and reasonably cynical. After the war I suppose it will be
> none of these things ... The war has ruined our little patch of civility
> as thoroughly as a revolution could have done.[33]

The resemblances between pre-war England and pre-Revolutionary
France are not really very striking. What *is* similar, though, and must
have brought the comparison to Bell's mind, is the sense of the
annihilating deluge that came after. Others of his generation thought in

those terms too; Rose Macaulay, sending a copy of one of her pre-war novels to a friend for Christmas 1917, wrote in it: 'You needn't read it — it's only a token of regard, & is ante-diluvian — i.e. just before the war.'[34] The post-war idea of the pre-war years as a *belle époque* begins here.

Both Leslie and Bell invoked civilization as the defining feature of their pre-war myths, though neither would have accepted the other's definition of what that word meant. They agreed, though, that civilization had existed before the war, and that it had died. In wartime, the word would have a bitterly ironic ring, as when Duhamel titled his Prix Goncourt war novel *Civilisation 1914–1917*. And though it would reappear after the war, it would retain some of that irony: how, one wonders, did the ex-soldiers feel when they were given their campaign medals in 1919, and found that they bore the inscription: 'The Great War for Civilization'? Was that what they had fought for? And if it was, had they won?

CHAPTER 13

11/11/18

I

November 11, 1918 was a dark, wet day in England, the sort of day that even Englishmen complain of. It was nonetheless a memorable day — at eleven o'clock that morning the war stopped — and every diarist recorded it.[1] But only to say that the weather was awful, and that out there in the rain other people, dreadful people, were celebrating in dreadful ways. 'London today is a pandemonium of noise and revelry,' Beatrice Webb wrote in her diary, 'soldiers and flappers being most in evidence. Multitudes are making all the row they can, and in spite of depressing fog and steady rain, discords of sound and struggling, rushing beings and vehicles fill the streets.'[2] Virginia and Leonard Woolf went up to town from Richmond that day, moved not by a feeling of rejoicing but by a kind of restlessness. On the train they looked on with distaste as a fat, half-drunk working-class woman kissed soldiers; 'she & her like possessed London,' Mrs Woolf observed, '& alone celebrated peace in their sordid way, staggering up the muddy pavements in the rain, decked with flags . . .'[3] At the Ministry of Information, Arnold Bennett noted that the staff was excited when maroons went off at eleven, but he went on working, and was pleased when the rain fell: 'an excellent thing to damp hysteria and Bolshevism.'[4]

Outside London, the celebrations were more violent; at Cambridge students rioted, looting shops and wrecking the premises of the pacifist *Cambridge Magazine*; in Dublin, civilians attacked British troops, and soldiers retaliated by breaking bank windows.

For men in uniform, it was a curiously muted occasion. Robert Graves, on training duty in North Wales, described the day to Nichols:

Things were very quiet up here on the 11th: London was full of buck of course but in North Wales a foreign war or a victory more or less are not considered much. Little boys banged biscuit tins and a Verey light or two went up at the camp but for the rest not much. A perfunctory thanksgiving service with nothing more cheerful in it than a Last Post for the dead; and then grouses about demobilization. Funny people *les anglais*.[5]

Sassoon, on sick-leave in Oxford, heard the church bells and thought: 'The war is ended. It is impossible to realise.' Like Virginia Woolf, he went restlessly up to town.

I got to London about 6.30 and found masses of people in streets and congested Tubes, all waving flags and making fools of themselves — an outburst of mob patriotism. It was a wretched wet night, and very mild. It is a loathsome ending to the loathsome tragedy of the last four years.[6]

Herbert Read, busy in London on *Art and Letters*, behaved not like a soldier but like a man of letters; he read Henry James's *Sacred Fount*, 'to the accompaniment of the rejoicings — with a savage zest'.[7]

It was the same for men at the Front, without the mob patriotism and the drunken charwomen. A gunner in the artillery recorded the scene in his diary:

Mon. 11th Nov 1918. Awaiting orders this a.m. & everybody full of hope & listening for the sound of any gunfire. We heard one or two. Then just before dinner the message came, saying 'Hostilities will cease at 11.00 11/11/18.' I could hardly think it was over and it was surprising how coolly everybody took it. Except for a determination not to work this p.m. nobody did anything extraordinary. Rotten miserable rainy day not likely to make one too cheerful even if it is the end of the war.[8]

It does seem odd. The end had come that English men and women had yearned and hoped for through the long war years, yet when it came it was not felt as an occasion for celebration. Nor for Art. There are no English Armistice Day paintings that I know of, no great images of Victory or Peace, and no significant celebratory music. The one great composer of wartime music, Elgar, was asked by Laurence Binyon to set a peace ode; but though he had had great success with Binyon's three *Spirit of England* poems earlier in the war, he curtly refused to deal with

the ode, and chose instead to work on chamber music, and then on his
cello concerto. That concerto has been called an elegy for the war dead,
and perhaps it is; certainly it has a brooding, elegiac tone. But perhaps
Elgar was grieving for more than the English dead; perhaps his concerto
spoke for all the other things that seemed to him to have perished in the
war: the Edwardian past, the musical tradition to which he belonged,
the audience that had wanted his music. It is certain, at any rate, that his
first major work after the war had no note of victory or celebration in it.

Only one poem in English records the complex emotions of that time
as contemporary private accounts record them. It is a poem written not
by a soldier-poet, but by a non-combatant who was old enough to
remember the Charge of the Light Brigade and the Franco-Prussian War
— Thomas Hardy, seventy-eight years old in 1918. Hardy's 'And there
was a great calm' celebrates nothing; it doesn't mention who won or
who lost, or why they were fighting. It says, rather, what Henry James
had said at the beginning, that the war destroyed the human dream of
progress, until 'old hopes that earth was bettering slowly/Were dead
and damned'. Rhetorically, the poem enacts the process that one sees in
the work of the war poets: it begins in abstractions, and proceeds by
emptying itself of them, until it ends in particulars, presided over by the
spirits that govern Hardy's world — the sinister Spirit of Irony, and the
Spirit of Pity — and in an unanswered question.

The last stanza of Hardy's poem seems to me to get the mood of
11/11/18 — at least as thoughtful Englishmen felt it — exactly right:

> Calm fell. From Heaven distilled a clemency;
> There was peace on earth, and silence in the sky;
> Some could, some could not, shake off misery:
> The Sinister Spirit sneered: 'It had to be!'
> And again the Spirit of Pity whispered, 'Why?'[9]

An empty peace on earth and a silent sky, continuing misery for some,
an empty fatalism, and an unanswered questioning of it all: those surely
were the elements of that mood with which men and women responded
to the end of the war.

One reason for that mood perhaps was that though the Armistice was
signed on November 11, the war did not end quite so precisely and
neatly. For some men, it had begun to wind down months earlier, when
they came home from the Front, to convalesce or to take some safe and
boring home-front assignment, or to be discharged. When Armistice
Day came, both Paul Nash and Lewis were in England, working at vast

war paintings for the British War Memorials Committee; Read and Osbert Sitwell were busy editing *Art and Letters*; Graves and Sassoon were hanging about awaiting discharge.

For other men, the war, the suffering, and the dying went on. *The Times* continued to print its Roll of Honour well into the next year, as men went on dying of old wounds, and men previously described as missing in action were declared dead. The war did not officially end until June 28, 1919, when the Peace Treaty was signed. But by then it was in the past, it was memory; it was too late for celebration.

As the war came to an end, as it changed from *now* to *then*, it began to take shape in men's and women's minds as a completed unit of history, a piece of time with a beginning and an end. Just as 'before-the-war' had assumed a wholeness as it receded and became history, so 'during-the-war' began to take on definition as peace neared. Myths of wartime began to emerge: not simply myths of the fighting, but of English wartime society, of generational and class behaviour, of politics and profiteering, of work and privation. Gradually these would coalesce into a collective sense of what it had been like — the whole myth of England's war.

It was clear, looking back, that some fundamental social changes had occurred. Women looked back and saw (or thought they saw) that they had become a new work force and a new political force; some had worked who had never worked before, and many who had been servants had found a new independence in war factories. They were different — a fact that Parliament seemed to acknowledge by passing the Representation of the People Act in June 1918, giving women over thirty the vote. Englishmen looked back at Ireland, and saw that the war that had threatened there in 1914 had become a reality, but that it was a different war from what they had expected. The working class looked back and saw four years of higher wages and higher living costs, years that had begun with an 'industrial truce' and were ending in a sudden wave of strikes. Some of them looked back, too, at the Russian Revolution, and saw in it a promise of things to come in Britain. (So did the upper social classes, though with less enthusiasm; Gilbert Murray, for example, thought that a 'Bolshevik cataclysm' was one possible end to the war.)[10]

Critics looked back too, at what had come to seem a 'period' in the arts, and tried to assess what had happened. Had the war been good for art, as some of them had predicted in 1914? Or had it destroyed art, as others had feared? Conservative art critics agreed that during the war the momentum of pre-war Modernist art had run down. Some also saw in the war years the end of academic art, which had proved inadequate to the rendering of the new reality of war. Looking back at the end of 1918, the *Annual Register*'s critic wrote that the work of the war artists

> has shown us how far the academical method of illustrating conventional heroics falls short of the insight and acute response to the opportunities offered by tremendous events displayed by artists who really are artists. Few, if any, of these works can in themselves be counted great pictures, or even such memorable embodiments of the sentiment of war as were Lady Butler's 'The Roll Call' or Detaille's 'Le Bourget.' But on the other hand, they are such intense realisations of the actuality of this hideous upheaval as to leave no doubt that when the time comes for them such pictures will far transcend anything that we have yet seen.[11]

By this account, the years of war had been a void, emptied of both the old and the significant new, a time of waiting, between an ending and a beginning.

That autumn Arthur Waugh, a respected conservative critic and reviewer, looked back at the poetry of the past four years, and wrote what amounts to the first history of war poetry of the First World War. Waugh gave that history a shape that has become the customary one: the war began with a flood of enthusiastic but meretricious verse; this changed when the young poets reached the Front and experienced war as it really was; from this point on their motive became 'an eager, almost passionate determination to picture War as it reveals itself, not to the outsider, but to the enlightened combatant himself'.[12]

Waugh was an historical critic, and his sense of history was sound. He saw, for example, that the new trench poetry had its roots in the pre-war realism of the Georgians, and he recognized also that a literary change had to occur when a war was fought not by professional soldiers, but by all classes of the community. But his most interesting remarks have to do with the influence of this war poetry on the future. Considering the question of whether the war had created the poetry, Waugh wrote:

> it would seem to be not so much a fact that the war has made poetry, as that poetry has, now for the first time, made War — made it in its

own image, with all the tinsel and gaud of tradition stripped away from it; and so made it perhaps that no sincere artist will ever venture again to represent War in those delusive colours with which Art has been too often content to disguise it in the past.[13]

What Waugh was saying was that language creates reality, and that this war poetry would shape the way that subsequent generations would imagine the war that they never saw, and their own wars, still unfought. And so, of course, it did.

Waugh took pleasure in pointing out that the dark prophecies of critics like Gosse had been wrong: far from coming to an end, as Gosse had predicted it would, 'current literature' had flourished in the war. But he followed Gosse in one thing: he too saw the war as a purifying force in English culture:

A comparison of the spirit of this new poetry with that of the generation which preceded it would seem to suggest that War has most certainly not been without its purging influence upon the artistic soul of youth. For the new poetry is honest; it is strong; and it is often very beautiful. Decadence, at any rate, has vanished; triviality is no more; eccentricity has almost disappeared.[14]

So the notion of pre-war decadence turns up again here at the end, purged from English poetry by the trials of war.

Waugh saw the history of the war's poetry as a process of rejection of the poetic past. The new poetry strove to be absolutely free of convention and of sentimentality; it set a new standard of truth-telling, and by telling truth it created the history of its own time in its own image. And that new-told truth justified the war, in Waugh's mind. Waugh was the father of a war poet: his son Alec had gone to the Front as a nineteen-year-old subaltern, had been a German prisoner of war, and had written poems from his experiences. Perhaps the father thought of that young soldier when he wrote the concluding paragraph of his essay.

We end, then, with the conclusion that Poetry, in spite of many tribulations, is well justified of its supreme ordeal. It has gone down into the darkness, and has carried light in its hand. Our young men, indeed, have grown old, as befits those who have been face to face with death. It may be true that the war has made Stoics of our Hedonists, but in the process it has also made men. And, being men, they have not feared to speak the truth about the bitter discipline under which they have emerged into manhood. It is a terrible truth, wounding the speaker and the hearer alike; but it is a truth that may yet help to set free the soul of humanity for nobler victories in the years of peace.[15]

Another way of looking back at what changes had taken place through the war is to consider what the war was called. Wells had called it 'The War That Will End War', and that phrase had been taken up by politicians and journalists as having the right idealistic ring to it; but it wasn't really a name, one couldn't imagine it in a list of British victories with the Crimean War and the Boer War, and it didn't enter into general use. Still, one had to call it something. In January 1915 the editor of *Burke's Landed Gentry* was perplexed enough by the problem to write to *The Times* about it. 'I wonder,' he wrote,

> whether you or any of your readers could give me any certain information as to what is or is going to be the official name for the present war. Those of us who have to record matters are in a difficulty with regard to it. The general opinion rather seems to point to the use of the term 'European War,' but this, of course, ignores a very important part of the fighting in which this country is concerned in China, South Africa, Asiatic Turkey, and elsewhere.[16]

A reader replied: 'Surely no better name could be found for the present contest than the "Great War".'[17] Both of these terms had some currency; *The Times* indexed war news under 'European War', and the government put 'Great War' on its campaign medal. But the question was still unanswered in September 1918, when one Major Johnstone, a Harvard professor who had been sent to England by the American government to plan an official history of the war, called on Colonel Charles à Court Repington, military correspondent for the *Morning Post*, to discuss what name the war should be given.

Colonel Repington recorded his conversation with the American major in his diary:

> We discussed the right name of the war. I said that we called it now *The* War, but that this could not last. The Napoleonic War was *The Great War*. To call it *The German War* was too much flattery for the Boche. I suggested *The World War* as a shade better title, and finally we mutually agreed to call it *The First World War* in order to prevent the millennium folk from forgetting that the history of the world was the history of war.[18]

Repington was saying, in his cynical, worldly way, that the war was neither great nor the last, but was simply the first in a new sequence of wars that would differ from those of the past only in geographical range. When he used *The First World War* as the title of his two volumes of war memoirs, some reviewers protested at his cynicism; but the title stuck.

In this transformation of the name of the war, we can see one more example of the process by which the war that Englishmen saw ahead of them in 1914 became the war that we, looking back, perceive it to have been, the process by which a turmoil of events became a myth. Like other backward glances that we have seen, it was an act of diminishment and of separation from the past: a myth of loss — in this case, the loss of the Big Words in the naming of the war, the emptying of abstractions.

II

From the day the war began, people speculated about what life would be like, or should be like, in the world after the war. Some speculations were simply day-dreams, like Graves's 'Letter to S.S. from Mametz Wood', a fantasy in verse of wandering freedom with his friend Sassoon; others were philosophical discourses on the reform of society and government, like Bertrand Russell's *Principles of Social Reconstruction*. Some were hopeful, others were apprehensive: after-the-war would be a world free of fear, class antagonism, and want; or it would be a violent, revolutionary time, a sinful time, a time of deprivation and barbarism. It would be a time of great creativity in the arts, or it would be the end of art. It would be a new civilization, or the grave of civilization. But whatever it was, it would not be like the world before the war, and it would not be like wartime.

The British Library is stuffed with the published texts of these speculations, some of them stout books from established publishers, others ephemeral pamphlets on brittle, brown wartime paper that crumbles to the touch. Some of the authors are familiar: Russell, Clive Bell, and H.G. Wells are all there, as evidences of this wartime need to foresee. Bell predicted a post-war England deprived of the things that made Bloomsbury pleasant, primarily money and privacy (see the passage from his *Peace at Once* quoted on p. 85 above). Russell hoped for a world changed in both its economic structure and its philosophy of life, probably under the pressure of Labour. Wells saw — or at least wanted to see — some kind of collective society, united in its devotion to a God that Wells was just in the process of inventing.[19] No conceivable future would have suited them all, and they would all have hated each other's.

The ephemeral pamphlets were by all kinds of people — clergymen, businessmen, land-reformers, educators — all of them forgotten now, if they were ever known. Their books have titles like *After the War*, *The War After the War*, *The War Against War*, and *After-War Problems*; or titles with *Peace* in them: *Peace and Victory*, *Peace at Any Price*, *Bulwarks of Peace*, *Peace: the Choice*; or sometimes *New*: *New Science*, *New Freedom*, *New Outlook*. All of them have their principles, their solutions, and their odd eccentricities. None, so far as I can discover, had any impact on anyone.

Russell's 1916 lectures were concerned with Social Reconstruction, and *reconstruction* continued to be the commonest term for what must happen in England after the war. It seems, at first glance, an oddly inapplicable term: the reconstruction that Belgium and north-western France would need was clear enough — those were devastated areas — but the war's destructiveness had scarcely reached England. What was there, then, that needed to be reconstructed? The world-before-the-war, mainly. The government's wartime powers, its economic control of industry and its curtailments of civil liberties would have to be dismantled, so that England might revert to its old laissez-faire ways. Labour was anxious that its pre-war restrictive practices should come back, and that wartime workers — that is, women — should be removed from the jobs that belonged to fighting men.

But the restoration of the English *status quo ante* was clearly not enough; Englishmen were not dying in France for the sake of Edwardian England. The nation after the war would have to be perceptibly better — more just, more orderly, more generous to the poor and the unfortunate. The question was: how was that to be accomplished? To find the answers, Asquith had appointed a small Reconstruction Committee; when Lloyd George became Prime Minister he first enlarged the Committee, appointing distinguished laymen like Beatrice Webb and Seebohm Rowntree to supplement the government members, and later (in 1917) made it a Ministry. There were many meetings, many sub-committees, and many reports. But as Mrs Webb crossly observed in her diary, 'no one seems to read the papers that pour into the office from government departments and from the litter of sub-committees',[20] and the Ministry was disbanded in 1919 with most of its plans unrealized. What had begun as the collective term for the war's idealistic goals was by then a huckster's cliché: 'And now for Reconstruction!' a patent medicine ad of December 1918 reads. 'But first Reconstruct Your Nervous System.'[21] (See page 264.)

Reconstruction is an important theme because it demonstrates how the burden of idealism weighed upon wartime England, and how it led to the cynicism of the post-war years. The war was being fought for a cause, to make the world — or at least the English part of it — a better place. But *how* better? The answer depended on whether you were an industrialist or a shop-steward, a Conservative or a Fabian or a Communist, an officer or a private. The pressure mounted as the Rolls of Honour grew longer, to somehow make the dying worthwhile, and to protect the dead against the words *in vain*. But there was no plan, no report of a sub-committee, that would accomplish ends that would be worthwhile in all eyes.

It might have been better for England if idealism had not been institutionalized in Committee and Ministry, and if promises had not been made in speeches and reports. But because those things were done, Reconstruction became an irony, like 'a fit country for heroes'[22] — one more official lie. It is used in that way by the Socialist poet W.N. Ewer, in 'A Ballade of Reconstruction', probably written during the last year of the war:

> Our masters — seeing us a little tired
>   Of war — for even wars begin to pall;
> Seeing us growing restless, are inspired —
>   Lest we should once again begin to call
>   For liberty and justice, and to bawl
> For things we've tended to forget of late —
>   To promise, lest some graver thing befall,
> They'll reconstruct our England while we wait.[23]

And Ford Madox Ford used it in 1919, less belligerently but just as ironically, in *No Enemy*. The book is a barely fictionalized memoir of a soldier-poet, living in poverty and neglect after the war; it is sub-titled 'A Tale of Reconstruction'.

Reconstruction was one way of looking to the post-war future, and one acknowledgement that that future would have to be different from both the present and the past. But there were also other, private ways: diarists confessed their hopes and anxieties to themselves, and letter-writers revealed them to their correspondents. The commonest

And now for Reconstruction!

But first Reconstruct Your Nervous System

One of the most distinguished of living scientists—formerly Assistant Professor of Physiology at Oxford University — was advised by his physician to take Sanatogen after an attack of Influenza.

He did so, and afterwards wrote as follows in the *Lancet:* " It is evident that Sanatogen acts as a strong stimulus so far as the recuperative powers of the blood are concerned, and that a building-up process goes on in the nerves."

SANATOGEN

expectation was of extreme social change, brought on by post-war economic ruin, or by the demands of returning soldiers — revolution or reaction, welcomed or feared, depending on the politics (and to a degree on the age) of the writer. As the end of the war grew perceptibly nearer, anxiety increased, and so did uncertainty. 'I am beginning to rub my eyes at the prospect of peace,' Cynthia Asquith wrote in her diary on October 7, 1918. 'I think it will require more courage than anything that has gone before. It isn't until one leaves off spinning round that one realises how giddy one is.'[24] Beatrice Webb, writing on November 4, 1918, put her apprehension into more explicitly political terms:

There is little or no elation among the general body of citizens about the coming peace ... The absence of public rejoicing and sombre looks of private persons arises, I think, from preoccupation as to the kind of world we shall all live in when peace has come. Burdened with a huge public debt, living under the shadow of swollen government departments, with a working class seething with discontent, and a ruling class with all its traditions and standards topsy-turvy, with civil servants suspecting businessmen and businessmen conspiring to protect their profits, and all alike abusing the politician, no citizen knows what is going to happen to himself or his children, or to his own social circle, or to the state or to the Empire. All that he does know is that the old order is seriously threatened with dissolution without any new order being in sight. What are the social ideals germinating in the minds of the five millions who will presently return from the battlefields and battle seas? What is the outlook of the millions of men and women who have been earning high wages and working long hours at the war trades and will presently find themselves seeking work? What are the sympathies of the eight millions of new women voters? The Bolsheviks grin at us from a ruined Russia and their creed, like the plague of influenza, seems to be spreading westwards from one country to another. Will famine become chronic over whole stretches of Europe, and will some deadly pestilence be generated out of famine to scourge even those races who have a sufficiency of food? Will Western Europe flare up in the flames of anarchic revolution? Individuals brood over these questions and wonder what will have happened this time next year. Hence the depressed and distracted air of the strange medley of soldiers and civilians who throng the thoroughfares of the capital of the victorious Empire.[25]

Two very different women — one young and one middle-aged, one social and one Socialist — yet they shared this feeling that something violent and unpredictable was coming, and that it *must* come, because the past was dead.

The war, in this account of English imaginings of it, began with a speech by Sir Edward Grey that may never have been uttered. It ends with an Armistice Night prophecy by D.H. Lawrence that was certainly spoken, but in words that are lost. Lawrence had lived through the war in a state of profound despair; the past was dead, England was finished, there would have to be a new heaven and a new earth. For him, the Armistice was not a significant ending, but the beginning of something else that would probably be worse. David Garnett, who was present at the party with Lawrence, remembered his remarks as going something like this:

> I suppose you think the war is over and that we shall go back to the kind of world you lived in before it. But the war isn't over. The hate and evil is greater now than ever. Very soon war will break out again and overwhelm you. It makes me sick to see you rejoicing like a butterfly in the last rays of the sun before the winter. The crowd outside thinks that Germany is crushed forever. But the Germans will soon rise again. Europe is done for; England most of all the countries. This war isn't over. Even if the fighting should stop, the evil will be worse because the hate will be dammed up in men's hearts and will show itself in all sorts of ways which will be worse than war. Whatever happens there can be no Peace on Earth.[26]

An extreme statement, certainly, by a man who had been maddened by the war. But that madness was not unique; England itself seemed mad that night, as an unendurable unit of history shuddered to an end, and an unimaginable new era began.

PART IV

THE WORLD AFTER THE WAR
1919–25

You must get your perspective right. There is no chance
of the future resembling the past. That is the first point.
England and the Empire can never again be the England
and Empire that you knew.

Reginald, Viscount Esher, letter to Sir Maurice Hankey

February 18, 1919

CHAPTER 14

Monument-Making

I

In November 1919 Katherine Mansfield was having trouble writing a book review, and wrote to her editor Middleton Murry (who was also her husband) about her difficulties. The book was Virginia Woolf's *Night and Day*, and the problem had to do with the war. 'I don't like it,' Mansfield wrote of Woolf's novel:

> My private opinion is that it is a lie in the soul. The war never has been: that is what its message is. I don't want (God forbid!) mobilisation and the violation of Belgium, but the novel can't just leave the the war out. There *must* have been a change of heart. It is really fearful to see the 'settling down' of human beings. I feel in the *profoundest* sense that nothing can ever be the same — that, as artists, we are traitors if we feel otherwise: we have to take it into account and find new expressions, new moulds for our new thoughts and feelings. Is this exaggeration? What *has* been, stands.[1]

The war had changed reality, she said, and so art must change. But how does art acknowledge that change? How does it give form and order to a new reality containing the war as a continuing presence? Not by pretending that the war had not occurred; not by writing as though the continuity of history had not been broken, and consciousness altered by four years of chaos and horror: 'Jane Austen could not write *Northanger Abbey* now,' Mansfield went on, ' — or if she did, I'd have none of her.'

Much of what happened in the arts in the years after the war can be seen as attempts of various kinds to deal with the issues that had troubled Katherine Mansfield. One immediate response was to build the war physically into post-war reality by creating monuments.

Monument-raising is an attempt by a society to deal with certain fundamental needs of those who survive a war. A monument records the dead, and so gives dignity to their undignified deaths. Poets since Homer have recognized this need, and the horror that survivors have felt at the thought of nameless annihilation in war, and of an unmarked grave. Old Priam in the *Iliad* fears that Hector's body will be thrown to the dogs, and the poem ends with a ritual funeral for the dead heroes. In 1918 there were half a million unmarked British graves in the war zones — not even graves, many of them, but shell holes and collapsed trenches and scattered bones among the other rubbish of the war. Somehow those random indignities would have to be ordered.

Monuments perform other functions, too. They reassure non-combatants that the dead died willingly and do not resent or repent their sacrifice. The classic example is the epitaph of Simonides of Ceos for the dead at Thermopylae:

> Go tell the Spartans, thou that passeth by,
> That here, obedient to their laws, we lie.

It was an epitaph widely adapted for English use in the early twentieth century: it stands on Waggon Hill, above Ladysmith in South Africa, to commemorate the Boer War dead there:

> Tell England, you who pass this monument,
> We died for her and rest here well content,

and it turns up on various memorials of the First World War, both in England and in foreign countries.[2]

One might also think of monuments as official acts of closure — the C-major chords that bring a war and its emotions to a grand and affirming conclusion. They embody, in permanent form, ideas about war — heroic, romantic, histrionic, occasionally tragic; they say, in effect, 'War has ideals: here they are, in stone, in bronze'. They have their own rhetoric, sometimes verbal, as in the epitaphs, sometimes gestural, in symbols and symmetries and allusions to the past. They belong to the discourse of Big Words, and by existing they affirm the meaning and value of those words, in spite of all the dying.

The idea of memorializing had been present in some minds, at least, from the beginning of the war.[3] The war had been going on only a few months when Fabian Ware, a Red Cross worker in France, began to locate and record graves of the dead. His amateur 'War Registration Commission' was recognized by the War Office in 1915, and eventually became the Imperial War Graves Commission. In 1916 it was decided that no bodies should be returned to England, but that they should be buried where they fell (more or less: there were more than twelve hundred patches of soldiers' graves in France alone at the end of the war, and these were eventually consolidated). In 1917 two English architects, Sir Edwin Lutyens and Herbert Baker, were sent to France to consider the whole cemetery problem, and to make recommendations.

The problems that they faced were considerable, and were not only logistical. What sort of monuments should each cemetery have? How symbolic should they be, and with what sort of symbolism? Should it be Christian? What about all those dead Jews, Moslems, Hindus, and atheists? Should there be inscriptions, and if so, what? Should individual monuments be allowed? Should officers be distinguished from enlisted men? In the end, the Commission agreed that all headstones should be identical, and should carry names but not ranks. Each cemetery should have two monuments: a Great War Stone — an altar-like horizontal block of stone,[4] raised upon three stone steps — and a Cross of Sacrifice. On the Cross a bronze sword would be mounted; on the Stone there would be an appropriate inscription. Lutyens asked Kipling to suggest what that inscription should be, and Kipling offered 'Their Name Liveth for Evermore'. The line comes from the familiar passage in Ecclesiasticus, Chapter 44, which begins 'Let us now praise famous men', and it has the right ring for a war memorial. But there is an irony in it too, if you look at the context. The verse immediately preceding the words that Kipling chose reads:

> And some there be, which have no memorial;
> Who are perished, as though they had never been;
> And are become as though they had never been born;
> And their children after them.

One can't help thinking of Kipling's only son, John, missing at Loos, his body never found.

It wasn't only the War Graves Commission that thought about monuments while the war went on. The government also appointed a General Committee for a National War Museum, and in 1917 received its first report. The Committee recommended a memorial consisting of a Hall of Honour, containing portraits and statues of figures pre-eminent in the war (generals and admirals, one assumes), and a Memorial Gallery containing the names of the dead, set in bronze. One can see what they were after: a hall to affirm that there had been heroes and heroism, and a gallery to record and preserve the names of the nameless, unburied dead. No such building, and no such rooms, were ever constructed.

Private individuals also thought about monuments, and especially if they were sculptors or architects. As early as March 1916 the sculptor W.R. Colton was looking forward, in a lecture, to the boom in his trade that the end of the war would surely bring.

> If this century is to have a real record of the war through its memorials that shall be worthy of the nation I imagine there is but one way. Never before, I am bold enough to say, has there existed such a mass of craftsmen anxiously awaiting to give expression to those feelings of patriotism, sorrow, and hero-worship, that when crystallised will produce its record in stone, marble, and bronze . . .
>
> A memorial must be a love gift spiritually ungrudged both by its promoters and by its artist if it is to be valued by succeeding generations. A utilitarian value detracts from its spiritual quality. A triumphal arch should be boldly nothing but an emblem of triumph. A war memorial should express simply the nobility of the individual or the common sacrifice in terms of Art. A thing of utility called a war memorial is but begging the question — beyond its usefulness it has no value in the history of the nation.
>
> We are fighting the greatest war the world has ever seen at untold sacrifice. Let us sacrifice a little more, and in our gratitude make sure that its commemoration shall stand for evermore a worthy tribute to our heroes.[5]

If Colton's speech sounded self-serving and greedy, that shouldn't have surprised anyone. There was going to be money to be made in memorializing the dead, and the living were determined to be in on it, when the time came. (Colton got commissions for a number of war memorials after the war, the best known of which is the Royal Artillery monument in the Mall, London.) But other, less unseemly motives were at work as well: a desire, on the part of serious, established architects and sculptors, to make certain that the nation woud be well served in its monuments, and that the objects that were raised to express the emotions of the bereaved and the values of the dead would be worthy of this great war. But what emotions? what values? and what sorts of objects? The symbolic particulars in these cases — the altar stone and the cross with its sword, the Hall of Honour and the Memorial Gallery, the triumphal arch — these were the symbols of the old tradition. But which of them would be appropriate for the dead of *this* war?

The Victoria and Albert Museum offered its answer to that question in the summer of 1919, with a 'War Memorials Exhibition'. The show was divided into two parts: a retrospective section of memorial objects and photographs from the museum's permanent collection, ranging from Greek stelae through sarcophagi and Renaissance memorial tablets to church furnishings, stained glass, and vestments, and a modern section of memorials recently executed or in hand — the same sorts of objects, only new. Clearly the whole exhibition amounted to a demonstration of what *tradition* meant; here were the forms in which the dead had been memorialized over the past two thousand years and more, and here was evidence that those forms were still alive — look in the modern section, you could see them all around you. But were they relevant? Could they express the way grieving men and women felt about the war and the dead in 1919? For many they were, and they could. People certainly went home from the V. and A. and commissioned windows and marble plaques, and had them installed in village churches and provincial cathedrals; one sees them everywhere in England. And no doubt the grieving families who put them there took comfort in the fact that their memorials looked like the others that commemorated earlier deaths in earlier wars.

But for many others, that show must have seemed as inappropriate as the Big Words that Owen's Preface proscribed. A Roll of Honour suitable for a public school; a memorial window for Gresham's School in Norfolk; another window, 'The Sacrifice of Motherhood', designed for a mothers' war memorial; endless St Georges and soldier-saints and enamelled angels — how could one relate those images to the dead at Bourlon Wood and Sedd-el-Bahr? For many viewers that exhibition must have demonstrated with appalling clarity how useless the tradition was for those who felt the uniqueness of the war that had just ended.

One thinks of monuments as made of stone or bronze; but the monumentalizing impulse took many other forms during the war years. There were, for example, a growing number of war paintings.[6] Masterman's Official War Artists had been at work for more than two years when the war ended, and pictures were piling up. There had been other collections of war art made, too: the Imperial War Museum Committee, with its mandate to accumulate everything connected with the war, had acquired a certain number of paintings among its trophies,

photographs, uniforms, medals and general detritus of war; there was
also an ambitious Canadian War Memorials project supervised by the
industrious Lord Beaverbrook, and from early 1918 a new British War
Memorials Committee, also under Beaverbrook. Some officials began
to think that these paintings, and others yet unpainted, might constitute
a monument in themselves, perhaps hung in the Hall of Honour of a
National (or why not *Imperial*?) War Museum, transformed from a
portrait gallery into a gallery of monumental war art.

But what should monumental war pictures look like? Members of
Beaverbrook's committee agreed that they should be large, and per-
haps uniform in size. Muirhead Bone later recalled that Robbie Ross
had proposed as a model 'the Mantegna series in the Duchess of
Mantua's bedroom'.[7] If he meant the frescoes in the Camera degli
Sposi in the Palazzo Ducale, he was proposing pictures slightly over
twenty-six feet long. Other suggested models were Velasquez's 'The
Surrender of Breda' (ten feet by twelve) and Uccello's 'Battle of San
Romano' (six feet by ten). Only one picture was painted that came
anywhere near the Mantegna size: John Singer Sargent's 'Gassed' is
seven and a half feet by twenty. But no other painting reaches these vast
dimensions, and there was no concerted effort even to be uniform on
a smaller scale; the pictures, like those in any other art gallery, came in
all sizes.

Those paintings were exhibited in December 1919 at Burlington
House, where the Royal Academy played host to the Imperial War
Museum's collection. The exhibition was much talked and written
about, partly because of the apparent dissonance between its contents
and its location. For the Royal Academy in 1919 was still closed against
Modernism; yet here was a show that was full of startlingly modern
pictures — by the Nash brothers, Wyndham Lewis, the Spencers,
Nevinson, William Roberts, Henry Lamb. For some reviewers it was
on this account an epoch-making event, comparable to Roger Fry's
'Manet and the Post-Impressionists' in 1910. Now, as then, something
radically new was entering English art; *les jeunes*, as one reviewer put it,
sont arrivés.

'The Nation's War Paintings' was in fact two shows which contradicted
each other, and which together raised fundamental questions about the
place and nature of art in post-war culture. The critic R.H. Wilenski put
the division clearly and simply: 'there are two kinds of pictures in the
present exhibition,' he wrote: 'the pictures by men who were tortured
by the war and the pictures by men who were not.'[8] But how does one

judge tortured paintings? Clive Bell, for one, could not; he could only dismiss them as existing outside his Bloomsbury aesthetic. They expressed, he said, only what had horrified the painters as men, not what had moved them as artists.

Middleton Murry, on the fringes of Bloomsbury, also worried about the content of the paintings. 'Art is not a protest,' he wrote; 'but the art that deals with war must be a protest. There is the dilemma.' His resolution of the dilemma was a conservative one:

> How shall we solve it? Only by waiting till the protesting part is calm, and using all the strength and subtlety of art to render the weariness that has descended upon our souls.[9]

In other words, just sit quietly, and Decadence will return.

But here and there, more acute critics saw that the protesting part would not go away, and that Decadence would not return. 'These war pictures', wrote one, 'are in themselves an object lesson. It has shown the so-called revolutionary artist as the one who has unquestionably expressed the true character and spirit of modern warfare.'[10] Modernism and hatred of the war were, he saw, the same; and traditional art and traditional views of war were on the other side together. What the 'War Paintings' show demonstrated was that the war's paintings could never be made to constitute a monument in the customary sense, that such a collection would continually refute itself, continually shift, in any viewer's eyes, from monument to anti-monument, from glory to death.

The will to create monuments also found expression in the other arts after the war. In music, for example, there was John Foulds's *World Requiem*, written in the years 1918–21, and performed for the first time on Armistice Night, 1923, in a commemorative service sponsored by the British Legion in the Albert Hall. Foulds, like some painters, seemed to equate monumentality with size: his *Requiem* was in twenty movements, required two hours to perform, and called for 1,200 singers and instrumentalists. The text was drawn from many sources — from the Bible, *Pilgrim's Progress*, and Hindu poetry, interspersed with passages that sound like contemporary free verse.

Foulds described his work, on the printed score, as 'a tribute to the memory of the Dead — a message of consolation to the bereaved of all countries'; that is to say, he intended it to do what monuments do, to affirm the value and significance of the war's sacrifices. The last movement, 'Consummatus', has this text:

Chorus

He hath blessed us from Whom all blessing flows: the living, loving
Father, in Whom, with Christ and the Holy Spirit, we are at peace for
evermore.

Soprano, Contralto and Tenor

Alleluia!

Chorus

He hath poured out His Spirit upon us,
He hath blessed us. Amen.

Soprano, Contralto, Tenor, Baritone and Chorus

Alleluia! Amen! Alleluia![11]

which sounds orthodox enough for any Christian, in spite of Foulds's
address to 'all countries', and the insertion of the Hindu passages.

The reviews were on the whole respectful but unenthusiastic.
Reviewers must have found the occasion difficult: how could one be
critically severe with so vast a work on such a solemn national occasion?
And yet, there seemed little to praise beyond the monumentality. The
Times's critic's cautious notice was typical. 'The scope of the work', he
wrote,

> is beyond what any one has dared to attempt hitherto. It is no
> less than to find expression for the deepest and most widespread
> unhappiness that this generation has known. As such it was received
> by a very large number of listeners, who evidently had felt that music
> alone could do this for them. They found perhaps in the communal
> note of that choir of 1,200 the sympathy of which they stood in need,
> and in the words, taken mainly from those parts of the Bible that we
> never can hear unmoved, the consolation they hoped for.[12]

In other words, it was large and it was long, and it used the best familiar
texts. But was it musically distinguished? The best that this critic could
say on that point was that 'the general spirit of it was the monotone,
such as grief and prayer both use'.

Foulds evidently expected that his requiem would be accepted as an
English institution, and would be performed ritually on every Armistice
Night; and for a time it was. But after 1926 the British Legion withdrew
its support, and Foulds was left with the printing bills for 1,200 parts,
and no royalties (he had assigned them to the British Legion). The
Requiem was never performed again, and Foulds left England, an angry
and disappointed man. His monument of musical remembrance had

held English audiences for four years, after which it had simply faded, as the two-minute Armistice Day silence faded, into oblivion. It is really fearful, as Katherine Mansfield said, to see the 'settling down' of human beings.

There was monument-making in the publishing world, too: anthologics of poems by dead young war poets, with monumental titles like *A Crown of Amaranth*, and *Valour and Vision*; volumes of brief lives of the dead (*Golden Deeds of Heroism*, *The New Elizabethans*); letters from the Front; reminiscences of dead sons, dead friends (like John Buchan's memoir of the Grenfell brothers, Francis and Riversdale); family memorials, like the *Book of Remembrance* of a Dorset County family for which Thomas Hardy wrote an introduction. How remote and faded those dead young men seem, how distant from the post-war world into which their memorials issued: the two fox-hunting Honourables, the man-about-town, the actor, the bishop's son, the Irish MP, the duke's grandson. Together these books commemorate not so much a number of individuals as one generation of a class. And they do something else: they preserve — artificially, anachronistically, like objects in a museum — the spirit in which these young men went to war. Look, for example, at the full title of the book for which Hardy wrote his introduction: *A Book of Remembrance, Being a Short Summary of the Service and Sacrifice Rendered to the Empire During the Great War by One of the Many Patriotic Families of Wessex, the Popes of Wrackleford, Co. Dorset*. There the words all are: Service and Sacrifice, Empire, the Great War, Patriotism, asserted not only in the face of the emerging contrary tradition, but of the known fact of the war, and the numbers of the dead.

The ultimate monument to an historical event will be a history of it — or perhaps in this case a heap of histories. In the years after the war there were many histories published: the serial histories that popular writers like Buchan, Conan Doyle and Le Queux had kept going through the war were brought to completion and published in sets; newspapers published their own (*The Times* and the *Manchester Guardian* each had one); Field Marshal Haig, in his collected *Despatches*, offered his version, and Churchill began his. By 1922 the British Museum, in its *Subject Index of Books Relating to the European War*, could list more than forty titles under 'General History'.

There are two things about these books — or about many of them at least — that suggest that *monumental* is the right word for them. One is the scale on which they were written. As with paintings, statues, and requiems, one measure of the monumentality of a history is its sheer

size. If you look at the British Museum's list you will find that 'General
Histories' came in all sizes, but that they tended towards the many-
volumed: eight volumes, nine volumes, ten volumes, fourteen volumes,
twenty-one volumes (*The Times*), twenty-four volumes (Buchan).
These were massive works that reported the war in copious detail; but
they also affirmed — that's the other monumental thing about them; it
was a good war, a just war, a *great* war (look at its scale, look at the
multitudinousness of its events, look at the length of the histories that
record it). The stories have their dark moments and their tragic losses,
but they swell with emotion and pride at the end, and the Big Words
sound out again, as though they had never been doubted.

Here, as an example, is the final paragraph of the second and
concluding volume of Philip Gibbs's collected dispatches, *Open Warfare:
The Way to Victory* (1919):

> And now the world in its heart must salute all our soldiers who
> through these four years and more of war have fought for this victory
> by great heroism through many years of horror and tragedy, with
> enormous sacrifice. I see only two figures in this war now that
> hostilities have ceased — the officers and men who have gained this
> victory on the British Front. One is the figure of the regimental
> officer, from subaltern to battalion commander, the boys and their
> elder brothers, who went over the top at dawn and led their men
> gallantly, hiding any fear of death they had, and who in dirty ditches
> and dug-outs, in mud and swamps, in fields under fire, in ruins that
> were death-traps, in all the filth and misery of this war held fast to the
> pride of manhood, and in the worst hours did not weaken, and for
> their country's sake and the game they play offered up their life, and
> all that life means to youth, as a free, cheap gift. And the other figure
> is Tommy. Poor old Tommy! You have had a rough time, and you
> hated it, but by the living God you have been patient and long-
> suffering and full of grim and silent courage, not swanking about the
> things you have done, not caring a jot for glory, not getting much,
> but now you have done your job, and it is well done.[13]

Gibbs was an experienced journalist, and he knew what his readers
needed in 1919: brave, consolatory language that would shore up their
faith in the war they had won, a monument of words.

There were other books published just after the war that one might
best call *self*-monuments — the memoirs of the commanders, the
generals and the admirals who had planned the battles, and won or lost

them, and who were swift into print to celebrate or to exculpate their judgements. Haig's *Despatches* appeared in 1919; so did Field Marshal French's version of his disastrous year of command, 1914, and Admiral Jellicoe's *The Grand Fleet, 1914–16*; so did memoirs by General Ludendorff, General von Falkenhayn, and Admiral von Tirpitz (all in print in English translation by the end of the year). General Hamilton's history of the Gallipoli campaign and Jellicoe's *The Crisis of the Naval War* followed in 1920.

In this great burst of historical monument-making, only the histories of surviving private soldiers and junior officers were missing. Their absence from publishers' lists was so noticeable that H.M. Tomlinson devoted an essay in the spring of 1920 to complaining about it.

> The publishers may send out what advice they choose [he wrote] to authors concerning the unpopularity of books about the War — always excepting, of course, the important reminiscences, the soft and heavy masses of words of the great leaders of the nations in the War which merely reveal that they never knew what they were doing. Certainly we could spare that kind of war book, though it continues to arrive in abundance; a volume by a famous soldier explaining why affairs went strangely wrong is about the last place where we should look for anything but folly solemnly pondering unrealities. But whatever the publishers may say, we do want books about the War by men who were in it.[14]

Perhaps 'we' did; but it was not a time for realism. In those years immediately after the war, the impulse, perhaps one should say the social need, was for affirming monuments.

II

The impulse to terminate the war finally and monumentally was expressed in public rituals on two post-war occasions. The first was July 19, 1919, a day designated officially as 'Peace Day'. The Versailles Treaty had been signed three weeks earlier, and this day would be a national celebration of the formal closure of the war. Bells were rung in the nation's churches, and there were fireworks in the evening; but it was mostly a day for parading. In London 18,000 troops marched, led by their wartime commanders — Haig, Foch, Robertson, Pershing, and

Jellicoe were all there. There was as yet no permanent cenotaph in Whitehall, but a temporary one was constructed for the occasion (see plate 17), and the troops saluted it as they passed. Along the pavements, crowds clapped and cheered, and women wept. This, at last, was peace.

The following year, on Armistice Day, there were other, and more final ceremonies. By then Lutyens's permanent Cenotaph was in place, and it was unveiled that day by the King. It was (and is) a plain structure — a plinth decorated only with stone wreaths (Lutyens did not favour religious symbolism in his monuments), with a terse inscription: 'The Glorious Dead'. On the same day the Unknown Warrior was buried in Westminster Abbey. The inscription in this case was more elaborate:

> BENEATH THIS STONE RESTS THE BODY
> OF A BRITISH WARRIOR
> UNKNOWN BY NAME OR RANK
> BROUGHT FROM FRANCE TO LIE AMONG
> THE MOST ILLUSTRIOUS OF THE LAND
>
> AND BURIED HERE ON ARMISTICE DAY
> 11 NOV: 1920, IN THE PRESENCE OF
> HIS MAJESTY KING GEORGE V
> HIS MINISTERS OF STATE
> THE CHIEFS OF HIS FORCES
> AND A VAST CONCOURSE OF THE NATION
>
> THUS ARE COMMEMORATED THE MANY
> MULTITUDES WHO DURING THE GREAT
> WAR OF 1914–1918 GAVE THE MOST THAT
> MAN CAN GIVE LIFE ITSELF
> FOR GOD
> FOR KING AND COUNTRY
> FOR LOVED ONES HOME AND EMPIRE
> FOR THE SACRED CAUSE OF JUSTICE AND
> THE FREEDOM OF THE WORLD
>
> THEY BURIED HIM AMONG THE KINGS BECAUSE HE
> HAD DONE GOOD TOWARD GOD AND TOWARD
> HIS HOUSE

This, surely, is the ultimate formulation of the official meaning of the war.

But there were aspects of these occasions that suggest a symbolism other than that intended. To celebrate Peace Day with marching troops and detonations in the night sky — is that peace? Or is it more like the world of the Western Front? As for the two monuments, one could find in both a symbolism that came closer to the war's reality than Lutyens and the King probably had in mind. For one contained an unidentified corpse, and the other no body at all — two sombre monuments to the half-million British soldiers whose bodies were still unidentified, or were never found, the eternally anonymous and unheroic dead.

Other events occurred on these solemn, official days that symbolize other realities of the post-war world, and that suggest the tensions that develop when a nation reduces complex emotions to the simplicities of monuments. At Epsom in June 1919, Canadian soldiers awaiting demobilization wrecked the local police station, and the station sergeant was killed; and in Luton, on Peace Day, ex-servicemen rioted because they had been excluded from public ceremonies, forced the doors of the town hall and wrecked and burned the building. This was outrageous behaviour in the peaceful streets of English towns, but it was what these men had been doing for four years, and for which they had been promised the treatment due to heroes. By the summer of 1919 both soldiers and ex-soldiers were beginning to see that the promises had been lies. As the Luton Town Council's Peace Day procession marched through the streets it passed disabled veterans who raised a banner reading: 'Don't pity us, give us work!'

There were similar conflicting pressures evident at the time of the Armistice Day unveiling in 1920. Beatrice Webb, always an acute observer of the social scene, wrote in her diary on November 29:

Our absorbing preoccupation during the last few weeks — alas! a symbol of what is happening — have been public funerals! The public pageant of the 'unknown warrior' symbolizing the ten million white men killed in the war, the funeral of the martyred Lord Mayor of Cork, and as a reprisal, the military parade through London of the corpses of the English Officers murdered in Dublin. Yesterday Downing Street was barricaded lest there should be yet another and still more impressive public ceremony — the funeral of an assassinated Prime Minister! It is said that he lives in fear of the Green Terror and is looking for a compromise with Sinn Fein.[15]

Mrs Webb's choice of words to describe the Unknown Warrior ceremonies — 'the public pageant' — suggests that she regarded such formalities as no more than empty public gestures. One war might have

ended, but other wars continued, and it would take more than pageants
to make the world peaceable indeed.

Nor was she alone in looking at such enactments with a dubious eye.
Osbert Sitwell wrote a poem for the Peace Day celebrations, and called
it 'Corpse Day'. And Charlotte Mew, thinking about the Cenotaph in
the autumn of 1919, wrote a poem about that monument that ends with
these lines:

> For this will stand in our Market-place —
> Who'll sell, who'll buy
> (Will you or I
> Lie each to each with the better grace)?
> While looking into every busy whore's and huckster's face
> As they drive their bargains, is the Face
> Of God: and some young, piteous, murdered face.[16]

Nothing can ever be the same, Katherine Mansfield had said: there *must*
have been a change of heart. The monuments and the ceremonies
existed to deny that assertion: nothing had changed, heroes were still
heoes, the Big Words retained their authority. But for many English
men and women that was not true. And because it was not true, post-
war art and culture would have to be different.

CHAPTER 15

Anti-Monuments

I

As the monuments rose, another, alternative version of the war's meaning was also taking form, a version that we might call collectively the anti-monuments. These were not buildings or statues or soldiers' graves, of course: those belonged to the state, or were the public gestures of private mourners. They were, rather, all the other forms in which judgements and conclusions about war could be expressed: paintings, poems, novels, histories, plays, music. These were works that rendered the war without the value-bearing abstractions, without the glory, and without the large-scale grandeur. Often they were conscious, aggressive rejections of the monument-making principles; they turned away from celebration, in search of war's reality.

This division of judgement is a fundamental fact in post-war English culture, a fact that has both social and aesthetic implications. It is not true, as is sometimes assumed, that a general wartime enthusiasm for war and its values was overwhelmed and replaced at the war's end by a total disillusionment that informs and defines English culture of the Twenties. Rather, both existed throughout the decade — two cultures, separate and mistrustful of each other, a conservative culture that clung to and asserted traditional values, and a counter-culture, rooted in rejection of the war and its principles. Each culture had its art, its literature, and its monuments; and each denied the other.

As an example of an anti-monument-maker, consider the case of Philip Gibbs. Gibbs is useful, because while the war went on he had served the war cause well. As the official correspondent for the *Daily Chronicle* on the Western Front, Gibbs was probably the most widely read, and most influential, of English journalists. His dispatches were vivid, but they were also consistently positive, even in the most disastrous circumstances (as, for example, in his report of the first day of the Somme offensive, quoted above, p. 110). Those dispatches were collected and published in book-form during the war, and made part of the mass of instant history that the war produced.[1] But once the war had ended, Gibbs's view of it changed; or rather, the view that he felt free to express changed, and he wrote a revisionary history that in England he called *The Realities of War*, and in the United States *Now It Can Be Told*.

Gibbs was aware of an apparent conflict between the story of war that he had told in his wartime dispatches, and the story he offered in his new, post-war book, and he insisted in a preface that the new version did not cancel or deny anything in the earlier narratives. But the two titles that he chose suggest otherwise; and so do his statements of his post-war intentions. *Realities of War*, he wrote, was 'a warning of what will happen again — surely — if a heritage of evil and of folly is not cut out of the hearts of peoples'. There, in the first sentence of the first page, the whole 'War That Will End Wars' notion is discarded. Further on, Gibbs explained his purpose in more detail:

> The purpose of this book is to get deeper to the truth of this war and of all war, not by a more detailed narrative of events, but rather as the truth was revealed to the minds of men, in many aspects, out of their experience; and by a plain statement of realities, however painful, to add something to the world's knowledge out of which men of good-will may try to shape some new system of relationship between one people and another, some new code of international morality, preventing, or at least, postponing, another massacre of youth like that five years' sacrifice of boys of which I was a witness.[2]

What is interesting here is the connection assumed between 'a plain statement of realities' and polemical effect. Truth-telling alone will persuade, if anything will. This is the aesthetic of description that one finds in the best of the trench narratives, and in trench poetry. Here, after the war, a journalist who had made his reputation out of heightened and emotive language comes to a soldier's style.

Gibbs's realities, the things that could now be told, were first of all the grotesque details of death and devastation that the censors would not have tolerated while the war was going on. Not details of actual fighting, of course — correspondents were not allowed to witness that — but of what was left after battle, the faceless corpses, the scattered limbs, the heaped-up bodies and the stench of death.

But there is another kind of particular in Gibbs's *Realities* that is, I think, equally important in the imagining of the war. Now he could name the regiments and the men to whom these disasters happened, and where. This act of naming is more than a matter of casting off censorship: for the men who fought, those names were symbols — Mametz and Fricourt Wood, the Menin Road, Thiepval, Contalmaison, the West Yorks, the Manchesters, and the Royal Welch Fusiliers all resonated with meaning, and so in other ways did the names of the commanders — French and Haig, Foch, von Arnim. Wilfred Owen must have been thinking of such resonances when he wrote in his draft preface, 'If I thought the letter of this book would last, I might have used proper names ...' — not, surely, to preserve memories of individuals, but as a further step towards absolute realism, and away from the lies. Ten years later, Hemingway's Frederick Henry thought it all through:

> I was always embarrassed by the words sacred, glorious and sacrifice and the expression in vain. We had heard them, sometimes standing in the rain almost out of ear-shot, so that only the shouted words came through, and had read them, on proclamations that were slapped up by billposters over other proclamations, now for a long time, and I had seen nothing sacred, and the things that were glorious had no glory and the sacrifices were like the stockyards at Chicago if nothing was done with the meat except to bury it. There were many words that you could not stand to hear and finally only the names of places had dignity. Certain numbers were the same way and certain dates and these with the names of the places were all you could say and have them mean anything. Abstract words such as glory, honor, courage, or hallow were obscene beside the concrete names of villages, the numbers of roads, the names of rivers, the numbers of regiments and the dates.[3]

Gibbs was neither an Owen nor a Hemingway, but he had come to something like their sense of what was real in the world of war: the end of the war had freed him to write like a soldier, in the language of fact.

The change was more than a change of language, though; it was also a change of tone. Like many of the soldier-writers, Gibbs found a new ironic voice for new kinds of stories that in wartime he had not told. He was free now to adopt the hatreds of the troops, and to attack their home-front enemies. He could describe how he walked through the

hospital at Corbie, known as the 'Butcher's Shop', and was horrified at
the suffering there:

> I never went again, though I saw many other butcher's shops in the
> years that followed, where there was a great carving of human flesh
> which was of our boyhood, while the old men directed their sacrifice,
> and the profiteers grew rich, and the fires of hate were stoked up at
> patriotic banquets and in editorial chairs.[4]

You can see, condensed in this short passage, the ideas that together
would compose the anti-monuments, and were already the objects of
soldiers' satires — the butchery, the sacrifice of the young by the old,
the mindless hatred and the cruel patriotism. These would become, in
time, the new Myth of the War.

Arnold Bennett wrote of *Realities of War* that 'it contains a few
goodish things, but I am perfectly certain that human nature was never
as he describes. He is incurably sentimental and inaccurate.'[5] Sentimental Gibbs certainly was; he retained his romantic feelings about the
common soldiers, and used the old heroic terms when he praised them
— *valour, sacrifice, love of country*. But even here there was a change:
Gibbs's sympathies extended, in this post-war book, to German soldiers
and to English cowards. He described the executions of two condemned
men — one enlisted, the other a young officer — with compassion, and
without judgement. The implications of this change are considerable:
war for Gibbs was no longer a struggle towards victory, but a cruel
thing done to young men.

Another significant change is in Gibbs's treatment of the Somme
offensive. He had published his wartime dispatches for that period, and
called them *The Battles of the Somme*; now he returned to the subject, but
called it this time 'Psychology on the Somme', and directed his attention
not to the winning and losing of ground, but to the effects of the
fighting on the combatants, and on their world. His conclusion is
another anticipation of the Myth.

> Modern civilization was wrecked on those fire-blasted fields, though
> they led to what we called 'victory'. More died there than the flower
> of our youth and German manhood. The old order of the world died
> there, because many men who came alive out of that conflict were
> changed, and vowed not to tolerate a system of thought which had
> led up to such a monstrous massacre of human beings who prayed to
> the same God, loved the same joys of life, and had no hatred of one

another except as it had been lighted and inflamed by their governors, their philosophers, and their newspapers. The German soldier cursed the militarism which had plunged him into that horror. The British soldier cursed the German, as the direct cause of all his trouble, but looked back on his side of the lines and saw an evil there which was also his enemy — the evil of a secret diplomacy which juggled with the lives of humble men so that war might be sprung upon them without their knowledge or consent, and the evil of rulers who hated German militarism, not because of its wickedness, but because of its strength in rivalry, and the evil of a folly in the minds of men which had taught them to regard war as a glorious adventure, and patriotism as the right to dominate other peoples, and liberty as a catchword of politicians in search of power.[6]

These are not the words of an embittered old soldier, but of a popular journalist, and one whose popularity extended to high places: he was knighted in the same year that *Realities* was published. One might conclude that his version of what the Somme had meant, and what the whole war amounted to, was already accepted as the truth, which could now be told.

Reviews suggest, however, that this was not entirely the case. 'We cannot honestly recommend anyone to read this book just now,' the *Saturday Review*'s critic wrote, 'valuable and interesting though it may be to the next and succeeding generations.' Why *not* now? Because Gibbs's version would 'stir up anger against the old men who planned and handled the war, and ... fan the flame of discontent and insubordination that are the dangers of the day.'[7] It is important to remember that in 1920 the war was still a political issue, and that there were those who regarded its realities as too dangerous to report 'just now'. There was still a war party and an anti-war party, and they were no more reconciled than they had been while the war lasted.

There is one last point to be made about Gibbs's book. His account of the war does not end with the Armistice, but continues into the post-war period: that is, the condition of England after the war is a part of the story. Gibbs's view of that condition was gloomy. He sensed that the war had brought about a radical change in Western society: there was no resemblance, he said, between Europe-after-the-war and Europe-before-the-war, though there were many political leaders who did not recognize that fact. Unless they did, he predicted a revolution; but he was not optimistic that they would: 'in a kind of madness that is not without a strange splendour,' he wrote, 'like a ship that goes down with drums beating and banners flying, we are racing toward the rocks.'[8]

Gloom like Gibbs's was perhaps the greatest change, and the greatest shock, in post-war England. It was felt most strongly by those who had accepted the war values most wholeheartedly, old men like Gosse, who wrote to his friend André Gide in 1920:

> We are passing through dreadful days, in which the pillars of the world seem to be shaken, all in front of us seems to be darkness and hopelessness. It is much harder to bear than the war was, because there is no longer the unity that sustained us, nor the nobility which inspired hope and determination.[9]

But younger men felt it too, as the end of an old order, an idea of civilization, a continuity. Lawrence spoke for his generation when he wrote that the old time could never come back, and that men and women would have to adjust themselves to a new world; 'England', he said, was 'changed inside.'[10]

The reception of *Realities of War* was both a symptom and an acknowledgement of that change: the book was criticized for its bitterness, and elderly reviewers wished that it had not been published, but nobody said it wasn't true. The fact that its 'realities' were accepted as such tells us something about how fundamental, and how wide-spread, the change in England was; the war — not only the way it was fought but the way it was exploited at home — had altered the ways in which people thought and talked about government, politicians, society, order, obedience; that is, it touched the most basic aspects of the relations between ordinary citizens and those who ruled them.

Another book published in 1920 had similar effects, though it told a very different war story. Colonel Charles à Court Repington's *The First World War* not only gave the war a new name, it also gave the public a new war — the war as it was experienced by the wealthy, influential upper classes of London, the 'insiders'' war. As an old soldier with military connections and something of a reputation as a military expert, Repington had access to the war's highest commanders; as a military correspondent, first for *The Times* and later for the *Morning Post*, he exercised considerable influence on policy, though his outspoken criticisms of the conduct of the war sometimes got him into trouble (he was arrested under DORA in February 1918, but got off with a fine). Repington was also a frequenter of London high society, a diner-out, a bridge-player, and a gossip, and his diary has as much in it of that wartime world as it has of the company of generals. (For Max Beerbohm's version of Repington see plate 20.)

Repington's world was the world of all the people whom the fighting soldiers hated: the Old Men, the idle, rich women, the politicians and profiteers. His book told the English, soldiers and civilians alike, that while men fought and died in France, the frivolities and trivialities of fashionable society went on, and that over dinner and bridge the privileged and safe gossiped about casualty figures, and played politics with reputations. But it also recorded the follies and stupidities that governed the direction of the war: how politicians interfered with military decisions, and how the War Cabinet dithered while the Allies intrigued against each other. Repington was a military man, and he saw war as the generals saw it; his only censures were of the politicians, who would make decisions for other than military reasons, men like Lloyd George who, when Repington complained of the shortage of man-power, replied angrily that he 'was not prepared to accept the position of a butcher's boy driving cattle to the slaughter'. Repington thought that was a sentimental thing to say, when the generals needed men.

Repington's diaries create a vivid and detailed picture of the English governing class in wartime — a class that was cynical, self-seeking, and indifferent to human suffering. Repington did not condemn this society — how could he, when he wrote from inside it? He simply recorded it. He would probably have defended his book, as Gibbs did his, by saying that it was a faithful account of 'realities of war', the more real for being cynical. When a friend asked him in 1917 when the war would end, he replied that he saw no reason why it should end until the Huns were more badly beaten:

> Since nations counted money no more than pebbles on a beach, and all would probably repudiate in one form or another at the end of the war, there seemed no reason for stopping, especially as so many people were growing rich by the war; the ladies liked being without their husbands, and all dreaded the settlement afterwards, industrial, political, financial, and domestic.[11]

There is no mention here of high ideals, or of poor little Belgium, or the world made safe for democracy, or war to end war. And no mention of the dead.

Repington savoured his world — the drama of the war part, and the gossip of the society part — and clearly did not wish it to be otherwise. But he was aware that others might judge it in other terms.

He records this conversation, from a country-house weekend in June 1917:

> Lady Ridley and I discussed what posterity would think of us in England. We agreed that we should be considered rather callous to go on with our usual life when we were reading of 3000 to 4000 casualties a day. But she said that people could not keep themselves elevated permanently on some plane above the normal, and she supposed that things round us explained the French Revolution and the behaviour of the French nobility.[12]

It was a startling comparison for a peeress to make in 1917. Was she prophesying the death of her class? She was not the only person in England to foresee a revolution: Gibbs had done so too, and so had many others. It was an important part of the apprehension with which many conservative Englishmen looked to the world-after-the-war.

Posterity's opinion would be a while in coming, but what Repington's contemporaries thought of him, his society, and his diary was made known very quickly. Reviewers praised the diary when it appeared, and compared it to Evelyn and Pepys, but they also hated it. The *Spectator* compared reading the diary to looking under a flat stone in the garden, and the *Nation* quoted passages of society gossip in order to condemn Repington and his friends for their arrogance and stupidity.[13]

Most critics recognized that the book told two stories: one story was about generals and field marshals, and how the war was planned, misplanned, muddled and in spite of all that, won; the other recorded lunch at the Ritz and dinner at Lady Astor's, how smart Lady Diana looked in her uniform, and what Lady Ridley said to the ambassador. It was, as a *Spectator* editorial remarked, 'an ugly, nay, a disgusting picture, but we should be hypocrites if we did not say at the same time that it is intensely interesting and intensely amusing.' But it was clearly also intensely disturbing; like Gibbs's book, it redefined the war and stripped it of its values, leaving that space of four years emptied of meaning, filled only with the particulars of private gossip and public folly. 'To read these volumes,' said one embittered critic, 'is to discover the unthinkable and the impossible. Nowhere will you find a period or a sentence of which you could say, "*There! that is what we fought for!*" The Cause finds no expression.'[14] And indeed it does not; for Repington, there was no cause, there was only a war, and society.

These two books, appearing within a few months of each other in the second year of the peace, were widely read and commented on; clearly they contributed to the shaping of post-war imaginations in England. But there is another document, from the preceding year, that was arguably far more influential — the Treaty of Versailles. Repington mentions it only in a sentence, the last in his book: '*Saturday, June 28.* This day the Treaty of Peace with Germany was signed at Versailles.' He took no interest in what it said; nations would repudiate it anyway. But Gibbs, the sentimentalist, gave the Treaty a paragraph, for its failure was a part of his argument that diplomats betrayed the causes that other men died for:

> When at last the Terms were published, their merciless severity, their disregard of racial boundaries, their creation of hatreds and vendettas, which would lead, as sure as the sun should rise, to new warfare, staggered humanity, not only in Germany and Austria, but in every country of the world, where at least minorities of people had hoped for some nobler vision of the world's needs, and for some healing remedy for the evils which had massacred its youth.[15]

Men had said, during the war, that the motives for fighting it had ceased to be idealistic, and had become low and evil; Sassoon said so in his protest, Lord Lansdowne said so in his letter, Mr Britling said so, and so did Rose Macaulay's Alix, and many war poets and many protesters at home. But the Versailles Treaty made that judgement public and official. It was punitive and vindictive; it spoke for economic interests and geographical ambitions and empires — all those shabby motives that men felt had destroyed the early idealism with which Englishmen entered the war.

Maynard Keynes saw what the Treaty meant for the future of Europe, and wrote his opinions in *The Economic Consequences of the Peace*, a book that belongs with Gibbs's and Repington's among those post-war documents — none of them strictly 'literary' — that shaped the way the world looked to post-war English imaginations. Keynes had supported the war in his role as an adviser to the Treasury, but he deplored the peace settlement. His book was ostensibly an economist's objective analysis of what that settlement would do to the European economy. But Keynes was a Bloomsburyite, and shared his friends' interest in art and literature (what other economist would have decorated his gloomy predictions with quotations from Hardy's *Dynasts* and Shelley's *Prometheus Unbound?*); and he was a gifted writer. The book that he wrote contains more than economics; it is also the testimony of a humane man.

Keynes offered his readers not only statistics but visions — of a stable pre-war world that had been lost, and of a post-war world that was threatened and uncertain; and these visions surely contributed to the way in which Englishmen imagined their world — their history, and their immediate reality.

Here is Keynes's pre-war England:

> What an extraordinary episode in the economic progress of man that age was which came to an end in August, 1914! The greater part of the population, it is true, worked hard and lived at a low standard of comfort, yet were, to all appearances, reasonably contented with this lot. But escape was possible, for any man of capacity or character at all exceeding the average, into the middle and upper classes, for whom life offered, at a low cost and with the least trouble, conveniences, comforts, and amenities beyond the compass of the richest and most powerful monarchs of other ages ... The projects and politics of militarism and imperialism, of racial and cultural rivalries, of monopolies, restrictions, and exclusion, which were to play the serpent to this paradise, were little more than the amusements of his daily newspaper, and appeared to exercise almost no influence at all on the ordinary course of social and economic life, the internationalisation of which was nearly complete in practice.[16]

This is not a description, but a fable of pre-lapsarian England, a bourgeois paradise lost. Into this perfection German ambition intruded — Keynes was entirely conservative in assigning blame for the war; but he added that in the Treaty the French and British ran the risk of completing the ruin of Europe that the Germans had begun.

The body of the book, concerned with the Treaty itself, reparations, and Europe after the war, is, as Keynes admits, pessimistic. But not as pessimistic as his conclusion:

> In this autumn of 1919, in which I write, we are at the dead season of our fortunes. The reaction from the exertions, the fears, and the sufferings of the past five years is at its height. Our power of feeling or caring beyond the immediate questions of our own material well-being is temporarily eclipsed. The greatest events outside our own direct experience and the most dreadful anticipations cannot move us ...
>
> We have been moved already beyond endurance, and need rest.

Never in the lifetime of men now living has the universal element in
the soul of man burnt so dimly.

For these reasons the true voice of the new generation has not yet
spoken, and silent opinion is not yet formed. To the formation of the
general opinion of the future I dedicate this book.[17]

One might say of these passages that they constitute the *Imaginative
Consequences of the Peace*: their images of paradise lost, and of an
emotionally exhausted, self-centred, unfeeling society, will appear in
many post-war literary works, and together constitute much of what
we mean by the spirit of the Twenties. The new generation, when it
spoke, would not restore idealism, as Keynes hoped; it would, rather,
confirm his pessimism.

II

Through the war years, critics had consoled themselves for the dearth of
impressive war art by saying that it would come later. In the second
month of the war, John Palmer advised readers of the *Saturday Review*
that the great poet of the war had probably not been born yet[18], and
variations on this notion turned up regularly until the war's end:

The poet who will write superbly of this war will not begin to do so
until the war has been at an end for a long time. (St John Ervine, July
1915)

Not for many years hence, then, will the enduring and fundamental
effects of the war upon literature be fully revealed. The work of the
next, the coming generation, will be its real harvest. (Walter de la
Mare, 1916)

The great war play has still to be written — it looks now as if the
greatest dramatic theme in history will have to wait for proper
treatment until peace has again returned to the world. (*Times* critic,
January 1917)

One thing seems certain: this immeasurable upheaval involves so
intense a concentration of energy that while it lasts we cannot expect
any great overflow of literary production . . . (S.K. Ratcliffe, October 1917)

> We must not look for much great poetry now, while the war lasts . . .
> after the war I think men will not write of the war nor think of it
> much for a long time. (John Masefield, March 1918)[19]

Those predictions seemed confirmed in the years just after the war: the
coming of peace did not energize England's writers and artists into an
immediate burst of definitive war art. There was time, there were
opportunities, even commissions for some; but the art that would fix
the realities of war in memorable images came slowly and fitfully. There
were no great war novels written in those first post-war years, no
powerful retrospective poems, no plays of lasting importance; a few
painters accomplished fine things, but in general it was a time of
waiting.

One reason for the difficulty may be discerned in the experience of
William Orpen, who had been an Official War Painter at the Front, and
was now commissioned by the Imperial War Museum to paint three
pictures of the Peace Conference. He went to Paris, and observed the
delegates in their frock-coats (he called the delegates 'frocks'), and he
was not favourably impressed. On the day of the signing of the Treaty
he was placed in a window at the back of the Hall of Mirrors at
Versailles, and from that vantage point he watched as the rearrangement
of the map of the world was made official. 'All the "frocks" did all their
tricks to perfection,' he wrote of that scene:

> President Wilson showed his back teeth; Lloyd George waved his
> Asquithian mane; Clemenceau whirled his grey-gloved hands about
> like windmills; Lansing drew his pictures and Mr. Balfour slept. It
> was all over. The 'frocks' had signed the Peace! The Army was
> forgotten. Some dead and forgotten, others maimed and forgotten,
> others alive and well — but equally forgotten.[20]

That bitter sense of the contrast between the occasion and the petty, vain
men who dominated it, got into Orpen's painting: he painted a tall
picture of a monumentally ornate room, with a row of insignificant
little figures in black — the 'frocks' — strewn across the bottom of the
picture like grit in the bottom of a birdcage. A second painting, 'A Peace
Conference at the Quai d'Orsay', has the same unstable, satiric quality
— a row of 'frocks', this time arranged before a vast, ornate fireplace,
above which is a tall female figure carved in marble (Peace, perhaps?)
surrounded by cupids.

Orpen had been commissioned to paint another formal group of delegates posed in the Hall of Peace, but though he worked at it for nine months, and painted thirty-six individual portraits on it, he found that he could not complete it. 'It all seemed so unimportant somehow,' he explained. 'In spite of all these eminent men, I kept thinking of the soldiers who remained in France for ever.'[21] In the end he painted out all the delegates and replaced them with a flag-draped coffin guarded by two mad-looking half-nude soldiers, with a pair of cupids floating above their heads (plate 25). He titled the picture 'To the Unknown British Soldier in France', and it was the hit of the Royal Academy summer exhibition in 1923. The War Museum Committee, however, was less impressed, and refused to accept it for the Museum's collection.

Orpen had felt a conflict between the conventions of monumentalism and his own anti-monumental feelings about the war, and he had painted that conflict into his pictures, in different ways. The two Peace Treaty paintings seem intentionally satirical, with their tiny drab figures in vast, ornate space, whereas the 'Unknown Soldier' painting is simply an unresolved dissonance (what are those naked men doing in that formal, gaudy room? do cherubs and soldiers really belong in the same frame? is there something grotesquely comic in the scene?). They are pictures that acknowledge a problem: how to render the complex feelings that the war had left, without falling back on the unacceptable conventions of monument-making. But they do not resolve that problem.

Two other English war artists were confronting that problem in 1919. Paul Nash and Wyndham Lewis, returned from France and out of uniform, were at work on the large canvases that the Imperial War Museum had commissioned. Nash had begun his 'Menin Road' in June 1918, but did not finish it until April of the following year. Some of his difficulties were logistical: he was moving about, and sometimes painting his large picture in a too-small room; but he was also trying to deal with questions of subject and treatment. In a letter written just after he began the job, Nash described the picture as a 'large memorial painting', and *memorial* here clearly has monumental associations. But in the same letter he described the conflict he felt living in the English countryside and painting the Western Front (where the final Allied offensive had just begun):

> France and the trenches would be a mere dream if our minds [he was painting alongside his brother John] were not perpetually bent upon those scenes. And yet how difficult it is, folded as we are in the

luxuriant green country, to put it aside and brood on those wastes in
Flanders, the torments, the cruelty & terror of this war. Well it is on
these I brood for it seems the only justification of what I do now — if I
can help to rob war of the last shred of glory the last shine of
glamour.[22]

But how does one paint a memorial painting and yet rob its subject of all
glory and glamour? Nash's letter contains his essential programme: he
would put aside luxuriant green country, and paint a picture that would
brood on war's wastes. It would be an anti-landscape, in the spirit of his
earlier war paintings; but it would be as architectural in its structure as a
monumental building.

Nash painted his waste land as a place emptied of living things.
Nothing grows on the ruined earth, and the trees are dead trunks — the
corpses of trees. The water in the foreground is dead water, standing
stagnantly in flooded shell-holes. Beside the water Nash has placed the
broken rubbish of war — toppled cement blocks and rusting corrugated
iron. In the background the smoke of war merges with the storm clouds
of the sky, to make a single threatening backdrop. The structure of the
picture derives not from natural forms but from the geometry of its
verticals and diagonals — the dead trees and their shadows, the beams
from the stormy sky, the tumbled masonry. The two central human
figures are so reduced, so trivialized, that one scarcely notices them;
they lean effortfully across the dominant diagonals, as though into a
strong wind. They have no place in the picture — no habitation, no
goal. Behind them, two other figures are frozen in gestures that cannot
be interpreted.

What is being memorialized in this 'large memorial painting'? None
of the Big Words, certainly: Nash succeeded in his goal of robbing war
of its glory and glamour. But the words that he had proposed as an
alternative language do not seem present either: there is no torment
here, no cruelty, and no terror. What there is, most powerfully and
oppressively, is simply annihilation, a natural world laid waste, emptied
of life and of old meanings, containing nothing except ruin, and a few
men who struggle towards nowhere. Nash wrote, when he had finished
'The Menin Road', that it was the best thing that he had yet done. And
he was right: it is a great painting, and a great solution to the problem of
making an anti-monumental monument: he had turned war into an
emptiness (plate 21).

Wyndham Lewis had been an artillery officer before he became a war artist, and it was artillerymen that he chiefly painted in his war paintings. His first one-man show after the war was a collection of scenes in a gunner's life; it was titled simply *Guns*, and opened in February 1919. Later that spring he began the large painting that the Imperial War Museum had commissioned. It too was an artillery picture: 'A Battery Shelled' (plate 22).

In a foreword to the catalogue of the *Guns* exhibition, Lewis described two kinds of war paintings: the passionate (his example was Goya's 'Desastres de la Guerra') and the aloof (as in Uccello's 'San Romano'). Both, he said, were great as paintings, but he clearly preferred the Uccello:

> It does not borrow from the *fact* of War any emotion, any disturbing or dislocating violence, terror or compassion — any of the psychology that is proper to the events of War ... The principal thing is that this is a purely inhuman picture, in the sense that the artist's attitude was that of the god for whom blood and death mean no more than bird's plumage and the scintillations of steel.

The artist of this cold and aloof type, he went on,

> would approach any disturbance or calamity with a child-like and unruffled curiosity and proceed to arrange Nissen huts, shell-bursts, elephants, commanding officers, aeroplanes, in patterns, just as he would proceed with flowers in a vase, or more delectable and peaceful objects.[23]

Clearly Lewis saw himself as this kind of painter, and it was in this spirit of detachment that he painted 'A Battery Shelled'.

The painting, like Nash's, is large — about the size of the Uccello, six feet by ten. The scene is an artillery position at the Front, with dugouts, camouflaged guns, piles of shells and duckboards all rendered in a recognizable though geometrical style. In the centre of the picture insect-like stick-figures are at work, while above their heads geometrical towers of smoke rise, apparently from shell explosions. In the left foreground are three officers: one stares indifferently at the scene, one looks at his feet, the third faces away from the action. You might say that they represent the Uccello-like artist: they are aloof. As Lewis later wrote, 'A gunner does not fight. He merely shells and is shelled.'[24] There is nothing here to be passionate about; it is only a war going on.

Both paintings were exhibited in the Royal Academy show of the nation's war paintings in December 1919, and were singled out for comment: praise by critics, condemnation by the general public. To ers, Nash and Lewis were revolutionary artists who had expressed the true character and spirit of modern war-fare'[25]; to detractors, they were subversives who insulted 'the fine men who fought in the great war'.[26] In either case, their work confirmed the separation in values, taste and understanding that existed at the war's end, between the monuments and the anti-monuments.

Having fulfilled their 'memorial' commissions, the two painters turned away from war as a subject. And so did everybody else. Masterman's war artists scheme, and the elaborations that followed from it, had produced an extraordinary number of fine paintings while the war lasted, and in the year that followed; but painting had no continuing role in the formulation of the ultimate Myth of the War. There was no later burst of retrospective versions of war, as there was in war literature, though there were one or two important later works.

Nevertheless, the Modernist painters' pictures of the war must be recognized as influential. Most obviously, they were a part of the nation's permanent collection, and so remained more or less permanently on show, thus ensuring that the visual images of the war that English-men were most likely to see — those that would eventually hang in the central gallery of the Imperial War Museum — would be *anti-monuments*. And many of the ex-soldiers who would later write their novels and memoirs and so compose the collective myth would surely see them there, and would remember their vivid, bitter images. But they were also influential in a less explicit way. These were paintings that seemed to announce the failure of two principal pre-war traditions in the visual arts: the old tradition of English romanticism, and the new tradition of English abstraction. If one followed the war careers of Nevinson, Nash, and Lewis, one saw a turning away from those traditions, as methods inadequate to the realities of war; and though in time both would re-enter English painting, there seemed at the war's end to be a gap in the history of English art, as in other aspects of history.[27]

War literature had no Burlington House exhibition to focus public attention upon its problems and its achievements in 1919; indeed it faced considerable difficulties in reaching the public at all. English publishers were persuaded that their readers were tired of war writing, or at least of writing of a realistic, anti-monumental kind, and books that are now considered classics of English war literature were refused publication. Herbert Read wrote *In Retreat*, his account of the British withdrawal of March 1918, in the spring of 1919, and tried to publish it then, but without success. 'The state of the public mind,' he later wrote, or at least, of that mind as localised in the minds of publishers and editors, refused anything so bleak. The war was still a sentimental illusion: it was a subject for pathos, for platitude, even for rationalisation. It was not yet time for the simple facts.[28]

That time did not come until six years later, when Leonard and Virginia Woolf published Read's book at their Hogarth Press.

Ford Madox Ford had even more trouble with his first war book, though he was an established writer of considerable distinction. He wrote *No Enemy*, a book that is half novel and half war memoir, in 1919, but had to wait ten years to find a publisher for it (and even then did not find one in England). It wasn't that publishers weren't publishing war books at all; many official histories and generals' memoirs appeared in the first months of the peace. But they were reluctant to publish books of an anti-war tone, perhaps feeling, as Osbert Sitwell put it in a post-war poem, that it was

> Very bad form
> To mention the war.[29]

Unless, that is, you could speak well of it.

There was one exception to this general rule: war poetry (including Sitwell's) did seem to have an audience: or rather, like the exhibition at Burlington House, it had two audiences, one that sought out traditional, celebratory, monumental poetry, and another that looked for its opposite. In the period immediately after the war, memorializing poetry continued to sell: *The Muse in Arms*, E.B. Osborn's 1917 anthology of poems by men in uniform, reached its fifth impression in 1919, and *Valour and Vision*, first published in 1920, was re-issued in an enlarged edition three years later. But anti-war anthologies also began to appear: *Poems Written during the Great War* in 1918, *Paths of Glory* and *The Minstrelsy of Peace* in 1920. These were collections that left out the praisers of war — the Brookes and the Grenfells and their imitators — and published instead Ewer and Sassoon and Sitwell (and in the case of *The Minstrelsy of Peace*, their anti-war ancestors, going back to the fifteenth century). These books were edited by Socialists, and their anti-war posture was clearly political; still, it is significant that they had an audience in that monument-making time — though not, presumably, a strictly literary one.

One can see this same division of judgement, the same two audiences, in the post-war histories of the three best-known war poets. Rupert

Brooke remained England's favourite war poet after the war, as he
had been through the fighting years. One might reasonably argue that
in fact Brooke was not a war poet at all, in the sense that men like
Owen and Rosenberg and Gurney were — he had never written from
direct experience, and the five '1914' sonnets were the only poems
he wrote that had anything at all to do with war. But it was those
sonnets that sold his books; and they sold in very large numbers. His
1914 and Other Poems, which was first published in 1915, reached its
twenty-eighth impression in 1920, and went on selling; his *Collected
Poems*, published in the last summer of the war, went through sixteen
impressions during the next ten years, and was then re-issued in a
new edition. Even in the bitter last years of the war he had remained
popular with soldiers at the Front: Herbert Read, for example, returning to the trenches for the second time, wrote home: 'I think my
gladness may be akin to that Rupert Brooke expressed in one of his
sonnets,' and he quoted 'Now God be thanked . . .', entirely without
irony.[30] Experience of war did not, apparently, dim the glamour of
those high-rhetorical lines, though it made it impossible for poets like
Read to imitate them. Nor did it affect the glamour of the golden-haired
Apollo himself, in his romantic Greek-island grave: Wilfred Owen kept
a newspaper photograph of Brooke's grave tucked into his copy of
1914, other poets wrote elegies to him, anthologists dedicated books
to him, and war novelists quoted his poems. Rupert Brooke had
become a monument.

Sassoon, on the other hand, had not. His last wartime volume,
Counter-Attack, was published in the same month as Brooke's *Collected
Poems*, July 1918, and it was as widely reviewed as Brooke's was. But
not as favourably. Here, in the last months of the war, one can
see reviewers leaning towards peacetime standards, and relegating
Sassoon's wartime realism and anger to the past, like last year's
newspapers. 'It is difficult', the *TLS*'s critic wrote,

> to judge him dispassionately as a poet, because it is impossible to
> overlook the fact that he writes as a soldier. It is a fact, indeed, that he
> forces upon you, as if it were a matter of indifference to him whether
> you called him poet or not.[31]

And the *New Age* took a similar view:

> Mr. Sassoon rules himself out from the realm of poetry on two
> grounds: first, he is quite indifferent to the creation of beauty; and,

second, he is a prey to the emotions which tend to satire. Hatred is the predominant impulse of Mr. Sassoon's expression, and without hatred it is probable that not more than one of these poems would have been written.[32]

But the cleverest dismissal came from that clever man, Middleton Murry. Murry was a keen judge of the literary climate, and was quick to adjust to it, so that his opinions can be read as indications of the direction in which a reputation is going. About Sassoon's poems he managed to be at once compassionate and condescending:

> It is the fact, not the poetry, of Mr. Sassoon, that is important. When a man is in torment and cries aloud, his cry is incoherent. It has neither weight nor meaning of its own ... Mr. Sassoon's verses — they are not poetry — are such a cry. They touch not our imagination, but our sense ... these verses express nothing, save in so far as a cry expresses pain.[33]

And Murry went on to argue that the recording of pain, chaos and horror was not enough; poetry was harmony and calm, and Sassoon had left *that* order to be created by the reader: 'it is Mr. Sassoon who is the martyr,' Murry wrote, 'and we ourselves who are the poets.'[34]

These were reviews written for reputable literary journals — two of them rather left-of-centre, the other conservative. They were also written, it must be noted, by civilians and for civilians. They seem agreed on two points: that the voice of the soldier was no longer sufficient to make a poem poetical; and that it was time to return to traditional ideas of poetry, and to begin talking once more about emotion recollected in tranquillity and all that. For the reviewers, at least, the war in poetry had ended before the war did.

It isn't surprising, then, that when Sassoon published a collection of *War Poems* in 1919, it went virtually unnoticed. Those journals that did review the book placed it in a special non-poetic category: 'a great pamphlet against war', said the *Nation*; much of it 'can only be described as journalism', said the *London Mercury*.[35] The war being over, the general critical impulse was to leave the memorializing of it to the monument-makers.

The post-war story of Wilfred Owen's reputation is more complicated. When he died, seven days before the Armistice, Owen had had only four poems published, and was quite unknown outside the circle of his friends — Sassoon, Graves, Robbie Ross. In the following year, his

reputation began to grow: poems appeared in journals, and Edith
Sitwell put seven into the 1919 volume of *Wheels* (which she also
dedicated to his memory). At the same time, she was hard at work
putting together a collection of his poems, an enterprise for which she
enlisted the aid of Sassoon. He stepped in, claiming the authority of
friendship (and, one must suppose, of gender and military experience
too), and when *Poems* by Wilfred Owen appeared in December 1920, it
was Sassoon's name that appeared on the title page as author of an
introduction (Miss Sitwell got an acknowledgement for her work of
preparation).

Poems contained only twenty-three of Owen's poems (as compared to
the 110 poems and 67 fragments in the 1983 edition) — Sassoon and
Sitwell had aimed, she said, at 'supreme quality, rather than quantity'.[36]
They had chosen well: most of the familiar Owen poems are there.
Reviews were numerous and admiring — Murry, for example, called
Owen 'the greatest poet of the war'[37] — though in many cases they
stressed the lost promise rather than the fulfilment. Critics were
particularly taken with Owen's draft preface, which Sassoon had
included in the book, and review after review quoted 'The Poetry is in
the Pity'. Sassoon could not have found a better way to attach his
friend's work to the post-war mood. Satire like Sassoon's was out of
date — one could not feel anger for a war that was past — but pity was
always in season.

Owen may have been the greatest poet of the war, but the reputation
that his work began to acquire was not confined to the category of war
poets. The journals in which his poems appeared were organs of
advanced literary taste — *Coterie, Arts and Letters, Wheels* — and he
appeared there with post-war Modernists like Aldous Huxley, Conrad
Aiken, and the Sitwells. After the appearance of his *Poems*, Owen's
work began to appear in anthologies, and not only collections of war
poems but general anthologies as well. Among all the war poets, it was
Owen who was taken most wholeheartedly into the company of the
Moderns — perhaps because he was the most experimental poet.

Yet his reputation did not make him popular in the sense that Brooke
was. Chatto & Windus printed only 730 copies of the 1920 *Poems* for the
English market, and 700 in the second impression in 1921; at the end of
the decade a hundred quires of the second impression were still
unbound. By that time Brooke's *Collected Poems* had sold 300,000
copies.

There is one other aspect of Owen's post-war reputation that is worth noting: his reputation as a soldier. In his introduction to *Poems* Sassoon had avoided any reference to Owen's war service beyond the barest facts, but Owen's friend C.K. Scott Moncrieff was not so protective. In a review of *Poems* he raised the question of Owen's mental health, and of his performance at the Front. He had met Owen, he wrote, at a wedding in January 1918 (it was the wedding of Robert Graves and Nancy Nicholson); Owen had returned from France six months earlier, Scott Moncrieff said, 'in a state of health which qualified him to write the terrible question and answer:—

> Who are these? Why sit they here in twilight? . . .
> These are men whose minds the dead have ravished . . .'

And he quoted on, through five more lines of Owen's 'Mental Cases'.[38]

Owen had spent his four months at Rivers's sanatorium, and he had grown happy again in England, Scott Moncrieff said; and though his dreams were still nightmares, and his hair was shot with white, his 'mental injury' seemed to have healed. Then in the summer of 1918 the Allied attack began that promised to end the war, and all available men were ordered to return to the Front. Owen's name was placed on a draft list, and then removed. It seemed he would be safe. But then, by Scott Moncrieff's account,

> the Military Secretary's Department claimed that, having been sent home a year earlier in a state which hinted at a loss of moral under shell-fire, it was under shell-fire alone that he could be entrusted with the command of men. The case was put more briefly, but in words which do not look well in print. He was again placed on a draft.[39]

When Owen returned to France with that draft he was in a shaky enough condition to worry his family and friends. In two of his last letters to his mother he explicitly assured her that his nerves were in perfect order, and he gave the same assurance to his friend Sassoon. Whether they were or not, he did his job well enough to win a posthumous decoration for valour.

But it was the first apparent cowardice, not the final courage, that was noticed. Middleton Murry picked up the story from Scott Moncrieff, and made it the dramatic ending for his review of *Poems*; Owen was sent home, Murry wrote, 'because his nerve had failed, and he was no longer considered fit to command soldiers in the field.' And Robert Nichols echoed the story in his review in the *Observer*. Sassoon, who must have known more about the case than any other of Owen's friends, said

nothing to deny the allegation. Only Edith Sitwell protested that it was
not a loss of morale that Owen had suffered, but only shell-shock. Ten
years later, Robert Graves put the story more baldly in *Goodbye to All
That*:

> Another patient at the hospital [Craiglockhart] was Wilfred Owen,
> who had had a bad time with the Manchester Regiment in France; and
> further, it had preyed on his mind that he had been accused of
> cowardice by his commanding officer. He was in a very shaky
> condition.[40]

The issue here is not whether or not Owen was a 'coward'; certainly he
had been severely affected by artillery fire and by his head injury during
his first tour of duty. The point is rather that he was perceived by his
acquaintances, and through them by others, as a 'damaged man'. If the
reader was an elderly civilian like Henry Newbolt, then Owen's
breakdown was reason enough to dismiss his poetry; 'Owen and the rest
of the broken men rail at the Old Men who sent the young to die,'
Newbolt wrote in a letter in 1924; '. . . I don't think these shell-shocked
war poems will move our grandchildren greatly.'[41] But if the reader was
a fellow-soldier, the charge did not seem to matter; shell-shock and
shaky nerves were simply part of the experience of war — a part that in
Owen's case had made it possible for him to write some of his most
moving poems, poems of other 'broken men', like 'S.I.W.', 'The Dead-
Beat', and 'Mental Cases'.

The damaged man began to appear as a sympathetic figure in war
literature in the middle of the war. The existence of 'Dottyville' is
evidence that he was also appearing in reality, in the trenches. If
Dottyville existed, then perhaps a fundamental idea about martial
behaviour was not true: perhaps bravery and cowardice were not within
men's control. After the war, this figure of the damaged man became a
frequent and dominant character in literature, and his presence radically
altered the whole idea of literary war. Consider, as an early and striking
example, A.P. Herbert's *The Secret Battle*, published in 1919. Herbert is
best known as a comic and satiric writer, but *The Secret Battle* is neither;
it is a plain, sober account of the military career of a young officer, first
at Gallipoli and later in France, and of his death. Herbert had served on
both of these fronts, and many of the novel's details are obviously from
direct observation, but the book is more than a disguised memoir. What
makes it more is that the central character, Harry Penrose, is shot for
cowardice, and that the novel does not condemn him for his action, but

rather condemns the military system that first destroys men's nerves, and then kills them for their failures. There had been other weak men in wartime writing, but Herbert was the first novelist to take a condemned coward for his hero.

The story that Herbert told was based very closely on the case of Edwin Dyett, the naval sub-lieutenant whose execution had also caught Bottomley's attention. Dyett had served in the same two theatres that Herbert had known, and perhaps this shared experience had sharpened Herbert's sympathy for the dead man. Or perhaps it was simply Herbert's sense of injustice done that moved him. Whatever his motive, he wrote Dyett's story, changing his name and inventing details of a personal life, but otherwise altering very little.

The Secret Battle is the story of a sensitive man who joins the army in 1914, endures the ordeal of Gallipoli, and is then sent to France. He does his duty there, but senior officers begin to doubt his courage, and so he is hounded into more and more dangerous jobs until he is wounded and evacuated to England. By then his nerves are gone, but he insists on returning to the Front (as both Sassoon and Owen did, one recalls), and there, on his first night in the line, he runs away from an artillery barrage. He is court-martialled, condemned to death, and shot.

Herbert's problem was to find a way of telling this story to an audience that had just lived through four years of martial rhetoric and heroic values, in a way that would make Harry Penrose an understandable, sympathetic figure. He accomplished this end mainly by choosing as his narrator an artless, ordinary fellow-officer, whose account is as plain as any common soldier's diary, and by telling the story through this plain, decent man, without decoration or high emotion. The narrator begins: 'I am going to write down some of the history of Harry Penrose, because I do not think full justice has been done to him' (what could be plainer than that?) and he ends with an equally plain conclusion:

> This book is not an attack on any person, on the death penalty, or on anything else, though if it makes people think about these things, so much the better. I think I believe in the death penalty — I don't know. But I did not believe in Harry being shot.
>
> That is the gist of it; that my friend Harry was shot for cowardice — and he was one of the bravest men I ever knew.[42]

The Secret Battle is a book that rejects the abstractions that sent men to the war, and Harry Penrose to his firing squad; bravery and cowardice are matters of nerves, not of morals. And this point of belief informs the language of the novel, so direct and ordinary that it seems to carry the authority of all ordinary soldiers, to be accepted without judgement because it is visibly true.

By writing an artless and unrhetorical novel, more in the style of trench letters and diaries than of 'literature', Herbert succeeded in constructing a new kind of war novel, and a new kind of memorial — an anti-monument to a condemned coward. Harry Penrose is not a hero in the traditional sense, but a victim, a man things are done to; in his war world, *heroism* is simply not a relevant term. Against the weight of war, the individual has no power of action; he can only suffer. It is Owen's point again: the Poetry is in the Pity.

This victim-figure anticipates the direction that later war literature will take, but it has a significance that stretches further. For once the idea of heroic action is denied, the whole conception of the hero, and of narratives that shape the actions of such figures, is called into question. The anti-hero, the victim, the passive man — these became conventions of post-war English writing; and it does not seem fanciful to argue that they had their literary beginnings on the Western Front, in the war that overwhelmed individuals, and denied them the power to be agents in their own lives and deaths. Herbert had found a structure, a language, and a subject for a new kind of narrative of human destiny.

I don't mean to suggest that Herbert was the sole inventor of the victim-as-hero, but simply that his novel was an early example of a kind that later became conventional. The earliness was not an advantage; in 1919 the English public was evidently not ready for the story that Herbert had to tell, and though the book received some favourable reviews (including one by Arnold Bennett, generally considered the most influential reviewer in England) it did not sell. When it was re-issued in 1928 the public was ready, and *The Secret Battle* took its place among the end-of-the-decade war books that defined the Myth.

The Secret Battle was not the only book of its time to render the victim-hero sympathetically. Herbert Read's *Naked Warriors*, also published in 1919, contains two such victims: 'The Execution of Cornelius Vane' is a poem about a man shot for desertion; 'Killed in Action' is a prose fragment about a trench suicide. Read's poems were no more successful than Herbert's novel had been (though Eliot praised them for their honesty), but like Herbert's book they thrust new characters into the stream of post-war war literature. These ruined figures would straggle through the novels, plays,[43] poems and memoirs of the rest of the decade and on into the Thirties: the deserters, the cowards, the suicides

NOTE.—The Pronouncements of Pope & Bradley are sometimes sympathetic.

AREN'T THE OLD MEN SPLENDID?

BY

H. DENNIS BRADLEY.

"The Hidden Hand"

IT is a cynical and unjust world. There is a grave danger that, on the outbreak of Peace, ungrateful Youth may forget in the stress and storms of Victory to pay tribute to the Old Men who have "carried on" so nobly during the interminable years of Armageddon.

Before it is too late, before their self-sacrifices are forgotten, before their little "bits" are ignored, before their rulings are over-ruled, before their public chatterings are drowned in the triumphant voices of returning Youth, let me pay homage to their elderly magnificence in war time.

Let us never forget their wonderful fight to make the world safe for Bureaucracy.

In their splendour the Old Men, too, have suffered.

Let not their self-denial be forgotten.

Leaving their businesses, their professions, their asylums—even their pleasures—with shaking fingers they buckled on their gout boots and hobbled forth to do their Bureaucratic duty.

Even the elderly and non-combatant clergy rallied to the standard of War, with tottering but determined steps ascended the dais of the tribunals, and preached patriotism, self-sacrifice, and self-denial—to others.

Who cannot admire these ministers of a new and martial Christus?

Did the working poor need beer? Then the Old Men heroically limited their cravings to Veuve Clicquot. Was there little mutton in the land? Then these aged heroes turned nobly to caviare and game. Were there super-taxes and excess profits to be paid? Then their hearts—and prices—rose valiantly to the occasion.

Were the women lonely? Then again the Old Men bravely "carried on" and sought to offer consolation.

And their reward? Virtue by necessity?

Alas, it is not in this world that men—even old men—should ask for their reward.

Venerable gentlemen, I commiserate you. But I congratulate you on your spirit if not on your flesh.

And if ingratitude and disappointment be your lot, summon your domestic fortitude, your placid omniscience, your Victorian and vicarious philosophy, summon your optimism, and remember, as Jimmy Whistler never said, "Old Age Must Come."

*   *   *   *   *   *   *   *   *   *   *   *   *   *   *

But comfort yourselves, for you is reserved the glory of a New Sacrifice.

I am grieved at the alarming wool shortage. Mufti manufacture has been reduced to a minimum. With Peace there will not be enough to go round. And, with delicate sadness, I am compelled to announce that :—

Pope & Bradley cannot receive any more orders for mufti materials from clients over the present military age of 51 until the war is over.

Knowing you so well, venerable sirs, I am sure you will bear this new deprivation with a proud and patriotic joy in the knowledge that you are helping your country.

Nevertheless, I am sorry for you. My heart bleeds when I think of you creeping shivering and naked to bed, with only the thought of your sacrifices to warm your vitals.

Hold fast, and stick it out, gallant hearts! It's a long tunnel through the Welsh mountains, but at the end of the steep gradient are green valleys and bad beer.

14, Old Bond Street, W. 1.

16   'Aren't the Old Men Splendid?', a tailor's advertisement from the *Cambridge Magazine*, November 2, 1918

27   Stanley Spencer, 'The Resurrection of the Soldiers'

and the self-wounded — all those unheroic, damaged men, present in the writing because they had been there at the Front, because they were a part of the war story, not Unknown Warriors but Unknown Victims.

But the theme of damaged men was more than a literary one: it was a troubling part of the general post-war reassessment of the values for which the war had been fought. From 1920 to 1922 a War Office Committee of Enquiry met in London to consider the whole question of 'Shell-Shock', and its relation to the army's traditional notions of cowardice. The Committee was heavily weighted towards the army (most of its members, including its doctors, were officers), though it listened to testimony by leading psychiatrists, including Rivers. Its conclusions were ambivalent and troubled: Committee members agreed 'that the military aspect of cowardice is justified', but they also agreed 'that seeming cowardice may be beyond the individual's control'. The idea of cowardice had to exist if there was to be an army, but it could no longer be identified or defined with any certainty. The damaged man had been recognized as a reality. And not surprisingly: when the Committee met in 1920, 65,000 former soldiers were receiving disability pensions for neurasthenia, and 9,000 of those were still hospitalized.[44]

III

Anti-monuments, whether they are histories or diaries, poems or paintings or novels, are monuments of loss: loss of values, loss of a sense of order, loss of belief in the words and images that the past had transmitted as valid. They testify to disconnection from the past, and to consequent dislocation, and to a sense of impoverishment. And they speak — even the paintings speak — the language of disillusionment and rejection. Such testimonies had appeared during the war, and they had stirred violent reactions, more violent even than the voiced hostility to conscientious objectors and pacifists. For they came from men who had believed, and who had lost their faith in the war, and to loyal war supporters they were most threatening.

It was not until four years after the war's end that the major monument of this turn of mind appeared — C.E. Montague's *Disenchantment*. Why was it delayed so long? I think because the post-war world had to take form before Montague could set down the whole process of loss. By 1922, 'Post-War' existed: not Reconstructed, as the

politicians had promised, not a land fit for heroes to live in, but a jumble
of the same old problems, made worse by the war — unemployment,
trade union discontent, Ireland, economic depression. This was the
present, the world-after-the-war. From this ruined place and time
Montague looked back, across the war years to England before the war,
and what he wrote was a history of the sad and disillusioning process by
which *that* England, so secure and so certain of its values, had become
this one.

Montague came to his task with a special set of qualifications. He was
forty-seven, and had been a journalist with the *Manchester Guardian* for
nearly twenty-five years, when he enlisted in 1914, dyeing his grey hair
to persuade the recruiting sergeant that he was young enough to fight.
In those early days he was very much the sort of Kitchener's Army
volunteer that Ian Hay wrote about in *The First Hundred Thousand*, a
civilian who was eager to serve, convinced of England's cause, and
willing to undergo hardship for the sake of those words that were on
everyone's lips. He served in France, and then was invalided out. Back in
England he turned to propaganda work, writing, among other things, the
texts that accompanied Muirhead Bone's war drawings. In that role he did
a good deal to bring the war to home-front civilians in a way that would
make it familiar-seeming and tolerable; he domesticated the foreign
landscape, explaining what was strange there and giving it familiar names;
he argued against the version of war that Barbusse offered; and he kept the
value-words in circulation. By the end of the war he had seen both the
realities of war and the home-front versions of it.

More than that, he had seen a change, and a betrayal of the high ideals
with which he and his fellow-volunteers had set out. That change he
called *disenchantment*: it, not the war itself, is the subject of his book. It
is a book about how England turned, and betrayed herself, her soldiers,
and her values. The war is at the centre, but not battle-scenes, not
victories or acts of heroism; his war is the stage for another kind of
drama, in which old regulars exploit the system and conscripts shirk
duty and danger, while in between, the volunteers lose their faith, and
learn the truth about war, armies, and profiteers. The war is won in
the end, but something more important is lost: a set of values that had
once clustered around the word *England*, and a connection with a past
that had been, in Montague's eyes, a good, moral, and decent time.

Montague divided his war, as I have, into an early and a late phase,
with a turning point in the middle. The tone in which he describes his
early war is suggested by the title of his first chapter, 'The Vision'; it is

a highly romanticized account of the state of mind of the men in Kitchener's Army. They felt, Montague says, 'the mental peace, the physical joy, the divinely simplified sense of having one clear aim . . . ' It was like a 'second boyhood', a time of tranquil hours and jocund days (the language gets very poetic at times). And because the pitch of enthusiasm and faith was so high, the fall was the greater: 'It seemed hardly credible now, in this soured and quarrelsome country and time, that so many men of different classes and kinds, thrown together at random, should ever have been so simply and happily friendly, trustful, and keen. But they were, and they imagined that all their betters were too. That was the paradise that the bottom fell out of.'[45]

Montague framed his war between two worlds: a world-before-the-war, and a world-after. His pre-war is a 'substantially stable' place, which seemed, at least, to work well enough. 'Surely,' he wrote, 'there never was any time in the life of the world when it was so good, in the way of obvious material comfort, to be alive and fairly well-to-do as it was before the war.'[46] It was a time when Englishmen accepted certain ideas as eternally true: that the ruling class ruled justly, that the social structure made for good, that human beings were decent, that civilization would last. Of course he would have to postulate such a world; one cannot be disenchanted unless one has been enchanted. And for Montague, that pre-war world had been a kind of enchantment, a bluff that nobody called. There is none of the condemnation of Edwardian England in his account that one finds in Gosse or Image, or any of the other wartime writers who looked back at peace and found it decadent. Montague saw it more or less as Keynes did, as a time when most Englishmen had been contented. There was only one trouble with that contented time, Montague said: it was based on a bluff.

Post-war was the world after the bluff had been called; a world in which all the comforting assumptions had been disproved. Montague characterized what had replaced them as a condition of mind composed of apathy, callousness, and lassitude. 'Some of the chief ingredients in the new temper', he wrote,

> are a more vigilant scepticism; a new impatience of strident enunciations of vague, venerable, political principles; a rough instinctive application of something like the new philosophy of pragmatism to all questions; and an elated sense of the speed and completeness with which institutions and powers apparently founded on rock can be scoured away.

In this world, even civilization itself, 'the at any rate habitable dwelling which was to be shored up by the war, wears a strange new air of precariousness,'[47] institutions shake, and no certainties remain.

Montague's book is less vivid about the war, and less profound in its analysis of its causes and consequences, than many others, but it had a powerful effect on English thought and feeling. Its power lay in the form that it gave to recent English history — to pre-war, and post-war, and the gap that the war had opened between them. Montague's pre-war past was a remote and unrecoverable time, a paradise lost (like Keynes's); his present was a negative space, emptied of everything good and secure that the past had held. This double vision, of what was lost and what was left, and of the gap in history between, was clearly what many Englishmen felt; they responded to Montague's disenchantment because they shared it. It was a vision that was not confined to any one post-war generation or class, or to the men who had fought, or to the bereaved at home: one finds it everywhere — in the universities and among the Old Men, in popular novels and in Modernist poems, among Socialists and in the reactionary British Empire Union. In 1922, it was the way the world was.

CHAPTER 16

The War Becomes History

I

Disenchantment is a condition of loss, and that was the way the war extended its presence into English culture after the Armistice — as forms of loss. Loss was there to be seen in the ordinary life of English streets, in the disabled and unemployed ex-soldiers, and the women in mourning, and in a great absence there — the absence of a million men. It was evident among the aristocracy in the dead heirs and the extinct titles that the war had caused, and among all the classes in a new impoverishment of life. To many Englishmen, post-war England seemed to exist as a sort of negative sum — the sum of all those losses, and of the war's ruins. Not only the physical ruins of destroyed landscapes, and dead and mutilated men, but the social, intellectual, and moral ruins of the old, pre-war society. Out of that view of reality came the mood that we think of as characteristic of 'the Twenties'. Post-war England stood, shakily and gloomily, on the rubble of the war's destruction.

One term for the sum of all that was ruined is *civilization*. That term had been much worried over at the war's beginning, and it returned again at the end. Civilization was what the war had been fought for: the official Victory Medal said so — 'The Great War for Civilization'. Now, with the war over, many writers took up that claim, to question it. If England had just caused a million of its men to die for civilization, then it seemed appropriate, indeed it seemed absolutely necessary, that the term and its recent history should be examined. What was civilization? Had it been destroyed by the war, as some said? If so, had it been guilty of its own destruction? If it survived, what form did it now take? Was it an absolute good? Or was it relative to the material conditions of existence?

These were questions that especially interested the intellectuals of Bloomsbury, who had invested so much of their lives in the idea of civility. They had worried about civilization in 1914, and the last shot of the war had scarcely been fired before they were at it again. Clive Bell dug out his notes for a book on the subject, begun in 1906 and put aside, and began again. 'Clive is writing a book called *Civilization*,' young David Garnett wrote to his mother in December 1918, 'but I don't know what it's about.'[1] Neither, I think, did Bell, quite. He knew what it *had* been about, back in 1906; it had been about aesthetic experience and personal relations and good states of mind — the essential values of pre-war Bloomsbury. But the war had intervened, and its violent actuality had altered reality, and so, presumably, had altered civilization. Bell fiddled with the term, in his ironic Bloomsbury manner, for ten years before he finally finished his book. What he at last produced was a curious museum piece, a bit of Edwardian Bloomsbury, perfectly preserved but quite removed from reality, like an arrangement of wax flowers under a bell jar.

Other artistic Bloomsburyites thought about civilization, too. Roger Fry, who had expected that it would end in August 1914, was still worrying about it in 1920. He was just back from a visit to France when he wrote in a letter:

> here one realizes the general instability better than in France; one feels the results of the war more sharply, the shocks from which our civilization is suffering, and one wonders with greater anguish where it will lead to, if civilization isn't too threatened, if the whole structure isn't too badly shaken for us to be able to prop it up.[2]

His image of civilization as a shaky structure, like a house damaged by a flood or an earthquake, was one that would recur.

Another member of the Bloomsbury circle, E.M. Forster, returned to England in 1919 from Egypt, where he had worked during the war, to find that the civilization he had known had disappeared while he was gone, leaving him a lonely last survivor. 'It's so puzzling and queer,' he wrote in a letter,

> to feel that one's the last little flower of a vanishing civilization, so exasperating to know that one doesn't understand what is happening, so chilling to realise that in the future people probably won't mind whether they understand or not, and that this attempt to apprehend

the universe through the senses and the mind is a luxury the next
generation won't be able to afford.[3]

This, like Bell's book, is essentially pre-war Bloomsbury, the gospel of
G.E. Moore. The war had not changed Forster's values, it seems; it had
only made him feel obsolete.

Not everyone who addressed the subject was as wan and flower-like
as Forster, but everyone agreed that civilization was in trouble. H.G.
Wells, for example, took upon himself the task of the salvaging of
civilization, and wrote a book with that title in 1921, in which he
announced that what mankind needed was a new 'Bible of Civilization',
and offered his recently published *Outline of History* as the new Book of
Genesis. Other writers took up the term in its social and economic
aspects; Beatrice and Sidney Webb wrote *The Decay of Capitalist
Civilisation*, and Bertrand Russell and his wife Dora wrote *Prospects of
Industrial Civilization* (both were published in 1923).

The ubiquitous Middleton Murry made his contribution to the
discussion in an essay that he wrote in January 1919. It is interesting not
because Murry was an original, or even a clear thinker, but because he
had an acute sense of what the literate, weekly-journal-reading public
was thinking, or wanted to think. During the war Murry had been fond
of the phrase 'the bankruptcy of civilization', scattering it through his
essays and reviews without explaining exactly what he meant by it; in
his essay on 'The Nature of Civilization' he spelled his meaning out.
'There would not be the faintest trouble,' he wrote,

> in reading modern history in such a fashion that the disaster of the
> war would appear not a terrible aberration of mankind, but the logical
> culmination of all that process of complicating and multiplying
> material satisfactions which began with the Industrial Revolution in
> England and has usurped the name of civilisation.[4]

And later in the same essay:

> So it came about that when the war burst upon the world, there was a
> general cry, equally convinced on both sides, that the war was being
> fought for civilisation; while no one who uttered the cry knew exactly
> what he meant. In the same way there were a few who protested that
> the war was the bankruptcy of civilisation, and though they knew
> what they meant, it was impossible for them to convey their meaning
> to the great majority who had been taught to understand something
> quite different by civilisation, and were compelled (if they were

honest) to admit that the war was rather a triumph of civilisation than the opposite.[5]

Forster's letter and Murry's essay were both written in the first year of the peace, and though they are different in tone and in direction, they make similar points. Forster looked back nostalgically to a fading, pre-war ideal — civilization understood as those products of the imagination by which the highest values are preserved and transmitted, and the community of people who addressed themselves to those goals. Murry agreed, but added an historical point: the cause of this change was not simply the war, but the whole cultural process that had begun with the Industrial Revolution — a process by which civilized society had destroyed its own civilization. Both Forster and Murry were right: a change had occurred, an ideal had vanished. And the war, if not the cause, had been the devastating expression of that change. The perception that this was true was a post-war commonplace; it was the cultural version of disenchantment.

Changes demand explanations: that is axiomatic. Men and women who perceive that their world has shifted have a need to report and interpret that shift, so that the new conditions of life may be understood, so that life may be lived. After the war, there were many analyses, many histories, and many theories of what had happened in the years before and during the war, and of what the war had done to England.

Among the many books in the post-war literature of change, one of the most significant is C.F.G. Masterman's *England After War* (1923). Masterman's work in wartime propaganda had given him unusual opportunities to observe wartime social changes. He had witnessed how public opinion had turned, how war idealism had dwindled and social divisions had opened, and how deaths and more deaths had darkened the nation's mood and cut off expectations. But he had another qualification: his *Condition of England* (1909) had analysed Edwardian change. He was, you might say, an authority on the subject.

In his earlier book Masterman had looked at England in the first decade of this century and had found it a troubled nation, spiritually empty and socially divided, with a greedy, insensitive plutocracy at the top exploiting a discontented proletariat at the bottom, and a vacuous, valueless middle class in between. His analysis, especially of the condition of the English upper classes, was not unlike Gosse's in 1914, but he did not see war as a cure for England's problems, as Gosse did.

He thought that two kinds of war were possible in the near future —
class war, or a European shooting war — and both seemed to him
frightful prospects. But what depressed him more than the threat of
war, or the reality of poverty and suffering among the poor, was the
spiritual state of the nation; for though Masterman was a Liberal, he was
also a Christian, and Edwardian England seemed to him a nation
without faith, and therefore without meaning.

Masterman began his analysis of post-war England, in *England After
War*, with a look back at that earlier England — a distant look, as though
across a vast empty space. 'Some fourteen years ago,' his preface
begins,

> I published a study of the Condition of England which received a
> kindly acceptance from the reviewers and those who honoured me by
> reading it. The world of which I then wrote had vanished in the
> greatest secular catastrophe which has tormented mankind since the
> fall of Rome. I have been invited to write a similar volume concerning
> the condition of an England but struggling with difficulty to survive
> and re-establish civilisation, in a Europe where it is still uncertain
> whether civilisation as we understood it will endure.[6]

The language and motifs of this passage are by now familiar: the
vanished world, the fall of a culture, the catastrophic war, the uncertain,
threatened post-war civilization. Masterman's odd phrase, 'secular
catastrophe', suggests an image of himself as like Noah after the flood,
looking at the absolute destruction of a world. This vision — of the
distant pastness of the pre-war past, and of its annihilation in the great
gap of the war — is the essential post-war myth of history.

The England that Masterman went on to describe in his book sounds
at first very like his Edwardian England: the same ostentation among
the rich, the same misery among the poor, the same mindless crowds at
football matches and music-halls, the same comedians in public office.
The English hadn't changed much, he remarked gloomily: the war
being over, they had simply reverted to type. (And so, one might add,
had he: he was still looking at England with an Edwardian Liberal's
eyes.)

Still, there were differences, and they were consequences of the war:
the rich were different — they were now the New Rich, the war
profiteers; the poor were different, too — having earned decent wages
for four years, they were grumbling against returning to the abyss of
poverty; even the middle classes were different — still contemptible

(Masterman despised the bourgeoisie as fiercely as any Socialist could), but pitiful in the new poverty that wartime prices had inflicted on them. The Church was different — in the doldrums, Masterman said, sapped of its strength by the war; love was different (and so was the birth rate — it was falling); patriotism was different. Seen as the sum of its classes and institutions, England was a shabbier, morally emptier place than it had been before the war.

But there were two changes in England that Masterman felt more strongly than any of these. One is described in a chapter titled 'The Fall of Feudalism', in which Masterman meditated on the consequences for a nation of the annihilation of its aristocracy. An aristocracy, he argued, is nourished and maintained by a nation for one purpose only — for war, and the British aristocracy was no exception. It had provided officers for the best regiments of the army, and once war had been declared those sons who were not soldiers volunteered. Masterman described what happened to them in a passage so striking as to be worth quoting at some length:

> If they did not woo darkness as it were a bride, they at least realized that all their life had been moulded for this hour, and many went into battle singing, without a trace of fear. They fought; if they were wounded, they returned as speedily as possible to the front; they allowed no health certificates to interfere with their ardour. Some knew with certainty that they would be killed, but cared nothing so long as they were facing the enemy. In the retreat from Mons and the first battle of Ypres perished the flower of the British aristocracy; 'playing the game' to the last, as they had been taught to play it all through their days of boyhood. They earned the extraordinary devotion of their men, and you may say with confidence nine-tenths of them thought of their men first . . . In the useless slaughter of the Guards on the Somme, or of the Rifle Brigade in Hooge Wood, half the great families of England, heirs of large estates and wealth, perished without a cry. These boys, who had been brought up with a prospect before them of every good material thing that life can give, died without complaint, often through the bungling of Generals, in a foreign land. And the British aristocracy perished, as they perished in the Wars of the Roses, or in fighting for their King in the great Civil War, or as the Southern aristocracy in America, in courage and high effort, and an epic of heroic sacrifice, which will be remembered so long as England endures.[7]

It is an extraordinary, extravagant eulogy of the upper classes, and it comes very oddly from a Liberal politician at the radical edge of his party, who had been a friend of the poor and the workers, and an enemy of privilege. But when he looked at England after the war, it seemed to him that without an aristocracy and its traditions it could not survive, and he lamented its loss in high rhetorical prose of the kind that one might expect to find in the editorial pages of some Tory newspaper. It is a case of a good writer made florid by feelings of loss — not his, but England's.

Masterman's paragraph articulates another part of the general myth of the war — the myth of the lost aristocracy, the death of an entire generation of the upper class. Masterman is a bit extravagant in his inclusiveness — of course not all of the aristocrats in arms perished. But if you look at the records you will see that enough of them did die to alter the structure of inherited power and wealth in England. Debrett's *Peerage* for 1918 contains a Roll of Honour that includes nearly 2,200 names, including a member of the Royal Family, 21 peers, 31 baronets, 11 knights, 562 companions, 149 sons of peers, 135 sons of baronets. In all 150 heirs to hereditary titles had been killed (and this includes only casualties to the end of 1917).

But Masterman was using the aristocratic dead as an example of something more than class: they stood for whatever in English society was the best — the oldest families, the most heroic traditions of soldiering — and was gone. This feeling, that the men who had died were the finest of their generation, and that the fact of their dying somehow proved their wasted excellence, is very common in post-war writing about the war of all kinds — anti-war and pro-war, written by soldiers and by civilian men and women. The effects of that assumption upon those who survived was obviously great; if one had survived, one must have been less than those who died.

Masterman wrote in his preface that he had spent the past fourteen years (the years, that is, since the publication of *The Condition of England*) 'in profound misery at the passing of the best life of England'; now, in the early 1920s, that life was gone. It wasn't only an aristocracy that had died; it was a culture, a civilization with all its civilities, the imaginations of men and women darkened and silenced by what they had witnessed. Masterman was at heart a literary man, and he most regretted this decline in English literature. England, he wrote, was 'so stunned by the war that so far as I can estimate, it is neither able to rejoice in the literature of the past or to produce any new spirit in literature which can voice its own miseries or aspirations in the present.'[8] (This was written in 1922, the year of *Ulysses* and *The Waste Land*.)

Even the war, Masterman felt, had been a disappointment in terms of its effects on imaginations; he compared it to the Napoleonic Wars, and found it sadly lacking. 'The extraordinary fact remains,' he wrote,

> that in both the two great interpreting branches of literature, fiction and poetry, not only has the war given no real inspiration and the great victory passed unsung, but among the young men, bitterness and cynicism and contempt of human life and of the foolishness of men is far more noticeable than any of such new inspiration, as filled the world, despite the defeat of the better cause, a hundred years ago.[9]

So the war, which ought to have inspired its own literature of celebration, had failed; it had not been greatly imagined. And the post-war world that followed the war was, in Masterman's view, even worse — was an imaginative desert. 'I cannot but believe,' he concluded gloomily,

> that this period of darkness and despair in literature is but the product on the one hand of the great loss whose immensity none of us yet realises, and on the other the time of sordidness and squalor which has succeeded the triumph of the fighting men.[10]

A product not of the war alone, you will notice; Masterman was saying that the war was one event — disastrous, but still only one — in a larger process of disintegration that had brought England to this ruined state.

England After War was not a success; only half of the five thousand copies printed were sold, and the reviews were at best lukewarm. Why, one wonders, was the book not taken up? Partly, perhaps, because of its tone; it was not an objective analysis of the post-war mood, it was the mood itself — defeated, despairing, and directionless. But also because of who the author was, and had been. Masterman titled his chapter on post-war literature 'How It Strikes a Contemporary': but he *wasn't* a contemporary, he was one of the Old Men. Though he was only fifty when he wrote *England After War*, he had been a member of Asquith's pre-war cabinet, and an official in the first wartime government. And now, in 1923, he was out of office. He had just stood as a Liberal in a coal-mining district, and had been badly beaten by a Labour candidate. The pre-war insider had become an outsider, a man whose present was the past.

In his book Masterman called contemporary England a 'New World', as though to imply that it held possibilities and promises; but he didn't believe it. His post-war world was a dark vacancy, emptied of values, emptied even of imagination. He could see no positive force there, no political movement, and no vital faith. The book that he wrote is a sensitive, intelligent, unsparing account of those post-war years; but when he spoke, nobody listened.

At the same time, another writer was writing his versions of England after the war, and was finding a large audience for his view. Harold Begbie was a writer of Masterman's generation (they were both born in the early 1870s), who had been around the London world of journalism since the turn of the century. He had published war poems during the Boer War, and again in 1914, he had worked for several London newspapers, and by 1919 he had written some forty books. But he did not make his reputation until after the war, when he began to appear in the *Pall Mall Magazine* as 'A Gentleman with a Duster', come to wipe away the dust and mists that concealed the truth about post-war England. As his articles accumulated, he published them in books: *The Mirrors of Downing Street* (1920), *The Glass of Fashion* (1921), *Painted Windows* (1922), *The Conservative Mind* (1924), *Declension* (1925). These books focus on different aspects of English post-war society — *The Mirrors* is about politicians, *The Glass* about class, *Painted Windows* about clergymen, *The Conservative Mind* about what its title names, *Declension* about national life — but all of them have one basic thesis, that a moral darkness was deepening over every aspect of English life that had profound consequences for the social, economic, and political future of the nation.

Masterman had written as an Edwardian Liberal; Begbie wrote as a Tory. He loved the aristocracy, and he hated Socialists; he also hated divorce, jazz, the rich, current fiction, and women who smoked. He was a harsh critic of high society and of politicians, and thought that the moral tone of both groups was pitiably low. But then, so was the tone of the nation as a whole. If, on the one hand, he criticized Colonel Repington and Margot Asquith for the moral shabbiness of their recorded lives, he was equally hard on ordinary citizens. Two quotations will give a sense of the 'Gentleman's' views:

We are a nation without standards, kept in health rather by memories which are fading than by examples which are compelling. We still march to the dying music of great traditions, but there is no captain of civilization at the head of our ranks. We have indeed almost ceased to be an army marching with confidence towards the enemy, and have become a mob breaking impatiently loose from the discipline and ideals of our past.

The fate of the country is largely in the hands of men and women who have lost the shrewd and natural instincts of ignorance without gaining the difficult and compensating wisdom of culture. We are an urbanised nation of half-educated people, and it is the mark of the half-educated to be sceptical, apathetic, unimaginative, and capricious.[11]

There is no mention in either of these passages of the war as a cause of England's decline. Begbie, like most Tories, had supported the war, and continued to regard it as a necessary defence against Prussianism. Yet when he described the war itself, it was in surprisingly strong and negative terms:

With a higher sensibility than was known to ancient warriors, with a far more delicate nervous organism, and with the greater tenderness of heart which we hope is one of the fruits of British civilisation, young Englishmen were called upon to take part in such a mangling of butchery, such an indiscriminate anarchy of slaughter and mutilation, such a filthiness of Bedlamite carnage, as no man had witnessed from the beginning of time.[12]

Begbie's post-war England was not so different from Masterman's — a country for which metaphors of sickness, darkness, and dying were appropriate, a leaderless country, a vulgar, valueless place. But where Masterman lamented, Begbie scolded; his task, he said, was the awakening of the nation to 'the true nature of the many great moral and economic changes confronting civilisation'; it was a difficult duty, but it was an urgent one, and he went about it with enormous enthusiasm. And with remarkable success: his books sold well, were reviewed approvingly, and went into cheap editions. One must conclude that the English didn't mind being told about the darkness of their post-war lives, so long as the telling was vigorous, and pointed, however vaguely, towards a light. Masterman had seen England's change as the irretrievable loss of what was best. Begbie was less thoughtful, but he was also less depressing; he saw the same lost Eden that other men had seen, but he seemed to promise that it could be regained, if only Englishmen would be *English*. As advice it does not seem useful — how

can one will oneself to be more English? — but at least it offered some
hope that the ruination of England might be reversible.

Diagnosing the present is one historical response to the feeling of
living in ruins. Writing historical narrative is another; for when you
construct a story of events from the past into the present, you construct
causation, and therefore meaning, and the ruins take shape, the strange
becomes the familiar. In the years after the war several histories
appeared that offered versions of the past, with varying degrees of
success.

The most important — indeed, the most important history in English
in the twentieth century — was Wells's *Outline of History* (1920). Wells
had set himself two ambitious goals, both of which are identified in his
sub-title: 'Being a Plain History of Life and Mankind'. By 'Life and
Mankind' he meant all life on earth, beginning when the flaming mass
that became our planet spun off from the sun, and ending with a view of
the future from 1920. 'Plain History' meant that it was intended as
reading that would be both instructive and entertaining to the general
reader, including the reader of modest means: the *Outline* was first
published in twenty fortnightly parts at one shilling and sixpence each,
and then in two volumes published at twenty-two shillings and
sixpence each, and in a one-volume edition at twenty-one shillings. All
but the very poorest class could afford it in one form or another.

Wells handled the historical problem of interpreting the 1914–18 war
primarily by simply putting it in scale. In an historical narrative that
reached back a notional 800 million years, four years in the early
twentieth century could scarcely matter very much; Wells gave the First
World War twenty-five pages out of a total of 761. But there was more
to it than that; the time-scale of the book placed Wells at a distance from
individual human events, as though he were looking down on the
war from a great height. So, for example, when he dealt with the
heated question of who was to blame, he could do it in this detached
way:

we may hazard the guess that when the passions of the conflict have
faded, it will be Germany that will be most blamed for bringing it
about, and she will be blamed not because she was morally and
intellectually very different from her neighbours, but because she had
the common disease of imperialism in its most complete and energetic
form. No self-respecting historian, however superficial and popular
his aims may be, can countenance the legend, produced by the

stresses of the war, that the German is a sort of human being more cruel and abominable than any other variety of men.[13]

And he could dismiss the issue of Belgian atrocities in a sentence:

A disproportionate fuss has been made over the detailed atrocities in Belgium . . . any people who had been worked up for war and led into war as the Germans were, would have behaved in a similar manner.[14]

From Wells's Olympian position, one soldier looked much like another, and even nations were not to be distinguished easily.

The war itself, as Wells narrated it, took a form that we have seen before. Wells began with an account of the German invasion of a Belgian border town on August 2, 1914. The German troops, in their first experience of behaving like soldiers, shot civilians and burned houses: 'And they had set alight,' Wells wrote, 'not a village, but a world. It was the beginning of the end of an age of comfort, confidence, and gentle and seemly behaviour in Europe.'[15] Here is the familiar theme of pre-war Europe as paradise lost that Keynes and the rest of Bloomsbury had felt, that Masterman had gloomily assumed, that Murry and Begbie had considered. It is a surprising view of the past for Wells to take, if you consider how he rendered pre-war England in novels like *Tono-Bungay* and *Boon*; but as he looked back across the abyss of the war to that earlier time, it looked better, more confident and seemly, than the present he stood in.

Wells's account of the fighting is remote and strategic: no tales of individual soldiers, only plans of attack, and the political schemes of nations. And technology: to Wells-the-scientist it was a war in which the scientists were — or should have been — the heroes, and in which the generals were the problem. Tanks, if they had been adopted, could have won the war in 1916; 'but the professional military mind is by necessity an inferior and unimaginative mind' and tanks were not used early enough, or in large enough numbers, and the war went on for two more years.

Well's version of the end of the war has a similar loftiness; he saw it not as a conflict of men, but as a conflict of interests:

. . . two mutually dangerous streams of anticipation were running through the minds of men in Western Europe towards the end of the war. The rich and adventurous men, and particularly the new war profiteers, were making their plans to prevent such developments as that air transport should become a state property, and to snatch back manufactures, shipping, land transport, the public services generally, and the trade in staples from the hands of the commonweal into the grip of private profit; they were securing possession of newspapers and busying themselves with party caucuses and the like to that end; while the masses of common men were looking forward naively to a new state of society planned almost entirely in their interest and according to generous general ideas ... By the middle of 1919 the labour masses throughout the world were manifestly disappointed and in a thoroughly bad temper ... There was to be no reconstruction, but only a restoration of the old order — in the harsher form necessitated by the poverty of the old time.[16]

That is a classic statement of the post-war myth, with a standard cast of characters: the expectant, naive soldiers, the greedy war profiteers, the New Rich and the New Poor. It is an anatomy of disenchantment.

Wells would go on to predict the future of the human race — being Wells, he couldn't stop at the present. But before he did, he paused to summarize 'The State of Men's Minds in 1920':

This *Outline* of our history would not be complete without at least a few words by way of a stock-taking of the state of mind in which we leave mankind to-day ... In the past six years there must have been a destruction of fixed ideas, prejudices, and mental limitations unparalleled in all history. Never before can there have been so great and so universal an awakening from assumed and accepted things. Never before have men stood so barely face to face with the community of their interests and their common destiny. We do not begin to realize yet how much of the pre-war world is done with for good and all, and how much that is new is beginning. Few of us have attempted to measure yet the change in our own minds.[17]

The passage is full of Wells's bustling, unsubstantiated optimism, but its essential message is not cheerful. The pre-war past is dead, its ideas and prejudices destroyed (and once again, the period of destruction is not confined to the war years — 'the past six years' includes the post-war years too). Post-war is an awakening (Wells reaches for a positive metaphor); but it is an awakening *from*, not an awakening *to*.

In the closing pages of his *Outline* Wells prophesied that what he wanted to happen would happen — that a World State would emerge; but when he looked at the present in 1920 he saw only what other Englishmen saw: a dead pre-war past, followed by a destructive gap, and a present that was simply the inheritor of ruins. No writer was more influential in establishing that mood than Wells. For he offered it as *history*, as the latest term in a 'Plain History of Life and Mankind', and he lent to it the immense authority of his name, his reputation, and his enormous sales.

The *Outline* sold better than even Wells had expected: more than two million copies in all. Critical judgements were mixed: scholars who were expert in fields that Wells touched on, and polemicists who objected to his treatment of their convictions, were harsh in their criticisms (Belloc, for example, published *A Companion to Mr Wells' Outline of History*, setting him straight on the Roman Catholic Church), but general readers praised it: Shaw found it 'enthralling', and Bennett called it 'a majestic success'.[18] Of the reviewers, the most perceptive and sympathetic was Forster. He devoted three reviews in the *Athenaeum* to the *Outline* — two to Part One, and the third to Part Two — and was lavish in his praise: 'a masterpiece', he called it, 'a wonderful achievement'. He had his criticisms to make: he objected to what he called 'a sort of Polytechnic glibness' in Wells's criticisms of the past, and he thought (quite rightly) that there was something essentially Victorian in Wells's faith in progress, but he did not doubt that Wells had written a great book.

Forster found the last chapters of the book the least satisfactory, and his reasons are worth pausing over. The final chapter, with its prophecies of a millennial future, Forster thought unconvincing; a writer simply couldn't be scientific and transcendental at the same time. The one before that, 'The International Catastrophe of 1914', displeased him for another reason:

> The chief events [he wrote] of the last six years have to be recorded, an impossible task, for no one yet knows what the chief events were. Our 'own' times, as they are ironically termed, are anything but ours; it is as though a dead object, huge and incomprehensible, had fallen across the page, which no historical arts can arrange, and which bewilders us as much by its shapelessness as by its size. The writer is intelligent, tender even, but how thin his voice sounds, as he comforts President Wilson or scolds Sir Edward Carson! Not now, not yet! The chapter is, as it was bound to be, journalistic jottings, which a new face or reaction will erase.[19]

I quote this passage not for its judgement of Wells, but for its version of contemporary history as a 'dead object, huge and incomprehensible'.

Forster is here rejecting the idea that the war *had* a history, that it could be shaped into narrative, and into meaning. Wells had tried to accomplish just that; but Forster objected: the gap in history was not to be filled with language: 'Not now, not yet!'

A few months after Wells's *Outline*, another unusual history book appeared. *Movements in European History* by 'Lawrence H. Davison' was ostensibly a school textbook, intended to replace the 'old bad history' of rote facts with a new history of

> the great, surging movements which rose in the hearts of men in Europe, sweeping human beings together into one great concerted action, or sweeping them apart for ever on the tides of opposition.[20]

The author, as the style of that passage may suggest, was in fact D.H. Lawrence, reduced to a pseudonym by the wartime censorship of *The Rainbow*, and the general feeling that he was too scandalous a man to address schoolchildren.

Lawrence's intentions were altogether less ambitious than Wells's. His time-scale was not cosmic but merely European: he began with the founding of Rome, and ended with the unification of Italy and Germany in the late nineteenth century. His length was modest — some hundred thousand words, roughly a fifth of what Wells had written — and he did without the pictures and maps and graphs and charts that Wells had needed to illustrate his vast project. And his audience was not everybody, as Wells's evidently was, but only adolescents, 'those who have had almost enough of stories and anecdotes and personalities, and who have not yet reached the stage of intellectual pride in abstraction'.[21]

A modest book, then; but nevertheless an interesting one, as the expression of a gifted man's sense of history at the end of the war. One notes, first of all, that Lawrence chose to end his history at the end of the nineteenth century, as though what happened after that point was not history, but something else. That sense of an ending is very clear in this valedictory passage, from the last page of the first edition:

> So the cycle of European history completes itself, phase by phase, from imperial Rome, through the mediaeval empire and papacy to the kings of the Renaissance period, on to the great commercial nations, the government by the industrial and commercial middle classes, and so to that last rule, that last oneness of the labouring people. So Europe moves from oneness to oneness, from the imperial unity to the unity of the labouring classes, from the beginning to the end.[22]

That end came with an apocalyptic finality that the publisher, Oxford University Press, found unsatisfactory: Lawrence was asked to add an epilogue telling what happened then, bringing the story up to date, for a new edition. He wrote, very rapidly, some additional pages in September 1924, and sent them on to OUP. (They were not included in the new edition, and were not published until 1971.)

Lawrence's 'Epilogue' is rather like *Women in Love* in its treatment of recent history: that is, it contains the war, but it does not describe it: as in the novel, 'the bitterness of the war may be taken for granted.' There are no narratives of military actions, no battle scenes, neither generals nor common soldiers, no mention of the Western Front, or of what nations were on either side: 'the War' is simply there as a vast disaster that changed the world. 'The War,' Lawrence begins, 'called now the Great War, came in 1914, and smashed the growing tip of European civilisation.'[23] That metaphor is carried on, endlessly: mankind is like a tree, with one trunk and many branches; every branch, every human race, has its 'growing tip'; and when that tip dies, the race dies. 'So the War came, and blew away forever our leading tip, our growing tip. Now we are directionless.'[24]

That sense of the dead past and the directionless present fills the Epilogue. The words that Englishmen believed in before the war, Lawrence says, words like *progress, expansion, free competition*, and *equal opportunity*, now 'make us feel sick, they have proved such a swindle'.[25] And there is nothing to replace them, no new ideals.

> No, the old ideal, the old leading tip was shot to smithereens, and we have got no new one. Nothing really to believe in. Only now, having lost our belief, we know inwardly that it would have been better to lose a war. Men cannot live *long* without a belief.
>
> Comes 'after the War'. The world after the War.
>
> We thought the old times were coming back. They can never come. We know now that each one of us had something shot out of him. So we have to adjust ourselves to a new world.
>
> Came 'after the War'. England ... changed inside ...[26]

The Epilogue was sent to two publisher's readers for assessment. One approved it, but the other wrote an angry rejection; he disliked the imagery ('at the twenty-seventh iteration of *growing tip* I almost screamed aloud'), but he disliked the argument more:

The doctrine that the war was either the cause or the effect of the sudden death of humanity [he wrote to the publisher] appears to me such vicious and cowardly nonsense that I am always tempted to suppose it an outbreak of injured vanity. But a great many people seem to hold this doctrine.[27]

This was a doctrine that Lawrence had been uttering in his letters for years; and no doubt, as the reader suggests, there was injured vanity in it. But it was also a *shared* doctrine; Lawrence was not alone in thinking that the war had killed something in Western society and in Western consciousness. And like many others — including Wells — he believed that a new political system would have to be imposed; the war he took to be proof that democratic capitalism no longer worked. His book, both the original text and the Epilogue, argues for an authoritarianism based on 'natural nobility', a system rather like Italian fascism but less bullying.

Lawrence's book was not a notable success; it offended many potential classroom users (Roman Catholic schools, for example, hated it), and its fact-free historical method did not appeal to teachers accustomed to thinking that history somehow had to involve facts. If it is nevertheless important, that is because Lawrence was important to his time, and because his view of the social and intellectual effect of the war on Western society was widely held. Many other post-war Modernists — Pounds, Yeats, Wyndham Lewis, for example — shared Lawrence's authoritarian politics, and would have agreed with him that the war had finally killed democracy as a feasible political system. The reactionary political side of Modernism had many roots, but one of them was certainly the war and its aftermath.

II

History is one way of ordering, and so making sense of, the past. Fiction is another. 'All novels are historical,' Ford Madox Ford wrote after the war, 'but all novels do not deal with such events as get to the pages of history.'[28] But after the war, many novels did; those events seemed unavoidable in fiction, because they had changed reality. That change became a primary literary theme, and the terms of change are those of the histories and analytical studies that we have been examining.

Such 'historical' novels had begun in the later years of the war, after the 'turn'; they continued in the post-war years. Novelists who had published wartime histories added post-war versions: Rose Macaulay wrote *Potterism* (1920), *Dangerous Ages* (1921) and *Told by an Idiot* (1923), Wells wrote *The Dream* (1924) and *Christina Alberta's Father* (1925). And books by new historical novelists began at once to appear: W.L. George's *Blind Alley* (1919), A.S.M. Hutchinson's *If Winter Comes*, Ernest Raymond's *Tell England*, and Michael Sadleir's *Privilege* (all 1921), C.E. Montague's *Rough Justice* and Osbert Sitwell's *Before the Bombardment* (both 1926). These novels vary enormously in quality, in point of view, and in the degree of their popular success; but they have these qualities in common: they are all located precisely in actual history, and they all contain the war at their centre — the disintegrating, transforming element that changed reality.

It would be easy to extract from these novels an anthology of remarks repeating and verifying the ideas that we have found in post-war historical studies: the world-before-the-war as a lost Eden, the war as a gap in history, the death of civilization, the post-war world as a valueless, directionless vacuum. Here is a small sample:

> Those of us who are old enough will remember that in June and July 1914, the conversation turned largely and tediously on militant suffragists, Irish rebels, and strikers ... It was a curious age, so near and yet so far, when the ordered frame of things was still unbroken, and violence a child's dream, and poetry and art were taken with immense seriousness. Those of us who can remember it should do so, for it will not return. (*Potterism*)

> 'It's queer,' she thought, 'the war goes on. Nothing much seems to happen. It might be going on for ever, and it's making a sort of ditch between what there used to be and what there will be.' (*Blind Alley*)

> The war had let him down, as it had let down most men of courage and clean heart who fought in it. All the early exaltation was out of them now, and the approach of victory was bringing nothing of what their innocence had expected — no sense of having freed or cleaned a world. (*Rough Justice*)

> The war had overstrained him, he realized, and left him too tired for a time to see new things. He had been one of the vast multitude of those who had come out of the war in the expectation of a trite and obvious old-fashioned millennium, and who expressed their disappointment by declaring that nothing had happened except devastation and impoverishment. (*Christina Alberta's Father*)[29]

All of these novels are concerned with loss, as these quotations show. And all of them express the sense of loss through characters that are by now familiar types: the executed coward, the woman war worker, the disillusioned veteran, the Old Men. Even their literary references are familiar: George mentions Masefield's *Gallipoli* and Haig's *Despatches*, Rose Macaulay's characters read a Begbie book, and wish that Lytton Strachey had written it, and Wells offers a bibliography of 'human books' about the war that includes Enid Bagnold's *Diary Without Dates* and Barbusse's *Le Feu*. These novels share a created reality, a set of ideas about their own world, and at the centre of that world is the war, which has changed the world and the conditions of existence in it. And that is where the imagination has to start from.

In most of the 'historical novels' I have mentioned, the war gives a structure to history, and therefore to the narrative. But it is a structure of a peculiar sort — disrupted and discontinuous, a Before and an After separated by a disruptive middle, the war itself. In these novels Pre-war and Post-war are more than two historical periods, or two sets of events — they are two sets of values, two worlds. The essential problem that the novels deal with is the causal relation between the two: what did we do, *then*, that led us to where we are *now*? or, what happened during the years between that made the past irrecoverable, and the disordered present inevitable? Of course the war itself is a cause of the post-war situation; but it is a *caused* cause, and novelists had to go behind it, to the world-before-the-war for origins. Almost no post-war historical novelist was content to begin with the war; the story had to begin further back.

Most post-war novels that treated the recent English past as history took this essential form: an Edenic pre-war time, a disvalued and depressed post-war, and in between, the war, a transforming chaos. But it was just possible to write another version of that history, in which the war was not a cause of radical change. Such novels seem now to have a curious anachronistic quality about them, as though they had somehow been written before the war, and written in Edwardian terms. The most striking example is Galsworthy's *Forsyte Saga*. Galsworthy published the first part of the *Saga*, *The Man of Property*, in 1906 as a single, self-contained novel, with no apparent thought of continuing it as a family chronicle. It was only after the war that he took it up again, and wrote *In Chancery* (1920) and *To Let* (1921), and then published the whole in one fat volume as *The Forsyte Saga* in 1922.

The surprising thing about *The Forsyte Saga* is that though its chronology runs from 1886 to 1920, there is no First World War in it. *The Man of Property* is set in the 1880s, *In Chancery* ends at the turn of the century, and *To Let* begins on May 12, 1920; the years from 1914 to 1918 are passed over in a few phrases in the mind of Soames Forsyte: 'Since the War', 'now that the War was over', 'during the War' — and that is all. In this vast novel of English society, the war is given no reality, and no social role.

One can infer Galsworthy's motive in this striking omission from remarks that he made during and just after the war. He wrote in an article on 'Art and the War' in 1915 that 'those of us . . . who are able to look back from thirty years hence on this tornado of death . . . will conclude with a dreadful laugh that if it had never come the state of the world would be very much the same'; and in 1919 he wrote to a hostile reviewer:

> I think if you were to use your eyes and nose and feelers generally, as novelists have to do, you would discover that under superficial differences human nature changes hardly at all, wars or no wars, revolutions or no revolutions, age in age out . . .[30]

Galsworthy was asserting, against the emerging mood of the time, that history, society, human nature itself were continuous, that there was no gap created by the war. His decision to take up his story after the war, and to make it a *Saga*, was an historical decision: he would demonstrate that history was unbroken, that Forsytes were still Forsytes.

One might argue, though, that his decision really verified the myth of diiscontinuity, that if there had not been a general sense of a break in history he would not have had to write a long novel denying it. And one could cite in support of this view the *Saga*'s concluding chapter, in which Soames, alone in Highgate Cemetery at the Forsyte family vault, meditates on his family and the past:

> The waters of change were foaming in, carrying the promise of new forms only when their destructive flood should have passed its full. He sat there, subconscious of them, but with his thoughts resolutely set on the past — as a man might ride into a wild night with his face to the tail of his galloping horse. Athwart the Victorian dykes the waters were rolling on property, manners, and morals, on melody and the old forms of art — waters bringing to his mouth a salt taste as of blood, lapping to the foot of this Highgate Hill where Victorianism lay buried.[31]

There is no war in this passage, but the terms of the post-war myth of history are all present: the destructive flood, the buried past, the radical changes in manners, morals, and art. Soames, the acquisitive, bloodless Man of Property in the first volume of the *Saga*, has become the sympathetic spokesman for a lost world in the last one — alone among the Victorian dead, facing backwards, into the irrecoverable past.

One might use the same image for Galsworthy himself, and say that he was a pre-war novelist in the post-war world, looking back to his Edwardian past and refusing to accept its pastness. That view of history made him an anachronism among Modernist writers; but it endeared him to the middle-brow middle class, made him rich and famous, and eventually an OM and Nobel laureate — all those rewards given, you could argue, for his comforting assurances that history was continuous.

While Galsworthy was completing his novel without a war, other historical novels containing the war were beginning to appear — novels, that is, in which the fighting is a central action, combatants' novels. None of these earliest post-war novels is very memorable, and none survives in the canon of First World War literature, but a number of them were extremely successful at the time, and these are interesting for what they suggest about how the war was first imagined, and what readers found to admire in such histories. Two in particular are worth looking at briefly: *Way of Revelation* (1921), and *Tell England* (1922) — both first novels, one by an ex-man-about-town, the other by an ex-army chaplain, both of them best-sellers.

The man-about-town was Wilfred Ewart, a young Guards officer who fought on the Western Front, was wounded at Neuve Chapelle, and was invalided home in 1918 with concussion. While he was still in France, Ewart had conceived the idea of writing a war novel, though curiously he first imagined it in home-front terms, as a book that would be truer to the reality of wartime London than *Sonia* or *The Pretty Lady* was. But as he thought about it, his ambitions expanded; he would write an English *War and Peace*. When he began to write, it seemed that his novel would indeed resemble Tolstoy's, in length at least: it grew to some 350,000 words. A prudent English publisher cut it by half, and it appeared in the late autumn of 1921, and was an immediate success.

Way of Revelation follows a young man of good family, Adrian Knoyle, from pre-war upper-class society in the summer of 1914 into and through heavy fighting in France, with intervening periods on leave in England. While he is at the Front his war is a convincing one; Ewart's accounts of battles — including Passchendaele and Cambrai — have that kind of vivid, plotless incoherence that the best war memoirs have. But he had not forgotten his idea of improving on Bennett and McKenna, and so there is also a home-front story, a plot. Home on leave, Adrian falls in love with a peer's daughter. When he returns to the Front she takes up with a circle of dissolute Bohemians, learns to use drugs, is seduced, betrays Adrian with a degenerate draft-dodger, and dies. The war ends, Adrian returns to England, marries a more virtuous peer's daughter, and assumes his family baronetcy.

Many familiar wartime themes are here: the faithful soldier and the unfaithful woman, the vileness of civilian males, the decadence of the upper classes. It is Ewart's notion of the latter that is most interesting. Decadence had been a wartime concern from the beginning (remember Gosse's stern condemnation in 1914); but it had generally been found in pre-war English society, and the war was seen as the purge that would cure it. Ewart saw it instead as a condition of wartime society, in which traditional restraints were cast aside and moral standards were lost, and Bohemianism (which Ewart identified with Futurism and Modernism generally) was set loose, to ruin peers' daughters and destroy the happiness of loyal chaps at the Front. It is another case of wartime home-front hating, but with a decadent difference.

The decadence and immorality that Ewart saw at home was, the novel tells us, filthy, but it was only temporary; after the war there are still country houses, with virtuous young women in them, there are still titles, England is still recognizable, familiar England. Adrian has been made to suffer dreadful things, and to witness a good deal of moral depravity, but nothing has really changed.

Ernest Raymond's *Tell England* is half a war novel and half a school story in the English tradition that runs from *Tom Brown's Schooldays* to *Stalky & Co* and *The Loom of Youth* and beyond. Three chums live together through five years in an English public school. When war is declared they all enlist; one is killed at Neuve Chapelle, the second at Cape Helles in Gallipoli. The third writes their story, and is then killed in France. The book is his narrative, edited by a sympathetic army chaplain.

Tell England breaks into two quite independent parts, divided at the war's beginning. One can see why Raymond told the story in that way: school life was his version of pre-war Eden, his paradise lost, and the war was the fallen world. Many young men like those in his novel must have felt the same, and quite understandably, for most of the subalterns who died so swiftly in action had come more or less directly from

school to war. One can find their sentimental feelings about the Old
School in any wartime anthology of soldiers' poems (*The Muse in Arms*,
for example, includes poems to Harrow, Marlborough and Winchester,
along with three to Oxford).

Out of the spirit of the English public school, with its subordination
of self to institution, its collective ethic, and its celebration of courage
and sacrifice, came the war spirit that filled the war's early days with
high emotion. Raymond makes the transition in a scene in which two
schoolboys travel from school to London to be received into the army
by an elderly territorial colonel. He asks how old they are, and when
they reply, 'Eighteen, sir,' he exclaims: 'Eighteen, by Jove! You've
timed your lives wonderfully, my boys. To be eighteen in 1914 is to be
the best thing in England . . . And now you enter upon your inheritance'
— and one hears the voice of Rupert Brooke: 'And we have come into
our heritage.' Later, when the first of the three boys is killed, and one of
the survivors suggests that a life has been wasted, the Colonel snaps,
'Nonsense,' and takes down Brooke's *1914* from a shelf and marks the
lines about pouring out 'the red sweet wine of youth'.[32] This spirit of
Brookeish, schoolboy patriotism never leaves the book.

Neither does the mixing of patriotism with religion: the chaplain wins
the two surviving boys back to the Christian faith on the way to
Gallipoli, and the last survivor's narrative ends on a note of high and
patriotic piety. All this was written after the war by a man who, if he
had not actually fought in it, had been a witness at Gallipoli to the
human consequences of war; yet his Rupert Brookeism and his Anglican
optimism never failed him. His title indicates as much; it is taken from
the Waggon Hill epitaph for the Boer War dead:

> Tell England, you who pass this monument,
> We died for her and rest here well content.

One must conclude — and it is a point worth noting — that though the
anti-war myth of the war had come to dominate post-war English
thinking, it had not entirely displaced the other, early-war one. It was
still possible, in 1922, to quote Rupert Brooke and the Waggon Hill
lines without irony — possible, that is, if you were Ernest Raymond.

Way of Revelation was received by the critics with a good deal of
approval, especially for the battle scenes. But *Tell England* was abused,
despised, and dismissed by virtually every reviewer. It was written,
Rose Macaulay wrote, 'apparently by a rather illiterate and commonplace
sentimentalist'; it was 'quite unreadable', said another critic. Even the

school-story part was attacked — Alec Waugh said that it showed the most profound ignorance of cricket he had encountered.[33] 'It is unconsciously a sentimental, coarse, and pretentious book,' the *Nation*'s critic remarked, — a vulgar book.'[34] And so it is.

Some critics (the *Nation*'s man was one) allowed that the book improved somewhat when Raymond wrote about Gallipoli; but *Tell England* is not a case of a bad book saved by good war writing, as one might argue is the case with *Way of Revelation*. Its appeal to its contemporary audience is rather expressed in the sub-title that Raymond chose; his book was, he said, 'A Study in a Generation'. 'You must write a book,' the chaplain tells the last surviving lad, '... about the dead schoolboys of your generation.'[35] Those were the terms in which the book was marketed: the dust jacket carried above the title the phrase 'A Great Romance of Glorious Youth', and below the title a picture of petals falling from a Red Rose of England into the flames of war. It must have been the right way to sell it: *Tell England* was reprinted fourteen times in 1922, and six times in 1923, and was still selling in its fortieth edition in the mid-1960s.

War novels like these, written after the war, are necessarily different from wartime narratives like *Le Feu*. Barbusse, caught in the uncertain middle of an unconcluded war, could only finish his story in a cloud of Socialist symbols. But post-war novelists knew how the story had ended, and their knowledge of the shape that history had taken had necessary formal consequences. Their novels are historical, in essentially the same way that novels like *Potterism* and *Christina Alberta's Father* are; they look back at a piece of the past that includes a completed war, and, like those other, 'civilian' novels, they attempt to deal with the problems of war and historical change, with the *before* and the *during* and the *after*. Ewart said that there had been a moral change in England in wartime, a descent into decadence, but he made it a temporary lapse, and so could restore Old England at the end. Raymond, a simpler-minded man, said that men had died, but had died gloriously, and that nothing had changed. In both cases, the permanence and continuity of pre-war values persist, the war passes, England remains as she was.

Reviewers seemed ill at ease, reviewing these books. They tended to praise the descriptions of actual war, which were mainly realistic and particular in the manner of late-war memoirs. To the parts that weren't about war, or the environments of war, they applied the standards of the fictional conventions that they recognized: Ewart's London plot was a trumpery society romance; Raymond's schooldays chapters were an

inaccurate, sentimental school story. This is not surprising: critics see
what they already know. What these didn't see was the connections
between these unsatisfactory conventional situations and the war itself,
though that is what both novelists were trying to establish. One might
say that the reviewers failed to read the novels *as history*.

A few of them tried, though. An anonymous reviewer of *Way of
Revelation* in the *Spectator* wrote:

> ... it is a thousand pities that so good a piece of work devoted to this
> particular theme should be published at this moment. Stories about
> the War have just got into the 'blind spot' of most readers. Three
> years ago they were immediately interesting. Seven or eight years
> hence they will be historically absorbing. Just now the world is taken
> with disgust at the doings of the last seven years, and certainly should
> not be reminded of them in the hours devoted to entertainment.

And after quoting a couple of strongly detailed passages describing the
trenches and the dead, he concluded: 'Is it not impossible to believe that
for four years a civilized world was entirely taken up with scenes so
terrible?'[36]

This is not so much a statement about war and history as it is about
the history of literary taste concerning war. But the critic had at least
recognized, somewhat dimly, that in 1921 there was no myth of history
existing in terms of which Ewart's novel could be understood and
judged. Ideas about the relations among pre-war, wartime, and post-
war, and between the Front and the Home Front, and between
generations — these ideas had been expressed, but separately; they had
not yet come together in a Myth of the War. Yet these two novels were
extremely popular, and one of them continued to be (*Way of Revelation*
faded in a year or two, and was never successfully revived). What did
they offer their ordinary English readers? Most obviously, a certain
amount of sex and scandal; decadence in high society was titillating, and
Raymond's schooldays story had a strong homosexual flavour (though
he professed not to have been aware of it when he wrote the book). But
the two books had more than that; they both had something of the
descriptive appeal that the war memoirs had — a sense of actual scenes,
on the Western Front or in Gallipoli.

But most of all, these novels must have given their readers the
comfortable feeling that the world-after-the-war was not as badly off as
pessimists said it was, that the war had caused no irreversible, disastrous
changes, and that civilization had survived. Soldiers survived, religion

survived, baronetcies and peers' daughters and parsons survived, even Rupert Brooke's sonnets survived; so England, as one had always known it, must have survived too. As a view of history it was against the evidence and against the cultural mood; but it must have been reassuring.

CHAPTER 17

'A Botched Civilization'

All wars divide — divide not only *our* side from *theirs*, but soldiers from civilians, men from women, one generation from another, war-lovers from war-haters. These divisions don't end with the war's last shot: they continue into the following years, and constitute those other conflicts, the wars after the war. These war-created divisions gave English culture of the Twenties its characteristic tone, and it is in this sense that one might say that the most important cultural event of that decade was nothing that happened within it, but the war that preceded it. The war was a presence in imaginations, even those that had not experienced the war directly; and it was a presence in society, dividing, separating, imposing oppositions.

One division that was already in place when the war ended was that between the civilian Modernist artists and writers and the war artists. To painters and poets returning from the fighting, it seemed that the stay-at-homes had not only avoided being shot at, but had managed to settle themselves into the best editorial jobs, the best journals and publishing houses. These men — men like Jack Squire and Middleton Murry, Pound and Eliot, Leonard Woolf and Edwin Muir, H.M. Tomlinson and Michael Sadleir — had had civilian jobs, or military administrative jobs that kept them in London, and they had gone on writing, reviewing, editing, exercising influence, and giving definition to what would come to be the major forms of post-war modern art and literature.

What these non-combatants had *not* done, and could not do, was to participate in the effort that engaged men like Owen, Read, Nevinson and Nash — the effort to bring the reality of the war directly into art, both as subject and as a determinant of form. 'I have been a disinterested spectator of the struggles of others with war and peace,' Eliot wrote to Read after the war[1]; and other civilian Modernists might have said the same thing. While the war went on, they had given it little heed. (Pound, for example, tried a couple of war poems in 1914–15, but didn't publish them; 'This war is not our war,' he wrote in one of them. 'Neither side is on our side.')[2] Once it was over, they turned to the new post-war world as their appropriate subject. The greatest, the most cataclysmic action of modern history had occurred, reality had been profoundly altered, and they had been merely onlookers. The war would enter their post-war work, but not as direct experience, not as incident and event.

Once the war was over, both Pound and Eliot surveyed the poetry it had produced, and concluded that it was not impressive. 'In the flood of "war" poetry, how much have we had that does not seem utterly inadequate from any possible angle of contact?' Pound asked in the summer of 1919. His answer was clear — very little. Writing at the same time, Eliot managed in the course of reviewing Herbert Read's *Naked Warriors* to define a war-poem aesthetic in terms of which Read passed, but most other poets didn't:

> Mr. Read's book is on a very high level of war poetry [Eliot wrote]. It is the best war poetry that I can remember having seen. It is better than the rest because it is more honest; because it is neither Romance nor Reporting; because it is unpretentious; and it has emotion as well as a version of things seen. For a poet to observe that war is ugly and not on the whole glorious or improving to the soul is not a novelty any more: but Mr. Read does it with a quiet and careful conviction which is not very common.[3]

You can see what Eliot was getting at in this passage, with his quiet denigration of 'Reporting' and 'a version of things seen': he was dismissing the principal English war poets — Sassoon and Owen and Graves — because they were Georgians. The Georgians, those poets who had gathered around Edward Marsh before and during the war, had aimed at a new realism of subject and diction: Masefield's use of *bloody* is an example, Brooke's poem about vomiting on a Channel ferry is another. That realistic aesthetic had transferred easily to war poetry; but with it had gone traditional notions of form and syntax that revealed what the Georgians really were, the last of the Romantics, even in war. These poets, and the poems they wrote, could have no place in a post-war Modernist agenda, and Eliot, in his sly way, was saying so.

The war poets felt a comparable lack of sympathy for the Modernists. Sassoon found Eliot aloof and chilling, with a 'cold-storaged humanity', and resented being told that Eliot was the most important of modern poets,[4] and Graves, though he professed to admire Eliot as a satirist, and even tried to collaborate with him on one occasion, disliked his work as a whole, and denigrated it all his life. As for Pound, Graves dismissed him flatly: 'I could never regard him as a poet, and have consistently denied him the title,' he wrote to Eliot.[5]

Graves's motive was as clear as Eliot's: here was a new movement that had largely emerged in English literary life while the war poets had been absent, and that seemed to have replaced the kind of poetry they practised. It was a movement that had something in common with the war poets: they were all in reaction against the pre-war world and its values, and they could all be described as iconoclastic, or disillusioned, or cynical, or disenchanted — those names for lost values that the elderly and conservative used against them. But their differences were greater, and were insurmountable. Those differences were partly formal — Georgian traditionalists vs. disjunctive Modernists; but a deeper difference was that basic sense that separates all old soldiers from their civilian contemporaries, the feeling that *I* was there, and fought, while *you* stayed at home and profited. That breach would never heal, and so the two literary lines did not become a single post-war literary movement. They remained separated by the experience that they did not share, and by the years that some of them had lost.

The war poets had another problem in placing themselves in the post-war literary world. Even as they returned to England, another, even younger generation — the post-war generation — was beginning to claim attention. A man like Graves, who was only nineteen when the war began, must have felt himself outrageously overtaken by time, deprived of his literary youth before he'd had it, and supplanted before he had begun to make a literary name — a poet who was too Georgian to make common cause with the home-front Modernists, and too experienced and war-weary to join the post-war young. Sassoon, though older, felt a similar disorientation after the war, groping for a place for himself in the literary world of London, but never really finding it. These men were the real Lost Generation, not the men who died; they had fallen out of the literary world of their own time, into the gap of the war. Or so, at least, it must have seemed to them.

The principal post-war Modernists distanced themselves from the war, and from soldier-poets like Sassoon and Graves, but they did nevertheless write their own forms of war literature. As Katherine Mansfield had said, they had to, or be traitors to their art.[6] But it was a war literature with a difference. Consider, as a primary example, the case of Pound. During the war years he had paid very little attention to the war, and one can extract no consistent attitude towards it from his letters and other writings (when he mentions it at all). But once it had ended he recognized that more than a war had come to an end: a movement in English art in which he had made a significant place for himself was also finished. Again and again in the years that followed Pound looked back, sometimes elegiacally, sometimes angrily, at a better time that was past.

You find him in this mood first in 'The Death of Vorticism', a brief essay in the *Little Review* early in 1919. Pound intended his title to be ironic; 'Vorticism has been reported dead by numerous half-caste reporters of Kieff, by numerous old ladies, by numberous [*sic*] parasites who having done their best to prevent the emergence of inventions later find it profitable to make copy out of the same, etc., etc.'[7] But in fact, he argued, it was alive and well: look at all those Vorticistically camouflaged ships, look at the war paintings of Lewis, look at William Roberts. But the reports were true, Vorticism *was* dead. Pound was losing the influence that he had had, and within a year would withdraw to Paris and fade from the London cultural scene; the *Egoist* would cease publication at the end of 1919; and Lewis, though he was back in London, would not resume the role that he had played before the war, and would in fact virtually stop exhibiting (he had no London show between 1921 and 1937). There would be no more *Blasts*.

'Hugh Selwyn Mauberley (Life and Contacts)' appeared in 1920 — the year in which Pound left London. The poem is, as Pound noted, 'a farewell to London', an angry and contemptuous rejection of the English literary life in which for ten years he had hustled in the interests of the new, and an obituary for 'E.P.', the man he had been then. But it is also a moving war poem, such as Pound had not written while the war was going on. Or perhaps it would be more accurate to say that it is an after-the-war poem, looking back on the war and its costs, and looking around at the post-war world that the war had created. No one got the retrospective sense of the war — the high motives of the beginning and the sense of betrayal at the end — better than Pound did in parts IV and V of this poem; appearing when they did, in 1920, and where they did, in a major poem by a major Modernist, they must have had a significant role in the shaping of the post-war Myth of the War. If so, Pound has the distinction of being the only non-combatant to have written an important war poem — or one of two if you count Hardy.

'Mauberley IV' is striking for Pound's understanding of the variety of motives for which men fought, and for the economy with which he renders the war and the world after. The whole Myth of the War is encapsulated in nineteen lines; first the motives for going:

> Some quick to arm,
> some for adventure,
> some from fear of weakness,
> some from fear of censure,
> some for love of slaughter, in imagination,
> learning later . . .
> some in fear, learning love of slaughter . . .

then the war itself, in three lines:

> Died some, pro patria,
>   non "dulce" non "et decor" . . .
> walked eye-deep in hell

and the 'turn', in a single line:

> believing in old men's lies, then unbelieving

and the return to England, disillusioned and betrayed:

> came home, home to a lie,
> home to many deceits,
> home to old lies and new infamy;
> usury age-old and age-thick
> and liars in public places.[8]

It is an extraordinary achievement, and especially for a man who had not apparently been much moved by or engaged in the war while his friends were fighting it, who had been, as he said, 'unaffected by "the march of events"'. One must conclude that it was only when Pound saw how the war had accelerated and confirmed the corruption of English culture that he took it seriously. Gaudier-Brzeska had died, Hulme had died, for *this*. The poem is in part an elegy for those dead friends; but it also mourns a larger death:

> There died a myriad,
> And of the best, among them,
> For an old bitch gone in the teeth,
> For a botched civilization.[9]

Pound wrote one more version of this 'botched civilization', in his two 'Hell Cantos', published in Paris in 1925. The Hell rendered in these cantos, he wrote to Wyndham Lewis, 'is a portrait of contemporary England, or at least Eng. as she wuz when I left her.'[10] This is the world that the war made — an Inferno peopled by all those damned English who stayed at home while the war went on, and benefited from other men's sufferings, and in the process corrupted culture, language, civilization. They are familiar figures: politicians, profiteers, financiers, perverters of language, vice-crusaders, orators, preachers, bishops, 'cowardly inciters to violence', Fabians, journalists — we have seen them all in the bitter writings of the war poets and the war painters, and in the letters and the diaries of the fighting soldiers.

There is a thesis in the 'Hell Cantos', and in 'Mauberley' too, that is important: the ruin of civilization that was post-war England was not a consequence of the fighting war, but of the war at home. Many others had said it; but none so powerfully, and with such fierce loathing, as this man who had scarcely noticed the war while it went on. Like Dante, Pound had filled his Hell with his enemies; but in his case, they were also the enemies of civilization. Hell was England-after-war — the ruin that Masterman saw, that Montague saw, that Lawrence saw, and that they all hated.

Eliot's *The Waste Land* is less explicitly a war poem than Pound's 'Mauberley' is, but it nonetheless belongs to the same category of post-war poems that render the action of the war upon human society, and in recent years that has been recognized. 'Seen in its immediate postwar context,' Paul Fussell writes in *The Great War and Modern Memory*, 'a work like *The Waste Land* appears much more profoundly a "memory of the war" than one had thought,' and he itemizes the echoes of war that are in the poem — some of them explicit, like the ex-soldier in the first part, others evocative images, like the rats and the dead men, the blasted landscape and the ruins.[11] It isn't that the poem describes the war; Eliot simply picked up the fragments that existed in post-war consciousnesses, and made a poem out of them, a poem that his contemporaries found haunting, even when they didn't understand it, because they shared its fragments.

But *The Waste Land* is more than an accumulation of image-fragments; it is a poem that takes fragmentation as its formal principle, as though the visual reality of the Western Front had imposed itself on language. This is a perception that the war poets never came to, and it makes Eliot's poem an expression of the war's impact on consciousness in a way that theirs weren't, and makes it Modern — or makes Modern whatever resembles the poem in form. From this perspective, the most important lines in the poem occur in 'The Burial of the Dead':

> What are the roots that clutch, what branches grow
> Out of this stony rubbish? Son of man,
> You cannot say, or guess, for you know only
> A heap of broken images . . .

and especially that last phrase. The idea that reality could be perceived, indeed *had* to be perceived, as broken and formless is one that many trench writers recognized, and adopted in their descriptions of the Front. Eliot saw that the war had imposed that vision upon the world after the war.

To say that is to say that Eliot had an historical vision, and wrote an historical poem in *The Waste Land*, and that is clearly the case. He carefully located the poem in the modern urban world, with images of gashouse and taxi and gramophone, and then made that world explicitly post-war by placing a demobilized soldier in it, and a phrase about 'the present decay of eastern Europe' in his notes, followed by a supporting quotation from Hermann Hesse: '*Schon ist halb Europa, schon ist zumindest der halbe Osten Europas auf dem Wege zum Chaos*' [Already half of Europe, at least the Eastern half, is on the way to chaos]. *The Waste Land* is not a timeless poem; it could not be about any other place or any other time. It is about post-war England as precisely as Masterman's *England After War* is.

Eliot's historical vision of that time was very clear. He described it in an essay that he wrote about Joyce's *Ulysses*, but that has as much to do with *The Waste Land* as with Joyce: Joyce's method, he wrote, was the right one, the only one, by which a writer might give form to 'the immense panorama of futility and anarchy which is contemporary history'.[12] Eliot's phrase would be equally apt as a description of the whole of the Western Front, and that is the point: the world of war and the world after had become mirrors of each other.

For that vision of contemporary history both the method of Eliot's poem and its title are metaphors, and it is not surprising that later writers picked up the title in their war writings. David Jones, for instance, wrote this description of drawings that he had made while in the trenches: 'They are without *any sense of form and display no imagination*. But the *War landscape* — the *"Waste Land" motif* — *has remained with me*, I think as a potent influence, to assert itself later.'[13] In this sense of the phrase, a painting like Nash's 'Menin Road' and Eliot's poem are images of the same condition — a ruined world, a botched civilization.

Other Modernist works show the way in which the war shaped and dominated post-war imaginations. Take Virginia Woolf's *Jacob's Room*, the first novel that she wrote after the war (it was published in 1922). In it she might be said to have taken Katherine Mansfield's advice — she *had* taken the war into account. But only just: war enters the novel furtively and unannounced, three pages from the end, when Betty Flanders thinks that her sons are fighting for their country, and then we learn, even more elliptically, that one of them — Jacob — has been killed. War is not the subject of the novel, but it is the termination of it, the event after which no story remains to tell.

Described in that way, *Jacob's Room* is clearly a novel about the first part of the emerging Myth of the War, the world-before-the-war, how there had been a time when English life was civil and secure, and how that time had ended, abruptly and for ever, when war came. It is the world that Virginia Woolf's brother-in-law Clive Bell had mourned in his 'Before the War' essay, and Maynard Keynes had evoked in his *Economic Consequences* — a world before the fall, a lost Eden. And so it is in *Jacob's Room*, and understandably; for those were the years of Virginia Woolf's young womanhood in Bloomsbury, years filled with promise for her and her friends. Her novel treats that time with a gentle nostalgia; but at the same time it dismantles it, breaking it into narrative fragments without a centre, until at the end of the book there is only a vacancy, which represents both the dead Jacob and his dead world, the 'civilization' of Edwardian England.

Virginia Woolf's next novel was also a 'war novel'. *Mrs Dalloway* shares the nostalgia for Victorian and Edwardian England that informs *Jacob's Room*: if you read no more than the first page you will feel it, as Clarissa Dalloway remembers her girlhood in her country house, and that mood continues through the novel as she and other characters recall their lives before the war. But *Mrs Dalloway* contains the war in a far more constant and insistent way than *Jacob's Room* does. The war is in many minds during the novel's one ordinary day; Mrs Dalloway thinks of women whose sons were killed, the tutor Miss Kilman thinks of how the war ruined her career, bystanders watching as a royal car passes think of the dead, boys in uniform lay a wreath on the Cenotaph, in Westminster Abbey people shuffle past the tomb of the Unknown Warrior.

But most of all the war is present in the mind of the suicidal ex-soldier, Septimus Smith. Smith is the archetypal damaged man, and it is a sign of the growing authority of the Myth that Virginia Woolf should choose him as her representative soldier. Word of his suicide comes to Mrs Dalloway while she is giving a party, and she thinks: 'in the middle of my party, here's death.'[14] But in fact the entire novel has been full of death, haunted by death and war as poor Septimus is haunted by his dead comrade Evans. War and death are there in the middle of everything because, in this world-after-the-war, they are part of reality.

Even more than *The Waste Land, Mrs Dalloway* is located precisely in time and space — on a June day in 1923, and not simply in London but in Westminster, the centre of government of England and the Empire. The novel is full of politicians, including the Prime Minister, and of government: Richard Dalloway is a Member of Parliament, and goes to a committee meeting; messages flash from the Fleet to the Admiralty; an official passes carrying a dispatch box; a Royal Personage drives to the Palace. One could scarcely call it a political novel, but it exists in a political world, where power is wielded, where the war was declared and administered. Politics, like war and death, is a part of its reality.

Out of this reality Virginia Woolf fashioned a very Bloomsburyish Myth of the War, a myth that has a first term, the remembered world-before-the-war, and a last term, the world after, but no middle. Unlike Rose Macaulay and Rebecca West, she did not try to imagine war itself. Perhaps it was beyond her (no one from her circle had fought); or perhaps it was simply not necessary for her vision, so long as war's victims, the damaged and the dead, were present in the person of Septimus Smith. Her subject was larger than a story of war; it was time, change, the irrevocability of loss, the ecstatic sharpness of the felt moment. But her novel is located in history, and like *The Waste Land* it has an historical vision. There was a time that was comfortable and happy, before war came with its cruelty and its madness, and ended all that. Now, in the world-after-the-war, the cruelty and madness remain; in the middle of the party, here's death.

In terms of the imagining of war, *Mrs Dalloway* confirms an historical vision: novels exist in history, and history includes the war, the extreme agent of destruction and change. You can't leave it out. This is more than a statement about content; it is a statement about form, too. It wasn't simply that something had been added to history; the *shape* of history had been radically altered. Virginia Woolf's most significant single utterance of this awareness, the sentence that expresses what that change was and what it meant, is Septimus's thought as he returns home from the war:

> It might be possible, Septimus thought, looking at England from the train window, as they left Newhaven; it might be possible that the world itself is without meaning.[15]

That statement has historical location; Septimus thinks it after the war, because of the war. And the fact that he can think it alters the world of the novel.

Every version of the war, even the versions of those who did not fight in it, is a personal response, a private act of the imagination. Pound and Eliot were displaced American civilians, and their images are coloured by that fact; Virginia Woolf was a Bloomsbury pacifist and a woman. D.H. Lawrence was in a more difficult situation than any of these — an English male, just over thirty when conscription was instituted and so subject to forced service, and the husband of a German woman who was the cousin of the German ace Baron von Richthofen. It was a situation made for persecution, and one can't be surprised that the narrative he wrote of his war is a paranoid version (though you might well argue that it can't be paranoia when the persecution is real).

When, just after the war, Lawrence wrote his *Movements in European History*, he avoided the war, first stopping his account at the end of the nineteenth century, and then, when asked to carry it forward, doing so in such a way that events of the war do not enter the story — as though he could deny the war historical existence. Two years later he corrected that curious omission in *Kangaroo*. That novel offers an odd context for a war story; it is set in Australia (where Lawrence and his wife were then living), and is concerned with post-war politics. Yet its longest chapter, 'The Nightmare', is Lawrence's personal narrative of his war years, a biographically accurate account, with only the names changed, and some of the Lawrences' many changes of address omitted. This narrative has nothing to do with the story of *Kangaroo*; it is a completely separate digression. Richard Somers, the Lawrence character in the book, says that he had suppressed his memories of the war years, and we must assume that the same had been true of Lawrence, and that now, five years after the Armistice, he was able to confront them.

Like most historians of the war, Lawrence divided the whole into two parts. His account in *Kangaroo* begins (as Pound's did in 'Mauberley') with an account of men's motives for enlisting:

Many men, carried on a wave of patriotism and true belief in democracy, entered the war. Many men were driven in out of belief that it was necessary to save their property. Vast numbers of men were just bullied into the army. A few remained. Of these, many became conscientious objectors.[16]

Somers/Lawrence remains, though he is not a CO: he simply will not join. Through 1915 he lives with his wife in the Vale of Health on Hampstead Heath, in a London that still retains some of its pre-war qualities — it is still the London of Asquith's Liberal government — though there are zeppelin raids, and recruits drilling on the Heath, and wounded soldiers. That London came to an end at the end of that year:

It was in 1915 the old world ended. In the winter 1915–1916 the spirit of the old London collapsed; the city, in some way, perished, perished from being a heart of the world, and became a vortex of broken passions, lusts, hopes, fears, and horrors. The integrity of London collapsed, and the genuine debasement began, the unspeakable baseness of the press and the public voice, the reign of that bloated ignominy, *John Bull*.[17]

And, one might add, of Lloyd George and his Coalition government, and Conscription. What followed, Lawrence said, was a reign of terror,

a true and deadly fear of the criminal *living* spirit which rose in all the stay-at-home bullies who governed the country during those years. From 1916 to 1919 a wave of criminal lust rose and possessed England ... Awful years — 16, 17, 18, 19 — and the years when the damage was done. The years when the world lost its real manhood.[18]

Lawrence had personal experience of that reign: he was called and recalled for physical examination by the army, and each time rejected as physically unfit (he was outraged by the intimacy of the examination, though it sounds standard enough as he tells it), and he and his wife were searched and spied on by police and by soldiers. But his conclusion is not a personal one; Lawrence generalized the turning of the English mood at the end of 1915 into an irreversible loss for the world. Individualism had been defeated, manhood was lost, and the people had demonstrated their unworthiness to govern themselves by choosing wartime leaders like Bottomley. Democracy was dead. Lawrence had reached the same conclusion in *Movements*, but by a different route; in 'The Nightmare' he made his own case an example of England's degradation.

There is no more actual war in 'The Nightmare' than there is in *Movements* or in *Women in Love*. But there is a version of war history — of the part of the story, that is, that took place in England. 'We hear so much of the bravery and horrors at the front,' Lawrence wrote:

> Brave the men were, all honour to them. It was at home the world was lost. We hear too little of the collapse of the proud human spirit at home, the triumph of sordid, rampant, raging meanness. 'The bite of a jackal is blood-poisoning and mortification.' And at home stayed all the jackals, middle-aged, male and female jackals. And they bit us all.[19]

It was a common enough view: civilians like Pound and H.M. Tomlinson shared it, and so did ex-soldiers like Montague and Ford. As the post-war Myth of the War formed, this was the story of the home-front war that became standard.

Eliot and Pound, Virginia Woolf and Lawrence — these are major Modernists, writers whose works define what is most valued in English writing of the 1920s. None of them had any experience of the war, and none wrote a war novel or a war poem in the customary sense of those terms. But they did something more interesting, and perhaps more important: they assimilated the war into their writing, both as concept and as form, made it a part of their idea of history, and of reality. The version of history that they shared is the post-war version; it renders recent history as discontinuous and fragmented, civilization as ruined, the past as lost. All four writers share the thought of Virginia Woolf's Septimus Smith: it might be possible that the world itself is without meaning. Their writings contain no battle scenes, no heroes, and no victories; they pick up from the war only the dominating negative themes — the death of civilization and the loss of Eden, and the negative characters — the damaged victims, and the tyrannous Old Men. And they construct out of this heap of broken images the forms of the history of their own time.

These themes and characters were not to be found only in the works of the great Modernists; they turn up everywhere in the popular literature of the Twenties. Which suggests what I take to be the case, that this version of history had entered widely into English imaginations, and that it appealed to the ordinary as well as to the sophisticated reader. Bits of it turn up in the most unexpected places: in *If Winter Comes*, for example, A.S.M. Hutchinson's best-seller of 1921, in which the damaged-man hero says to his friend late in the war:

> When the peace comes, you look out for the glide down into the trough. They talk about the nation, under this calamity, turning back to the old faiths, to the old simple beliefs, to the old earnest ways, to the old God of their fathers. Man ... what can you see already? Temples everywhere to a new God — Greed — Profit — Extortion. [20]

And he expands on this theme:

> Where's that making to, Hapgood? ... I'll tell you ... You'll get the people finding there's a limit to the high prices they can demand for their labour: apparently none to those the employers can go on piling up for their profits. You'll get growing hatred by the middle classes with fixed incomes of the labouring classes whose prices for their labour they'll see — and feel — going up and up; and you'll get the same growing hatred by the labouring classes for the capitalists. We've been nearly four years on the crest, Hapgood — on the crest of the war — and it's been all classes as one class for the common good. I tell you, Hapgood, the trough's ahead; we're steering for it; and it's rapid and perilous sundering of the classes. [21]

This is striking, not because it is particularly acute — it's more or less what everyone else was saying in the years just after the war — but because it comes in the middle of a novel that has nothing to do with class hatred and economics after the war, and which ends, not with this vision of unrest confirmed, but with the assurance that the war has ended with England 'at peace, victorious; those dark years done. England her own again.'[22] *That* was Hutchinson's essential attitude: he was a patriotic, conservative, Rupert-Brooke-quoting Englishman, to judge from this novel. Yet the common vision of post-war chaos caught his imagination, and he thrust it into the middle of an otherwise unprophetic, unspeculative novel.

Warwick Deeping's *Sorrell and Son* had the sort of success in 1926 that *If Winter Comes* had in 1921, and with much the same audience. Unlike Hutchinson's novel, *Sorrell and Son* is an after-the-war story, in which an ex-public-school ex-officer with a Military Cross struggles to support himself and his son (his wife has left him), first working as a hotel porter, and gradually rising to proprietorship. In this story there are several familiar elements: the left-over officer with no place in society, the New Poor, the apparent obsoleteness of pre-war virtues in the post-war world. Deeping states his theme in the first pages; his book is about

> all that scramble after the war, the disillusionment of it, the drying up of the fine and foolish enthusiasms, the women going to the rich fellows who had stayed at home, the bewilderment, the sense of bitter wrong, of blood poured out to be sucked up by the lips of a money-mad materialism.[23]

We must believe that Deeping felt all of that himself, and that it was the sincerity of his bitterness, and the fact that many English readers shared his feelings, that made his unremarkable, plodding novel popular. There must have been a great many English men and women who read the book and found there a demonstration and confirmation of their own feelings of displacement and disenchantment.

The ultimate novel of post-war disenchantment is Michael Arlen's *The Green Hat* (1924). Novels like Deeping's and Hutchinson's spoke to the middle classes, the yearners after past values and 'England her own again'; Arlen's addressed and defined a new audience, the self-consciously post-war generation. He expressed post-war attitudes — despair, ennui, cynicism, romanticized promiscuity and drunkenness, the sentimentalizing of dissolute and meaningless existence — that became the clichés of the decade, and turn up in the works of better writers like Huxley, Coward and Waugh, and he created a model of the de-sexed, de-classed Twenties woman in Iris Storm. It was as though the London fashionable world had been waiting for a displaced Armenian to define it, or perhaps to invent it.

But even though *The Green Hat* is feverishly post-war, it depends on the war for an explanation of its existence, for it is out of the war and its corruption that Arlen's beautifully disenchanted people have come. Iris Storm and her brother, Gerald Marsh, are ruined aristocrats — not financially ruined (there is always plenty of money about), but spiritually ruined. Arlen's narrator explains:

> I was what Gerald was not, and what she [Iris] obviously was not. I could somehow 'cope with' my time and generation, while they were of the breed destined to failure. I was of the race that is surviving the England of Horatio Bottomley, the England of lies, vulgarity, and unclean savagery; while they of the imperious nerves had failed, they

had died that slow white death which is reserved for priv
defeat.[24]

Gerald has been in the war, and apparently served creditably; but Iris,
telling her brother's story, says, 'Then the war, and that, of course,
buried him.'[25] 'Of course'? Presumably because the war was too vulgar,
too unheroic for him. Iris has also been 'buried' by the war; she is the
widow of a war hero with a VC, who has been killed in the Irish
Troubles. Both brother and sister live directionless lives, which the
narrator finds romantic, or tragic. And both die by their own hands.

There is, in *The Green Hat*, a version of the corruption of the war that
is by now familiar — it goes back to the mid-war years, to Sassoon's
later poems and his letter of resignation, and to *Mr Britling*. But there is
also a version of pre-war England, the lost Eden, the 'Careless-Days-
Before-The-War', as Arlen named them. Arlen saw those days in terms
of the gifted men who were young then, and were now dead:

> To youth of this decade, grown now a little impatient of the careless-
> wise seeming pastime of indulging 'sound' scepticisms or catholic
> idealisms, those youths of the days before the war must seem to
> have been the most gifted of God's creatures who ever walked this
> earth . . . they would verily seem, those few dead young men, to have
> a certain god–like quality of immortality, denied to the multitude that
> died with them and for whom cenotaphs and obelisks and memorials
> must do duty for memory . . .[26]

There is an important point made here; for Arlen, and for his imitators
and followers, the cynicism and the boredom of the Twenties generation were founded on loss. It was because the dead young men were
dead and their promise scattered that one must be disillusioned, bored,
promiscuous or drunk. Arlen had found a way of making amorality
seem tragic and doomed.

One could go through examples of popular writing in the Twenties,
pointing out the themes and attitudes and stock characters that the
war had created — how Agatha Christie's first detective story, *The
Mysterious Affair at Styles* (1921), is set in wartime, with a convalescent
soldier as narrator, and Hercule Poirot making his first appearance as a
Belgian refugee, how Dorothy Sayers's Lord Peter Wimsey is a shell-
shocked, damaged man. But these examples are surely sufficient for the
point made: that the war was a shaping presence in post-war writing of
all kinds, and that the assumptions made in writing on the highest level

were also made in the most popular works. These assumptions we know well enough by now. Some of them have to do with the shape of recent history: that the world before the war was a lost Eden; that the war began honourably, but was corrupted by the greed and ambition of the Old Men at home; that the world after the war was a ruined place, where dishonourable forces had triumphed, and the war's good men had been defeated and ignored. Some of them have to do with divisions in English society: between the New Rich and the New Poor, between ex-soldiers and non-combatants, between generations. The sum of these assumptions was a version of history that became, and remains, the dominant account of the war's effects on England — of what was lost, and of what remained, in the botched civilization of the Twenties.

CHAPTER 18

The Wars After the War

Out of so many testimonies, out of histories and memoirs, letters and diaries, poems and novels and paintings, a version of post-war England emerges: an England isolated in its moment in history, cut off by the great gap of the war from the traditions and values of its own past. It is a damaged nation of damaged men, damaged institutions, and damaged hopes and faiths, with even its language damaged, shorn of its high-rhetorical top, an anxious fearful bitter nation, in which civilization and its civilities will have to be re-invented.

For brevity's sake we might call that version The Waste Land Myth of the War, noting that as in Eliot's poem it is not essentially a myth of the war itself but of its aftermath, that its subject is not the fighting but ruin, loss, and fear of life. And noting also that its continuing currency has seemed to validate the art and literature of High Modernism, which in turn has validated the Myth as the authentic expression of post-war reality; and that this process of cross-validation has had significant consequences for cultural history as well as for the literary canon.

We should not be too quick to accept the Myth in its entirety. The past may have *felt* like a heap of broken images, but in fact much that had been established and secure in 1914 was still intact in post-war English society, and in post-war English minds. The same King reigned, the same man was Archbishop of Canterbury, and the same politicians — Asquith and Balfour, Lloyd George and Bonar Law — still dominated Parliament, which was composed of pretty much the same men who had declared war (of the members of Asquith's Liberal cabinet of August 1914, every one was still an MP in 1920, except for poor Masterman). Society (with a capital S) was much the same: there were still top hats at Ascot, and young ladies were presented at Court, and Parliament still adjourned for the grouse and salmon season. The Royal Academy still had its Summer Exhibitions, Henry Wood went on conducting Proms (the Wagner Nights had been restored, and were very popular), Thomas Beecham and grand opera returned to Covent Garden, and German conductors like Felix Weingarten were once more conducting English orchestras. The prominent Edwardian writers went on writing — Bennett, Galsworthy, and Wells all published novels in the years just after the war, and the post-war London theatre was dominated by Edwardian playwrights — Barrie, Bennett, Galsworthy, Henry Arthur Jones, and Shaw all had plays in West End theatres between 1919 and 1921.

Galsworthy, that permanent Edwardian, found a phrase for the continuing presence of pre-war things in the preface that he wrote for his novel of continuance, *The Forsyte Saga*, in 1922:

'Let the dead Past bury its dead' would be a better saying if the Past ever died. The persistence of the Past is one of those tragi-comic blessings which each new age denies, coming cocksure on to the stage to mouth its claim to a perfect novelty. But no Age is so new as that! Human Nature, under its changing pretensions and clothes, is and ever will be very much of a Forsyte, and might, after all, be a much worse animal.[1]

The persistence of the past: that also is a reality of the post-war world, as much a part of that world as the contrary perceptions of radical newness, ruin, and futility. The old were older, but they were not dead, and neither were their institutions, their values, or their powers: it was, after all, the *young* who had died.

The past persisted, but with a difference. Edwardian ideas and values had survived, and were palpably there, in the post-war world. But post-war culture could not be taken as simply a resumption and continuation of Edwardian culture (as Galsworthy would have liked his readers to believe), because the war had interposed its denying force between *then* and *now*, and that force was a new part of what persisted. Edwardian past and wartime past seemed contradictory realities, one refuting and cancelling the other. But both existed in the minds and imaginations of post-war survivors, and both together defined the troubled post-war world.

This complex mixing of present and past is evident in the directions taken after the war by those other wars — the social conflicts that had divided England before and during the 1914–18 fighting. The Labour War, the Irish War, the Women's War, the War against Modernism, even the Professors' War — these all carried over from Edwardian England into the post-war years, and were fought again. But they were fought differently — on different battlefields and with different weapons — because the Great War gaped between the present and the past.

We can see the differences readily enough if we compare the troubles that Edwardians feared — with the Irish, the working class, women — with what England actually got after the war. In 1914 British political leaders had expected a civil war in Ireland, probably initiated by Ulster Unionists. What they got instead, five years later, was a nationalist revolution against British occupation. For that struggle the British had a new force to call upon that they had not had in the pre-war days — the demobilized veterans. Auxiliary police (called 'Black and Tans' or 'Auxies') were recruited — largely from among ex-officers — and sent to Ireland. Many of these recruits had learned brutality on the Western Front, and they brought that knowledge to their new task. The trouble in Ireland became not so much a war as a conflict of terrorisms, symbolized for both sides by 'Bloody Sunday' (November 21, 1920), when in the morning IRA Volunteers assassinated eleven suspected British intelligence agents, and in the afternoon Black and Tans fired into an Irish football crowd, killing twelve people. And when that war was settled in an Anglo–Irish treaty in 1921, the Irish fell upon each other in a civil war as bloody as the uprising had been. The troubles that had been feared before the war had happened, but worse — more violent and more fratricidal than anyone had expected.[2]

The same description — the old, expected troubles, but worse — also characterizes what happened in the Labour Wars. The industrial unrest of the Edwardian years had been suspended by a truce in 1914, but that truce had begun to unravel in the later war years. In 1918 there were strikes by miners, railwaymen, munitions workers, cotton spinners, even the London police, and in the post-war years there were more strikes, as workers struggled to preserve their wartime gains, and employers tried to return wages and hours to peacetime levels. But things were different. Unemployment grew in England after the war — by 1921 there were more than two million men and women out of work. Trade union membership grew too, and so did the political party that represented the unions; where there had been 42 Labour MPs in Parliament in 1914, there were 142 in 1922. From 1920 there was also a new workers' party on the Left: the Communist Party of Great Britain.

Neither its membership nor its power was impressive, but it was nevertheless a presence, a reminder that in post-war Europe there was a new nation in which the workers ruled, and a new international force called Bolshevism that threatened the peace and troubled the dreams of Conservative souls.

Strikes and threats of strikes were a part of English life in the post-war years. Virginia Woolf recorded them in her diaries, along with the weather and the latest gossip: the Tube strike in February 1919, the rail strike in September, the miners' strike in 1921. These actions were more than simply news, they were disturbances in her world: 'The strike', she wrote of the railwaymen's stoppage, 'broke in to our life more than the war did.' And when unions threatened collective action in 1921 she felt 'a queer sort of stillness ... settling down on us, as of Sunday. This is the foreboding of the General Strike.'[3] That sense of foreboding ran through the years after the war, even in Bloomsbury, until at last it came true in the General Strike of 1926.

The Labour Wars, like the Irish Wars, were the same but different. One difference in both was the presence, on both sides, of veterans of the Great War. The fact that there were now workers trained in military combat made some employers nervous; and on the other side there were ex-officers, loyal to the nation and the social system for which they fought. Some of these had gone to Ireland with the Auxiliaries, but there were others on hand when the rail strike began, to volunteer as strike-breakers. From the ranks of such men another new political party was created in 1923: the British Fascisti, later the British Fascists.[4] One of this party's first acts was to offer its assistance to the government in the maintenance of order during strikes (the government declined the offer). So on the Right, as on the Left, there was a party that had not been there before the war, and it too had its foreign model — of an alternative to democratic government — in Fascist Italy. The British political spectrum had been stretched, leaving the centre less stable, and less certain.

Ex-soldiers figure prominently in post-war fiction. In the more serious novels, as we have seen, they are usually damaged men; but in popular novels they appear as soldier-heroes, the last survivors of the tradition of the early war years. The home-front battles that these heroes fight are fought in defence of an idealized Old England, and their antagonists are a medley of villains who threaten all that — foreigners, Jews, radicals, Irishmen, Bolsheviks, profiteers, and intellectuals. Here, as examples, are passages on enemies from three of the most popular post-war novels:

The moral imbecile, he said, had been more or less a sport before the War; now he was a terribly common product, and throve in batches and battalions. Cruel, humourless, hard, utterly wanting in sense of proportion, but often full of perverted poetry and drunk with rhetoric — a hideous, untamable breed had been engendered. You found it among the young Bolshevik Jews, among the young entry of the wilder Communist sects, and very notably among the sullen murderous hobbledehoys in Ireland.

John Buchan, *The Three Hostages* (1924)

'A terrible fellow's after it [an English country house]. One Dunkelsbaum. Origin doubtful — very. Last known address, Argentina. Naturalized in July, 1914. Strictly neutral during the War, but managed to net over a million out of cotton, which he sold to the Central Powers *at a lower price than Great Britain offered* before we tightened the blockade. Never interned, of course.'

Dornford Yates, *Berry and Co.* (1921)

[An international villain addresses three millionaires — two Germans and an American]: 'There is a force in England, which, if it be harnessed and led properly, will result in millions coming to you . . . It is present now in every nation — fettered, inarticulate, unco-ordinated . . . It is partly the result of the war — the war that the idiots have waged . . . Harness that force, gentlemen, co-ordinate it, and use it for your own ends . . .'

'Sapper', *Bull-Dog Drummond: The Adventures of a Demobilised Officer Who Found Peace Dull* (1920)[5]

The enemies portrayed in these passages are all foreigners, and some of them are Jews. But there is more to these portraits than xenophobia and anti-Semitism. These foreigners serve ugly foreign causes, like Bolshevism, which they hope to impose on England. Or they have no cause at all, but are simply out to exploit gullible Englishmen. In either case, they are enemies not simply of Hannay and Berry and Drummond, but of England — an England that these books define as a pre-war idealized nation, county and upper-class. And they are powerful. Their wealth and their power have increased during the war, as though the possibilities for doing evil in England had multiplied. But domestic villains have increased, too — un-English Englishmen, profiteers and draft-dodgers, social climbers and unscrupulous politicians. Collectively, these antagonists represent the forces of change in the post-war world, perceived as evils. Insofar as these books externalize evil in such villains, and concentrate virtue in heroes, they are simply repeating the habits of melodrama. But they also make evil un-English and extra-territorial, and that is surely a habit of the war.

The 'wars' that are fought in these novels are patriotic, nationalistic wars, which was no doubt one reason for their great popularity. But they are also class wars: the foreign villains appeal to English workers, and are abetted by trade unionists, and the forces that defeat them are mostly upper-class, or at least gentlemen. One feels in such books the class conflict that had marked the pre-war years resurfacing in the post-war years. While the war went on, that conflict had been sup-pressed for patriotic reasons; but when it ended that fragile national unity ended, too. In the years of political and economic trouble that followed, each class felt itself to be threatened and declining, while the other classes were greedily rising, or trying to, and they blamed it on the war.

When older Englishmen, and particularly members of the middle and upper classes, looked back across the abyss of the war, they saw what seemed an idyllic time, when life in England was secure, comfortable and easy. (We have seen that nostalgic version in Keynes's *Economic Consequences* and Montague's *Disenchantment*.) The war had destroyed that security, and had left people with an anxious feeling that the entire English class structure was breaking up. That feeling was common enough to generate a kind of post-war class myth. Here is one formulation, by a prominent interpreter of the English scene, W.R. Inge, the Dean of St Paul's; it is from an essay titled 'The Future of the English Race', written in 1919:

> We have seen that the destruction of the upper and professional classes by taxation directed expressly against them has already begun, and this victimisation is certain to become more and more acute, till these classes are practically extinguished. The old aristocracy showed a tendency to decay even when they were unduly favoured by legisla-tion, and a little more pressure will drive them to voluntary sterility and extermination. Even more to be regretted is the doom of the professional aristocracy, a caste almost peculiar to our country. These families can often show longer, and usually much better pedigrees than the peerage; the persistence of marked ability in many of them, for several generations, is the delight of the eugenist. Yet they have no prospects except to be gradually harassed out of

existence, like the *curiales* of the later Roman Empire. The power will apparently be grasped by a new highly privileged class, the aristocracy of labour.[6]

For the middle classes in particular it was an unsettled and unsettling time. They had been comfortable, and now they felt sunk into poverty. So widespread was this feeling that a new name for the class was coined: 'The New Poor'. It turns up in newspaper articles, and even in books: in *The Nouveau Poor: A Romance of real life in West London after the Late War*, a satirical novel by 'Belinda Blinders' (who was a comic novelist named Desmond Coke), and as a chapter title in Bennett's 1922 satire, *Mr Prohack*.

The best and fullest account of the state of mind of the New Poor is in Masterman's *England After War*, the chapter titled 'The Plight of the Middle Class'. Masterman was ostensibly writing social history, and he did what he could to make his chapter seem objective and detached. He repeated the accepted economic explanations of the class's decline — the rise in prices and taxes after the war, the fall in the value of securities, and the failure of middle-class salaries to rise with the cost of living — and he cited such statistics as were available. But Masterman was at heart an emotional and literary writer, and a melancholy man, and he saw the plight of the middle class as his own. By the end of the war his promising political career had ended; his Liberal Party was collapsing, he was out of office and out of work, he drank too much, and he was broke. His chapter on his class is a dirge for himself, a middle-class Edwardian adrift in post-war England.

In this sad meditation on failure, Masterman did not really attribute middle-class decline to economic factors, nor to political errors such as might have been avoided by wise leaders; what he described was simply a turn of fortune's wheel, as inevitable as a Greek tragedy. These two passages are typical:

> The efforts of those who still maintain the civilized standards of pre-war times are tremendous, and yet the general impression is that of a whole body of decent citizens slipping down by inexorable God-made or man-made or devil-made laws into the Abyss: as if a table was suddenly tilted slanting and all the little dolls and marionettes were sent sliding on to the floor. Some cling wildly to the edges, some get their feet into crooks and crannies and retain their hold for a moment; but in bulk the whole mass, despite resistance, is falling through the bottom of the world.

Here, then, is a complete and startling transformation of values; not slowly changing from one to another, but suddenly and almost brutally forced upon the life of millions by causes altogether outside their control ... Misfortune has come upon them as if deflected by unknown malignant powers, like the four winds, which, in conformity with the request of Satan, destroyed the prosperity of the blameless Patriarch Job.[7]

Masterman was depressed and defeated when he wrote *England After War*, but so was the class for which he spoke. It was, you might say, a damaged class, as ruined by the war as the individual damaged men who came out of it. One finds the sense of damage and decline expressed in many post-war newspapers[8], and there are many examples in post-war fiction. Warwick Deeping's Sorrell is one, an ex-officer with a Military Cross (like Bull-Dog Drummond), out of work in the post-war world. 'Before the war,' Deeping wrote,

he had sat at a desk and helped to conduct a business, but the business had died in 1917, and deny a business man his office chair and he becomes that most helpless of mortals — a gentleman of enforced leisure.[9]

Sorrell has fallen, like Masterman's marionettes, through the bottom of his world, into the working class.

Sorrell is an example of a new element in the class wars, the ex-officer. In Edwardian society officers had been assumed to be gentlemen — to have come, that is, from established, land-owning families. But during the war the officer corps had been compelled to accept 'temporary gentlemen', officers who had risen from the ranks, or had enlisted from shops and offices. If they were gentlemen while they were in uniform, what were they after the fighting stopped? What class did they belong to then? And how would they support themselves without that requisite of the traditional 'officer and gentleman', a private income?

In a class-conscious society those were worrying questions, and a novel that dealt with them conservatively and reassuringly, as *Sorrell and Son* did, allowing the fallen bourgeois to pull himself up by his own bourgeois values, his industry and his rectitude, was bound to be a popular success. Another novel of the Twenties that confronted the same questions from a rather different angle was less successful, unless you consider notoriety a form of success. *Lady Chatterley's Lover* is as

class-conscious and as post-war in its themes as *Sorrell and Son* is. It has
in its central love-triangle two war-damaged men, both ex-officers.
Clifford Chatterley is a baronet's son, born to the class that *officer*
traditionally implied; he has been paralysed in the war. Oliver Mellors is
working-class, a blacksmith at the coal mines before the war, who left
Tevershall to join the army and was commissioned in the field, and was
by that change declassed and isolated, neither lower-class nor gentry.
He too returns damaged by illness.

Ivy Bolton, the Chatterleys' housekeeper, recalls Mellors's career:

> He'd been a clever boy, had a scholarship for Sheffield Grammar
> School, and learned French and things: and then after all had become
> an overhead blacksmith shoeing horses ...

And then the war began:

> For years he was gone, all the time of the war: and a lieutenant and all:
> quite the gentleman, really quite the gentleman! — Then to come
> back to Tevershall and go as a game-keeper! Really, some people
> can't take their chances when they've got them! And talking broad
> Derbyshire again like the worst, when she, Ivy Bolton, knew he
> spoke like any gentleman, *really*.[10]

He can speak like a gentleman, but he isn't one; he can do a working-
class man's job, but he isn't one of them, either. Mellors is a character
made by the war; one can't imagine him in a pre-war novel.

The war affected both the labour wars and the class wars, making the
old oppositions and divisions more acute, more bitter and more
belligerent, more like real wars than metaphorical ones, resolving no
issues and reconciling no antagonisms. But in one before-the-war
combat zone some battles did appear to have been won: the condition of
women had changed for the better, and in their case the war had surely
been the catalyst.

Women's victories were of two kinds. In the social and political world
they had gained opportunities and privileges that had not been theirs
before the war. The Representation of the People Act of 1918 gave the
franchise to women over thirty who were occupants of their own
houses (or of their husbands'), and in the following year another act, the
Sex Disqualification (Removal) Act, opened a number of professions to
women for the first time: they could become barristers, solicitors,
auctioneers, surveyors, or architects, they could stand for Parliament

and sit on the judge's bench and in the jury box, and they could be admitted to the universities.

With these legal victories came a flurry of women's accomplishments. Lady Astor, the first woman to be an MP, entered the Commons in November 1919. In 1920 110 women graduates were admitted to membership of the University of Oxford. The first women jurors in the High Court were appointed in 1921. Mrs Swynnerton, a painter, was elected to the Royal Academy in 1922, the first woman to be elected in the Academy's history (though two women had been in at the founding in 1769). There was an exhibition of women artists at Olympia in 1923, and a British Women's Symphony Orchestra was founded in 1924. For women of talent and ambition it was a liberating time.

One should not make that time sound too euphoric for women, though; not all of their battles had ended in victory. In the labour market, women who had worked during the war were swiftly pushed aside as the men who had held their jobs before the war returned; by the autumn of 1919 three-quarters of a million women who had held jobs at the Armistice had been dismissed, and by 1921 the proportion of employed women was smaller than it had been before the war.[11] From May 1920 women at Oxford were allowed to take all degrees except theology, but Cambridge continued to deny degrees to its women students. There were no women on the Stock Exchange or in the clergy, and the London Hospital refused to take any more women students, on the grounds that it was difficult to teach 'certain unpleasant subjects of medicine' to mixed groups. The British Women's Symphony Orchestra was conducted by a man — Malcolm Sargent. In post-war England the liberation of women was a patchy and partial affair.

It was widely believed that another kind of liberation had taken place during the war years — that those years had been a time when women cast off moral restraints in sexual matters. A common view, but how does one test it? Not with statistics about actual sexual practices: in those pre-Kinsey days there were none. There is, however, some statistical evidence that changes in sexual behaviour were occurring: though the legitimate birth rate declined during the war, the number of illegitimate births did not and there were more cases of venereal disease. One might conclude from this that there was more illicit sexual activity.

That this was the case was in part simply a matter of opportunity: because of the war, a large number of young women found themselves outside customary social controls for the first time in their lives. During

the war years nearly half a million female domestic servants left service
to take jobs in industry, and so escaped the censorious scrutiny of their
household employers; and though attempts were made to police the
private lives of women war workers by placing them in dormitories and
restricting their free time, it must have seemed a glorious step towards
freedom for all those cooks and scullery maids. It was a step that they
were reluctant to reverse when the war ended: hence the post-war
'servant problem', which was surely the consequence of a sexual choice
by working-class women as well as a choice of employment.

Middle-class and upper-class girls had also escaped, into volunteer
work in hospitals and into the auxiliary services, where they were
continually in the company of men in circumstances that their mothers
would never have approved in peacetime — bathing the wounded,
dressing their wounds, working with men, driving them about. At the
war's end there were 61,000 women in the VAD and the forces. They
knew more about men than pre-war young ladies had been allowed to
know, and the idea of chaperoned innocence could not be revived.

There is one source of information about women's sexual lives in
wartime that is neither scientific nor statistical, but is nevertheless worth
examining — the representations of women's wartime existence that
were offered in fiction. Here, if I read the examples correctly, an
interesting change occurs. If you look at the ways in which sex is
rendered in serious wartime novels like *Non-Combatants*, *Mr Britling Sees
It Through*, and *The Tree of Heaven*, you will find flirtations and early
marriages, but nothing in the way of extra-marital sex among the young
characters; it is as though while the war continued novelists avoided
writing about irregular sex lives for patriotic reasons. Once the war
ended, that side of sex began to appear in novels about wartime
England, but mainly as seduction. There is the débutante seduced by the
cad in *Way of Revelation*, and a series of seductions in W.L. George's
Blind Alley (1919) — a servant girl by a soldier and a munitions worker
by her employer, but also a seduction the other way round — a young
gunner by an officer's wife. George's novel is instant history, in the
manner of Rose Macaulay and Wells, as its sub-title makes very clear:
'Being the picture of a very gallant gentleman; the adventures of his
spirit in war and peace; the tale of his daughters, his son, their friends; of
their lives and miseries; of the way of the world through the Great War
into the unexplored regions of peace'.

Blind Alley is especially interesting for its account of the impact of the
war on private lives. George assumes that the war is both the cause of

the sexual crises in the lives of his characters and the bond between lovers, and that the over-heated sexual atmosphere will dissipate when the war ends. 'What a mess we're in!' the employer-seducer thinks:

> If only she were another sort of girl! But she's not a working girl. I can't take her away from her people, and set her up in a cottage outside Chatham. She wouldn't, she couldn't. But then? I say after the war . . . but what after the war?

And George adds: 'He knew that the war was their bond, that nothing could come after the war.'[12]

Novels written later in the Twenties and early Thirties were more likely to make wartime extra-marital sex a freely chosen act than a seduction, but an act performed under great emotional pressure from the time itself. In Sylvia Thompson's *The Hounds of Spring* (1926) a married woman leaves her husband to live with a soldier, and the novel's young heroine defends the action as necessary in wartime:

> . . . perhaps, Mummie, she may never have known what it was to be in love before. Daddy said he believes it was a sort of *mariage de convenance*; and then she met this man, who's probably going to the Front. And in the stress of war how could anything else in the world matter to her?[13]

In another war novel by a woman, Helen Zenna Smith's *Not So Quiet . . .*, the heroine, just returned to England from duty as an ambulance driver in France, takes a young second lieutenant into her bed before he leaves for the Front

> not only because he was whole and strong-limbed, not only because his body was young and beautiful, not only because his laughing blue eyes reflected my image without the shadow of war rising to blot me out . . . but because I saw him between me and the dance orchestra ending a shadow-procession of cruelly-maimed men . . .[14]

In both of these passages, war — the stress of war, the shadow of war — is offered as a credible and sufficient sexual motive. It is the same in what is probably the best-known expression of this theme, the scene in Hemingway's *A Farewell to Arms* in which Catherine Barkley, the English VAD, tells Frederick Henry that she didn't make love to her fiancé before he left to be killed on the Somme:

I wanted to do something for him. You see I didn't care about the other thing and he could have had it all. He could have had anything he wanted if I would have known. I would have married him or anything. I know all about it now. But then he wanted to go to war and I didn't know ... I didn't know about anything then. I thought it would be worse for him. I thought perhaps he couldn't stand it and then of course he was killed and that was the end of it.[15]

All of these quoted passages, and the novels from which they are taken, articulate ideas of sexual freedom, and ignore conventional sexual morality. Here there is a new morality of — what shall I call it? — sexual generosity, perhaps, or the sexual necessity of wartime. In none of the examples is sex associated with pleasure, or with the liberation of the senses. Quite the contrary: the tone is dutiful, self-sacrificing, and generally rather depressed. This association of sexual freedom and low spirits became a part of the Myth of the War, but it was not confined to the war years only: it continued into the Twenties, and is evident in many of the most characteristic literary works of the post-war years — in *The Green Hat*, for example, and *Point Counter Point*, and *The Vortex*, and in the most central of post-war texts, *The Waste Land*. Only at the very end of the decade, when Lawrence's Connie and Mellors perform their flower-decked rain dance, does something approaching joy, or even fun, enter the literary sexual scene.

It was not only in fiction that sex, the ever-interesting topic, was discussed in post-war England. Those were the years in which psycho-analysis first reached a general English public. Freud's writings had only begun to appear in translation before the war — three were published in 1913–14. During the war the writings in German of a Viennese Jew were works of an enemy, and no more volumes were translated, though psychologists like Rivers who were working with shell-shock cases were aware of Freud's importance. But once the war ended, there was a flood of Freud-in-translation, thirteen volumes between 1919 and 1925.

Not all of these books were concerned with sexual psychology, of course, but it was Freud's treatment of sex that captured the attention of English intellectuals. A group called the British Society for the Study of Sex and Psychology met in Hampstead to discuss Freud early in 1918 — another instance of 'post-war' ideas appearing while the war was still being fought. Lytton Strachey was there, and reported the discussion to Virginia Woolf, who recorded it in her diary:

they were surprisingly frank; & 50 people of both sexes and various ages discussed without shame such questions as the deformity of Dean Swift's penis: whether cats use the w.c.; self abuse; incest — Incest between parent & child when they are both unconscious of it, was their main theme, derived from Freud . . . Lytton at different points exclaimed *Penis*: his contribution to the openness of the debate.[16]

A year later her friend Roger Fry read Ernest Jones's book on Freud, and wrote to Vanessa Bell:

I'm deep in Jones's new Freudian book. It's very fascinating, especially the study of anal-erotic types; anal-erotic complexes appear to account for everything one does or doesn't do. But it's a fine corrective to nobility and edification to realize that our spiritual nature is built upon dung.[17]

T.E. Lawrence, back in the army in 1923, turned to Freud to reconcile himself to the gross carnality of his fellow-soldiers: 'A filthy business all of it,' he wrote to a friend, 'and yet Hut 12 shows me the truth behind Freud. Sex is an integer in all of us . . .'[18] The *other* Lawrence, D.H., was also thinking about Freud then; he published two books about psychoanalysis, rewriting Freud to make him more Lawrentian.[19] The *New Statesman* summed up the situation in a 1923 essay:

we are all psycho-analysts now. That is to say that it is as difficult for an educated person to neglect the theories of Freud and his rivals as it would have been for his father to ignore the equally disconcerting discoveries of Darwin.[20]

The most popular and influential post-war book on sex, however, was neither by Freud nor about him. Its author was a woman scientist whose training was not in psychology but in botany, and whose sources were not Viennese psychologists but the English Edwardian writers Edward Carpenter and Havelock Ellis. *Married Love*, by Marie Stopes, was published in March 1918 (like her exact contemporary, Lytton Strachey, she was 'post-war' before the war had ended). It sold immediately and very well — far better than any of the novels I have mentioned above — and it went on selling. In the next nine years it went through eighteen editions in England alone, and sold more than half a million copies, making it by far the most-read book on sex of its time — perhaps of any time.

Married Love is sub-titled 'A new contribution to the solution of sex difficulties'. The difficulties are those that arise from ignorance: women's ignorance of biological facts, and men's ignorance of women's physical and emotional needs. *Victorian* ignorance, one might say: if Stopes was right, there had been no advance in general understanding of sex since the old Queen's prudish days. 'It has become a tradition of our social life,' she wrote, 'that the ignorance of woman about her own body and that of her future husband is a flower-like innocence,' and she blamed that ignorance on the English educational system:

> ... the whole education of girls, which so largely consists in the concealment of the essential facts of life from them; and the positive teaching so prevalent that the racial instincts are low and shameful; and also the social condition which places so many women in the position of depending on their husband's will not only for the luxuries but also for the necessaries of life, have all tended to inhibit natural sex-impulses in women, and to conceal and distort what remains.[21]

Stopes recognized that 'often the man is also the victim of the purblind social customs which make sex-knowledge tabu';[22] but *Married Love* is a woman's book, and its arguments centre on women's needs, and women's ignorance.

In addressing the women of her time, as she perceived them, Stopes had two apparently incompatible tasks: she had to explain both male and female biology to them, but she had to do it in a way that would not offend or frighten them, or make sex seem too coldly scientific, or too grossly animal. She solved the problem by adopting two attitudes, and two styles. The first style — you might call it the poetical-soulful style — is the one in which the book begins:

> Every heart desires a mate. For some reason beyond our comprehension, nature has so created us that we are incomplete in ourselves; neither man nor woman singly can know the joy of the performance of all human functions; neither man nor woman singly can create another human being. This fact, which is expressed in our outward divergencies of form, influences and colours the whole of our lives; and there is nothing for which the innermost spirit of one and all so yearns as for a sense of union with another soul, and the perfecting of oneself which such union brings.[23]

Nothing frightening in that opening paragraph, nothing even very physical, only hearts and souls. That style — metaphorical, soulfully vague, vaguely inspirational — dominates the first half of the book, and continues intermittently throughout. There is no point at which the reader is not aware that the subject is married *love*, not sex, and that married love is spiritual as well as physical.

The other style does not appear until well into the book, where Stopes announces that 'to describe the essentials, simple, direct and scientific language is necessary',[24] and turns from hearts and souls to penises and vaginas, and a straightforward, plain-language account of what happens in intercourse, in pregnancy and in childbirth, what sperm does and how a douche works — the 'embarrassing' subjects that a couple in sexual difficulties would want to know about, treated with a calm scientific detachment as though the author was describing reproductive processes in plants. One can see that this two-style method was exactly right both for the time and for the audience that Stopes was addressing: facts were cushioned with romance, and nothing was too graphic, yet everything was clear. It was a brilliant rhetorical strategy.

There is another explanation for the double style that is not strategic. In her preface Stopes hinted what the 'sexual difficulties' of her sub-title meant to her personally: 'In my own marriage I paid such a terrible price for sex-ignorance that I feel knowledge gained at such a cost should be placed at the service of humanity.'[25] In 1911 she had married an impotent man, and when the marriage was finally nullified five years later she was still a virgin, at the age of thirty-six. Her story confirms her assumption of the vast sexual ignorance of women of her time, even the educated ones. It was that married virgin who wrote the book, not out of experience, but out of her dreams of what marriage might be.

Married Love succeeded as it did, when it did, because its two styles linked the poetical attitude towards sex with a new scientific attitude, and made poetry and science seem to confirm and support each other, and both to march together in the service of sexual love. Not *real* science, a scientist might protest, only charts and graphs and scientific terms (not all of them accurately used); not real poetry either, for that matter, only the language of a vague spirituality. Nevertheless, those two modes of discourse combined to articulate two crucial claims for women: that women's role in sexual love was equal to men's but different, with a difference that men must learn; and that women's desires and satisfactions would also be equal, if only men would be sensitive to them.

For all its inadequacies and limitations, for all its sentimental yearning and inexact science, *Married Love* is a work of enormous importance in

English cultural history. It changed the way that English people, and especially English women, thought about love and marriage, and about their own sexual natures. It merits a place with books like *Eminent Victorians* and *The Economic Consequences of the Peace*, and with legislation like the Representation of the People Act and the Sex Disqualification (Removal) Act, as one of the documents that shaped post-war imaginations. *Married Love* is a milestone in the history of women's rights — the right, in this case, to be fully sexual.

There was another factor besides the restlessness of women at work in England at the end of the war that made the time ripe for the discussion of sexual difficulties. One finds, in the press, in records of public meetings, and in private writings, an anxious sense of a crisis in the sexual aspects of national life. Marie Stopes acknowledged it in *Married Love* whenever she turned from the personal to the social aspects of sex, whenever she considered the problems of venereal disease, prostitution, or the relations between poverty and infant mortality. And especially when she mentioned, as she did cautiously but insistently, the importance for both individual couples and society at large of a widespread knowledge of methods of contraception. At these points her theme ceased to be married love, and became social — the public problems of sex in post-war England.

After *Married Love*, Stopes's work focused on these social problems, and especially on birth control. She published *Wise Parenthood*, a guide to contraception, in the autumn of 1918, *A Letter to Working Mothers: on how to have healthy children and avoid weakening pregnancies* in 1919, *The Truth About Venereal Disease* in 1921, and *Contraception, Its Theory and Practice* in 1923, and in 1921 she opened a birth-control clinic in London (the first in the British Empire) and founded the Society for Constructive Birth Control to publicize her teachings. She even wrote a birth-control play, *Our Ostriches*, in which a well-bred young woman takes up the cause, and rejects a titled suitor for a sympathetic doctor. The play ran briefly at the Royal Court Theatre in the autumn of 1923, but was not a critical success. 'With the production of last night,' the *Times* reviewer wrote, 'dramatic criticism is not concerned. There is no play to criticize; it is mere propaganda.'[26] That, of course, is what Stopes intended it to be.

The climactic scene in *Our Ostriches* is one in which the heroine testifies before a Commission which is meeting to discuss the birth rate. That Commission, made up of bishops, doctors, clergymen, gentlewomen and government officials ('our amiable ostriches,' Stopes calls them), had an actual historical existence — had several, in fact. Its presence there in Stopes's play, and in post-war England, is an important part of the sex wars in England.

The story begins in the year Queen Victoria died, with the establishment of the National Social Purity Crusade, a committee of clergymen, medical men, and other persons in established positions, dedicated to encouraging sexual purity among the young, raising the English birth rate, regenerating the English race, censoring contemporary literature, and reducing the costs of public welfare by eliminating sin among the lower classes. The Crusade in time became the National Council of Public Morals, which in turn spawned the National Birth Rate Commission, the National Council for Combating Venereal Diseases, and the National Council for the Promotion of Physical and Moral Race-Regeneration. All of these were substantially the same organization, with the same Permanent Secretary (a clergyman named James Marchant), and one Anglican bishop or another as President — interlocking directorships, you might call them, in the morality business.

During the war years the Council and its subsidiaries kept themselves busy worrying about morality among the troops, the incidence of venereal diseases, and the rise in illegitimacy. After the war they returned to pre-war issues like the birth rate, continued their campaign against venereal disease, and began discussions of divorce, the problems of adolescence, and birth control. Through the post-war years the various Commissions and Councils met and heard evidence, and issued annual reports (the Venereal Disease Council also had an annual dinner), and were given a good deal of publicity by the conservative press. What influence they had on English thought and behaviour is, of course, impossible to judge; certainly they were a visible conservative moral presence. If one looks at a list of the members of one of these Commissions one can get a sense of just what a conservative force they were. In 1922 the sixty-member Birth Rate Commission included three bishops, General Sir Robert Baden-Powell, six doctors (including Caleb Saleeby, the Edwardian eugenicist), Sir Rider Haggard, two doctors of divinity, and three ladies — Lady Baden-Powell, Lady Leslie Mackenzie, and a Mrs Burgwin. There were no reformers, no radicals, and no Marie Stopeses.

The crisis that these Councils perceived in post-war England can be summed up in a few contentious propositions: the birth rate is falling among the middle and upper classes, and rising among the poor (many of whom are diseased and feeble-minded, and morally degenerate);

venereal disease is rampant, especially among the poor (many of whom, etc.); the family is failing as the moral centre of English life (look at the divorce rate, look at the illegitimacy rate, look at the middle-class men who are not marrying); the English race has been weakened eugenically by the loss of its best young men in the war. Taken together, these propositions add up to a single dark conclusion, which we have seen before in the post-war opinions of many writers: that England after the war was a fallen and corrupted place, a civilization in danger of self-destruction.

The difference between the Councils and other post-war analysts of England's condition was that the Councils tried to be objective and even scientific in their procedures. They held hearings, they questioned expert witnesses, and they gathered statistics. Some of the evidence did support their collective sense of a society in trouble. The birth rate was indeed declining, though this was nothing new: it had been falling fairly steadily in Britain since the middle of the nineteenth century, and after a temporary rise in 1918–20, it fell again. Venereal disease was a problem: infection had been widespread among the troops in France, and now four million soldiers had returned to England, and it was widely believed that one in five of them brought back a disease. Statistics on this point are hard to find, but figures on infant deaths from syphilis show a sharp rise in 1917, and perhaps these were children of syphilitic soldier-fathers. The divorce rate had risen dramatically at the end of the war: there were three times as many divorces in 1919 as in 1913, twice again as many in 1920, even more in 1921. As for illegitimate births, there were roughly ten per cent more of them in 1918 and 1919 than there had been in the last pre-war year, and even more in 1920 (after which the number dropped towards the pre-war level); but there were also more legitimate births, which is not surprising, considering those four million returning men. As for the rate of marriage, it peaked in 1915, when marriage was a way of avoiding military service, and again in 1919, after which it levelled off, well above the 1913 figure.[27]

These social statistics seem to indicate a set of problems that were worth worrying about, but were not peculiar to post-war England, and did not constitute a crisis. Men and women were doing more or less what they had always done, dying and being born (both in and out of wedlock), contracting and transmitting diseases, marrying and repenting marriage. The only striking statistical change was in the number of people who sought a solution to their marriage problems in divorce.

If nevertheless a crisis existed for the Moral Councillors, it was an emotional, not a statistical one. They looked about them and saw change and decay in moral standards and in sexual behaviour, old values questioned and principles abandoned. They looked back to the world before the war as a time when these things had not been so, and they blamed the gap of the war for morality's decline. And they tried to reverse that decline by talking about it.

One must not despise their efforts. They were establishment conservatives, but they sought expert testimony, and some of what they heard was liberal and enlightened. Here are two examples among many: Miss Norah Marsh testifying in an inquiry into the problems of adolescence, in October 1920:

> She said that whether chastity was the best preparation for parenthood seemed to be a point on which medical and psychological thought was not yet agreed. Personally holding the view that love should be the basis of marriage, she also held that as a general social guide the tenet of chastity was the ideal, recognizing, of course, that there might be individual cases wherein some other decision in regard to the rule of life might be a matter of responsible choice. If marriage was delayed till late in life, chastity might be a matter of supreme difficulty to many, while those whose circumstances made marriage impossible were confronted by the problem of entire celibacy. Our social code on these matters was obviously undergoing a change. It was possible that the future might see some forms of extra-marital sex relationships and parenthood finding a recognized place in our social code. There were many more women than men in this country. The wider education of girls, their entry into the world of labour, in short, their general emancipation, all tended towards a liberation of natural impulses and a desire for freedom of choice. The right to motherhood was a doctrine which was rapidly gaining ground.[28]

Sir Arthur Newsholme, MD (Principal Medical Officer of the Local Government Board), testifying on venereal disease before the National Council for the Promotion of Physical and Moral Race-Regeneration, in April 1922:

> With a simpler kind of life one of the main obstacles to protection from these diseases would disappear. He did not think that fathers and mothers of the well-to-do classes realized that they were responsible for the continuance of prostitution. Until they got the abolition of the

dual standard of conduct in regard to men and women in this matter they would not succeed in abolishing venereal diseases.[29]

The Councillors heard testimony that acknowledged change and reasoned from it. But though they heard it, they were not moved; for them, change was error, to be deplored and corrected by moral actions. In the end we must take all these solemn meetings, all these hearings and reports, as simply counter-propaganda to the efforts of people like Marie Stopes, and as further evidence of that force in post-war English life that Galsworthy had identified — the persistence of the past.

You can see the past persisting in another meeting of the early Twenties — the Lambeth Conference of the English bishops in 1921. Bishops had customarily presided over the various Moral Councils, and it is not surprising that when they gathered together they discussed some of the same moral issues, including birth control and divorce. To guide them in their deliberations, Marie Stopes sent each bishop a copy of her pamphlet, *The New Gospel to All Peoples*, in which she argued that birth control was Christian. The bishops resisted her arguments, and passed one resolution condemning 'the use of unnatural means for the avoidance of conception', another affirming the life-long and indissoluble nature of marriage, and a third forbidding the participation of women in the administration of the sacraments of the Church.

The Lambeth Conference was another defeat in the women's war: faced with the suggestion that women might live freer lives, that they might control their own reproductive functions, escape from intolerable marriages, and even serve the Church in sacramental roles, the bishops said 'No!'

Women fared no better in the Houses of Parliament than they had across the river in Lambeth. Two pieces of legislation debated in the early Twenties especially affected women's lives. The first, the Criminal Law Amendment Bill, contained two clauses of particular interest. One, which proposed raising the age at which sexual relations with a female minor became indecent assault to sixteen, was supported by women's organizations, but opposed by many MPs on the grounds that you couldn't always tell. The other was a proposed new clause to be attached to the existing clause governing 'acts of gross indecency between males'; it was to extend the legislation to women, in the following terms:

Any act of gross indecency between female persons shall be a misdemeanour and punishable in the same manner as any such act committed by male persons . . .[30]

(The original Act of 1885 had not recognized that female homosexuality existed.) What is interesting about this bit of equal rights legislation is the ideas about lesbianism that MPs expressed — not that any MP used that term, or came anywhere near being explicit about what kind of behaviour he was alluding to. Here are a few quotations from the Commons debate:

. . . all lawyers who have had criminal and divorce practice know that there is in modern social life an undercurrent of dreadful degradation, unchecked and uninterfered with . . . This House, which has the care of the law and to a large extent the morals of the people, should consider it to be its duty to do its best to stamp out an evil which is capable of sapping the highest and the best in civilisation.

Mr Macquiston

This vice does exist, and it saps the fundamental institutions of society. In the first place it stops child-birth . . . It debauches young girls, and it produces neurasthenia and insanity . . . [It is] a vice that must tend to cause our race to decline.

Sir E. Wild

They [lesbians] are examples of ultra-civilisation, but they have the merit of exterminating themselves, and consequently they do not spread or do very much harm to society at large . . . To adopt a Clause of this kind would do harm by introducing into the minds of perfectly innocent people the most revolting thoughts . . .

Lt.Col. Moore-Brabazon

. . . as far as I can see, it is very nearly what I may call a class Measure, a fight between the male and the female.

Rear-Admiral Sir R. Hall[31]

In these confused minds, sex between women was modern and ultra-civilized yet was a threat to civilization, was self-exterminating yet would destroy the race. Most commonly it was seen as a force in the general degeneration of the English people that was so much on conservative minds, a force to be feared and suppressed. We have seen that fear before, in Pemberton Billing's campaign against the Cult of the Clitoris in 1918. But in that case the campaign was primarily against a class; here, the fear seemed rather to be directed against female sexuality itself. At a time of women's liberation, how could their sexuality be kept confined? It was, as Admiral Hall ventured to say, a fight between the male and the female.

In the end, the Bill was defeated. But who won? Women who were homosexual continued to be free of the charge of gross indecency, but only because men found it too gross to deal with. One must conclude, I think, that in this battle between the sexes there was no victory at all.

The other Bill, the Matrimonial Causes Bill, was left over from before the war. In 1909 a Royal Commission on Divorce and Matrimonial Cause had been appointed to examine British law on divorce. That law dated from 1857; it provided that a husband might divorce his wife on grounds of adultery, but that a wife must prove her husband guilty of incestuous adultery, or of bigamy with adultery, or of rape, or of sodomy or bestiality, or of adultery coupled with such cruelty as without adultery would have entitled her to a judicial separation, or of adultery coupled with desertion. Divorce without proven adultery by one party — and only one party — was not possible.

The Commission brought in its report in 1912; it recommended that the grounds for divorce should be made the same for men and women, and that those grounds should be extended to include desertion, cruelty, incurable insanity and habitual drunkenness. The Bill was a contentious one, with powerful opponents, especially in the Church, and Asquith delayed bringing it to a vote through two Parliaments. Then the war came, and all such liberal proposals became impossible.

And so, in 1920, divorce in England was still Victorian. In that year a bill based on the Commission's Majority Report was introduced; it was debated and amended and debated again over the following three years. When it finally passed and became law it had been divested of nearly all of its liberal changes, though one important reform remained—that women and men should have equivalent rights. But there would continue to be only a single acceptable ground—adultery.

Divorces had nevertheless become a fact of life in post-war England — 'as common as flies in a hot summer', Beatrice Webb remarked disapprovingly.[32] And because they were common in society, they were common in literature: divorce is contemplated or accomplished, for example, in *Sorrell and Son*, *If Winter Comes*, *Point Counter Point*, and *Lady Chatterley's Lover* — works of very different levels of sophistication, and appealing to very different audiences.

But the most important post-war literary text on the subject is surely

A Bill of Divorcement, the play by Clemence Dane that opened in March 1921 to critical acclaim, and ran for more than eight months. The date of the opening is significant: it fell between the reintroduction of the Matrimonial Causes Bill and its final feeble enactment — a time, that is, when divorce law was a matter for debate, and for discussion. The play is set, however, at a later date; a stage direction to the opening scene reads:

> SCENE. — *A small house in the country. The action passes on Christmas Day, 1933. The audience is asked to imagine that the recommendations of the* Majority Report of the Royal Commission on Divorce *v*. Matrimonial Causes *have become the law of the land.*[33]

The new, as-yet-not-enacted law plays a crucial part in the plot of the play. Margaret Fairfield is a woman whose husband is one of the war's damaged men, long confined to an asylum. She has divorced him, on the new grounds of incurable insanity, and is about to remarry, when he escapes from the asylum and appears at her door, apparently recovered, and claiming that their marriage is still valid. The wife hesitates, is half-persuaded, and is only able to leave him and seize happiness with her suitor when her daughter assumes responsibility for her father, recognizing that she has inherited his instability, and cannot marry.

It seems a melodramatic and not very original play. What made it a hit? The currency of the divorce debate, surely, and the sense the play gives of what was at stake in that debate, and especially for women. *A Bill of Divorcement* is built on women, three generations of women: an elderly aunt, who speaks for the old, religious view that marriage is inviolable and married happiness irrelevant; the wife, damaged by what the war did to her life, and afraid of her freedom; and the daughter, who sees the rightness of her mother's divorce, and accepts the burden of her father for the sake of her mother's future. Three generations and two moral worlds confront each other: Miss Fairfield, the old aunt, has the Church on her side (and in the audience's world the law as well); Sydney, the young daughter, has the reality of post-war life with her; Margaret, the mother, is in the middle, confused and frightened, as many persons of her class and age were, caught between tradition and change.

Other pertinent themes appear, too. The war is there as a cause of human actions and miseries, articulated, for example, in this exchange between mother and daughter:

SYDNEY. I'm not actually engaged, if you mean that — [*Watching their faces mischievously*] but I'm going to be.

MISS FAIRFIELD. Engaged at seventeen! Preposterous!

SYDNEY. [*Instantly*] Mother was married at seventeen.

MARGARET. That was the war . . .

SYDNEY. It's extraordinary to me — whenever you middle-aged people want to excuse yourselves for anything you've done that you know you oughtn't to have done, you say it was the war. How could war make you get married if you didn't want to?

MARGARET. [*Groping for words*] It was the feel in the air. They say the smell of blood sends horses crazy. That was the feel. One did mad things. Hilary — your father — he was going out — the trenches — to be hurt. And he was so fond of me he frightened me. I was so sorry. I thought I cared.[34]

It's very like Hemingway's Catherine Barkley — a common feel in the air that affected both sexuality and reason.

The war as a cause enters again when the family doctor tries to explain why the laws of divorce had to be changed.

D'you remember [he asks Hilary, the husband] — can you throw your mind back to the beginning of the agitation against the marriage laws? . . . Well, as the result of that agitation — and remember, Hilary, what thousand, thousand tragedies must have had voice in such an out-cry — a commission was appointed to enquire into the working of the divorce laws. It made its report, recommended certain drastic reforms, and there, I suppose, as is the way with commissions, would have been the end of the subject, if it hadn't been for the war — and the war marriages . . . Never, I suppose, in one decade were there so many young marriages. Happy? that's another thing! Marry in haste —[35]

Because of the war, marriages were different, more unhappy — and so the divorce laws *must* change. For this new, unhappy world the old laws won't do.

Young women like Sydney Fairfield, independent in their thought and speech, and unhappy in their lives, are common in post-war literature — common enough to constitute the decade's most familiar female type, 'The Modern Girl'. ('The Modern Young Woman' would be a more accurate term, since they range over two generations, those who came of age during the war, and those who came of age in the

Twenties.) Sydney is brash, irreverent and independent, opposed to all
that is old and repressive, and committed to openness and honesty. Her
great-aunt says of her and her kind: 'They know too much, the young
women'; and 'She's like the rest of the young women. Hard as nails!'[36]
But she is neither knowing enough nor hard enough to accomplish her
own fulfilment. The lives of these young women offer a puzzling
paradox: why are they at once so liberated and so unhappy? At a time
when women were claiming freedom in their public and private lives,
asserting their equality with men, and taking control of their own
existences, one might expect to find a buoyant, affirmative literature of
women. But one doesn't: the Modern Women we meet in Twenties
fiction and drama are not free and not self-affirming, but bitter, sad,
cynical, wistful, lost. Look at some of the decade's most vivid and
characteristic woman characters: Iris Storm in *The Green Hat*, Fleur
Forsyte in Galsworthy's *A Modern Comedy*, Lady Brett Ashley in
Hemingway's *The Sun Also Rises*, Lucy Tantamount in Huxley's *Point
Counter Point*, Lawrence's Constance Chatterley, the women in *The
Waste Land* and in Noël Coward's plays. And one could add many
others that are similar, if less well known: Lydia Clame in C.H.B.
Kitchin's *Streamers Waving*, Paula in Norah James's suppressed novel,
Sleeveless Errand, Smithy in Helen Zenna Smith's *Not So Quiet . . .*, most
of the women in Mary Butts's *Speed the Plough*. These women are quite
various — young and not-so-young, married, single, divorced and
widowed, rich and poor — but they have certain characteristics in
common. They are disengaged from life: they have failed marriages or
none, they have no children, they are alienated from their parents and
their parents' generation. They don't work, or do much of anything
else, except perhaps drink too much, and engage in casual and unsatisfactory relationships with men. They are all unhappy — three
commit suicide. But the thing that they most evidently share is a feeling
that lies behind all the other details — a feeling of personal failure, of
worthlessness and waste. They are damaged women, as the male
survivors of the war are damaged men.

    This feeling is a defining element in the post-war mood as it involves
women. How is one to explain it? One cause, obviously, is the war. All
of these women characters are in some sense products of the war: 'I
came out of the chrysalis during the War,' Lucy Tantamount says,
'when the bottom had been knocked out of everything.' And Norah
James's Paula: 'I can't fit in — I suppose I was born bored, or maybe it
was the war. It threw our generation out. Things were so hectic and

unreal just when we were arriving at our adolescence.'[37] War — any war
— is for women an inevitably diminishing experience. There is nothing
like a war for demonstrating to women their inferior status, nothing like
the war experiences of men for making clear the exclusion of women
from life's great excitements, nothing like war casualties for imposing
on women the guiltiness of being alive and well. We have seen such
feelings in the war writings of many women — in Rose Macaulay and
Rebecca West, in May Sinclair and Cynthia Asquith and Enid Bagnold;
they seem an inseparable part of women's experience of war. It would
be unreasonable to assume that such strong feelings would simply
evaporate when the war ended.

But if women were excluded from the men's game of war, they
were sustained during those war years by the thought that they
were proving their worth in other ways — working long hours in
hospitals and factories, driving trains and buses, serving in the auxiliary forces — and that when the war ended they would be rewarded
with the rights that they deserved. And then peace came, and they
were not; or were in some ways and not in others. The defeats that
came with the victories in their women's war must also have contributed to the feeling of low esteem that characterizes the Modern
Girl.

There is one other explanation that is simply statistical. In the 1921
census there were 19,803,022 females in England and Wales, and only
18,082,220 males — a difference of a million and three-quarters women.
This situation was not indeed a new phenomenon: there had been
more women than men in England for nearly a hundred years — a
million more in the last pre-war census. But in 1921 that number had
nearly doubled, by a figure that was almost exactly the number of the
English war dead. If you look at the numbers for persons of child-
bearing age, the point is even more striking: there were more than nine
and a half million women between the ages of fifteen and forty-four in
1921, and less than eight and a half million men. More than a million
women — one in nine of the child-bearing group — would not marry or
bear children. For them, the war would be a continuing reality in their
lives until they died.

One might argue that the Sex Disqualification (Removal) Act was
designed for such women: they could have professional careers. But
they couldn't all be barristers or auctioneers, and some observers
worried that in their numbers they would not be a liberating force, but a
reactionary one. A leader-writer in *The Times* saw this monstrous

regiment of single women as constituting a serious social problem. 'Though the problem', he wrote

> has in some degree been mitigated by the expansion of woman's opportunities, which has followed the war, it has lost none of its true seriousness.
>
> It may even be that the effects of feminine enfranchisement, now so widely evident, will encounter strong counteracting influence.[38]

What he feared was that too many women would seek fulfilment outside of marriage, because they *had* to, and that male-dominated society would react against them, and obstruct and perhaps reverse their advances. The only solution that the *Times* man had to propose was that single women should emigrate, and take their problem to the Commonwealth.

That *Times* leader was titled 'Surplus Women'. The editor who chose that title was presumably referring simply to a statistical fact. But *surplus* has strong emotional connotations, too: to be a surplus woman was to be redundant, left-over, superfluous. More than a million women were, in post-war society's eyes, unnecessary to society's needs; so it is not surprising that a sense of worthlessness should permeate much post-war writing by and about women, even in that time of enfranchisement and liberation. A good example of this woman's mood is Vera Brittain's poem, written in July 1920, and titled 'The Superfluous Woman':

> Ghosts crying down the vistas of the years,
> Recalling words
> Whose echoes long have died,
> And kind moss grown
> Over the sharp and blood-bespattered stones
> Which cut our feet upon the ancient ways.
>
> *   *   *   *   *   *   *
> *But who will look for my coming?*
>
> Long busy days where many meet and part;
> Crowded aside
> Remembered hours of hope;
> And city streets
> Grown dark and hot with eager multitudes
> Hurrying homeward whither respite waits.
>
> *   *   *   *   *   *   *
> *But who will seek me at nightfall?*

> Light fading where the chimneys cut the sky;
> Footsteps that pass,
> Nor tarry at my door.
> And far away,
> Behind the row of crosses, shadows black
> Stretch out long arms before the smouldering sun.
>
> *   *   *   *   *   *   *
>
> *But who will give me my children?*[39]

Vera Brittain was as liberated, as militantly feminist, as any woman of her time. But her poem is not about activism, but about emptiness. In post-war England, there were a million such empty women. And how do women win *that* women's war?

Compared to those vast battlefields of sex and war, the professors' war-after-the-war was a trivial matter, scarcely more than a footnote. It blew up in October 1920 when a group of Oxford professors, doctors, and miscellaneous intellectuals, led by Robert Bridges, published the following letter in the *The Times*:

> To the Professors of the Arts and Sciences and to Members of Universities and Learned Societies in Germany and Austria:
>
> Since there will be many of you who fully share our heartfelt sorrow and regret for the breach that the war has occasioned in our friendly intercourse, and since you cannot doubt the sincerity of the feeling which engendered and cherished that old friendliness, you must, we believe, be sharing our hope for its speedy re-establishment.
>
> We therefore, the undersigned doctors, heads of houses, professors, and other officers and teachers in the University of Oxford, now personally approach you with the desire to dispel the embitterment of animosities that under the impulse of loyal patriotism may have passed between us.
>
> In the field where our aims are one, our enthusiasms the same, our rivalry and ambition generous, we can surely look to be reconciled, and the fellowhip of learning offers a road which may and if our spiritual ideals be alive, must lead to a wider sympathy and better understanding between our kindred nations.
>
> While political dissensions are threatening to extinguish the honourable comity of the great European States, we pray that we may help to hasten that amicable reunion which civilization demands. *Impetret ratio quod dies impetratura est.*[40]

The sixty-six signatures included those of Bridges, Gilbert Murray, and
T.E. Lawrence.

It seems a mild enough professorial gesture in a time of peace, but it
stirred up fierce opposition. There were angry letters from other dons in
The Times, and a leader titled 'An Ill-judged Appeal', which protested
that

> the whole character and tone of this document will shock the feelings
> of many in all classes of the British peoples. Their attitude throughout
> the war was wonderfully free, in the face of unparalleled provocation,
> from hatred and vindictiveness, and they recognize to the full the
> catholic nature of art, of literature, and of science. But they do not
> forget, as these professors and others seem ready to forget, the unjust
> and wicked war forced upon them, which has swept away a whole
> generation of their youth . . . The 'fellowship of learning' is very fine,
> and forgiveness to the truly repentant wrongdoer is a lofty 'spiritual
> ideal' and a Christian duty. But justice is the first of human virtues,
> and justice demands that there shall be no pardon . . .[41]

There would be no forgiveness and no forgetting; the war had occurred,
and had made the pre-war fellowship of learning irrecoverable. Once
that point had been made, the controversy died away.

In the wars after the war, there were both old battles and new ones.
Class still stood against class, Ireland against England, men against
women. There were changes, advances even, in these causes, but every
advance created a new conflict, and there were no resolutions. We think
of the decade of the Twenties as a new era in English culture, cut off
from pre-war values and conventions by the great devastation of the
war; and that is a part of the truth. But only a part. The other,
countering truth is the persistence of the past.

The past persisted in two ways. The world-before-the-war remained
in the representatives of the Edwardian generation, who retained great
power, and used it to continue in power. But there was also another
past: the war remained, too — a memory of ruin and loss that survived
in post-war lives that had been darkened and damaged by it. England
did not begin afresh in 1919: it picked up the burden of its pasts, and
moved, uncertainly and anxiously, towards its future.

CHAPTER 19

The Generation Wars

A generation exists when it thinks it does: that is, when it identifies itself as distinct from other generations. Generation-consciousness is weakest in the most stable societies, in which each age group succeeds the one before it, inheriting property, class, occupation and values, and is strongest when continuities fail, and age groups see themselves as in conflict with others, and as separated from them by some unique generational experience.[1]

In the Edwardian world, generation lines do not seem to have been very clearly drawn until just before the war, when a confrontational avant-garde appeared, and a sharp opposition of old against young became visible and audible, the established conservative elders against a younger generation of Vorticists, Futurists, Imagists, Suffragists, Socialists and various otherists. During the war that opposition of old and young continued, but in different terms: then it became the Old Men, who had caused the war and who controlled it, versus the young, who did the fighting and the dying. But in both cases the division was binary and adversarial, one self-defined generation confronting its antagonist.

The war exploded that generation sense, as it exploded so many other social patterns; in the post-war years one finds not two generations, but many groups — cohorts, or factions, or parties — divided partly by age, partly by experience, partly by values, each thinking itself separate and distinct, and the others radically different, competitive, and more or less hostile. Within single generations there were sharp divisions and conflicts, and in some cases the separations within a generation were greater than those between generations. Even where generations seemed sharply different from each other, the chronological lines between them were overlapping, and blurred by the variables of experience and values. But what is clear is that generation-consciousness, or something like it, the sense of belonging to *this* group and in conflict or competition with others, was very strong in the post-war years, as English men and women of different ages and experiences struggled to define themselves, and to claim their place in the new, fragmented English society.

One can distinguish five distinct groups in post-war England that might be called, in inverted commas, 'generations'. They are, from the oldest to the youngest:

The Old Men: these were the generals and the politicians, the bishops and the newspaper proprietors, all those conservative elders who were established in their professions before the war, and who saw the war as a continuation of their pre-war values — men like Newbolt and Gosse, Ricketts, Asquith and Balfour. To themselves, they were survivors of a nobler and more ordered past; post-war England seemed to many of them incoherent and threatening. 'It is not so much the war as the peace that I have always dreaded,' Balfour said as he set off for the Paris Peace Conference, and many of his contemporaries shared his dread. 'What is to come of the angry, distracted world?' Gosse asked Gide in 1920. 'I feel very old and helpless.' And Ricketts wrote to Yeats, in 1922: 'I must confess to moments of acute depression and fear of the future ... I know I am a quite useless survival from another age, and because the future has no use for me I look at it like a sheep in a railway truck.'[2] But if they seemed helpless and useless to themselves, to the young they remained the hostile power that they had always been, and the phrase 'the Old Men' continued in post-war rhetoric as the name for the repressive forces of society: 'yet when we achieved and the new world dawned,' T.E. Lawrence wrote,

> the old men came out again and took our victory to remake in the likeness of the former world they knew. Youth could win, but had not learned to keep: and was pitiably weak against age. We stammered that we had worked for a new heaven and a new earth, and they thanked us kindly and made their peace.[3]

This sense of anger and betrayal, this bitter feeling that it was the Old Men who had won the war, and so retained their power over the young, is an important continuing element in the mood of the Twenties.

Edwardians: as a generation, they overlapped the Old Men, but writers like Bennett and Wells and social thinkers like the Webbs thought of

themselves as different, more advanced and modern than the men who
had prosecuted the war. They remained active, and strove to exhibit
their up-to-dateness in their work, but they too were apprehensive. The
war, to them, had been a great social and cultural disruption, and the
world that they saw around them after the war seemed impoverished,
unpredictable, and sometimes threatening. Bennett's *Mr Prohack*, in
which the hero is first made poor by the war and then accidentally rich,
is typical of this mood; Mrs Webb's *Diary* has the same quality of
uncertainty, but is gloomier about it.

The Pre-war Avant-Garde: writers and artists such as Lewis, Pound,
Nevinson and Ford had separated themselves from the Edwardian
establishment, and had declared war on conservative art; in the brief
period before the war began they defined avant-garde art in England. A
decade later they did not exist as a movement, but only as a few
scattered survivors. Of the circle around Pound and Lewis and *Blast* in
1914, Hulme and Gaudier-Brzeska were dead in the war; Pound had
denounced England and English culture and moved to Paris in 1920;
Ford had departed (also for Paris) in 1922; Nevinson had resigned from
Modernism; Lewis was back in London, but withdrawn from the art
world. Without a surviving centre there could be no continuity with the
old, pre-war avant-garde; Futurism was dead, Vorticism was dead;
Imagism was dead. If there was to be a post-war Modernism, it would
have to begin afresh.

The War Generation: another, more emotional term for this group is
'The Lost Generation', and one might argue that in that form it is the
most important of the post-war categories. The phrase entered the post-
war mythology of the war quickly with two distinct meanings. One
meaning refers to the dead, and implies that those who died would have
been their generation's leaders, and that they died in such numbers as to
leave their generation emptied of the men who would have given it
significance — so that what it named was not so much a generation as an
emptiness *between* generations.

This seems at first glance an unlikely interpretation of the war
statistics. After all, six million men served in the British forces, and
fewer than a million died: surely some leaders must have survived. If,
however, you accept the proposition that England's leaders — not only
in politics, but in the arts — had traditionally come from the educated
and upper classes, then the notion of a lost generation becomes credible.
Consider the following facts: of all the young men who matriculated at
Oxford and Cambridge between 1910 and 1914 and entered the army,

one in four was killed in the war; of public-school old boys, about twenty per cent died; of peers and their sons under the age of fifty in 1914, nearly a fifth were killed; the death rate of officers (where most of the public-school and university men were) was twice that of the other ranks, most of whom were working-class.[4] It would appear that the people like Masterman who mourned the death of a class had some evidence on their side: certainly the upper and middle classes had lost something like a fifth of their young men.

The other meaning of 'lost generation' is what Gertrude Stein had in mind when she said (apparently to a garage mechanic in France), 'You are a lost generation,' and what Hemingway intended when he picked up Stein's remark and made it an epigraph for *The Sun Also Rises*, and what Ford meant when he wrote that 'our martyred generation was lost for good'.[5] Here *lost* means not *vanished* but *disoriented*, *wandering*, *directionless* — a recognition that there was great confusion and aimlessness among the war's survivors in the early post-war years, much moving about, much changing of plans, many beginnings without endings, and comparatively little solid work done.

One explanation of this uncertainty has to do with the age of this 'lost' war generation. Some of them were established adults when the war began: among English artists and writers, for example, Lewis and Ford were both known in 1914. But the core of the war generation was made up of younger men — Graves, Sassoon, Blunden, the Nash brothers, Stanley Spencer — who had had no reputation before the war (some of them had been boys when the war began), and who had come of age as artists during the war years. They were in their twenties when the war ended, ready, one would have thought, to enter the mainstream of modern English art and letters. But they had difficulty in doing so; they felt out of step with what was new. A psychologist I know once drugged a hatching of baby ducks at the stage in their developing when ducklings learn to follow their mother, and so these never did so, but wandered off in all directions. The war generation's young artists were like that: they had been drugged by war at the moment when they might have been learning the experimental gestures of their time, and so they never learned, but went off in their own eccentric directions, no two alike and none a canonical Modernist. They were none the worse as artists for their eccentricity, one might add; but they were less certain, and less secure in their sense of where they belonged in the world-after-the-war.

Nor did they find it easy to locate themselves in the post-war cultural world. Sassoon tried working as Literary Editor of the Socialist *Daily Herald*, quit, and went off to America on a poetry-reading tour; Graves went up to Oxford, and opened a village shop on Boars Hill (which failed); Paul Nash moved to the country to paint landscapes, then tried theatrical design, went to Paris, returned to London, travelled to the Riviera and Italy, went back to the English countryside; Robert Nichols left England for three years as a professor of English literature in Tokyo; poor Ivor Gurney, war poet and composer, wandered the streets of London and the roads back to Gloucestershire until he was declared mad and put into an asylum. Nash's phrase for his own restless situation describes them all: 'Struggles of a war artist without a war.'[6] It took time for them to shed the war as a subject; some never did — Gurney went on writing war poems in the madhouse until he died there in 1937. But it also took time to cast off the war's style — the plain, blunt representation of broken things; some never managed that, either — Sassoon wrote like a war poet for the rest of his life, and only wrote well when war was both his subject and his style.

These were the essential war generation, the men who had fought; yet in the world after the war they were the least noticeable of the many cultural groups on hand. Some of them wrote, or painted, or composed, or edited journals, but none made much of an impression. They had the most dramatic of subjects — the war they had endured — but when they tried to write about it they either failed to find a publisher (as Ford and Herbert Read did), or were published and ignored (as A.P. Herbert was). It is an odd fact, but a true one, that in those years, so full of the war's surviving presence, there was little work of importance produced about the war itself by those who had fought it. In that sense there certainly was a Lost Generation — and a Lost War as well.

But what about the other members of their age group, the ones who stayed at home and wrote their books and painted their pictures, and moved into positions of power in the English cultural world — people like Murry, Edwin Muir, J.C. Squire, Eliot, Huxley? They certainly thought of themselves as members of the same generation as their ex-soldier contemporaries. When Huxley's father wrote to his son, expressing his extreme distaste for *Antic Hay*, son Aldous replied:

> I will only point out that it is a book written by a member of what I may call the war-generation for others of his kind; and that it is intended to reflect — fantastically, of course, but none the less faithfully — the life and opinions of an age which has seen the violent

disruption of almost all the standards, conventions and values current in the previous epoch.[7]

That is a good example of an acute generation sense; but was Huxley really a member of the war generation? Certainly he was the right age — a year younger than Wilfred Owen, a year older than Graves — but because of his near blindness he had not shared the war experience that had shaped their sensibilities and bound them to each other; he had shared instead the experiences of the civilian wing of the generation. From the soldier's point of view this must have seemed to have been mainly a matter of getting on with his career — writing, getting published, making useful connections. By the end of the war he was established in the emerging new avant-garde, was publishing poems in *Wheels* and reviews in the literary journals, weekending at Garsington, dining with the Eliots and the Woolfs. But one can't doubt that he also felt the war in the way that he described it to his father, as a violent disruption of everything that had made life and thought orderly in the world before the war.

A generation, I said, is an age group defined by a common experience; but here was an age group not all of whom did share in the great rite of passage that the war had been, or didn't share in it in the same way. So the war generation divided, as war generations do, into those who fought, and so could imagine the war in its actuality, and those who hadn't, and could only imagine its consequences. But for all of them, soldiers and civilians alike, the war was there, in their consciousnesses, to be carried into the peace, and to be imaginatively dealt with.

The Post-War Generation: these were the young people who came of age after 1918, were Oxford and Cambridge students in the post-war years, the Bright Young Things of Twenties mythology. Their memories of the war were school memories — of cold rooms and no sweets and Rolls of Honour on chapel walls, and their memories of the Edwardian world-before-the-war were of early childhood. Theirs was a present without any normal, ordinary, stable past.

The first attempt to define this generation came very early, in 1921, when Evelyn Waugh wrote 'The Youngest Generation', and published it in the *Lancing College Magazine*. He was still a schoolboy, eighteen years old, but he had a strong sense that he belonged to a generation that was separate and distinct. 'During the last few years,' his essay begins,

a new generation has grown up; between them and the young men of
1912 lies the great gulf of the war. What will they stand for and what
are they going to do?

The men of Rupert Brooke's generation are broken. Narcissus-
like, they stood for an instant amazedly aware of their own beauty;
the war, which old men made, has left them tired and embittered.
What will the young men of 1922 be?

They will be, above all things, clear-sighted, they will have no use
for phrases or shadows ... And because they are clear-sighted, they
will not be revolutionaries and they will not be poets and they will
not be mystics; there will be much that they will lose, but all that they
have will be real ...

It is a queer world which the old men have left them and they will
have few ideals and illusions to console them when they 'get to feeling
old.' They will not be a happy generation.[8]

There are a number of interesting things in this passage. First, how
quickly the adolescent Waugh picked up aspects of the myth of the war:
the 'great gulf of the war', and the 'old men who made it'.[9] And second,
that in one respect he got it wrong, taking Rupert Brooke as the
defining figure, and not as the type of romantic, idealistic innocence that
the war disproved and destroyed. And third, that his view of the world
after the war contains the same language of disillusionment that one
finds in the post-war writings of the soldier generation. It seems
unlikely that this was simply a case of a literary youth adopting the
attitudes of current war literature; in 1921 the 'anti-monuments' were
only beginning to be written, and Montague's influential *Disenchantment*
had not yet appeared. Rather, Waugh had compounded a generation
myth of his own, part romanticism and part disillusionment, as though
he and his generation were the heirs of both Brooke and Owen. In those
terms they too had their war.

When Montague wrote of disenchantment, he meant disenchantment
with the war, and with the motives of those who had directed it. But
that mood spread over English society after the war, and persisted
through the years that followed; it was as though disenchantment was
a disease, contracted in the trenches but transmittable to persons who
had not been there. The younger generation seemed particularly suscep-
tible, and that is not surprising; for it is generally true that the first
generation to come along after any war will be influenced by the war
that it was born too late to fight, will envy older brothers and resent

fathers who fought it, and will shape its own behaviour in reaction to it.

At Oxford that behaviour took the form of a revival of interest in Decadence, aestheticism, and Oscar Wilde. Undergraduates wrote Wildean poems (and were rebuked by Lord Alfred Douglas for doing so), published a previously unpublished poem by Wilde, drew in the manner of Aubrey Beardsley, and wrote essays in praise of decadence.[10] Young aesthetes like Harold Acton and Brian Howard became celebrated Oxford figures; the novels of Ronald Firbank were read and admired. Beverley Nichols put the neo-decadent movement into an Oxford novel, *Patchwork* (1921), in which his hero returns from the war to re-create a pre-war, decadent Oxford modelled on *Dorian Gray* and Compton Mackenzie's *Sinister Street*, as an antidote to the post-war preoccupation with Modernism and the war. He explains his motives in a conversation with a friend:

> '. . . I want people to be charming again and not go about in standard suits and look horribly earnest and put cubist paintings on their walls and talk about the war . . . If you wear futurist jumpers and join the Labour Party and say that Chopin is out of date, and that nobody's any good but Stravinsky, and if you read 'Wheels', and adore Robert Smillie, and talk about skyscrapers, it shows one thing quite clearly, and that is that the war has deprived you of your mental balance.'
>
> 'But don't you see that you *ought* to have been deprived of your mental balance? You ought to be mad. You can't ignore these things.'
>
> 'Oh yes, I can.'[11]

The co-existence of so many 'generations', each with a style and a history and a war of its own, makes the cultural life in England in those early post-war years seem as fragmented and disparate as *The Waste Land* or *Jacob's Room*. Some examples will give an impression of the cultural situation.

1919 in the art world: Two exhibitions of war paintings, Wyndham Lewis's *Guns* in February, Lady Butler's *Some Records of the Great War* in August.

1922 in the literary world: The Modernist *annus mirabilis*. *The Waste Land* and *Ulysses* were published. But so was *The Forsyte Saga*.

1923 in the musical-theatrical world: In March, the first performance of *Arthur*, a tragic drama by Laurence Binyon (age fifty-four), with music by Elgar (age sixty-six); and in June, the first public performance of

Façade, poems by Edith Sitwell (age thirty-six), music by William Walton (age twenty-one).

1924 in the theatre world: The first London performances of Shaw's *Back to Methuselah* and *Saint Joan*, and of Noël Coward's *The Vortex*. Shaw was sixty-eight, Coward was twenty-five.

There is nothing unusual, of course, in writers and artists of different ages producing works at the same time. What *is* unusual about the post-war situation is how different the works were, how various in style, in tone, and in values, and how disconnected from each other. Lewis and Lady Butler, Joyce and Galsworthy, Elgar and Walton, Shaw and Coward — in each pair the individuals come from entirely different worlds. There is no possible continuity between older and younger, no influence, no shared values or ideas. Each generation stands apart, each with its own version of reality.

Yet these diverse generational examples do have one element in common: they all contain the war, though each contains it differently — or one might even say contains a different war. I can explain this point best simply by commenting on my examples in order:

The two art shows: Lewis was showing the last of his war paintings in the popularized Vorticist style that he had adopted for the war, and would now abandon. Lady Butler had been painting battle pictures since the 1870s, and had made her reputation with heroic Napoleonic War subjects, like 'Scotland Forever!', the cavalry charge of the Scots Greys at Waterloo. In the First World War she had continued to paint cavalry charges, though they were hard to find. Both shows were explicitly exhibitions of war art, but how different — Lewis's Vorticist war, rendered with a cold and value-denying aloofness, Lady Butler's Victorian war, full of galloping horses and heroic men.

The Waste Land and *The Forsyte Saga*: they have little in common, but both in the poem and in the conclusion of the novel the war is present as an historical gap, and as a cause of fragmentation and loss.[12]

Ulysses: One doesn't look for the war here, in a novel set on June 16, 1904; but Joyce wrote it during the war, and though war is furtive, it is present. And particularly in the second chapter, 'Nestor', written in the autumn of 1917 (season of Passchendaele and the Russian Revolution). In this chapter Stephen Dedalus gives a history lesson and then talks with Mr Deasy, his headmaster. The lesson concerns Pyrrhus and the Battle of Asculum in 279 BC. A student repeats Pyrrhus's famous remark after the battle: 'Another victory like that and we are done for'; and Stephen thinks:

That phrase the world had remembered. A dull ease of the mind.
From a hill above a corpsestrewn plain a general speaking to his
officers, leaned upon his spear. Any general to any officers.[13]

So war is present here, bloody and cynical, *any* war — at Asculum or on
the muddy flats at Ypres, it was all one.

In Stephen's conversation with Mr Deasy, a Young Man confronts an
Old Man. Three of their remarks are relevant to our considerations
here. Two are Stephen's: 'History . . . is a nightmare from which I am
trying to awake,' and 'I fear those big words . . . which make us so
unhappy'; one is Mr Deasy's: 'Old England is dying.'[14] To anyone at
all familiar with the rhetoric of the war, these sentences are familiar,
and are appropriately assigned to Young Man and Old Man; they
represent the opposing attitudes towards language, towards history, and
towards the idea of England that Old and Young held in the war's later
years.[15]

The two musical dramas: one in blank verse, traditional and entirely
Georgian in spirit, the other satirical, outrageous, and altogether
Modern. Binyon's tragedy concerns the last days of King Arthur's reign
and, like *Ulysses*, it would seem to be not subject to the war's influence
by reason of its location in time. But one war may stand for any war,
and *Arthur* is as much an expression of a post-war view of the Great War
as *Disenchantment* or *The Secret Battle* is. There is not much actual
fighting in the play, but there is much grief for those who have fought
and died (Binyon was the author, you recall, of the much-quoted war
elegy, 'For the Fallen'), and the best speeches are elegiac. Here, as an
example, is Guenevere's last speech, after Arthur's death:

> I am the cost. They are fallen, those famous ones
> Who made this kingdom glorious, they are fallen
> About their King; they have yielded up their strength
> And beauty and valour.
> (*The convent bell begins to toll.*)
> The grieving bell begins,
> As if it were the mouth and voice of Death
> Emptying the earth of honour and renown.[16]

Who, hearing those lines in 1923, would not remember 1918? And who,
hearing Elgar's elegiac incidental music, would not be aware of Elgar's
grief for a dead past?

Façade: very much a Modern, post-war work, into which war enters only as an object of mockery — soldiers and sailors, a captain and an admiral, Attila and Balaclava, swords and drums, all treated with fantastic disrespect (which applies to Walton's music, too).

The two plays: *The Vortex*, like *Façade*, an entirely up-to-date work. In it the war occupies only a single sentence in a conversation between a young man and a young woman:

TOM: How many years ago is it since we . . .
BUNTY: During the War — the last time I saw you, you were at Sandhurst.[17]

Tom is the lover of an older woman, Florence Lancaster; Bunty is the fiancée of Mrs Lancaster's artistic, neurotic son, Nicky. From this exchange we know that by the end of the play Tom will be off with Bunty, leaving mother and son to their neuroses, because Tom has been a soldier, and soldiers are virile, but Nicky is merely modern, and is not.

Back to Methuselah: Shaw's play is sub-titled 'A Metabiological Pentateuch', which for Shaw meant that it is a vast speculative fantasy, reaching from 4004 BC, Archbishop Ussher's calculation of the date of Creation, to AD 31,900. One of its five parts is located in the historical present: Part Two is set in the 'Present Day', and has at its centre two historical figures, disguised only in their names: Joyce Burge (who is Lloyd George), and Lubin (who is Asquith). Shaw, being Shaw, explained exactly why he set this Part when he did: it is all in a section of his preface headed 'POLITICAL INADEQUACY OF THE HUMAN ANIMAL'. Shaw has been describing an occasion in 1906 when he delivered a lecture deriding Darwin and his followers. The next paragraph reads as follows:

Ten more years elapsed. Neo-Darwinism in politics had produced a European catastrophe of a magnitude so appalling, and a scope so unpredictable, that as I write these lines in 1920, it is still far from certain whether our civilization will survive it. The circumstances of this catastrophe, the boyish cinema-fed romanticism which made it possible to impose it on people as a crusade, and especially the ignorance and errors of the victors of Western Europe when its violent phase had passed and the time for reconstruction arrived, confirmed a doubt which had grown steadily in my mind during my forty years' public work as a Socialist: namely, whether the human animal, as he exists at present, is capable of solving the social problems raised by his own aggregation, or, as he calls it, his civilization.[18]

Much of that is familiar by now — the doubts about civilization, reconstruction, the romantic folly of the young men, the duping of the people; many other writers in the post-war years were saying very similar things. But for Shaw it was the fact of this catastrophe that made his play necessary: if man could create the war, then he could not be trusted to deal with other human problems; he would have to evolve.

In the dialogue of the play the war appears again and again, always as the atrocious crime of elders like Lubin/Asquith and Burge/Lloyd George. 'I shall clear out,' Conrad Barnabas, the play's Shavian biologist, announces:

> It was hard enough to stand the party politicians before the war; but now they have managed to half kill Europe between them, I can't be civil to them, and I don't see why I should be.[19]

And Franklyn Barnabas, the play's Shavian metaphysician, tells Lubin:

> You will go down to posterity as one of a European group of immature statesmen and monarchs who, doing the very best for your respective countries of which you were capable, succeeded in all-but-wrecking the civilization of Europe, and did, in effect, wipe out of existence many millions of its inhabitants.[20]

At the age of sixty-eight, Shaw was as bitter a hater of the Old Men as any ex-subaltern.

Among such various versions of war, from artists so diverse in age and in attitude, one might expect to find no common denominator, and indeed one doesn't. They do, however, fall into two categories that express two different answers to a crucial post-war question: What shall we do with the past? These categories are not strictly generational (Shaw marches with the young here), but with that one exception they do divide chronologically. One group — the older — treats the past (and the war as a part of the past) with nostalgic regret for lost values and lost security, and regards art as a vessel in which what has been lost in society can be preserved. That is the mood of *Arthur*, certainly — both the text and the music — and of Galsworthy at the end of his *Saga*, and even of Lady Butler, who looked back fondly to the days of the Victorian army, when artillery pieces were not camouflaged, and cavalrymen were armed with sabres, and were picturesque.[21]

The younger artists were less likely to be reverent and nostalgic about the past, and more likely to confront the ruins of history in the spirit of a wrecking crew at a bomb-site, levelling in order to build something new, or of an archaeological team at a dig, sorting through the midden of the past. That view of the past is evident in the major Modernist texts — in the 'heap of broken images' of which *The Waste Land* is constituted, and in the archaeological reconstruction of June 16, 1904 that is *Ulysses*. It is equally evident in *Façade*, where the sounds of words and their inherited references are systematically separated, as though language had been violently detached from past meanings, and in a non-experimental way in *The Vortex*, which almost completely excludes the past from its frame of reference, and creates a play-world that contains only its present.

There are two war stories here: one of lost values amd lost glories, fading like the end of a bright day; the other simply a tale that takes the destruction of the past for granted. Though *war* story isn't quite the right term, for one must take as a part of the story that perception that Henry James uttered at the war's beginning, that the war, simply by occurring, proved the whole pre-war liberal vision of the world to be wrong. That pre-war world is the thing destroyed or lost in *both* stories. What the two stories have in common is that neither pretends that the past can be recovered; post-war must be a starting over, whether you are Laurence Binyon or Noël Coward.

In those younger artists starting over again in the twenties there is an element in common beyond their shared sense of the fragmented past; there is also a common tone — they are all in some sense *satirists*. Of my examples above, *The Waste Land*, *Ulysses* and *Façade* are clearly satires; Lewis's war paintings satirize the troops by representing them as insects; Coward assumes an aloof and mocking attitude towards most of his characters. One might venture to propose from these examples that the post-war period was a satiric time.

And one would be right. I remarked earlier that at the end of the war, as opposition to the war grew, satire began to emerge as the voice of that opposition — a bitter, often angry voice that divided society, and distanced one part from another. And I called that emergence 'the beginning of post-war'. Satire continued to be a prominent mode in the years after the war, expressing the conflicts between generations and between values, and emphasizing, and perhaps intensifying, social divisions. We saw some examples among the 'anti-monuments', in the paintings of Orpen and Lewis, and in the poems of Osbert Sitwell and Sassoon. There are many others; indeed, the years from, say, 1916 to the end of the Twenties can reasonably be described as a single period in English culture, dominated by the dividing, alienating forces of satire.

A history of English satire in the post-war years might begin with two books written during the last year of the war, but published in the first year of the peace: Rose Macaulay's *What Not*, and Galsworthy's *The Burning Spear*. They resemble each other in one aspect — they are both satires of wartime, but neither is about the war itself. The target of *What Not*'s satire is wartime bureaucracy. The title comes from a report of a food-hoarding case, in which the defendant had angrily exclaimed:

> It has come to a fine thing if people cannot live in their homes without being interfered with by the police . . . You are upsetting the country altogether with your Food Orders and What Not.[22]

— a remark that Macaulay adopted as her epigraph. Interfering ministries and officials swarm through the book (there is even a Ministry of Brains, dedicated to improving English intelligence by genetic control), and DORA is anthropomorphized into a foolish female who does foolish things. *What Not* is not set in wartime, however, but in the immediate post-war future. It is ostensibly a prophetic vision of England at peace, and its depressing thesis is that the end of the war would not mean the end of bureaucratic follies, that the habits of regimentation and suppression would live on. She was, of course, quite right.

Galsworthy's book appeared in 1919 under a pseudonym, as by 'A.R. P-M.' One can see why he might have wished to conceal his authorship, for he had been a public-spirited man of letters during the war, giving generously of both his money and his literary talents to war causes, and *The Burning Spear* is about a public-spirited man who tries to support the war with words (he makes speeches), and who finds that his words contradict themselves, and that in the end there is no way of getting beneath the rhetoric of war to the truth. This radical loss of confidence in the medium of language itself is an important element in the post-war mood, a part of the questioning, doubting, denying mood of the Twenties. Galsworthy's lapse was only temporary; he recovered, and went back to writing the conventional novels that he had always written; but others didn't. And it is interesting to find that even into a mind as ordinary as Galsworthy's was, the acid of inevitable lying had bitten deep.

Both *What Not* and *The Burning Spear* are anti-war satires: not, that is, against the actual fighting, but against what the penetrating presence of the war spirit in English society had done to basic human values — to privacy, to freedom, and to truth-telling. In the two books the sense of the war's consequences spreads out, both in space and in time, from the actual war to its world: if this is what war does to human existence, how will its effects ever end?

In the years that followed there were many other satires published, most of them not directly concerned with the war. Here are some representative titles — a few well known, most quite forgotten — from 1919 to 1924. G.A.M., *Six Satires*; Osbert Sitwell, *The Winstonburg Line*; Rose Macaulay, *Potterism*; J.B.M., *Gorgeous Poetry 1911–1920*; Rose Macaulay, *Dangerous Ages*; Belinda Blinders [Desmond Coke], *The Nouveau Poor*; anon., *Cranks 1921*; Osbert Sitwell, *The Jolly Old Squire, or Way-Down in Georgia*; Aldous Huxley, *Crome Yellow*; Bennett, *Mr Prohack*; William Kean Seymour, *A Jackdaw in Georgia*; Wells, *Men Like Gods*; Louis Golding, *The Sea Coast of Bohemia*; Huxley, *Antic Hay*; Noël Coward, *Poems by Hernia Whittlebot* and *Chelsea Buns by Hernia Whittlebot*; A Lady of Quality [Enid Bagnold], *Serena Blandish; or The Difficulty of Getting Married*; Reginald Berkeley, *Unparliamentary Papers*; John Cournos, *The New Candide*; J.C. Squire, *A Grub Street Night's Entertainment*; Rose Macaulay, *Orphan Island*.

If most of these books were short-lived, that is partly because their satire is particular and topical. Most frequently they turn their ridicule upon notable individuals of the time, on Churchill, Lloyd George, and Balfour in the political examples, on a range of writers from Hardy and Kipling to the Sitwells in the literary ones. Most of these objects of satire are older than those who satirize them, and so the satire becomes generational, and demonstrates those divisions in post-war English culture with which this chapter began. Of the literary satires, most are parodic — they satirize style, and the literary movements that those styles identify. So Sitwell and Seymour mock the Georgians and their *Georgian Poetry* anthologies, and Coward and *anon.* mock the Sitwells and *Wheels*. Here, too, the divisions become generational, each generation ridiculing the manner of its elders; and so the spirit of rejection and animosity that grew during the war flowers here after the war — if *flowers* is the correct term for writing which is not on the whole very good.

Satire is the spirit of the post-war years, and that is perhaps the reason for the extraordinary success of the early novels of Aldous Huxley. 'We are grateful to Mr Sitwell,' Huxley wrote in a review of Osbert Sitwell's *Argonaut and Juggernaut* in 1919, 'for having revived one of the most respectable of our home industries, the writing of satire.'[23] It was a home industry that Huxley himself pursued with vigour; his novels of the 1920s — *Crome Yellow*, *Antic Hay*, *Those Barren Leaves*, and *Point*

Counter Point — all express the satiric spirit of the time; if any novel is typical of the Twenties, it is one of these.

Huxley's first novel, *Crome Yellow* (1922), belongs to the well-established English tradition of the country-house novel, and particularly to a sub-division of that tradition, the country-house satire (with Peacock and Evelyn Waugh, among others). The house was modelled closely on Ottoline Morrell's Garsington, the favourite retreat of the Bloomsbury circle and a centre of wartime pacifism; in keeping with the generational point that I have been making, the youngest member of that circle took the first opportunity to satirize his elders. Bertrand Russell, Middleton Murry, Ottoline herself, they are all there, and all are mocked.

Crome Yellow is in one way like the novels of Wells and Rose Macaulay: it has a strong historical location, given it by the numerous contemporary references scattered over its pages. But the point with Huxley is different; he is not concerned with immediate history, but with contemporariness. The references to current ideas and current literary figures are a way of showing his credentials as a thoroughly up-to-date young man. And where historical events and issues do arise, they do so as subjects for conversation: birth control, the Black and Tans, the possibility of state control, these are present not as pressing problems, but as table talk. History itself, the continuum of human events, seems to have come apart; in the now of *Crome Yellow*, there are only current events.

The war enters in the same way — as an occasion for witticisms, for conversational decoration and satiric mockery. 'Personally,' says Gombauld the painter, 'I found the war quite as thorough a holiday from all the ordinary decencies and sanities, all the common emotions and preoccupations, as I ever want to have.'[24] And Huxley tells us little war jokes, like his story of the woman who ate peaches during the war because the government needed peach stones. War is never imagined as fighting and dying; Huxley's imagination does not reach, as Macaulay's and Wells's had both reached during the war, from civilian safety to the actual Front. The war does exist in the novel in one other way, however — Huxley is keenly aware of the war as a gap in history, separating a *before* from an *after*. 'Before the war' means 'In an earlier, innocent, totally different society'; 'Since the war' means 'Having got used to horrors . . .' This is the difference, perhaps, between wartime and post-war imaginations: Huxley, in this as in so much else, was a sensibility of his time.

By the time that Huxley had written his next two satires — *Antic Hay*
and *Those Barren Leaves* — he was recognized as an authentic voice of his
time, and was identified with the emerging myth of the Twenties
(which of course he had helped to create). Here is Conrad Aiken
reviewing *Those Barren Leaves* in the *Criterion*:

> And what could be more appropriate in this post-war world of
> sad, gay disillusionment and scientific luxury, than Mr Huxley's
> macaronic *mélange* of the classical and the up-to-date, of Peacock and
> the *fin-de-siècle*, of Folengo and Freud? Mr Huxley's affinities, in this
> respect, are easy to find. During the last decade there has been what
> one might almost call a macaronic school — an international school
> concerned with satire, with burlesque, and, in the absence of any
> stable convictions concerning art or morals, with the breakdown of
> forms and the extensive use of reference and quotation. If Mr Huxley
> does not go as far as some in the direction of the *cento*, he at any rate
> shares in that tendency.[25]

This is both a version of Huxley and a version of post-war English
culture — sad, gay, disillusioned, satirical, and emptied of convictions.
And, you will note, it is identified as 'this *post-war* world': the war, that
is, is the force that made the world like this. In this world, Huxley and
writers like him are consequences of war, or symptoms of its power.

In this world-after-the-war, satire is more than a literary form; it is an
attitude towards the world, and towards the past — a mocking,
rejecting, dismissive attitude that is the spirit of the post-war time. One
finds it in all literary forms, and in some paintings, and some music
(Walton's score for *Façade* is an obvious example). And one finds it in
other, less likely places — in the documents, for example, in the most
famous literary war of the post-war years, the controversy between
Virginia Woolf and Arnold Bennett.

That war extended over many years, from 1917 until Bennett's death
in 1930, and divided the post-war novel-writing world. One shot in
particular has become a classic of Modernist criticism, and has had a
remarkable effect on the shape of English literary history — that is,
Virginia Woolf's 'Mr. Bennett and Mrs. Brown'. More than any other
critical piece of its time, that essay taught post-war readers how to think
about their fiction-writing contemporaries, and how to divide them into
generations.[26]

Two aspects of this literary battle are notable: the historical terms that
were adopted, and the tone in which it was fought. From the beginning,

Woolf's argument was essentially historical; she treated Bennett and his contemporaries, Galsworthy and Wells, as figures from an outmoded past whose methods were useless for present-day writers, while Bennett defended their work as valid and current. For Woolf, a gap in history had opened in the recent past, and Bennett and novelists like him were on the other side, out of touch and out of reach. For Bennett, no such gap existed; history, including literary history, was a continuous process.

Woolf's view of the past is, of course, the vision of history that is at the heart of the Myth of the War. It is striking, then, that the war never entered her argument as a factor. For her, human character changed not in August 1914, or July 1916, or even November 1918, but 'on or about December 1910'; it was the First Post-Impressionist Show, and the English discovery of the great Russian novelists, that separated the present from the past. In her version of literary history, the military history of millions of men was not a recognized force. Katherine Mansfield had written, in regard to Woolf's *Night and Day*, that 'the novel can't leave the war out'; and indeed Woolf had not left it out of her post-war novels. But she could and did leave it out of her critical polemics; there the past was simply a distant place cluttered with outmoded novels.

The effect of this curious sense of history was to make the post-war English novel an entirely new beginning. There is no immediate past, no continuity with previous generations, no inherited subject: the novel begins again, *now*. And Woolf explained to her contemporaries how reality must be rendered in this new present, and how it must not be. One can see how such a critical stance would appeal to young writers after the war, and why Virginia Woolf took such a prominent place among theorists of Modernist fiction. But there was more to it than theory, I think; she had also found the right post-war tone. She did not argue with Bennett, she satirized and parodied him. Her summaries of his novels, and of those of Galworthy and Wells, are inaccurate and unjust, but they are very clever, and devastatingly dismissive. 'I asked them,' she writes in 'Mr. Bennett and Mrs. Brown'.

> I asked them — they are my elders and betters — How shall I begin to describe this woman's character? And they said: 'Begin by saying that her father kept a shop in Harrogate. Ascertain the rent. Ascertain the wages of the shop assistants in the year 1878. Discover what her mother died of. Describe cancer. Describe calico. Describe — ' But I cried: 'Stop! Stop!'[27]

The terms of the quarrel did not require this ridiculing tone: differences in literary methods had been debated before in less demeaning ways. But the *time* required it: reject, reject the past, the time said; ridicule it, annihilate it with mockery. Choose as your themes discontinuity and destruction, use as your figure of the past the ruins and splinters of a tumbled mansion. Begin again.

There is one other thing about the controversy that is worth noting. Beginning with the first version of 'Mr. Bennett and Mrs. Brown', in 1923, Woolf referred to Bennett and Co. as 'Edwardians' and her contemporaries as 'Georgians', and treated both as generations. 'Georgian' didn't last, no doubt because of the pejorative associations with Edward Marsh and his *Georgian Poetry* anthologies; but 'Edwardian' did, and tied the novelists of Bennett's generation — who were still active and productive in post-war England — to a remote, pre-war past and a fat, dead king:

> Our minds fly straight to King Edward. Surely that was the fatal age, the age which is just breaking off from our own, the age when character disappeared or was mysteriously engulfed, and the culprits, happily still alive, active, and unrepentant, are Mr. Wells, Mr. Galsworthy, and Mr. Bennett himself.[28]

And so a gap in history became a gap in literature, and all of the literature of the past that could be identified with an English monarch was dismissed. The post-war generation would have to start over again, without a monarch to call their own, and without a usable historical past. Between them and their elders a condition of war would exist.

That generation war is commonly perceived as a literary revolution. In that revolution, a principal weapon of the young was satire. But where there is a revolution there will be counter-revolutionaries, the old and the established, and they too had their weapons, which were what they had always been — control, suppression, and censorship.

The story of post-war censorship begins with the same book that began the story of post-war satire — Rose Macaulay's *What Not*. That novel was ready for publication in November 1918, 'when', as Macaulay explained in a note to the published text, 'it was discovered that a slight alteration in the text was essential, to safeguard it against one of the laws of the realm.'[29] Pages were removed, and new pages were tipped in, and the novel finally appeared in 1919 (the British Library copy is dated March 17). To judge from the replacement pages, the offending matter must have had to do with recruiting and censorship during the war, and perhaps with some actual English newspapers. We may conclude that *What Not* was DORA's last wartime victim.

Two years later the London firm of Kegan Paul announced a new book, to be published anonymously: *The Autobiography of a Child*. The unnamed author was a man whom we have come upon before in this study — Cyril Scott, the theosophical young composer who had found Schönberg's music so discordant on the Astral Plane. He was also, coincidentally, the husband of Rose Allatini, whose novel, *Despised and Rejected*, had been suppressed in 1918.[30]

The full title of Scott's book was *The Autobiography of a Child. Written from the Psycho-Sexual-Analytical Standpoint: For Doctors, Parents, Teachers, and Psychologists*. His object, he explained in a preface, was 'to present the child in its entirety, with all its moods (both grave and frivolous), its emotions and passions laid bare . . .'[31] It is a curious book, part Freud and part Edward Carpenter, part post-war, you might say, and part Victorian-Edwardian. In it Scott tells the story of his sexual feelings and experiences, from infancy to maturity; along the way he pauses to urge the legalizing of mutual masturbation between men, and to defend openness in sexual matters generally, arguing that Christ would have agreed.

No sooner had the *Autobiography* appeared than an action was brought against it for obscenity, filed by (who else?) Lord Alfred Douglas. In the trial, which was before the Lord Mayor of London, Lord Alfred conducted his case personally. Against him the defence brought witnesses, including a number of doctors, all of whom testified to the decency and usefulness of the book. The Lord Mayor was unconvinced, and found the book to be obscene; all copies were destroyed, and the type was distributed.

Other suppressions of books during the Twenties have become notorious events in the history of English censorship: *Ulysses* in 1923, *The Well of Loneliness* in 1928, *Lady Chatterley's Lover* in 1929 — each case evidence that the wartime fear of sexuality had not ended with the war. At the same time, there were censorious gestures made towards a number of works of art that extend the range of subjects that post-war conservative society wished to forbid. In 1923 a drawing by Max Beerbohm of King Edward VII in Heaven had to be withdrawn from a Leicester Gallery exhibition after protests; in 1925 Jacob Epstein's memorial to W.H. Hudson caused a great uproar, both in the press and in Parliament, when it was unveiled in Hyde Park (it includes the nude figure of Rima, the bird-girl in *Green Mansions*); in 1926 a painting titled

'The Breakdown', by John B. Souter (see plate 23), was removed from the Royal Academy's summer show (it represented a nude white woman dancing before a seated Negro musician); in 1928 paintings by D.H. Lawrence were confiscated from a London art gallery.

Obscenity was the offence in the Epstein case, but in the others there were further issues at stake. Beerbohm had offended by caricaturing a British monarch, and Lawrence had committed a sacrilege by including among his nude paintings one of the Holy Family. In the case of 'The Breakdown' the offence was not sexual but racial — or perhaps Imperial: the complainant was not the Home Office but the Colonial Office. Souter had clearly intended that his picture should be read as a moral parable: the woman is dancing a breakdown (which the *OED* defines as 'a dance in the peculiar style of the negroes'); but there is another, vaster breakdown represented too. The black saxophonist is seated on the helmeted head of a colossal fallen statue (Britannia, perhaps, or Minerva): what has broken down is classical art, order, values, morality, Western civilization. Reviewers got Souter's point, though they didn't like it[32]; but the Colonial Office saw only a black man (seated and clothed) and a white woman (naked and dancing).

All of these complaints might have been heard in 1900, or for that matter in 1850; they suggest a pre-war sense of propriety. One might conclude from this recital of cases that the spirit of suppression was as strong as it had ever been, and that it was attacking the same kinds of offences. And that does seem to have been true: in the decade beginning with the Armistice writers and artists got into trouble for criticizing kings and governments, for speaking frankly about sex, for representing sexual organs on canvas, for condoning homosexual acts (both male and female), and for painting a black man with a nude white woman. The spirits of DORA, Lord Alfred Douglas, and Queen Victoria seemed to reign on, uninterrupted by the 'liberations' that the war was said to have brought about.

The embattled post-war liberal, in search of some ray of encouragement, might have argued that these cases were not all complete defeats; Rima remained on her site in Hyde Park, and banned books got published in Paris. But these aren't really very consoling points. Rima stayed, but was splashed with paint and otherwise abused; and not all of the banned books were printed elsewhere — Scott's *Autobiography* has never been reissued, not even in Paris (which is a pity, because it has considerable value as a narrative of late-Victorian childhood, and merits a place among the works of English amateur sexologists, with Havelock

Ellis and Carpenter). No, there is not much to cheer the liberal heart in the history of Twenties censorship. Those forces that had been powerful before the war were still powerful.

What was different in the post-war situation was the strength and the articulateness of the opposition to the censoring powers, and the certainty with which the opposing lines were drawn. If the spirit of pre-war censorship continued strong, that other spirit, the spirit of satire, was also strong, clear in its views, and vocal in its protests. The balance of Old and Young had shifted.

PART V

MYTH-MAKING
1926–33

Here we, and the post-war generation too, must leave
it, stunned as we still are from war shock, stumbling
alone perforce as we must among the ruins of happier
times, picking our way among the barren harvest of
war delusion, trying to build homes fit for heroes out
of strewn wreckage.

Caroline E. Playne, *Society at War* (1931)

I think that the only literature of any value my generation (which began to write in 1919) will have to leave is
its War books.

Storm Jameson, *No Time Like the Present* (1933)

CHAPTER 20

The Ten Days' War

A reader who opened his *Times* at breakfast on Saturday, May 1, 1926, would have thought — for a time, at least — that England was at peace, and going about its spring rituals in its usual way, subject only to the hostilities of the English weather. He'd have read about scheduled openings of the polo, cricket, and rowing seasons (all cancelled, as it turned out, because of heavy rain); he'd have seen that the Royal Academy had had its private view of the annual Summer Exhibition, and that the grand opera season at Covent Garden would begin in ten days. Among the theatre notices he would have read that the Astaires were at the Empire and Paul Whiteman was at the Tivoli, and that *The Student Prince, No No Nanette, Saint Joan,* and *White Cargo* were all playing in the West End. The Court Calendar would have told him that the King had returned to Windsor, and that the Duchess of York was gaining strength after the birth of a daughter — Elizabeth, the future Queen.

Only when he reached page 14 would that reader have found any sign that things in England were not altogether serene. There he would have come upon this headline:

COAL CRISIS
NO SETTLEMENT REACHED.
LAST PEACE REPORTS
UNION LEADERS' ATTITUDE.

And as he read on he would learn — if he did not already know it — that beyond his breakfast table, out there in the streets of London and in the mining villages of Wales, disturbing forces were gathering that threatened England's peace. Before May Day was over the Trades Union Congress would do what no TUC had done before: it would order a General Strike, to begin at midnight on Monday, May 3.

During the week that followed, the Strike disrupted English life in many ways. It closed coal mines, halted public transportation, silenced newspapers, and stopped postal deliveries. Individually, such disruptions were not new in post-war Britain: there had been many stoppages since 1918. But occurring together in a General Strike they seemed to be something different and more dangerous — an attack by British workers on British society at large, on British institutions, on Parliamentary government itself. It was not a strike, people said, it was a revolution; it was Bolshevism, it was Communism let loose.

The fear of revolution had hung over English society ever since the Russian Revolution of 1917, thrusting itself into consciousnesses whenever the people came out into the streets *en masse*, or seemed about to do so. Many English men and women thought that a revolution might come in England once the war was over. Arnold Bennett felt a *frisson* on Armistice Night at the sight of the mobs outside; Beatrice Webb thought revolution a possible consequence of the peace, and so did Gilbert Murray. And when popular writers like Buchan and Sapper looked round for anti-English villains to frighten their readers, they chose Bolsheviks. So it is not surprising that once the Strike had begun, government spokesmen fed the nation's fear with inflammatory words, and spoke, in Parliament and out of it, of revolution.

A revolution was a fearful thing because it was unknown, a bloody sequence of events that happened over there on the continent, among foreigners. A *war*, on the other hand, was familiar; Englishmen had recently survived one, and they could surely survive another. And so it was with a kind of relief that people saw that England caught up in a General Strike was very like England in wartime. Certainly it looked like a war. The ordinary Londoner, walking the streets during the days of the Strike, might well have felt that he was back in the days of 1914–18. There were men in khaki uniforms on street corners, special constables patrolling in tin helmets, troops guarding the docks, and naval ratings running the electrical and power services. Volunteers queued at recruiting stations, and armoured cars passed carrying armed soldiers. Tent-camps went up in Hyde Park; there were rumours of food shortages.

Rhetorically, too, the Strike was a reversion to the days of the war. 'It is a conflict,' Winston Churchill declared in the Commons on the 3rd, 'which, if it is fought to a conclusion, can only end in the overthrow of Parliamentary government or in its decisive victory.'[1] And Labour, the opposing force, was even more bellicose. 'We are willing to face the music,' Labour MP Jack Jones declared,

> We have faced it before. The men who fought from 1914 to 1918, 40,000 of them have come back and are in the East End, are quite as ready to put their back to the wall in opposition to those who want to force wages down, as they were to fight the Germans. We are willing to fight now. Bring out all your horse, foot and artillery. Threaten us with what you like. We are going to have peace if we can get it, but we are not going to be told that we are to be starved into submission; we are not going to be told that all the power of the State is to be organised against us ... No, we are willing to go through anything necessary. We may be strong enough before this fight finishes. You have declared war upon us by these Regulations. If it is to be war, we are ready to face the issue. Do your damnedest; we are out to fight![2]

Asquith, too, saw the Strike as a war though, being an ironic man, he saw it as an ironic one. 'Can there be a more singular and a more lamentable fact,' he asked in the House of Lords,

> than that at a time when we are all, in the international sphere, hymning the praises and propagating the doctrine of disarmament, here at home in England and in Scotland, in the freest of all the free countries of the world, we should be witnessing a resort to an unexampled step — one of the cruellest, because the most undiscriminating, of all forms of warfare?[3]

And the Prime Minister, Stanley Baldwin, took up the rhetorical figure of war when he addressed the people on the BBC: 'Good citizens', he said, '... will "keep steady" whatever happens, as steady as they kept during the worst days of the war.'[4]

Only one voice was raised against the rhetorical battle. 'Let us avoid the language of war,' Lord Henry Cecil cautioned the Commons:

> Do not let us speak about people having victories, or beating one another. We do not want to beat anyone. Do not let us indulge, though we are all susceptible to it in these times, in excessive suspicion ... Let us avoid the language of suspicion

and let us avoid the analogy of war, which one is so tired of in these matters.[5]

But if Lord Henry was tired of that language, no one else seems to have been. It continued throughout the Strike, inflaming and simplifying the issues.

One reason for its continuance was the fact that the government had put Churchill, then Chancellor of the Exchequer, in command of its retaliatory forces. Churchill was a military leader by nature, and he led his government forces into battle like a cavalry commander leading a charge. When the printers struck, and closed down most British newspapers, Churchill launched his own, the *British Gazette*, which by the end of the week had the largest print-run of any newspaper in the world — nearly two and a quarter million copies.[6] This does not necessarily mean that its readership was the largest, since distribution was apparently a matter of dumping bundles of papers on to street corners and from RAF planes on to mining villages, but, in the absence of competition, it must have had a considerable audience.

The *British Gazette* was a wartime publication, and Churchill filled its columns with recruiting propaganda and official statements. Those statements seem modelled on wartime dispatches, and some are extra-ordinary for the wartime powers they assigned, like this one:

> The following announcement is made by his Majesty's Government:
> All ranks of the Armed Forces of the Crown are hereby notified that any action which they may find it necessary to take in an honest endeavour to aid the Civil Power will receive, both now and afterwards, the full support of his Majesty's Government.[7]

Churchill even found space for war poems: not new ones for the occasion, but poems that had inspired Englishmen in other wars, like Kipling's 'For All We Have and Are', which had first appeared in *The Times* in September 1914. And in the last issue, when it was all over, he proclaimed the government's victory in military terms: 'General Strike Off ... Surrender Received by Premier in Downing Street.'[8]

The rhetoric was the same in Parliament: belligerent, confrontational, uncompromising, and heavy with the words of war. It was as though, after the difficult issues of the post-war years, Englishmen in general, and their leaders in particular, had turned with relief to a familiar vocabulary of conflict. For the ten days of the Strike, Members of

Parliament postured like generals and roared like cannons, and fought a war without leaving the House.

Because the combatants imagined that they were engaged in a war, they thought of its end, as they had thought of the end of the Great War, as necessarily a matter of absolute victory or absolute defeat. And so it turned out to be. The TUC surrendered unconditionally on May 13, and though the miners doggedly continued their fight alone for another six months, they too capitulated at last, and returned to the pits on the mine-owners' terms, to work longer hours for lower pay.

While it continued, the Strike drove other problems out of English minds: like the war, it created a present in which nothing customary seemed to happen, and only the Strike was real. Diaries and letters of the time read very much like civilian records of August 1914. 'An exact diary of the Strike would be interesting,' Virginia Woolf wrote on May 5; and she kept one, and it *is* interesting. 'For instance,' she continued,

> it is now a 1/4 to 2: there is a brown fog; nobody is building; it is drizzling. The first thing in the morning we stand at the window & watch the traffic in Southampton Row. This is incessant. Everyone is bicycling; motor cars are huddled up with extra people. There are no buses. No placards. No newspapers. The men are at work in the road; water, gas & electricity are allowed; but at 11 the light was turned off ... It is all tedious & depressing, rather like waiting in a train outside a station. Rumours are passed round — that the gas wd. be cut off at 1 — false of course. One does not know what to do. And nature has laid it on thick today — fog, rain, cold.[9]

That brown fog will serve as a metaphor for a state of mind that continued while the Strike lasted. Woolf reported those days fully in her diary, and wrote virtually nothing in her entries that was not about the Strike, yet there are no *facts* in her account: what she wrote was a record of a wartime state of mind — of uncertainty and ignorance and waiting, of rumours and counter-rumours. 'One believes nothing,' she wrote on the 6th; '. . . So we go on, turning in our cage. I notice how frequently we break off with "Well I don't know".' She groped for metaphors that would describe the feeling of living in that uncertain crisis: 'more than anything,' she decided, 'it is like a house where someone is dangerously ill.' But no metaphor was adequate. 'It beggars description,' she wrote to her sister, Vanessa Bell; the only way to imagine it was to 'recall the worst days of the war'.[10]

Other personal responses have much the same quality — of a strange existence, of crisis beyond definition, for which the war offered the only analogy. 'I have lost my day-dreams,' Beatrice Webb wrote in her diary at the end of the Strike, 'I have only the nightmare left — the same sort of nightmare I had during the Great War; that European civilisation is in the course of dissolution . . .'[11] Such responses suggest that it was not only public services that the Strike had disrupted; it had shaken such hopes and expectations as had survived the war.

One lost illusion was the dream that many working-class men had brought home from the Front — the dream that the war, in which working men had fought beside men of the middle and upper classes, would make a difference in the nature of the English class system. Surely now that the war was over, men who had survived it would carry their wartime spirit of comradeship into peacetime. The events of 1926 showed them how wrong and how innocent they had been: the 'land fit for heroes' would be as class-ridden as it had been before the war began. Some had also hoped that returning soldiers would be a political force that would work for peace; 1926 showed that no such force, no such unity existed. Others — the most radical — had hoped for revolution, now that Russia had shown that it might be done; that, too, the failure of the Strike denied. For such reasons as these, the end of the Strike was more than simply the end of an industrial action; it was the end of hope that the war might still have some positive consequences in the lives of the men who had fought it.

It is not surprising that English novelists whose works dealt with immediate history should have turned at once to the General Strike as a subject. Within two years, General Strike novels had been written by the two most popular English novelist-historians: H.G. Wells's *Meanwhile* (1927) and John Galsworthy's *Swan Song* (1928). Here were two novelists who saw the world in very different terms — Wells a heterodox Socialist, Galsworthy an Edwardian Liberal. But they agreed on two central points: that the Strike was a social crisis of great importance for Britain, and that the way to treat it in fiction was in the language of war.

Meanwhile begins in the spring of 1926 in a villa in Italy, where a young English coal-mine owner, Philip Rylands, has gathered a party of talkative guests, and for a time it proceeds as a house-party novel in the manner of *Crome Yellow* and the early chapters of *Women in Love* — garrulous, opinionated people talking about large issues. But the General Strike interrupts the party, and Rylands returns to London to

observe events, and to write long letters to his wife — which are Wells's
analyses and judgements of the whole affair, and amount to nearly a
quarter of the novel's length.

Those letters are written partly by the Wells of *The Outline of History*
and partly by the Wells of *Boon*. *Outline*-Wells provides the cosmic-
historian's view of the Strike as the expression of a stage in British
history — capital and labour reacting to the post-war decline of the
British Empire, each side trying to impose the cost of that decline on the
other, 'a world change being treated as a British political and social
row'. Workers and employers call each other 'the enemy', Wells
observes, but the enemy is in fact time and fate, geography and
necessity.[12]

That is *Outline*-Wells being Olympian. *Boon*-Wells enters whenever
the subject shifts from world change to the particulars of the political
and social row as it was being enacted in London. Observing the trade
unionists and the politicians at their battle-stations, Rylands remarks:
'I am disposed to call this General Strike the Silliest Thing in the
History of England,' and he goes on to enumerate the follies of both
sides — the government dressing its citizens up in tin helmets; the
strikers closing down the newspapers in which their appeals to the
public might have been printed; soldiers and police going about looking
for a revolution that wasn't there; and rushing around in the midst of the
confusion, doing everything everywhere, Winston Churchill, 'gone
clean off his head'. And at this point Wells turned from words to
sketches, as he had done in *Boon*, to render the follies that were beyond
language:[13]

Winston doing anything

Meanwhile is characteristic of Wells in its unstable mixing of the detached historian and the exasperated prophet: we have seen them both before. But there are elements in this novel that are new to the Wells vision. One is that though the book is concerned with large movements in history, the historical scale is a very short one. 'After the war,' Rylands writes to his wife, 'to go back to the beginnings . . .'[14] However one defines England's problems, Wells seemed to be saying, they began at the war's end, and what happened before then was simply not relevant to an understanding of the present.

There is another note in *Meanwhile* which, if not entirely new to Wells, is new to his post-war writing. One finds it in Rylands's conclusions about the Strike, and about England. Here the voice of Wells speaks not in words of prophecy and vast projections and world religions, but in anger and confusion. This is also the concluding note of *Boon*, and one might perhaps conclude that in *Meanwhile* Wells once more felt himself to be the one rational man in a nation irrationally stumbling into war. 'This muddle,' Rylands writes from London,

> this dislocated, leaderless country, finding its level in a new world so clumsily and dangerously, this crazy fight against a phantom revolution, is Reality. It is England 1926.[15]

And in a later and angrier passage:

> Is all life a comedy of fools? Am I *taking myself too seriously* and all that? Here is a crisis in the history of one of the greatest, most intelligent, best educated countries in the world, and it is an imbecile crisis![16]

A sub-plot in *Meanwhile* expresses another new theme, and looks ahead to crises still to come. While Rylands is in London witnessing the collapse of the Strike, his wife back in Italy is dealing with Fascism. Into her garden one night an Italian liberal politician staggers, on the run from Fascist thugs. She shelters him, and later smuggles him across the border to freedom. Wells offers this episode not simply as an incident in Italian politics but as a foreshadowing of a new kind of world conflict — an international war between murderous reactionaries and the progressive spirit. The Italian fugitive draws Wells's moral:

> Nothing is safe in life. Now I know. What has happened in Italy may happen all over the world. The malignant, the haters of new things and fine things, the morally limited, the violent and intense, the men who work the State against us, are everywhere. Why did we not see

it? Man civilises slowly, slowly. Eternal vigilance is the price of civilisation.[17]

As far as I know *Meanwhile* is the first English novel to treat Fascism as a world force of future violence; in this respect it is, one might say, the first novel of the Thirties. But what does Italian Fascism have to do with an English General Strike? The connection, in Wells's mind, seems to have been something like this. The Strike was a late stage in the post-war disintegration of the old order: the old England, the old Empire, the old world-before-the-war — those systems that lost their authority and their justification in the events of 1914–18. Reality in 1926 was disloca-tion and muddle; and into that vacuum a new ordering force was flowing: authoritarianism, Fascism. Wells's performance as a prophet continued to be impressive.

If *Meanwhile* is the first Thirties novel, Galsworthy's *Swan Song* is the last Edwardian one. And that is appropriate enough; for of all the novelists of their generation, Wells looked most persistently forward, and Galsworthy most determinedly back. *Swan Song* is a contemporary novel, in the sense that it is located in 1926, and begins with the General Strike. But it also has another kind of location: it stands at the end of the long chronicle of Forsyte fortunes that began with *The Man of Property* in 1906, and it ends with a death — the death of Soames Forsyte, the man of property himself.

The essential subject of *Swan Song* is permanence and change — what can survive, and what cannot. Galsworthy wanted to believe that history was coherent and continuous, that the past persisted, that the war had changed nothing essential in English life, that England would always be England. He said those things again and again in essays, and in the earlier Forsyte novels, and he said them in *Swan Song* — a bit desperately now, perhaps, but he said them. But he also grappled with change, for this novel concerns the death of Soames, the last represen-tative of Victorian and Edwardian values, and the succession of the next generation.

The General Strike appears in the novel as an attempt to change England, an attempt that fails because the English character will not allow it to succeed. Here is Soames's son-in-law, Michael Mont, responding to the news that the Strike has ended:

> There it was! For a minute he sat motionless with a choky feeling, such as he had felt when the news of the Armistice came through. A sword lifted from over the head of England! A source of pleasure to

her enemies dried up! People passed and passed him, each with a
news-sheet, or a look in the eye. They were taking it almost as
soberly as they had taken the strike itself. 'Good old England! We're a
great people when we're up against it!' he thought, driving his car
slowly on into Trafalgar Square.[18]

For Galsworthy, the Strike is simply another national war, which
England has won; he even refers to it as 'the Great Strike', in direct echo
of 'the Great War', and the analogy continues through the Strike
chapters; in terms of causes, of loyalties, of emotions the two 'wars'
are alike. And if that is so, then the collapse of the Strike means
that England will remain England — Galsworthy's England, Soames
Forsyte's England, bourgeois, property-owning England. Revolution,
the threat of violent and destructive change, has been defeated.

Towards the end of the novel Soames travels westward to visit the
countryside of his Forsyte forebears in Dorset, and there, in a field
that ancestral Forsytes had owned, he meditates on the past, and on
change:

> In the old time here, without newspapers, with nothing from the
> outer world, you'd grow up without any sense of the State or that
> sort of thing. There'd be the church and your bible, he supposed, and
> the market some miles away, and you'd work and eat and sleep and
> breathe the air and drink your cider and embrace your wife and watch
> your children, from June to June; and a good thing, too! What more
> did you do now that brought you any satisfaction? 'Change, it's all on
> the surface,' thought Soames; 'the roots are the same. You can't get
> beyond them — try as you will!' Progress, civilisation, what were
> they for?[19]

You might expect that Soames's thoughts about permanence and
change would close the novel, and bring the final episode of the Forsyte
chronicle to an end with an affirmation of essential permanence, for by
now Soames was Galsworthy. This had not always been the case.
Soames had begun life in *The Man of Property* as the embodiment of the
man Galsworthy most detested, his wife's first husband; but as the
chronicle grew, through six volumes and twenty years, he had changed,
until at the end he spoke with his inventor's own unmistakably
Edwardian voice.

But it is not Soames who has the last word; it is Michael Mont, a
representative of the new generation, the new man of property. In the

climactic scene, in which Soames's house is destroyed by fire and
Soames is fatally injured, it is Mont who points the moral:

> He looked back at the house, still marked and dishevelled by fire and
> water. And melancholy brooded in his heart, as if the dry grey spirit
> of its late owner were standing beside him looking at the passing
> away of his possessions, of all that on which he had lavished so much
> time and trouble. 'Change,' thought Michael, 'there's nothing but
> change. It's the one constant.'[20]

Like Wells, Galsworthy was a double man, though in his case it was
a different duality, part Edwardian traditionalist and part reluctant
modern man. The traditionalist saw the war and the General Strike as
two vast efforts to disorder England. Both had failed: there had been no
German victory and no workers' revolution. Those threats had been
defeated, not by strategies or tactics or high principles, but simply by
the intransigent Englishness of the English. *Swan Song* says this clearly
enough, but when Galsworthy reprinted the novel in the second Forsyte
trilogy, *A Modern Comedy*, in 1929, he took the occasion to make the
point even more explicitly in a preface. The war, he wrote, had been a
four-year earthquake in which everyone had lost the habit of standing
still. 'And yet,' he went on,

> the English character has changed very little, if at all. The General
> Strike of 1926, with which the last part of this trilogy begins, supplied
> proof of that. We are still a people that cannot be rushed, distrustful of
> extremes, saved by the graces of our defensive humour, well-
> tempered, resentful of interference, improvident and wasteful, but
> endowed with a certain genius for recovery. If we believe in nothing
> much else, we still believe in ourselves.[21]

That is Edwardian Galsworthy, asserting that the English tradition is a
national characteristic, a sort of dominant English gene (but one not
found in the working class, apparently). Further on in the Preface the
other Galsworthy speaks, in a series of anxious questions: 'What is to
come?' he asks:

> Will contentment yet be caught? How will it all settle down? Will things
> ever again settle down — who knows? Are there to come fresh wars,
> and fresh inventions hot-foot on those not yet mastered and digested?[22]

These questions have no answers in the Preface, as they had none in
Galsworthy's mind; they simply express the feeling that he put into

Michael Mont's thought: 'there's nothing but change. It's the one constant.'

For both Wells and Galsworthy the post-war years were a period of disordered confusion and division, in which the General Strike took on symbolic significance, and became a little war in itself. It was a war the outcome of which was less clear than the World War had been; Galsworthy saw it as a victory for England, Wells as a war that both sides lost. But what is important, in this history of English imaginations, is that both writers, their minds full of the recent war, took the Strike to be another war, to be rendered in the same language, the same images. And by imagining it as a war, they turned it into the termination of something — a disruption that was simply the violent end of a conflict in society.

Other writers more Modern than either Wells or Galsworthy looked back to the time of the General Strike and saw an end there. Wyndham Lewis, introducing a volume of his memoirs in 1937, wrote:

> I find a good way of dating after the war is to take the General Strike, 1926, as the next milestone. I call 'post-war' between the War and the General Strike. Then began a period of a new complexion. It was no longer 'post-war'. We needn't *call* it anything. It's just the period we're living in to-day.[23]

And Eliot took the same date as an end, though he was more precise as to what had ended:

> The period immediately following the war of 1914 is often spoke of as a time of disillusionment: in some ways and for some people it was rather a period of illusions. Only from about the year 1926 did the features of the post-war world begin clearly to emerge — and not only in the sphere of politics. From about that date one began slowly to realise that the intellectual and artistic output of the previous seven years had been rather the last efforts of an old world, than the first struggles of a new.[24]

That output included Eliot's own *Waste Land*, as well as *Ulysses*, *Mrs Dalloway*, *Façade*, and the post-war paintings of Nash and Lewis: the heart of what is usually thought of as English Modernism. And, said Eliot, it had come to an end.

One might describe the period that ended in 1926 in various ways. It was a time of disillusionment with the war and its leaders and, as Eliot added, of illusions too, a time of muddle and disunity. In the arts it was, as Eliot recognized, a period of experiment and formulation, when artists sought for the forms of this new disunity in art, and offered them to society as images of society's condition. It was a period in which the war seemed continuously present, but in which it did not find great expression, so that it seemed to some thoughtful people to have become already a dead subject. Virginia Woolf, keeping her 'exact diary' of the Strike in 1926, wrote: 'I believe it is false psychology to think that in after years these details will be interesting. The war is now barren sand after all.'[25] Eliot agreed. 'Perhaps the most significant thing about the war', he wrote in the *Criterion*, 'is its *insignificance*.'[26]

If the war was finally over in 1926 — over, that is, as an urgent imaginative problem — then perhaps English artists could turn their imaginations to other issues. And did they? Some certainly did. It was after the Strike, for example, that Virginia Woolf turned and looked back to the world before the war, and came to terms with her parents, and her own Victorian family life, in *To the Lighthouse*. It was after the Strike that Eliot turned to the Church, announced his new institutional loyalties — Anglo-Catholic, Royalist and Classicist — and began the series of religious poems that became *Ash Wednesday*. And it was in 1926 that Wyndham Lewis began to publish the series of aggressive books that defined his philosophical position and attacked his enemies: *The Art of Being Ruled* (1926), *Time and Western Man* (1927), *The Childermass* (1928) and *Paleface* (1929). 'During the "post-war" I was incubating and was pretty silent,' Lewis later wrote. 'I buried myself. I disinterred myself in 1926, the year of the General Strike — but as a philosopher and critic.'[27] For these writers, at least, a new era, with new necessities and possibilities, opened in the mid-Twenties. Something had ended, something had begun.

A similar sense of new directions is evident in an important critical book published in the year after the Strike — *A Survey of Modernist Poetry*, by Laura Riding and Robert Graves. The *Survey* is the first book in English, so far as I can discover, to use *Modernist* as an adjective identifying avant-garde writing, but it has other and more important significances. It is the first critical book in English to give scrupulous literary definition to the post-war movement in poetry; and it is the first to demonstrate a new critical method for dealing with Modernist texts — the method that would come to be called 'The New Criticism'. If Modernism was created in the earlier part of the decade, it was defined, analysed, and located in literary history in the latter part, beginning here.

The *Survey* is also important in another way, as a document in the history of imagining the war. For most of its length the book scarcely mentions the war as a literary event at all — as though it had indeed been proved 'barren sand'. The authors note in passing that 'a great many poets were carried through to popular recognition on the wave of the war who would otherwise never have been heard from again', but they have little to say about war poems, and quote only one — Owen's 'Dulce et Decorum Est ...' Their Modernism is largely a post-war phenomenon, and their examples from poets like Cummings, Marianne Moore, Eliot and Pound have little to say about the war.

Nevertheless, the war does enter the argument — or rather, elements of the emerging Myth of the War do. Riding and Graves assumed, for example, that a gap in history opened between the pre-war and post-war years, and that literary movements from before the war — movements like Georgianism and Imagism — sank into that gap, and were dead and irrelevant to post-war imaginations. But most significantly, they hypothesized a generation, created by the war, which in their argument became synonymous with the Modernist sensibility. Their account of this generation begins with Hemingway's *The Sun Also Rises*, and continues in this defining paragraph:

> Above all things, [this generation] is interested in self-preservation. It is therefore an intensely serious generation in its way, whose wilful cheerfulness is often mistaken for drunken frivolousness: a generation that the War came upon at its most impressionable stage and taught the necessity for a self-protective scepticism of the stability of all human relationships, particularly of all national and religious institutions, of all existing moral codes, of all sentimental formulas for future harmony. From the War it also learned a scale of emotional excitement and depression with which no subsequent variations can compete; yet the scale was too nervously destructive to be wished for again. The disillusion of the War has been completed by the Peace, by the continuation of the old regime patched up with political Fascism, by the same atmosphere of suspense that prevailed from 1911 to the outbreak of nationalistic war and now again gathering around further nationalistic and civil wars.[28]

Here, in a book on modern poetry, a book that seemed determined to avoid the war, the war enters as a most powerful defining force for the authors' generation. There is no better statement of that generation's state of mind at that point, just past the end of 'post-war'.

What are we to make of these examples of self-definition and re-direction in the years just after the General Strike? Are they simply separate instances of creative adults, approaching their middle years, attempting to organize and clarify their lives? Or was there something new and unifying here, a sense of a time and place and state of mind out of which new modes of creation might come? Had these people learned, through the war and the post-war years, how to live, how to imagine, and how to create in a discontinuous world cut off from history? Had Modernism become not a revolutionary fragmentation of reality, but simply the way things are, the new Condition of England? Yes, I would say, to those last three questions.

One might argue, I think, that two things had happened to bring this state of mind into being, and into focus. First, the war and the years that followed immediately after it had dismantled the securities and values of the past, and had made the world before the war seem irrelevant; and then the Strike, war's echo in society, had occurred, and had forced another gap in the continuity of history. Once that gap had opened, the past was sufficiently distanced to leave a space in imaginations for new ideas to fill. A social war, and beyond that gap the Great War, had receded into history and had become the past. And because that past was cut off from the present, one could look away from it. Though as we shall see, one could also look back with a new mythologizing eye.

For the war generation, the General Strike had come as an ending. But for the next generation, the one that had come of age since the war, it was a beginning — the first political event of their adult — or nearly adult — lives. Those who were university students, or recent graduates, took the Strike mainly as a sort of rag, an opportunity to abandon studies or work and play at soldiering — in a mood that was like the mood of some of their student-elders in 1914. Most of them went with their social class, to support the government, and drove trams and lorries, or unloaded cargos on the docks, or became special constables. Rex Warner went to Hull and drove trams there; Alec Waugh enrolled himself as a special constable; his brother Evelyn was too drunk on the first day of the Strike to do anything except drink, but he signed up a week later, and was given a tin hat 'and such military necessities', just in time to hear that the Strike had ended.[29] Graham Greene, just settling in to a job on *The Times*, stayed at his work (*The Times* was the only London paper that continued to appear throughout the strike, though in a reduced form), and so became a strike-breaker, a blackleg. He also became a special constable, and walked up and down Vauxhall Bridge, defending it against an enemy that never appeared.[30]

Many of these young men would in the following decade become militant supporters of the Left and the working class; but in 1926 they were politically innocent: 'the middle-class', as Greene later wrote, 'had not yet been educated by the hunger marchers.'[31] Some of them nevertheless joined the workers' cause. W.H. Auden drove his car in London for the Trades Union Congress, Day Lewis drove between Oxford and the TUC's London headquarters, and Hugh Gaitskell drove for the Oxford Strike Committee. For some of them, and particularly for those who sided with the workers, the experience was more than a lark. 'The impact of the Strike', Gaitskell later wrote,

> was sharp and sudden, a little like a war, in that everybody's lives were suddenly affected by a new unprecedented situation, which forced us to abandon plans for pleasure, to change our values and adjust our priorities.
>
> Above all we had to make a choice, and how we chose was a clear test of our political outlook . . .[32]

Again the comparison is to a war; but this one is a *political* war. The political Thirties may be said to have begun here, for this generation at least. And with the intrusion of politics, and especially of left-wing politics, into the intellectual lives of the young, Modernism changed direction, and became something else — a literature of engagement that faced forward, towards the next world war.

CHAPTER 21

The War Becomes Myth

I

In English art and literature of the years that Lewis called 'post-war', there were many ideas that had their origins in the war, and many oblique manifestations of the war's continuing presence. But there were very few enduring images of the actual war: no imagined version of the war from the years between 1919 and 1926 has entered the canon. The great war poems and most of the major English war paintings already existed — they had been created during the war years or, in the case of a few paintings, in the first year after the Armistice. But the important prose works had yet to be written. For a period of nearly a decade, there was a curious imaginative silence about the greatest occurrence of recent history.

That silence is not simply an historian's after-the-fact creation: writers noticed it at the time, and speculated on its causes. A matter of taste, said Osbert Sitwell: it was 'Very bad form/To mention the war'. Eric Partridge agreed: 'with the Armistice', he wrote, 'came a violent reaction, against not so much war as the Great War, applying equally to art, literature and conversation: it was "bad form" to mention it.' H.M. Tomlinson thought it was a publishers' conspiracy, and the *Annual Register*'s reviewer insisted that 'for ten years there had been a hushed taboo on the expression of war-feeling'.[1]

For some writers the silence had a psychological explanation. 'All who had engaged in the war,' Herbert Read wrote,

all who had lived through the war years, had for more than a decade refused to consider their experience. The mind has a faculty for dismissing the debris of its emotional conflicts until it feels strong enough to deal with them. The war, for most people, was such a conflict, and they never 'got straight' on it.[2]

Robert Graves used a physiological metaphor to make a similar point: the danger and noise of war filled the blood with a kind of drug, he said, and ten years had to elapse 'before the blood is running fairly clear again'.[3] For others, the cause lay in the difficulty of the subject itself. 'Those who have attempted to convey any real war experience,' Richard Aldington wrote,

> sincerely, unsentimentally, avoiding ready-made attitudes (pseudo-heroic or pacifist or quasi-humorous), must have felt the torturing sense of something incommunicable ... It wasn't a question of anyone's being brave; it was a question of trying to communicate the incommunicable.[4]

But however the explanation was expressed, one fact was accepted — that for most of the Twenties the war had not been significantly imagined, in any form.

At about the time of the General Strike this situation began to change, and the great period of English prose-writing about the war began. In the years that followed, the classic war books were published, and the Myth of the War was defined and fixed in the version that still retains authority. You can see this process of emergence in a simple calendar of the publications of those years:

> 1926: Ford Madox Ford, *A Man Could Stand Up*; T.E. Lawrence, *Seven Pillars of Wisdom* (the private printing); Herbert Read, *In Retreat*;
>
> 1927: Lawrence, *Revolt in the Desert* (the public version of *Seven Pillars*); Mark VII (Max Plowman), *A Subaltern on the Somme*;
>
> 1928: Ford, *Last Post*; Edmund Blunden, *Undertones of War*; Siegfried Sassoon, *Memoirs of a Fox-hunting Man*; E.E. Cummings, *The Enormous Room*; Arnold Zweig, *The Case of Sergeant Grischa*;
>
> 1929: R.C. Sherriff, *Journey's End*; Erich Maria Remarque, *All Quiet on the Western Front*; Richard Aldington, *Death of a Hero*; Robert Graves, *Good-bye to All That*; Ernest Hemingway, *A Farewell to Arms*; Ernst Jünger, *Storm of Steel*; Charles Carrington (Charles Edmonds), *A Subaltern's War*;
>
> 1930: Henry Williamson, *Patriot's Progress*; Sassoon, *Memoirs of an Infantry Officer*; Private 19022 (Frederic Manning), *Her Privates We*;

1931: *The Poems of Wilfred Owen* (Blunden's new edition, with his memoir);

1933: Vera Brittain, *Testament of Youth;* Herbert Read, *The End of a War.*

Why did these war books come when they did, to break the conspiracy of silence? Various explanations might be ventured. One might simply say that narrative is a retrospective and deliberate mode, that the past takes its time in becoming history, and that in the case of the First World War ten years was the necessary gestation period. Or that the horrors of the war had to be distanced in time before they could merge into narrative shape and become a story. Or perhaps one might argue that it is only after the passage of years that recollection can become an act of exorcism. Or that the presence, there at the end of the decade, of a possible future war made the telling of the past war's story both possible and imperative. Perhaps all of these explanations are parts of the truth.

The classic narratives of the war that were written in the late Twenties share many elements: common themes, a common language, a common range of tones. But perhaps most importantly, they share a sense of history, and it seems best to enter the great myth-making period on this point, for it is here that the Myth most clearly connects with the Modernist tradition as a whole, and so participates most directly in the imaginative world of art and literature that we still inhabit.

There are two basic narrative forms into which war narratives divide: call them the Autobiographical and the Historical, or the Personal and the General, or the Small Picture and the Large. Autobiographical narrative takes individual experience of war as its entire subject, beginning when the narrator's personal war begins and ending when it ends, and excluding all other modes of existence, whether before or during or after the war, as fundamentally different from war and so irrelevant. History is rendered as discontinuity: *now* does not follow from *then,* war is not a consequence, and the world before the war is not a cause. The war simply *is,* and when it ceases to be, the story ends. The individual's experience will have the same discontinuity, for a single soldier cannot comprehend the war in which he fights. Incoherence therefore must be an aspect of war's reality, to be represented, not ordered.

The great example of the autobiographical mode in war fiction is Erich Remarque's *All Quiet,* which was published in England in March 1929. The novel begins in the mind of a young recruit as he enlists in the

German army, apparently in 1915, and ends in the last month when he is
killed by a sniper's bullet. The events in between occur in a linear
chronological order, but the story is not a continuous narrative. It is
told, rather, in short fragments, ninety-two of them by my count,
which constitute a narrative model of individual experience in war.
Shells explode, men die, new recruits appear, an attack is made, the war
goes on. Nothing here causes what follows; everything is broken and
fragmentary, and the relations between fragments are not logical or
causal, but ironic, as in this example:

> One morning two butterflies play in front of our trench. They are
> brimstone-butterflies, with red spots on their yellow wings. What can
> they be looking for here? There is not a plant nor a flower for miles.
> They settle on the teeth of a skull.[5]

Remarque's irony, which is evident everywhere in the book — in the
title, in the largest organization of episodes, in vignettes like this one,
and in the smallest particulars of style — creates a tone that is the
dominant tone of the classic war books. This war-world, with its
butterflies and skulls, its quiet fronts on which men die violently, is
ironic in its essential nature. War has disturbed the familiar world of
values and meanings, leaving only contradictions, denials, conflicts,
tensions, incoherences. Irony does not resolve these confusions;
it simply acknowledges them, leaving the whole idea of values in
question. The book ends when the young narrator dies, not when its
issues are resolved (the war is still being fought on the last page: only
Paul Bäumer's war is over).

Among English non-fiction narratives of this kind, one of the best is
Edmund Blunden's *Undertones of War,* published a few months before
All Quiet. Blunden was a very young, very naive officer (he was only
nineteen when he first went into action); he obeyed orders, did his duty
without any claim to particular distinction, and survived, as he put it, by
luck. His story is the whole of his war, and no more: it begins when he
is ordered to France (the first sentence is 'I was not anxious to go'), and
ends not with the Armistice, but in March 1918, when he is ordered
back to England; as with Remarque's Paul Bäumer, the end of the war is
the end of *his* war. The intervening events are told simply and without
judgement, as a naive young man overwhelmed by the vastness of war
might tell them, episodically, discontinuously, as he experienced them.

Throughout the book Blunden shows a self-conscious awareness of
the confusions that must necessarily attend upon his telling. Of bitter

fighting on the Ancre he writes: 'the singular part of the battle was that no one . . . could say what had happened, or what was happening,'[6] and later, near Ypres:

> In this vicinity a peculiar difficulty would exist for the artist to select the sights, faces, words, incidents, which characterised the time. The art is rather to collect them, in their original form of incoherence.[7]

Incoherence appears again in the 'Preliminary' note that he wrote for the book:

> Why should I not write it?
>   I know that the experience to be sketched in it is very local, limited, incoherent; that it is almost useless, in the sense that no one will read it who is not already aware of all the intimations and discoveries in it, and many more, by reason of having gone the same journey. No one? Some, I am sure; but not many. *Neither will they understand* – that will not be all my fault.[8]

Discontinuity, incoherence, irony: these terms define a conception of history that the individual, autobiographical narratives of war assume and render.

The other kind of war narrative — the historical or general narrative of war — offers what seems at first a very different model of history. In this kind of book the historical range is spacious, reaching back to the world before the war, and forward to the world after, and placing the war in the space between those worlds, as the agent of historical transformation. We have seen that before-during-after narrative model before, in novels of the early Twenties that attempted to render the social changes that the war brought to English society — novels like Rose Macaulay's *Potterism* and Wells's *Christina Alberta's Father*. It is also the model on which some of the most important war narratives were constructed.

A classic example is Robert Graves's *Good-bye to All That*. We think of Graves's book as a war memoir, but in fact only a little more than half of it is directly concerned with Graves's wartime life. It is, rather, a record of historical change in England during the first three decades of this century: Edwardian England in the first hundred pages, Twenties England in the last hundred, and between those radically different decades the transforming force — the great disruption of the war. Because Graves was a child in the first of these worlds, a soldier in the second, and a young adult in the third, the process of change that he recorded was personal; but it was also general and social; while he looked on, a comfortable middle-class life came to an end, a generation's expectations died, and a disordered new society came into being. Seen in its entirety, the beginning and the end together with the wartime middle, *Good-bye to All That* is a paradigm of the process of social and cultural transformation that is the subject of this book.

The Edwardian world-before-the-war, in Graves's telling, was like a Victorian novel: the dominant, elderly father, the pious mother, the siblings with their rivalries and their problems, the endless uncles and cousins, the servants, the family holidays and outings, and behind all that the worries about money, about religion, about duty. For the young Graves the emotional centre of this life was his public school, a place, as he tells of it, of strict hierarchies of power, of bullies and games-playing heroes, and of homoerotic yearnings and shame. It was a completely authoritarian world, and a completely male one; when the war came its structure and values were transposed, virtually intact, to that other womanless world, the Western Front — a process that explains much about the wartime officer class, and about the things that they wrote about the war, from Owen's poems to Sherriff's *Journey's End*.

Graves's version of his life in the world after the war is the antithesis of this first world — an irresponsible, impecunious, polyphiloprogenitive bohemian life in which Graves recovered from the war's effects, and made a name for himself as a poet. It was a life in which the war continued as a reality; Graves was shell-shocked and haunted by death, and had many incapacitating phobias: he could not use a telephone, or travel by train, and any unusual smell set him trembling (it might be German gas). But it was a free life; the rules and structures that had bound his Edwardian existence had been dispersed and cancelled by the war.

Graves's account of the war is vivid and particular and beyond summarizing; but there are two events at its centre that must be noted for their symbolic suggestiveness. One occurred on July 20, 1916, during the Battle of the Somme, when Graves 'died'. What happened in fact was that he was severely wounded, but his family was notified that he had been killed, and he had the peculiar experience of reading a notice of his own death in *The Times* as he lay recuperating in a London hospital. Graves saw that death as in some sense actual; he wrote a poem about it, shortly after the event, which begins: 'But I *was* dead, an hour or more,' and later he wrote a verse letter to his friend Sassoon in which he took the death to be a reality that raised a question of identity: if he had died, then who *was* he?[9]

The other symbolic event in Graves's war narrative concerns Sassoon's notorious letter of protest and Graves's response to it. Sassoon wrote the letter because he believed that the ideals for which the war was declared had been betrayed. Graves agreed with Sassoon, but saw that he risked court martial, to his discredit and the shame of the regiment to which they both belonged (the Royal Welch Fusiliers). He therefore intervened at the medical inquiry into Sassoon's condition, and persuaded the 'mad old men' of the board that his friend was shell-shocked, and should be sent not to be tried by a military court but to be treated at Craiglockhart.

The historical point of these two episodes is that both contain contradictions of what was apparent and, to the ordinary world, natural: a man died and yet survived, another man was sane and yet mad. The rules by which existence had been understood had given way under the pressure of war. Here, at the centre of Graves's narrative of his war, were two enactments of the war's destruction — not merely of lives, but of order and reason.

Graves explained his motives for writing *Good-bye to All That* at the beginning of his book, in a paragraph that has since disappeared from the text:

> The objects of this autobiography, written at the age of thirty-three, are simple enough: an opportunity for a formal good-bye to you and to you and to you and to me and to all that; forgetfulness, because once all this has been settled in my mind and written down and published it need never be thought about again; money.[10]

This is partly an expression of that general rejection of the past that marks the post-war period — goodbye to *all* that, the Edwardian comforts and the post-war confusions as well as the war itself. But it also suggests another motive that Graves shares with many other ex-soldiers of that time, a decade after the war's end: the impulse to exorcize the war by mythologizing it. If you could turn your war into a story, you might quiet its uproar, might give it some order, perhaps even some significance. And then maybe you could turn away from it and get on with life. Graves wrote his war book so that he could stop writing about war.

There is support for that reading of his motives in the fact that at roughly the same time he was saying goodbye to his past in another way. He put together his first *Collected Poems* in the late Twenties (it was published in June 1927), and for that volume he gathered together his best war poems, in a section headed 'War: 1915–1919'. Then he forgot about them. Not a single one of his war poems appears in any of his many subsequent collections — only one memory poem, the melancholy 'Recalling War', which he wrote in the early Thirties. It was as though Graves decided that the man who wrote those poems was the Captain Graves who had been declared dead on the Somme. The other man, the one who survived, had moved on, to be a different (and a better) poet.

Good-bye to All That ends with another passage that is also absent from recent editions, a passage in which Graves reviewed what he had thus far accomplished in his life, ending with the claim that he had 'learned to tell the truth — nearly'. That process, he implied, had taken him the ten years that had elapsed since the war ended, and even so he had only 'nearly' achieved it, because it was a myth that he had made, and not the war itself — a distanced, post-war myth of a war that grew more distant as his narrative moved on into peacetime, until by the end it seemed remote and fabulous, like Thermopylae or Agincourt, and so at last the narrator could say 'Good-bye' to it.

Remote, but not erased from memory: the forgetfulness that Graves named among his motives for writing never came to him. At the end of his long life, when he could no longer recall the events of the previous day, he remembered his war, grieved for the men he had killed, and was proud of his regiment. In a televised interview shortly before his death he could still quaver out, in his thin, old man's voice, a soldier's song from his army days: 'Hanging on the Old Barbed Wire'. His war had become his last reality.

Graves gave his war story the form of a long historical narrative — the war located in history, between the pre-war and post-war worlds. But not a continuous one: his book is a series of lost worlds, all of them separated from the present by radical changes in both personal and public life. The greatest English novel of the war, Ford Madox Ford's four-volume *Parade's End,* takes the same general form, and with similar consequences. Like *Good-bye to All That, Parade's End* is full of war; and yet one might say of it, as one might say of Graves's book, that it is not a war book but something more comprehensive — a novel of twentieth-century historical change.

In the simplest narrative terms Ford's intention was, he said, to tell the story of the war as it might have appeared to the eyes of an anachronistic figure, Christopher Tietjens, the Last English Tory. In his dedication to *No More Parades,* the second volume of the tetralogy, he explained:

Some Do Not — of which this one is not so much a continuation as a reinforcement — showed you the Tory at home during war-time; this shows you the Tory going up the line. If I am vouchsafed health and intelligence for long enough I propose to show you the same man in the line and in process of being re-constructed.[11]

But Ford had another intention — or another way of formulating that one — that was more expansive. Looking back at *Parade's End* in 1934, he described his ambitions in this way:

> The work that at that time — and now — I wanted to see done was something on an immense scale, a little cloudy in immediate attack, but with the salient points and the final impression extraordinarily clear. I wanted the Novelist in fact to appear in his really proud position as historian of his own time. Proust being dead I could see no one who was doing that . . .[12]

This is hindsight, of course, and one must mistrust the hindsight of artists. But Ford had been thinking about the novelist-as-historian for a long time — at least since the end of the war. In 1919, when he made his first attempt at a war novel with *No Enemy,* he wrote this passage in the manuscript:

> If, before the war, one had any function it was that of historian. Basing, as it were, one's morality on the Europe of Charlemagne as modified by the Europe of Napoleon. I once had something to go upon. One could approach with composure the Lex Allemannica, the Feudal System, problems of Aerial Flight, the price of wheat or the relations of the sexes. But now, it seems to me, we have no method of approach to any of these problems.[13]

So in the first year after the war Ford was worrying about what had happened to history — not to particular historical events or processes, but to the *idea* of history. Continuity had been disrupted, the past no longer offered a basis for morality, there was nothing for the novelist–historian to go on. He still had to confront history: the novelist's function was still 'that of historian'; but that function could not be performed in the old, pre-war way. History was not simply there to be told; it would have to be remade.

Parade's End is that new kind of history-in-faction, a novel that begins in the ostensible security of pre-war England (as *Good-bye to All That* also does) and moves through the dispersals and destructions of the war to

end in the fragmented, disoriented post-war world. The book opens
with a memorable image of Edwardian security:

> The two young men — they were of the English public official class
> — sat in the perfectly appointed railway carriage. The leather straps to
> the windows were of virgin newness; the mirrors beneath the new
> luggage racks immaculate as if they had reflected very little; the
> bulging upholstery in its luxuriant, regulated curves was scarlet and
> yellow in an intricate, minute dragon pattern, the design of a
> geometrician in Cologne. The compartment smelt faintly, hygienically
> of admirable varnish; the train ran as smoothly — Tietjens remembered
> thinking — as British gilt-edged securities.[14]

It is a security built on class, and on securities: in the course of the novel
all of that will crumble, until at the end, in the world after the war,
nothing is left that a life or a morality can be built on except love
between a man and a woman, and love of England.

'The "subject"', Ford later wrote of his vast novel, 'was the world as
it culminated in the war.'[15] He rendered that subject with a fine
historical inclusiveness: in the first volume, *Some Do Not . . .* , the
venality of Edwardian politics, the greed of the rich, the blind stupidity
of the upper class, the troubles with the Suffragists and the Irish are all
present, and all participate in the disintegration of which the war is the
culmination, not the cause. This is the version of the world-before-the
war that we have seen evolving since 1914. In Ford's novel it finds its
fullest formulation.

That disintegrating society continues in the two wartime volumes,
No More Parades and *A Man Could Stand Up:* politicians advance their
careers, bankers exploit their soldier–clients, society-women posture,
and generals blunder, while in France men suffer and die. And in the
post-war volume, *Last Post,* it is the bankers, the society-women and the
generals who have triumphed and who own England.

Ford's sense of the disintegration of England and English culture
appears in the novel in disintegrated forms and vivid impressionistic
fragments. Narrative point of view is broken down, chronology is
disrupted, and characters and events are constituted by accumulation,
out of the shards of experience. This fragmentation is Ford's vision of
immediate reality — pre-war and wartime life broken and intermixed,
incidents left incomplete, returned to, left again, the whole disrupted
narrative becoming a complex image of the world's disorder. In this
model the war is not the cause of the decay; Ford saw that English

society was disintegrating before the war began, and that the war was at most an acceleration and a symptom of that process. He expressed that understanding by making the entire novel, from pre-war railway carriage to post-war rural cottage, a model of disunity.

Other metaphors sustain and expand the sense of disruption and loss that the form itself renders. Telephone connections don't connect, military communications fail, letters are not delivered, a map is soaked in blood. Tietjens, at the Front, is half-buried by an exploding shell and suffers amnesia, forgetting his vast store of knowledge and his own history (as the soldier did in Rebecca West's *Return of the Soldier*), and has to reconstruct his own mind. Ford ends his war with a brilliant Armistice Night scene in which Tietjens returns to his London house to find it emptied of furnishings, as his mind is; and there, in the company of other soldiers — the maimed and the mad, the ruins of war — he celebrates the peace. In *Last Post,* the final volume, Tietjens goes into self-exile in a country cottage, where he supports himself as an antique-dealer, selling pieces of the English past to rich Americans. It is an odd resolution: a novel that began in the sophisticated society of pre-war London ends in pastoralism. But Ford's pastoral vision was a peculiarly post-war one, a vision of England emptied of history and beyond social conventions, pastoralism seen as the defeat of civilization, all that is left after the apocalypse.

Parade's End is a great historical novel — inaccurate in many details (Ford was hopelessly careless about facts) but exact in its intricate rendering of the myth of history that would henceforth describe what happened in England during the first quarter of this century. It does what other fictional versions of that historical period (Galsworthy's *Forsyte Saga,* for instance) had not done: it embodies the whole historical myth — the world-before-the-war, the gap of the war itself, and the world-after-the-war — in one intelligible story, and in a form that is appropriate to the Myth: a fragmented, elliptical, difficult form. That is to say, it is Modernist. *Modernism* means many things, but it is most fundamentally the forms that post-war artists found for their sense of modern history: history seen as discontinuous, the past remote and unavailable, or available only as the ruins of itself, and the present a formless space emptied of values. *Parade's End* is a masterly expression of that mythic view.

A particular, definable sense of history is a central element in these major narratives of the war — a conception of history as discontinuous, fragmented, and subjective. In these examples, history-writing is not a

matter of establishing causes and consequences, but of charting the
fractures in the continuity of recent time. That sense of radical breaks in
recent history entered the language in the years after the war when the
phrases 'before the war' and 'after the war' became the names of distinct
and entirely separated historical realities. 'The War is such a tremendous
landmark,' Wyndham Lewis wrote, 'that locally it imposes itself upon
our computations of time like the birth of Christ. We say "pre-war" and
"post-war", rather as we say B.C. or A.D.'[16] Charles Carrington made
much the same point in the Epilogue to his *A Subaltern's War:*

> Throughout Europe the phrases 'before the war' and 'since the war'
> are the commonest on men's lips. They are used to divide the age into
> three periods, the world of men into three generations.[17]

'Before the war' and 'after the war' were territories in time, in terms
of which history could be thought about. But they were also divisions in
the histories of individual selves — the self-before-soldiering and the
self-after. One finds in the classic personal war stories a marked sense of
the narrators' separation from the earlier selves about whom they write.
'This is the story', Graves wrote at the end of *Good-bye to All That,* 'of
what I was, not what I am.' And Carrington looked at his own memoir
and noted 'the rather romantic tone, taken (if I read him right) by that
lad who ten years ago was I'.[18] It is not simply that these, like all
memoirs, are retrospective; it is that they look back across an abyss in
which extreme changes had occurred. The self that remembers is not
merely older; he is fundamentally different.

A change of self not only alters the present, it alters the past; for it is
the changed self who remembers. This point is clearest in those cases in
which both a wartime version and a later recollection of the war exist.
Graves provides one such case. I have quoted (p. 255 above) his letter
describing Armistice Day as he experienced it in a North Wales army
camp, in which he reported simply that 'things were very quiet up here
on the 11th', and that 'a perfunctory thanksgiving service' was held,
'with nothing more cheerful in it than a Last Post for the dead . . .' It is
the letter of a young man posing as an old soldier — tough, cynical,
disdaining emotion. Ten years later *Good-bye to All That* offered a rather
different and more personal story of the same occasion:

> Armistice-night hysteria did not touch the camp much, though some
> of the Canadians stationed there went down to Rhyl to celebrate in
> true overseas style. The news sent me out walking alone along the

dyke above the marshes of Rhuddlan (an ancient battle-field, the Flodden of Wales) cursing and sobbing and thinking of the dead.[19]

This is a highly emotional passage, but it is more than that: it is, with its invocation of ancient battlefields and their ancient dead, a highly self-conscious, constructed, *literary* passage — Graves the war poet generalizing his experience into a 'war book'.

Vera Brittain is another writer who remade her wartime records of the war into a canonical war book. The diary that she kept during the war years recounts the war as it was experienced by a very young, provincial, middle-class girl. There is war reality in it — her brother was first wounded and then killed, her lover died in the trenches, and she worked with the wounded in military hospitals — but there is also ignorance and naiveté, and the conventional patriotic language and values of the journalists and politicians (and Rupert Brooke, whom she went on quoting even after the deaths). Here is a typical passage; she has just learned that her brother, wounded on the first day of the Battle of the Somme, is in her hospital, and she goes to his bedside:

> We could neither of us say much . . . but he smiled & seemed gayer & happier than he had been all through his leave. I think the splendid relief of having the great deed faced & over was uppermost in his mind then, rather than the memory of all he had been through on that day — hereafter to be regarded as one of the greatest dates in history.[20]

Seventeen years later she rewrote the passage for *Testament of Youth,* her 'Autobiographical Study of the Years 1900–1925':

> Even then, neither of us could say much. He seemed — to my surprise . . . gayer and happier than he had been all through his leave. The relief of having the great dread faced and creditably over was uppermost in his mind just then; it was only later, as he gradually remembered all he had been through on July 1st, that Victor and Geoffrey and I realised that the Battle of the Somme had profoundly changed him and added ten years to his age.[21]

Not much has been changed, and yet the tone is radically different. The older Vera Brittain looks back across the years, no longer with pride but with pity. The poetry is in the pity, Owen had said; by 1933 there was pity in the prose too — pity had become the standard, conventional attitude towards the war and its victims.

Sassoon offers a somewhat more complicated case. Like Brittain, he kept a wartime diary; like Graves, he looked back, from the end of the Twenties, to write a classic historical narrative of his pre-war and wartime life. But unlike the others, Sassoon acknowledged the distorting power of memory by fictionalizing his narrative. In his books — *Memoirs of a Fox-hunting Man, Memoirs of an Infantry Officer,* and *Sherston's Progress* — the man who lives Sassoon's life is called George Sherston, Robert Graves is David Cromlech, the Royal Welch Fusiliers become the Royal Flintshire Fusiliers, and so on. Why the transparent disguise, one wonders, since the events all seem to be so factually accurate — the pre-war country house and the hunting, the regiment, the fighting, the medals, the Protest, Dottyville, the return to the Western Front and the final wound all there, and evidently narrated as they happened?

The answer lies, I think, in the one fundamental difference between the life and the narrative of it: in fictionalizing himself, Sassoon omitted one essential aspect of his identity: his George Sherston is not a poet. One might argue that it was the poet who wrote the book; but the young man at the centre of it is an un-poetic self — a fox-hunting man, an infantry officer, and no more. Sassoon was not writing about the sensitive, articulate, angry man who emerged from the war, but of another, earlier, more ordinary self, living through his experiences, and being changed by them.

All of these memoirs — Graves's, Brittain's and Sassoon's — share that central point: their common subject is the power of the war to change individuals in radical ways. Each offers an earlier self, seen from a distance in time, and seen primarily in one intense relationship — the individual's relationship to war. This, each book tells its reader, is what war did to that person who, ten or fifteen or twenty years ago, was I, but is I no longer. They are all disjunctive memoirs for a disjunctive time, parts of the myth of disruption and fragmentation that is the Myth of the War. And they were all written within the five- or six-year period over the end of the Twenties when the Myth was given its ultimate formulations.

Another influential text was not, strictly speaking, a work of those years at all. *Poems of Wilfred Owen,* edited by Edmund Blunden, was published in 1931, thirteen years after Owen's death. It was the first full collection of Owen's verse, with nearly three times as many poems as Sassoon and Edith Sitwell had put into their 1920 volume, and it created the canon by which Owen is known as a poet. It was not a best-seller, as some of the war books in prose were; indeed Owen sold no better through the Thirties in the new edition than he had through the Twenties in the earlier one. Nevertheless, it was Blunden's edition that established Owen in the position that he has held ever since, as the best of the British war poets, and the model to whom later poets turned when war was their subject. *Poems by Wilfred Owen* took its place among the classic myth-making texts, as the truest and most sensitive record in verse of a modern poet's war.

The importance of Blunden's edition to the myth-making process was not a matter of its poetry alone. Indeed one might argue that in terms of the Myth the prose in the book was more important than the poetry was. There was, first of all, the long biographical memoir of Owen. Blunden had made it almost entirely out of Owen's letters home from the Front, and the text speaks in Owen's voice rather than in Blunden's. It is the autobiographical narrative that Owen might have written in 1930, if he had lived.

Out of that narrative, out of Owen's own words, Blunden created what Owen had never had — a poetic character of his own. Blunden's Owen is a sensitive, compassionate young officer whose experience of war and suffering made him a kind of Christian pacifist, but who nevertheless returned to the trenches out of love for his men, and was killed there, ironically and pointlessly, a week before the Armistice. He is neither a hero nor a coward, but a sacrifice, and his life as Blunden constructs it is an exemplum — the story, in one life, that the Myth tells. In that story the episodes that became Owen's poems — the blinded sentry, the coward, the self-inflicted wound case — appear as actual trench incidents, thus giving the poems that authority of fact that war narratives depend on for their validity, and making them not so much acts of the imagination as testimonies.

There are two other prose texts in Blunden's edition, and they are among the most important texts of the myth-making years. One is Owen's draft of his preface (which Sassoon also published in the 1920 edition, and which I have quoted in full on p. 182). From it subsequent generations would take a single phrase, 'the Poetry is in the pity', and would make that phrase a touchstone for war poetry. They might well have taken more; for in his preface Owen had sketched the whole aesthetic of the Myth of the War: that it would not be about heroes, that it would not use the big abstractions, that it would not be 'literary', that it would be elegiac. No other single document says so much about how to imagine the war.

The other important document in Blunden's edition had not previously been published. It is the plan of a table of contents that Owen had made for his book of poems, no doubt at the time that he wrote the preface. I quote it here in its entirety as Blunden transcribed it:

Poem	*Motive*		DOUBTFUL
Miners	How the Future will forget the dead in war	*Protest*	Greater Love. A Ponderous Day.
Arms & the Boy / Sonnet	The unnaturalness of weapons	*Protest*	Greater Love. Identity Disc.
The Chances	Madness		Heaven.
Aliens	"	*Protest*	Soldier's Dream.
Letter	Heroic Lies		The Seed.
Inspection / Last Word	Inhumanity of war.		The End.
Dulce et Decorum / Dead Beat	Indifference at Home.		
Parable	Willingness of old to sacrifice young.		
S.I.W.	The insupportability of war.		
Draft	Mentality of Troops and vastness of Losses, with reflections on Civilians.		
The Show	Horrible beastliness of war.		
Next War	Cheerfulness and Description and Reflection.		
Apology	" "		
Nothing happens / The Light	*Description* "		
Conscious / Ode / Anthem / Hospital Barge / Futility	Grief.		
Strange Meeting.	Foolishness of War.		
Killed Asleep / *A Terre* / The Woman and the Slain	The Soul of Soldiers.		Descriptive. Reflective. Allegorical. Lyric.
		Philosophy.	Disgust.[22]

This is, as Blunden remarked, a perplexing document, and some of the connections between 'Poem' and 'Motive' are obscure. But the motives themselves are not: 'The unnaturalness of weapons', 'Madness', 'Heroic Lies', 'Inhumanity of War', 'Indifference at Home', 'Willingness of old to sacrifice young', 'Horrible beastliness of war' — these amount to an index of principal themes of the Myth, as found in the great war narratives, and in war poems, war paintings and war films too. And embracing these particular formations, the one word that was the most inclusive and powerful motive of all: *Protest Protest Protest.*

II

The Myth of the War: that phrase has recurred in these pages, as elements of the emerging whole have appeared. Some of those elements acquired catch-phrase identities: the Old Men, the Big Words, the Turning Point, Disenchantment — identities that they still retain. Others remain submerged in the characteristic lines of the narratives. But together they compose one story — the received, accepted version of what happened in the First World War, and what it meant in human terms.

The elements of that story are everywhere in the war narratives published in the myth-making years. We know them all by now: the idealism betrayed; the early high-mindedness that turned in mid-war to bitterness and cynicism; the growing feeling among soldiers of alienation from the people at home for whom they were fighting; the rising resentment of politicians and profiteers and ignorant, patriotic women; the growing sympathy for the men on the other side, betrayed in the same ways and suffering the same hardships; the emerging sense of the war as a machine and of all soldiers as its victims; the bitter conviction that the men in the trenches fought for no cause, in a war that could not be stopped.

The way that this story was told makes another point: that the old high rhetoric of war had been emptied of its meaning and its values, and that the truth about war could only be told in the plainest, most physical words. To this, women's stories added their own perception: that in the arguments of armies women are useless, and their stories marginal.

But the Myth that took shape at the end of the Twenties was more than simply a story of what the war *was:* it was also a story of what it *did* — to history, to society, to art, to politics, to women, to hopes and expectations, to the idea of progress, the idea of civilization, the idea of England. It expanded as it evolved, from a myth of war to a myth of ruination that included life among the ruins, a myth of the world that the war had made.

One can see that larger myth taking form in the reviews that war writers wrote of other men's war books. Such reviews characteristically begin with the rendering of war, but move on to describe the post-war destinies of the generation that had fought it. Herbert Read, for example, began his review of *All Quiet* with high praise for Remarque's war: 'it is the first completely satisfying expression in literature of the greatest event of our time,' he wrote; it was the greatest of all 'war books'. But he soon moved on to quote a passage that many soldier-reviewers noted, in which Remarque's soldier, Paul Bäumer, prophesies the future lives that his generation will live:

> Had we returned home in 1916, out of the suffering and strength of our experiences we might have unleashed a storm. Now if we go back we shall be weary, broken, burnt out, rootless, and without hope. We shall not be able to find our way any more. And men will not understand us — for the generation that grew up before us, though it has passed these years with us here, already had a home and a calling; now it will return to its old occupations, and the war will be forgotten — and the generation that has grown up after us will be strange to us and push us aside. We shall be superfluous even to ourselves, we shall grow older, a few will adapt themselves, some others will merely submit, and most will be bewildered; the years will pass by, and in the end we shall fall into ruin.[23]

It is this theme in Remarque's book, of a war generation adrift in the post-war world, that appealed to soldier-critics like Read, a decade after the war. They saw themselves as members of a generation that had survived the war and yet were casualties, and their sense of what they had lost was absolute. That sense of loss is the real subject of Read's review, which ends with this paragraph:

> No idealism is left in this generation. We cannot believe in democracy, or Socialism, or the League of Nations. To be told at the front that we were fighting to make the world safe for democracy was to be driven to the dumb verge of insanity. On a mutual respect for each other's sufferings we built up that sense of comradeship which was the war's only good gift. But death destroyed even this, and we were left with only the bare desire to live, although life itself was past our comprehension.[24]

An incomprehensible world, emptied of values and beliefs, in which life is lived alone and without hope: this is no longer a war story that is being reviewed and judged. Read has made it a myth of his own generation, a personal, plotless narrative of modern existence in the world after the war.

That complex myth was fixed by the narratives that were written at the end of the Twenties and the beginning of the Thirties, including the narratives that I have been considering by writers like Graves, Sassoon, Blunden and Ford. But not by narratives alone: there were other important myth-making forms — plays, films, a posthumous edition of poems, paintings. One of the most influential texts of the late Twenties was an amateur play, written by an amateur playwright for his rowing club's dramatic society — *Journey's End,* by R.C. Sherriff. The play was quickly recognized as a potential hit; it was first given a short run by the Stage Society (with the young Laurence Olivier and Maurice Evans in the starring roles), and then transferred to the Savoy Theatre, where it ran for sixteen months and 600 performances.

Not many critics thought that *Journey's End* was a great play, or even a very good one, but most recognized that it had qualities that would hold audiences. One such quality was the realism — one might better say the literalism — of its situation, its language, and its set (see plate 24). The action is played out on a single set — a dugout on the Western Front near St Quentin, in a few days before the German army's attack in March 1918. In the dugout are Captain Stanhope, the Company Commander, and four of his officers: Osborne, Hibbert, Trotter, and a new lieutenant, Raleigh. During the play Stanhope shows himself to be a hard, steady drinker, and Hibbert shows himself to be a coward. A raid is planned and carried out, Osborne and Raleigh are killed, Hibbert recovers his nerve, and the German attack begins as the play ends.

Old soldiers recognized in all this what they had seen and heard on the Western Front, and were affected by it. The *Times's* reviewer (almost certainly Charles Morgan) wrote of the Savoy production:

> 'How like it all is!' we say, looking round the dugout in the support trench near St Quentin. It is not alone of pit props, of earthen walls, or of the other realistic but inessential details of the scene that we are thinking. The life of the dugout, with its terrible excitements, its boredom, and its humour, is represented no less faithfully than its trimmings ... We never lose our first impression of actuality ... and when the expected attack has broken with more than expected fury on the trenches above, and the play ends, we say again, 'How like it all is. How again and again it has recalled this incident or that character in our own experience.'[25]

Morgan did not think that the play would live; it was like letters from the trenches, he said, and it needed the same sort of naturally responsive audience. But for men like himself, who had known the war, it was an experience of reality itself.

Sherriff's play had another quality that guaranteed its success: in his effort to render the reality of the Front, Sherriff had collected the basic elements of the Myth. The characters are the stock figures of the war stories — the brave, hard-drinking commander, the steady, quiet second-in-command, the innocent new lieutenant, the coward, the lower-class New Army officer, even the comic servant. The actions, too, are familiar — the entrance of the staff officer with the impossible plan of attack, the raid that fails, the death scene. And so are the set speeches — the 'Don't you think I care?' speech and the 'I drink to forget' speech. The historical situation was also, by this time, almost a convention: the last great German offensive, the last British defeat.

There is one further element in *Journey's End* that makes it a canonical example of the Myth. That is the analogy that is drawn — unintentionally, one feels, but nonetheless persistently — between the world of the trenches and the world of the public schools. Stanhope, we are told, was skipper of rugger at his school, and kept wicket for the eleven; he is the schoolboy idol. Osborne, the wise older officer, tells young Raleigh that 'rugger and cricket seem a long way from here', but in fact they don't. The company lives by a set of rules, unspecified but rigid, that are very like what public school seems to have been (as described, for example, in *Good-bye to All That*). There is the same idolizing, the same adolescent emotionalism, the same team spirit and self-sacrifice, the same hovering note of homosexuality. That model of behaviour — so English, so male, and so anachronistic — was killed on the Western Front. In Sherriff's play it was resurrected and sentimentalized.

Men like Charles Morgan who had served in the war were moved by what they found of themselves in Sherriff's play; they ignored the conventions and the sentimentalities, and stressed its fidelity to actuality. Others, Morgan wrote, might say that it was not a work of art, but 'we, who have not their detachment from St Quentin and the month of March, 1918, cannot afford their aesthetic didacticism.'[26] For them it was reality, and they filled the stalls of the Savoy.

Other critics were able to step back, and to look at it with more detachment, and to see what it meant, sentimentalities and all. Rebecca West put *Journey's End* together with Sassoon's *Memoirs of a Fox-hunting*

Man, and was touched by both. Of Sassoon's book she wrote: 'to us (the English) it seemed the most heartrending portrait of a class that was allowed to play at being children until the war came, and then was delivered, bound hand and foot, to the forces of hell' — and she found essentially the same motif in *Journey's End.* 'Considering these two works together,' she continued,

> one recognises that they have the same theme; the precipitation of a class bred from its beginnings to eschew profundity, into an experience which only the profoundest thinking could render tolerable, with no words to express their agony but the insipid vocabulary of their education, no gods to guide them save the unhelpful gods of Puritan athleticism.[27]

West saw that Sherriff's very inadequacies of imagination and maturity made his play as moving and as descriptive as it was. He *was* one of those English schoolboys delivered to war, and his story of that experience was truer than he knew.

One other myth-making medium exercised a powerful influence on the Twenties and early Thirties. War films had been a part of the myth-making process since the war's beginning; nearly fifty titles were released in England and the United States between 1914 and 1918, and they continued to appear throughout the following decade. In England the principal producer was British Instructional Films, a company formed specifically to make 'factual films' of important events of the war. During the Twenties, BIF made six war films: *The Battle of Jutland* (1921), *Armageddon* (on Allenby's campaign in Palestine) (1923), *Zeebrugge* (1924), *Ypres* (1925), *Mons* (1926), and *Battles of the Coronel and the Falkland Islands* (1927). These were commercial films, but they were also intended to be educational, as the firm's name indicates. They were made up partly of actual archival footage, and partly of re-enactments and various explanatory aids — diagrams, moving models, maps. For the re-enactments of military engagements, BIP had the cooperation of both the War Office and the Admiralty, which supplied personnel and equipment; in the *Coronel and Falklands* film, for example, 4,000 naval ratings were involved, as well as thirty-five ships of the Navy. There was so much cooperation that questions were asked in the Commons: what exactly was the government's policy? And was it getting a decent return on its investment? The questions were taken seriously enough to be answered by the Prime Minister, Stanley Baldwin:

It is the policy of the Board of Admiralty, the Army Council and the Air Council to give assistance, by way of loan of personnel and material, to approved British film companies engaged in making war films, provided that

(1) the method of production is entirely approved by the Department;
(2) nothing secret is divulged;
(3) the films are submitted unconditionally for censorship;
(4) they involve no undue interference with the normal duties of the personnel concerned;
(5) any additional expenditure incurred by the Department is repaid by the company;
(6) a reasonable charge is made to the company for the facilities granted to them, in the form of a fee or a percentage of the profits. [28]

As Baldwin's reply shows, the questioner had missed the point: the government was not concerned with profit-making but with monument-making, and controlled the entire film-making process to that end, approving the method and censoring the result.

One can see the monumentality of these films in their titles alone: they are historical in the traditional sense — narratives about battles and campaigns, rather than about individuals. *Ypres,* for example, is a history of the Salient from the autumn of 1914 to the final retaking of the ground by the British in August 1918. Many historic episodes are represented: the first use of gas by the Germans, the great Messines mine, the Battle of Passchendaele, the German offensive of March 1918. There are also scenes of ordinary trench life, using what appears to be archival material: men shaving, bathing, reading their mail, and a curious scene of Indian troops arriving at the Front pushing bicycles (what scenario-writer could have invented that incident?).

That much of the film is documentary; but interspersed among the factual events are spots of sentimental fiction, as when a returning soldier is met at his garden gate by his wife and infant child, and when ex-soldiers meet after the war (in an odd out-of-chronology scene) to recite together Binyon's 'For the Fallen'. These alter the film's tone in a direction that the final caption epitomizes: 'Laughing they came upon the great adventure, these men from the mine, the field and the office . . . laughing and singing still they march on — to Victory!' And the film ends with Binyon's poem on screen again.

Mons, made in the following year, is if anything more monumental,

though in a special way. It is the story of the great British retreat of
August 1914, and is dedicated 'to the memory of the Old Army which
came triumphantly through a great ordeal and gave a new and noble
meaning to the word "Contemptible"'. The original title of the film was
The Retreat from Mons, but that had to be changed: *retreat* is not a
monumental word. Yet the film remains a story of heroic losing against
odds, the sort of story that so dominated boys' papers and boys' minds
at the war's beginning. In *Mons* the Germans have the advantage in men
and material (as indeed they had), but the British fight bravely: one man
with a machine gun holds a bridge against a swarm of Germans, a gun-
crew continues firing until the last man is killed. And once more the
final caption makes the film-makers' intentions clear: 'Pass by once
more, you "Old Contemptibles!" — and burst into our hearts afresh the
meaning of your sacrifice.'

The BIF films were commercially very successful, but critical
responses were somewhat qualified. Reviewers acknowledged the
educational value of the enterprise, and admired the makers' epic
aspirations, but they quibbled over historical accuracy, and disliked the
farce and melodrama of the invented episodes. In Dublin, the critics
were more severe: when *Ypres* was about to be shown there armed men
broke in to the cinema and stole the film; and when another print was
procured they returned and blew up the theatre.[29] The grounds of their
disapproval was, apparently, that the film was 'British propaganda'.

The same thought seems to have occurred to Members of Parliament;
in December 1927 a spokesman for the Secretary of War has to reassure
the Commons that the films were not war propaganda, but merely
'instructional', and two days later a group of Labour Members placed
the following motion on the Notice Paper of the House of Commons:

> That, in the opinion of this House, the granting of assistance to
> commercial cinematograph film producers by the loan of officers and
> men and material belonging to His Majesty's Services is derogatory
> to His Majesty's uniform and is open to grave objection as mischie-
> vous propaganda.[30]

The motion was not debated — it was an expression of opinion only —
but the men who had moved it were obviously right: the films *were*
propaganda, intended to tell the story of the war in the heroic, value-
affirming terms that monuments traditionally express. As the decade
moved towards its end, that version of the war was coming more and
more under critical scrutiny, and not only in the House of Commons. In

1925 the *Times*'s reviewer of *Ypres* complained that the actual footage used was too 'moderate', and the reviewer of *Mons* the following year observed a tendency 'to give too much prominence to examples of individual valour . . .'[31] Neither of these reviews was a frontal attack on monumentalism in war films, but one senses a growing restlessness with the heroic, patriotic tradition.

That restlessness is the spirit of the emerging Myth of the War. One finds it in reviews in the national press, but it is also evident in more serious film criticism. The English novelist who called herself Bryher is an example. Bryher had moved to Switzerland after the war, and there, with her husband, she edited an avant-garde film journal called *Close Up*. She was an unusually knowledgeable film critic for her time, familiar with the new work being done in France, Germany and Russia as well as in England, and she wrote well about what she saw; her *Film Problems in Soviet Russia* (1929) is the first book in English to treat Russian films critically and seriously.

Bryher reviewed two BIF war films — *Mons* and *The Battles of Coronel and the Falkland Islands* — and what she had to say about them expressed an idea of what war films should and should not be that was new to film criticism, though it resembles current writing about war literature. She thought that *Mons* was badly photographed; but that wasn't the worst of it:

> beyond the photography was the film itself — full of the kind of sentimentality that makes one shudder, a sentimentality that Hollywood even would not dare offer to a Middle Western audience . . . mixture of a Victorian tract for children and a cheap serial in the sort of magazines one finds discarded on a beach.[32]

She continued her attack in her review of *Coronel and the Falkland Islands*:

> What I and many others (according to reviews) object to . . . is that war is presented *entirely* from a romantic boy-adventure book angle, divorced from everyday emotions and that thereby the thousands who desire unreality are forced further and further away from the actual meaning of battle. In a time of danger the 'We Want War' crowd psychology may destroy a nation. We want a race that understands what acceptance of warfare means. By all means let us have war films. Only let us have war straight and as it is; mainly disease and discomfort, almost always destructive (even in after civil life) in its effects. Let us get away from this nursery formula that

to be in uniform is to be a hero; that brutality and waste are not to be condemned provided they are disguised in flags, medals and cheering.[33]

This was not the voice merely of a sophisticated film critic of European taste. Certainly she disliked crude and old-fashioned film techniques when she saw them, but the foundations of her criticisms were not aesthetic, but moral. These films were bad, in her judgement, because they told the wrong story. They were heroic, patriotic, to-the-last-man films, and such films could not be works of art. For Bryher, as for so many other intellectuals of her time, anti-war had become avant-garde.

It had also become popular. As the anti-war books began to appear at the end of the Twenties, so also did the anti-war films — not documentaries, not monuments like the BIF films, but imagined stories of imagined individuals, intended for the world's mass audiences. Consider, for example, five memorable films released in 1930: *All Quiet on the Western Front, The Dawn Patrol, Hell's Angels, Journey's End,* and *Westfront 1918.* The first thing to be said of these films is that they were international: three were American, one was a British film made in Hollywood for technical reasons, the fifth was German. Yet they were all part of the myth-making process in Britain, and one must suppose that more British men and women formed their ideas of the Great War from these films than from all the war books put together.

These five films differed widely in particulars of story and tone. *Hell's Angels* was the most romantic, with its brilliant flying sequences and its to-the-last-man ending, and *Dawn Patrol,* also a flying film, shared the romance that war in the air had; *Journey's End* was a faithful transcription of Sherriff's play, part dugout literalism and part sentiment; *All Quiet* and *Westfront 1918* were closest to the realism of the great war memoirs. Yet each shared something of the essential Myth: each told a war story that was individual, violent, and mortal — a story not of battles won, but of lives lost. It was an international story — not because American actors played German soldiers and Germans played Frenchmen, but because there was only one story, in which young men went to war, fought there, and died. Audiences of any nationality could see that story and respond to it.

Of the five, *All Quiet* and *Westfront* have become classic war films. They are classics in part because they are the most anti-war, the nearest to the dark realism of the great war memoirs. The stories that they tell are of ordinary infantrymen in the trenches of the Western Front, and that is the story that the Myth tells. These films are indeed two major contributions to the making of the Myth. Nothing like them had been, or could have been done before.

That they could be made in 1930 was partly a matter of film technology. Sound had been introduced, and soldiers in war films could now speak. More importantly, the noise of battle could be reproduced (that was why *Journey's End* had to be made in Hollywood: there was no sound equipment in England equal to the demands of artillery barrages). The volume of noise did more than add to the realism; it altered the balance in war films between men and the machinery of war. As a reviewer of *Hell's Angels* remarked: 'the noise of the propellers and machine guns keeps dialogue in its place.'[34] It was another aspect of the Myth, in which the personal and the human were subordinated to the vast cacophonous machine.

There were other technological changes, too, involving the range and mobility of cameras. This was most striking in the flying sequences: 'I have never seen anything more beautiful or exciting on the screen,' the *London Mercury*'s critic wrote of the *Hell's Angels* combat scenes, 'and I have never seen anything like the scenes above our earth, which the pilots seem so at home in.'[35] And there were other effects: entire towns built so that they could be reduced to ruins, acres of land turned into shell-pocked, trench-slashed desolation to make a battle scene. By the end of the Twenties film-makers could create devastation almost as efficiently as generals.

But the classic war films were mythic in more than the reality of their technology. They told their stories in the same terms that the novels and memoirs used — stories of victims and damaged men, of cowards and sufferers, but not of heroes. And they told them in the same structures, beginning when a man's war began, and ending when it ended in death (and not when the actual war ended). They told the same story of the soldier's alienation from home and family, and of his sense of comradeship with the enemy. And they employed the same ironic modes of closure: in *All Quiet*, the ghosts of the dead super-imposed upon the military graves, in *Westfront* the final scene between the wounded Frenchman and the German in hospital, in which the Frenchman says: '*Moi, camarade. Pas ennemi*' — but to a man who is already dead.

Reviewers came to these films in the spirit of the time, looking for the Myth, praising films in which they found it and rebuking those film-makers who had told their stories differently, and expecting above all that a war film would be a gesture against war. Here are a few examples:

of *Journey's End:* 'Old soldiers, with that terrifying memory of Western Front details which will only die with them, may find themselves looking for things which are not there; but they will come away with the conviction that this film will combat war, in the hearts of the millions who will see it, with overwhelming force. The effect of nightmare is obtained in every glimpse of grey and smoking battlefield that varies the interplay of those doomed beings in the dugout . . .'

of *Hell's Angels:* 'It is difficult to justify war films unless they contribute something towards a peace psychology, and I cannot say that *Hell's Angels* does this, although there were moments during this film, for instance, when the Zeppelin came down in flames, which made one wonder why it was necessary to witness so horrible a representation.'

of the zeppelin scene in *Hell's Angels:* 'It is never suggested that such a thing must never happen again.'

of *All Quiet:* '. . . no film yet produced has depicted the horror and waste of war more forcibly.'[36]

Occasionally a reviewer paused to note that the film under review was like the current literature of war. But the point didn't need making: among the people who told the war stories, and the people who reviewed them, and the people who read the reviews, there was general agreement that there was only one story to tell, whether one told it in prose or in visual images, and only one motive for telling it. By 1930 the Myth was in place.

III

But though the Myth took firm definition in those years, there was not a complete, miraculous conversion of all of English society to Wilfred Owenism. War writers themselves were critical of the emerging version of the war, and drew back from a too-complete identification with it. Charles Carrington, writing an epilogue to his *Subaltern's War* in 1929, explicitly rejected the Myth's central thesis:

a legend has grown up, propagated not by soldiers but by journalists, that these men who went gaily to fight in the mood of Rupert Brooke and Julian Grenfell, lost their faith amid the horrors of the trenches and returned in a mood of anger and despair. To calculate the effect of mental and bodily suffering, not on a man but on a whole generation of men, may seem an impossible task, but it can at least be affirmed that the legend of disenchantment is false.

And even Graves denied anti-war intentions.

I was surprised [he wrote of the reception of *Good-bye to All That*] at being acclaimed in headlines of daily papers as the author of a violent treatise against war. For I had tried not to show any bias for or against war as a human institution, but merely to describe what happened to me during a particular and not at all typical one in which I took part.

And the cautious, scholarly Eric Partridge took note of 'that appalling inaccuracy and that ridiculous lack of proportion which invalidate the claims made for so many books that they "tell the truth about the War"'.[37]

More organized, and often angrier opposition came from other directions: from war historians, from senior army officers, and from some older and more conservative literary critics — so much opposition that journalists began to refer to a 'War Books Controversy', and generals hinted at a pacifist conspiracy. Here are some extracts from newspaper reports of speeches made in the first two months of 1930, when the controversy was at its loudest:

Brigadier-General John Carteris . . . said we were experiencing an inundation of war books and war plays, some of which seemed to be going out of their way to show all the bad and horrible things about war. War was bad and horrible, and no one who was in France would wish to see war again, but one could not help feeling a large measure of resentment as book after book came out showing the murky side of war and the bad side of human nature. He did not say that the books were exaggerated, but they were sensational. Many men went through the War and came back ennobled by the fact that they had taken part in it and had put into actual practice towards their fellow men some of the finest instincts in human nature.

General Sir Ian Hamilton . . . said that '. . . on several sides we are tempting reaction by overdoing peace propaganda.' It was rather odd that at the very moment when there were more people in the world who had fought in war; been shelled almost out of their skins; been shot at like Aunt Sallies; been wounded; gone over the top — surely it was extra queer that these elaborate attempts to exclude virtue, nobility and even valour from war should choose this time to begin to flourish like toadstools on the tombs of our dead heroes. The blazing and largely deserved success of 'All Quiet on the Western Front' and *Journey's End* had shown publishers how, by employing finer writers and by cutting out more thoroughly any touches of self-sacrifice, devotion, or love of adventure, they could go one better with the pacifist public.

Colonel John Brown: Referring to recent war books, he said these purported to show the horrors of war and were put forward as propaganda for peace. If these books were true they would be an insult to ex-Servicemen and none of them would be fit to walk the streets and mix with decent women.[38]

Well, you might say, they would say that, wouldn't they? But it was not only senior army officers who objected to the war books. Librarians thought they were obscene (*All Quiet* was banned from the Northampton Public Library), conservative critics deplored their scatological details (J.C. Squire headed his editorial remarks on German war books 'The Lavatory School'), and one military reviewer complained that 'literature of disillusionment' and 'War Books' had come to mean the same thing.[39] The feeling was widespread that this sort of thing ought not to be said: the spirit of DORA, it appeared, had not died.

Two books — or to be more precise a pamphlet and a book — published early in 1930 gave the war-books opposition its most authoritative utterance. Douglas Jerrold and Cyril Falls were both official military historians with personal experience in the wartime army: Jerrold was the author of *The Royal Naval Division* and *The War on Land, 1914–1918,* and had served with the Royal Naval Division in Gallipoli and in France; Falls was a former staff officer and liaison officer with the French, had written *The History of the 36th (Ulster) Division* and *The History of the Royal Ulster Rifles,* and worked for the History Section (Military Branch) of the Committee on Imperial Defence.

Jerrold's pamphlet, *The Lie About the War: A Note on Some Contemporary War Books,* appeared first, in February. It is ostensibly a criticism of sixteen recently published war books, nearly all of them now considered classic texts: *All Quiet, A Farewell to Arms, Good-bye to*

All That, *The Case of Sergeant Grischa*, *The Secret Battle*, *The Spanish
Farm* trilogy, *The Enormous Room* and *Le Feu* are among them. But
though Jerrold conceded that many of these books had great merits, he
had virtually nothing to say about them individually, and as literary
criticism the book is without interest (except perhaps for the occasional
blimpish remark, like the judgement that Hemingway's Frederick
Henry is an 'unspeakable cad'). What is interesting is Jerrold's effort to
persuade his reader that these war books collectively tell one consistent
lie about the war — that it was a futile, meaningless horror — and to
offer in place of that lie a 'truth', which was that

> the war of 1914–18 was a great tragedy because it was a great
> historical event. It was a great drama, because neither in its origins, its
> actions or its results was there any element fundamentally accidental
> or ultimately without meaning. It can only be right, or even useful, to
> deny the element of greatness to the struggle of 1914–18 if that
> element was absent. To deny the dignity of tragic drama to the war in
> the interests of propaganda is not only unworthy but damnably silly
> and incredibly dangerous.[40]

In support of his case for tragic meaning, Jerrold summarized the 'lie'
of the war that current war books provided, in order to refute it. In the
war books, he said, strong men are brutalized by horrors, brave men are
shot for cowardice, and doomed men become convinced that war is
futile, and is only prolonged out of mere callousness, or for personal
gain by politicians, contractors and generals. That was the lie. The
truth, he said, was that war — any war — turns idlers into men,
accelerates the pulse of life, is a great adventure (and not really a very
dangerous one, if you consider the odds). Furthermore, this particular
war had accomplished many good things: it had destroyed empires,
liberated the German people, and created the League of Nations.

It is impossible to say how large a portion of the British population
Jerrold spoke for, but it must have been substantial. The pamphlet was
favourably reviewed in serious journals, and was praised by other war
writers: Partridge, for example, wrote that

> This notable brochure, refreshing in its sanity, decency and penetration,
> is just what is needed by the general public to enable it to distinguish
> the genuine from the spurious, the normal from the abnormal.[41]

And one must note that it appeared under the sponsorship of T.S. Eliot:
it was published as *Criterion Miscellany No. 9* by Faber & Faber.

Cyril Falls's *War Books: A Critical Guide,* appeared a few months later. It is primarily a critical bibliography of war writings — 728 titles by French, German, American, Italian and Romanian writers as well as by English men and women — and as such it still has considerable scholarly value. One can get a sense of the qualities of Falls's judgements from his comments on a few familiar examples:

> of Blunden's *Undertones of War:* 'It is probably the only single book of its kind we have had in English which really reaches the stature of its subject.'

> of Graves's *Good-bye to All That:* 'His war scenes have been justly acclaimed to be excellent; they are, in fact among the few in books of this nature which are of real historical value. His attitude, however, leaves a disagreeable impression.'

> of Graeme West's *Diary of a Dead Officer:* 'Arthur Graeme West and his type are ill represented among those who have left personal records of the war, though there were probably many who felt like him of it . . . He had none of that protective armoury of callousness or use, which was so valuable to most of us, and his life must have been miserable.'

> of Remarque's *All Quiet:* 'a good novel of the more brutal naturalistic school, and at times reaches considerable heights,' but 'unnecessarily coarse' and 'frank propaganda'.[42]

Falls was a more generous and sensitive critic than Jerrold was, but he wrote from essentially the same point of view. Like Jerrold, he believed that the flood of recent war books had falsified the story of the war in the interests of a dangerous propaganda for peace. His book, like Jerrold's pamphlet, was a polemical work, written against the Myth.

Falls offered, in his introduction, a summary of the myth-makers' war that is similar to Jerrold's:

> The writers have set themselves, not to strip war of its romance — for that was pretty well gone already — but to prove that the Great War was engineered by knaves or fools on both sides, that the men who died in it were driven like beasts to the slaughter, and died like beasts, without their deaths helping any cause or doing any good. So much for the theme; the incidental details are of like nature. Shooting for cowardice — in fact exceedingly rare, in the British Army at least — is painted as a common occurrence; drunkenness among officers often

appears to have been the rule rather than the exception; every dirty little meanness — of which in truth you will meet more in a month of peace than in a year of war — leaps into the foreground ...

But the falsest of false evidence is produced in another way: by closing-up scenes and events which in themselves may be true. Every sector becomes a bad one, every working-party is shot to pieces; if a man is killed or wounded his brains or his entrails always protrude from his body; no one ever seems to have a rest. Hundreds of games of football were played every day on the Western Front, by infantry as well as other arms, but how often does one hear of a game in a 'War book'? Attacks succeed one another with lightning rapidity. The soldier is represented as a depressed and mournful spectre helplessly wandering about until death brought his miseries to an end.[43]

He then goes on to argue the other side, as Jerrold had done: the high British motives and the political fruits of victory in Europe.

Professional soldiers shared in this opposition to the Myth — understandably enough — and some of them wrote about it. Sir Ian Hamilton, asked to comment on *All Quiet* in Desmond MacCarthy's *Life and Letters,* replied:

There was a time when I would have strenuously combated Remarque's inferences and conclusions. Now, sorrowfully, I must admit, there is a great deal of truth in them. Latrines, rats, lice; smells, blood, corpses; scenes of sheer horror as where comrades surround the deathbed of a young *Kamerad* with one eye on his agonies, the other on his new English boots; the uninspired strategy; the feeling that the leaders are unsympathetic or stupid; the shrivelling up of thought and enthusiasm under ever-growing machinery of an attrition war; all this lasting too long — so long indeed that half a million souls, still existing in our own island, have been, in Remarque's own terrible word, 'lost'. Why else, may I ask, should those who were once the flower of our youth form today so disproportionate a number of the down and out?[44]

But even Hamilton, sensitive and intelligent as he was, could only concede so much: he had been, after all, the Commanding General of the disastrous Gallipoli expedition. And so, having made his concessions to the Myth's truths, he went on to argue his objections to it:

All the same, this German goes too far. As there is more in Easter than hot-cross-buns, so there is more in Patriotism than 'beans and bacon'. Even in the last and most accursed of all wars — the war 'on the Western Front' — was there not the superb leading of forlorn hopes; the vague triumphs, vague but real, of dying for a cause? Was there not also that very patriotism which Remarque treats much as he treated the goose his hero murdered in the officers' mess? Above all, is there not the victory of those, and they were many, who survived everything; profited even by Passchendaele; and afterwards still found courage enough to turn themselves to making the world a better place for themselves and everyone else, including their ex-enemies?[45]

This passage has a defeated tone, like a 'forlorn hope' charge against an already victorious enemy. By the time Hamilton posed his rhetorical questions, a hundred soldiers' testaments had answered them: and the answer was 'No'.

One can see easily enough why military historians and generals deplored the version of war that the war books told. It was not simply that in that version the war was bloody and cruel; it was that it was meaningless. If the myth-making authors of those books were right, then the war had no history, in the sense of a story expressing the meaning of events, but was anti-historical, apocalyptic, an incoherence, a gap in time.

The Myth accomplished this demolition of meaning, as Jerrold acutely observed, by telling the story of the war not in the traditional way — that is, in terms of the big battalions — but through the stories of individuals, and obscure ones at that: junior officers and men in the ranks. But to the individual personally, Jerrold wrote, 'all operations of war are meaningless and futile'. The story that he wanted told instead was the *other* story, of 'the conflict of *armies*', where the meaning was clear, and the values unambiguous.

The War Books Controversy was a quarrel over history; but it was also a literary dispute. Critics like Partridge, Williamson, Blunden and Read, the ex-soldiers who first treated war books extensively and critically, shared the conviction that the best of the books they wrote about were *literature*. But they also agreed that these books could not attain to that high status by the old means. One is constantly aware, reading their critical assessments, of the literary problems that the war-book genre posed for them: problems of technique, of style, and of relation to past literary traditions. Consider, as examples, the following remarks made by war writers about other men's war books:

Graves on Mottram and Blunden: 'Mr Mottram's command of literary technique is all against him ... Mr Blunden too is not helped in his task by his mastery of traditional literary technique.'

Williamson on Blunden: 'Mr Blunden writes with restraint, which is a necessary attitude for the artist; but too much restraint, like too much tranquillity in a young writer, may result in sterilisation.'

Read on Barbusse: 'Barbusse was never quite satisfactory because one felt the presence always of the humanitarian Socialist; it was realistic enough, but it was also rhetorical, and rhetoric, in this context, was always false.'

Graves on Carrington: '... he spoils its force by quoting familiar passages of Shakespeare, Carlyle, Wordsworth, Kipling, and Bunyan. And he seems reticent about the really shameful things that happened.'

Read on Sassoon: 'It is not the literary skill I object to; obviously, once your aim is clear, the more skill you can bring to bear on its expression the better. What I feel rather is that the aim is nothing but literary; it is art for art's sake, and the horrors and the human misery are there so as to make what Mr Sassoon calls "an impressive picture of 'Despair'".'[46]

The literary implications are clear enough: the literary tradition is an obstacle, reticence and restraint inhibit the truth, rhetoric lies. These provide principles for writing about war, but they are principles that extend far beyond that subject, into the literary rendering of all reality. If this is the way to write about war, it must also be the way to write about the world that the war made.

Of these principles, far the most important is that concerning rhetoric: for these writers, the war's great betrayal had been a betrayal of language. 'The whole war was fought for rhetoric,' Read wrote:

— fought for historical phrases and actual misery, fought *by* politicans and generals and *with* human flesh and blood, fanned by false and artificially created mob passions; a war 'waged' by rhetoricians, with rhetoric, for the sake of more rhetoric. Is it any wonder that some men not wholly caught in that windy blast, and not altogether torn in body and mind, should challenge the whole concept of history which subordinates the individual mind to the events it endures. The pen is mightier than the sword, and is now turned against the sword. Here is a different kind of rhetoric ...[47]

There is an ontological opposition here that I have remarked before, between the *words* of war and the *things* of war, between rhetoric and flesh and blood, and a turning away from the Big Words that Owen proscribed, and towards a language that will approach as closely as possible the actual physical reality of war.

The extreme example of that effort is the double-page spread in *Goodbye to All That* in which Graves went beyond narrative to reproduce directly documents drawn from his own military career, as though any account of these records would filter and so falsify reality. In his 'List of Illustrations' these documents are identified as 'VARIOUS RECORDS, MOSTLY SELF-EXPLANATORY', and are described as follows:

> The Court of Inquiry mentioned in the bottom left-hand message was to decide whether the wound of a man in the Public Schools Battalion — a rifle shot through his foot — was self-inflicted or accidental. It was self-inflicted. B. Echelon meant the part of the battalion not in the trenches. IDOL was the code-name for the Second Battalion the Royal Welch Fusiliers. The notebook leaf is the end of my 1915 diary only three weeks after I began it; I used my letters home as a diary after that. The message about Sergeant Varcoe was from Captain Samson shortly before his death; I was temporarily attached to his company.[48]

How circumstantial and located it all is: the battalion duties, the dead captain, the dated notebook and, in the lower left-hand corner, the self-inflicted wound. The two pages are a war story, a version of the Myth made out of actual things, and a paradigm case of the reaction against rhetoric and against language itself that was so significant a part of the war-books controversy.

More is at stake here than how to write a war story. If you remove from literary discourse all abstract propositions — about values, about history, about heroism, freedom and sacrifice, about the nation and its institutions; if you distrust language, and make that distrust the basis of your style; if you fragment narrative structure, and accept incoherence as reality's image; and if you shift narrative inward, to the confinement of subjective experience, then what you have is something very like High Modernism. This is not to say that war writing and Modernism were the same movement: they weren't, and their differences are important. Most obviously, the war writers did not indulge in formal difficulty, nor seek the minority audience that the cult of difficulty presumed. They shared that sense of urgency that Owen expressed when he wrote that 'all a poet can do today is warn', and though they were not all peace-propagandists, as men like Falls and Jerrold believed them to be, they were all concerned to tell the truth — their truth — about war to the world, and especially to the next generation, and that aim implied a large general audience, and an open, available style.

But if war writing and Modernism were not identical, they were more closely connected than is commonly assumed. Perhaps the best way to describe that connection is to say that during the later years of the Twenties, war writing and Modernist writing interpenetrated each other. Look, for example, at the ways in which war is a part of the reality of major Modernist novels of those years — of *Lady Chatterley's Lover,* and of Ford's *Last Post,* two Condition-of-England novels of the late Twenties, neither rendering the war directly, yet both containing the war and its destructive consequences for individuals, for society, and for England. Or consider Virginia Woolf's *To the Lighthouse,* a novel which takes its form quite explicitly from the Myth of the War: a first part set in the world before the war, a third part in the changed world after the war, and separating those parts 'Time Passes', in which the war occurs as a parenthetical example of time's destruction:

> [A shell exploded. Twenty or thirty young men were blown up in France, among them Andrew Ramsay, whose death, mercifully, was instantaneous.]⁴⁹

Or look at the ways in which images of war penetrate the poetry of the period — Eliot's *Sweeney Agonistes* and *Coriolan,* Yeats's *Winding Stair* poems, Pound's *Cantos* — as though it was a subject too great and too insistent to be ignored, whatever the ostensible subject might be.

The interpenetration worked in the other direction, too. When Read reviewed *All Quiet* in 1929, and quoted Remarque's passage about his doomed generation, he went on to comment on it as follows:

> It might seem, that in expressing the point of view of a generation, the author had fallen into the same error as Barbusse, and foregone that universality which is the essential condition of great art. That is not so, because a man who is 'burnt out' has no prejudices: he is either all or nothing, generally nothing. Hollow men. Why Herr Remarque should rise out of this 'cactus land' and speak so powerfully is perhaps difficult to understand.⁵⁰

Reaching out for metaphors for the war's ruined generation, Read found them in Eliot's 'Hollow Men', a poem that has no evident connection with

the war, and used them without explanation or justification, as though it
were self-evident that the figures described in the poem occupied the same
ruined post-war world, and suffered the same spiritual annihilations, as
Remarque's young soldiers did. By the end of the Twenties, the War Myth
and the Waste Land Myth were simply two versions of the same reality.

The implications of the War Books Controversy reached far beyond
the events of the war, into society at large, into politics and art, history
and literature, into the future; its subject was not simply the truth about
the war, but the truth about the world. Read recognized that fact when
he wrote of the controversy:

> Generally, I think, it may be said that two things are involved; a
> conception of history, and a scale of values ... The opposing
> historical conceptions may be represented simply in this manner: are
> we to regard history as a determinate process to which the individual
> contributes merely one iota of significance; or is history the record of
> human sensibility in the very toils of this determinate process? —
> more briefly: is history to be written from the point of view of God or
> of Man? The opposing moral values are simply these: political
> idealism and human life.[51]

Read's formulation seems, in the most general terms, correct; it was
history and values that were at stake, with all the issues that stem from
those large terms — issues involving social structures and institutions,
continuity and discontinuity, tradition, culture, civilization, nation-
hood. These were not issues having only to do with the rendering of the
war; they concerned the post-war world generally. The history of
English art and thought in the Twenties is a record of attempts to
reconstruct history and values, and so build a new culture out of the
broken images left by the war. Only at the end of that decade was the
war itself remade, the vast loss described and mythologized, in the prose
narratives that became the war-book canon. As the Twenties turned and
became the Thirties, the future would be different — anticipated
differently and imagined differently, because that canon had been formed.

IV

By the time the decade of the Thirties began, the Myth of the War
had been constructed in its essential and persisting form, and that

construction may be regarded as an act of closure, both for the war and for the decade that followed it. The closure was primarily a matter of printed books and films, but not entirely: two painters completed projects during the myth-making years that were also, in their ways, concluding statements about the war's meaning.

One was yet another revision of Orpen's 'To the Unknown British Soldier in France'. Orpen had begun the picture as a commissioned painting of the Versailles Conference, and had then painted out the dignitaries and painted in a coffin, cherubs, and mourning soldiers, a version that the Imperial War Museum refused to accept. In 1928 he reopened negotiations with the IWM, offering to repaint the picture and submit it again as a memorial to Field Marshall Earl Haig, who had just died. This time he painted out the soldiers, the cherubs, and the hanging garlands; what was left was simply a coffin, draped with a flag and surmounted by a soldier's helmet (see plate 26).

The IWM accepted this version of the picture, and rightly I suppose; it is beautifully painted, and it no longer contains anything likely to mystify or offend old soldiers. Still, it is an odd kind of memorial for a famous commander: an ornate painting of a gaudy room, centred on an anonymous coffin and an empty space. This, Orpen seemed to be saying, is what it all amounted to: the armies, the victories, the medals and the titles are all gone, even the poor, mad soldiers have departed; nothing is left but a nameless dead soldier in a cold emptiness. It is a disturbing picture.

A year earlier, in 1927, another English painter, Stanley Spencer, began a war-memorial commission that would occupy him for five years — a series of paintings that would cover the walls of a memorial chapel especially built to house them. They are the last important war paintings of the First War, the largest, and the greatest.

Spencer's chapel, dedicated as the Oratory of All Souls and commonly known as the Sandham Memorial Chapel, was built at Burghclere, Berkshire, between 1923 and 1927. Spencer began work on the paintings as soon as the building was completed, and finished the last in 1932, when the whole series was installed. For his subjects, Spencer drew on his own experiences of the war, and the pictures taken together constitute a kind of autobiography, 'a sort of Odyssey' as he said, like the war memoirs of Graves and Sassoon. Spencer had served as a private soldier, in two humble roles; he had first been an orderly in a Bristol war hospital, and had then transferred to the Royal Berkshire Infantry and had served in Macedonia on the Salonika front, part of the time as an ambulance man. He had known the suffering of war, though he had not taken part in any major battles, or been distinguished in a military way.

Like some of the great Italian fresco-painters, Spencer ranged his pictures along the side walls of the chapels on three levels. The lowest range of panels represents scenes from the military hospital: men scrubbing floors, sorting laundry, filling tea urns and serving tea, making beds, treating patients — the sorts of duties that Spencer performed as an orderly. The middle range of panels, a series of arched lunettes, includes further hospital scenes, but also reaches out to the Salonika front with pictures of men in camps, at reveille, filling water bottles, reading maps, burning off the grass around a bivouac. The two uppermost paintings, each running the entire length of a side wall, represent on one side morning in a camp in Macedonia and on the other a Macedonian landscape in which troops are building roads, playing cards, and making mosaic designs on the ground, using coloured pebbles.

The story that these pictures tell is of army life, but not of war; there are no military formations, no enemy forces, no battle lines, no guns, and only one officer. Men work, eat, and play together, and serve their comrades in simple ways; they do not try to kill each other. The spirit of the paintings is of comradeship, kindness, caring, and love, and in the landscapes there is a kind of pastoral innocence, as though the news of the death of landscape on the Western Front had not yet reached the outskirts of the war in Macedonia.

Spencer's war story, as these paintings tell it, is different from most of the canonical memoirs in two fundamental ways: in its spirit of gentle humility, and in its visionary religiousness. In Spencer's mind, these qualities were intimately connected. Describing his scheme in a lecture in 1923 he said: 'In this scheme there are many pictures of very ordinary moments in the kind of life I was living at the time ... All these activities will reveal in each of these pictures a kind of spiritual meaning.'[52] And in a letter to his wife Hilda he explained how this could be, in war paintings:

I would like to explain what was at the back of my mind when I began to want to do these pictures. Well, when I first enlisted ... after about three weeks, I began to feel ... I was dying of starvation, spiritual starvation, and this feeling intensified my desire for spiritual life. 'I must find it. Where is it? I used to find it in painting pictures. Where is it now?'

And then suddenly I began to see and catch hold of little particles of this life in the scrubbing of a floor or the making of a bed and so, gradually, everything began to reveal to me. Everything I did meant a spiritual revelation to me. Everything I had to do became a key to my conception of spiritual life. Just cutting up bread and butter in the kitchen ward revealed to me as much of the spiritual life I longed to attain to, as if I had sat down and had half an hour's talk with God.[53]

That sense of the spiritual meaning of ordinary acts informs and connects the paintings in one central theme. 'In every picture in the scheme,' Spencer wrote in a letter in 1929, 'there is a feeling of joy and hopeful expectancy, as though what they were doing was all a part of a graduated course, leading distinctly and logically to the resurrection.'[54] Resurrection appears in these paintings on three levels: as the ordinary daily resurrection of men from sleep, as the great resurrection of the Armistice, and as the Christian Resurrection. Several of the side-wall paintings are morning scenes, and in two of them — the two lunettes nearest the east wall of the chapel — the morning is that of November 11, 1918. 'The idea . . . occurred to me,' Spencer wrote in a letter in 1928,

> in thinking how marvellous it would be if one morning, when we came out of our dug-outs, we found that somehow everything was peace and that war was no more . . . It is a sort of cross between an 'Armistice' picture and a 'Resurrection'.[55]

Resurrection in the Christian sense is the subject of the great east-wall painting (see plate 27). Spencer had thought of this picture from the beginning as 'the resurrection of soldiers in Salonika', and it has some of the spirit of a church altarpiece, with Christ as the central figure; but it also contains the other senses of resurrection. In the picture dawn breaks over Macedonian hills, and in the foreground dead soldiers climb out of stony graves, in a tangle of white crosses. They greet each other warmly, while other soldiers (are they living or dead?) prepare them-selves as though for an inspection, polishing buttons and wrapping puttees. Behind these figures is a collapsed wagon, with men and mules around it; both men and mules are waking, from sleep or death, and turning towards the central space above and beyond them, where the resurrected dead gather around Christ, each carrying his own white cross. 'The part . . . where Christ is,' Spencer explained,

> and where the men are handing their crosses in, (symbolic of the way that on being demobilised one handed in one's equipment) is perhaps

the main subject notion . . . meaning that in the resurrection they have even finished with that last piece of worldly impedimenta.[56]

Still further back, the landscape rises past a stone fortress towards the distant horizon. On these hillsides men are sleeping wrapped in blankets, or are just waking. It is a picture of soldiers' dawn, of Armistice Day, and of the Day of Resurrection, a picture at once particular and joyous, physical and spiritual.

These two works, Orpen's revised 'memorial' and Spencer's Oratory, may be seen as two visual acts of closure, at the end of the period of First World War paintings. Both have a kind of finality about them, as though the artist had taken his vision of war as far as it would go. Orpen had reached an extreme and empty cynicism, beyond mourning soldiers and guardian angels. Spencer had moved in the opposite direction, to a spiritual vision that was free of the darker emotions of the Myth, a vision of the occasions in his own war when he had been happy serving others, and of the companionship of ordinary soldiers, and of the resurrection of the dead. With the completion of these two enterprises, the story of the war had come to its dissonant conclusion, and the war was finally over.

EPILOGUE

Remarque described his war generation as 'burnt out', and many other ex-soldiers felt as he did, that they were a 'missing generation' in post-war culture, an interruption in the course of modern art and thought. 'We are not only "the last men of an epoch",' Wyndham Lewis wrote in 1937,

> ... we are more than that, or we are that in a different way to what is most often asserted. *We are the first men of a Future that has not materialised.* We belong to a 'great age' that has not 'come off'. We moved too quickly for the world. We set too sharp a pace. And, more and more exhausted by War, Slump and Revolution, the world has *fallen back.*[1]

This sounds odd, coming from an important and productive artist and writer, but what he said of his generation was true. As a generation they did not develop, or if they did, it was not in the direction that modern English culture as a whole was taking. Poets like Graves, Blunden, and Sassoon did not advance formally beyond their early styles, Read and Williamson remained minor imaginative writers, Lewis was never again as avant-garde as he had been in 1914, Nevinson abandoned his early Vorticism for a conservative representational style.

Nor did they easily find secure places in English literary and artistic circles. At the end of the Twenties Graves had gone off to Majorca, Aldington was in Paris, and Ford was in New York. Williamson was in a Devon cottage trying to live by his writing, and Blunden, just back from three years of teaching in Japan, was struggling to survive as a journalist in London. Carrington was teaching in a provincial school;

Manning, seriously ill, was avoiding London and writing nothing. Nevinson and Nash moved restlessly back and forth between London and France; Lewis stayed in London and wrote, but did not paint much. Only Sassoon had achieved a notable degree of success: his *Memoirs of a Fox-hunting Man* had won both the Hawthornden and the James Tait Black Prize in 1928; but he lived an unsettled, outsider's life, in and out of London, writing and hunting. None of these old soldiers had penetrated to the centre of either the literary establishment or the avant-garde. Together they had achieved a place in English cultural history: they had imagined war. But as a generation they had not rooted.

At that time, as the Myth was coming into its fullest expression, a new decade was beginning. That decade would acquire a strong identity of its own, and 'the Thirties' would come to be as evocative a phrase for a tone, a style, and a set of problems as 'the Twenties' had become. But history is not metric, and decades do not begin from nothing when the numbers change; the new decade would build its identity on elements inherited from the decade before.

One of those elements was a spirit of urgent, anxious pacifism — the spirit that in the Thirties would produce the Peace Ballot and the Peace Pledge Union. That spirit had been strengthened by the general anti-militarist tone of the war books, but it had not been created by them. It had been building throughout the Twenties, and manifested itself in many forms besides the novels and memoirs at the decade's end. One can see it, for example, in two issues raised in the House of Commons.

One is the debate on questions of military discipline that continued through the Twenties. In 1923 Parliament abolished Field Punishment No. 1, the infamous 'crucifixion' in which the prisoner was tied spreadeagled to the wheel of an artillery piece. At the same time the question was raised and debated of reducing the number of capital offences under military law, though no action was taken. In 1925 that debate was renewed, and two offences were eliminated. The debate continued in subsequent years until in 1928 eight further offences were dropped from the list, leaving only mutiny, treachery, cowardice, and desertion as firing-squad crimes. In 1929 a motion was made to abolish the death penalty for cowardice and desertion. The debate that followed recalls the discussions just after the war as to the nature of cowardice and its relation to shell-shock. On this occasion, as on the earlier ones, strong speeches were made arguing that cowardice was a psychological state to be treated, not a moral lapse to be punished by death. The amendment failed; but it was renewed in 1930, and this time passed.[2]

A second issue involving attitudes towards war arose in October 1929 when a Tory MP, Captain Sir George Bowyer, asked the Home Secretary during Parliamentary question time whether the Armistice Service at the Cenotaph that year would be the usual ceremony. The Home Secretary replied that the arrangements generally would follow the lines adopted in previous years, but that the number of troops on duty would be substantially reduced. Why was that being done? Bowyer asked. 'Because', the Home Secretary replied, 'there is an increasing public feeling that, while we should continue to pay our tribute to the dead, as far as possible these ceremonies should partake of a civilian aspect more and more,' and he cited the wishes of the deceased men's relatives. Major Cohen, MP, then asked: 'Does the right hon. gentleman imply that when there are no relatives of ex-servicemen left the Armistice Service will be dropped?' The Secretary of State for War responded: 'I cannot answer hypothetical questions, but I hope that when there are no relatives left we shall have forgotten what war is.'[3]

In European diplomacy this pacific spirit expressed itself most obviously in the League of Nations and in international treaties: the Locarno Conference and Treaty in 1925, guaranteeing non-aggression between Germany, France, and Belgium; the Kellogg-Briand Pact in 1928, renouncing war as an instrument of national policy; and the London Conference on Naval Disarmament and Treaty in 1930. One might have been justified in thinking, as the decade turned, that Europe had learned the lesson of the First World War, and that peace would thereafter be maintained because the people and their leaders wanted it.

But there was another, contrary spirit rising in Europe — an authoritative, violent spirit. In Italy, Mussolini and his Fascists had been in power for most of a decade; in Spain a right-wing coup had made General Primo de Rivera dictator; in Germany Hitler's National Socialists had won more than a hundred seats in the Reichstag; in the Soviet Union Stalin controlled the state. In response to all this authoritarian energy, the democracies of the West drew back defensively. In 1930 France began the construction of the Maginot Line, a line of defence that would come to symbolize the West's failure to act, and that in the end did nothing to stop German aggression.

It is not surprising, in these circumstances, that the First World War began to recede from English imaginations, to be replaced by the fearful image of a different war, the Second World War. That war had begun to be imagined earlier, in the Twenties: there are references to it as a possibility in both Wells's *Meanwhile* and Galsworthy's *Swan Song,* for example, and as the decade of the Thirties proceeded it even entered the old war's myth, as a melancholy coda. 'It is sad to think', Williamson wrote in 1934,

> that in a few years, perhaps, the literature of the war of 1914–1918 will be forgotten, like that of other wars, in a European war arising not because the last war was forgotten, but because its origins and contributing causes in each one of us in Europe were never clearly perceived by ourselves.[4]

Williamson was wrong in thinking that the literature of his war would be forgotten; but he was right about the European war that was coming.

There would be another war — by the early Thirties most thoughtful Englishmen believed that. And it would be fought by a new generation. That generation is another significant difference between the Twenties and the Thirties. Its members had been children while the First World War was being fought, and had come of age in its aftermath, in the post-war atmosphere of ruination and public chaos. These young people would differ from their elders in many ways, but perhaps most importantly in the fact that for them the Myth of the War had already taken form when they reached maturity; it was a part of their world, it was the truth about war.

That truth turns up everywhere in the writings of the Thirties generation — in the poems of Auden, Spender, and Day Lewis, in the reportage of George Orwell, in the novels of Graham Greene and Evelyn Waugh. A vivid example is in Waugh's *Vile Bodies,* published in 1930. Waugh's novel ends on a battlefield of the Next World War, a scene that has clearly been composed out of details from recent war books and films.

> The scene all round him was one of unrelieved desolation; a great expanse of mud in which every visible object was burnt or broken. Sounds of firing thundered from beyond the horizon, and somewhere above the grey clouds there were aeroplanes.[5]

But Waugh had got more than descriptive details from the Myth: he had learned a tone, neither bitter nor angry, but accepting, taking the war that was coming for granted as a black ironic joke that was waiting to be played on him and his generation. This is the Myth, transformed by a new generation for a new war. Men of Waugh's generation would go to war in a mood very different from that in which their elders had volunteered in 1914. They would go without dreams of glory, expecting nothing except suffering, boredom and perhaps death — not cynically, but without illusions, because they remembered a war: not the Great War itself, but the Myth that had been made of it.

Much had changed in English culture in the years between the war and the time when Waugh wrote his novel. Ideas about war had changed; morality had changed; ideas about art had changed; language had changed. At the end of the Twenties, Virginia Woolf meditated on the nature of change in *A Room of One's Own,* a book that is yet another product of the myth-making years. At the book's beginning she describes a university luncheon party — a recent, post-war occasion. The food is good, and the talk flows freely and amusingly; and yet, she thinks, something seems lacking, something is different.

> But what was lacking, what was different, I asked myself, listening to the talk? And to answer that question I had to think myself out of the room, back into the past, before the war indeed, and to set before my eyes the model of another luncheon party held in rooms not very far distant from these; but different. Everything was different.[6]

The difference is between pre-war and post-war society. When Woolf sought a name for the quality in the earlier party that is missing from her present occasion, the word that she found was *romance*. Romance is something that one finds in the poetry of Tennyson and Christina Rossetti, she said, something that 'celebrates some feeling that one used to have', back then, before the war. It is not a very precise definition, but we can supplement it from Woolf's other post-war books, for that sense of lost emotions is in all of them. Her women — Betty Flanders, Mrs Dalloway, Mrs Ramsay — feel it; and so do her men — Mr Ramsay, Septimus Smith, Peter Walsh. In their minds memories hover of an earlier time before the war, a time that seemed to hold more promise, and a sad sense that that time is gone.

The name for that sense of loss is *nostalgia*. Virginia Woolf felt it; Forster felt it when he returned to England after the war and found himself obsolete; Keynes felt it when he looked back across the abyss of war to Edwardian England and saw peace and contentment there; Clive Bell felt it, and called that lost world *civilization*. It was not a feeling confined to Bloomsbury sensibilities; one finds it in the minds and works of many other artists of the time — in Galsworthy and Ford, Nash and Elgar, the Sitwells, Sassoon, Graves. It is as much a part of post-war consciousness as its companion feeling, disillusionment.

What catastrophe had caused this sense of loss? Virginia Woolf asked:

Shall we lay the blame on the war? When the guns fired in August 1914, did the faces of men and women show so plain in each other's eyes that romance was killed? Certainly it was a shock (to women in particular with their illusions about education, and so on) to see the faces of our rulers in the light of the shell-fire. So ugly they looked — German, English, French — so stupid. But lay the blame where one will, on whom one will, the illusion which inspired Tennyson and Christina Rossetti to sing so passionately about the coming of their loves is far rarer now than then. One has only to read, to look, to listen, to remember. But why say 'blame'? Why, if it was an illusion, not praise the catastrophe, whatever it was, that destroyed illusion and put truth in its place? For truth ... those dots mark the spot where, in search of truth, I missed the turning up to Fernham. Yes, indeed, which was truth and which was illusion, I asked myself?[7]

Past and present, romance and loss: which was the truth, which the illusion? Virginia Woolf did not answer the questions that she asked; she simply expressed her feeling, which was the feeling of her contemporaries, that there had been a time, before the war, when emotions ran deeper and life seemed richer and more certain. That time was past, and she would live in the world that was left, the world after the war, because there was no alternative. But she would go on expressing her nostalgia for that other, lost world.

Shall we lay the blame on the war? No, one does not blame history for its events and consequences. One tries instead to understand it, and to understand the ways in which men and women, faced with the new and terrible realities of history, have striven to comprehend them by imagining them. In our reality, here at the century's end, the First World War remains a powerful imaginative force, perhaps the most powerful force, in the shaping not only of our conceptions of what war is, but of the world we live in — a world in which that war, and all the wars that have followed it, were possible human acts. Our world begins with that war. If, as Virginia Woolf said, it killed romance, that is a part of our reality too, to be comprehended, to be imagined, and to be understood in the imaginings of others.

NOTES

Introduction

1. George Orwell, *The Road to Wigan Pier*, (London: 1937), p. 170.
2. Stephen Spender, *The Struggle of the Modern* (London: 1963), p. 168.
3. F.R. Leavis, *For Continuity* (Cambridge: 1933), p. 158; Spender, *The Creative Element* (London: 1953) p. 142.
4. Paul Fussell, *The Great War and Modern Memory* (New York: 1975), p. 21.

PART I
Chapter 1

1. The remark was not made in print, so far as I can discover, until ten years after the event, when Grey put it into his memoirs, but very tentatively:

> A friend came to see me on one of the evenings of the last week — he thinks it was on Monday, August 3. We were standing at a window of my room in the Foreign Office. It was getting dusk, and the lamps were being lit in the space below on which we were looking. My friend recalls that I remarked on this with the words: 'The lamps are going out all over Europe; we shall not see them lit again in our lifetime.' (Viscount Grey of Fallodon, *Twenty-Five Years 1892–1916* [New York: 1925], vol. II, p. 20.)

A decade later, when G.M. Trevelyan wrote the life of Grey, the tentativeness had evaporated: Grey said it, and he said it on the night of

August 3. (George Macaulay Trevelyan, *Grey of Fallodon* [Boston: 1937], p. 302.) Dictionaries of quotations have been more cautious: they attribute the remark to Grey, but tend to avoid identifying sources.

2. *The Letters of Henry James*, ed. Percy Lubbock, vol. ii (London: 1920), p. 398.

3. *The Letters of Virginia Woolf*, vol. ii (New York: 1976), p. 51. The letter, addressed to Katherine Cox, is dated Aug. 12, 1914.

4. *The Times*, Jan. 19, 1914, 8 and March 16, 13.

5. Emmeline Pankhurst, *My Own Story* (London: 1914), p. 299.

6. *The Times*, July 18, 1914, 10.

7. Quoted in Joshua C. Taylor, *Futurism* (New York: 1961), p. 124.

8. *Vorticism and Its Allies*, the Hayward Gallery, London, March 27–June 2, 1974.

9. Pound, 'The New Sculpture', *Egoist*, vol. i (Feb. 16, 1914), 68.

10. Pound, 'Wyndham Lewis', *Egoist*, vol. i (June 15, 1914), 234.

11. E.P., 'Chronicles', *Blast*, no. 2 (July 1915), 86.

12. 'Manifesto', *Blast*, no. i (June 20, 1914), 30–31.

13. Lewis, 'Futurism, Magic and Life', *Blast*, no. i, 133.

14. *Letters of Roger Fry*, ed. Denys Sutton, vol. ii (London: 1972), p. 380; H.V. Marrot, *Life and Letters of John Galsworthy* (London: 1935). p. 396; P.N. Furbank, *E.M. Forster: A Life*, vol. i (London: 1977), p. 259; *Letters of D.H. Lawrence*, ed. George J. Zytaruk and James T. Bolton, vol. ii (Cambridge: 1981), p. 211; Evan Charteris, *Life and Letters of Sir Edmund Gosse* (New York and London: 1931), p. 365; *Letters of Rupert Brooke*, ed. Sir Geoffrey Keynes (London: 1968), p. 607.

15. James, *Letters*, vol. ii, p. 462.

16. Edmund Gosse, 'War and Literature', *Edinburgh Review*, vol. 220 (Oct. 1914), 313.

17. Rupert Brooke, 'Peace'. The poem was first published in December 1914, in *New Numbers*, no. 4.

18. Gosse, 'War and Literature', 321.

19. Gosse, 'War and Literature', 331.

20. Selwyn Image, *Art, Morals, and the War* (Oxford: 1914), p. 18.

21. *Art, Morals and the War*, p. 19.

22. Charles V. Stanford, 'Music and the War', *Quarterly Review*, no. 443 (April 1915), 393.

23. 'War and Poetry', *Times Literary Supplement*, Oct. 8, 1914, 448. The article is unsigned, but *TLS* files identify Clutton Brock as the author.

24. S.P.B. Mais, 'Literature and the War', *Journal of Education*, vol. 37 n.s. (April 1915), 208.

25. C.H. Collins Baker, 'Art and War', *Saturday Review*, vol. 118 (Aug. 22, 1914), 220.

26. Hilaire Belloc, *A General Sketch of the European War: the Second Phase* (London: 1916), p. 17.

27.   Wells, 'The Most Splendid Fighting in the World,' *Daily Chronicle*, Sept. 9, 1914, 4.

28.   *The Times*, Aug. 8, 1914, 9.

29.   *The Times*, Oct. 31, 1914, 9.

30.   *Henry James and H.G. Wells*, ed. Leon Edel and Gordon N. Ray (London: 1958), p. 264. The quotation is from a letter from Wells to James, dated July 8, 1915.

31.   Preface to vol. XIII, *The Atlantic Edition of the Works of H.G. Wells* (London: 1925), p. x.

32.   *Atlantic Edition*, p. x.

33.   Wells, *Boon* (London:1915), pp. 270–71.

34.   E.B. Osborn, 'The Heroic Spirits', *Morning Post*, Dec. 26, 1914, 4. Wells quoted at length from Osborn's article in the first edition of *Boon*; he removed the quotations from later editions.

Chapter 2

1.   *Later Life and Letters of Sir Henry Newbolt*, ed. Margaret Newbolt (London: 1942), p. 189. 'The Vigil' was first published in *The Island Race* (London: 1898).

2.   'War Poems from "The Times",' *The Times*, Aug. 6, 1915, 7.

3.   *The Journals of Arnold Bennett*, vol. II, ed. Newman Flower (London: 1932), p. 99.

4.   The quotation is from Hardy's journal, as quoted in Florence Emily Hardy, *The Later Years of Thomas Hardy* (London: 1930), p. 163. See also Bennett's *Journal*, vol. II, p. 103 (where he dates the meeting as Sept. 3), and Lucy Masterman, *C.F.G. Masterman* (London: 1968), p. 272. Also D.G. Wright, 'The Great War, Government Propaganda and English "Men of Letters" 1914–16', *Literature and History*, no. 7 (Spring 1978), 70–100.

5.   *The Times*, Sept. 18, 1914, 3.

6.   The apparent exceptions to this generalization are Winston Churchill who went out as a war correspondent, though he characteristically managed to get involved in the fighting, and Kipling, who was present as a civilian observer. See Malvern Van Wyck Smith, *Drummer Hodge: The Poetry of the Anglo-Boer War (1899–1902)* (Oxford: 1978).

7.   Herbert Blenheim, 'Song: in War-Time', *Egoist*, vol. I (Dec. 1, 1914), 446.

8.   Letter from Charles Morgan to his father, dated April 6, 1916; in *Selected Letters of Charles Morgan*, ed. Eiluned Lewis (London: 1967), p. 44.

9.   'Varia', *Poetry and Drama*, vol. 2 (Sept. 1914), 251.

10.   These phrases are taken from the following reviews and articles: John

Palmer, 'The Poetry of the War', *Saturday Review*, vol. 118 (Sept. 12, 1914), 290–92; 'War and Poetry', *TLS*, Oct. 8, 1914, 448; review of *Poems of the Great War*, *Athenaeum*, Sept. 19, 1914, 279; 'National Poetry', *Saturday Review*, vol. 118 (Oct. 3, 1914), 375–6; reviews in *TLS*, Sept. 24, 1914, 435, and Dec. 24, 1914, 583.

11. 'War and Poetry', *TLS*, Oct. 8, 1914, 448.

12. 'The Poetry of the War', *Saturday Review*, vol. 118 (Sept. 12, 1914), 291.

13. Clutton Brock, 'War and Poetry', *TLS*, Oct. 8, 1914, 448; R.K.R. Thornton, ed., *Ivor Gurney War Letters* (London: 1983), p. 28. Gurney's letter is dated April 8, 1915.

14. 'August 1914', *English Review*, vol. 18 (Sept. 1914), 145.

15. Masefield's notebook is in the Bodleian Library, Oxford.

16. Masefield, *The Old Front Line* (London: 1917), p. 31.

17. *The Poems and Plays of John Masefield*, 2 vols. (New York: 1918), vol. I, pp. viii–ix.

18. Albert Chevallier Tayler (1862–1925), a painter, mainly of 'official' portraits, and illustrator. He was painter for the permanent collection of the Corporation and London Guildhall Art Gallery, and his work was also represented in corporation galleries of other English cities. His portrait subjects include Admiral Earl Beatty and Field Marshal Earl Haig.

19. *The Times*, May 1, 1915, 5.

20. 'New English Art Club. Three Remarkable Works', *Morning Post*, Dec. 2, 1914, 3.

21. Letter to Ethel Sands, quoted in Wendy Baron, *Sickert* (London: 1973), p. 149. The letter is undated, but was clearly written while Sickert was at work on 'The Soldiers of King Albert'.

22. *The Times*, Aug. 18, 1914, 8.

23. *Letters of Virginia Woolf*, vol. II, p. 57; the letter is dated 3 Jan. 1915. Bell, 'Art and War', *International Journal of Ethics*, vol. 26 (Oct. 1915), 2.

24. Mrs Novello was not the only musician who disliked the song. Early in 1915 Sir Charles Stanford approached Kipling to urge him to write a marching song for the New Army that would be as popular as 'Tipperary', but more decorous in its allusions. Kipling considered the matter, but didn't write the song. The exchange is reported in the *Cambridge Magazine*, vol. 4 (Feb. 20, 1915), 271.

25. There are two, for instance, in the September 1914 issue of *The Musical Times*: 'The Comrades' Song of Hope', words by J.S. Stallybrass, music by Adolphe Adam; 'Our Island Home', words by Shapcott Wensley, music by Eaton Faning, *Musical Times*, vol. 55 (Sept. 1914), Supplement.

26. The poem is titled '*Après Anvers*'. These lines read, in Tita Brand-Cammaerts's translation:

> Sing, Belgians, sing!
> Although our wounds may bleed,
> Although our voices break,
> Louder than the storm, louder than the guns,
> Sing of the pride of our defeats,
> 'Neath this bright autumn sun,
> And sing of the joy of courage,
> When cowardice might be so sweet.

Both the French text and the translation are from Emile Cammaerts, *Belgian Poems* (London: 1915), pp. 14–15.

27.   *Musical Times*, vol. 56 (Jan. 1, 1915), 41.

28.   *The Times*, Dec. 8, 1914, 7. The piano score of the music was printed in *King Albert's Book*, a collection sold to benefit Belgian charities; it was also recorded on gramophone discs, with the actor Henry Ainsley reciting the poem, and sold very well. (Jerrold Northrop Moore, ed., *Elgar and his Publishers* [Oxford: 1987]), p. 787n.

29.   *The Times*, May 15, 1915, 11.

30.   Percy M. Young, ed., *Letters of Edward Elgar* (London: 1956), p. 229.

31.   Elgar letter to Colvin, April 13, 1915; quoted in Michael Kennedy, *Portrait of Elgar* (London: 1968), p. 225.

32.   *The Times*, Sept. 9, 1914, 3.

33.   The incident is reported in Edward Knoblock, *Round the Room* (London: 1939), p. 203. Knoblock anglicized his name from Knoblauch during the war, as many Englishmen with German-sounding names did.

34.   *The Times*, Dec. 22, 1914, 8.

35.   Virginia Woolf, *Diary*, vol. 1 (London: 1977), p. 19. The entry is dated Jan. 16, 1915.

36.   'Der Tag', *The Times*, Dec. 22, 1914, 11.

37.   J.M. Barrie, *Der Tag* (London: 1914), pp. 11–13.

38.   *The Times*, June 2, 1915, 9.

39.   Stephen Phillips, *Armageddon* (London: 1915), pp. 15 and 27–8.

40.   'The War in Fiction', *TLS*, Dec. 9, 1915, 458.

41.   His model was clearly the prolific G.A. Henty, author of numerous late-Victorian and Edwardian boys' books, including *With Clive in India* (1884), *With Moore at Corunna* (1898), *With Roberts to Pretoria* (1901), and *With Kitchener in the Soudan* (1903).

42.   Escott Lynn, *In Khaki for the King* (London: 1915).

43.   *Chums*, Aug. 15, 1914: a loose plate, tipped in facing the title-page in the British Library copy.

44.   *The Times History of the War*, 21 vols. (1914–20); *The Manchester Guardian History of the War*, 9 vols. (1914–20); Buchan, *Nelson's History of the War*, 24 vols. (1915–19); Conan Doyle, *The British Campaign in France and Flanders*, 8 vols. (1916–20); William Le Queux and Edgar Wallace, *The War*

of the Nations, 11 vols. (1914–19); Sir Edward Parrott, The Children's Story of the War, 10 vols. (1915–19); Elizabeth O'Neill, The War: A History and Explanation for Boys and Girls, 5 vols. (1914–17). For other 'instant histories' see Subject Index of the Books Relating to the European War, 1914–1918, Acquired by the British Museum, 1914–1920 (London: 1922, re-issued 1970).

45. 'Sapper', Sergeant Michael Cassidy, R.E. (London: 1915), p. 34.

46. Sergeant Michael Cassidy R.E., p. 177.

47. Spectator, vol. 115 (Dec. 25, 1915), 919.

48. Saturday Review, vol. 120 (Dec. 11, 1915), 566.

49. Saturday Review, vol. 120 (Dec. 11, 1915), 566.

50. Major-General Sir George Younghusband, A Soldier's Memories in Peace and War (London: 1917), pp. 187–8.

51. Ian Hay, The First Hundred Thousand (Edinburgh and London: 1915), p. 342.

52. Official Book of the German Atrocities (London: 1915), p. [7].

53. Report of the Committee on Alleged German Outrages [Cd. 7894], 1915, p. 6.

54. Report, Appendix, pp. 145, 133, 84.

55. See, as examples, J.H. Morgan, 'A Dishonoured Army. (I) German Atrocities in France: with Unpublished Records', R.S. Nolan, 'A Dishonoured Army (II). The Report of Lord Bryce's Committee', Nineteenth Century, vol. 77 (June 1915), 1213–33 and 1234–48; and anon., 'The Black Record of Germany', Saturday Review, vol. 119 (June 5, 1915), 569–70.

56. Arthur Machen, The Angels of Mons: The Bowmen and other Legends of the War (London: 1915). In his Introduction, and again in a Postscript, Machen denied that any of the stories in the volume had any basis in fact.

57. Including the historian Arnold Toynbee, who published two books in 1917 based on published atrocity sources: The German Terror in Belgium and The German Terror in France.

Chapter 3

1. W.R. Colton, 'The Effects of War on Art', The Architect, vol. 45 (March 17, 1916), 200. Colton's works included a statue of King Edward VII in King's Lynn and a drinking fountain in Hyde Park.

2. 'Art after Armageddon', Athenaeum (Sept. 12, 1914), 269.

3. Connoisseur, vol. 40 (May 1915), 56.

4. The Times, March 10, 1915, 8.

5. Noel Carrington, ed., Mark Gertler: Selected Letters (London: 1965), p. 106.

6. Cyril Scott, 'The Connection of the War with Art and Music', The Monthly Musical Record, vol. 46 (March 1, 1916), 68–70.

7.   St John Ervine, 'The War and Literature', *North American Review*, vol. 202 (July 1915), 98. The essay was published in England in *The Englishwoman* in October 1915.

8.   'The War and Literature', *Book Monthly*, vol. 12 (April 1915), 436 & 437.

9.   James Douglas, 'Books and Bookmen: "The Rainbow"', *The Star* (London), Oct. 2, 1915, 4.

10.   John Galsworthy, 'Art and the War', *Fortnightly*, vol. 98 (Nov. 1915), 928.

11.   Gosse, 'War and Literature', in *Inter Arma: Being Essays in Time of War* (London: 1916), p. 38.

12.   R.H.C. [Orage], 'Readers and Writers', *New Age*, vol. 15 (Sept. 10, 1914), 449.

13.   'Readers and Writers', *New Age*, vol. 15 (Oct. 8, 1914), 549.

14.   W.K. Rose, ed., *The Letters of Wyndham Lewis* (Norfolk, Conn.: 1963), p. 70.

15.   For a discussion of this process, see my *Edwardian Turn of Mind* (Princeton: 1968), Chapter X.

16.   For a fuller discussion of the British scholarly community during the war see Stuart Wallace, *War and the Image of Germany: British Academics 1914–1918* (Edinburgh: 1988).

17.   'Scholars Protest Against War with Germany', *The Times*, August 1, 1914, 6.

18.   Gilbert Murray, 'Thoughts on the War', *Hibbert Journal*, vol. 13 (October 1914), 80–81. The essay is dated 'August 1914'. It was later included in Murray's collection of lectures and essays, *Faith, War and Policy* (London: 1918).

19.   It was a vision that Murray's friend George Bernard Shaw shared. Shaw wrote to Murray in November 1914, shortly after Murray's 'Thoughts' had appeared:

> . . . I have a strong feeling that if we start making international assurances of good feeling, we should begin with the Germans, to shew that in the republic of Art & Literature, & the Humanities generally, there are no frontiers and no wars. Only, the war seems to prove that this is a lie, and that the professors, saving your chair, are the worst of the lot. *The Letters of George Bernard Shaw* (London: 1985), vol. III, p. 261.

20.   W.P. Paterson, ed., *German Culture: The Contributions of the Germans to Knowledge, Literature, Art, and Life* (London: 1915), p. vi.

21.   'Germany and the Neutrals', *The Times*, Aug. 25, 1914, 5.

22.   'Today's Call', *Daily Call*, October 7, 1914, 8; Gilbert Murray, 'German Scholarship', *Quarterly Review*, vol. 223 (April 1915), 339; John Cowper Powys, *The Menace of German Culture* (London: 1915), p. 69; Ford Madox Hueffer, *When Blood is Their Argument* (London: 1915), p. xvi.

23.   Preface to Violet Hunt, *The Desirable Alien at Home in Germany*. With Preface and Two Additional Chapters by Ford Madox Hueffer (London: 1913), pp. 3n., 113n., and x.

24.   *When Blood is Their Argument*, p. vii.

25.   C.F.G.M., *Nation*, vol. 16 (March 27, 1915), 838.

26.   'Right and Left Among the Professors. Sir Arthur Quiller-Couch on Huns and Historians', *Cambridge Magazine*, vol. 4 (Nov. 14, 1914), 119.

27.   Bertrand Russell, 'The Future of Anglo-German Rivalry', in *Justice in War-Time* (Chicago and London: 1916), p. 69. The essay was first published in the *Atlantic Monthly* in July 1915.

28.   'Music and the War', *Spectator*, vol. 114 (Jan. 16, 1915), 74.

29.   Charles V. Stanford, 'Music and the War', *Quarterly Review*, vol. 223 (April 1915), 397.

30.   H.C. Colles, 'Music in War-Time', *Proceedings of the Musical Association*, 41st Session, 1914–15 (London: 1915), p. 1.

31.   Quoted in Thomas Russell, *The Proms* (London: 1949), p. 46.

32.   Dan Laurence, ed., *The Letters of George Bernard Shaw*, vol. III (London: 1985), p. 289.

33.   Newman Flower, ed., *The Journals of Arnold Bennett*, vol. II (London: 1932), p. 130.

34.   'The British Music Campaign', *The Times*, April 24, 1915, 11.

35.   *The Times*, April 24, 1915, 11.

36.   Ernest Newman, 'The War and the Future of Music', *Musical Times*, vol. 55 (Sept. 1, 1914), 571; Edmonstoune Duncan, 'Music and War', *Musical Times*, vol. 55 (Sept. 1, 1914), 573.

37.   4 & 5 Geo. 5, Bill 359 (1914). 'A Bill to Confer on his Majesty in Council power to make Regulations during the present War for the Defence of the Realm.'

38.   A. Fenner Brockway, *The Devil's Business. A Comedy in One Act* (London: 1926), p. 19.

39.   *Parliamentary Debates* (Commons) 1915, vol. 75, cols. 1994–5 (Nov. 19, 1915).

40.   *Parliamentary Debates* (Commons) 1915, vol. 77, cols. 481–2 (Dec. 22, 1915).

41.   *Parliamentary Debates* (Commons) 1915, vol. 70, col. 289 (Feb. 24, 1915).

42.   For example, the poems of W.N. Ewer, including 'Five Souls', *Nation*, vol. 16 (Oct. 3, 1914), 17, reprinted in *Five Souls and other War-Time Verses* (London: 1917), and frequently included in anti-war collections. The early war poems of W.W. Gibson, though not polemically anti-war, are also worth noting; in their realistic treatment of violence and death they anticipate the work of later poets. (See, for example, his 'Battle', *Nation*, vol. 16 (Oct. 17, 1914), 65, later included in *Battle* (London: 1916).

43.   Francis Meynell, 'War's a Crime', *Herald*, Dec, 19, 1914, 7.

44.   See Francis Meynell, *My Lives* (London: 1971).

45.   Clive Bell, *Peace at Once* (Manchester and London, n.d. [1915]), pp. 12–13. A pencilled note on the cover of the British Library's copy reads: 'Seized by the Police. This copy forwarded by the Public Prosecutor. July, 1916.'

46.   Clive Bell, 'Art and War', *International Journal of Ethics*, vol. 26 (October 1915), 7.

47.   Bell, 'Art and War', 4.

48.   Bell, 'Art and War', 5.

49.   'Women Denounce War', *Daily Herald*, Aug. 5, 1914, 2.

50.   Emmeline Pankhurst, *My Own Story* (London: 1914), p. 363.

51.   Christabel Pankhurst, *The Great War* (London: 1914), pp. 15–16.

52.   'I admit that the silly campaign of arson and violence which was in full swing at the beginning of the war, must have contributed to the effect of lawlessness which made Germany think it a propitious moment for the outbreak of hostilities. I admit that one bows one's head with shame when one hears of former officials of the Women's Social and Political Union mobbing Lord Haldane with idiot cries of treachery. But if the suffragettes and suffragists had not conducted their campaign there would not have been the vast and willing army of women which is taking men's places all over the country.' Rebecca West, 'Socialism in the Searchlight', *Daily Chronicle*, Nov. 6, 1916; quoted in Jane Marcus, ed., *The Young Rebecca* (London: 1982), p. 392.

53.   According to Sylvia Pankhurst, *The Home Front: A Mirror to Life in England during the World War* (London: 1932), p. 199. Sylvia's accounts of the Suffrage movement are not always trustworthy, and it may be that Lloyd George did not in fact provide funds for the march, but it was obviously done with the government's approval.

54.   Mary Lowndes, 'Women's Suffrage in War-Time', *The Englishwoman*, vol. 27 (July 1915), 9.

55.   B.L. Hutchins, *Women in Modern Industry* (London: 1915), pp. 253–4.

56.   For statistics on women's employment see Ministry of Reconstruction, *Report of the Women's Employment Committee* [Cd. 9239], 1919; and *Report of the War Cabinet Committee on Women in Industry* [Cd. 135], 1919.

57.   Lady Cynthia Asquith, *Diaries 1915–1918* (New York: 1969), p. 34. The entry is dated May 31, 1915.

58.   See Ministry of Reconstruction, *Report on the Women's Employment Committee*, p. 8.

59.   Enid Bagnold, *A Diary Without Dates* (London: 1918), pp. 27 and 64. Also Vera Brittain, *Chronicle of Youth* (London: 1982). The *Chronicle* is Brittain's actual wartime diary and letters; the later *Testament* was written

with the hindsight of some fifteen years, and belongs with the other myth-making versions of the war (see part V, Chapter 21 below).

60.   Florence L. Barclay, *My Heart's Right There* (London: 1914), p. 58.
61.   Cicely Hamilton, 'Non-Combatant', first published in J.W. Cunliffe, ed., *Poems of the Great War* (New York: 1916). Reprinted in Catherine W. Reilly, ed., *Scars Upon My Heart* (London: 1981), p. 46.
62.   May Sinclair, *A Journal of Impressions in Belgium* (London: 1915), p. 122.
63.   Rebecca West, 'Miss Sinclair's Genius', *Daily News* (London), August 24, 1915; reprinted in Jane Marcus, ed., *The Young Rebecca* (London: 1982), p. 305.
64.   *Young Rebecca*, p. 307.

PART II
Chapter 4

1.   H. Perry Robinson, *The Turning Point: The Battle of the Somme* (London: 1917), p. 280.
2.   The Somme offensive was not the first battle to be declared a turning point by supporters of the war. Early in 1916 Hilaire Belloc published *The Second Year of the War*, in which he remarked:

> I think one can write it down in this spring of 1916 with a fair measure of confidence that human history as a whole will see one of its great turning-points in the BATTLE OF THE MARNE. (p. 21)

Later in the book he explained what this turn (in Sept. 1914) had meant:

> The Battle of the Marne secured Europe not from an external peril, as did Tours and Chalons from the Arab and the Hun, but from one internal and spiritual. It decided that most profound of all issues which can appear within a man's own soul or within that of a nation, or within that of a whole vast tradition, such as is the tradition of Christendom — I mean whether the lesser should conquer the greater, the viler the more noble, the more changeable the more steadfast, the baser the more refined. (p. 400)

The significance of Belloc's remarks is less that he chose a preposterously early occasion for his turn than that in 1916 he felt the need to reassure English readers that a turn had indeed taken place.

3.   Timothy Materer, ed., *Pound/Lewis: The Letters of Ezra Pound and Wyndham Lewis* (London: 1985), p. 39. The letter is dated June 24, 1916; Valerie Eliot, ed., *The Letters of T.S. Eliot*, vol. I (London: 1988), p. 144 (Aug. 21, 1916).

4.   Caroline E. Playne, *Society at War* (Boston: 1931), p. 242.
5.   'Miss Asquith on Art and the War', *Morning Post*, Oct. 10, 1916, 7.
6.   'The Theatrical Year. Playwrights in War-time', *The Times*, Jan. 1, 1917, 11.
7.   See F.W.T. Lange and W.T. Berry, *Books on the Great War*, 4 vols. (London: 1915–16). Volume I of this annotated bibliography covers the period from August to December 1914, and contains more than 600 titles. Volume II runs through March 1915, and includes slightly over 500 titles. Volume III, covering the next four months, has 600 titles, and Volume IV runs through the end of April 1916, with more than 1,200 titles — nearly 3,000 titles altogether, in a period of twenty-one months (after which the series ended). English production of new books during these years was approximately 8,000 volumes per year.
8.   A. St John Adcock, 'British Authors and the War', *Bookman*, vol. 49 (Dec. 1915), 87.
9.   Alec W.G. Randall, 'Poetry and Patriotism', *Egoist*, vol. 3 (Feb. 1, 1916), 26. During the previous year Randall had been assigned by the government to work with Ford Madox Hueffer on his two propaganda books, *When Blood is Their Argument* and *Between St. Denis and St. George*
10.   The essay was first published, under the title 'Arms and the Mind', by Ford Madox Ford, in *Esquire*, vol. 94 (Dec. 1980), 78–80; the passage quoted is on p. 79.
11.   'Arms and the Mind', 80.
12.   *TLS*, Feb. 3, 1916, 50.
13.   E.T., ed., *Keeling Letters and Recollections* (London: 1918), pp. 279–80. Keeling's Christian name was Frederic, but he was always called 'Ben', and is so named in references to him by Shaw, Russell and Wells.

Chapter 5

1.   Philip Gibbs, 'The Historic First of July', *Daily Chronicle*, July 3, 1916, 1.
2.   Dispatch dated July 16; reprinted in Gibbs's *The Battles of the Somme* (London: 1917), p. 130.
3.   Gilbert Murray, 'The Evil and the Good of the War', in *Faith, War and Policy* (London: 1918), pp. 91–2.
4.   John Buchan, *Greenmantle* (London: 1916), p. v.
5.   Quoted in Vera Brittain, *War Diary 1913–1917. Chronicle of Youth*, ed. Alan Bishop and Terry Smart (London: 1981), p. 272.
6.   *War Diary*, pp. 327–8.
7.   Lady Cynthia Asquith, *Diaries 1915–1918* (New York: 1969), p. 91.

8. *The Diary of a Dead Officer: being the posthumous papers of Arthur Graeme West* (London: 1918), p. 67. The entry is dated Sept. 20, 1916.

9. [The Hon. R.G.A. Hamilton], *The War Diary of the Master of Belhaven 1914–1918* (London: 1924), pp. 226–7.

10. Private Sydney Thomas Fuller, Suffolk Regiment, *War Diary*, entry for Sept. 26, 1916. An unpublished manuscript in the Imperial War Museum, London.

11. 'Some Reflections of a Soldier', *Nation*, vol. 20 (Oct. 21, 1916), 104.

12. 'Some Reflections', 105.

13. 'Never Again! Battle Cry of the Allies', *The Times*, Sept. 29, 1916, 7.

14. *The Great Advance: Tales from the Somme Battlefield Told by Wounded Officers and Men on their Arrival at Southampton from the Front, and Published by Permission* (London: n.d. [Aug. 1916]), p. 24.

15. 'Some Reflections', 106.

16. 'Some Reflections', 105.

Chapter 6

1. In the discussion that follows I have drawn on essays by two members of the Imperial War Museum staff: S.D. Badsey's 'Battle of the Somme: British war-propaganda', *Historical Journal of Film, Radio and Television*, vol. 3 (1983), 99–115, and Roger Smither's "A wonderful idea of the fighting": the question of the fakes in *The Battle of the Somme'*, *Imperial War Museum Review*, no. 3 (1988), 4–16.

2. *Bioscope* (Aug. 17, 1916), 579.

3. *The Times*, Sept. 6, 1916, 9.

4. Quoted in Rachael Low, *The History of the British Film*, vol. 3 (1914–1918) (London: 1950), p. 29.

5. *The Times*, Sept. 1, 1916, 7.

6. *The Times*, Sept. 4, 1916, 11.

7. *The Times*, Sept. 2, 1916, 3; Sept. 6, 1916, 11.

8. D.S. Higgins, ed., *The Private Diaries of Sir H. Rider Haggard* (London: 1980), p. 84.

9. John Jolliffe, ed., *Raymond Asquith: Life and Letters* (London: 1980), p. 294.

10. Peter Vansittart, ed., *John Masefield's Letters from the Front 1915–1917* (London: 1984), p. 116. The letter is dated Sept. 1, 1916.

11. Rose Macaulay, *Non-Combatants and Others* (London: 1916), p. 149.

12. Wells, *Boon*, p. 284.

13. *Non-Combatants*, p. 69.

14. *Non-Combatants*, p. 71.

15. *Non-Combatants*, p. 305.

16.   *TLS*, Aug. 31, 1916, 416; *Westminster Gazette*, Sept. 2, 1916, 3; *Outlook*, vol. 38 (Sept. 23, 1916), 306; *Nation*, vol. 19 (Sept. 16, 1916), 768.

17.   H.G. Wells, 'The Most Splendid Fighting in the World', *Daily Chronicle*, Sept. 9, 1914.

18.   Wells, *Mr Britling Sees It Through* (London: 1916), p. 206. (The novel had been serialized in the *Nation*, May 20-Oct. 21, 1916.)

19.   *Mr Britling*, p. 282.

20.   *Mr Britling*, p. 351.

21.   *Mr Britling*, p. 431.

22.   Shaw: letter to Wells Dec. 7, 1916, in *Letters*, vol. III, p. 442; Cynthia Asquith: *Diaries 1915–1918*, p. 230 (entry dated Oct. 25, 1916); Sassoon: Rupert Hart-Davis, ed., *Siegfried Sassoon Diaries 1915–1918* (London: 1983), pp. 109–10 (entry dated Dec. 27, 1916); Hardy: in Vere Collins, *Talks with Thomas Hardy at Max Gate* (London: 1928), p. 41 (dated Dec. 29, 1920); Bennett, letter to Wells dated July 8, 1916, in *Letters*, vol. III, p. 17.

23.   Tawney, 'Some Reflections of a Soldier', *Nation*, vol. 20 (Oct. 21, 1916), 106n.

24.   *Non-Combatants*, pp. 32–3.

25.   *Women in Love* and *Heartbreak House* are discussed in relation to the war in Anne Wright's *Literature of Crisis, 1910–22* (London: 1984).

26.   George J. Zytaruk and James T. Bolton, eds., *The Letters of D.H. Lawrence*, vol. II (Cambridge: 1981). p. 441; James T. Bolton and Andrew Robertson, eds., *The Letters of D.H. Lawrence*, vol. III (Cambridge: 1984), pp. 142–3.

27.   See below, pp. 346–8.

28.   D.H. Lawrence, *Women in Love*, Ch. I. In the Cambridge Edition of the novel, ed. David Farmer, Lindeth Vasey and John Worthen (Cambridge: 1987), p. 10.

29.   *Women in Love*, Ch. I, p. 11 and Ch. XI, p. 127 (Cambridge Edition).

30.   *Women in Love*, Ch. XI, p. 127.

31.   Letter to J.B. Pinker, Oct. 31, 1916, *Letters*, vol. II, p. 669; letter to Martin Secker, May 24, 1920, *Letters*, vol. III, p. 531.

32.   *Women in Love*, Ch. XIV, p. 173.

33.   'Foreword to *Women in Love*', *Women in Love*, Cambridge Edition, p. 485.

34.   *Letters*, vol. II, pp. 389–90 (dated Sept. 9, 1915).

35.   *Letters*, vol. III, p. 25 (Nov. 7, 1916) and p. 143 (July 27, 1917).

36.   Bernard Shaw, *Heartbreak House, Great Catherine*, and *Playlets of the War* (London: 1919), p. 102.

37.   *Heartbreak House*, p. 108.

38.   *Heartbreak House*, p. 106.

39.   In a manifesto issued on July 31, 1915, on the first anniversary of the beginning of the war in Europe, the Kaiser said: '*Ich habe den Krieg nicht*

gewollt . . .' *The Times* published a translation of the manifesto on August 2nd. For a fuller account, see the explanatory note to the passage in the Cambridge Edition of *Women in Love*, p. 585.

40.   *Women in Love*, Ch. XXII, p. 479.

41.   *Heartbreak House*, p. 90.

Chapter 7

1.   Norman and Jeanne MacKenzie, eds., *The Diary of Beatrice Webb*, vol. III (London: 1984), p. 244.

2.   For an important debate on the issue of freedom of expression, see *Parliamentary Debates* (Commons), vol. LXXXIII, cols. 1086ff. (June 29, 1916).

3.   As reported in Michael Holroyd, *Lytton Strachey*, vol. II (London: 1968), p. 179. Robert Graves offers a similar version in *Good-bye to All That*, p. 308.

4.   *The Times*, June 27, 1916, 12.

5.   Rose Waugh Hobhouse, *An Interplay of Life and Art* (Broxbourne, Herts.: 1958), p. 147.

6.   *The Diary of a Dead Officer*, p. 50.

7.   Miles Malleson, *'D' Company and Black 'Ell* (London: 1925), pp. 31 and [3].

8.   *'D' Company and Black 'Ell*, pp. 63–4.

9.   *Parliamentary Debates* (Commons) 1916, vol. XXXVI, cols. 1531–2 (Oct. 31, 1916).

10.   *Parliamentary Debates* (Commons) 1916, vol. LXXXVII, col. 32 (Nov. 7, 1916).

11.   A more extreme form of Malleson's opposition to the war was the aid that he gave to deserters from the army. One such deserter, F. Beaumont Wadsworth, walked away from an English training camp in the summer of 1917, and later wrote the story of his escape and published it anonymously in the *Atlantic Monthly* ('The Deserter', *Atlantic*, vol. 146 [Sept. 1930], 300–310). In Wadsworth's account, Malleson (whom he calls 'X') sheltered him and provided him with civilian clothing, and then passed him on to Edward Carpenter, the old Socialist simple-lifer, who passed him on to a third man, who gave him introductions to friends in Ireland. Wadsworth spent the remainder of the war in Dublin, unharassed by police, and then returned to England without trouble.

12.   Robert Graves, *Good-bye to All That* (London: 1929), p. 224.

13.   *The Times*, Jan. 15, 1916, 7. Later versions have an additional line, and some variations in punctuation.

14.   Sassoon, 'The Hero', *Cambridge Magazine*, vol. 6 (Nov. 18, 1916), 145.

15.   'A Protest', *Cambridge Magazine*, vol. 6 (Dec. 2, 1916), 199.

16.   Sassoon, 'The Poet as Hero', *Cambridge Magazine*, vol. 6 (Dec. 2, 1916), 199.

17.   Graves, 'Big Words', *Over the Brazier* (London: 1916), p. 27.

18.   *Diary of a Dead Officer*, pp. 79–80. The Feston poem that West quotes is 'O Fortunati':

> O happy to have lived these epic days!
>   To have seen unfold, as doth a dream unfold,
>   These glorious chivalries, these deeds of gold,
> The glory of whose splendour gilds death's ways,
> As a rich sunset fills dark woods with fire
>   And blinds the traveller's eyes. Our eyes *are* blind
>   With flaming heroism, that leaves our mind
> Dumbstruck with pride. We have had our heart's desire!
> O happy! Generations have lived and died
>   And only dreamed such things as we have seen and known!
> Splendour of men, death laughed at, death defied,
>   Round the great world, on the winds, their tale is blown;
> Whatever pass, these ever shall abide:
>   In memory's Valhalla, an imperishable throne.

H. Rex Feston, *The Quest for Truth and Other Poems* (Oxford: 1916), p. 30.

19.   For examples see footnote 42 of Part One, Chapter 3.

20.   This is Mrs Masterman's version: see Lucy Masterman, *C.F.G. Masterman* (London: 1968), pp. 286–7. A rather different account, in William Rothenstein's *Men and Memories* (London: 1932), vol. II, p. 307, makes Rothenstein the initiator of the scheme. For a full account of English war artists see Meirion and Susie Harries, *The War Artists* (London: 1983), a book to which I am much indebted.

21.   C.E. Montague, 'The Western Front', in *The Western Front. Drawings by Muirhead Bone*, Part I (London: 1916), [p. 1]. The pages of the text are not numbered.

22.   Harold Owen and John Bell, eds., *Wilfred Owen: Collected Letters* (London: 1967), p. 429. The letter is dated Jan. 19, 1917.

23.   Ian Hamilton, 'Mr Nevinson's Pictures', *Catalogue of an Exhibition of Paintings and Drawings of War by C.R.W. Nevinson* (London: 1916), pp. 3–4.

24.   'Mr Nevinson's Pictures', p. 5.

25.   O.R.D., 'Mr Nevinson's War Pictures', *Westminster Gazette*, Oct. 2, 1916, 7.

26.   'Personality or Process. Mr. Nevinson's Pictures of Men as War Machines', *The Times*, Sept. 29, 1916, 9.

27. John Gould Fletcher, 'On Subject-Matter and War Poetry', *Egoist*, vol. 3 (Dec. 1916), 189.

28. Peter Vansittart, ed., *John Masefield's Letters From the Front 1915–1917* (London: 1984), p. 186. The letter is dated Oct. 15, 1916.

29. *Masefield's Letters*, p. 211 (March 11, 1917).

30. As an example of Masefield's prose vision of the war, consider the opening paragraph of *The Old Front Line*, his book about the Somme battlefield, published in 1917:

> This description of the old front line, as it was when the Battle of the Somme began, may some day be of use. All wars end; even this war will some day end, and the ruins will be rebuilt and the field full of death will grow food, and all this frontier of trouble will be forgotten. When the trenches are filled in, and the plough has gone over them, the ground will not long keep the look of war. One summer with its flowers will cover most of the ruin that men can make, and then these places, from which the driving back of the enemy began, will be hard indeed to trace, even with maps. It is said that even now in some places the wire has been removed, the explosive salved, the trenches filled, and the ground ploughed with tractors. In a few years' time, when this war is a romance in memory, the soldier looking for his battlefield will find his marks gone. Centre Way, Peel Trench, Munster Alley, and these other paths of glory will be deep under the corn, and gleaners will sing at Dead Mule Corner.

This is the conservative dream of war as a temporary, erasable event. Once the war is over, the world will revert to its prior condition, nature will again be Nature, the earth will be Landscape, the war will become Romance, and poems will once more be possible. It didn't happen; and because Masefield believed it would, he was an alien in the post-war world.

PART III
Chapter 8

1. Eiluned Lewis, ed., *Selected Letters of Charles Morgan* (London: 1967), pp. 46–7.

2. 'A Parable of the War', *TLS*, Aug. 2, 1917, 361. The essay was published anonymously, as was the *TLS* custom.

3. 'Co-ordination of Allies' War Aims', *Daily Telegraph*, Nov. 29, 1917, 5–6. Lansdowne had held important government posts for some forty years; he had been Governor-general of both Canada and India, War Secretary, and Foreign Secretary. During the early years of the war he was a member without portfolio of Asquith's Coalition Cabinet.

4.   *Parliamentary Debates* (Commons) 1918, vol. CIII, col. 161 (Feb. 13, 1918).

5.   Rupert Hart-Davis, ed., *Siegfried Sassoon Diaries 1915–1918* (London: 1983), p. 176. The entry is dated June 19, 1917.

6.   *Sassoon Diaries*, p. 171 (May 21, 1917).

7.   [Virginia Woolf], 'Mr. Sassoon's Poems', *TLS*, May 31, 1917, 259: 'What Mr. Sassoon has felt to be the most sordid and horrible experiences in the world he makes us feel to be so in a measure which no other poet of the war has achieved.' E.B. O[sborn], 'A Soldier Poet', *Morning Post*, May 11, 1917, 2: 'His poems from the Front are grimly humorous, making no armistice with conventional patriotism ... But all that is fancy or fretfulness vanishes when, as in his most beautiful 'Absolution,' the true meaning of this iron time is as clear and calm as a night of stars, as a morning of roses ...'

8.   Quoted in *Sassoon Diaries*, p. 173–4.

9.   Paul O'Prey, ed., *In Broken Images: Selected Letters of Robert Graves 1914–1946* (London: 1982), p. 80.

10. *Sassoon Diaries*, p. 183 (July 26, 1917).

11. Gosse, quoted in note to 'The Rear Guard', Hart-Davies, ed., *Siegfried Sassoon: The War Poems* (London: 1983), p. 76; Ross, letter to Gosse, July 19, 1917, quoted in *Sassoon Diaries*, p. 182.

12. *War Poems*, p.85. The title is also the title of a paper by W.H.R. Rivers that he read at a meeting of the Royal Society of Medicine on Dec. 4, 1917; presumably it was a phrase that he used with his patients.

13. W.H.R. Rivers, *Instinct and the Unconscious*, 2nd ed. (Cambridge: 1922), pp. 1–2.

14. Rivers, 'War Neurosis and Military Training', *Instinct and the Unconscious*, p. 208. Originally a report to the Medical Research Committee, London, and published in *Mental Hygiene*, vol. 2 (Oct. 1918), 513–33.

15. Rivers, *Conflict and Dream* (London: 1923), p. 167.

16. *Conflict and Dream*, p. 168.

17. *Conflict and Dream*, p. 171.

18. *Sassoon Diaries*, p. 197 (Dec. 19, 1917).

19. *War Poems*, p. 108. The poem is date-lined: 'Craiglockhart, 1917'.

20. *Sassoon Diaries*, p. 246 (May 9, 1918).

21. Harold Owen and John Bell, eds., *Wilfred Owen: Collected Letters* (London: 1967), p. 484 (Aug. 15, 1917).

22. *Owen Letters*, pp. 485–6 (Aug. 22, 1917).

23. Jon Stallworthy, *The Poems of Wilfred Owen* (London: 1985), p. 192. Owen's draft is reproduced as the frontispiece to this edition.

24. Max Plowman, *Bridge Into the Future: Letters of Max Plowman* (London: 1944), p. 44. The letter was written on Aug. 1, 1916; Plowman was with his regiment near Albert.

25. Max Plowman, *A Lap Full of Seed* (Oxford: 1917), p. x.
26. Plowman, *Bridge Into the Future*, p. 92. The sentiments of the third paragraph had been in Plowman's mind while he was at Bowhill; his last war poem, 'The Dead Soldiers', was written there in April 1917, and ends with these lines:

> God in every one of you is slain;
> For killing men is always killing God,
> Though Life destroyed shall come to life again
> And loveliness rise from the sodden sod.
> But if of life we do destroy the best,
> God wanders wide, and weeps in his unrest.
>
> *A Lap Full of Seed*, p. 76.

27. *Bridge Into the Future*, p. 94 (Jan. 26, 1918).
28. *Bridge Into the Future*, p. 127 (July 4, 1918).
29. *Sassoon Diaries*, p. 261.
30. *Owen Letters*, p. 580 (Oct. 4 or 5, 1918).
31. *Sassoon Diaries*, p. 189 (Oct. 4, 1917).

Chapter 9

1. Edmund Gosse, 'Some Soldier Poets', *Edinburgh Review*, vol. 226 (Oct. 1917), 311
2. Gosse, 'Some Soldier Poets', 313.
3. Gosse, 'Some Soldier Poets', 315.
4. Gosse, 'Some Soldier Poets', 315.
5. Robert Graves, 'A Dead Boche', *Fairies and Fusiliers* (London: 1917), p. 33.
6. Paul O'Prey, ed., *In Broken Images: Selected Letters of Robert Graves* (London: 1982), p. 83 (Sept. 13, 1917).
7. Isaac Rosenberg, 'Returning, we hear the larks', *Collected Works*, ed. Ian Parsons (London: 1979), p. 109 (the poem is dated 1917).
8. *Poems of Wilfred Owen*, p. 156.
9. *Fairies and Fusiliers*, p. 24.
10. Letter to Edward Marsh dated Feb. 24, 1916; *In Broken Images*, p. 40.
11. Lucy Masterman, *C.F.G. Masterman* (London: 1939), p. 287.
12. Quoted in Andrew Causey, *Paul Nash* (Oxford: 1980), p. 62. The letter is postmarked March 21, 1917.
13. Wyndham Lewis, *Rude Assignment* (London: 1950), p. 128.
14. Paul Nash, *Outline* (London: 1949), pp. 210–11. The letter, to his wife, is dated Nov. 16, 1917.

15.   *Outline*, p. 211.

16.   Margery Ross, ed., *Robert Ross, Friend of Friends* (London: 1952), p. 331 (June 11, 1918).

17.   Robert Graves, 'The British Soldier', introduction to 'The British Soldier: Exhibition of Pictures by Eric H. Kennington' (London: Leicester Galleries, 1918), pp. 4–5

18.   Arnold Bennett, 'Introductory Note', '"Void of War": An Exhibition of Pictures by Lieut. Paul Nash' (London: Leicester Galleries, 1918), pp. 4–5.

19.   T.E. Hulme, 'Diary from the Trenches', in S. Hynes, ed., *Further Speculations by T.E. Hulme* (Minneapolis: 1955), p. 164 (March 2, 1915).

20.   *Keeling Letters & Recollections*, p. 275 (March 22, 1916).

21.   Herbert Read, 'The Innocent Eye, A War Diary 1915–1918', in *The Contrary Experience* (London: 1963), p. 95 (May 22, 1917).

22.   'War As It Is', [C.E. Montague], preface to 'The Western Front: Drawings by Muirhead Bone', vol. II (London: 1917), [p. 3].

23.   Owen, *Collected Letters*, pp. 431–2 (Feb. 4, 1917).

24.   Quoted in Meirion & Susie Harries, *The War Artists*, p. 108.

25.   Wilfred Owen, *Collected Letters*, p. 521. The letter is dated Dec. 31, 1917.

26.   Timothy Materer, ed., *Pound/Lewis: The Letters of Ezra Pound and Wyndham Lewis* (London: 1985), p. 76.

Chapter 10

1.   Henri Barbusse, *Under Fire* (London: 1917), p. 254.

2.   *Under Fire*, p. 266.

3.   *Robert Ross, Friend of Friends*, p. 329 (May 25, 1918).

4.   *Sassoon Diaries*, p. 184; *Poems of Wilfred Owen*, p. 133 (note to 'The Show'); *Pound/Lewis: The Letters of Ezra Pound and Wyndham Lewis*, p. 93.

5.   *The Western Front*, p. [3].

6.   For a German judgement see Rudolf Binding, *A Fatalist at War* (London: 1929), pp. 231–2.

7.   Gerald Gould, in *New Statesman* (Sept. 8, 1917), 546.

8.   Georges Duhamel, *The New Book of Martyrs* (New York: 1918), pp. 10–11.

9.   *New Book of Martyrs*, p. 221.

10.   *TLS*, June 7, 1917, 270. Reprinted in Murry's *The Evolution of an Intellectual* (London: 1920).

11.   Letter to Robert Ross, Jan. 9, 1918, in *Robert Ross, Friend of Friends*, p. 323.

12.   *Sassoon Diaries*, p. 255 (May 22, 1918).

13. Wyndham Lewis, *Men Without Art* (London: 1934), p. 22.
14. Pvt. A. H. Hubbard. The diary is in the Imperial War Museum.
15. *Sassoon Diaries*, p. 188 (Oct. 4, 1917).
16. Bernard Adams, *Nothing of Importance* (London: 1917), p. xvii.
17. *Nothing of Importance*, p. 125.
18. *Nothing of Importance*, pp. 227–8.
19. *Nothing of Importance*, p. 181.
20. *Nothing of Importance*, pp. 304–5.
21. Rebecca West, *The Return of the Soldier* (London: 1918), pp. 5–6.
22. *Return of the Soldier*, pp. 187–8.
23. 'Shot at Dawn!' *John Bull* (Feb. 23, 1918), 6–7.
24. 'Shot at Dawn!', 7.
25. *Parliamentary Debates* (Commons), vol. CIII, col. 851 (Feb. 20, 1918).
26. See *Statistics of the Military Effort of the British Empire During the Great War* (London: 1922), Part XXIII: 'Discipline'. Anthony Babington examines many cases in detail in his *For the Sake of Example* (London: 1983). For French statistics, see Guy Pedroncini, *Les Mutineries de 1917* (Paris: 1967) and Philippe Bernard and Henri Dubief, *The Decline of the Third Republic* (Cambridge, 1985). Italian statistics are from Martin Clark, *Modern Italy 1871–1982* (London: 1984). German statistics are from *Das Werk des Untersuchungsauchsschusses der Verfassunggebenden Nationalversammlung und des Deutschen Reichstages 1919–1928*, Band 11–2 (Berlin: 1929).
27. The issue was debated in the Commons on July 7, 1915, and again on Nov. 13, 1917, when the following exchange took place:

> Mr. HOGGE (to the Under-Secretary of State for War): Is the hon. Gentleman aware that the next-of-kin are informed by a very brutal letter, and will my hon. Friend consider whether these cases could not be put in the casualty lists, so as to avoid this kind of communication to the parents? In many of these cases the boy is suffering from shell shock.
> Mr. MACPHERSON: My hon. Friend must be aware of the facts. As I think I have stated, to put these cases in the casualty lists would not be stating the true facts. It is a polite letter which is sent, stating what is necessarily a brutal fact. *Parliamentary Debates* (Commons), vol. 99, cols. 191–2.

Basil Liddell Hart in his *Memoirs* describes a period of convalescent duty during which he wrote such letters:

> A nauseating feature of it was the despatch of formal letters to the widows or parents of men who had been sentenced to death by a field court-martial, notifying them of the sentence and that it had been carried out. Until then I imagined, like most soldiers, that such executions were camouflaged in some way as accidental death. When I protested at the callousness of these bald announcements, I was told that it was a means of saving the Government's money on pensions. *The Memoirs of Captain*

Liddell Hart, vol. I (London: 1965), p. 27. Quoted in Anthony Babington, *For the Sake of Example*.

28.   Rudyard Kipling, 'Epitaphs of the War', *Rudyard Kipling's Verse: Inclusive Edition 1885–1918* (Garden City: 1922), p. 441.
29.   W.B. Yeats, Introduction, *The Oxford Book of Modern Verse* (Oxford: 1936), p. xxxiv.

Chapter 11

1.   See, for example, John Cournos, 'The Death of Futurism', *Egoist*, vol. 4 (Jan. 1917), 6–7.
2.   W.H.D. Rowse, letter to *New Witness*, vol. 10 (May 31, 1917), 114; Chesterton, 'At the Sign of the World's End: Concerning Cambridge Pacifists', *New Witness*, vol. 10 (May 31, 1917), 106–7; letter to *Morning Post*, Feb. 24, 1917, 6. Fight for Right members included the Poet Laureate, Robert Bridges, Viscount Bryce, author of the Bryce Report on German atrocities; Henry Newbolt; the poet–novelist Maurice Hewlett; composer Sir Hubert Parry; Gilbert Murray; the Revd William Temple (late Archbishop of Canterbury), and the Belgian poet Emile Cammaerts, whose 'Carillon' Elgar had set to music with such success in 1914.
3.   *The Times*, July 5, 1917, 9.
4.   Doris Arthur Jones, *The Life and Letters of Henry Arthur Jones* (London: 1990), p. 297. The letter is dated Dec. 8, 1917.
5.   Harold Owen, *Common Sense About the Shaw* (London: 1915).
6.   Harold Owen, *Loyalty* (London: n.d. [1918], pp. 79–80, 47, 83, 126–7, 166–7.
7.   *Court Journal*, quoted in back matter of *Loyalty*, p. [170]: Chesterton, 'At the Sign of the World's End. The Lost Point of "Loyalty"', *New Witness*, vol. 11 (Dec. 6, 1917), 130–1.
8.   'An Anonymous Play at the St. James's,' *The Times*, Nov. 22, 1917, 9.
9.   Owen, *Loyalty*, p. xxi.
10.   Lt. Col. C. à Court Repington, *The First World War 1914–1918* 2 vols. (London: 1920), vol. II, p. 320.
11.   Harold Owen, *Disloyalty: The Blight of Pacifism* (London: 1918), p. 51.
12.   Quoted in *Annual Register for 1918* (London: 1919), part I, p. 27.
13.   *Disloyalty*, p. 222. Owen is quoting A.G. Gardiner, the editor of the *Daily News*.
14.   'God's Lovely Lust', *The Antidote*, no. 4 (June 12, 1915), 15.
15.   John Buchan, *Greenmantle* (London: 1916), pp. 83–4.
16.   *Manual of Military Law* (London: HMSO, 1894), p. 136.
17.   John Jolliffe, *Raymond Asquith: Life and Letters* (London: 1980), p. 290.

18.   *Vigilante*, April 13, 1918.

19.   Billing published a verbatim report of the proceedings in the *Vigilante* for April 6, 1918, 1–5; April 13, 1–3; and June 15, 1–8; he later issued the report as a pamphlet, *Rex v. Pemberton Billing* (London: 1918). The quotation is from the *Vigilante*, April 13, 3.

20.   *Vigilante*, April 13, 1918, 3.

21.   *Vigilante*, June 15, 1918, 7.

22.   'Vanoc' [Arnold White], 'An Old Bailey Thunderstorm: The Wider Issues', *Referee*, June 9, 1918. The term *urning* is taken from the German writer on sex, Iwan Bloch.

23.   Arnold White, 'Efficiency and Vice', *English Review*, vol. 22 (May 1916), 450; reprinted in *Vigilante*, April 20, 1918, 4.

24.   James Hepburn, ed., *Letters of Arnold Bennett*, vol. III (London: 1970), p. 60. The letter is dated May 24, 1918.

25.   'The Unclassed', *Athenaeum* (June, 1918), 277.

26.   'The War in Patchouli', *Nation*, vol. 23 (May 11, 1918), 154.

27.   H.M. Richardson, 'An Ignoble New Novel', *Sunday Chronicle* (April 14, 1918), 2.

28.   The story of Bennett's troubles with censors is told in Kinley E. Roby, *A Writer at War: Arnold Bennett 1914–1918* (Baton Rouge: 1972).

29.   Margery Ross, ed., *Robert Ross, Friend of Friends*, p. 333. The letter is dated 'June 1918'.

30.   Lady Cynthia Asquith, *Diaries 1915–1918*, p. 445 (June 2, 1918); Arnold Bennett, 'There is No Smoke Without Fire', *Lloyd's Sunday News*, June 9, 1918, 4.

31.   Artemis Cooper, ed., *A Durable Fire: The Letters of Duff and Diana Cooper 1913–1950* (New York: 1984), pp. 67–8 (June 3, 1918).

32.   *A Durable Fire*, p. 70 (June 5, 1918).

33.   *Sassoon Diaries*, pp. 259–60 (June 2, 1918).

34.   A.T. Fitzroy [Rose Allatini], *Despised and Rejected* (London: n.d. [1918]), p. 348.

35.   '"Despised and Rejected." Publisher of Pacifist Novel Fined', *The Times*, Oct. 11, 1918, 5.

36.   *The Diary of Virginia Woolf*, vol. 1 (London: 1977), p. 246 (Feb. 25, 1919).

Chapter 12

1.   Fry's show opened in Birmingham, and moved to the Mansard Gallery at Heal & Sons, London in October 1918.

2.   Clive Bell wrote of 'the new spirit in a little backwater called English

vorticism, which already gives signs of becoming as insipid as any other puddle of provincialism,' in 'Contemporary Art in England', an essay first published in the *Burlington Magazine* in July 1917, and later collected in *Pot-Boilers* (London: 1918), pp. 209–30. The quoted passage appears on p. 229.

3.   See Frances Spalding, *Roger Fry: Art and Life* (Berkeley: 1980), p. 199.

4.   *Annual Register, 1917* (London: 1918), Part II, p. 139.

5.   'Extracts from a Diary', in Herbert Read, *The Contrary Experience* (New York: 1973), p. 141. Lewis repeated the remark in *Blasting & Bombardiering* nearly twenty years later: 'The War, of course, had robbed me of four years, at the moment when, almost overnight, I had achieved the necessary notoriety to establish myself in London as a painter. It also caught me before I was quite through with my training. And although in the "post-war" I was not starting from nothing, I had to some extent to begin all over again.' (p. 212).

6.   *Wheels: An Anthology of Verse* (Oxford: 1916): Osbert Sitwell, 'Night', p. 20; Nancy Cunard, 'Uneasiness', p. 35; Edith Sitwell, 'A Lamentation', p. 42; Arnold James, 'All day he moved not', p. 58; Iris Tree, 'Now is the evening', p. 62.

7.   Review of *Wheels* (1916) in the *Oxford Chronicle*; quoted *Wheels* (1916) 2nd edition (March 1917), p. 91.

8.   *Art and Letters* vol. 1 (July 1917), 1–2.

9.   Francis Bickley, 'Some Tendencies in Contemporary Poetry', *New Paths* (May 1918), 1–11; M.T.H. Sadler, 'The Young Novel', 75–92; J.G. Fletcher, 'Tendencies in Present-Day English Art', 112–19.

10.   Richard Aldington, 'The Blood of the Young Men', *New Paths* (May 1918), 24.

11.   Lady Cynthia Asquith, *Diaries 1915–1918* (New York: 1969), p. 366 (Nov. 15, 1917).

12.   Grover Smith, ed., *Letters of Aldous Huxley* (London: 1969), p. 141.

13.   Cynthia Asquith, *Diaries*, p. 379 (Dec. 12, 1917).

14.   *The Journal of Arnold Bennett* (New York: 1933), p. 639.

15.   For example, the poems of W.N. Ewer.

16.   Edmund Gosse, 'Some Soldier Poets', *Edinburgh Review*, vol. 226 (Oct. 1917), 314; Robert Lynd, 'The Young Satirists', *Nation*, vol. 26 (Dec. 6, 1919), Supplement, pp. 351–2.

17.   See above, p. 197.

18.   The libretto of *The Tigers*, with an introductory essay by Thomas Hubbard, was published in Aberdeen in 1976 by the Havergal Brian Society of that city. See also Reginald Nettel, *Havergal Brian and his Music* (London: 1976).

19.   Often assumed to have been Strachey, but I can find no contemporary evidence that he actually said it, nor can Michael Holroyd, Strachey's

biographer. The first published version that I know of is in Wyndham
Lewis's play 'The Ideal Giant' (*Little Review*, V [May, 1918], 13), where the
remark is attributed simply to 'one of the "Café Royalties"' (that is, the
habitués of the Café Royal in Regent Street). Lewis repeated the story in his
war memoir, *Blasting & Bombardiering* (London: 1937), p. 183: 'Then there
were the tales of how a certain famous artist, of military age and militant
bearing, would sit in the Café Royal and addressing an admiring group back
from the Front, would exclaim: "*We* are the civilization for which you are
fighting!"'

20.   Virginia Woolf recognized Strachey's modernity; in 'Mr. Bennett and
Mrs. Brown', in 1924, she placed him with Joyce and Eliot as examples of
contemporary writers who were 'led to destroy the very foundations and
rules of literary society'. The book by Strachey that she compared to *Ulysses*
and *The Waste Land* was *Eminent Victorians*. The essay appears in *The
Captain's Death Bed* (London: 1950).

21.   Mrs Humphry Ward, letter to the editor, *TLS*, July 11, 1918, 325.

22.   Lytton Strachey, *Eminent Victorians* (London: 1918), p. vii.

23.   *Eminent Victorians*, p. 309.

24.   Arthur Quiller-Couch, *The Oxford Book of Victorian Verse* (London:
1912). Quiller-Couch explained in his Preface: 'I have thought it no insult to
include any English poet, born in our time, under the great name
'Victorian', (pp. viii–ix); *Blast*, no. 1 (June 20, 1914), p. 18, Ezra Pound,
'Wyndham Lewis', *Egoist*, vol. I (June 15, 1914), 234; Graves to Marsh,
quoted in Martin Seymour-Smith, *Robert Graves His Life and Work*
(London: 1982), p. 33; Wilfred Owen, *Collected Letters*, p. 426; Alec Waugh,
The Loom of Youth (London: 1917), p. 234.

25.   'A Word to the Middle-Aged', *Cambridge Magazine*, vol. 4 (May 1,
1915), 380; Richard King, 'With Silent Friends', *Tatler*, no. 797 (Oct. 4,
1916), 16; 'A Young Man's War', *Nation*, vol. 20 (Feb. 10, 1917), 649; Mrs
Victor Rickard, *The Fire of Green Boughs* (London: 1918), p. 138.

26.   'Miles' [Osbert Sitwell], 'The Modern Abraham', *Nation*, vol. 22 (Feb.
2, 1918), 567; Owen, 'The Parable of the Old Man and the Young', *Poems*,
p. 151. Stallworthy gives the probable date of composition as July 1918.

27.   Ford Madox Hueffer [Ford], *The Good Soldier* (London: 1915), p. 9.
The passage was published in *Blast* no. 1. (July 1914).

28.   H.G. Wells, *Joan and Peter* (London: 1918), pp. 717–18.

29.   Stephen McKenna, *Sonia: Between Two Worlds* (London: 1917), p. 258.

30.   *Sonia*, p. 402.

31.   *Sonia*, p. 404.

32.   Shane Leslie, Preface to *The End of a Chapter*, rev. ed. (London:
1917), p. iii.

33.   Clive Bell, 'Before the War', *Cambridge Magazine*, vol. 6 (May 12,
1917), 581, 582.

34.   Inscription in *The Making of a Bigot* (London: 1914), in the Princeton University Library.

Chapter 13

1.   For a detailed account of Armistice Day in London see Stanley Weintraub, *A Stillness Heard Round the World: The End of the Great War* (London: 1986), Chapter 8: 'Having a Knees-Up'.

2.   Norman and Jeanne MacKenzie, *The Diary of Beatrice Webb*, vol. III (London: 1984), p. 318.

3.   *Diary of Virginia Woolf*, vol. I, pp. 216–17.

4.   *Journal of Arnold Bennett*, p. 674.

5.   *In Broken Images*, p. 104.

6.   Sassoon, *Diaries 1915–1918*, p. 288.

7.   Herbert Read, *The Contrary Experience*, p. 146.

8.   Unpublished diary of Gunner W.R. Acklam, RFA, in Imperial War Museum, London.

9.   Thomas Hardy, '"And there was a great calm" (On the Signing of the Armistice, Nov. 11, 1918)', *Late Lyrics and Earlier* (London: 1922), pp. 55–8.

10.   Gilbert Murray, Preface, *Faith, War and Policy* (London: 1918), p. ix.

11.   *Annual Register* for 1918 (London: 1919), Part II, p. 69.

12.   Arthur Waugh, 'War Poetry (1914–18)', *Quarterly Review*, vol. 230 (Oct. 1918), 382. Reprinted in *Tradition and Change* (London: 1919), p. 42.

13.   'War Poetry', 381.

14.   'War Poetry', 399.

15.   'War Poetry', 400.

16.   *The Times*, Jan. 15, 1915, 9.

17.   *The Times*, Jan. 16, 1915, 9.

18.   Lieut.-Col. C. à Court Repington, *The First World War 1914–1918*, vol. II p. 391. The entry is dated Sept. 10, 1918.

19.   Bertrand Russell, *Principles of Social Reconstruction* (London: 1916); Clive Bell, *Peace at Once* (London: 1915); H.G. Wells, *War and the Future* (London: 1917).

20.   *The Diary of Beatrice Webb*, vol. III, p. 280 (June 3, 1917).

21.   *New Statesman*, vol. 12 (Dec. 28, 1918), 263. The product is Sanatogen.

22.   The phrase is from a speech made by Lloyd George at Wolverhampton on Nov. 23, 1918: 'What is our task?' he asked. 'To make Britain a fit country for heroes to live in.' 'Mr Lloyd George on His Task', *The Times*, Nov. 25, 1918, 13.

23.   W.N. Ewer, 'A Ballade of Reconstruction', *Satire and Sentiment* (London: 1918), p. 4.

24.   Cynthia Asquith, *Diaries 1915–1918*, p. 480.

25.   *Diary of Beatrice Webb*, vol. III, pp. 315–16.

26.   David Garnett, *The Flowers of the Forest* (London: 1955), pp. 190–91. Garnett, writing nearly forty years after the event, prefaces the passage with this sentence: 'What he said was something like this, though I do not suppose that a single phrase reproduces his actual words.'

PART IV
Chapter 14

1.   J. Middleton Murry, ed., *The Letters of Katherine Mansfield* (New York: 1932), p. 247. The letter is dated Nov. 10, 1919.

2.   The Waggon Hill epitaph is quoted in E.B. Osborn, *The Muse in Arms* (London: 1917), p. xiii. The eleventh edition of Bartlett's *Familiar Quotations* (Boston: 1941) cites uses of the same epitaph on a grave in Luderitzbucht Cemetery in German Southwest Africa and on the Southport, England war memorial, both from the First World War.

3.   For the account of the War Graves Commission that follows I am indebted to Fabian Ware, *The Immortal Heritage* (Cambridge: 1937), and to the unsigned introductory essay in *Silent Cities: An Exhibition of the Memorial and Cemetery Architecture of the Great War* (London: 1977). The exhibition was organized by John Harris and Gavin Stamp.

4.   'Too long for an altar,' wrote the *Connoisseur*'s critic of Lutyens's design, 'it presents the appearance of a shop-counter executed in stone, and one cannot look at it for any length of time without expecting a trim salesman to appear on the other side saying, "And what is the next article, please?"' 'War Memorials Exhibition at the Royal Academy', *Connoisseur*, vol. 55 (Dec. 1919), 260.

5.   W.R. Colton, A.R.A., 'The Effects of War on Art', *The Architect*, vol. 45 (March 17, 1916), 201.

6.   For a detailed account of the accumulation of these paintings see Meirion and Susie Harries, *The War Artists*.

7.   Muirhead Bone, in the *Manchester Guardian*, 1931; quoted in Lucy Masterman, *C.F.G. Masterman* (London: 1968), p. 304.

8.   R.H.W., 'The Nation's War Paintings at Burlington House', *Athenaeum*, Dec. 19, 1919, 1375.

9.   Middleton Murry, 'The War Pictures at the Royal Academy', *Nation*, vol. 26 (Dec. 20, 1919), 420.

10.   A.M. Berry, 'Art and Reconstruction', *Ploughshare*, vol. 5 (Jan. 1920), 20.

11.   John Foulds, *A World Requiem* (London: 1923), p. v.

12.   'A World Requiem', *The Times*, Nov. 12, 1923), 7.

13.   Philip Gibbs, *Open Warfare: The Way to Victory* (London: 1919), pp. 551–2.

14.   H.M. Tomlinson, 'The South Downs', in *Waiting for Daylight* (London: 1922), pp. 193–4.

15.   *Diary of Beatrice Webb*, vol. III, p. 371.

16.   Charlotte Mew, 'The Cenotaph', *Collected Poems* (London: 1953), p. 65. The poem, dated Sept. 1919, was first published in 1921.

Chapter 15

1.   Gibbs's dispatches were collected in *The Battles of the Somme* (London: 1917), *From Bapaume to Passchendaele* (1918) and *Open Warfare: The Way to Victory* (London: 1919).

2.   Philip Gibbs, Preface, *Realities of War* (London: 1920), p. v.

3.   Ernest Hemingway, *A Farewell to Arms* (New York: 1929), p. 196.

4.   Gibbs, *Realities of War*, p. 307.

5.   *Letters of Arnold Bennett*, vol. III, p. 130. The letter is dated Sept. 10, 1920.

6.   *Realities of War*, p. 363.

7.   'A Bitter Book', *Saturday Review*, vol. 129 (April 10, 1920), 349–50.

8.   *Realities of War*, p. 453.

9.   Letter to Gide written in 1920; quoted in Ann Thwaite, *Edmund Gosse: A Literary Landscape, 1849–1928* (Chicago: 1984), p. 497.

10.   D.H. Lawrence, 'Epilogue', *Movements in European History* (Oxford: 1971), p. 313. The book was first published in 1921 under the pseudonym 'Lawrence H. Davison'; the first edition did not include the 'Epilogue', which was written for a second edition that was not printed. It first appeared in the 1971 re-issue.

11.   Lieut.-Col. C. à Court Repington, *The First World War 1914–1918*, vol. II. p. 68. The entry is dated Oct. 4, 1917.

12.   *The First World War*, vol. II. p. 3. Dated July 22, 1917.

13.   'The Soldier and the Politicians', *Saturday Review*, vol. 130 (Sept. 25, 1920), 260; 'Under the Stone', *Spectator*, vol. 125 (Oct. 2, 1920), 434; 'How We Did It', *Nation*, vol. 27 (Sept. 25, 1920), 790.

14.   'Some Problems of Publicity', *Spectator*, vol. 125 (Sept. 25, 1920), 393; 'A Gentleman with a Duster' [E.H. Begbie], *The Glass of Fashion: Some Social Reflections* (London: 1921), p. 32.

15.   *Realities of War*, p. 444.

16.   John Maynard Keynes, *The Economic Consequences of the Peace* (New York: 1920), pp. 10–11.

17.   *Economic Consequences*, pp. 297–8.

18.   John Palmer, 'The Poetry of the War', *Saturday Review*, vol. 118 (Sept. 12, 1914), 291.

19.   St John Ervine, 'The War and Literature', *North American Review*, vol. 202 (July 1915), 92–3; Walter de la Mare, lecture on 'The Effect of the War on the production and reading of Literature', published in *The English Association Bulletin*, no. 29 (July 1916), 6; 'The Theatrical Year', *The Times*, Jan. 1, 1917, 11; S.K. Ratcliffe, 'The English Intellectuals in War-time', *Century*, vol. 94 (Oct. 1917), 832–3; John Masefield, 'Poets of the People: A Discussion of War and Poetry', *Touchstone*, vol. 2 (March 1918), 591–2.

20.   Sir William Orpen, *An Onlooker in France 1917–1919* (London: 1921), pp. 118–19.

21.   The quotation is from a letter quoted in P.G. Konody and Sidney Dark, *Sir William Orpen Artist & Man* (London: 1932), p. 254. The two soldiers in Orpen's picture are copies from his wartime drawing, 'Blown up — Mad'; in the letter quoted Orpen refers to them as 'dead comrades'. All three paintings are in the Imperial War Museum.

22.   Letter to Gordon Bottomley, dated July 16, 1918, in Claude Colleer Abbott and Anthony Bertram, eds., *Poet and Painter* (London: 1955), p. 99.

23.   Wyndham Lewis, Foreword to catalogue of *Guns*, an exhibition at the Goupil Gallery, London, Feb. 1919; reprinted in Walter Michel and C.F. Fox, eds., *Wyndham Lewis on Art* (London: 1969), pp. 105–6.

24.   Wyndham Lewis, *Blasting and Bombardiering* (London: 1937), p. 131.

25.   A.N. Berry, 'Art and Reconstruction', *Ploughshare*, vol. 5 (Jan. 1920), 20.

26.   *The Morning Post*, Dec. 24, 1919; quoted in M. and S. Harries, *The War Artists*, p. 152.

27.   Fifteen years later, Nash wrote: 'The immense intervention of the War left very little of the substance or spirit of Vorticism surviving, although some of its chief exponents made valuable pictorial War records.' 'Unit One', *The Listener*, July 5, 1933, 14.

28.   Herbert Read, *In Retreat* (London: 1925), p. 7.

29.   Osbert Sitwell, 'The War-Horse Chants', *Out of the Flame* (London: 1923), p. 57.

30.   Herbert Read, 'Extracts from a Diary', *The Contrary Experience*, p. 89. The passage is dated April 12, 1917.

31.   'Two Soldier-Poets', *TLS*, July 11, 1918, 2.

32.   'Recent Verse', *New Age*, vol. 24 (Nov. 21, 1918), 41.

33.   'Mr Sassoon's War Verses', *Nation*, vol. 23 (July 13, 1918), 398.

34.   'Mr Sassoon's War Verses', 400.

35.   Robert Lynd, 'The Young Satirists', *Nation*, vol. 26, Supplement (Dec. 6, 1919), 352; *London Mercury*, vol. 1 (Dec. 1919), 206.

36.   John Lehmann and Derek Parker, eds., *Edith Sitwell: Selected Letters 1919–1964* (New York: 1970), p. 23. The letter, to Owen's mother, is dated 'late January 1920'.

37.   J. Middleton Murry, 'The Poet of the War', *Nation & Athenaeum*, vol. 28 (Feb. 19, 1921), 705.

38.   C.K. Scott Moncrieff, 'The Poets There Are III — Wilfred Owen', *New Witness*, vol. 16 (Dec. 10, 1920), 575.

39.   Scott Moncrieff, 575.

40.   Robert Graves, *Good-bye to All That* (London: 1929), p. 326.

41.   Margaret Newbolt, ed., *The Later Life and Letters of Sir Henry Newbolt* (London: 1942), pp. 314–15.

42.   A.P. Herbert, *The Secret Battle* (London: 1919), pp. [1] and 243

43.   For war plays concerning damaged men, see Harry Wall's *Havoc* and Allan Monkhouse's *The Conquering Hero* (both 1924).

44.   *Report of the War Office Enquiry into 'Shell-Shock'* [Cd. 1734], 1922, p. 189. The report is analysed by Ted Bogacz in his essay, 'War Neurosis and Cultural Change', *Journal of Contemporary History*, vol. 24 (1989), 227–56.

45.   C.E. Montague, *Disenchantment* (London: 1922), p. 15.

46.   *Disenchantment*, p. 267.

47.   *Disenchantment*, pp. 112 and 248.

Chapter 16

1.   David Garnett, *The Flowers of the Forest* (London: 1955), p. 194.

2.   Denys Sutton, ed., *Letters of Roger Fry* (London: 1972), vol. II, p. 494. The letter is dated Nov. 12, 1920.

3.   Mary Lago and P.N. Furbank, eds., *Selected Letters of E.M. Forster*, vol. I (Cambridge, Mass.: 1983), pp. 305–6.

4.   John Middleton Murry, 'The Nature of Civilisation', reprinted in *The Evolution of an Intellectual* (London: 1920), p. 168.

5.   'Nature of Civilisation', p. 175.

6.   Charles F.G. Masterman, *England After War* (London: 1922), p. ix.

7.   *England After War*, pp. 31–2.

8.   *England After War*, p. 177.

9.   *England After War*, p. 192.

10.   *England After War*, p. 195.

11.   'A Gentleman with a Duster', *The Mirrors of Downing Street* (London: 1920), pp. 207–8; *The Conservative Mind* (London: 1924), pp. 11–12.

12.   *The Glass of Fashion* (London: 1921), p. 16.

13.   H.G. Wells, *The Outline of History* vol. II (London: 1920), p. 710.

14.   *Outline of History*, II, pp. 711–12.

15.   *Outline of History*, II, p. 712.

16.   *Outline of History*, II, p. 727.

17.   *Outline of History*, II, p. 748.

18.   Shaw, *Letters*, vol. III, p. 725; Bennett, *Letters*, vol. III, p. 132.

19.   E.M.F., 'Mr Wells' "Outline"', *Athenaeum* (Nov. 19, 1920), 690. Readers familiar with *A Passage to India* will notice the similarity to that novel's last page which ends: "No, not yet" ... "No, not there".'

20.   D.H. Lawrence, 'Introduction', *Movements in European History* (Oxford: 1971), p. xxvi.

21.   *Movements*, p. xxvi.

22.   *Movements*, p. 306.

23.   *Movements*, p. 307.

24.   *Movements*, p. 310.

25.   *Movements*, p. 310.

26.   *Movements*, p. 313.

27.   Quoted in 'Introduction to the New Edition', *Movements*, p. xiv.

28.   Ford Madox Ford, dedication to *No More Parades* (London: 1925), p. 5.

29.   Rose Macaulay, *Potterism* (New York: 1920), p. 6; W.L. George, *Blind Alley* (Boston: 1919), p. 140; C.E. Montague, *Rough Justice* (London: 1926), p. 360; H.G. Wells, *Christina Alberta's Father* (London: 1925), pp. 361–2.

30.   Galsworthy, 'Art and the War', *Fortnightly*, vol. 98 (Nov. 1915), 927; *Life and Letters of Galsworthy*, pp. 461–2.

31.   John Galsworthy, *To Let* (London: 1921), p. 311.

32.   Ernest Raymond, *Tell England* (London: 1922), pp. 167–8.

33.   The unfavourable reviews are all cheerfully quoted in Raymond's autobiography, *The Story of My Days* (London: 1968), pp. 182–4.

34.   'War', *Nation & Athenaeum*, vol. 31 (Apr. 29, 1922), 160.

35.   *Tell England*, p. 314.

36.   *Spectator*, vol. 127 (Dec. 10, 1921), 790–1.

Chapter 17

1.   Valerie Eliot, ed., *The Letters of T.S. Eliot*, p. 386. The letter is dated June 20, 1920.

2.   The two poems, 'War Verse' and '1915: February', are quoted in James Longenbach, *Stone Cottage: Pound, Yeats, and Modernism* (Oxford: 1988), pp. 115 and 119–20. The quotation is from '1915: February'.

3.   T.S. Eliot, 'Reflections on Contemporary Poetry', *Egoist*, vol. 6 (July 1919), 39.

4.   Sassoon, *Diaries 1920–1922*, pp. 132–3; *Diaries 1923–1925*, p. 79.

5.   Graves, *In Broken Images*, p. 342, letter dated April 5, 1946.

6.   *Letters*, p. 247.

7.   Ezra Pound, 'The Death of Vorticism', *Little Review*, vol. 5 (Feb.-Mar. 1919), 45.

8.   *Hugh Selwyn Mauberley* was first published in London in 1920. My text is from *Personae* (New York: 1926), p. 190, in which one typographical error is corrected, and lineation and spacing are altered.

9.   *Hugh Selwyn Mauberley*, p. 91.

10.   *Letters*, p. 191. The letter is dated Dec. 3, 1924.

11.   Paul Fussell, *The Great War and Modern Memory* (New York: 1975), pp. 325-6.

12.   T.S. Eliot, 'Ulysses, Order and Myth', *Dial*, vol. 75 (Nov. 1923), 483.

13.   David Jones, an account of his early life printed in the catalogue of a Memorial Exhibition of Jones's work, Kettle's Yard, Cambridge, Feb. 1975; reprinted in Rene Hague, ed., *Dai Greatcoat* (London: 1980), p. 21.

14.   *Mrs Dalloway*, p. 276.

15.   *Mrs Dalloway*, p. 134.

16.   D.H. Lawrence, *Kangaroo* (London: 1923), pp. 238-9.

17.   *Kangaroo*, p. 243.

18.   *Kangaroo*, pp. 238, 239.

19.   *Kangaroo*, p. 244.

20.   A.S.M. Hutchinson, *If Winter Comes* (London: 1921), p. 326.

21.   *If Winter Comes*, p. 327.

22.   *If Winter Comes*, p. 413.

23.   Warwick Deeping, *Sorrell and Son* (London: 1924), p. 5.

24.   Michael Arlen, *The Green Hat* (London: 1924), p. 15.

25.   *The Green Hat*, p. 14.

26.   *The Green Hat*, p. 93.

Chapter 18

1.   John Galsworthy, *The Forsyte Saga* (London: 1922), p. x.

2.   See Roy Foster, *Modern Ireland 1600-1972* (London: 1988), and Charles Townsend, *The British Campaign in Ireland 1919-1921* (Oxford: 1975).

3.   Woolf, *Diary*, vol. I, pp. 238 and 309; vol. II, pp. 109 and 111.

4.   Not to be confused with Oswald Mosley's British Union of Fascists, which was founded in 1932. See Robert Benewick, *The Fascist Movement in Britain*, revised edition (London: 1972), p. 28.

5.   John Buchan, *The Three Hostages* (London: 1924), pp. 26-7; Dornford Yates, *Berry and Co.* (London: 1922), p. 225; 'Sapper' (Cyril McNeile), *Bull-Dog Drummond* (London: 1920), p. 17.

6.   William Ralph Inge, 'The Future of the English Race', *Outspoken Essays*, First Series (London: 1919), pp. 98-9.

7.   Masterman, *England After War*, pp. 85 and 102–3.

8.   For example in a *Daily News* correspondence on middle-class problems, quoted extensively in Masterman, pp. 88–95, and in 'Death of the Middle Classes', *The Times*, Nov. 11, 1919, 11.

9.   Deeping, *Sorrell and Son*, p. 15.

10.   D.H. Lawrence, *Lady Chatterley's Lover* [1928] (New York: 1957), p. 172.

11.   See Vera Brittain, *Women's Work in Modern Britain* (London: 1928) and A.J.P. Taylor, *English History 1914–1945*, p. 139 n.1.

12.   W.L. George, *Blind Alley* (London: 1920), p. 197.

13.   Sylvia Thompson, *The Hounds of Spring* (London: 1926), p. 92.

14.   Helen Zenna Smith, *Not So Quiet . . .* (London: 1930), pp. 173–4. The marks of elision are authorial.

15.   Ernest Hemingway, *A Farewell to Arms* (New York: 1929), p. 19.

16.   Woolf, *Diary*, vol. I, pp. 110–11 (dated Jan. 21, 1918).

17.   Fry, *Letters*, vol. II, p. 449 (dated March 17, 1919).

18.   David Garnett, ed., *The Letters of T.E. Lawrence* (London: 1938), p. 414 (dated March 27, 1923).

19.   *Psychoanalysis of the Unconscious* (New York: 1921, London: 1923), and *Fantasia of the Unconscious* (New York: 1923, London: 1923).

20.   Raymond Mortimer, 'New Novels', *New Statesman*, vol. 21 (April 28, 1923), 82. I am indebted for this reference, and for much information about Freud in post-war England, to Professor Dean R. Rapp, of Wheaton College, Illinois. See his essay, 'The Reception of Freud by the British Press: General Interest and Literary Magazines, 1920–1925', *Journal of the History of the Behavioral Sciences*, vol. 24 (April 1988), 191–201.

21.   *Married Love* (London: 1918), pp. 22 and 27.

22.   *Married Love*, p. 22.

23.   *Married Love*, p. 1.

24.   *Married Love*, pp. 39–40.

25.   *Married Love*, p. xiii.

26.   *The Times*, Nov. 15, 1923, 10.

27.   These figures are from *The Registrar-General's Statistical Review of England and Wales, for the year 1921* (London: 1923).

28.   'The "Right to Motherhood"', *The Times*, Oct. 2, 1920, 7. The *Times* report of Miss Marsh's testimony brought angry responses from the Mothers' Union and from the chairman of the Church Penitentiary Association. (*The Times*, Oct. 20, 1920, 11, Nov. 25, 1920, 8 and Nov. 26, 11).

29.   *The Times*, April 7, 1922, 14

30.   *Parliamentary Debates* (Commons) 1921, vol. 145, col. 1799 (Aug. 4, 1921).

31.   *Parliamentary Debates* (Commons) 1921, vol. 145, cols. 1799, 1800, 1804, 1805, 1846 (Aug. 4, 1921).

32.   Beatrice Webb, *Diary*, vol. III, p. 401 (dated July 10, 1922).
33.   Clemence Dane, *A Bill of Divorcement* (London: 1922), p. [v].
34.   *A Bill of Divorcement*, p. 6.
35.   *A Bill of Divorcement*, p. 54.
36.   *A Bill of Divorcement*, pp. 91, 92.
37.   Aldous Huxley, *Point Counter Point* (London: 1928), p. 186; Norah C. James, *Sleeveless Errand* (Paris: 1929), p. 59.
38.   'Surplus Women', *The Times*, March 25, 1921, 9.
39.   Vera Brittain, *Testament of Youth* (London: 1933), pp. 491–2.
40.   *The Times*, Oct. 18, 1920, 8.
41.   *The Times*, Oct. 18, 1920, 13.

Chapter 19

1.   See Annie Kriegel, 'Generational Difference: The History of an Idea', *Daedalus*, vol. 107 (Fall 1978), 23–38, and Alan B. Spitzer, 'The Historical Problem of Generations', *American Historical Review*, vol. 78 (Dec. 1973), 1353–85.
2.   Balfour, quoted in Angela Lambert, *Unquiet Souls* (New York: 1984), p. 223; Ann Thwaite, *Edmund Gosse* (London: 1984), p. 497; Ricketts, *Self-Portrait* (London: 1939), p. 343.
3.   'The Suppressed Introductory Chapter for *Seven Pillars of Wisdom*', in *Oriental Assembly*, ed. A.W. Lawrence (London: 1939), pp. 142–3.
4.   These figures are taken from J.M. Winter, 'Britain's "Lost Generation" of the First World War', *Population Studies*, vol. 31 (Nov. 1977), 449–66.
5.   Ford Madox Ford, *It Was the Nightingale* (London: 1934), p. 68.
6.   Paul Nash, *Outline*, p. 218.
7.   Grover Smith, ed., *Letters of Aldous Huxley* (London: 1969), p. 224.
8.   First published in the *Lancing College Magazine* (December 1923); reprinted in Donat Gallagher, ed., *The Essays, Articles, and Reviews of Evelyn Waugh* (London: 1983), p. 11.
9.   It wasn't only at Lancing that the Myth was becoming current. Waugh's Oxford friend Brian Howard said much the same thing in a poem, 'To the Young Writers and Artists Killed in the War: 1914–18', published in the *Eton Candle* in 1922, when Howard was 17. It is reprinted in Marie-Jaqueline Lancaster, ed., *Brian Howard: Portrait of a Failure* (London: 1968), p. 579.
10.   The undergraduate poem, 'The Heathen's Song', was printed in the May 25, 1921 issue of *Isis*. Lord Alfred expressed his disapproval in an editorial, 'An Oxford Outrage', in his journal *Plain English*, June 4, 1921, 443. Beardsleyish drawings appear in *Coterie*, a journal edited at Oxford

and published in London by the wartime radical bookseller-publisher, The Bomb Shop. The unpublished Wilde poem, 'To M.B.-J.', is in the Winter 1920–21 issue of *Coterie*. The essay in praise of decadence is Beverley Nichols's 'Decadence in Art', *Oxford Outlook*, vol. 1 (Nov. 1919), 254–71.

11. Beverley Nichols, *Patchwork* (London: 1921), p. 145.

12. I have discussed both above, pp. 343–4 and 330–1.

13. *Ulysses*, 'Nestor'. In the Bodley Head edition (London: 1986) the quotation is on p. 20.

14. *Ulysses*, 'Nestor', The quotations are on pp. 28, 26 and 28 of the Bodley Head edition.

15. For a full analysis of this theme see Robert E. Spoo, "Nestor" and the Nightmare: The Presence of the Great War in *Ulysses'*, *Twentieth Century Literature*, vol. 32 (Summer 1986), 137–54.

16. Laurence Binyon, *Arthur: A Tragedy* (London: 1923), p. 126.

17. Noël Coward, *The Vortex* (London: 1925), p. 43.

18. George Bernard Shaw, Preface to *Back to Methuselah*, (London: 1921), p. x.

19. Shaw, *Back to Methuselah*, p. 46.

20. Shaw, *Back to Methuselah*, p. 69.

21. Elizabeth Butler, *An Autobiography* (Boston and New York: 1923), pp. 325–7.

22. Rose Macaulay, *What Not: A Prophetic Comedy* (London: 1918 [1919]).

23. Huxley, 'Satires and Native Woodnotes', *Athenaeum* (Nov. 28, 1919), 1255.

24. Huxley, *Crome Yellow* (London: 1921), p. 276.

25. Conrad Aiken, *Criterion*, vol. 3 (April 1925), 450.

26. For a fuller account of the controversy, see 'The Whole Connection Between Mr. Bennett and Mrs. Woolf', in my *Edwardian Occasions* (London: 1972).

27. 'Mr. Bennett and Mrs. Brown'. First published as 'Character in Fiction' in *The Criterion*, vol. 2 (July 1924), 409–30; then as a pamphlet in the Hogarth Essays series (1924). Reprinted in *The Captain's Death Bed* (London: 1950), where the quoted passage is on p. 106.

28. 'Mr Bennett and Mrs Brown' (the first version), *Nation and Athenaeum*, vol. 34 (Dec. 1, 1923), 342–3.

29. This note is tipped in to the British Library copy, but is not in all first-edition copies.

30. See above, pp. 232–4.

31. [Cyril Scott], Introduction, *The Autobiography of a Child* (London: 1921), p. viii.

32. See 'Royal Academy/Some Successful Portraits/An Elderly Show', *The Times*, May 1, 1926, 15–16.

PART V

Chapter 20

1. *Parliamentary Debates* (Commons) 1926, vol. 195, col. 124 (May 3, 1926).
2. *Parliamentary Debates* (Commons) 1926, vol. 195, cols. 467–8 (May 6, 1926).
3. *Parliamentary Debates* (Lords) 1926, vol. 64, col. 16 (May 4, 1926).
4. *The Times*, May 6, 1926, 3.
5. *Parliamentary Debates* (Commons) 1926, vol. 195, col. 342 (May 5, 1926).
6. See G.A. Phillips, *The General Strike* (London: 1976), Chapter VIII.
7. *The British Gazette*, May 8, 1926, 1.
8. *The British Gazette*, May 13, 1926, 1.
9. Virginia Woolf, *Diary*, vol. III, p. 77.
10. Virginia Woolf, *Diary*, vol. III, pp. 78–9; *Letters*, vol. III, p. 260 (May 12, 1926.
11. Beatrice Webb, *Diary*, vol. IV, pp. 82–3.
12. H.G. Wells, *Meanwhile* (London: 1927), pp. 198, 194.
13. *Meanwhile*, pp. 176, 177, 178.
14. *Meanwhile*, p. 181.
15. *Meanwhile*, p. 199.
16. *Meanwhile*, p. 230.
17. *Meanwhile*, p. 258.
18. John Galsworthy, *Swan Song* (London: 1928), p. 54.
19. *Swan Song*, p. 299.
20. *Swan Song*, p. 344.
21. Galsworthy, 'Preface', *A Modern Comedy* (London: 1929, p. viii.
22. 'Preface', p. x.
23. Wyndham Lewis, *Blasting and Bombardiering* (London: 1937), pp. 1–2.
24. T.S. Eliot, 'Last Words', *Criterion*, vol. 18 (Jan. 1939), 271.
25. Virginia Woolf, *Diary*, vol. III, p. 83. Entry of May 11, 1926.
26. Eliot, 'A Commentary', *Criterion*, vol. 9 (Jan. 1930), 183.
27. Lewis, *Blasting and Bombardiering*, p. 5.
28. Laura Riding and Robert Graves, *A Survey of Modernist Poetry* (London: 1927), p. 226.
29. Michael Davie, ed., *The Diaries of Evelyn Waugh* (London: 1976), p. 253.
30. Graham Greene, *A Sort of Life* (London: 1971), pp. 172–5.
31. *A Sort of Life*, p. 175.
32. Hugh Gaitskell, 'At Oxford in the Twenties', in Asa Briggs and John Saville, eds., *Essays in Labour History in Memory of G.D.H. Cole* (London: 1960), p. 9.

Chapter 21

1. *Annual Register* for 1928 (London: 1929), Part II, p. 24.

2. Herbert Read, 'Books of the Quarter', *Criterion*, vol. 9 (July 1930), 764.

3. Robert Graves, 'French History', *Nation & Athenaeum*, vol. 44 (Dec. 15, 1928), 420.

4. Richard Aldington, in a review of Read's *In Retreat*, *Criterion*, vol. 4 (April 1926), 363.

5. Erich Remarque, *All Quiet on the Western Front* (London: 1929), p. 142.

6. Edmund Blunden, *Undertones of War* (London: 1928), p. 100.

7. *Undertones*, p. 194.

8. *Undertones*, p. vii.

9. Graves, 'Escape' and 'A Letter from Wales', *Poems (1914–26)* (London: 1927).

10. Graves, *Good-bye to All That*, 3rd impression (London: 1929), p. 13.

11. Ford Madox Ford, *No More Parades* (London: 1925), pp. 7–8.

12. Ford, *It Was the Nightingale* (London: 1934), p. 180.

13. Quoted in James Longenbach, 'Ford Madox Ford: The Novelist as Historian', *Princeton University Library Chronicle*, vol. 45 (Winter 1984), 161.2.

14. Ford, *Some Do Not . . .* (London: 1924), p. 1.

15. *It Was the Nightingale*, p. 195.

16. Lewis, *Blasting and Bombardiering*, p. 1.

17. Charles Carrington (Charles Edmonds) *A Subaltern's War* (London: 1929), p. 192.

18. Graves, *Good-bye to All That*, p. 440; Carrington, *A Subaltern's War*, p. 8.

19. *Good-bye to All That*, p. 342.

20. Vera Brittain, *War Diary 1913–1917. Chronicle of Youth*, p. 327.

21. Brittain, *Testament of Youth* (London: 1933), pp. 282–3.

22. Edmund Blunden, ed., *The Poems of Wilfred Owen* (London: 1931), p. 41.

23. Herbert Read, 'A Lost Generation', *Nation & Athenaeum*, vol. 45 (April 27, 1929), 116. The quotation is slightly inaccurate: see *All Quiet*, pp. 317–18.

24. Read, 'A Lost Generation', 116.

25. 'Savoy Theatre./"Journey's End"', *The Times*, Jan. 22, 1929, 10.

26. 'The Stage Society./"Journey's End"', *The Times*, Dec. 11, 1928, 14.

27. Rebecca West, '"Journey's End" Again', *Ending in Earnest* (Garden City, N.Y.: 1931), p. 77.

28. *Parliamentary Debates* (Commons) 1927, vol. 211, col. 1174 (Dec. 6, 1927).

29. *The Times*, Nov. 10, 1925, 4 and Nov. 21, 1925, 12.

30. House of Commons *Notices of Motions* (1927), p. 3403.

31. *The Times*, Oct. 6, 1925, 12 and Sept. 21, 1926, 12.

32. Bryher, 'The War from Three Angles', *Close Up*, vol 1 (July 1927), 19.

33. Bryher, 'The War from More Angles', *Close Up*, vol. 1 (Oct. 1927), 45.

34. *The Times*, Oct. 29, 1930, 12.

35. Robert Herring, 'Movies and Talkies', *London Mercury*, vol. 23 (Jan. 1931), 287.

36. *Nation & Athenaeum*, vol. 47 (April 26, 1930), 112; Celia Simpson, 'The Cinema', *Spectator*, vol. 145 (Nov. 8, 1930), 665; 'Movies and Talkies', *London Mercury*, vol. 23 (Jan. 1931), 287; C.S., 'The Cinema', *Spectator*, vol. 144 (June 28, 1930), 1045.

37. Carrington, *A Subaltern's War*, pp. 192–3; Graves, *But It Still Goes On* (London: 1930), 16; Eric Partridge, 'The War Continues', *The Window*, vol. 1 (April 1930), 63.

38. *The Times*, Jan. 11, 1930, 5; Feb. 10, 1930, 9; Feb. 17, 1930, 8.

39. J.C. Squire, 'Editorial Notes', *London Mercury*, vol. 21 (Nov. 1929), 1; 'The Garlands Wither', *TLS*, June 12, 1930, 485.

40. Douglas Jerrold, *The Lie About the War* (London: 1930), p. 10.

41. Partridge, 'The War Continues', 63.

42. Cyril Falls, *War Books: A Critical Guide* (London: 1930), pp. 183, 202, 237–8, 294.

43. *War Books*, pp. x–xi.

44. 'The End of War?' *Life and Letters*, vol. 3 (Nov. 1929), 403.

45. 'The End of War?', 403–4.

46. Graves, 'French History', *Nation & Athenaeum*, vol. 44 (Dec. 15, 1928), 420; Henry Williamson, 'Reality in War Literature', *London Mercury*, vol. 19 (Jan. 1929), 300; Read, 'A Lost Generation', *Nation & Athenaeum*, vol. 45 (April 27, 1929), 116; Graves, 'More War Books', *Nation & Athenaeum*, vol. 45 (Aug. 10, 1929), 629; Read, 'The Pity of War', *Adelphi*, vol. 1 (Oct. 1930), 71.

47. Read, 'Books of the Quarter', *Criterion*, vol. 9 (July 1930), 767–8.

48. *Good-bye to All That*, p. 8.

49. Virginia Woolf, *To the Lighthouse* (London: 1927), p. 207.

50. Read, 'A Lost Generation', 116.

51. Read, 'Books of the Quarter', 765.

52. Quoted in Richard Carline, *Stanley Spencer at War* (London: 1978), p. 149.

53. *Stanley Spencer at War*, p. 153.

54. *Stanley Spencer at War*, p. 194.

55. *Stanley Spencer at War*, p. 184.

56. *Stanley Spencer at War*, pp. 190–91.

Epilogue

1.   Lewis, *Blasting and Bombardiering*, p. 258.

2.   *Parliamentary Debates* (Commons) 1930, vol. 237, cols. 1564ff. (April 3, 1930); *Public General Statutes*, 20 & 21 George 5 (1929–30), Ch. 22; 'An Act to provide during Twelve Months, for the Discipline and Regulation of the Army and Air Force. (Army and Air Force (Annual).)'

3.   *Parliamentary Debates* (Commons) 1929, vol. 231, cols. 319–20 (Oct. 31, 1929).

4.   Henry Williamson, *The Linhay on the Downs* (London: 1934), p. 262.

5.   Evelyn Waugh, *Vile Bodies* (London: 1930), p. 248.

6.   Virginia Woolf, *A Room of One's Own* (London: 1929), p. 18.

7.   *A Room of One's Own*, pp. 23–4.

INDEX

Acton, Harold 390
Adams, Bernard 209–11, 216
  Nothing of Importance 209,
  211
Aiken, Conrad 101, 302, 399
Aldington, Richard 239–40,
  424, 464
  'Blood of the Young Men,
  The' 239
Allan, Maud 226, 229, 232
Allatini, Rose: *Despised and
  Rejected* 232–4, 248, 402
Allen, Clifford, 174
Archer, William 27, 163
Arlen, Michael: *Green Hat,
  The* 350–1, 365, 378
Art and Letters 236, 238, 255,
  257, 302
Asquith, Cynthia 61, 91, 113,
  133, 157, 183, 231, 241,
  245, 265, 379
Asquith, Elizabeth 102
Asquith, Herbert 228, 245
Asquith, Margot 163, 228,
  319
Asquith, Raymond 126, 225–6
Astor, Lady 362
Auden, W.H. 422, 467
'Authors' Declaration' 27, 69
Ayre, Ruby M.: *Richard
  Chatterton V.C.* 104

Bagnold, Enid 92, 379
  Diary Without Dates 329
Bailey, John 81

Baker, Herbert 271
Bantock, Granville 76
Barbusse, Henri: *Le Feu* 178,
  203–5, 211, 329, 334, 452
Barclay, Florence L.: *My
  Heart's Right There* 92
Baring, Maurice 189, 245
Barker, Granville 27, 39, 104
Barrie, James M. 26, 44, 104,
  354
  Der Tag 40–2, 58, 121, 142
  Kiss for Cinderella, A 102
Battle of the Somme 122–6
*Battles of Coronel and the
  Falkland Islands* 446
Bax, Ernest Belfort: *German
  Culture Past and Present* 70
Beecham, Thomas 76, 354
Beerbohm, Max 244, 402,
  403
Begbie, Harold 28, 319, 320,
  322
Bell, Clive 36, 84, 174, 252,
  253, 275
  'Before the War' 344
  Civilization 312
  Peace at Once 84–6, 261
Bell, Vanessa 84, 366, 411
Belloc, Hilaire 19
  *Companion to Mr Wells'
  Outline of History* 324
Bennett, Arnold 4, 5, 26, 39,
  103, 104, 133, 175, 194,
  199–200, 242, 254, 286,
  354, 384, 399, 400, 408

Mr Prohack 359, 385
Pretty Lady, The 229–30
Benson, A.C. 26
Benson, Hugh 26
Besier, Rudolph 104
Bevan, Robert 65
Billing, Noel Pemberton 146,
  226–31
Binyon, Laurence Arthur 25,
  391
  Spirit of England, The 255
Blast 8–10, 59, 65–7, 101,
  166, 385
Blunden, Edmund 81, 167,
  386, 436–8, 441, 455, 464
  Undertones of War 426–7,
  453
Bone, Muirhead 159, 274,
  308
  'Battle of the Somme, The'
  160, 196
  Somme Battlefield, The
  161
  Western Front, The 161,
  205
Book of Remembrance, A 277
Bottomley, Horatio 146, 213,
  214
Bowyer, Captain Sir George
  466
Boy Scout with the Russians, A
  43
Brancusi, Constantin 236
Brand, Tita 38
Brereton, Captain F.S. 44–6

With French at the Front 44, 46
With Joffre at Verdun 104
Brian, Havergal: *Tigers, The* 243
Bridge, Sir Frederick 37
Bridges, Robert 25, 26, 28, 381, 382
  Spirit of Man, The 103
Brighouse, Harold 104
  Hobson's Choice 102
British Artists at the Front 198
Brittain, Vera 112, 113, 150, 158, 436
  'Superfluous Woman, The' 380–1
  Testament of Youth 435
Brock, Arthur Clutton 17, 30, 31, 34, 164
Brockway, Fenner 81
  Devil's Business, The 80
Brooke, Rupert 5, 11, 25, 42, 58, 65, 105, 119, 127, 190, 213, 299–300, 333, 336, 338, 389, 435, 450
  1914 and Other Poems 109, 112, 189, 300
  'If I should die' 113
  'Peace' 13
Bryher 446
Buchan, John 47, 277, 408
  Battle of the Somme: First Phase, The 125
  Greenmantle 104, 111, 224
  Nelson's History of the Great War 45
  Thirty-Nine Steps, The 45
  Three Hostages, The 357
Butler, Lady 391
  'Roll Call, The' 258
  Some Records of the Great War 390
Butts, Mary: *Speed the Plough* 378
Byles, Sir William 151, 152

Caine, Hall 26
Cameron, Basil 77
Cammaerts, Emile 37, 38
Carpenter, Edward 86, 176, 366, 404
Carrington, Charles 464
  Subaltern's War, A 434, 449
Carson, Sir Edward 6, 324

Cecil, Lord Henry 409
Chapell, Henry: 'Bath Railway Porter, The' 28
Chesterton, G.K. 26, 28
Children's Story of the War 47
Christie, Agatha: *Mysterious Affairs at Styles, The* 351
Churchill, Winston 6, 109, 163, 277, 410, 413
Colefax, Sibyl 241, 244
Collins Baker, C.H. 18
Colton, W.R. 58, 272
Colvin, Sidney 39
Conan Doyle, Sir Arthur 26, 40, 47, 277
Condition of England, The 314, 317
Condy's Fluid 13, 35, 175
Conrad, Joseph 22, 103, 163
  'Secret Sharer, The' 4
Cooper, Diana 231
Cooper, Duff 231, 245
Coward, Noël 350, 378
  Vortex, The 365, 391, 393
Cummings, E.E. 420
Cunard, Nancy 236

Dane, Clemence: *Bill of Divorcement, A* 376–7
Daniel, C.W. 233
Darling, Mr Justice 227, 228
Davidson, Lawrence H. *see* Lawrence, D.H.
de la Mare, Walter 293
de Lara, Isidore 76
Deeping, Warwick: *Sorrell and Son* 349, 360, 375
Delius, Frederick 76
Detaille: Édouard 'Le Bourget' 258
Douglas, James 61
Douglas, Lord Alfred 16, 223, 390, 402, 403
Duhamel, Georges
  Civilisation 1914–1917 253
  Vie des Martyrs 206–8
Dyett, Edwin 213, 305
Dyson, Will 34, 42, 67, 101
  'Kultur Protector' 68

Elgar, Sir Edward 391, 468
  'Carillon' 37–8
  'For the Fallen' 38
  'Fourth of August, The' 38

'Le Drapeau belge' 38
'Pomp and Circumstance' 39
'To Women' 38
'Une Voix dans le desert' 38
Eliot, T.S. 65, 67, 101, 236, 242, 244, 338, 339, 344, 346, 348, 387, 420
  Ash Wednesday 419
  Coriolan 458
  Sweeney Agonistes 458
  Waste Land, The 24, 143, 238, 318, 342–3, 345, 365, 378, 391, 395, 418
Ellis, Havelock 366, 403–4
England Expects 39–40, 121
Epstein, Jacob 59, 402
Ervine, St John 59, 293
Eucken, Rudolph 70
Ewart, Wilfred: *Way of Revelation* 331–5, 363
Ewer, W.N.: 'Ballade of Reconstruction, A' 263

Falls, Cyril 451, 453
Firbank, Ronald 390
Fitzroy, A.T. *see* Allatini, Rose
Fletcher, John Gould 165
Ford, Ford Madox 22, 71–2, 107, 109, 327, 385–7, 441, 468
  'Day of Battle, A' 105–6
  Good Soldier, The 249
  Last Post 458
  No Enemy 263, 299, 431
  Parade's End 430, 431, 433
  When Blood is Their Argument 72
Forster, E.M. 11, 25, 65, 84, 312, 314, 324, 325
  Howards End 13, 136, 251
Forster, H.W. 151–2
Foulds, John: *World Requiem* 275–6
Freston, H. Rex: *Quest for Truth, The* 157
Freud, Sigmund 365
Fry, Roger 4, 5, 10, 16, 22, 62, 235, 245, 274, 312, 366
  'German General Staff' 236
Fussell, Paul 342

Gaitskell, Hugh 422

Galsworthy, John 4, 11, 25, 26, 64, 103, 104, 136, 137, 163, 354, 373, 391, 400, 468
'Art and the War' 62
Burning Spear, The 396
Forsyte Saga, The 329–31, 354, 433
In Chancery 329
Man of Property, The 329, 330, 415
Modern Comedy, A 378, 417
Swan Song 412, 415, 466
To Let 329
Garnett, Constance 4
Garnett, David 65, 84, 266, 312
Gaudier-Brzeska, Henri 65, 66, 341, 385
George, W.L.: Blind Alley 328, 363
Georgian Poetry 4, 5, 103, 202, 397, 401
Gertler, Mark 236
'Eve' 59
Gibbs, Philip 110, 283
Battles of the Somme, The 286
Open Warfare 278
Realities of War, The 284–91
Gide, Andre 288, 384
Gilman, Harold 65, 236
Ginner, Charles 65, 236
Gosse, Edmund 11–14, 16–18, 20, 25, 34–5, 58, 62–4, 84, 96, 131, 136, 154, 175–6, 189, 191, 219, 241–2, 259, 288, 309, 314, 384
'War and Literature' 12, 83, 128
Grainger, Percy 76
Grant, Duncan 84
Graves, Robert 65, 67, 157–8, 167, 175–6, 179, 181–3, 199, 202, 209, 235, 241, 243, 246, 254, 257, 301, 303, 338, 386–8, 424, 436, 441, 464, 468
'Big Words' 156, 166
Collected Poems 429–30
'Dead Boche, A' 192
Fairies and Fusiliers 189
Good-bye to All That 153,

304, 427–31, 434, 442, 451–3, 457
'Letter to S.S. from Mametz Wood' 261
Over the Brazier 153, 156, 189
'Sorley's Weather' 194
Survey of Modernist Poetry, A 419–20
Great Advance, The 118
Greene, Graham 421, 467
Grein, J.T. 227
Grenfell, Julian 450
Grey, Sir Edward 3, 5, 266
Gris, Juan 236
Grosz, George 198
Gurney, Ivor 31, 65, 167, 300, 387
Severn and Somme 189

Hackel, Ernest 70
Hackett, Sir John: Profession of Arms, The 125
Haggard, Sir Rider 27, 125, 370
Haig, Douglas 160
Haig, Field Marshall: Despatches 277, 279, 329
Hamilton, Cicely 134, 210
'Non-combatant' 92–3
Hamilton, Sir Ian 162–3, 454
Hamilton, R.G.A. 114–15, 183
Hamnett, Nina 236
Hardy, Thomas 26, 28, 103, 133, 175, 256, 277
Dynasts, The 39
'Men Who March Away' 27
Harrison, Austin 223
Harrison, Jane Ellen 27
Hawkins, Anthony Hope 26
Hay, Ian 50, 52, 118
First Hundred Thousand, The 48–9, 51, 226, 308
Hemingway, Ernest 285
Farewell to Arms, A 364, 451
Sun Also Rises, The 378, 386, 420
Henty, George Alfred 45, 203
Herbert, A.P. 387
Secret Battle, The 304–6
Herbert, Colonel Aubrey

172, 191, 216, 228
Hewlett, Maurice 25, 26, 28
Hicks, Seymour 39
Holbrooke, Josef 76
Howard, Brian 390
Hudson, W.H. 402
Hueffer, Ford Madox see Ford, Ford Madox
Hulme, T.E. 5, 65, 200, 341, 385
Hunt, Violet: Desirable Alien at Home in Germany, The 71
Hutchinson, A.S.M. If Winter Comes 328, 349, 375
Huxley, Aldous 174, 236, 242, 302, 350, 387–8
Antic Hay 387, 397, 399
Crome Yellow 397, 398, 412
Point Counter Point 365, 375, 378, 397–8
Those Barren Leaves 397, 399

Image, Selwyn 14–17, 96, 128, 136, 309
In Khaki for the King 43
Inge, Dean W.R. 109
'Future of the English Race, The' 358

James, Henry 3–4, 5, 11, 12, 18, 20, 22, 24, 25, 103, 126, 135, 225, 256, 395
Sacred Fount, The 255
James, Norah: Sleeveless Errand 378
Jellicoe, Admiral John 279
Jerrold, Douglas 451, 453, 454
Joad, C.E.M. 148
John, Augustus 66
John Bull 146, 213
Johnstone, Major 260
Jones, David 65, 167
Jones, Ernest 366
Jones, Henry Arthur 27, 104, 219, 354
Pacifists, The 218
Jones, Jack 409
Joyce, James 236, 246, 391
Portrait of the Artist as a Young Man 235
Ulysses 143, 235, 318, 343, 391, 392, 395, 402, 418

Junior Sub. *see* Hay, Ian

Keeling, Ben 107, 108, 200, 210
  Letters and Recollections 209
Kennington, Eric 194, 198–9
Keynes, John Maynard 309, 322, 468
  Economic Consequences of the Peace, The 291–3, 344, 358
King, Richard 247
Kipling, Rudyard 25, 26, 28, 42, 103, 118, 203, 271
  'Coward, The' 214
  'Epitaphs of the War' 214
  'For All we Have and Are' 410
  Fringes of the Fleet, The 38
  Light That Failed, The 250
  Soldiers Three 49–50
  Stalky & Co. 250
Kitchen, C.H.B.: *Streamers Waving* 378
Knoblauch, Edward 39, 104

Lamb, Henry 194, 231, 274
Lankester, E.Ray 123, 125
Lansdowne, Lord 172, 191, 223, 291
Lavery, John 198
Lawrence, D.H. 5, 11, 25, 65, 236, 266, 288, 325–7, 366, 378, 403
  'Crown, The' 61
  'England My England' 61
  Kangaroo 137, 346–7
  Lady Chatterley's Lover 360, 375, 402, 458
  Look! We Have Come Through! 235
  Movements in European History 325, 346, 348
  Rainbow, The 60–1, 137, 140, 325
  Trespasser, The 4
  Women in Love 136, 137, 138–43, 326, 348, 412
Lawrence, T.E. 366, 382, 384
Le Queux, William 47, 277
  German Atrocities: A Record of Shameless Deeds 52
Lee, Sidney 219
Leighton, Roland 112, 134,

150, 157, 158, 166, 183
Leslie, Shane 252, 253
Lewis, C Day 422, 467
Lewis, Wyndham 5, 7, 8, 22, 59, 62, 63, 66, 101, 194, 195, 199, 202, 204, 205, 208, 237, 256, 274, 295, 296–8, 327, 340, 342, 385, 386, 391, 395, 418, 423, 434, 464
  Art of Being Ruled, The 419
  Battery Shelled, A 297
  'Enemy of the Stars, The' 9
  Childermass, The 419
  Guns 297, 390
  Paleface 419
  'Plan of War' 9
  'Slow Attack' 9
  Time and Western Man 419
  'Vortices' 9
Lloyd George, David 6, 89, 100, 117, 122, 123, 222, 262, 289, 294, 347, 353
Locke, W.J. 26, 60
Lucas, E.V. 26
Lutyens, Sir Edwin 271, 280, 281
Lynn, Escott
  In Khaki for the King 45, 46
  Oliver Hastings V.C. 104

Macaulay, Rose 134, 135, 138, 253, 291, 329, 333, 345, 379
  Dangerous Ages 328
  Non-Combatants 126–7, 128, 129–30, 136, 141, 204, 212, 251, 363
  Potterism 328, 334, 427
  Told by an Idiot 328
  What Not 396, 401–2
MacCarthy, Desmond: *Life and Letters* 454
MacDonald, Ramsay 86, 163
Machen, Arthur: *Angels of Mons, The* 55
Mackail, J.W. 26
McKenna, Stephen: *Sonia* 249–52
Mackenzie, Compton: *Sinister Street* 390
McLeod, Irene 241
McNeile, Herman Cyril: *Sergeant Michael Cassidy, R.E.* 47–8, 51

Mais, S.P.B. 17
Malleson, Constance 148
Malleson, Miles 81, 148, 166, 167, 174
  Black 'Ell 150, 152, 167
  Cranks and Commonsense 24, 149
  'D' Company 149
  Out-and-Outer, The 152
  Two Short Plays: Patriotic and Unpatriotic 149, 152
Manning, Frederic 465
Mansfield, Katherine 269, 277, 282, 340, 344, 400
Marchand, Jean 236
Marinetti, F.T. 7, 62, 162
Marsh, Edward 175, 202, 246, 338, 401
Marsh, Norah 372
Masefield, John 26, 103, 126, 165, 166, 294, 338
  'August 1914' 31–3
  Battle of the Somme, The 32
  Gallipoli 32, 329
  Old Front Line, The 32
Mason, A.E.W. 26
Masterman, C.F.G. 26–9, 72, 159, 194, 273, 314–20, 322, 353, 386
  Condition of England, The 13, 314, 317
  England After War 314, 315, 318, 359–60
Mew, Charlotte 282
Meynell, Francis 84, 147, 175
  'War's a Crime' 83
  Minstrelsy of Peace, The 299
Moncrieff, C.K Scott 303
Monro, Harold 5, 29, 30, 65
Mons 444–6
Montague, C.E. 160, 200, 205, 307–10
  Disenchantment 307, 358, 389
  Rough Justice 328
Moore, G.E. 313
Moore, Marianne 420
Morel, E.D. 216–7
Morgan, Charles 171, 191, 223
Morrell, Lady Ottoline 5, 6, 140, 149, 154, 174, 176, 186, 398

Morrell, Philip 149, 151, 174, 214, 217
Moulton, James Hope: *British and German Scholarship* 70
Muir, Edwin 339, 387
Murray, Gilbert 26, 68, 71, 111, 112, 257, 382, 408
'First Thoughts on the War' 69
Murry, J. Middleton 61, 174, 207, 236, 269, 275, 301, 303, 314, 322, 337, 387, 398
'Nature of Civilization, The' 313
Muse in Arms, The 299, 333

Nash, John 65, 194, 295
Nash, Paul 194–9, 204, 256, 298, 339, 387, 465, 468
'Landscape: Year of Our Lord 1917' 197, 201
'Meadow with Copse' 197
'Menin Road, The' 295, 296, 344
'Void' 196
Void of War 196, 199–200
'We are making a New World' 197
Nevinson, C.R.W. 34, 59, 66, 162–6, 187, 194–5, 199, 274, 298, 339, 385, 464, 465
'Doctor, The' 197
'He Gained a Fortune but He Gave a Son' 198, 243, 247
Modern War Paintings 198
'Paths of Glory' 198
Pictures of War 243
'Returning to the Trenches' 166
'War Profiteers' 197–8, 243
Nevinson, H.W. 165
New Age 4–5, 22, 63, 65, 300
New Paths 236, 238–9, 240
Newbolt, Henry 26, 34, 42, 219, 304, 384
'King's Highway, The' 37
'Vigil, The' 25
Newman, Ernest 77
Newsholme, Sir Arthur 372
Nichols, Beverley: *Patchwork* 390
Nichols, Robert 207, 235,

241, 303, 387
Ardours and Endurances 189
Nicholson, Nancy 303
No-Conscription Fellowship 86, 147, 174
Novello, Ivor 36

O'Neill, Norman 76
Ogden, C.K. 155
Orage, A.R. 4, 63, 64
Orpen, William 187, 395
'Dead Germans in a Trench' 198
'Peace Conference at the Quai d'Orsay, A' 294
'To the Unknown British Soldier in France' 295, 460
Orwell, George xii, 467
Osborn, E.B. 23–4, 128, 174, 299
Our Common Humanity 147
Owen, Harold 219–22
Loyalty 219–21
Owen, Wilfred 65, 67, 81, 161, 180–3, 185, 186, 196, 201, 202, 215, 239, 243, 285, 300–6, 338, 339, 388
'A Terre' 193
'Anthem for Doomed Youth' 182
'Chances, The' 187
'Dead-Beat, The' 181, 208, 304
'Dulce et decorum est' 182
'Greater Love' 182
'Insensibility' 182
'Mental Cases' 208, 303, 304
'Parable of the Old Man and the Young, The' 247
Poems 302, 436, 437
Poems and Fragments 181
'The Show' 205
'S.I.W.' 182, 208, 304

Palmer, John 30, 293
Pankhurst, Christabel 88, 89
Pankhurst, Mrs Emmeline 6, 87, 88, 89
Pankhurst, Sylvia 89, 216, 217
Parker, Louis Napoleon 104
Partridge, Eric 423, 450, 452, 455

Paterson, W.P.: *German Culture* 69–70
Paths of Glory 299
Phillips, Stephen
Armageddon 42–3
Pinero, Sir Arthur 27, 104
Plowman, Max 81, 183–5, 216
Poems Written During the Great War 299
Poetry and Drama 5, 29, 65
Pollard, Professor A.F. 172, 191, 223
Pound, Ezra 5, 7, 8, 62, 65, 67, 101, 205, 235, 236, 246, 327, 337, 339, 346–8, 385, 420
Cantos 458
'Death of Vorticism, The' 340
'Hell Cantos' 342
'Hugh Selwyn Mauberley (Life and Contacts)' 340–1, 342
Ripostes 4
Powys, John Cowper 71

Quiller-Couch, Sir Arthur 26, 73–4

Randall, Alec 105
Ratcliffe, S.K. 293
Raymond, Ernest: *Tell England* 328, 331, 332–3, 334
Read, Herbert 200, 237, 255, 257, 298, 339, 387, 440, 455, 456
'Execution of Cornelius Vane' 306
'Killed in Action' 306
Naked Warriors 306, 338
Remarque, Erich Maria: *All Quiet on the Western Front* 425–6, 440, 451, 453, 454
Repington, Colonel Charles à Court 221, 260–1, 289–91, 319
First World War, The 261, 288
Richardson, Dorothy: *Honeycomb* 235
Rickard, Mrs Victor 247, 248
Ricketts, Charles 58, 163, 231, 384

Riding, Laura: *Survey of Modernist Poetry, A* 419–20
Rivers, W.H.R. 176–7, 179, 185, 186, 365
  Conflict and Dream 177
Roberts, William 66, 194, 274, 340
Robinson, H. Perry
  Turning Point: The Battle of the Somme, The 99
Rosenberg, Isaac 65, 167, 189, 192, 300
  'Returning, we hear the larks' 193
Ross, Robert 16, 175–6, 181, 194, 197, 205, 225, 231, 241–2, 274, 301
Rothenstein, William 194
Rowntree, Seebohm 262
Rowse, W.H.D. 217
Russell, Bertrand 74, 83, 86, 108, 147, 148, 149, 174, 216, 245, 262, 398
  'German Peace Offer, The' 217
  Principles of Social Reconstruction 261
  Prospects of Industrial Civilization 313
Russell, Dora 313
Rutter, Frank 236

Sadleir, Michael 70, 339
  Privilege 328
Sapper (*see* McNeil, Herman Cyril) 49, 50, 52, 118, 408
  Bull-Dog Drummond 357
Sargent, John Singer:
  'Gassed' 274
Sargent, Malcolm 362
Sassoon, Siegfried 65, 67, 81, 133, 154–8, 161, 167, 173–87, 194, 202, 207–9, 216, 223, 235, 239, 241–3, 245, 255, 257, 291, 301–3, 305, 338, 339, 351, 386, 387, 395, 437, 441, 464, 468
  'Atrocities' 180
  'Ballad, A' 208
  'Banishment' 179–80
  'Counter-Attack' 179, 205, 300
  'Died of Wounds' 208
  'Does it Matter?' 179

'Fathers, The' 179
'Fight to a Finish' 179
'Glory of Women' 179
'Hero, The' 154, 156, 158, 166
  Memoirs of a Fox-hunting Man 436, 442–3, 465
  Memoirs of an Infantry Officer 436
  Old Huntsman, The 174, 189, 190
  'Poet as Hero, The' 155
  'Redeemer, The' 154
  'Repression of War Experience' 176
  Sherston's Progress 436
  'Suicide in the Trenches' 208
  'Survivors' 179, 187
  'To Victory' 153, 154, 156
  War Poems 301
Sayers, Dorothy 351
Schonberg, Arnold 5, 58, 59, 74, 75
Scott, Cyril 59, 76
  Autobiography of a Child, The 402, 403
Seaman, Owen 26
Shaw, Bernard 22, 75–6, 104, 108, 163, 219, 324
  Back to Methuselah 391, 393
  Common Sense About the War 72, 83
  Heartbreak House 136, 141, 142, 143
  Perfect Wagnerite, The 142
  Pygmalion 103
  Saint Joan 391, 407
Sherriff, R.C.: *Journey's End* 441–3
Sickert, Walter 5, 34, 35, 163
  'Integrity of Belgium, The' 36
  'Soldiers of King Albert the Ready, The' 35
  'Tipperary' 36
  'Wounded' 36
Simon, Sir John 81
Sinclair, May 27, 379
  Journal of Impressions in Belgium, A 93–5
  Tasker Jevons: The True Story 93–5
  Tree of Heaven 248, 363
Sitwell, Edith 236, 242, 244,

302, 304, 436
  Argonaut and Juggernaut 397
  Façade 391, 392, 395, 418
Sitwell, Osbert 239, 241, 242, 257, 299, 395, 423
  Before the Bombardment 328
  'Corpse Day' 282
  'Modern Abraham, The' 247
Sitwell, Sacheverell 242
Smith, Helen Zenna *Not So Quiet. . .* 364, 378
Smyth, Ethel 76
  'Song: in War-Time' 28
Sorley, Charles 167
  Marlborough and Other Poems 194
Souter, John B.:
  'Breakdown, The' 403
Spencer, Gilbert 194
Spencer, Stanley 65, 194, 386, 460–2
  Sandham Memorial Chapel 460–2
Spender, Stephen x–xi, 467
Squire, Jack C. 337, 387
Stanford, Sir Charles 17, 37, 76
Stanley, Venetia 133
Steel, Flora Annie 27
Stein, Gertrude 386
Stephen, Adrian 84
Stopes, Marie
  Contraception, Its Theory and Practice 369
  Letter to Working Mothers, A 369
  Married Love 366–9
  New Gospel to All Peoples, The 373
  Our Ostriches 369–70
  Wise Parenthood 369
Strachey, James 146
Strachey, Lytton 84, 146, 252, 365, 366
  Eminent Victorians 244–6
Strang, William 34, 42
Strauss, Richard 74–5, 243
Sutro, Alfred 104
Swynnerton, Mrs Annie Louisa 362

Tawney, R.H. 116–17, 118, 119, 210, 243

'Some Reflections of a
    Soldier' 116, 134
Tayler, A. Chevallier 33
Tennyson, Alfred Lord: 'A
    Call to Arms' 37
Tennyson, Emily Lady 37
Tennyson, Lord 37
Thomas, Edward 244
Thompson, Sylvia: *Hounds of
    Spring, The* 364
Thomson, Arthur 70
*To Christ's Disciples
    Everywhere* 147
Tomlinson, H.M. 339, 348,
    423
Tovey, Donald 70
Trevelyan, G.M. 26

Vachell, Horace Annesley 104
Valour and Vision 299

Wadsworth, Edward 66
Wallace, Edgar 47
Walpole, Hugh: *Dark Forest,
    The* 107
Walton, William: *Façade*
    391, 392, 395, 399, 418
*War: A History and
    Explanation for Boys and
    Girls, The* 47
Ward, Mrs Humphry 22,
    27, 245
Ware, Fabian 270
Warner, Rex 421
Watson, William 25
Waugh, Alec 334, 421
    Loom of Youth 246, 248
Waugh, Arthur 60, 258–9
Waugh, Evelyn 350, 389, 421
    Vile Bodies 467
    'Youngest Generation,
    The' 388
Webb, Beatrice 145, 254,

262, 265, 281, 385, 408,
    412
*Decay of Capitalist
    Civilisation* 313
Webb, Sidney
*Decay of Capitalist
    Civilisation* 313
Weingarten, Felix 354
Wells, H.G. 5, 24, 26, 108,
    111, 135, 137, 138, 175,
    252, 260, 261–2, 329, 354,
    384, 400, 417
Ann Veronica 21
Boon 21, 22–4, 58, 127,
    128, 129, 130, 322, 413
Christina Alberta's Father
    328, 334, 427
Dream, The 328
'If England is Raided' 20
Joan and Peter 248, 249
Marriage 4
Meanwhile 412, 414–15,
    466
Mr Britling Sees It Through
    130, 136, 141, 171, 222,
    251, 351, 363
'Need for Strength and
    Clearness at Home, The'
    20
Outline of History, The 313,
    321–4, 325, 413
Tono-Bungay 13, 136,
    322
'War That Will End War,
    The' 20
West, Arthur Graeme 114,
    134, 147, 148, 150, 183,
    216
Diary of a Dead Officer 209,
    453
'God! How I hate you, you
    young cheerful men!'
    157–8

West, Rebecca 94, 95, 345,
    379, 442
Return of the Soldier, The
    212–13, 433
Wheels 236, 237, 244, 302,
    397
Whibley, Charles 245
Wilde, Oscar 16, 17, 181,
    228, 234, 390
Dorian Gray 58
Salomé 227, 229, 232
Wilenski, R.H. 274
Williamson, Henry 455, 464,
    467
With French at the Front 43
Wood, Henry 5, 74, 77, 354
Woodville, R. Caton 33
Woolf, Leonard 84, 254, 299,
    339
Woolf, Virginia 4, 36, 41, 84,
    174, 233, 236, 255, 299,
    346, 348, 356, 365, 411,
    419, 469
Jacob's Room 143, 344
Mark on the Wall, The 235
'Mr Bennett and Mrs
    Brown' 399–401
Mrs Dalloway 344–5, 418
Night and Day 269, 400
To the Lighthouse 419, 458
Room of One's Own, A
    468

Yates, Dornford: *Berry and
    Co.* 357
Yeats, W.B. 103, 215, 327,
    384
Winding Stair, The
    458
Younghusband, Major-
    General Sir George 50

Zangwill, Israel 26

DATE DUE
